THE HISTORY OF BROADCASTING
IN THE UNITED KINGDOM
VOLUME II

THE GOLDEN AGE
OF WIRELESS

THE HISTORY OF BROADCASTING
IN THE UNITED KINGDOM

VOLUME II

THE
GOLDEN AGE OF
WIRELESS

BY

ASA BRIGGS

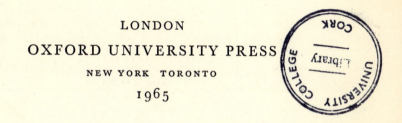

LONDON
OXFORD UNIVERSITY PRESS
NEW YORK   TORONTO
1965

Oxford University Press, Amen House, London E.C.4

GLASGOW NEW YORK TORONTO MELBOURNE WELLINGTON
BOMBAY CALCUTTA MADRAS KARACHI LAHORE DACCA
CAPE TOWN SALISBURY NAIROBI IBADAN ACCRA
KUALA LUMPUR HONG KONG

PRINTED IN GREAT BRITAIN
AT THE UNIVERSITY PRESS, OXFORD
BY VIVIAN RIDLER
PRINTER TO THE UNIVERSITY

This History is dedicated to

J. H. WHITLEY

Chairman of the Board of Governors of
The British Broadcasting Corporation
(1930–1935)

'He was all to us that a chairman could be'

PREFACE

THIS volume follows chronologically *The Birth of Broadcasting* which appeared in 1961. In writing it I have had extremely generous help from everyone I have consulted within the BBC. I have had the fullest access to the voluminous records of the Corporation, and I have benefited greatly from interviews, conversations, and the opportunity of meeting collectively groups of people associated with particular aspects of broadcasting. The record I present and the conclusions I have reached are, however, entirely my own.

Outside the BBC I remain deeply grateful for the friendly and invaluable co-operation of Lord Reith, who has placed at my disposal all his private papers and his extremely full and informative Diary. The use of this unique source has greatly enlivened the writing of this volume of the history, just as it enlivened the writing of the first. My debt to Lord Reith goes beyond this, however, for it is in discussing people and problems with him that I have learnt a great deal, not only about broadcasting, which could have been learnt in no other way. I cannot conceive how this history could have been written without the interest he has shown in it and the help he has given.

I am also grateful to the late R. C. Norman, who gave me a vivid and illuminating first-hand account of the Governors of the BBC in the late 1930s, and to Oliver Whitley, who lent me press cuttings and papers relating to his father, J. H. Whitley, a previous Chairman of the Board of Governors, to whom this book is respectfully dedicated. Through the kindness of T. W. Tallents I have been able to use many of his father's papers and press cuttings. These, indeed, constitute a major historical source. I am also greatly indebted to Ralph Wade, whose manuscript history 'Early Life in the BBC' is full of interesting and unique information. Stuart G. Williams kindly made available to me papers and books relating to his stepfather, Sydney Moseley, and among a large number of former officials of the BBC who have offered me their fullest co-operation I must mention Sir Noel Ashbridge, Sir Basil Nicolls, Sir Adrian Boult, Mrs. Mary Adams, Donald Boyd, Gerald Cock, F. H. Dart, the late Peter Eckersley, H. Lynton Fletcher, J. W. Godfrey, Maurice Gorham, John Green, Julian Herbage, Owen Mase, W. E. Gladstone Murray, Norman Luker, W. St. J. Pym, A. P. Ryan, Charles Siepmann, the late Mary Somerville, Roger Wilson, Kenneth Wright, and the Hon. R. T. B. Wynn. I was also able to talk with Lady Ogilvie, to acquire useful material about the building of Broadcasting House from Marmaduke T. Tudsbery, to study microphones and studios with the help of Dr. F. W. Alexander, to make use of Mungo M. Dewar's Variety Day Book, to examine a file of articles by S. J. de Lotbinière, to collect information about programme finance, a subject where some of the BBC's own files have been destroyed, from P. E. Cruttwell, and, most important of all these debts, to study the rich private papers of Sir Beresford Clark which carefully document the whole development of empire and overseas broadcasting. I have also been able to make use of relevant Post Office archives, and I would particularly like to thank the Post Office for willing co-operation.

It would be invidious to single out people within the BBC, but a number of people who were of great help to me have subsequently left the Corporation and some of them have read through parts of the manuscript. Sir Gerald Beadle, Val Gielgud, and Eric Maschwitz all provided me with valuable information. Sir Harold Bishop took immense pains to advise me about the technical complexities of radio history, and gave me much other help. Sir Lindsay Wellington sketched out details of policies which have never been given full expression on paper, and saved me from serious errors. The Controllers of the Midland and North Regions, and Scotland, sent me valuable papers. Kenneth Adam read through the first draft and made necessary criticisms. H. Davies, T. H. Eckersley, Laurence Gilliam, H. A. Hanlon, L. F. Lewis, A. P. Monson, R. C. Patrick, Martin Pulling, R. J. E. Silvey, Donald Stephenson, and D. B. Weigall all proved helpful in various capacities.

To R. L. W. Collison, the BBC's Librarian, and to Miss M. S. Hodgson, the Archivist, I owe an immense debt. Mr. Collison not only provided me with a fund of bibliographical information, but prepared the index of this volume. Miss Hodgson, in the process of planning and arranging BBC papers, has acquired a prodigious detailed knowledge without which

I would often have been lost. In addition, Dr. Harold Spivacke of the Library of Congress gave me useful information about popular music across the Atlantic and B. G. Cooper, author of an Oxford B. Litt. thesis, on the BBC and religion; while Mrs. Healing helped me with material on BBC programmes during the few months before the outbreak of the Second World War. Miss Marjorie Whitaker, my secretary, helped me to organize and pursue the whole enterprise, an often difficult undertaking, as smoothly and efficiently as possible. Above all, my friend D. H. Clarke, with his wide experience and knowledge, has assisted me at every stage, setting me on the right paths and guiding me towards the destination. Dr. Barry Supple and Dr. Bryan Wilson very kindly read through the final proofs.

Contemporary history, particularly institutional history, is a necessary but hazardous enterprise. I have tried in this volume, as in the first volume of this history, to keep a careful watch on perspective and not to allow current fashions of thought to dominate either arrangement or conclusions. I have also kept a close watch on scale. There are certain problems in broadcasting history, as in other kinds of history, where unless the historian explores in considerable depth he can offer little but meaningless detail and useless generalization. I have tried to penetrate as deeply as I can where this is possible—it is not always possible—and where I think it is necessary. I am sure, however, that more monographs are needed in relation to problems both in broadcasting history and in the social history of which this volume is also a part. Like Volume I, this volume is designed to be read in itself or to be treated as one volume in a bigger series. It will be followed up by a third volume on broadcasting during the Second World War.

ASA BRIGGS

The University of Sussex
August 1964

I MUST apologize to Brigadier R. F. Johnson for misspelling his name on p. 254 of Volume I, where, as author of a series of broadcast talks under the title 'My Part of the Country', which began in 1924, he is referred to as Captain Johnston. In my reference to Miss F. I. Shields, Reith's secretary, I wrote that she was a graduate of Newnham. She was, in fact, a graduate of Girton.

CONTENTS

LIST OF ILLUSTRATIONS

The author would like to acknowledge with thanks the kind permission given to reproduce illustrations belonging to individuals and corporate bodies. Items marked with an asterisk are by permission of the BBC. Pictures of wireless receivers are from the catalogues of the National Association of Radio Manufacturers and Traders.

I

INTRODUCTION

PERSONALITIES AND PERFORMANCE

———

. . . yet hath modern cultur enrich'd a wasting soil;
Science comforting man's animal poverty
and leisuring his toil, hath humanized manners
and social temper, and now above her globe-spredd net,
of speeded intercourse hath outrun all magic,
and disclosing the secrecy of the reticent air
hath woven a seamless web of invisible strands
spiriting the dumb inane with the quick matter of life:
Now music's prison'd raptur and the drown'd voice of truth
mantled in light's velocity, over land and sea
are omnipresent, speaking aloud to every ear,
into every heart and home their unhinder'd message,
the body and soul of Universal Brotherhood. . . .

ROBERT BRIDGES
Lines 721–33 from *The Testament of Beauty* (1930), Book I

Introduction

PERSONALITIES AND PERFORMANCES

ON 1 January 1927 the British Broadcasting Corporation took over the work of the four-year-old British Broadcasting Company. The principle of public service, which had dominated the development of the work of the Company, was given full institutional expression in the Charter of the new Corporation. So secure had the principle become and so directly had the old régime of the Company become associated with it that the change of constitution and title entailed no sharp break in the life of the BBC: it was generally considered as a 'logical and inevitable result' of the policy adopted from the foundation of the Company in 1922.[1] The announcers, indeed, had to be warned to 'remember the change' and not to refer over the air to the Company instead of the Corporation 'by inadvertence'.[2]

There was only one change in the domestic nomenclature of the BBC. Sir John Reith, who, as Managing Director of the old Company, had directed broadcasting towards its new public status, was given the title of Director-General. He was then thirty-eight years old, adventurous and forthright. It was Reith himself who told a later generation of BBC employees that 'the transition from Company to Corporation was hardly obvious inside the BBC to anyone other than myself, nor to anyone outside either. Those of us who were with the old Company are sorry when we hear people talking of the BBC as if it began in January 1927.'[3]

Reith remained as Director-General of the new BBC for most of the period described in this second volume of British Broad-

---

[1] The phrase 'logical and inevitable result' is that of Lord Clarendon, the first Chairman of the Governors of the new Corporation. See his Foreword to the *BBC Handbook* (1928), p. 29. Cf. the memorandum circulated to Members of Parliament by the BBC just before the transfer of authority: 'The policy of the BBC during its stewardship of the Service has led logically and indeed inevitably to the creation of a Public Corporation as the permanent Broadcasting authority.'

[2] *Memorandum to Station Directors and Head Office, 31 Dec. 1926. [An * in front of a footnote means that the letter or document is among the BBC's Records.]

[3] *Talk to the BBC Staff Training School, 2 Oct. 1936.

casting history. When he retired in June 1938, to be succeeded
by Frederick Ogilvie, he had spent sixteen years of his life in
creating one of the most distinctive and impressive of modern
British institutions. He discovered wireless when its use for
entertainment was thought of at most as a fad, at least as a
toy. He left the world of broadcasting when everyone agreed
that wireless was a great 'medium' of communication. 'This
age of broadcasting', Ernest Barker called the 1930s.[1] 'Of the
external forms that are helping to shape human life and behaviour,' another commentator remarked in 1939, 'none I
should say, is more ubiquitous and permeating than radio. Men
and women have arrived at the point where they feel that, be
it grand or ever so humble, no place is like home that has no
radio. That gentle or not so gentle murmur of music or talking
which people summarily refer to as "the wireless" has become
as necessary a background to home life as was once the loud tick
of the grandfather clock or the singing of the kettle on the hob.'[2]

The acceptance of wireless as a part of the homely background of life and the acceptance of the BBC as the 'natural'
institution for controlling it distinguish the period covered in
this second volume from that of the first. The main theme of
that volume was the control of broadcasting. The successful
effort to achieve public control gave unity to the period and
still provides a tidy case study with general implications.
Between 1922 and 1927 there had been a struggle to establish
both the medium and the institution, and out of the struggle
there emerged a system of public control over what only a few
people had the imagination to realize was an invention of major
social importance. From 1927 to 1939, however, that system
of public control was never seriously in jeopardy. The one big
official inquiry of the period, the Ullswater Report, published
in 1936, started and ended with declarations that no major
constitutional changes were necessary.[3] When Reith gave way
to Ogilvie the balance of power changed, but the constitutional
strength of the BBC was not undermined.

For this reason the main theme of this second volume is a
different one. It may be called the extension and the enrich-

[1] E. Barker, 'This Age of Broadcasting' in the *Fortnightly Review*, 1935, pp. 417–29.
[2] B. Maine, *The BBC and Its Audience* (1939), p. 7.
[3] See below, pp. 476 ff.

ment of the activity of broadcasting. The theme was once used as the starting-point of a provocative article by George Bernard Shaw. 'I leave to others the discussion of the political control of the BBC', he began. 'They are sure to forget all about the instrument the BBC controls, colloquially known as the Mike; and it is the Mike that interests me.'[1] It is amazing how frightened many people were of the 'Mike', although a few, the 'natural broadcasters', loved it. The fear is well communicated in a passage from Thomas Jones's diary:

Put into Studio 3B. . . . The red light quivered, then stopped and before I knew I was away. Up to that moment I had been thoroughly at ease, but then I began to feel very 'artificial', as if the voice did not belong to me at all. At the end of my first five minutes I could see I was about eight lines behind and about this time I rested my hand on the table and it bumped away, up and down, at a great rate and I could *not* keep it still. . . . I tried hard to get out of the reading manner to a more natural speaking key, but for the life of me, could I? But I saw I was keeping fairly to my time until the last five minutes when I realized I was going to be a trifle behind. In fact I ended a minute over—which the announcer thought was very good for a first go off.[2]

1. A Cheap Wireless Set of 1927

Thomas Jones's friend, Stanley Baldwin, a natural broadcaster, would never have behaved like this. Yet many music hall stars did. No television camera could have created greater anxiety.

[1] G. B. Shaw, 'The Tell Tale Microphone' in the *Political Quarterly*, Oct.–Dec. 1935.
[2] Thomas Jones, *A Diary with Letters, 1931–1950* (1954), p. 118.

To begin this book with the impact of the microphone directs attention from the start to two aspects of broadcasting history. First, the activity of broadcasting depended upon co-operation between engineers and programme builders. The terms of co-operation changed frequently as the engineers carried through some of the biggest projects in the history of the BBC—the introduction of the Regional Scheme; the provision of Empire and Overseas broadcasting; and the first launching of a television service. Yet the programme builders had their influence on the engineers also. They asked, for example, for better acoustics and, in the later 1930s, for cheaper and more efficient means of recording programmes.

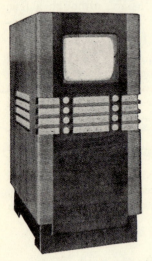

2. A Television Set of the late 1930s

The second aspect of broadcasting history is the relationship between broadcaster and audience. The number of broadcasters and the number of people working for the BBC increased with the increasing size of audience. On 1 January 1927 the BBC employed 773 people. There were then 2,178,259 wireless-licence holders. On 1 September 1939 the BBC employed nearly 5,000 people and there were 9,082,666 wireless-licence holders. To put the matter simply, in 1927 the BBC was still a small organization, catering for a minority, if a large and growing minority, of the British public. In 1939 the BBC was a large organization, and it was catering for a majority of the British public.

Beginning with the 'Mike', therefore, there are two possible ways of approaching 'the golden age of wireless'. The first would be to concentrate on the development of the BBC as an institution—to trace the intricate pattern of its organizational growth, comparing it with growth in organizations of other kinds. The second would be to concentrate on the impact of broadcasting on society, the divided society of the inter-war years, divided by age, by class, by education, and by region, yet more and more coming to accept radio as a part of life's routine. Did radio help to hold British society together as it was or did it introduce new leaven? Children born after 1922 increasingly took wireless for granted so that they could hardly conceive of a pre-broadcasting age. Did any of them see the influence of the medium, as Bridges saw it, with poetic vision, as the weaving of 'a seamless web of invisible strands spiriting the dumb inane with the quick matter of life'? Or did they think rather of 'the kettle singing on the hob'?

The second line of approach is extraordinarily difficult. For, despite all the talk of wireless being 'permeating' and 'ubiquitous', it is almost impossible to separate its social and cultural consequences from the tangle of social forces which were changing Britain during the 1920s and 1930s. The influence of broadcasting was neither exclusive nor necessarily paramount. Obvious social changes, like the end of the isolation of rural life, owed as much to the internal combustion engine as they did to the BBC. The revolution in popular entertainment did not start inside the BBC. Interest in drama or opera and the extension of the appreciation of classical music owed much to the BBC, but it is not easy to say how much. In politics the BBC diffused information but did not usually give a lead: it registered and reinforced. There is always a temptation for writers on radio to exaggerate its influence. For the most part it reflected the society and the culture in which it developed rather than reshaped them.

When it did not reflect, as it often did not in Britain, it was largely because Reith and his colleagues deliberately stood out against some of the tendencies of the age. 'Broadcasting in this country', Reith told a conference in 1928, 'is a striking example of the advantages which are gained through being able to be definite—it may even appear arbitrary—in the pursuit and execution of a line of policy capably but deliberately chosen.'[1] The religious policy of the BBC during the period stood out against many of the tendencies of the age, and in economic matters the BBC always remained outside the market complex. It did not help to sell the products of an expanding technology, except for wireless sets. Motor-cars,

[1] * Speech to the Adult Education Conference, Cambridge, Oct. 1928.

lawn-mowers, and kitchen-sinks were quite outside its province. Stuart Hibberd, the distinguished and popular Chief Announcer of the BBC, noted in his diary in April 1936 that Professor Lloyd James, who had just returned from a visit to the United States, made a 'startling point' to a BBC announcers' meeting when he told them that 'the American Universities regarded broadcasting in America as having no cultural value at all, but looked upon the programmes put out by the various networks solely as instruments for selling goods'.[1]

In the United States radio, the cinema, the gramophone record industry, even the press, all belonged to the same world of 'mass entertainment'. In Britain the BBC did not belong to that world. It was not 'a factory of dreams'.[2] It reflected life, even if it reflected it imperfectly. Given the wide social and geographical divisions in Britain, it had a limited if useful role as the interpreter of one part of 'the great audience' to another. It is fair to say that it was more effective in its geographical than in its social mediation, in pulling together the different parts of the country rather than in pulling together the different classes. It was during the Second World War rather than before it that it fully achieved what had always been its aim, that of informing, inspiring—and diverting—a whole community. Yet because it always set out to do this, it is necessary at every point in the history of British broadcasting to turn back from social history to institutional history, to the strategic decisions taken inside the BBC, to the relations between the BBC and the controllers of the other media, and to the philosophy of communication which Reith and his staff upheld.

The BBC conceived of broadcasting-licence holders as a 'public' and not as a 'market'. It was technically permitted, by the Licence and Agreement of 1926, to broadcast 'sponsored programmes', although direct advertisement was barred. No use was made of this power, however, and sponsored programmes, along with direct advertising, were prohibited in the new Licence and Agreement of 1936. The BBC's opposition to

[1] S. Hibberd, *This—is London* (1950), p. 130.
[2] Compare the remark of F. L. Allen, the American social historian. 'If a dozen or two feature pictures [of the 1930s] selected at random were to be shown to an audience of 1960, that audience would probably derive from them not the faintest idea of the ordeal through which the United States went in the 1930s.' *Since Yesterday* (1961 edn.), p. 222.

systems of finance based on advertising was supported not only by most British writers during this period but by the powerful interest of the press. 'People have a horror of introducing into England some of the systems of radio advertising to be found in certain foreign countries', a writer who favoured a 'more open mind' admitted in 1936.[1]

The system was distinctive. The wireless licence was a yearly obligation, more like rates and taxes than a cinema ticket. It provided you with very mixed fare, a different kind of fare from that provided in the United States, where business set the pace and the terms, or in Germany, where broadcasting became an engine of propaganda after 1933, an instrument of totalitarian government.

These three broadcasting systems were diverging—not converging—during the 1930s, yet Reith did not hesitate to advocate the merits of the British system even to Americans and Germans. In his advocacy he always stressed that while there was public control or the possibility of public control in Britain, there was at the same time no public interference in management. The standards were set by the managers themselves. The BBC was an autonomous institution, as unlike a government department as it was unlike a retail store.

The kind of fare provided, therefore, is the subject of the first part of this volume, which, beginning with the 'Mike', assumes that it is wisest for the historian to start where broadcasting ends—with the programmes themselves, the final product of the activity of broadcasting. Here is all the colour of broadcasting—and also a great deal of the routine—a cavalcade of names and, for those who remember, of memories. On Sunday, 2 January 1927, the first day to appear in the *Radio Times* after the advent of the Corporation, B. W. O'Donnell was conducting the Military Band, J. C. Squire reading *The Ancient Mariner*, and Stanford Robinson conducting the Wireless String Orchestra; and on the following Saturday night Tommy Handley was appearing in an Ernest Longstaffe revue.[2] On Sunday, 3 September 1939, the programmes listeners would have heard, had it not been for the war, included the first

[1] 'Broadcasting in a Democratic State' in the *Round Table*, June 1936.
[2] *Radio Times*, 31 Dec. 1926.

instalment of *The Four Feathers*, Reginald Foort at the theatre
organ, J. B. Priestley reading the first instalment of *Let The
People Sing*—and the BBC Military Band.[1]

Behind the cavalcade of programmes was a multiplicity of
decisions taken within the BBC. Some of the decisions came
from above, encouraging as well as restraining: most came from
below. Some reflected general programme policy: most bore the
imprint only of scriptwriter, producer, and performer. At this
level, as at any other, broadcasting rested on a partnership
between studio and control-room engineers and programme
builders, words and music being converted into electrical currents and voltages before they could become words and music
again in listeners' homes.

The second detailed chapter of this volume moves to 'the
other side of the microphone'. It is concerned with the listeners,
and the various ways in which their needs were met (or not
met) as the broadcasting system was expanded. The most
vocal of the listeners begin—and end—by holding the stage.
'As a student and lover of music, may I appeal for greater
simplicity in the music that is broadcast', a listener wrote to the
Radio Times in the first week of the Corporation.[2] 'I have just
heard the first Wagner Prom of the season', another listener
wrote in the last week before the war, 'and there must be a
large number of musical cranks at large to tolerate such meaningless tripe.'[3] All things connect, or, as the BBC quickly
learned from listeners' letters, cancel out. Organized listener
research began late, only after a struggle.[4] The tardiness of the
development reflected the philosophy of control. If listeners
were not thought of as a market, why worry about market
research?

Both the Regional Scheme and the Empire Scheme find their
place in this chapter on listeners, for both schemes, bold and
enterprising as they were as engineers' exploits, were designed,
above all else, to provide the kind of service listeners required.
The partnership between engineers and programme builders
continued at all times. High-quality lines were necessary
to carry BBC programmes from their point of origin in the
studios to the transmitters, and an elaborate transmitter net-

[1] *Radio Times*, 1 Sept. 1939.   [2] Ibid., 7 Jan. 1927.
[3] Ibid., 1 Sept. 1939.   [4] See below, pp. 256 ff.

work was necessary to ensure satisfactory reception both at home and abroad. At the same time, British schemes had to fit into a European and a world framework, and, in relation both to wavelengths and to programmes, there was competition as well as co-operation. Zeesen and Radio Luxembourg must both have their place, therefore, in any account of broadcasting in Britain. Both were interested in British listeners, the first to influence their opinions, the second to shape their buying habits.

From the makers of programmes and the listeners to them, it is natural to turn to organization and control. Although these are not the major themes of this volume, they cannot be left out. Even when the BBC was small, it needed a formal structure of control, and the terms 'controller' and 'control committee' were soon used in relation to administration.[1] As the organization grew, there was greater specialization and differentiation. There were also greater difficulties in 'communication'. Frequent experiments were made in organization, culminating in a major change in 1933 when the 'creative' work of the BBC —that relating directly to programmes—was separated from the 'administrative' work. Each division had its own formal hierarchy, the first described as 'blue tab', the latter as 'red tab'. Engineering, it is interesting to note, was grouped with the 'red tab' side, although Reith, who always recognized that the imagination and vision of engineers were needed as well as their expert knowledge, admitted that in his language of colour engineering 'was more blue than red'.

This division of control, which lasted until 1942, characterized an era of extreme centralization in the institutional history of the BBC.[2] The system was vigorously defended by Reith, although it was widely criticized during the 1930s and has continued to be criticized since. The division between 'creative' people and 'administrative' people was designed to liberate the 'creative' people from tasks in which they felt little interest and for which they often had little aptitude. Yet dividing lines were difficult to draw, and there was sometimes resentment against administrative 'rules'. Far too much emphasis,

[1] See Vol. I of my History, *The Birth of Broadcasting*, p. 207.
[2] See below, pp. 442 ff.

according to Reith's critics, seemed to be placed on institutional machinery, and even while committees were taking up too much time, they often seemed to have little real power.

It is organizational issues of this kind rather than the bigger public issue of the BBC's constitution or the more publicized and sensationalized problems of BBC staffing, which are of greatest interest during this period. As the BBC grew, both in the size of its staff and the range of its functions, what was its shape to be? Were the strains and stresses of growth which it registered, sometimes painfully, the kind of strains and stresses which are common to all growing organizations or were some of them, at least, peculiar to the BBC?

There are three other aspects of 'organization' which must be considered carefully in the third detailed chapter. The first is the public reaction to the BBC. One of the features which distinguished the BBC from many other large and growing organizations was the publicity it received not only as a purveyor of programmes but as an institution. News of its internal changes was seized upon with avid interest: its personalities were personalities in the press, whether they liked it or not. 'As far as the newspapers are concerned,' the well-known journalist Tom Clarke wrote in 1932, 'the BBC has become news.'[1]

Corresponding to the 'shape' of the BBC, therefore, there was an 'image'. The favourite image of the BBC during the 1930s was that of a great British institution, as British as the Bank of England, an institution which was different from other institutions, which took decisions that quite deliberately diverged from the decisions many—perhaps most—listeners would have taken. The image of the institution and the image of its Director-General became blurred, and even after Reith had left—and some very different kinds of people had begun to emerge as important figures in the BBC's hierarchies—the BBC remained 'Reithian' in most people's eyes.

Attitudes towards the BBC as a national institution require not only social analysis but psychological study in depth. Such study was not made during the 1930s. The historian, therefore, must sift superficial evidence. One point he must emphasize is the danger of reading back into the past attitudes which

[1] *Daily Mail*, 17 Jan. 1932.

belong to a later period, to the Second World War, for example, or to the period of uncertainty after the war. Nobody referred to the BBC as 'Auntie BBC' in the period covered in this volume, just as very few people queried the constitution of public service broadcasting. More emphasis was placed then than later both on the 'inspirational' power and on the 'consoling' power of radio, both of which the BBC was thought to cherish and defend.

> . . . consoling voices of the air
> Soothing the sightless, cheering the bedridden.
> The lighthouse-watchers, men who bravely bear
> The burden of captivity unbidden—
> Voices that calm the heart and ease the strain
> Of those who live in loneliness or pain.[1]

This aspect of radio—neither as the broker of ideas nor as the purveyor of culture, not even as the source of entertainment, but as the instrument of 'solace'—remained important so long as there was an older generation who remembered what it was like before the days of radio and did not take their wireless sets for granted. It was left to a later generation to demand from the BBC soul-searching 'face to face' interviews and ruthless social and political exposure.

The 'inspirational' power of radio was felt most strongly not by the listeners but by the broadcasters themselves. Throughout the late 1920s and the early 1930s the BBC attracted to its service a considerable number of men and women who 'believed in broadcasting' almost as a social and cultural crusade. They included a high proportion of young people and of men 'who had served in the War but who, on account of some awkward versatility or some form of fastidiousness, idealism or general restlessness, never settled down to any humdrum profession after war was over'.[2] Many of them have described their approach to the new medium. 'We really believed', Lionel Fielden has written, 'that broadcasting could revolutionize human opinion'.[3] They also believed that it could develop or transform taste. Their influence was felt not only in school broadcasting or in adult education but in news, talks, music, and drama. Music, indeed, was often picked out as the test case

[1] *Punch*, 11 May 1932.   [2] H. Matheson, *Broadcasting* (1933), p. 52.
[3] L. Fielden, *The Natural Bent* (1960), p. 100.

of cultural penetration. 'The plain man', Ernest Newman wrote, 'can now get in two or three years a knowledge not only of the acknowledged masterpieces, but of fine works of the second rank which his father could scarcely have acquired in a lifetime.'[1] However uncertain the historian may be about the extent of the social and cultural influence of broadcasting, there were many broadcasters who felt no doubts.

Some of the people who joined the BBC never completely settled down once they had got there. It is interesting, indeed, that most of the accounts of the BBC during the period covered in this volume were written by 'rebels', by people who were forced to leave it, who did not like its ethos or who criticized its organization. Their accounts are useful evidence, like the press accounts of the BBC's activities, but they need to be supplemented and set in perspective. What you thought of the BBC in the 1930s, if you were a member of it, depended not only on your temperament, character, and experience—and the conditions and date at which you entered the Corporation—but on the place which you occupied in the system. Your perspective would often change as you moved upwards, downwards, or across. The historian has less difficulty in interpreting the institution than in interpreting the society in which it developed. He has the advantage of being able to look at the scene from more than one angle, to take into account evidence which was hidden from partial view at the time, and to trace complex sequences of cause and consequence.

The chapter on organization in this volume ends with the one public inquiry into broadcasting which was made during this period—the Ullswater Committee investigation—and the reactions to it inside and outside the BBC. It was to meet the needs of this committee that a great deal of BBC evidence was assembled in 1935, and the year provides an excellent vantage point from which to look back over the period from the foundation of the Corporation and forward towards the Second World War.

The other vantage point in the period covered in this volume was the move in 1932 from the cramped premises at Savoy Hill to the imposing new building, Broadcasting House. All BBC

[1] Quoted in R. S. Lambert, *Ariel and All His Quality* (1940), p. 57.

history can be dated pre- or post-Broadcasting House. The change of building became identified not only with growth and all the problems which went with it but with a change of mood, even of style. Jack Payne, for example, has written: 'Yes, it was a chummy atmosphere in the old Savoy Hill days. There was some slovenliness about it too, or so it would appear against the punctiliousness of the present regime.'[1] Even listeners felt that the end of Savoy Hill was a break, and it was natural that one of the big programmes of the inter-war years should be Lance Sieveking's *The End of Savoy Hill*, broadcast on 14 May 1932. What happened in 1932, therefore, has a place in several chapters in this volume, not only in the chapter on organization.

To move from Savoy Hill to the BBC's first television centre at Alexandra Palace requires a less dramatic leap of the imagination than to move from Savoy Hill to Broadcasting House, for the early days of Alexandra Palace had much in common with the early days of Savoy Hill. There was a certain inevitability about the coming of television which did not escape letter-writers to the early issues of the *Radio Times*. As early as October 1923, indeed, the winner of the BBC's 'Brighter Britain Essay Competition' began by describing somewhat fearfully the genie who lived inside his 'magic wireless box' and who could see everything which he translated into words. He ended more confidently, however, that 'one day I shall be able to see through similar eyes'.[2] People were prepared for television long before the apparatus or the programmes were available, and the fifth detailed chapter of this volume is concerned with the steps that led up to the development of the world's first regular television service in 1936. Here again, the detail is more revealing than the generalization, the detail of the mass of separate decisions taken by engineers, administrators, and programme builders.

One of the first internal memoranda on television related not to techniques but to nomenclature. 'May I suggest', a prominent BBC official, V. H. Goldsmith, wrote in May 1928, 'that the first of the three articles on Television which are to go

[1] J. Payne, *Signature Tune* (1947), p. 39.
[2] *Radio Times*, 19 Oct. 1923.

into the *Radio Times* should define Television as distinct from Telephotography? . . . It may be just as well, if you agree the right definition, to get away in the Press with a clear standard of what the words mean.'[1] Seven years later, nomenclature was still raising difficulties. 'The question has been raised', wrote Ralph Wade, 'as to what the equivalent to a listener should be called in the case of television. I do not know whether anybody has ever considered this, but it might be a good thing to get it settled before some horrible name creeps in.'[2] The Television Committee of 1934, the first official inquiry into television, recommended the word 'looker'; Basil Nicolls, the Director of Internal Administration, suggested 'televiser'; and V. H. Goldsmith, Director of Business Relations, was in favour of 'viser'. None of these words appealed to Reith, who added that he had never liked the word 'listener' either.

The word 'viewer' made its début as an abbreviated version of the more formal 'televiewer', with the *Radio Times* itself arguing that the abbreviation was inevitable. 'As for "tele-viewer", that may be the authorised word, but we don't see it entering into the vocabulary of the masses all the same. We would back the "viewer" to shed the "tele" at the first fence.'[3] There was no hint that 'telly' by itself would establish independent usage naturally and with affection. The whole question of terminology was referred to A. Lloyd James and through him to the authoritative Advisory Committee on Spoken English. 'Glancer', 'witnesser', 'telobservist', and even 'visionist' and 'teleseer' were formidable alternatives to 'viewer'. Rose Macaulay favoured 'looker-in', and Lascelles Abercrombie stated boldly that this was 'the word which will win in the long run'. Logan Pearsall Smith, however, thought that nothing better than 'viewer' could be found, although the word 'gazer' rather attracted him.[4]

The chapter on television is concerned with more basic questions than these interesting if archaic issues of terminology —with the BBC's attitude towards Baird, for example, and with the planning of the first regular television programmes. There is a contrast at the end of the chapter between what

1 *V. H. Goldsmith to P. P. Eckersley, 16 May 1928.
2 *R. Wade to B. E. Nicolls, 5 Feb. 1935.
3 *Radio Times*, 12 Apr. 1935.
4 *Logan Pearsall Smith to A. Lloyd James, 5 June 1935.

happened to television and what happened to sound radio. The history of sound radio in 'the golden age of wireless' leads directly into the history of the Second World War, when sound radio through the BBC became a recognized international force. The history of television, the lesser medium during the 1930s, leaps the war, however, almost as if the studios at Alexandra Palace had never been closed down in September 1939. There is a note of irony in the pages of the issue of the *Radio Times* for 1 September 1939 which set out the details of television programmes for the week that never was. It was to begin with *The Circle* by Somerset Maugham and to end with Alice de Belleroche playing the guitar.

The last chapter in this volume is concerned with the shadows of war and the way they fell over 'the activity of broadcasting'. It is a short chapter, for much of the detail is more relevant to the next volume of this History (a volume concerned solely with the Second World War) than to the present one. There was one major event, however, in the months leading up to the war which was so important that it, rather than the outbreak of war, might have been made the last event in this volume.[1] When Reith left the BBC for Imperial Airways in June 1938 this was the end not only of a régime but of an era. New forces were re-leased inside Broadcasting House which were to produce changes with which Reith was often out of sympathy, and the manner of the break had its profound sadness. Yet there could be no doubt whatever concerning the extent of Reith's contribution not only to the history of the BBC but to the development of broadcasting as an agent in human history. 'The BBC is not without its critics', *The Times* wrote, 'and never should be. But Sir John can leave Broadcasting House with the knowledge that his pioneer work, now brought to maturity, has not to wait for posterity. His con-temporaries can measure their debt to his vision, his energy and even his obstinacy.'[2] The verdict stands. Reith dominates history as he dominated the contemporary scene.

Without Reith British broadcasting would have been differ-ently organized and, more important, differently guided throughout the whole of the period covered in this volume. He, in the last instance if not in the first, was the man who determined what 'the activity of broadcasting' should be. 'A decade and a half ago', wrote *The Economist*, which always took an independent line on BBC matters, 'a few discriminating people

B.B.C.

D.G.   *Editor, Ariel .*

Thank you for your message.
The work to which I have been asked
to go is of great importance — but you
can maybe imagine how I feel about
leaving the B.B.C. and B.B.C. Staff.
I try not to think about it.

J. C. W. Reith .

June 16.1938.

3. Sir John Reith's Farewell Message to the Editor of *Ariel*

realised that a monopoly of the use of the air for broadcasting might have very serious hidden dangers. Today . . . as a result of Sir John's work . . . it is clear to the whole world that the right of expressing opinion through the microphone may be one of the most powerful, if not *the* most powerful instrument for good or evil; and that the power of controlling the know-ledge of events which is vouchsafed to the people of a country may spell the difference between their being slave or free.'[1]

Such tributes were universal. Reith was only forty-eight years old when he left the BBC for pioneer work of a different kind. Yet the decision to end this volume with the war and not with Reith's departure is a recognition of the fact that by 1938 the BBC was something more than a projection of Reith. It was an institution which had a dynamic of its own. Some, at least, of the conflicts of personality, which followed his departure,

[1] *The Economist*, 18 June 1938.

had antedated it, and battles were already being waged about issues, particularly about listener research and the finance of television, which have a curious element of topicality about them.[1] There was even a serious discussion of sponsored television in 1939, not only in the BBC but in the Cabinet.

Reith was the outstanding personality in the BBC throughout the period from 1927 to 1938. Broadcasting is a co-operative activity, however, and behind the anonymous façade there were many other personalities who left their mark on major policies and many others whose coming—or going—altered institutional arrangements. Peter Eckersley, the Chief Engineer, who left for personal reasons in 1929, had more ideas about broadcasting than any other man in the country. Some he put into effect, some were never realized, and some never could have been. His successor, Noel Ashbridge, knighted in 1935, had worked with Eckersley since 1926 and represented the continuity which lies at the centre of the BBC. He made far-reaching projects possible, not least the start both of Empire broadcasting and of television. One of Reith's successors, Sir William Haley, thought so highly of him that he made him Deputy Director-General in 1943. Reith's choice for that office when Vice-Admiral Sir Charles Carpendale left the BBC a few months before Reith left it himself was Cecil Graves, knighted in 1939: he thought of Graves, indeed, as his own successor as Director-General.

Basil Nicolls, knighted in 1953, moved from Manchester to London in 1926, and was given the key post of Director of Internal Administration in 1933 when the division between the 'blue tab' and 'red tab' was put into effect. Later called Controller (Administration), he had great power within the hierarchy, and when Graves became Deputy Director-General, Nicolls took over his post as Controller of Programmes. Gladstone Murray, who had been with the BBC since 1924 in charge of a shifting empire of publicity and public relations, did not leave until 1936: part of his work then passed to Sir Stephen Tallents, who became Controller of Public Relations, a position from which he exerted increasing influence. He later brought in with him A. P. Ryan, who had been with him at the Empire Marketing Board, as Assistant Controller. Another man whose

[1] See below, pp. 616–19, 644.

brief sojourn at the BBC involved many changes of organization, if not of policy, was Colonel Alan Dawnay, who was appointed Controller of Programmes over the two 'Output Heads', Roger Eckersley, Peter's brother, the Director of Entertainment, and Charles Siepmann, the Director of Talks. Dawnay came from and returned to the Army. For a time he had seemed to Reith to be the answer to many problems.

Names can be multiplied, and many others figure frequently in these pages. Most operated at the level where the BBC was most properly judged by the public—at the level of programme production. Some were young men who were to acquire positions of influence in the future. There were others, however, who seemed in some sense to 'represent' the institution almost permanently—H. L. Chilman, the strict and forceful House Superintendent, and H. A. Plater and M. Arbuckle, to name only two of the Commissionaires. No organization becomes an institution until it has characters like these. They are, as a retired officer of the BBC has aptly called them, 'cornerstones'.[1] For the public, however, it was the programmes that counted, and it is with the production of programmes that this book begins.

[1] R. Wade, Manuscript History, *Early Life in the BBC*, p. 95.

II

PROGRAMMES AND THE PUBLIC

The elemental fact about broadcasting is its tremendous output. You may have all the authorities and restrictions and committees and regulations: but they are all defeated by the rapidity of successive programmes.

LIONEL FIELDEN
The Natural Bent (1960), p. 104

1. Programme Parade

THE social and cultural consequences of broadcasting depended not only on the philosophy of control which determined the decisions and actions of the controllers of the BBC but on the cumulative impact of daily programmes on a growing audience. The decisions of the controllers were often hidden from the public: the 'output' of the producers was the 'stuff of radio'. It was in terms of the range, the balance, and the quality of programmes that most people judged the BBC, whether they were press critics, like Sydney Moseley, Collie Knox, Gale Pedrick, or Jonah Barrington,[1] or ordinary listeners beside their own firesides. The *Radio Times*, which set out the details of weekly programmes, sold a million copies for the first time at Christmas 1927 and had a regular weekly circulation of three million by 1939.[2] Each day the popular newspapers had their regular ration of information and comment about programmes, backed by gossip about broadcasters.[3] There was a difference of degree rather than of kind between such information and comment and that provided in more specialized journals like *Popular Wireless*. The first number of one of the new journals of the period, *Radio Pictorial*, published in January 1934, well reflects the shift in interest from wireless as a technical hobby to radio as a social activity. A free crayon portrait of Henry Hall was issued to every reader, and in addition to a friendly message from Reith there were contributions from A. J. Alan, Christopher Stone, and Captain Wakelam. Arthur Henderson wrote on the theme 'Broadcasting Will End War' and Oliver Baldwin speculated ambitiously on what he would do if he were 'Governor of the BBC'. There was even a comic strip 'introducing the Twiddleknob Family'.[4]

---

[1] For Moseley, see S. A. Moseley, *Broadcasting in My Time* (1935); Collie Knox, who wrote regularly for the *Daily Mail*, touches on broadcasting in his *People of Quality* (1947).

[2] *Note by G. V. Rice, 1 Feb. 1928; *BBC Handbook* (1939), p. 146. For the history of the *Radio Times*, see below, pp. 281–6.

[3] The press had threatened in the early days of broadcasting to boycott BBC programme information. See *The Birth of Broadcasting*, p. 142, where the consequences of this attempt are discussed.　　　　[4] *Radio Pictorial*, 19 Jan. 1934.

Much of the information contained in the wireless columns and in some, at least, of the wireless journals was unauthoritative and even unreliable. A distorting mirror was being held up which accentuated the glossy and the bizarre. Yet broadcasters and producers themselves found it difficult to resist the temptation of seeing themselves as others saw them. 'If you were to see the interest with which producers and all who are engaged

4. The Twiddleknob Family as depicted by Arthur Ferrier

in the production of programmes at Savoy Hill rush for the morning papers to see what the critics have to say,' Eric Maschwitz, then editor of the *Radio Times*, told the first meeting of the Broadcast Critics' Circle in 1931, 'you would be amazed.'[1] Reith himself deliberately remained aloof. He was shocked by what he frequently regarded as deliberate 'misrepresentation', and he urged incessantly the need for 'honest criticism' of programmes which would concern itself not with gossip but with 'standards'.

The volume of criticism, fair or unfair, trivial or sensible, welcomed or resented, based on general criteria or on personalization, increased sharply during the 1930s, far more sharply than the volume of programme 'output', as the BBC inelegantly called it. According to BBC statistics, 65,800 hours of programmes were broadcast in 1927, great emphasis being placed on the fact that 'breakdown' time was only 0·07 per cent. of the total.[2] It is difficult to make precise comparisons between these figures and those of a later date because of the reduction in the number of transmitters and the increase in their range.

[1] Quoted in *Broadcasting in My Time*, p. 65. For the founding of the Circle, see S. A. Moseley, *Private Diaries* (1960), p. 310. Collie Knox proposed Moseley as President.

[2] *BBC Handbook* (1928), p. 55. The First Annual Report (Cmd. 3123, 1928) gives a figure of 'over 68,000'.

In 1935, however, the 'aggregate time for all transmitters', excluding the Empire Service, was not very different—68,796 hours, with a 'breakdown' time of 0·026 per cent. In 1938 the comparable figure was 79,525.[1] Behind these figures was an engineering achievement, none the less remarkable because it was increasingly taken for granted. The term 'technical hitch', which had been born in the early years of the Company, ceased to inspire easy jokes. The development of a hidden network of telephone landlines transformed the techniques of transmission. As the interchange of programmes became more complex, the engineers never failed to accomplish what was required of them.

Both at the beginning and the end of the period the hours of broadcasting were severely restricted. The main Daventry station (5XX) did not begin its daily programme in January 1927 until 10.30 a.m., when the shipping forecast was read twice—once at normal reading speed and then slow enough for long-hand dictation. There was then a gap until the mid-afternoon, when school broadcasts took place in term time, with a variation on Thursday afternoons when there was a broadcast of Evensong from Westminster Abbey. On Saturday afternoon there was no broadcasting at all except for occasional outside broadcasts of outstanding special interest, and Sunday broadcasting was kept to a minimum. In January 1927 it did not begin until after the end of the evening service in church and chapel. Proposals made by the Assistant Controller of Programmes at a Control Board meeting in December 1926—that both Daventry and 2LO (London) should provide daily morning music at 10.45 a.m. and on Saturday light music between 1 p.m. and 2 p.m.—were not accepted.[2]

During the course of 1927 there was some extension of hours, including an extra hour of light music from London between noon and 1 o'clock, but the new experimental station at Daventry, 5GB, the first transmitter in the world designed to provide an alternative programme, was on the air only from 3 p.m. to midnight. Morning programmes took shape only slowly with the morning religious service, introduced in January 1928, providing a 'fixed point' which still remains.[3] Morning talks

---

[1] Cmd. 5088 (1936), p. 22; Cmd. 5951 (1939), p. 25.
[2] *Control Board Minutes, 7 Dec. 1926.
[3] For the history of the morning service, see below, pp. 229–33.

started on 5XX in January 1929, and a year later 5GB began
to operate at noon instead of 3 o'clock. In 1930 the programme
from Daventry 5XX became known as the 'National' programme, and that from 'Daventry Experimental 5GB' as the
'Regional' programme.

Yet the beginning of the main Regional programme along
with the extension of regional programmes from the provinces
did not add significantly to the hours of broadcasting.[1] It was
not until the end of 1932 that 'continuous' broadcasting took
place every Saturday from noon to midnight: a few months
later, in September 1933, a 'silent period' between 6.15 p.m.
and 8 p.m. on Sundays was filled in. The opening of a new
transmitter at Droitwich in 1934 meant that listeners had the
choice of alternative programmes from Monday to Friday from
10.30 a.m. to 6 p.m. and from 6.30 p.m. until 11.15 p.m., but
in the same year an important Programme Revision Committee
stated that there was no case, 'on programme grounds', for
beginning general programmes before 10.45 a.m., the hour
agreed upon as a 'concession' to the radio manufacturers, or for
extending the hours of transmission beyond midnight. Alternative afternoon programmes also were primarily provided not
to satisfy the listening habits or preferences of the 'great audience' but to meet 'the requirements of the trade'.[2] When war
broke out in 1939 there was still no broadcasting before the
daily service at 10.15 a.m., and there were no regional variations in the afternoons before the start of Children's Hour.

The gradual increase in programme output over the whole
period was associated with the provision of more 'alternative'
programmes as more transmitters became available and with
changes in 'balance' between different types of programmes.
In January 1927 not only was output restricted, but there was
little choice. Daventry (5XX) and London (2LO) in no sense
provided alternative programmes for those listeners who could
receive both stations: 5XX, indeed, was intended to extend
coverage, not to provide choice. Yet there had been talk of
alternative programmes as early as September 1924, when it had

---

[1] For the technical and organizational aspects of the development of 'National'
and 'Regional' broadcasting, see below, pp. 293 ff.
[2] *Report of the Programme Revision Committee (1934), pp. 2, 3.

been suggested, without much thought, that a second London station should cover 'high brow education and better class material' while old 2LO should transmit a 'popular programme'.[1] A. R. Burrows, the first Director of Programmes, actually went so far as to produce a scheme based on the assumption that there should be 'two opposite types of programme each night'. This was turned down after Carpendale had called it 'a drastic and expensive change in our present procedure'.[2]

Talk of alternative programmes had scarcely affected current programme policy by the time that the Corporation took over from the Company, but it shaped the idea of the 'Regional Scheme', based on the transmission of alternative programmes —one 'universal' and one 'regional'—and it was in Reith's mind in all his private and public deliberations. Peter Eckersley made it the cornerstone of his engineering policy.[3] While the *Observer* was still heading its weekly wireless column 'The Programme and the Listener', the BBC was beginning to promise 'contrasting' programmes. 'Universal' programmes would be offered which would not call 'fundamentally' for the undivided attention of the listener: 'speciality' programmes, whether talks, music, news, or variety, would require fuller and more deliberate and sustained listening.[4]

This was, however, a pledge for the future. The local stations of the BBC in January 1927 were not providing their programmes as alternatives: indeed, the Corporation placed emphasis rather on the extent to which local stations were adopting 'simultaneous broadcasting', what would now be described as simultaneous 'network' programmes. The first Programme Board of the BBC was a by-product not of the development of 'alternative' programmes but of the growth of simultaneous broadcasting, and its first name was the Simultaneous Programmes Board.[5] It was admitted in 1928 that while the conception of a balance of programmes had been known for years to the BBC programme builders, 'the possibilities of contrast are as yet for the most part unexplored. . . .

[1] *Control Board Minutes, 23 Sept. 1924.
[2] *Memorandum from the Controller to the Managing Director, 28 Oct. 1924: 'With reference to Two Programmes Operating from London.'
[3] See below, pp. 295–6.   [4] *BBC Handbook* (1928), p. 67.
[5] See *The Birth of Broadcasting*, p. 217.

It is a principle only less concrete than the principle of "balance" because the latter has been clothed with flesh and blood by experience.'[1]

It is tempting to trace the development of what happened to alternative programmes after 1928 with the contemporary problems of television in mind. There was, indeed, in 1928 and 1929 a growing recognition inside the BBC that much popular criticism of BBC programmes would be softened if listeners had a real choice. 'We want entertainment, not instruction', a listener calling himself 'A Sufferer' had written during one of the frequent anti-BBC campaigns of 1928. 'Cannot a meeting of protest be called? I am afraid it would require a very large space.'[2] Although the BBC did not lack eloquent defenders in this press controversy, it was clearly more likely to attenuate controversy if both entertainment and what 'A Sufferer' had called over-comprehensively 'instruction' were both on offer. It is possible, however, to make too much of the comparison between sound radio and television and of the distinction between 'entertainment' and the rest. It is perhaps more useful to note that it was not until after the end of the period covered in this volume—not until 1945 and 1946—that the sound audience was divided into 'home, light, and third'. As regional broadcasting developed, alternative programmes were devised not on the basis of broadcasting for different types and sizes of audience, ranging from the 'popular mass audience' to the 'cultural minority', but of offering to listeners everywhere a choice of two programmes, each of which was felt to be balanced.

The framers of policy in 1928 asked the question 'By what principle of contrasted programmes is it possible to ensure that the great majority of listeners will be able to find one of the two programmes available at a given time suited to their tastes?' The distinction between 'high brow' and 'low brow' was once again explicitly rejected: so too was the distinction between a 'spoken word' programme and a 'continuous music' programme. Instead, emphasis was placed on a choice, at any given time, between a programme demanding 'concentrated listening' and a programme suited to 'more casual listening'. No assumptions were made about patterns of taste. The principle of contrast

[1] *BBC Handbook* (1928), p. 74.   [2] *Evening Standard*, 19 July 1928.

was designed rather to meet changes of mood, to satisfy people who might usually prefer 'serious chamber music' or reading, but who might also want to have the chance of relaxing with 'a military band or musical comedy programme which would normally leave them uninterested'.[1]

After 1930, therefore, when National and Regional programmes were both being transmitted, it was assumed that on each wavelength, at any given time, a cross-section of the 'great audience' would be listening. The National programme and the composite Regional programme were compounded of the same elements. Given such assumptions, the role of the 'programme builder' was of strategic significance. Assembling ideas for the week's programmes, injecting new ideas of his own, organizing them into a coherent whole, which would set out to please the listener rather than the producer, was a task at least as interesting and important as that of the producer himself. Yet by its nature it was bound to be as hidden from the public eye as the work of the engineers.

It was also bound by its nature to be something of an irritant to independent minded or idiosyncratic producers. Nicolls used to quote within the BBC the tart remark of the creative writer: 'Now Barabbas was a publisher.' Lindsay Wellington, who joined the BBC in 1924, became Presentation Director in October 1933 and was Director of Programme Planning in 1935 —early stages in a long and distinguished BBC career—emphasized the need for diplomacy in the task of programme planning, for maintaining 'a firm web of confidence and respect'. 'The whole operation', he has stated, 'was rather like doing a jig-saw puzzle in such a way that the final picture not only worked in the sense of pieces fitting together, but also made the particular pattern willed by the chief policy makers who neither cut the pieces themselves nor knew much about them.' He thought of himself as a middleman between administrators and the makers of 'high policy' on the one hand and 'creative artists' on the other, but he recognized that the 'editorial or sub-editorial' function had considerable effect on policy as it was actually carried out.[2] Planning was not made the easier in that it was carried out eight weeks in advance.

[1] *BBC Handbook* (1929), p. 58.
[2] Oral evidence and Notes supplied in June 1963

Some flexibility was possible, but inevitably a sense of immediacy was not always easy to achieve.

Two of the most interesting and revealing articles on 'programme building' appeared in the special Broadcasting Number of *The Times* in 1934.[1] It was pointed out definitively by the writer of one of them that 'you cannot compile programmes as you would a Bradshaw', and some of the difficulties—and opportunities—were listed by him. 'One thing only is certain', he concluded, 'and that is that it is quite impossible to please listeners all the time, and it would be a help if those who are regular, or even intermittent, listeners, would pick their programmes, instead of turning on at random and expecting to get what they want.' The writer of the second article examined the concepts of 'contrast' and 'balance' with some care. 'Every broadcaster is permanently engaged on the search for positive programmes which have positive content, and positive programmes tend to annoy those whom they do not delight. Their very existence in a programme plan depends, therefore, on the success of a parallel search for programmes to offset them which will allay the irritation which might otherwise end by driving them out of existence altogether.' There was, however, no obvious formula. The oldest idea that speech should be balanced by music 'pushed simplification to the point of nonsense'. The newest ideas of 'robust alternatives' were not very helpful either, for definitions of robust alternatives were almost as various as definitions of 'a good programme'. There were only two principles to which the programme builder should usefully cling—first, 'to contrast an extreme with a mean and not with the opposite extreme', and second, 'to refuse in the last resort to sacrifice good programmes to good contrast'.

Given that each programme had to be balanced within itself, in what did the balance consist? 'There is a satisfaction both to the builder and to the listener when the component parts of an evening's programme follow smoothly on one another with the links between them accentuated by careful presentation. On the other hand, if careful listening is, as has been said, a reasonably arduous occupation, is it not better that the component parts should contrast with one another? The latter view tends to hold the field at present, because it seems im-

[1] *The Times*, Broadcasting Number, 14 Aug. 1934.

possible for any one to listen carefully to the whole of an evening's broadcasting without suffering from mental indigestion.
The BBC has always held the belief (or hope) that the critical
listener will make his own choice from what is offered and will
not swallow broadcasting whole.'

The position did not change substantially between 1934 and
1939, although the number of regional stations increased and
there was intermittent—and often highly vociferous—pressure
throughout the period for what later became known as a 'light
programme'. The one official reference to BBC policy on 'alternative programmes', in 1938, was less illuminating than *The
Times* articles of 1934.

The alternative programme service consists of a National and a
Regional programme [listeners were told in 1938]. The National
programme, transmitted by the high-power, long-wave station at
Droitwich and by three auxiliary medium-wave stations, is intended
for reception throughout Great Britain and Northern Ireland. There
is one main programme alternative to the National programme . . .
which originates largely in London, but to which Regions contribute. This 'Regional' programme is always transmitted by the
London Regional Station. Parts of it are included in the programmes
of other Regions, and broadcast simultaneously by their transmitting
stations. The programmes of the individual Regions are planned so
as to contrast as far as possible with the National programme, and
contain certain items of particular interest to listeners in various local
areas. Each Region can work independently or in conjunction with
any other Region as required.[1]

For most of the period covered in this volume the weekly
organization of programmes was considered weeks ahead by a
Programme Board or Committee which had held its first meeting in May 1924.[2] From April 1926 until the reorganization of
1933, its chairman was Roger Eckersley, who was styled
Assistant Controller (Programmes) and later Director of
Programmes. Meetings of the committee were attended by the
heads of 'the output departments' as they were called, along
with other full-time or part-time members of the BBC's staff,
including Filson Young, who was employed for many years as
an outside critic, and representatives of other BBC departments

[1] *BBC Handbook* (1938), p. 59.
[2] See above, pp. 26–27 and *The Birth of Broadcasting*, pp. 207–8, 217, 260.

—Engineering, Public Relations, and Administration. The average attendance was between twelve and fifteen. It was the main task of this committee to shape the programmes of the week under review in the light of suggestions already considered 'at a lower level'. A subsidiary task was to comment on programmes which had been broadcast during the previous week. The fact that programmes had to be planned so far ahead was primarily due to the *Radio Times* arrangements for printing and distribution, and also to the need for projected plans to circulate around the regions. The weekly programme sheet was not complete, indeed, until contributions had been asked for from the regions.

After the meeting of the Programme Committee ended, it was left to individual producers and programme builders to clothe the skeleton with flesh—to collect scripts, to hire artists (with the help of the contracts executives), and to rehearse. The work was continuous. While the script-writing, hiring, and rehearsing went on, the individual producers would also be hatching new ideas which, if they survived scrutiny at the lower level, would ultimately make their way up to the Programme Committee.[1]

Unfortunately, the minutes of the Programme Committee do not survive for the period from 1927 to 1933. We have it on Roger Eckersley's authority, however, that 'in scrutinising the programmes, the lay-out, content, contrast between alternative programmes, financial implications and balance as between the various ingredients had to be considered. Each departmental head would quite properly try to get as much representation of his own material as possible. Argument was encouraged, and some of the comments made on someone else's programme might be extremely caustic and as hotly defended.'[2] Eckersley adds discerningly that while his brother Peter was very critical in the press and in his books after he left the BBC concerning the programmes broadcast, he was not particularly critical while he was at the BBC, either at the meetings of the Programme Committee or the Control Board.

The Control Board, set up as early as 1923, was the final

1 *The procedures are set out in an undated note by Graves called 'Notes on the Preparation of a Broadcast Programme'.
2 R. H. Eckersley, *The BBC and All That* (1946), p. 97.

factor in the reckoning. It carried out its deliberations at the apex of the BBC's internal committee structure, surveying 'high policy', which always included major developments or changes in programme policy. It was attended by 'controllers', any of whom could take along with him departmental chiefs for the discussion of special items. It was at this meeting that some of the most interesting and important general discussions about programmes took place—what part, for instance, to assign to the regional stations, whether to change the shape of broadcasting on Sundays, or how to deal with political, industrial, and religious controversy.

There was no agenda for the meetings, but minutes were kept and circulated. They cover a wide range of items of almost every kind. In January and February 1927, for example, there were discussions not only about education, talks, regional engineering, relay stations, and whether or not to abolish the Programme Board, but about whether to revert to the practice, only recently abolished, of referring in Children's Hour programmes to 'aunts' and 'uncles': it was suggested that the titles of 'aunt' and 'uncle' were not objectionable in themselves, but only when they were applied to men and women 'who had to carry outside the dignity of senior organising officials'.[1] In January and February 1938 there were protracted discussions not only about wireless exchanges and the opening of the Latin American service but about George Black's ban on his theatre artists taking part in television.[2]

The pattern of Programme Board (or Committee) plus Control Board did not survive unchanged throughout the whole of the period covered in this volume. As a result of the appointment of Colonel Alan Dawnay as Controller (Programmes) in 1933 and the major organizational changes which followed in consequence,[3] Control Board meetings were terminated and 'the Director-General's Meetings' took their place. The Programme Board ceased to exist in its old form at the same time, but a 'Programme Meeting' remained under the chairmanship of

[1] *Control Board Minutes, 5 Jan. 1927, 15 Feb. 1927. For the decision of Nov. 1926 to drop the titles of 'aunt' and 'uncle', see *The Birth of Broadcasting*, p. 261.
[2] *Control Board Minutes, 18 Jan. 1938, 22 Feb. 1938. For some of these developments, see below, p. 613.
[3] See below, pp. 443–9.

Dawnay himself.[1] By then the organization of programmes had become far more specialized than it had been in 1927, and there were 'Directors' of Entertainment, of Talks, of Religion, of Information and Publicity, of Empire and Foreign services, and, as we have seen, of Presentation.[2] In addition there was a scattered regional organization,[3] which later entailed monthly meetings with Regional Directors and quarterly meetings with Regional Programme Directors.

Dawnay's sojourn at the BBC was short, and there was a further reorganization in 1935 when he left the BBC to return to the Coldstream Guards.[4] Thereafter until 1939—and throughout the Second World War—two programme meetings were held each week. The first—on Thursdays—was called the Programme Committee,[5] and the second, held on Fridays, was called the Programme Board. The second body was the largest in the history of programme planning. It included, under the chairmanship of the new Controller of Programmes, Cecil Graves, the new Controller of Public Relations, Sir Stephen Tallents; it was at one of the early meetings of the reconstituted Board that it was agreed to recommend to the Director-General that a scheme of 'listener research' should be started.[6]

An analysis of the range of programmes broadcast shows how far the BBC was successful in realizing its objectives. The early balance of programmes may be illustrated from the table opposite, which gives a breakdown of the kind of programmes broadcast in the third week of October in 1927, 1928, 1929, and 1930. Some of the programme constituents remained remarkably constant—the time devoted to Children's Hour, for instance, or the proportion of transmission hours given over to the 'spoken word'. There are some surprises. Drama and features took up little of programme time, and school broadcasting always accounted for more hours than religion. A place

[1] See below, p. 435.
[2] For the process of differentiation, see below, pp. 445–6.
[3] See below, p. 336.
[4] *Programme Board Minutes, 4 Oct. 1935.
[5] For its first few meetings it was known as the Programme Sub-Committee.
[6] *Programme Board Minutes, 2 Oct. 1936. For the history of Listener Research, see below, pp. 256–80.

PROGRAMME CONSTITUENTS

One week in October 1927, 1928, 1929, and 1930

		1927	1928	1929	1930 Nat.	1930 Reg.
Total hours and minutes of transmission		77 hrs. 35 m.	80 hrs.	78 hrs. 55 m.	*Nat.* 78 hrs.	*Reg.* 68 hrs.

PERCENTAGES OF PROGRAMME TIME

		1927	1928	1929	1930 Nat.	1930 Reg.
Classical Music	Opera (whole or part, not excerpts)	..	..	..	..	6·22
	Orchestral (with soloists)	10·10	5·63	7·38	7·45	6·59
	Chamber Music	0·64	3·13	3·27	..	1·83
	Instrumental Recitals	4·73	5·94	4·12	2·98	5·37
	Song Recitals	0·32	1·15	0·95	3·30	..
	Cantatas, Oratorios, Church Music	..	..	..	..	..
	Total:	15·79	19·40	19·32	14·69	20·01
Light Music	Orchestral, Band, Small Combination (with soloists)	21·28	7·60	11·30	7·02	18·49
	Operetta, Comic Opera, Musical Comedy	1·83	..	..	1·59	1·22
	Ballad or Chorus Song Recitals	..	4·58	0·85	0·64	2·20
	Café, Restaurant, or Cinema Organ	6·34	9·69	11·72	11·58	13·93
	Total:	29·45	21·87	23·87	20·83	35·84
Dance Music		16·43	11·56	9·92	11·48	19·76
Gramophone Records		1·29	7·50	6·96	2·55	0·73
Drama		..	0·63	2·53	1·49	3·05
Features		..	1·04	1·27	..	..
Light Entertainment	Music Hall, Vaudeville, Cabaret	3·97	3·44	3·06	3·19	..
	Revue	..	..	..	2·55	1·83
	Star Entertainer or Celebrity	1·29	1·25	0·32	0·32	..
	Total:	5·26	4·69	3·38	6·06	1·83
Children's Hour		5·80	5·63	5·70	6·08	..
Spoken Word	News and Weather Forecasts	4·51	6·24	4·75	9·05	9·02
	Ministry and Society Bulletins	0·75	0·52	0·85	0·64	..
	Talks and Discussions	9·13	7·92	8·87	11·17	6·83
	Poetry and Prose Readings	0·21	0·31	0·64	0·64	0·37
	Appeals	0·11	0·10	0·11	0·11	0·12
	Total:	14·71	15·09	15·22	21·61	16·34
Outside Broadcasts	Running Commentaries	1·29	..	..	1·38	..
	Ceremonies	..	..	0·76	..	..
	Speeches	..	..	0·64	0·64	..
	Total:	1·29	..	1·40	2·02	..
Religion		2·25	4·05	3·80	5·32	2·44
School Broadcasts		7·09	8·54	6·65	7·87	..
Interludes	'Fill ups' advertised in *Radio Times*	0·64	..	..	..	..
	TOTAL:	100	100	100	100	100

was deliberately left for chamber music 'of an advanced and difficult order' and for talks on 'intricate subjects'.[1]

While the BBC was considering the implications of the Regional Scheme, it envisaged some differences in the 'balance' between programmes on the Regional and the National transmitters. In fact, however, the difference did not develop as had been anticipated. The Daventry 'experimental' station, 5GB, had devoted more of its experimental time in 1928 and 1929 to light entertainment than 5XX, which later became the National transmitter: by 1934, however, there was more light entertainment on the National than on the Regional service. Gramophone records had accounted for only 0·25 per cent. of 5GB's experimental time in 1928 and 1929—an exceptionally low figure—as against 9·67 per cent. of 5XX's time, but by 1934 the National figure was 7·12 per cent. and the Regional figure 10·87 per cent.

There was a notable extension of the use of gramophone records in 1934, not only for background or interval music but for whole programmes of serious, light, and dance music. Surprisingly, however, they were not referred to as such in the comprehensive Report of the Programme Revision Committee in that year. What the Report, like *The Times* articles, did show was that the same conception of 'programme balance' dictated the pattern of evening broadcasting from both National and Regional transmitters. Many programmes, indeed, were 'diagonalized', that is to say they were sent out first on the National or Regional wavelengths and then repeated—live —on the other wavelengths on a different evening and usually at a different time. 'Diagonalization' was thought of as a means not only of giving listeners the chance of hearing a programme which they had missed at the first broadcast, but of 'conserving effort' and 'controlling finance'.

The role of specifically regional broadcasting from the various regional stations was severely limited in practice,[2] but the close association between the National and the composite Regional programme transmitted on 5XX was something more than the reflection of centralizing prejudice or financial stringency. It derived in part, at least, from Reith's desire not to divide 'the great audience' more than was necessary. Britain

[1] *BBC Handbook* (1929), p. 58.   [2] See below, pp. 306 ff.

was a small country: could it not be held together as one? Every part of it deserved not what it was getting through the media of existing cultural and entertainment facilities, but 'the best'. It was in an effort to give it 'the best' that 'diagonalization' was supplemented by what was known as the 'Phi' system. By this system, which went back to 1924, programmes of outstanding public interest or artistic value—a national talk by a national celebrity or a concert by Toscanini—were made obligatory for all BBC stations. These 'three-star' programmes were 'universal'. Two-star programmes were recommended to the regions by Broadcasting House, but could be argued about: it was open to regions to suggest acceptable alternatives. One-star programmes could either be accepted or rejected by the regions.[1] 'Thus,' according to Reith, 'with due regard, financial and otherwise, to what regions could efficiently and worthily do—national and regional interests, characteristics and capabilities were reconciled.'[2]

There was also a deeper level of the argument. The 'great audience' was conceived as an audience whose tastes and interests could develop over time. Listeners hearing the 'best things' might begin by condemning and end by demanding. Segmentation would reflect tastes and interests as they were: 'national' programmes would develop tastes and interests dynamically, changing some minorities into majorities or, at the least, increasing their size and influence. Broadcasting could enlarge horizons, both artistically and politically. Artistically Reith believed that it could do much to engender new cultural interests—in music and drama, in particular: politically it could serve as an instrument of integration in a divided community.

The contrast in these respects between the work of the BBC and the work of the other agencies of mass communication was often pointed out during the period. Music was usually taken as the classic case, and there was powerful evidence later, during the Second World War, that radio had in fact helped to bring into existence a new audience for serious music.[3] As

[1] The system is briefly described in J. C. W. Reith, *Into the Wind* (1949), p. 299.
[2] Ibid.
[3] See B. Ifor Evans and M. Glasgow, *The Arts in England* (1949); Lord Bridges, *The State and the Arts* (Romanes Lecture, 1958).

early as 1930, indeed, Reith had pointed out that 'whereas *x* hours of good music in the old days brought forward one hundred letters of protest, one hundred *x* hours of good music today bring forward not ten thousand letters of protest but only fifty'.[1] Drama provided an equally good example. When in 1929 a number of West End theatre managers sought to limit or even eliminate all radio criticism of the stage, some of their most influential colleagues, led by C. B. Cochran, replied that 'we are confident that BBC criticism brings the theatre to the notice of many people into whose lives the theatre has not hitherto entered, and this creates an audience which did not before exist'.[2] In the political world *The Economist* once stated that BBC news had 'helped to give the British public a power of discrimination which has exercised a salutary influence on the Press and the screen'. And 'if unbiased information tends to break down the barriers of party feeling and thereby to make the traditional organization of democracy on a party basis more difficult and uncertain, it has unquestionably helped to consolidate the feeling for democracy itself'.[3]

Many writers generalized from particular instances and argued that the development of the power of discrimination was also assisting the emergence of a 'common culture'. Every listener was given equal access to the best, and although some rejected it—unheard or hearing without listening—others learned how to appreciate and to understand. If in 'the Age of the Cinema' 'the most amazing perfection of scientific technique' was all too often being devoted 'to purely ephemeral objects, without any consideration of their ultimate justification',[4] sound radio was seeking to reinforce what was lasting. Not that the influence moved in one direction only. Experts were learning how to communicate not with other experts but with the 'public', and 'minorities' which otherwise would have been forced into increasing segregation were being subjected to 'the contagion of the majority'. There was an obvious sense in which sound radio contributed to a revival of what J. L. and Barbara Hammond called 'common enjoyment', an enjoyment

---

[1] Speech given in December 1930.
[2] Letter to *The Times*, 26 Oct. 1929.   [3] *The Economist*, 18 June 1938.
[4] A phrase of Christopher Dawson, quoted in R. C. Churchill, *Disagreements* (1950), p. 6.

which had been imperilled in industrial society since the great technical and social changes of the eighteenth and nineteenth centuries.[1]

One limitation and one qualification must be taken into the reckoning in assessing the weight of this interesting social argument. The limitation would have been true in any society. Broadcasting carries with it not only the opportunity of pushing forward the idea of a 'common culture' but the danger of 'standardization'. When Beatrice Webb visited Savoy Hill in 1925, she wrote of the 'admirable way in which the BBC is using this stupendous influence of wireless over the lives of the people—in some ways greater than the written word because it is so amazingly selective and under deliberate control—and on the whole an eminently right control'. She added, however, 'what a terrible engine of compulsory conformity, in opinion and culture, wireless might become'.[2] Hilda Matheson made the same point eight years later when sound radio had greatly extended its hold on the British public. 'Broadcasting may spread the worst features of our age as effectively as the best; it is only stimulating, constructive and valuable in as far as it can stiffen individuality and inoculate those who listen with some capacity to think, feel and understand. . . . Broadcasting is a huge agency of standardization, the most powerful the world has ever seen.'[3]

The BBC avoided the worst dangers of standardization during the inter-war years, particularly the kind of fragmentary and ephemeral standardization inherent in commercialized 'mass culture', but it avoided them only by deliberately following a conscious and continuous policy. It allowed for a broad, if not unlimited, exchange of views and a wide variety of programmes. The very fact, however, that the medium of sound radio permits centralized transmission to millions of people must always imply a threat as well as a challenge.

The qualification relates not so much to all societies as to

[1] For the idea of 'common enjoyment', see J. L. Hammond, *The Idea of Common Enjoyment* (The Hobhouse Memorial Lecture, 1930) and J. L. and B. Hammond, *The Age of the Chartists* (1933).

[2] M. Cole (ed.), *Beatrice Webb's Diaries, 1924–1932*, p. 81: entry for 25 Dec. 1925.

[3] H. Matheson, *Broadcasting* (1933), quoted in D. C. Thomson, *Radio Is Changing Us* (1937), p. 4.

British—or more particularly English—society as it was constituted during the 1920s and 1930s. It was a divided society,
divided both by bitterness and by complacency, and effective
social controls were always in the hands of 'privilege' of one
kind or another. Cultural configuration was itself an expression
of economic inequality and social and educational privilege.
Covent Garden was distinguished by its diamonds as well as
by its music; only 2 per cent. of the Second World War
audiences who watched plays sponsored by the Council for the
Encouragement of Music and the Arts had been to a stage play
before.[1]

The BBC, by the nature of its social context, never found
it easy fully to penetrate the working-class world which provided it with by far the largest part of its audience. It was
partly a matter of personnel. Roger Eckersley, for example,
once feigned complete ignorance of the fact that by far the
largest section of British society ate high tea and not dinner.
It was also a matter of posture and attitude. BBC announcers
wore dinner jackets; their enforced impersonality clashed
sharply with the powerful working-class instinct to stress the
personal in every aspect of human relationships.[2] The language
of discourse—accent, vocabulary, style—was so separate that
it was always a matter of 'them and us'. There were excellent
reasons for paying special attention to the training of announcers
and for the encouragement of good standard English—G. B.
Shaw was, after all, a member of the Spoken English Advisory
Committee[3]—but there were also, as Shaw never failed to point
out, all kinds of social and cultural complications.

In such circumstances to talk of common culture is exaggerated, and at its most rhetorical the talk is dangerously misleading. In an early contribution to the *Radio Times* G. K.
Chesterton expressed the view that it was 'a good thing indeed'
for the 'masses'—a dangerously patronizing word—to listen to
the words of Lord Curzon: he did not add that it would have
been at least equally good 'if his lordship could, by means of
radio, have listened to the views of the people'.[4] There was

[1] *The Arts in England*, p. 44.
[2] See R. Hoggart, *The Uses of Literacy* (1957), ch. iv, 'The Real World of People'.
[3] See below, pp. 467 ff.
[4] *Radio is Changing Us*, p. 19.

always a difficult problem of human communication, even if it was never of the BBC's making, and it was well stated, where we would expect it to be well stated, if it was to be stated at all, in the BBC's schools broadcasting service. One of the most influential members of the Central Council for School Broadcasting, G. T. Hankin, an Inspector of Schools, frequently warned against a 'middle-class point of view'. 'Historically we have long believed in games and sports for the rich and are only just beginning to realize the need for organized leisure for the poor' was one of his comments on a suggestion that the full weight of BBC persuasion should be employed to press working-class children to join youth clubs.[1] On a different occasion he objected strongly to a proposed history pamphlet. 'Herewith the typescript of the English history pamphlet with a good many criticisms. The whole attitude in the script seems to me middle-class. Our History is for the children of the workers.'[2]

Given the difficulties of social communication, the BBC did much if not to break the barriers down, at least to make one part of the community aware of the existence of other parts. It did not gloss over the cracks with a thin veneer of 'hearti-ness'. The period covered in this volume was one of quite exceptional economic and social strain—with a crisis in the world economy and alarming waves of mass unemployment. Against this background there were a number of radio talks and programmes which genuinely sought to explain the plight of the unemployed. Sir William Beveridge gave six talks on unemployment in 1931, following on a general series on the same subject; 'I feel that I should have liked leisure to make them a little more human', he commented after the last of his efforts.[3] There were no complaints of lack of humanity concerning talks on the same subject given by John Hilton from 1933 onwards. Hilton, indeed, knew how to talk not only about the unemployed but to them, in his own words 'making them laugh, teasing them and saying occasionally a silly thing and occasionally a wise one' but, above all, being just himself.[4] Hilton's range of subjects was wide, from industrial relations

[1] *Hankin to Miss Gibbs, 7 Apr. 1938.
[2] *Hankin to A. C. Cameron, Oct. 1938.
[3] *Sir William Beveridge to C. A. Siepmann, 26 June 1931.
[4] E. Nixon, *John Hilton* (1946), p. 162.

to football pools: *This and That* was the title of the most successful of his series. He was never patronizing, and what N. G.
Luker, then a talks producer, called his 'great belief in the man
in the street' was a sincere belief and not a pose. There were
many other people who felt, however, as did one speaker
deliberately chosen to confront him in debate, that 'all this
talk about Tom, Dick and Harry is largely rubbish'.[1]

There is evidence that the BBC was far more anxious than
many of its critics genuinely to probe 'the condition of England' during the divided 1930s. In 1931 Beveridge was preparing conscientiously for a series of discussions on *Changes in
Family Life*, which entailed thorough social research by questionnaire.[2] The questionnaires themselves, which greatly interested
R. S. Hudson, then the Minister of Labour,[3] produced what
Beveridge called 'a splendid detonation in the press'.[4] There
were also vigorous protests against some of the talks in a *Whither
Britain?* series in 1934, the first of many series of talks arranged
by the BBC to plot the national destiny. The complaints were
certainly not stilled by H. G. Wells's opening talk in the series
in which he stated in his first sentence that what he said was
uncensored. 'The BBC is responsible for giving me this half
hour with you—but nobody on earth, except myself, is responsible, and nobody's approval has been asked, for the things I have
to say.'[5] Wells was an active controversialist, a dealer in provocative ideas. There was no dearth of BBC social reporting
either, although it always provoked far more vigorous protest
than social reporting does in the 1960s.

The protest, which must be examined in more detail,[6] often
expressed itself in political rather than social form. This was
inevitable, given the social basis of much of British politics.
Moreover, in an age when there was usually as much tension
between 'establishment' and *avant-garde* as between rich and
poor, there was a tendency on the right to confuse all forms
of novelty, including artistic and cultural novelty, with 'left-
wingism' and on the left to associate 'stuffiness' with all forms

[1] *N. G. Luker to Sir Richard Maconachie, 13 Oct. 1937.
[2] *Mary Adams to Beveridge, 29 July 1931.
[3] *Mary Adams to Beveridge, 1 May 1933.
[4] *Beveridge to Siepmann, 4 Feb. 1932 (copy sent to Reith).
[5] *The Listener*, 10 Jan. 1936.   [6] See below, pp. 128 ff.

of authority. 'An impression of left-wing bias is always liable to be created by any agency which voices unfamiliar views', Hilda Matheson wrote in 1933—in the light of experience. 'It does not always follow that the ideas themselves are of the left. In practice, they usually hail from every point of the compass. How is the inevitable fear they provoke to be reconciled with the spirit of open-minded enquiry which is inseparable from all education, from any search after truth?'[1]

The notion that all new ideas *inevitably* provoke fear is an alarming comment on the mood of the 1930s. Yet programme planners within the BBC, particularly planners of talks, were often confronted with inevitable reactions which they had to challenge or to ignore. They were also subject to attack from the left for not going far enough or for imposing an internal censorship on broadcasters whose views were thought to be dangerous. In 1932, for example, the *New Statesman* complained that 'official and orthodox pressure' inside the BBC was constantly permitted 'to keep out the expression of new ideas', although it sugared its complaint with congratulations to Reith for preserving the BBC from 'commercial influences' and paid a tribute to the BBC as a whole for offering 'a striking example of a self-governing autonomous Corporation'.[2] At the very time this complaint was being made, Reith was being attacked in private as well as public for allowing the BBC to 'subvert established ideas and spread left-wing propaganda'. Lord Hailsham was long convinced that the BBC was 'a disruptive influence',[3] and Sir Waldron Smithers was about to begin a long and tempestuous correspondence with the BBC. 'Cannot Parliament compel the BBC to abstain from using their monopoly for the purpose of socialist propaganda?'[4] Not all the critics were as far to the right as Sir Waldron Smithers.

In meeting the double-pronged attack, the BBC perhaps accepted too easily the simple test that if criticisms came from both left and right or from both highbrow and lowbrow, they somehow or other cancelled each other out. The test made it easy to defend the BBC in Parliament, but it did not follow that to limit argument or to promote the 'middle-brow' were

[1] *Broadcasting*, p. 199.   [2] *New Statesman*, 19 Nov. 1932.
[3] Reith, Diary, 22 Apr. 1934.
[4] *Sir Waldron Smithers to the Postmaster-General, 10 Mar. 1935.

proper objectives of programme policy. Cancelling out gives no guarantees of quality. In marginal matters, however, it is not easy to think of a more satisfactory test. There is always a genuine question as to the extent of freedom which 'a public corporation like the BBC can permit itself in exorcising . . . the sins and follies of Establishments of all kinds'. This was the language of another writer in the *New Statesman*, thirty years later, who concluded that 'there is a line to be drawn somewhere', and that somehow or other criticisms from both sides have not only to be met but to be encouraged.[1]

The implications of this argument were—and are—cultural as well as political. At a time when a number of young artists were grumbling that the BBC favoured safer and less unorthodox forms of expression, the BBC was being assailed from the opposite angle on the grounds that it presented too much 'modern music' or grand opera or even that it fostered '*avant-garde* philosophies'. 'We may sometimes feel', Ernest Barker remarked, 'that our broadcast programmes entertain us too loftily, and that a young and advanced aesthetic *élite*, encamped in the Parnassus of Broadcasting House, is seizing us by the hair of our heads to draw us into a modernist Paradise in which our feeble spirits faint.'[2]

What Barker noted professorially—from Cambridge—was often expressed quite unprofessorially outside. In one sense the programmes from Radio Luxembourg were an implicit comment.[3] A more explicit comment was made by a committee of the Radio Manufacturers' Association in a memorandum of 1935. For a year before this the R.M.A. had been strongly criticizing the content and timing of BBC programmes.[4]

The R.M.A. claimed that there was a 'public apathy' about radio which merited a careful testing of 'public reactions'. 'The fundamental contention is made that the general public—as distinct from any select section—demands a greater proportion of light entertainment and evinces a lesser interest in cultural broadcasts, education or serious entertainment.' No doubts

---

[1] *New Statesman*, 14 Dec. 1962.
[2] E. Barker, 'This Age of Broadcasting' in the *Fortnightly Review*, vol. 138 (1935).
[3] See below, pp. 362 ff.
[4] *Programme Board Minutes, 22 Feb. 1934.

were expressed as to whether such public demands provided adequate criteria for programme policy: it was simply assumed that they did.

A proper programme policy, the committee of the R.M.A. contended, should be concerned with light entertainment above all else. The key days of the week were Saturday and Sunday. On Saturdays there should be a proper choice of alternative programmes in the afternoon, with a concentration on 'Music Hall' in the evenings. On Sundays there should be no silent periods, and there should always be musical or dramatic alternatives to religious services. The fact that the increasingly active wireless relay exchanges were broadcasting foreign commercial programmes on Sundays was 'proof that the public desire that kind of broadcast'. On weekdays there should be early morning broadcasting from 6.30 a.m. with 'physical exercises, followed by a news survey, today's headlines and bright "tonic music" by the Military Band or Theatre Orchestra or records'. In the evening, 'if Athlone with a negligible revenue can broadcast a variety show every night, the BBC should be able to do one also'. There should be regular 'star features' each day on American lines, and fixed points within the week when the public would 'make its date with radio'. 'It is noted that the BBC already subscribe to, and practise this policy, but it is very significant that this applies only to such 'heavy' subjects as "Foundations of Music" and "Talks".'

Far too little money, it was suggested, was being spent on 'popular programmes'. Indeed no attention was paid to what should have been the guiding principle, that 'of spending most on that type of entertainment that has greater public appeal and least on those with minimum appeal'. 'It is our experience, based on close contact with the purchasing public, that of the two chief categories of listener—those who want entertainment which requires no special training to appreciate it, constitute eighty per cent of the public, and those who have a cultivated capacity for appreciating serious drama, talks, grand opera, chamber music and symphonies, represent no more than twenty per cent.' Perversely the BBC got its priorities upside down. *Wozzeck* cost 'well over a thousand pounds to broadcast' and four classic symphonies conducted by Toscanini more than £2,000: 'the Royal Command Performance was not broadcast because £750 was all the BBC would offer'. Money and hours went together. 'The incidence of time values should also be reversed and entertainment of popular appeal should occupy at least sixty per cent of the air time.'[1]

It is not difficult to construct a week's programmes along the lines envisaged by the R.M.A. They are familiar enough, and they would undoubtedly have had an obvious and immediate appeal. Had broadcasting taken this shape, however, there would have been an even greater element both of escapism and waste during the 1930s than there already was. Radio would not have been different from the other mass media: it would have been fully representative of them.

Some of the individual charges made by the R.M.A. were fair—a financial skimping, for example, in the provision of certain kinds of popular programme—and some of the individual changes it suggested have come about, notably the extension of broadcasting hours in the early morning. There was no philosophy at all behind the proposals, however, except the dubious pragmatism of giving the people what you believed them to want. There is certainly no evidence that 'commercialism' of this kind, particularly if practised by a public corporation, would have freed England from the invidious control of the 'Establishment', a post-war argument which was influenced as much by war-time experience as by memories of the pre-war BBC.

The matter was stated bluntly in the early 1930s by R. J. Smith of the Yale School of Law, in relation to the kind of influence exerted by commercial broadcasting in the United States. 'To the extent that private interests become more and more entrenched in this method of communication, it will be possible for them to exert more and more a censoring influence upon the types of all programmes which go before the public. If the question resolves itself between private censorship and public censorship, I take it that it is in the interests of the country that the censorship be public rather than private.'[2]

Although this view was challenged in 1934 by the National Association of Broadcasters in the United States, which echoed

[1] *Committee of the Radio Manufacturers' Association, Memorandum on Programmes, 1935.
[2] Quoted in *Broadcasting*, p. 236.

Winston Churchill in accusing the BBC of 'pontifical mug-wumpery', the National Association hardly put up an attractive case. It was not merely the London *Times* which pointed out that American strictures against the BBC 'emanated from an associa-tion which represents the American broadcasting trade gener-ally and had a vested interest to protect'.[1] However much some of the members of the Radio Manufacturers' Association might disagree with aspects of BBC policy, they had an immense respect for Reith's tenacity of purpose. At an R.M.A. lunch attended by Reith, he was loudly applauded, to his 'amaze-ment', when he said that there would never be jazz or variety on Sundays. He was told afterwards that while they quarrelled with what he said, they greatly respected him for saying it.

Throughout the period styles of American broadcasting con-tinued to generate far more criticism than praise in Britain.[2] At the height of the 1928 press debate, already mentioned,[3] one 'average listener' sharply attacked the view that America provided a model. 'American broadcasting', he stated, 'is designed for people who cannot concentrate.' He personally did not like 'sentimental songs, poetry reading, most talks, the news bulletins and Walford Davies'. Yet he did like the BBC. 'On my simplest set I am always able to hear what I like from 2LO or 5GB.'[4] This was before the days of alternative pro-grammes and when there was less range of BBC programmes than there was to be ten years later.

There is a fascinating account in Reith's Diary of a visit he paid in 1931 to the office of the Chairman of the Federal Radio Commission, General Sultzman, in Washington:

I told him roughly what the English arrangement was and asked him whether he did not think something of the sort would be possible here, beginning with the Federal Radio Commission taking more power and applying the public interest clause far more than the no censorship one. In other words could the Commission not assert itself now. At that point three of the four Federal Radio Commis-sioners trooped in. . . . This, I thought, is the Federal Radio Com-mission, of which one had heard so much, or rather four fifths of it. I was not impressed by them. They were all of a different type to

[1] *The Times*, 30 Jan. 1934.
[2] For criticism before 1927, see *The Birth of Broadcasting*, p. 347.
[3] See above, p. 28.   [4] *Evening Standard*, 11 July 1928.

the Chairman, and just what I would have expected political nominees to look like. . . . They all sat in a row and I facing them. I said I had just asked the Chairman an important question, which I then repeated; their reply was significant. He (Sultzman) said that it was for the other gentlemen to say. The meeting might well have reached a deadlock, because obviously they were all embarrassed. They did not know how much I knew of their position and of conditions generally in America, and there was considerable reserve. I thought the only way to clear it was to make a statement myself, showing that there was not much that I did not know. They exchanged looks with each other, smiled, settled themselves more easily in their chairs and we got properly down to it . . . they were immensely tickled with the idea that they should exert their powers.[1]

Two internal BBC committees took up positions radically different from that of the Committee of the Radio Manufacturers' Association and the National Association of Broadcasters in the United States. A Programme Revision Committee, headed by Colonel Dawnay just after he had been appointed to the new key post of Controller (Programmes), held thirty meetings in 1934 between the middle of January and the end of March. Its terms of reference were to review the suitability of programme timing, 'the correctness or otherwise of the present ratio between one type of programme and another', and the 'efficiency' (a curious word to choose) of the programmes as a whole. Dawnay was assisted by Roger Eckersley, who then held the post of Director of Entertainment, Siepmann, the Director of Talks, G. C. Beadle, the Entertainment Executive, and Lindsay Wellington, the Presentation Director.

The committee endorsed most aspects of existing BBC policy, including 'control' of the regions from London,[2] 'balance' of both National and Regional programmes, and refusal to determine the shape of programmes 'solely or even mainly by numerical consultations'. A few minor changes were suggested, however, in the light of outside comment. The Bach cantatas, which had been broadcast at regular times since May 1928, were to cease to have a 'fixed spot' on Sundays; adult education talks were to be reduced from five to three a week; an alternative to dance music was to be offered from 10 o'clock until 11.15 in the late evening; and continuous alternative programmes were

[1] Reith, Diary, May 1931.   [2] For this policy, see below, pp. 314 ff.

to be provided on National and Regional wavelengths from 10.45 a.m. to noon on all week-days and from noon to 6 o'clock on Mondays to Fridays, 'to meet the requirements of the wireless trade'. The committee also welcomed 'the recent relaxation' of Sunday broadcasting and 'considered that it might well be extended to admit of still lighter material for which there was a widespread demand. There might even be a talk at 9.5 p.m. on regular matters of national or international importance.' This anticipation of one of the great features of war-time broadcasting was treated very cautiously by Dawnay. 'The selected topic should not by its nature inspire or exacerbate acute or drastic controversy among listeners.'

Dawnay also had strictly limited interest in a 'brighter Saturday'. 'I am still extremely dubious with regard to any extension of alternatives on Saturday afternoons. The day-time alternatives agreed on working days, as a concession to the Trade, will be of the cheapest and simplest kind, gramophone records, cheap musical combinations and so forth, introduced purely for service purposes and without the general listener in view. If we were to have more alternatives on Saturdays, they would have to be of a totally different order, such as Symphony Concerts, plays and the like, which would be very expensive and for which it would be difficult to secure the additional material of the necessary quality.'[1]

The Report is hardly an exciting document, and Dawnay's comments are even less so. The suggested changes were timorous —they were too much like extorted concessions—and there was no clear policy about the scale or cost of light entertainment. The Regional Directors complained that they were insufficiently consulted.[2] Reith himself queried the tendency of the committee to reject all 'fixed points'—not only the fixed point of the Bach cantatas. 'As a listener I welcome fixity of a time; as a programme builder I should dislike it, but the programme builders must take at least as much cognisance of the convenience of listeners and the general efficiency of the service, which would, I think, lead to more fixtures than you have recommended.'[3] The argument about 'fixed points' was

[1] *Dawnay to Reith, 7 May 1934.
[2] *Dawnay to the Regional Directors, 30 July 1934.
[3] *Reith to Dawnay, 25 Apr. 1934.

to be put before the public in the Broadcasting Number of *The Times* in August 1934. 'There is undoubtedly a large class of listeners who like to know when to expect certain items. They look forward to their variety programme on Saturday night, their Symphony Concert on Sunday night. They would like to know that talks would always be given at the same time, and that they can turn on at the same time each night for the news. A certain amount of fixity of this kind is not only welcome but necessary, yet on the general grounds of good programme building the fewer fixed points the better chance there is of keeping the programmes changing and, therefore, fresher.'[1]

One of the Programme Revision Committee's recommendations marked a definite stage in the evolution of programme policy. 'During the early and more experimental days of broadcasting', the committee concluded, 'there was a tendency towards deliberate complexity in the techniques of presentation, which is now regarded as highly undesirable in itself': 'simplification' should now be the order of the day.[2] It is possible to read a certain complacency in this judgement also. Programme policy must always be experimental. The fact that some of the earlier experiments had been excessively complex and self-conscious did not mean that 'simplification' was the answer, even though the heads of all the departments of the Programme Division were said to be convinced of the case for 'simplicity in methods of production'.[3]

On the crucial question of balance, the Dawnay Committee thought that the ratios were 'about right'. Their breakdown of programmes (opposite page) related only to broadcasts given after 5.15 p.m. so that it is not strictly comparable with the figures given in the Table on p. 35. To make comparison easier, an independent breakdown of the programmes in the second week of October 1934 is given alongside the Committee's own figures.

The Committee suggested only one change—that there should be a slight decrease in the proportion of music on Sundays. The independent statistics suggest, however, that if balance was the objective throughout the week, there was far too much light music, far too little light entertainment, far too little drama,

---

[1] *The Times*, Broadcasting Number, 14 Aug. 1934.
[2] *Report of the Programme Revision Committee, 1934.
[3] *Note on General Programme Standards, 14 May 1935.

and far too few outside broadcasts. It should be added that one of the reasons why outside broadcasting figures seem so low was that there were considerable fluctuations from week to week and the week in question had an exceptionally small number. More important, however, was the unwillingness of many outside interests to allow the BBC to stage outside broadcasts at all.[1]

PROGRAMME CONSTITUENTS
One Week in October 1934
PERCENTAGES OF PROGRAMME TIME

	Dawnay Committee's figures	National Programme	Regional Programme
Classical Music	14	17·46	14·81
Light Music	16	29·08	43·02
Dance Music	13	8·55	9·97
Gramophone Records	Not given	7·92	10·87
Drama	3	2·79	0·90
Features	Not given	0·54	2·15
Light Entertainment	6	2·16	0·81
Children's Hour	8	..	4·85
Spoken Word	21	18·45	9·33
Outside Broadcasts	Not given	0·27	0·54
Religion	6	5·76	2·75
School Broadcasts	6	7·02	..
Miscellaneous	7	..	..
Total	100	100	100
Total Hours Broadcast	..	92 h. 35 m.	92 h. 50 m.

A detached scrutiny of the alternatives offered by the National programme and the composite Regional programme suggests that there was too little contrast. This was an important point which Dawnay's Committee completely overlooked. Some of the Regional Directors, who were asked their views after the committee had reported, made the point clearly. 'The feeling here is that the contrast as between National and Regional programmes is not entirely satisfactory', wrote G. L. Marshall from Belfast. 'It would seem that frequently the contrast is only between one type of music and another, say

[1] See below, pp. 77–79, 92–93.

for instance, the symphony as against a lighter type of concert, which does not seem to be sufficiently marked.' Marshall also suggested very pertinently that there was too much music of all kinds. 'It is the simplest form of entertainment to devise and produce but it is tending to encroach too much upon programme time as a whole.'[1]

Other regional officials complained that the main or composite Regional programme was being elevated at the expense of the subsidiary provincial programmes,[2] while one of the most enterprising young Programme Directors in the provinces, R. A. Rendall in Bristol, argued that for all the committee's certitude, 'we have little or no direct evidence that the present structure of programmes is satisfactory or otherwise. By direct evidence I mean overwhelming correspondence on any particular point, or anything in the nature of a statistical survey.'[3]

This was one of the chief points made in the second BBC Report, which was written by Dawnay's successor, Cecil Graves, in June 1936. Graves's Report was based on evidence collected from four committees, one dealing with Sunday programmes, the second with day-time programmes, the third with the main evening programmes, and the fourth with forward planning. Siepmann and Wellington were members of all four committees. Graves had made it clear on taking over his post that he wished to make changes. There was, he felt, 'insufficient live controversy in Talks' and 'subjects of a more provocative nature' should be discussed as they had been when Siepmann was Director of Talks from 1931 to 1935. There should be at least one straight variety programme of the music-hall type once a week. The Sunday evening concerts should be more 'popular' than they had been in the past. The 'monotony' of day-time programmes should be attacked, and there should be 'a gradual insertion of more programmes of other types than cinema organs, restaurant orchestras, and the like which fill the bulk of the day'. *Foundations of Music* had to go: 'I cannot allow general programme building to be blocked by the daily insertion at a fixed time of a feature which has now had a

---

[1] *Marshall to Dawnay, 19 Dec. 1935.

[2] *H. J. Dunkerley (Midland Region Programme Director) to Siepmann, 13 Dec. 1935.

[3] *The comments are quoted in E. R. Appleton (West Regional Director) to Siepmann, 17 Dec. 1935.

sufficiently long innings in its present form.' Finally he looked to 'an increased Regional contribution to the National and London (composite) Regional Programmes in 1936/7'.[1]

It was no surprise, therefore, that Graves's Report was far less complacent than the Report of 1934. It was recognized that programme planning required a much closer knowledge of listeners' backgrounds, habits, and preferences, even if the planners were not tied to the rule of giving the people what they wanted. 'In considering programme revision as a whole those concerned were faced at every turn with an absence of reliable evidence on which to base their judgments and recommendations.' Listener research was necessary if 'the Corporation was to rely mainly on its own professional judgment to produce the widest possible range of programmes, each good of its own kind . . . and to meet the reasonable demands of a considerable audience'. It was necessary also to have a more clearly defined programme policy. 'It seems evident that at present Heads of Departments and Regional Programme Directors are not conscious of a general Corporation policy and are uncertain as to the parts that they, individually, are expected to play.'

Future policy, it was suggested, should not ignore the style of treatment. 'The importance of presentation—or "showmanship"—should not be underestimated. Concentrated listening to broadcast programmes is not easy, and the devices of presentation should be used to catch and hold the attention.' Finally, the claims of the regions to a fuller life were acknowledged. 'Regions are neither separate entities nor . . . mere appendages of London. British Broadcasting regards itself as one unit, and all our plans are made co-operatively. Regional centres have two very important functions to fulfil: firstly, to take their share—and their share is on the increase—in contributing to the National Programme, and secondly, they have the important task of providing broadcasting material of a specialised and local kind for the benefit of listeners in their area.'[2]

Programme balance in the years after 1936 reflected to some extent at least the influence of this last big internal Report of the inter-war years.

[1] *C. G. Graves, Note on Programmes, 25 Mar. 1936.
[2] *C. G. Graves, Report of Programme Revision, June 1936.

PROGRAMME CONSTITUENTS
One Week in October

PERCENTAGES OF PROGRAMME TIME

	1936		1938	
	National Programme	*Regional Programme*	*National Programme*	*Regional Programme*
Classical Music	19·96	15·03	17·83	16·84
Light Music	21·90	38·81	23·02	31·84
Dance Music	8·88	8·00	4·59	9·24
Gramophone Records	10·73	9·18	6·93	11·71
Drama	1·32	1·62	3·03	1·65
Features	..	..	1·30	2·11
Light Entertainment	3·96	2·97	6·84	6·76
Children's Hour	..	4·86	..	6·58
Spoken Word	16·45	13·13	19·23	9·15
Outside Broadcasts	1·85	1·53	2·68	0·37
Religion	6·24	3·33	4·76	3·75
School Broadcasts	8·71	..	9·70	..
Interludes: Fill Ups, &c.	..	0·54	0·09	..
Total	100	100	100	100
Total Hours Broadcast	94 h. 45 m.	92 h. 35 m.	96 h. 15 m.	91 h. 5 m.

There was more light entertainment, an increase in outside broadcasting, and a fall, if not a substantial fall, in the proportion of light music. For purposes of comparison, it is interesting to examine a typical Sunday programme from one of the foreign commercial radio stations, Radio Normandie.[1] Sunday was the day when the BBC was most vulnerable:[2] it is a fair day to choose, however, since Radio Normandie was concentrating then on what it felt that the British listener really 'wanted'.

7.00 Radio Reveille
8.00 Sacred Music
8.15 Sing Song
8.30 (French News)
8.40 Astrology
8.45 'Musical Adventure' for Children
9.00 Cabaret
9.15 'Hit' Songs
9.30 Dance Music
9.45 Sports Review

10.00 Dance Music
10.30 Variety
11.00 Soloist
11.15 Variety
11.45 (French Programmes)
1.30 'Singing, Fun and Music'
2.00 Sponsored Show
2.30 'Teaser Time'
2.45 Light Music
3.00 Dance Music
3.30 Theatre Organ

[1] The day chosen is 18 June 1939.   [2] See below, p. 272.

4.00	Variety	10.00	'Motor Magazine'
4.45	'Personalities'	10.30	Cinema Organ
5.00	Sing Song	10.45	'Hit' Songs
5.15	'Discoveries'	11.00	'Musical Comedy Memories'
5.30	Variety	11.15	Variety
5.40	Dance Music	11.45	Light Music
6.00	Songs	12.00	'Melody at Midnight'
6.30	Variety	12.30	Dance Music
7.00	Crime Serial	1.00	'Goodnight Melody'
7.15	Light Music		Close Down
7.30	(French Programmes)		

Among the British artists who performed on Radio Normandie on this 'spot' day were George Formby, Tommy
Handley, Jack Warner, Vic Oliver, Bebe Daniels, Leonard
Henry, Olive Groves, Donald Peers, Anne Ziegler and Webster
Booth, Phyllis Robins, and Reginald Foort. The bill of fare
revealed what could be done if conceptions of balance were
thrown to the winds. It is interesting to add that at least one
attempt was made to capture John Hilton:[1] it failed because
Hilton had great respect for Reith's views.

Determining the balance of particular BBC programmes
was the work of the programme planners. They were the people
working 'in the line' who implemented general policies agreed
upon at a higher level. Their work was an art, not a science, a
difficult art which is not easily traceable in documents. It
rested, nonetheless, on certain general principles—first, that
different tastes should be catered for, including the tastes of
minorities, and second, that different views should be expressed.
'Experience has evolved a practical working rule', it was stated
in 1930. 'Give the public something slightly better than it now
thinks it likes': in consequence, 'the public becomes not less but
more exacting'.[2] Yet it was always impossible adequately to
cater for all minority tastes or to express all opinions. There
were limits set not only by time but by policy. Before scrutiniz-
ing the policy, it is important to note that it was the BBC itself
which determined it. The limits, it was felt both by Reith and
the programme builders, should be imposed neither by the Post
Office nor by the radio trade, and certainly not by government:
they should be determined within the BBC itself. The whole

[1] *Roger Wilson to Sir Richard Maconachie, 25 May 1937.
[2] *BBC Handbook* (1928), p. 71.

theory of the public corporation—with its monopoly powers—
was basic to this conception of autonomous programme policy.[1]
Freedom from government interference was one aspect of the
BBC's situation: freedom from the pressures of a market in
'mass culture' was the other. Yet freedom by itself does not
make policy. 'The BBC must lead, not follow, its listeners, but
it must not lead at so great a distance as to shake off pursuit.'[2]

The viability of this conception of broadcasting depended
upon four factors—first, a sense of responsibility on the part of
the BBC, responsibility coupled with enterprise, resource, and
confidence, equally necessary ingredients; second, the acceptance by Parliament of the 'system' of public service broadcasting, and, behind Parliament, on the acceptance of the 'system'
by a preponderance of the forces of opinion and interests which
Parliament reflected; third, the pressure of honest criticism and
the ability of the BBC to meet it; and fourth, so Reith would
always have said, the 'brute force of monopoly'.[3]

Monopoly made it possible for Reith successfully to resist the
kind of competitive pressures which, if unchecked, might have
turned broadcasting simply and solely into a provider of
entertainment: competition would have determined automatically the balance of programmes rather than leaving the
determination to policy-makers. Given that 'policy' was the
crucial factor, a combination of enterprise and responsibility
was essential. Responsibility without enterprise would have been
stuffy and uncreative: enterprise without responsibility would
have magnified criticism. It is interesting to note that press
critics like Sydney Moseley, who based their argument on quite
different premises from those of Reith, supported the general
policy. 'I am myself satisfied', Moseley wrote in a book with a
very wide circulation, 'that the early policy of the BBC, based
on the belief that the needs of broadcasting were specialized
and distinct from those of any other form of entertainment
whatever, was the right policy. And I am sure that Sir John
Reith was equally right in his determination to elevate the
public taste rather than play down to it.'[4]

[1] For the theory of the public corporation and its critics, see below, pp. 413 ff.
[2] *J. C. W. Reith, Draft on Broadcasting for a Blattnerphone Recording, 1931.
[3] J. C. W. Reith, *Into the Wind*, pp. 99–100. See also *The Birth of Broadcasting*, p. 238.
[4] *Broadcasting in My Time*, p. 223.

Collie Knox, the *Daily Mail* critic, did not go so far: he realized that 'public opinion polls'—very unscientifically conducted —were a good stick with which to beat the BBC. With Rugby and Sandhurst behind him, he was fascinated by the world of show business, which impinged directly on the BBC without ever controlling it.[1] *The Times* had a different angle: 'To the British way of thinking, a service privately conducted and indirectly financed offers no attractions. It seems no more natural to receive the amenities of the microphone as a by-product of publicity than to accept a book, a play, a film, a concert or an educational course on the same terms. In the last resort the listener retains direct control, and it is common knowledge that he does not hesitate to let the BBC hear his opinions. The British system, in short, is one of those social institutions over which the man in the street has some right to a little complacency, and when it is attacked it will not lack defenders.'[2]

This was general support for a policy based on a philosophy: it was support given by Parliament in all the important debates on broadcasting during the period. As far as individual programmes were concerned, however, or the balance between them, there was scope for criticism both of programme builders and of programme producers. 'Output' is a quantitative term: the most interesting aspects of programme policy are qualitative. The great themes of broadcasting history can be understood only if the attitudes and approaches of producers are understood—and the relation between producers, programme planners, controllers, critics, and the public. The BBC's philosophy owed an immense amount to one man: the BBC's programmes were the work of many men of extremely varied experience and outlook.

The most remarkable development of the period was the growing sense that the production of wireless programmes was an art, not a business. Talks producers had begun in the 1920s by looking for 'Voices to Fill the Hours'—mellifluous 'golden voices' were specially prized—but they ended by treating the broadcast talk as a distinctive art form. The most distinguished thinkers, artists, writers, and academics were expected to state their opinions in an approved form, to have their scripts scored

[1] See *We Live and Learn* (1951).   [2] *The Times*, 30 Jan. 1934.

like pieces of music, and to rehearse as diligently as actors preparing for a West End opening. The medium had to be respected.[1] In drama, and even more particularly in 'features',
the bounds of theatrical form and stage convention began to be
thought of as shackles: what radio could do distinctively began
to be prized. Experiment was felt to be a necessary part of the
exploitation both of sound and, though the new medium was
still young, of television. The daring and creative mind of Lance
Sieveking was early applied to such productions as *Kaleidoscope I* (1929), 'a play too purely radio to be printed for reading', and *The Man with the Flower in His Mouth* (1930), a specially
designed version of a Pirandello play for Baird's experimental
television.[2]

It is remarkable, indeed, to see how quickly, perhaps too
quickly, fascination with the art of radio, which led to original
and exciting experiments with sound, like Lynton Fletcher's
Pieces of Sound (1933) with its sequence of related and contrasting
sounds, was merged in concern for the prospects of television.
Tyrone Guthrie, for example, who wrote and produced *The
Squirrel's Cage* in 1929—'a definite use of a new medium dealing
with a story after a fashion which no other medium could have
employed'—commented in 1931 that he felt that the future lay
along the lines of television, 'of co-ordination with other arts
—a vista of ever-growing elaboration, mechanisation, centralisation, most depressing to contemplate, but quite inevitable'.[3]

It was not for many years, however, that television was to
threaten the position of sound radio, and it was primarily to
the arts of sound radio that the writers of the 1930s devoted
themselves. The mood of the period is captured in Sieveking's
book *The Stuff of Radio* (1934) where, after talking of the
'ghastly impermanence of the medium', he seized on the 'feature
programme'—'an arrangement of sounds which has a theme
but no plot'—as the distinctive art form of radio. The rest of the
programmes, with the possible exception of running commentaries, were not specifically 'radio-centred': they provided
material which could be handled equally effectively by other

[1] For Talks, see below, pp. 125-6, 200.
[2] For *Kaleidoscope I*, see L. Sieveking, *The Stuff of Radio* (1934); for the performance of the Pirandello play in its setting, see below, pp. 550-1.
[3] *BBC Year Book* (1931), pp. 185-90.

media—in the newspaper or on the concert hall or theatre stage. Another writer called the use of such material 'the reproductive side of broadcasting', by which he meant 'the distribution of entertainment and cultural matter that exists in the world already', a very wide definition.[1]

By contrast, the radio feature, whatever form it took, was dependent not on reproduction but on invention, not on one form of art but on several. As early as 1928 Cecil Lewis, one of the pioneers of the British Broadcasting Company,[2] had drawn attention to features as 'radio at its best'. 'Such programmes', he pointed out, 'mean research and study . . . the absorption of the subject and, what is more important, the ability to select the striking views which illuminate it best and are suitable to the microphone.'[3] The obstacle in the way of more features, he suggested, was a shortage of the right kind of people to write and to produce them. Within a few years the interest of this work was more generally appreciated. It was at its most intricate in 'the kaleidoscopic use of multiple studios, music and poetry being employed as protagonists'. The feature gave unprecedented opportunities to the producer, who through broadcasting could achieve not only invention but 'intensive concentration and continuity'. 'There is no other training or experience comparable to that of a radio producer unless it be that of the producer to a repertory company in the theatre.'[4]

The other aspect of programme presentation which was unique to radio had less to do with the producer than with the commentator, and, behind the commentator, the engineer. Radio acted as a kind of magic carpet enabling the listener to feel that he was participating in events which he could not attend and which in many cases he would never have been permitted to attend. Not only did the outside broadcast carry the listener over great distances but, as S. J. de Lotbinière put it, 'it took him past "sold out" notices to some of the best seats in the house'.[5] While Lance Sieveking was concentrating on the ingenuities of the studio, particularly on the dramatic control

[1] Filson Young, *Shall I Listen?* (1933), p. 5.
[2] For Cecil Lewis, see *The Birth of Broadcasting*, pp. 138 ff., 206 ff.
[3] *The Observer*, 19 Feb. 1928.
[4] *The Stuff of Radio*, p. 31.
[5] Private Notes by S. J. de Lotbinière on the development of Outside Broadcast programmes.

panel, which was to him like 'a flexible musical instrument', permitting a subtle blending of voice, music, and effects, de Lotbinière thought that there was an 'art' of quite a different kind associated with perfect commentating. It also rested on 'a subtle mixture of description and interpretation'.

'The man who does these things [running commentaries] properly', Roger Eckersley told Station Directors as early as 1927, 'probably will be difficult to find, as he should have the journalistic instinct, a decent voice, a sound communicable knowledge of the subject, and the power to make listeners feel as though they were present at the event.'[1] The same point was made clearly in the *BBC Handbook* for a much later date, 1939, in which de Lotbinière complained that most people failed to realize that 'commentary is an art and that its successful practice depends on attention to a specifiable technique'. 'That few people have the ability and application to succeed in this new art', he went on, 'is apparent from the fact that first class commentators are still scarce.'[2]

More than anything else, commentators had to learn how to play a variety of parts. At boxing matches they were all important: at Guildhall lunches they were 'only incidental'. On big national occasions, when broadcasting pulled 'the great audience' together more effectively than at any other time, the events could 'more or less speak for themselves'. 'The commentator's virtuosity will be held in check.'[3] Already by 1939 a number of BBC commentators, notably John Snagge and Howard Marshall, had learned the art of combining restraint and excitement in a way that commentators in no other part of the world had been able to achieve.

It is not easy to describe in words either the 'arts' of the feature or of the commentary. Not only do both date, so that, when recordings exist, neither the restraint nor the excitement is always fully convincing; but more often there are no records. The output has been lost in the air. Sieveking was haunted not only by the 'ghastly impermanence' of particular programmes but by the thought that the medium of sound radio itself might prove equally impermanent. 'Perhaps it *never can happen again*. Perhaps, and it is more than likely, this present decade will be

[1] *R. H. Eckersley to Station Directors, 7 Jan. 1927.
[2] *BBC Handbook* (1939), pp. 64–67.   [3] Ibid.

the only decade in the history of the human race which will know the radio play, that strange curiosity which appeals to the ear alone, just as three preceding decades may be the only ones to know the silent film. Of course, they may survive, these two struggling, limited forms of art; survive and move on side by side with fuller developments appealing to more senses— sight, scent, touch, indeed the whole "five parts of knowledge".[1]

In approaching radio as an art, BBC producers during the 1930s were not always able to discover the right set of relationships with planners and controllers, critics and the public. The controllers sometimes seemed to be too distant and to be operating at a quite different level; the critics seemed to be less interested in BBC programmes than in theatre productions, films, or concerts; and the public included millions of listeners who did not seek to discriminate or to judge. 'The only way to enjoy broadcasting', Filson Young wrote, 'or to get out of it the art which it has to give you is to decide what you mean to listen to, and listen carefully and critically to that.'[2] He admitted, however, as did other writers on broadcasting, that large numbers of listeners used wireless merely to provide 'a new type of auditory background for home life'. 'The housewife is tempted to perform her household chores to the accompaniment of music or speech; at most times a background of sound accompanies the process of eating; reading, writing, sewing and playing games are all done with the background provided by broadcasting.'[3]

Leaving on one side the response of the public, the organizational shape of broadcasting was changed on many occasions throughout the late 1920s and 1930s. There were some people who felt that while the 'output' of the BBC increased, its 'immense and intricate organization' was destructive both of creative art and vision.[4] At least one of the biggest changes— that of 1933—was designed 'to enable the creative staff to concentrate on their creative work',[5] but complaints continued

[1] *The Stuff of Radio*, p. 41.   [2] *Shall I Listen?*, p. 16.
[3] M. Dinwiddie, 'The Influence of Broadcasting on Modern Life' in the *Transactions of the Royal Philosophical Society* (Glasgow, 1936).
[4] *Shall I Listen?*, p. 2.
[5] *Memorandum on Re-Organization, 21 Sept. 1933. For the background of the new policy and the details of the changes, see below, pp. 439–46.

—and have continued since—that the actual rules under which 'creative work' was carried out were made and applied by people who were responsible for administration but not for the work itself. The 'hierarchy' was inevitably a hierarchy of control, more interested in order than in creation. 'Luckily', one critic has written, 'there were always plenty of obscure people on the production side who did their jobs according to their lights and not according to the book.'[1] Peter Eckersley, the Chief Engineer of the BBC during the 1920s, has gone further. 'The BBC Governors have, up till now, been appointed by the highest governmental authorities; these gods have made Governors in their own image. I would suggest men whose background was in the arts instead of "public service", however worthy. This would ensure the appointment of an executive staff likely to have originality and enthusiasm rather than an ability to "fit in" to a large organisation.'[2]

Such opinions have been countered, of course, by many others. Reith himself, for example, always argued firmly that BBC Governors should not include 'delegates' from music or letters. The validity of the conflicting opinions can best be judged at the many points in this History where specific decisions are being discussed. Yet Reith as Director-General was never complacent about organization, and had no illusions about the ability of committees or hierarchies to achieve 'the best'. He genuinely admired 'creative power' and did his best to allow it to develop. It is interesting to note that Lance Sieveking, who demanded the most imaginative experiments, should have dedicated his *Stuff of Radio* to Reith 'who, like a patron in the Middle Ages, has made it possible for an art to flourish, by enabling artists and craftsmen to devote their lives to its practice and development in freedom from any limitations save those which have seemed, to an ever modifying degree, inherent in it'.

It was a just and warm tribute, and it rightly directed attention to the element of patronage which broadcasting carried with it. In the absence of state patronage of the arts, the BBC did much to provide it, subsidizing many cultural activities more generously than many of its more 'philistine' critics

[1] M. Gorham, *Sound and Fury* (1948), p. 54.
[2] P. P. Eckersley, *The Power Behind the Microphone* (1941), p. 18.

wished it to do. The patronage in music, for example, was
reflected not only in the taking over of the Promenade Concerts in 1927—thereby ensuring their survival[1]—but in subsidy
to opera and in the commissioning of new works, including an
Elgar symphony in 1933. 'Most powerful of all the agencies
extending interest in music,' Sir Henry Hadow wrote in 1931,
'both in the width of its range and in the concentration of its
authority, is the BBC which affords to our composers their due
share of opportunity and gives them the whole civilized world
for audience.'[2] To the university world also the BBC provided
much indirect patronage and far greater opportunities to influence the public than lecturers or professors had ever enjoyed
before, either intra-murally or extra-murally.

There were, of course, problems concerning patronage which
were at least as difficult as problems concerning show business.
Were the speakers whom the BBC employed a kind of clique?
Was independent music in danger when a public corporation
could build up the strength of the new orchestra while the
London Symphony Orchestra was passing through a difficult
phase of its history?[3] There was almost as much rumour surrounding the answers to questions of this kind as there was tittle-
tattle about 'radio personalities'. In fact, the files of the Talks
Department of the BBC reveal not only a relentless search for
new speakers but a great unwillingness to 'over-work' particular
speakers, including its best-known speakers like Hilton. Similarly, although the Board of the London Symphony Orchestra
had taken the initiative in 1930 in 'bombarding the Press with
letters of protest against the BBC',[4] four years later, when it
turned to the BBC for help, the help was willingly given.[5] In
both 1930 and 1934 the BBC was consistent in seeking to lower
admission charges to concerts, a policy which was extremely
unpopular with existing musical institutions. It also fought for
cheaper opera, and on at least one occasion in 1934 Reith
said that he would be prepared to consider a bigger subsidy to
Covent Garden if cheap performances were arranged as part of
the regular season.[6]

[1] See below, pp. 172–3.
[2] W. H. Hadow, *English Music* (1931), p. 173.
[3] See H. Foss and N. Goodwin, *London Symphony* (1954), p. 129.
[4] Ibid.   [5] Ibid., p. 145.
[6] *Geoffrey Toye to V. H. Goldsmith, 9 Oct. 1934.

In discussions with outside people and outside interests the BBC was anxious to recruit the best. Some of the discussions —at the highest level—were carried out by Reith himself who was a superb negotiator. Others, like the complex discussions on opera, brought in T. Lochhead, the BBC's Chief Accountant, or V. H. Goldsmith, who in 1933 was given the title of Director of Business Relations. Some were initiated at the departmental level by the Director of Talks or the Head of Outside Broadcasts. There was a fascinating correspondence, for example, in 1936 between the Director of Religious Broadcasting, the Rev. F. A. Iremonger, and the contributors to a series on Church, Community and State, who included T. S. Eliot. 'You will see', Eliot wrote, 'that the group of problems that has been handed to me is extremely bristly, and likely to become more so— I can't help feeling that the lot has fallen on me to go down the drain after the man-eating tiger.'[1]

Many more discussions, however, some of them quite informal, were carried on at a lower level by individual producers, the best of them men who were brave enough to make independent judgements as well as to rely on speakers' records from the past. Some of the comments on speakers were refreshingly frank. Sir Thomas Beecham, for instance, who had often made devastating comments about the BBC—music on the wireless, he once said, was 'the most abominable row that ever stunned and cursed the human ear, a horrible gibbering, chortling and shrieking of devils and goblins'[2]—was given a very candid report by George Barnes on his first BBC performance as a speaker in April 1939. 'Title of Talk—The London Musical Festival: Script—Obvious, but lively towards the end: Delivery —Supercilious: Production—Nervous, Difficult.'[3]

Occasionally there were difficulties between producers and the directors of their departments and even with people higher up in the BBC's organization. More frequently, however, the difficulties—and the pleasures—of personal relationships were appreciated most keenly by the producers. It is fascinating to trace in the personal files of BBC speakers and artists the development of relationships. In July 1925, for instance, C. A.

[1] *T. S. Eliot to Rev. F. A. Iremonger, 12 Nov. 1936.
[2] Quoted in C. Reid, *Thomas Beecham: An Independent Biography* (1961), p. 196.
[3] *Producer's Report on New Speaker, 1 May 1939.

Lewis had a telephone conversation with George Bernard Shaw just after he had installed a Burndept four-valve wireless set and loudspeaker: his opinion of plays broadcast by the BBC was

5. A Postcard from George Bernard Shaw

expressed in one word: 'damnable'.[1] Early in 1928 Shaw was refusing an invitation from Lance Sieveking to take the chair at a debate on the grounds that he never took the chair: 'the listeners-in cannot see me sitting and do not want to hear my silence'.[2] Reith himself was drawn into correspondence, as he

[1] *G. B. Shaw to C. A. Lewis, 10 July 1925.
[2] *Note by G. B. Shaw appended to letter from L. Sieveking to Shaw, 10 Feb. 1928.

F

was on many occasions with individual broadcasters, in 1932. Asked by Reith to take part in a series called *Rungs of the Ladder*, Shaw replied, 'if ever there was a man who succeeded in spite of his incompetence for helping himself that man is myself. I never put my best foot forward, because I never put my foot forward at all.'[1]

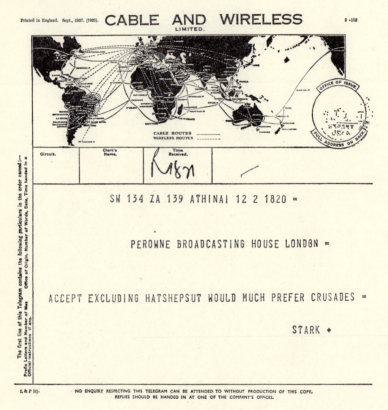

6. A Cable from Freya Stark

If Shaw's correspondence with producers and BBC officials, including the Director-General, brings out the fascination of a developing relationship, there are other files which bring out the colour. Freya Stark's file is as full of postcards as Shaw's, but whereas Shaw's are often postcards with terse and cryptic

[1] *G. B. Shaw to Reith, 2 May 1932.

messages, Freya Stark's postcards from Italy announce her return from exciting journeys. The romance was contagious. Lionel Fielden wrote to her in 1934 about a programme which would begin with a man ringing up Imperial Airways about a journey to Persia. 'One could then work through anecdote and description from Baghdad to Teheran with some description of the Shah; from Teheran down the Caspian; from the Caspian to Meshed and across the Salt Desert to Ispahan. Then we could take in Luristan and through to Shirez and Bushire.'[1]

While programmes were being initiated and assembled through widening circles of personal contact, letters about programmes were pouring in from unknown listeners. The result was a running commentary on what the BBC was doing, a commentary supplemented by the comments of radio critics and the opinions of a number of paid advisers, of whom Filson Young was the most important.

From May 1924 onwards listeners' letters had been scrutinized by a Programme Correspondence Section, started by Ralph Wade. Letters were answered with punctilious care, not only for reasons of public relations, but because they were felt to provide some indication of the views of minorities.[2] By 1927 letters were reaching Savoy Hill at the rate of over 50,000 a year. Most of them were appreciative: 'very few indeed of the critics really intend to be rude or cross.' In a representative week in 1931, 699 letters concerning the National Programme were appreciative and fifty-seven strongly critical. A tiny minority consisted of short, simple messages on postcards like 'Your programmes are rotten' or more picturesque descriptions of mood, like 'I hope your face is getting red with temper as you read this.' Among the appreciative letters, it is interesting to note how phrases like the 'wonder of wireless' or the 'miracle in the home' persisted long after broadcasting had developed its routines.

Appreciative or critical, however, few letter-writers admitted that they were speaking for themselves alone. 'One will speak on behalf of his whole circle of wireless friends; another for the overwhelming majority of listeners in his vicinity; others—yet

[1] *Lionel Fielden to Freya Stark, 7 June 1934.
[2] See *The Birth of Broadcasting*, pp. 203–4.

more confident—voice the views of anything from 90 to 99 per cent. of the entire audience. The latter is a very favourite percentage and is applicable impartially to any type of matter broadcast.'[1]

According to an early analysis of the letters, the impression was overpowering that anything which anyone particularly disliked predominated in BBC programmes. 'To those to whom dance music is anathema, it appears to be broadcast in every programme. A listener who does not care for talks cannot switch on without finding one in progress, and another who longs for variety entertainment is utterly bewildered at the interminable transmissions of symphony concerts.'[2]

The limitations of readers' letters as a source of constructive criticism or as a 'representative sample' of listeners' opinions were clearly recognized in the 1930s: so too, however, was their sociological interest. 'It is clearly not enough to count heads in dealing with such correspondence', Hilda Matheson wrote: 'it amply repays scrutiny, and deserves to be charted, indexed and kept for reference not only by a remote statistical department, but by those who devise programmes, talks and plays.'[3] The comments made by listeners are very similar to the comments recorded by Mass Observation in its surveys of the last three years of peace. Values obtruded in almost every sentence, and there was great confusion between opinion and prejudice. The number of letters received revealed a curious pattern of preoccupation and protest, and there were certain set reactions to particular stimuli. A broadcast of *The Emperor Jones* in May 1937 evoked eighty criticisms, practically all being directed against 'the frequency of swearing': any references to vivisection or to inoculation were immediately followed by a spate of angry letters.[4]

The responses of one week in March 1936 have survived in full. Nineteen complaints against a Roman Catholic service were evoked by controversial references in the sermon to the Reformation; an item called 'Handel in Harlem' provoked thirty-seven criticisms as against six letters of appreciation; a talk by John Hilton on football pools elicited seventy-seven

[1] *BBC Handbook* (1928), p. 79.   [2] Ibid.
[3] H. Matheson, 'Listener Research in Broadcasting' in the *Sociological Review*, vol. xxvii (1935).   [4] *R. W. P. Cockburn to R. J. Silvey, July 1937.

appreciations and thirteen criticisms.[1] Hilton subsequently published a selection of comments from letters which provide
fascinating sociological evidence. 'The answer to "why do
people bet?",' one of them read, 'is easy. In the early days
man sought the Elixir of Life. . . . Today it's the Irish Sweep and
the Football Pool, in other words, the *impossible*. Getting something for nothing.'[2]

Some of the letters received by the BBC, far from dwelling
on attack, had a ring of Samuel Smiles about them. 'I write to
you as a music lover, and I owe my love of the best in music to
you entirely.' 'Ten years ago I was a schoolboy and my favourite
music was Jazz. Symphony orchestras just faintly bored me.
Then I began to listen to light overtures and Military bands. . . .
Through shorter pieces like overtures etc., I came to find that
I could listen to a full Symphony Orchestra with pleasure.'
'Please let me know the dates of the Toscanini Concerts next
summer; it would enable me to decide on my summer holidays.'

In retrospect, letters of this kind are among the most interesting. During the late 1930s, however, the public relations aspect
of correspondence came to dominate BBC thinking in this field,
and in 1935 the Programme Correspondence Section was transferred to the Public Relations Division and placed under the
supervision of Maurice Farquharson.[3] Ten years earlier C. R.
Wade had written that 'even though a listener may be almost illi-
terate and very vituperative in his comments he has probably
many friends, and far more may depend upon the conciliatory
nature of our reply than may appear on the surface'.[4] In other
words, diplomacy was at least as necessary as analysis. The
diplomacy became more sophisticated as the number of listeners grew. At the same time, listeners' opinions were communicated to the Programme departments. A summary sheet
of correspondence received was circulated daily to heads of
departments, giving details of criticisms and appreciations, and
a weekly summary was produced centrally. In the office of
Assistant Director of Programmes—from 1930 onwards—a
large wall chart was kept, giving the figures for a whole year.[5]

---

[1] *The information in BBC Archives relates to the week ending 7 Mar. 1936.
[2] *Why I Go In For The Pools* (1936), p. 63.
[3] *Internal Memorandum of 10 Oct. 1935.
[4] *C. R. Wade, undated note, probably written late in 1925 or in 1926. C. R.
Wade was Ralph Wade's brother.   [5] *The system was perfected in February 1930.

Listeners' letters were always supplemented by press comment, with questions of public relations overlapping from the start with considerations of criticism. 'Newspaper criticism has increased considerably during the last twelve months', a BBC spokesman remarked in 1932. 'It is a valuable addition to the BBC's sources of information. In many instances it is well-informed and constructive. Its chief limitation, which should tend to disappear, is that it is hardly seasoned enough to stand completely on its own feet without too close a reference to the preferences, real or imagined, of its readers. It has not yet won for itself the independence of the best kind of general dramatic and musical criticism.'[1]

The spokesman was referring to the 'preference polls' which newspapers felt that it was useful to conduct. Not surprisingly, they showed 'the public's preference for entertainment'. An early *Daily Mail* ballot of February 1927, for instance, showed that of the 1,285,083 votes cast, 238,489 (nearly 20 per cent.) put 'variety and concert parties' at the head of their programme preferences, whereas 78,781, perhaps a surprisingly high figure, put symphony concerts first, and only 30,919 talks. 'We must remember', Basil Nicolls wrote, 'that the results were based purely on first choices with no proportional representation of other tastes and, therefore, whether they confirm us or otherwise, they are fallacious.'[2]

Eight years later, Hilda Matheson made similar points in greater detail. 'The fact that the largest number of entrants give their votes for variety programmes does not mean that even they want to hear variety programmes all the time; it does not indicate what kind of variety programme they want, nor their relative preference for musical items, for comic dialogue, for humorous sketches and the rest.'[3] Miss Matheson made the further point that listeners' reactions were influenced not only by content but by style of presentation.

Technique in broadcasting, like style in literature, is not trimming, but the essence of its quality. It is, of course, of less importance in connection with straightforward concerts than with entertainment, plays, discussions, talks and general programme planning and

[1] *BBC Year Book* (1932), p. 106.
[2] *Nicolls to Roger Eckersley and W. E. G. Murray, 28 Feb. 1927.
[3] 'Listener Research in Broadcasting', loc. cit.

presentation. . . . It is possible to make unduly lofty claims for the art of broadcasting, but it is equally misguided to deny that broadcasting is in any way different from other kinds of popularisation. Broadcasting is not mass projection, though it seems to be so. It is an individual, even intimate, business. It has, moreover, its own technical limitations and properties. An interesting line of research would aim at discovering how far the popularity and unpopularity of items was due to presentation as opposed to content.

Miss Matheson had left the BBC when she made this penetrating observation on the nature of listeners' response to programmes. The press critics seldom probed so deep. Their comments on particular programmes—plays or variety especially —often cancelled each other out far more convincingly than did political opinions on the content of 'controversial broadcasting'.

Similar observations to those made by Miss Matheson were often made behind the scenes, however, by the paid advisers whom the BBC consulted from time to time both about particular programmes and programme balance. Filson Young, who wrote a weekly column in the *Radio Times* from 1926 onwards, was employed as a 'programme consultant' from September 1926 until his death in 1938. His letters and criticisms, often highly idiosyncratic, provide a fascinating gloss on the programmes of a whole era.

At first Filson Young attended meetings of the Programme Board, and he was encouraged not only to express any views 'constructive or destructive' about what the BBC was doing but to suggest new ideas for the future;[1] later, the scope of his work was greatly restricted, and he became a far from popular figure with many people inside Broadcasting House. He had as much trouble with the Commissionaires as he had with the programme builders. The range of his interests was wide, and two of his own ideas for programmes were as far apart as the *Foundations of Music* series and the BBC 'National Lectures'.[2] He could also make acute, if one-sided, comments about Variety and urge the BBC to broadcast racing odds: 'I do not think that any moral objection can attach to letting people know the

---

[1] *V. H. Goldsmith to Filson Young, 27 July 1926.

[2] For those two programmes, see below, pp. 177, 127, 144. *For an acknowledgement of Filson Young's part in their initiation, see Reith to Filson Young, 24 Apr. 1929. Filson Young also devised the Bach Cantatas and the St. Hilary programmes from Cornwall.

price at which a winning horse ran.'[1] He could be devastatingly destructive, particularly about theatre organs, but he could also be disarmingly flattering. One summer's evening in July 1937 he found everything to his satisfaction from a 'little symphony concert conducted by Edward Clark to "Our Hour" with Flotsam and Jetsam. One could not expect to have such programmes every evening, but they stood out in such striking contrast to the general level as to give one rather seriously to think. This especially applies to the Flotsam and Jetsam programme—perfectly delightful entertainment, full of music and variety and fun and presented in an unpretentious way, which proves that it is not necessary for this kind of programme to succeed, to be blatant and vulgar. It is also interesting to notice that for three out of these first-rate features we were indebted to no outside assistance, but to the internal resources of Broadcasting House.'[2]

Lindsay Wellington, who was then Presentation Director, agreed, adding that 'it is difficult to know precisely why the same ingredients, mixed in the same way, can sometimes give different or inferior results'.[3] The mystery remains, and because it remains, men like Filson Young have always been necessary if occasionally exasperating. Roger Eckersley found his assistance invaluable.[4] At a later date Graves considered that he was always 'useful in being constructively critical during the development of any particular branch of our work'.[5] In between, Dawnay agreed with this verdict,[6] not knowing that just after he (Dawnay) had been appointed to a job of which he knew so little, Filson Young wrote to a BBC colleague: 'Do you think that it would be a graceful, helpful and useful act on your part to send Dawnay a copy of my book "Shall I listen?" It would at least give him some kind of grasp of the job he has to tackle.'[7]

Filson Young felt that as the BBC grew in size, 'the science of administration' had 'to some extent overlaid the essentially

1 *Filson Young to R. H. Eckersley, 13 Dec. 1933.
2 *Filson Young to Eckersley, 1 July 1933.
3 *Note on Filson Young's letter.
4 *Eckersley to Carpendale, 2 Dec. 1931.
5 *Graves to Carpendale, 23 June 1937.
6 *Dawnay to Carpendale, 18 Sept. 1933.
7 *Filson Young to W. E. G. Murray, 6 July 1933.

creative side of broadcasting, to its disadvantage'.[1] At the same time he maintained, in face of new moves inside Broadcasting House, that the programme policy of the BBC did not need drastic revision. 'On the contrary, if it were suddenly to be placed in the control of any other body, I believe that after some years of experiment and experience they would arrive at very much the same point to which the present organisation has attained.'[2]

In 1925 he had once suggested to Reith that 'any intelligent person' could have taken the previous week's programmes together and 'rearranged them in a way that would deserve and secure the appreciation of the majority of listeners without adding a single item'.[3] He took up the same theme in 1934. 'If I were asked what, in my opinion, would be the most advantageous single extension or change in the present programme policy, it would be to break up the time plan which has now become more or less standardized. I would advocate a monthly change in the time-table of standardized features so that listeners who are governed in their habits by Time should have a chance of greater variety.'[4]

He did not add that some of the staleness came from the fact that the better the broadcaster, the more he tended to be 'used', and eventually the more stale he became. Individuals as well as programme sequences could wilt. The BBC has never completely mastered the intricacies of either of these two sets of problems, and when it has tried, it has more often alienated the listener than raised the level of programmes.[5] When Hilton was rested in 1937, for example, on the grounds that he was 'in danger of being ruined by excessive publicity and success', there was talk in the press about political pressure—which was certainly not there. Hilton himself received many letters suggesting that he had been 'stood off from the microphone because of capitalist wire pulling'.[6]

Filson Young's interest in listeners' habits went as deep as

[1] *Filson Young to Dawnay, 5 Mar. 1934.   [2] Ibid.
[3] *Filson Young to Reith, 24 Mar. 1925.
[4] *Filson Young to Dawnay, 5 Mar. 1934.
[5] For an instance of difficulties, see below, p. 241.
[6] *Roger Wilson to Sir Richard Maconachie, 9 July 1937; Hilton to N. G. Luker, 10 Feb. 1938.

that of the first sponsors of listener research. He was intuitive, however, where they tried to be scientific, speculative rather than sociological. 'What is to be the attitude of the ordinary listener towards broadcasting? Is he going to regard it simply as a means of filling the vacuum of idle hours, carping at everything which does not make immediate and facile appeal for him and being amazed when the programmes are not continually filled with the kind of items that do so appeal?'[1] So much pivoted on the answer to this question. It haunted the Programme Revision Committees and stimulated the search for information about listening habits. It led Dawnay to dismiss from the reckoning 'the tap listener who wants to have one or more very light programmes available at all hours between breakfast and bedtime'.[2] Two years later Graves concluded that while the 'serious listeners', who selected their programmes carefully, demanded the most serious attention, the demands of 'tap listeners' warranted 'no further provision in programmes'.[3]

It is impossible to understand the programmes of the period from 1927 to 1939 without realizing that a special service for 'tap listeners' was explicitly rejected. So was a special service for 'highbrows'. So too was the idea of 'continuity' itself. 'The BBC definitely aims at having an interval of four or five minutes between programmes', it was stated officially in 1932. 'It is obvious that it is irritating to a listener who switches on his set to hear, say, the News to find himself listening to the last five minutes of an opera or a vaudeville turn. The News is what he switched on to hear, and he does not want to listen to a fraction of some other programme which for him has no beginning and no middle.'[4]

It was not that no one thought of special continuous services for listeners who had not appreciated the power of the switch. Lionel Fielden in his reminiscences says that he and his colleagues in the early 1930s had definite plans for a 'continuous news programme always on the air, always available, always being added to by the latest events', a programme of light music and waltzes 'without the intervention of any announcer', a pro-

[1] *Shall I Listen?*, p. 16.   [2] *Programme Revision Committee, 1934.
[3] *C. G. Graves, Report on Programme Revision, 1936.
[4] *BBC Year Book* (1932), p. 115.

gramme of continuous readings from the classics, and a 'Third' programme 'essentially highbrow'. He adds characteristically: 'Reith, however, was very much against such specialisation, and I think now that he was right.'[1]

2. Entertainment

ANY detailed consideration of the pattern of programmes must begin with popular entertainment. Some listeners wanted the BBC to entertain them all the time, most listeners wanted the BBC to entertain them most of the time, all listeners wanted the BBC to entertain them some of the time. 'Variety is the "bread-and-butter" of broadcasting', one writer on radio remarked in 1934, but not all listeners agreed that it was perfect entertainment.[2] There was no agreement, indeed, about what constituted 'entertainment', particularly when it was entertainment before the listeners' own firesides.

Leaving on one side philosophical questions about the relationship between 'education' and 'entertainment',[3] there had been immense changes in 'popular entertainment' during the fifty years before the BBC came into existence.[4] The 'amateur' had given ground to the professional, the theatre to the cinema; spectator sport had become highly organized; music hall had travelled far from its humble Victorian origins. As early as 1912, the year of *Hullo Ragtime* at the Hippodrome, there had been a Royal Command Performance, with Harry Lauder, Vesta Tilley, George Robey, and Wee Georgie Wood; Oswald Stoll and Edward Moss had created formidable institutions in 'show business'; and huge London theatres like the Coliseum (1904) and the Palladium (1910) staged spectacular entertainment on a lavish scale. The gramophone-record industry had grown

[1] *The Natural Bent*, p. 108.
[2] *The Times*, Broadcasting Number, 14 Aug. 1934.
[3] See below, pp. 185-6.
[4] See my *Mass Entertainment: the Origins of a Modern Industry*, Joseph Cowen Memorial Lecture, University of Adelaide (1960). There are not many detailed monographs, but there is much of interest in E. Short, *Fifty Years of Vaudeville* (1946) and A. E. Wilson, *Half a Century of Entertainment* (1951).

prodigiously since the time of Edison's first discoveries. When Edison died at the age of eighty-two in 1929, enormous concentrations of economic power were becoming almost as common in the entertainment world as they were in heavy industry.

The merger of the Victor Talking Machine Company and the Radio Corporation of America in 1930 demonstrated that across the Atlantic there were strong business links between radio manufacture, the gramophone-record trade, broadcasting, and the cinema. In Britain two years later E.M.I. (Electric and Musical Industries Ltd.) was formed as the result of a merger between the Columbia Graphophone Company and the Gramophone Company—it was to be the first company to produce cathode-ray tubes for television sets[1]—while in the same year Gaumont-British Picture Corporation, the parent company of the General Theatre Corporation, took over control of Moss Empires Ltd. *The Performer* wrote of 'a movement towards monopoly in the entertainment world', and hoped that this 'new and huge combination' between screen and stage would encourage the artist rather than ruin him.[2]

These massive forces behind so-called 'mass entertainment' were usually hidden from the public view. So too was the growth of the 'agency business' and of the trade unions. In the foreground of the public view, spotlighted on and off the stage, were the 'stars'. Again, it was often forgotten that for every star, there were scores of performers about whom the public knew nothing at all.

The BBC had given its first variety programme in January 1923 and its first programme of dance music, from the Carlton Hotel, in May 1923. Light music, musical comedy, revue, and gramophone-record programmes were very early features of the broadcasting week.[3] Stanford Robinson, whose BBC career spans the whole history of broadcast music, had been a member of the staff since 1923 and had been given charge of a BBC Chorus as early as September 1924; Albert Sandler and his orchestra had first broadcast from the Grand Hotel, Eastbourne

[1] L. White, *The American Radio* (Chicago, 1947), p. 32; S. G. Sturmey, *The Economic Development of Radio* (1958), p. 42.
[2] *The Performer*, 7 Dec. 1932.
[3] See *The Birth of Broadcasting*, esp. ch. V, section 2.

in July 1925.[1] Comedians like John Henry, 'Blossom', and Helena Millais, 'our Lizzie', had quickly established their radio reputations.[2] Christopher Stone, the first of the British 'disc jockeys' and thereby 'founder of a very exclusive profession',[3] did not broadcast, however, until July 1927, and because of the restrictive clauses in the BBC's agreement with the news agencies there were no running commentaries on sporting events until the same year.[4]

Quiz contests and competitions were also held in check. A resolution of the Control Board at a meeting in January 1926 had read that 'the conduct of competitions should be carefully considered by the Programme Board before they were entered into by any department' and that under no circumstances was more than one a month to be held.[5] In 1930 a note was sent to all heads of programme branches stressing that the Board of Governors was 'in principle not in favour of competitions in our programmes' and that all suggestions for competitions, outside the scope of the Children's Hour, were to be referred to the Director-General.[6]

'Live' broadcasts from theatres and music halls had been banned—with only occasional exceptions—from 1923 to June 1925, when a strictly limited agreement had been signed with Walter Payne, the chairman of Moss Empires and the president of the Society of West End Theatre Managers: individual artists had hitherto found their broadcasting activities severely curtailed by clauses in their contracts forbidding them to broadcast while their contracts were in force, or by intimidating letters threatening no future theatre contracts should they perform on the air.[7] The 1925 agreement provided for the setting up of an 'Entertainment Organizations Joint Broadcasting Committee', including BBC representatives and members of the four 'Entertainment Associations'. Unfortunately the agreement did not clear the air. Although its purpose was to 'eliminate friction', in fact it continued to circumscribe the BBC's field of enterprise.

[1] Ibid., p. 278. [2] Ibid., pp. 285–8.
[3] *Rex Palmer, in an interview with Christopher Stone, BBC Light Programme, *These Radio Times*, 25 Apr. 1952.
[4] For the agreement, see *The Birth of Broadcasting*, pp. 130–4, 262–7.
[5] *Control Board Minutes, 13 Jan. 1926.
[6] *Assistant Director of Programmes, Memorandum of 9 July 1930.
[7] See *The Birth of Broadcasting*, pp. 251 ff.

Moreover, Variety was left completely outside the terms of the agreement, since the Variety Artistes' Federation would not sign it. Walter Payne interpreted the Federation's position to mean that variety managers would have nothing to do with the BBC unless generous compensation was paid for the use of their artists. He saw no possibilities either of broadcasting enhancing the value of the artist to the variety theatre manager or of the BBC creating artists itself.[1]

His views were expressed even more forcibly in 1926 when Charles Gulliver of the London Theatres of Variety threatened to take legal proceedings against the BBC if it broadcast his artists without his consent. And Gulliver was totally unimpressed by a letter from Roger Eckersley of the BBC in January 1927 in which Eckersley wrote somewhat plaintively that he wished he could persuade Gulliver that broadcasting should not be thought of as a serious rival of the theatre: 'the fact that we can give no representation of the visual sense makes it to our minds so tremendously non-competitive that it should not be considered nearly so much a rival as, shall we say, the cinema'.[2]

A further agreement with the four 'Entertainment Associations' in January 1927 did little to improve the position. It certainly did not break the stranglehold which the Association could place on the BBC's programmes. In March 1927 a furious campaign against the BBC was launched by Gulliver, Sir Oswald Stoll of the Palladium, and R. H. Gillespie of Moss Empires. Abandoning their unqualified opposition to broadcasting as such, they demanded large block sums for the 'use' of their artists and threatened that they might seek to open a broadcasting station of their own. A statement issued by the Joint Committee of the Entertainment Protection Association, another of the 'combinations' involved in the bargaining of this period, remarked that 'either the music hall industry should be allowed to broadcast from a station of its own or that it should control the broadcasting of variety from BBC studios'. If the industry broadcast from BBC studios it should be paid by the Corporation 'so much of the BBC's net income as represents the proportion that Variety entertainment bears to the rest of the matter broadcast'. The statement at first sight

---

[1] *Oral evidence of Walter Payne to the Crawford Committee, 18 Dec. 1925.
[2] *R. H. Eckersley to Gulliver, 3 Jan. 1927.

looks reasonable enough, but the emphasis was being placed on the demands of the 'industry' not on the interests of the artist—or the public.

Popular entertainment, at this time, was the responsibility within the BBC of no single knowledgeable and experienced person. This was a great organizational weakness. In January 1927 R. E. Jeffrey, the first Productions Director of the BBC, was dealing with popular entertainment very much as a side-line—under the general direction of Roger Eckersley who had taken over the chairmanship of the Programme Board in May 1926. George Grossmith ('Gee-Gee' in the world of the foot-lights) was an experienced 'entertainment adviser', recruited direct from the theatre. Two other men with interesting careers before them had already been brought in. Bertram Fryer, for-merly the Station Director at Bournemouth, had been given charge of popular music hall and variety productions: he was a shrewd organizer and after leaving the BBC in 1932 he was later to be connected with the production of 'sponsored pro-grammes' from Radio Normandie. His assistant was John Sharman, 'a perfect type of the real pro': he had been on the halls for several years 'and his cat act was a surefire success at the annual staff pantomime'.[1] Sharman joined the London organization temporarily at first, but then permanently, to help with studio work and light programmes. He and Fryer were the two people most directly involved in daily problems of production, and Stanford Robinson[2] with the musical arrangements.

Although there was much sharing of offices in the Savoy Hill days—Jack Payne, for example, sharing an office with Stanford Robinson, and enjoying good relations with the Music Department[3]—there was perhaps insufficient exchange of views and ideas between the forceful group of people inside the BBC who were concerned with 'education'[4] and the few who were concerned with popular entertainment. There was a tendency

[1] M. Gorham, *Sound and Fury* (1948), p. 33.

[2] For Stanford Robinson, see below, pp. 94–95, 182.

[3] 'I rather expected the cold shoulder from the Music Department, which handled straight and serious music,' Jack Payne wrote, 'but everyone was most helpful.' *Signature Tune*, p. 42.

[4] See below, p. 187.

for 'Talks' to think that 'Variety' was vulgar and 'Variety' that 'Talks' should not exist.[1]

One of the most lively, tough, vigorous—and knowledgeable—persons inside the BBC on its entertainment side was Gerald Cock, the man who first broke the deadlock with entrenched sporting and entertainment interests. Cock had enjoyed an interesting and adventurous life before he joined the BBC in 1925 as Director of Outside Broadcasts: he was later to be placed in charge of the BBC's Television Service, in 1935, one year before the first regular television service began.[2]

As Director of Outside Broadcasts, Cock dealt with everything from royal broadcasts to the Cup Final and the Boat Race. The year 1927 saw an enormous increase in the work of his department, since from 1 January onwards the Corporation was permitted for the first time to give full running commentaries on sporting events. The first commentary on a rugby match, between England and Wales, was given on 15 January and on a soccer cup-tie on 29 January. During the following month several commentaries on international matches were broadcast. The Grand National followed in March—with the Inter-Varsity Sports a day later—the Boat Race on 2 April, the Amateur Golf Championship on 28 May (with Bernard Darwin), and Wimbledon in July (with J. C. Squire as one of the commentators).

At first it was felt, in a very erudite simile, that 'the perfect commentator, like the economic man, so convenient to the hypotheses of the nineteenth-century philosophers, does not exist'.[3] Yet the BBC soon brought many of them into existence —Captain H. B. T. Wakelam, who was the very first rugby commentator on 15 January 1927 and covered, in addition, soccer, cricket, and tennis (the last-named along with Colonel R. H. Brand); John Snagge, first employed by the BBC at its Stoke-on-Trent studio, and one of the most versatile as well as the most distinguished of all the BBC's commentators; Freddie Grisewood, still loved by broadcast audiences; George Allison

---

[1] L. Fielden, *The Natural Bent* (1960), p. 103; cf. M. Gorham, *Sound and Fury*, p. 33. 'In that small building, we were always running across the popular broadcasters of the time . . . even administrators were always meeting them in the lift and in the corridors.'

[2] See below, pp. 596–604.

[3] See above, p. 60. *BBC Handbook* (1928), p. 140.

of Arsenal fame; and Howard Marshall, records of whose voice still recapture the forgotten thrill of test matches.

Gerald Cock was the man behind all these other men. But it was not only with sporting events that he was concerned. It was his task also to give the ordinary listener the feeling that he was participating in great events and sharing in unseen pleasures—events like the ceremony and service at the unveiling of the Memorial Arch at the Menin Gate at Ypres in July 1927 or the Westminster Abbey Thanksgiving Service for the recovery of King George V from serious illness in July 1929, and pleasures like the Royal Command Variety Performance in February 1927, a Gracie Fields excerpt from *The Show's the Thing* in January 1930, or the Promenade Concerts.[1] It was not until Cock left Outside Broadcasts for television in 1935 that the responsibilities of the Outside Broadcasts Department were cut to exclude outside dance music, 'restaurant, cinema and other O.B. orchestras, cinema organs and O.B. light music generally'.[2]

Not only was Cock the man behind the increasingly popular announcers and commentators on outside events, the people who had a ringside view of great occasions of state and every sporting event in the calendar: he was also the negotiator behind the scenes, completely hidden from public view, in the complex bargaining with sporting and entertainment interests which made the broadcasting of sport and variety possible. Cock was 'an indomitable worker', as Roger Eckersley once described him:[3] in the words of another writer, he was the man who had given to broadcasting 'many realistic touches'.[4] Yet he worked with slender resources both in Outside Broadcasts and later in Television. In 1927 he had only one programme assistant to help him and in 1934 only five.

Inevitably much of his work depended on the skill and enterprise of Outside Broadcasts engineers, who played a large part in the development of the wide range of activities associated with outside broadcasting. H. H. Thompson was in charge, and R. H. Wood, who started outside broadcasting work with the

---

[1] For Promenade Concerts, see below, pp. 172–3.
[2] *Director of Internal Administration, *Internal Instruction*, no. 313, 27 Aug. 1935.
[3] R. H. Eckersley, *The BBC and All That* (1946), p. 85.
[4] S. A. Moseley, *Who's Who in Broadcasting* (1933), p. 36.

BBC in 1923, was in charge of the London Outside Broadcasts Engineering Unit after him: through his long record of continuous service, he has been able to meet and know large numbers of people in all walks of life. He has also been able to take part in the development of outside broadcasting techniques from the early days of the cumbersome carbon microphone and the first large Outside Broadcasts lorry of 1929.

It was as a result of Cock's initiative and energy that an agreement was prepared in February 1928 whereby Reginald Foort was allowed to broadcast a series of theatre-organ recitals from the Palladium.[1] In October 1928 a much more important general agreement was signed with George Black, recently appointed Director of the General Theatre Corporation, a man of great drive and enthusiasm, who subsequently in 1932 made a merger with the Moss Empires organization and thereby became controller of most of Britain's best music halls. Although Walter Payne tried to persuade Black to stand out against the BBC—as he had already stood out against the idea of variety performances inside cinemas—regular fortnightly broadcasts from Black's biggest theatre, the Palladium, began in October 1928. They were popular from the start with listeners, but they were bitterly criticized by the Variety Artistes' Federation.[2] Broadcasters were accused of 'giving their talents away', although, as Black pointed out, they had the option of refusing the BBC if they wished and they were paid an additional fee by the BBC if their turns were broadcast. 'Our new policy with regard to the General Theatre Corporation is one of benevolence', Eckersley wrote gratefully later in 1928.[3]

The agreement with Black was so much more satisfactory to the BBC than the 1925 agreement with Walter Payne, as modified in 1927, that in November 1928 Roger Eckersley told Payne that the Corporation did not intend to renew their agreement with him when it lapsed on 31 December.[4] Payne was in an 'explosive mood', and a stormy meeting followed in

[1] *Cock to Castleton Knight, 21 Feb. 1928. The agreement was signed in April and Foort gave his first broadcast on 14 April.

[2] *The Performer*, 10 Oct. 1928.

[3] *Undated Memorandum, 'General Theatre Corporation'.

[4] *R. H. Eckersley to Walter Payne, 16 Nov. 1928. The full text of the letter is missing from the BBC Archives.

January 1929.[1] The BBC stood by its decision, however, and the Entertainment Organizations Joint Broadcasting Committee lapsed. A separate agreement was also signed with Sir Oswald Stoll in December 1928 whereby relays were to be arranged from the Alhambra, Leicester Square. Stoll had approached the BBC through a useful intermediary, Archibald Haddon, his chief publicity officer, who had previously been a dramatic critic with the BBC.[2]

The first broadcasts from the Alhambra were arranged in February 1929 and the Coliseum broadcasts a fortnight later. 'It is a mistake to suppose that Sir Oswald has at any time been opposed to broadcasting', a press release conveniently stated; 'indeed, he has himself broadcast in America with gratifying results.'[3] Stoll himself recognized, as he told his shareholders later in 1929, that 'history is being rapidly made in the entertainment world: variety theatres, dramatic theatres, sound theatres, silent theatres, new theatres and old theatres, and in circumstances which are changing almost daily'.[4]

Personal relations with Stoll remained good, as they did also with Walter Payne and H. M. Tennent, who was also connected with Moss Empires until he founded the enterprising firm which bore his name. 'I got to know Payne very well', Roger Eckersley wrote, 'and he was always a very good friend to me and very helpful.' George Black, he thought, was 'one of the most immaculately dressed people I ever met'.[5] Other members of the BBC staff often complained about his 'Napoleonic' postures—the phrase recurs—but few denied that, as one BBC Director of Variety was to put it, he was a great man, 'one of the very greatest that ever graced the lighter side of the theatre'.[6]

As a result of these agreements and understandings, well-known variety turns began to be brought before the listener in broadcasting seasons which assured him of at least one outside

[1] The meeting was held on 17 Jan. 1929. R. H. Eckersley, George Grossmith, and Cock represented the BBC. *For a note on Payne's mood, see Cock to Eckersley, 22 Nov. 1928. 'It is not exaggerating to say that he "blew up" . . . and that we, from the Governors down, ought to be ashamed of ourselves.'
[2] *R. A. M. Dix to Cock, 21 Nov. 1928.
[3] Stoll Theatres News Service, Press Release, 24 Jan. 1929.
[4] Ibid., 31 Oct. 1929.
[5] *The BBC and All That*, p. 149.
[6] Eric Maschwitz, *No Chip on My Shoulder* (1960), p. 72.

performance from a London music hall each week. In 1929 he could hear popular artists like Jackie Coogan, Marie Burke, and Flotsam and Jetsam. Not all the stars and programmes, however, were of the Palladium and Coliseum type. Some well-known stage variety artists were surprisingly temperamental, finding broadcasting 'a much greater strain than artists do on the legitimate stage'.[1] There was long felt to be a dearth of comedians, particularly of comedians who could write their own material. 'In these days, when songs are only written in the first instances as dance music, with the lyrics added after, the so-called humour that these songs contain is often pitiful.'[2] Some promising comedians complained also that their material, which under old conditions would last the length of a tour of the whole country, was killed by a single broadcast. Clapham and Dwyer, for example, who first broadcast as a pair in 1926, were not very keen at first: 'we had only one act at that time and we really didn't want to give it away to thousands listening in'.[3]

Given such limits, there had to be a persistent search for talent. Between 1,500 and 2,000 aspiring artists were given auditions each year in the late 1920s and early 1930s, with less than 1 per cent. reaching the standard required.[4] Fortunately, some new artists made their mark with the BBC. The *BBC Year Book* for 1931, for example, describing the previous year's programmes, referred to Gillie Potter and Ronald Frankau as comedians 'worthy of the intelligence of the public': they provided, it said, 'the type of comedy that deserves and gets success, the type that will become more and more prevalent'. It added that 'broadcast vaudeville has attracted a large public which does not in the ordinary course of events patronise the music halls. It is for these listeners as well as the others that the quieter type of vaudeville is broadcast.'[5]

The difficulties of successfully presenting 'theatre turns' were never minimized. Juggling, dancing, trick cycling, and

---

[1] *BBC Handbook* (1928), p. 119. There was also a problem of straight nervousness. Elsie and Doris Waters, who became such expert broadcasters, were so nervous on their first broadcast that they called down 'stern reprimands on the spurious mirth with which they essayed to conceal it'. Another artist actually fainted when she saw the light flick her signal to start. See J. Payne, *Signature Tune* (1947), p. 38.

[2] *BBC Year Book* (1931), p. 207.

[3] *These Radio Times*, BBC Light Programme, 6 Oct. 1951.

[4] *BBC Year Book* (1931), p. 209.

[5] Ibid., pp. 207–9.

acrobatics were obviously ruled out, like ballet: there was, in fact, one conjurer billed in 1927, presumably a conjurer with a running commentary. This was a period when people talked of 'hearing' the Derby or the Cup Final, a habit that would have been meaningless to people of any other age except the blind.[1] The hearing was far from 'straight', for broadcasting was still beset with technical and production difficulties. In retrospect they usually seem as distant as the difficulties of the silent screen, although they were serious enough at the time. Roars of laughter, we are told, ruined an act by Will Hay from the Palladium in 1929 by 'overwhelming the microphone': if this had not been so, the turn would have 'ranked high'.[2]

There had been earlier trouble of a different kind at the Palladium in 1928, when the police complained that theatre-organ recitals interfered with the work of the nearby magistrates' court. Copyright was also a perpetual problem, this time to lawyers, not to engineers. There was a lawsuit in 1928, for example, over the BBC production of the musical comedy *The Little Michus*; and because owners of the copyright of musical comedies feared that broadcasting would harm them, such popular musical comedies as *The Geisha* and *The Merry Widow* could never be broadcast. Nor could full performances of Gilbert and Sullivan.

Dance music was easy to broadcast, but there were awkward problems in this kind of programme also. Complaints of 'song plugging' were made frequently in 1928 and 1929, the first Control Board minute on this subject dating back to February 1928. The minute suggested that to deal with the possible 'use' of dance-band leaders—through subsidy—by the writers and publishers of songs, the aid of the Popular Music Publishers' Association should be enlisted.[3] In fact, dozens of meetings were held during the following decade—the first of them in April 1928[4]—scores of resolutions passed, and many different procedures adopted without the problem of song plugging being solved. Questions were even asked in the House of Commons. One of Gerald Cock's most drastic solutions was physical.

[1] M. Gorham, *Broadcasting and Television Since 1900* (1952), p. 68.
[2] *BBC Year Book* (1930), p. 238.
[3] *Control Board Minutes, 9 Feb. 1928.
[4] Ibid., 12 Apr. 1928. There is a vast amount of material in the BBC Archives on this subject.

He suggested in February 1929 that dance-band leaders should not be allowed to use announcing microphones. 'This will prevent leaders from telling the public what number they have played or are about to play.' 'Should there be any tendency to shout the number into the announcing microphone,' he added, 'the latter can be faded down between each number.'[1]

Neither the dance orchestras, the Performing Right Society, the newspapers, nor presumably the song writers liked this drastic arrangement, which was dropped in October 1929.[2] Gerald Cock was annoyed that the editor of the *Radio Times* had left unexplained why the practice of not announcing numbers had been adopted. It looked like cussedness, he complained, and roused the annoyance of a public which was clamouring for more light entertainment. In the same complaint he criticized his colleagues in public relations for not making clear that the BBC's refusal to pay a sum of £50 to charity for the right to broadcast the Cup Final was based on principle and not on a miserly desire to starve the public of the kind of entertainment it wanted.[3]

Despite all the difficulties, there were important developments in broadcast popular entertainment during the late 1920s and early 1930s. Without ever being caught up in the bigger world of show business, the BBC successfully organized its own enterprises and created its own artists, not only comedians but artists of all kinds, in face of outside restraints and criticisms.

In February 1928 Jack Payne was given the title of Director of the BBC Dance Orchestra: he took with him to Savoy Hill the band which had previously broadcast frequently from the Hotel Cecil. It consisted of ten players (as against Sidney Firman's six), and his signature tune 'Say it with Music' quickly became popular throughout the country. Jack Payne has told his own story with great skill and colour—of how he took up

[1] *Memorandum by Gerald Cock, 19 Feb. 1929.

[2] *Control Board Minutes, 12 Mar. 1928; Memorandum from Cock to Station Directors, 15 Oct. 1929. In July 1933 the quite different procedure was followed of having a special BBC official to watch over programmes and 'empowered, if need be, to take positive action, including the banning of offenders from the microphone for a period of at least six months'. (Memorandum by Nicolls, 14 July 1933.)

[3] *Memorandum by Cock, 9 Apr. 1929.

dance-band leadership in the Midlands when the post-war
public was asking for more and more dance music, of his engagement at the Hotel Cecil in London, of how he yearned to
be travelling along 'the new road' of broadcasting himself, and
of how he worked his way into the BBC with Roger Eckersley's
help.[1]

From

THE BRITISH BROADCASTING CORPORATION,

Telephone: TEMPLE BAR 8400   SAVOY HILL,

Telegrams: ETHANUZE, LONDON   LONDON, W.C.2.

DATE AS POSTMARK

---

*Mr. Jack Payne has asked us to thank you very much for
your letter of recent date and he is glad that you appreciate
the work of his dance orchestra. All requests are noted,
but it is not always possible to include them on particular
days owing to the great numbers received.*

7. Jack Payne's Popularity

His first contract covered much more than the broadcasting
of late-evening dance music: he was expected also to provide
a light orchestra for revues and vaudeville programmes and
incidental music for radio plays, if necessary with augmented
numbers.[2] The orchestra was entirely his own, and he paid his
musicians. At first it was called, misleadingly, 'the BBC Dance
Orchestra, personally conducted by Jack Payne'. In August
1928 it became 'Jack Payne and the BBC Dance Orchestra',
and in November 1929, correctly, at his request, 'Jack Payne
and his BBC Dance Orchestra'. By then the orchestra was felt
to have a well-known 'collective personality', outside as well as
inside the BBC, and the number of players had risen to fourteen.
Payne's contractual position had greatly improved also. The
orchestra had two more members by February 1932, when
Payne left the BBC to begin a successful career on the stage and
in the dance halls.

[1] J. Payne, *Signature Tune*, particularly pp. 118–37. Cf. Eckersley, *The BBC and
All That*, p. 147.

[2] Firman's band had also been used at first for Variety and Revue accompani-
ments, but it had dropped out of this work by Aug. 1927.

Jack Payne's move from the BBC was treated as a 'sensation' on many of the newspaper placards. An artist who had made his name with the BBC was going into 'show business'— a reversal of what was still felt to be the normal procedure. Yet Payne was now in a position to make far more money commercially than he had ever done through sound radio.[1] His successor at the BBC was Henry Hall, then thirty-three years of age and the controller of thirty-two bands playing at London, Midland, and Scottish Railway Hotels.[2] Hall started with an orchestra of fourteen players, including an oboe player, the first time one had ever been included in a dance orchestra. Changes were quickly made, however, the oboe player being dropped and the brass section being extended.[3] Seven hundred applications had been received for the first fourteen places in the band.[4]

Hall's first broadcast was on 15 March 1932, the first occasion on which a Broadcasting House studio was employed: it started two minutes late because the preceding programme had run over, and consisted of ten tunes which Hall considered would provide rhythm, harmony, and variety and give adequate expression to the capabilities of the new combination.[5]

Before long the scope of his programmes had been considerably widened, for he believed that the surest way of forfeiting listeners' good opinions was to lead them to believe 'he had only one shot in his locker'. He was always looking for what the press called 'Hall Marks'.[6] His 'guest nights', first broadcast in 1934, were popular not only in Britain but were occasionally rebroadcast in the United States and Canada. Jack Payne's orchestra continued to broadcast from time to time, but Henry Hall himself quickly became a popular and versatile radio 'personality'. He even appeared on the stage at Radiolympia in 1933. His signature tune 'Here's to the Next Time' was composed by Roger Eckersley: it was also the first piece of music played from the BBC's new Broadcasting House.[7] Hall admitted later in life that he owed almost everything to the BBC, a remark which inspired a comment from Collie Knox that he

[1] *Signature Tune*, p. 71.
[2] H. Hall, *Here's to the Next Time* (1955), p. 83.
[3] *BBC Year Book* (1933), pp. 166–7.
[4] *BBC Press Release, 24 Feb. 1932.   [5] *Ibid., 14 Mar. 1932.
[6] *Here's to the Next Time*, pp. 111, 115.
[7] *The BBC and All That*, p. 79.

was probably the only human being alive or dead 'who has got out of that extraordinary institution exactly what he wanted'.[1]

The second big development in the BBC was the creation of a separate 'Revue and Vaudeville Section' of the Production Department in March 1930. This was part of a bigger reorganization. In January 1929 R. E. Jeffrey had been transferred from the Productions Department to the Production Research Section, a little group of people, with Lance Sieveking in their midst, browsing through the whole range of BBC programmes and initiating experiments wherever they could.[2] Jeffrey left the BBC soon afterwards.[3] His successor as Productions Director was Val Gielgud, who had been working as an assistant on the *Radio Times*—his first job was editing a page of listeners' letters —but who, after graduating through BBC amateur dramatics, was quickly caught up in professional radio drama, in both production and research.[4] Although it was serious drama rather than variety which interested Gielgud most, it was he who was responsible for staging the first variety programmes in a proper theatrical setting, with floodlights, chorus girls, and even (controversially) a studio audience.

It was Gielgud and Gladstone Murray who brought from Belfast to London John Watt, a young and energetic producer, who had made a mark with 'shoe-string' revue productions in the Belfast studio. Watt was given charge of the new Revue Section in 1930. The Vaudeville Section consisted of Fryer, Sharman, and Denis Freeman, and Watt worked alongside Gordon McConnel and Doris Arnold. McConnel had worked in the Research Section with Sieveking and Gielgud;[5] Doris Arnold, who was to become well known to listeners everywhere with her programme *These You Have Loved* (1938), had started her career as a BBC stenographer.[6] Doris Arnold and McConnel

---

[1] Collie Knox, *People of Quality* (1947), p. 234.

[2] For the Research Department, see below, pp. 160 ff.

[3] For Jeffrey and his work, see V. Gielgud, *British Radio Drama, 1922–1956* (1957), pp. 20–21, 24 ff.; *The Birth of Broadcasting*, pp. 281–3.

[4] For Gielgud's work in radio drama, see below, pp. 160–9.

[5] His position there had been considered 'a little anomalous', but he insisted when he moved to his new post that 'the theoretical freedom which he had enjoyed had rendered his routine work much less arduous'. *Internal Memorandum by V. H. Goldsmith, 9 Jan. 1930.

were joined in 1932 by Harry S. Pepper, a great character in show business, born and brought up in it. His father, Will C. Pepper, had founded the famous Concert Party, 'The White Coons', on Mumbles Pier in the summer of 1899, and Harry was proud to revive the show in radio form in August 1932.[1] The performers included Elsie and Doris Waters, Wynne Ajello, and C. Denier Warren. Pepper and Doris Arnold shared the pianos and quickly became broadcasting partners in song and music acts. They were to marry in 1943.

There were many new 'departures' both in revue and vaudeville under the new régime. The most significant of them in retrospect were the first 'series' programmes. John Watt's *Songs From the Shows* began its long run in April 1931, *Music Hall* its even longer run in March 1932.[2] Harry S. Pepper's *White Coons' Concert Party* was the third of the series.

Music Hall was one of the first programmes to be broadcast with an invited audience, and it brought to the microphone both well-established artists and new ones. Among the latter were Flanagan and Allen, who were first heard in 1932. The curious link between amateur and professional in the early history of BBC light entertainment is demonstrated by the fact that the stage equipment for the first performance of *Music Hall* was borrowed from the BBC Amateur Dramatic Society.

The first White Coons' Concert Party broadcast was followed in January 1933 by the Kentucky Minstrels: only Doris Arnold and Harry S. Pepper had much confidence in the idea behind the new show, that of reviving a 'real old-time black-faced, "Sit around" show, as in the days of Moore and Burgess', but their confidence soon proved abundantly justified. Pepper wrote the signature tune and the hit song of 1934, 'Carry me back to green green pastures'. Leslie Woodgate was also associated with the show from the start as conductor of the choir of thirty singers, and Scott and Whaley were the two extremely popular comedians.

Revivals of this kind have always had a place in show business. Val Gielgud, however, planned to write a new style of radio operetta, 'musicals' particularly adapted to sound radio. It was with this in mind that he approached Eric Maschwitz,

[1] *Radio Times*, 25 Aug. 1932.
[2] *These Radio Times*, BBC Light Programme, 13 Oct. 1951.

who had been his editor while he worked on the *Radio Times*, was passionately interested both in writing and in the stage, and was married to Hermione Gingold. Maschwitz had started work in the BBC as a member of the Outside Broadcasts Department in 1926, and his first nine months had been spent in 'uproarious occasions with Gerald Cock at theatres, football matches and the like' and church services, which were his special responsibility. On the death of Walter Fuller, the talented and cultured editor of the *Radio Times*, in September 1927, Maschwitz had taken over, first as acting and then as established editor.[1]

The *Radio Times* then and later was a centre of inspiration in relation to the entertainment side of broadcasting. In addition to Gielgud, Maschwitz also had under his direction Laurence Gilliam, who later became Head of Features,[2] and Maurice Gorham, his art editor, who was to have an extremely varied and lively BBC career as editor of the *Radio Times*, Director of the North American Service, Head of the Light Programme, and Head of Television. Gorham has also written copiously about the history both of the BBC and of broadcasting as a whole.[3]

The milieu was favourable, but Maschwitz had individual gifts which would have pushed him to the forefront in a quite different kind of organization. He wrote the words of the best-selling popular song, 'These Foolish Things', with melody by Jack Strachey and went on to co-operate with George Posford in the kind of operetta about which Gielgud had dreamed. The result was *Good Night, Vienna*, finished in 1932. The operetta was broadcast for the first time—with great success—in 1932. The BBC was not to have the monopoly of the new kind of musical. Maschwitz was rung up the day after the broadcast by Herbert Wilcox, the film producer, with an offer to buy the film rights. The result was the first musical talkie made in Britain, with Anna Neagle and Jack Buchanan

[1] For Fuller's contribution to BBC history, see M. Gorham, *Sound and Fury*, particularly pp. 11–12, 22, 27–28; *No Chip on My Shoulder*, p. 51; *The Birth of Broadcasting*, p. 306.

[2] For Gilliam and his work, see below, pp. 112–13, 167–9.

[3] See particularly the two books frequently cited in the footnotes of this History —*Sound and Fury*, an autobiography, and *Broadcasting and Television since 1900*, a general survey.

as stars. 'So', writes Maschwitz, 'I became, almost by accident, a lyric writer and in a sense a musical playwright too.'[1]

There was no accident about his later career. He continued to write radio shows and to take an interest in films, visited Hollywood, and through both his social life and his work on the *Radio Times* met many of the people whom he was later to employ. In the meantime, Val Gielgud was finding himself overworked in the Production Department. There was more than enough to do with radio drama by itself 'without troubling himself with ukelele players and comedians'.[2] In 1933, therefore, there was a change in internal organization within the BBC, which marked the beginnings of really effective machinery for the development of popular entertainment. A quite separate Variety Department was created, and Maschwitz was put in charge of it.

Roger Eckersley has said that he 'seduced' Maschwitz from the *Radio Times*.[3] In fact, there had been long and heart-searching discussions in the BBC during the year 1932 about the whole future of its policy for popular entertainment. After the move to Broadcasting House, it was decided that the popular entertainment side of broadcasting should receive much more attention: the development of the Empire Service gave added force to the decision.[4] So too did the increasing public appeal of commercial programmes broadcast from Radio Normandie and Radio Luxembourg.[5] Finally, there was a new crisis in the BBC's dealings with outside entertainment interests.

George Black had been extremely irritated in 1931 when the BBC proposed, for reasons of economy during the financial crisis, that relays from the Palladium should cease, at least as a temporary measure.[6] Perhaps in consequence, in October 1931 he reimposed the broadcasting ban on his artists which he had lifted in 1928.[7] Cock understood Black's 'point of view as a businessman' and warned Roger Eckersley that 'the whole of my original six months of difficult negotiations to remove "bans" from stage artists in vaudeville threatens now to be nullified'.

[1] *No Chip on My Shoulder*, p. 57.   [2] *The BBC and All That*, p. 79.
[3] Ibid., p. 64.   [4] For the Empire Service, see below, pp. 369 ff.
[5] See below, pp. 350 ff.
[6] *Cock to Black, 7 Oct. 1931. For the financial crisis and its effects, see below, p. 556.
[7] *Lance Sieveking to Cock, 7 Oct. 1931.

He argued rightly that the decision to cease the Palladium relays had been a 'false economy', and had led to what Black thought was a breach of faith.[1] Gielgud backed him up. 'Either we must undertake a battle to the death with Black and the G.T.C. for the complete independence of our vaudeville artists', he told Eckersley, 'or else we must admit a blunder and get out of it as best we can.' A battle would be both wasteful and futile. 'We are not in a position to offer any artiste a complete livelihood, and an attempt to mobilise public opinion on our side would be a double-edged weapon.'[2] Black controlled one-third of the BBC's artists, and he was, after all, 'representing an organisation' just as the BBC was.

With these considerations in mind Cock persuaded Black, with Gielgud and Eckersley's approval, immediately to cancel the ban on condition that the relays restarted.[3] Unfortunately Black remained suspicious and throughout the rest of the 1930s, as his power increased, his suspicions of the BBC increased. The merger between the General Theatre Corporation and Moss Empires in 1932 gave Black control over both circuits, and he imposed bans intermittently—and somewhat arbitrarily —on many of the army of artists whose livelihood he controlled. Despite his ostensible lifting of the ban in October 1932, by the end of the year he had withheld permission to broadcast from Dajos Bela's Orchestra, Layton and Johnstone, Norman Long, and Max Miller, though their performances had all been advertised in the *Radio Times*.[4]

Confronted by Black, the BBC looked around for allies— other managements, some of the independent theatrical agencies, the gramophone-record companies, Equity, and the Variety Artistes' Federation—but above all, it searched for its own artists. In January 1933, a few months before Maschwitz was appointed to his new post, a BBC memorandum read, 'we should definitely refuse either to pay the G.T.C. a subsidy or

[1] *Cock to R. H. Eckersley, 7 Oct. 1931. 'Seeing that I held Black with us against the strongest possible pressure from the managements wishing to exercise a general ban on BBC Variety [cf. Gillespie and Stoll's threats and even Walter Payne's prophecies] I feel I have to a certain extent personally been obliged to break faith with him.' [2] *Gielgud to R. H. Eckersley, 8 Oct. 1931.
[3] *Cock to R. H. Eckersley, 8 Oct. 1931.
[4] *Memorandum by Cock, 'Resumption of G.T.C. studios' bans on Vaudeville Artists', 16 Dec. 1932; further Memorandum of 19 Dec. 1932; *Daily Express*, 21 Dec. 1932.

fee per artist, and further refuse to make any commitment which would in effect make BBC vaudeville a publicity medium for G.T.C. . . . We can pull through quite comfortably, with the recording companies' co-operation as a trump card.'[1]

It was around this time that a long cool look at 'entertainment' policy was beginning to clarify what the BBC could and could not do. It shared with the theatre a shortage of 'entertainment material', yet it could not or would not call upon the financial resources of the largest theatre managers. Whereas in the United States commercial sponsors were willing to spend up to 25,000 dollars on a single hour's programme, and 'professional broadcasters' of light entertainment were able to make large incomes by concentrating on radio work alone, in Britain the costs of individual broadcasts were severely restricted. The BBC thus had little chance of creating and retaining performers who would remain radio artists, developing their performances on lines most suited to broadcasting. There were genuine difficulties not only in business dealings with the theatre but in the adaptation for radio of a basic tradition of popular entertainment which was visual, gregarious, and ribald. The slicker and more sophisticated side of entertainment, associated with the revue, could easily become so slick and sophisticated that it ceased to be popular at all.

As a result of the changes of 1933, Gielgud remained Head of the Productions Department with four producers and a team of three researchers, while Maschwitz had seven producers—McConnel for light opera and old-time musical comedy, Watt and Pepper for revue and concert-party work, Freeman and Mark Lubbock ('one of the few old Etonians who can ever have danced in the chorus of a London show')[2] for radio operettas and 'light productions', and Sharman and Webster for vaudeville and music hall, the latter concentrating on Empire programmes. In addition he had Stanford Robinson as Music Director,[3] Henry Hall and the Dance Orchestra, Doris Arnold as Musical Assistant to Watt and Pepper, and Jean Melville as an extra accompanist. The responsibility for 'studio

[1] *Memorandum by Cock, 'Resumption of G.T.C. studios' bans on Vaudeville Artists', 2 Jan. 1933.   [2] *No Chip on My Shoulder*, p. 65.
[3] He did not get this title until Sept. 1934. See below, p. 182.

management, effects, balance and control' was left with Gielgud, but Brian Michie and his 'effects staff' and Askew and his 'balance and control staff' were to work equally with both departments.[1]

The 'effects staff' was one of the most interesting units in the BBC. Beginning with hand effects only, the members of the effects unit soon guaranteed to produce any noise required. Some of them were to have distinguished careers in production. Brian Michie was an ex-L.C.C. schoolmaster; C. A. Ladbrook and George Inns had started their BBC careers as messengers. They provided an invaluable link between drama and features on the one hand and light entertainment on the other.[2] Michie was very warmly praised by Maschwitz when the changes of 1933 took place. 'He knows studio work backwards, has a calm nerve, an occasional touch of inspiration and, very important, an unassuming manner which is greatly appreciated by our artists.'[3] With such a testimonial, it is not surprising that Michie was soon transferred to production work and became an interviewer in *In Town Tonight*.

The 'balance and control staff' had been entrusted since the earliest days of broadcasting with the responsibility of placing microphones in the studios so that they would achieve the correct balance and of regulating volume so that it did not overload the transmitters. After 1933 the stage managers and members of 'the balance and control section' were known as 'studio assistants' and the 'effects staff' as 'junior studio assistants'.[4] Changes in title involved, in this case, some real changes in function. They reflected developments in studio technique, which are far from easy to trace in exact chronological sequence. Rex Haworth, working with Stanford Robinson and Gordon McConnel, showed great ingenuity in dealing with the technical presentation of musical comedy and light opera. Work of this kind called upon the imagination of the engineer as well as his technical knowledge, and by 1939 'the balance and control staff' were working directly under F. W. Alexander as Head Programme Engineer.

[1] *Memorandum from the Controller, 31 Mar. 1933.
[2] See also below, pp. 165–8.
[3] *Memorandum by Maschwitz, 'Variety Department Staff', 10 May 1933.
[4] *Internal Instruction*, no. 291, 2 Jan. 1935.

One of the basic developments of the 1930s was the improvement of studio acoustics. The earliest studios at Savoy Hill had
been very heavily damped with felt on the walls and ceilings,
and there had been a lavish use of curtains. It was not until
1927 that attempts were made to increase reverberation by
covering the felted walls with paper so that sound quality
would be lighter and more lively. In the preparations for the
move to Broadcasting House, H. W. L. Kirke and R. Howe
of the Engineering Research Department experimented with
sound-absorbing materials, which were later used in the new
studios, and when additional studios were opened at Maida
Vale in 1934, resonant floors were introduced along with
resonant dados of wood with an air space between panel and
wall.[1]

Acoustics was—and is—a very inexact science, the study of
which had been long neglected in Britain. Some of the best acoustic conditions were associated with buildings where no special
precautions had been taken. The lounge of the Grand Hotel
at Eastbourne, for example, where Albert Sandler played, was a
model in this respect. The desirable 'echo effect' there led to
attempts to introduce 'artificial echo' to BBC studio output, and
echo-room techniques were developed by the BBC's Engineering Research Department long before they became essential to
the equipment of certain kinds of 'pop' singer.[2] Many other
special devices were associated with the Production Group of
studios on the sixth and seventh floors of Broadcasting House.
Studio 6D, like the Effects Studio at Savoy Hill, was equipped
with machines for the production of every conceivable noise,
including a large tank for water noises, a wind machine,
suspended sheets for thunder, and even a barrel organ. Studio
6E, with elaborate electrical controls, contained six gramophone
turntables to be used for 'mixing' a variety of noises, including
applause.[3]

Within the studios, much depended on the evolution of
'microphone techniques'. Four different designs of microphone

---

[1] Paper by Kirke and Howe to the Institution of Electrical Engineers, 1936.
See also paper by H. Bishop,
[2] *BBC Handbook* (1929), pp. 298–301.
[3] *BBC Year Book* (1932), p. 74. It was the policy of the BBC throughout the 1930s
not to introduce artificial applause into studio programmes.

were employed between 1927 and 1939.[1] The Round–Sykes electro-dynamic microphone, which had been a very valuable instrument because of its silent background, had been in general use since the earliest days of broadcasting. It had, however, a small angle of sensitivity, in front only, and outside this angle it was sensitive only to low frequencies. This did not prevent it from being disturbed by draughts and movement. The Reiss carbon granule microphone was introduced in 1926. It had a good frequency response, but had trouble with 's's and was prone to 'blasting' in loud passages and hiss in weak passages. Yet it was more sensitive than the Round–Sykes microphone, and it remained in service until the late 1930s. The moving-coil microphone—of American origin—was smaller and had a silent background. It was used experimentally in 1932, and in greatly improved form is still used in outside broadcasts—most of which require multiple-microphone techniques.[2] The angle of sensitivity was not so wide as the Reiss, but its frequency response was better and it did not 'blast'.

Lastly, the BBC ribbon microphone, designed by F. W. Alexander of the BBC in 1934, represented a revolutionary advance. It had the enormous advantage of being sensitive for about 120 degrees both at the front and the back, and of having two dead sectors of about 60 degrees on either side. The frequency response did not vary, however, in the horizontal plane. Its value in variety—as in drama and radio discussion work— was obvious, and it became the standard studio microphone in 1936. It had the additional advantage of being cheap. The Marconi Company sold it for about £9 as against the price of £40 for the moving-coil microphone.

Advantageous though the new microphone obviously was, its development by engineers was not fully co-ordinated with the work of the producers, and there was some friction between producers, who had become used to less highly developed microphones, and engineers who were interested in technical perfection. The eventual result, however, was closer liaison between engineers and producers. R. T. B. Wynn, Senior

[1] There was also a fifth, the condenser microphone, used in various forms experimentally between 1927 and 1939. The first example, the Western Electric Microphone, is illustrated in the *BBC Handbook* (1929), p. 302. The condenser microphone was to become a service microphone during the 1950s.

[2] See *BBC Year Book* (1932), 'The Technique of Outside Broadcasts', pp. 345–7.

Superintendent Engineer in charge of Operations and Maintenance, was appointed as the representative of the Engineering Department to maintain close liaison formally through a Microphone Committee and informally in many ways. This side of BBC engineering has a special fascination of its own.

One main problem in liaison was not solved until the Second World War. There was no adequate control of 'continuity'. The centralization of continuity and control in the main Control Room on the eighth floor at the top of Broadcasting House could often lead to tension between programme producers and junior engineers—and incidentally to strange incongruities for the listener, like the fading back to dance music after the first bulletin on King George V's serious illness in 1936. The broadcasting of the unforgettable remarks of Lieut.-Commander Woodrooffe at the Spithead Review of May 1937, beginning with the phrase 'The Fleet is all lit up', was a further demonstration of the inflexibility of the centralized Control Room. It was not until after 1939, however, that a new de-centralized continuity system came into operation.[1] It had been suggested first by Wynn as a direct result of the Woodrooffe incident, and it was designed by C. H. Colborn. The system consisted essentially of two rooms separated by a glass panel and sound-insulated from each other. One was manned by a technical operator who was provided with technical facilities for selecting and mixing programmes and checking quality. The other was an announcing studio manned by the presentation announcer for the programme or network. The latter was responsible for making quick decisions about the running of the programme and for making stop-gap announcements. Other countries followed the BBC in developing this 'continuity system', which was so efficient that it quickly became taken for granted, like so many of the achievements of the engineers.

Other aspects of the relationship between engineers and programme producers centred on the development of recording.[2] The idea of 'bottled programmes' had been mooted as early as 1927—partly as a device for ensuring the provision of repeat

[1] For this account, which cannot be traced in the Archives, I am grateful to the Hon. R. T. B. Wynn. For information on microphones I am grateful to Dr. F. W. Alexander.

[2] See also above, p. 6.

programmes in an Empire Service so that in different time
zones listeners could listen at convenient hours[1]—and dicta-
phones were used in 1927 to record both a rugby match between England and Wales and the Grand National. It was not,
however, until after Blattner's development of the 1925 Stille
electro-magnetic machine for recording programmes on steel
wire or tape that recording became a practical possibility, if
still a very cumbrous one.[2] The value of the machine lay in the
fact that immediate play-back was possible along with electrical
editing and 'wiping' of the tape for re-use. Carpendale and
Ashbridge visited the Blattner studios at Elstree in 1929,[3] and
in 1931 a Blattnerphone recording machine was installed at
Savoy Hill. It was transferred in 1932 to the seventh floor of
Broadcasting House and supplemented by other machines of
improved design. H. L. Fletcher, who became first Recorded
Programmes Executive in January 1934,[4] was the kind of
imaginative person who could see a direct link between engineering techniques and programme production, even though the
Blattnerphone was an awkward piece of apparatus and the
cutting of steel tapes was a hazardous procedure, requiring
'battleship'-driving machinery.

Fletcher used the new apparatus to experiment with sound.
Pieces of Tape (1932) was produced from a number of Blattnerphone tapes recorded during the year. *Stars in their Courses*
(1933) featured Dame Irene Vanbrugh, Fay Compton, Sir
Frank Benson, and Matheson Lang. The use of the technique
in news programmes was obvious,[5] and *Radio Gazette* (1935)
pointed the way forward to such popular programmes of the
future as *Radio Newsreel*. 'We have built a number of pro-

[1] *Beadle to Reith, 12 May 1927. Beadle referred in this interesting memorandum on the 'General Principles of an Empire Broadcasting Scheme' to 'Captain
Eckersley's "bottled programme" idea'. Eckersley was thinking of recording on
iron wire at this time. A BBC engineer was sent to Berlin to investigate German
developments in 1927. Reith's Report to the Board of Governors, 15 June 1927.

[2] See J. W. Godfrey, 'The History of BBC Sound Recording' in the *Journal* of
the British Sound Recording Association.

[3] *Control Board Minutes, 9 Dec. 1929.

[4] *Internal Memorandum, no. 254. Fletcher, who had been transferred in March
1933 from Programme Routine to a new Recorded Programmes Section, was
assigned the task of providing a link between the Technical Recording Section (in
the Engineering Branch) and the Programme Services Executive, R. J. F. Howgill.
At the same time a separate Gramophone Section was set up.

[5] See below, p. 155.

grammes from records', Fletcher wrote as early as January 1934, including 'guessing games' and 'retrospective programmes' like *What's On In Town?* 'in which an overseas visitor returns to the Dominions and describes his experiences'. 'The use of recorded material', he added, 'involves a definite *working* knowledge [on the part of producers] of a new and special technique which arises from the special nature of the new machinery employed.'[1] When Thomas Jones first heard of it in 1933 he was more guarded in his reception of the new invention, which he described as 'new marvels in the behaviour of electrons in recording human wisdom—and folly'.[2]

If Blattnerphone made recording feasible, it also left it expensive, and even after the introduction of the Marconi–Stille machine in 1934[3]—six machines were installed in pairs, at Maida Vale—the search for alternative methods of recording continued. There were technical difficulties, too, associated with 'wow', the wavering of pitch, and 'plop', extraneous disturbances. BBC engineers were always searching for a better process, and the development of flat-disc recording produced in 1933 what in many ways was a far more flexible system. Cecil Watts, the Managing Director of the Marguerite Sound Studios in Old Compton Street, worked with zinc or aluminium disc-recording—the discs had a lacquer or acetate surface—and the BBC began to co-operate with Watts in October.[4] The results were found to be sufficiently satisfactory for the BBC to prefer his apparatus to that of German competitors. The number of Watts discs used inside the BBC in 1936 was double that in 1935. Disc editing became possible, and John Lock of the Engineering Division developed a mechanism to locate the exact groove on each disc on which an incident or even a word was recorded.

George Inns was one of the first highly skilled operators of this equipment as of so much else, and one of the first deliberate uses of editing was in the recording of the speech of the Garter King at Arms at the proclamation of George VI. With only the original voice being used, a repeated spoonerism—'our right

1 *Fletcher to Dawnay, 12 Jan. 1934.

2 T. Jones, *A Diary with Letters* (1954), p. 89.

3 *On 9 Nov. 1933 MacLarty, Howe, and Patrick visited Chelmsford to inspect this model.

4 *Bishop to Watts, 24 Oct. 1933.

liegeful Lord' instead of 'our rightful liege Lord'—was cor-
rected, after the Garter King at Arms and the Director-General
had given their consent. The record was long used as a test of
editing skill for trainees.[1] Such selective editing was also used
in the Empire Service to cut recordings of home programmes
which would otherwise have taken up too much time.

It is interesting to note that while editing was being used
for these innocent purposes in Broadcasting House, its more
sinister possibilities were being recognized in Germany. The
more general use of recording was held back in Britain, partly
for reasons of cost—gramophone disc-recording and excerpts
from the sound track of films were particularly expensive[2]—
partly because there was a very powerful feeling in almost all
programme departments that it was better to broadcast 'live'.
'If an hour's programme requires to be recorded on wax for
any special reason', the Variety Executive wrote in 1936, 'it
must be borne in mind that this is a very costly business and
cannot be done unless there are some very special reasons for
it.'[3] 'If artists know they are being recorded and a re-take can
be made if they "fluff",' another BBC official put it, 'they tend
to give a mediocre performance. A live broadcast, with the
artist having a "this is it" feeling when the red light comes on,
gives the most satisfaction to listeners.'[4]

Recording, nonetheless, made producers more conscious of
'quality production' and ultimately may have made some of
them, at least, less afraid of working without scripts. 'In the
Savoy Hill days, we never had scripts', one of the Houston
Sisters recalled later.[5] Yet by 1935 scripts were almost obligatory
in light entertainment as elsewhere.[6] Another aspect of recording, which later revolutionized light entertainment, was
very slow to develop before 1939—the recording of outside
broadcasts. A 30-cwt. Morris Commercial truck was bought in

[1] For this story, which cannot be traced in the Archives, I am grateful to Mr.
H. L. Fletcher, who has also provided me with much other useful information about
recording.
[2] In 1935 the BBC realized that it would be useful to have engineers with
gramophone-company experience, and F. H. Dart was brought in with this in
mind.
[3] *Note by M. M. Dewar, 25 Mar. 1936.
[4] Note by R. C. Patrick, to whom I am grateful for information on this subject.
[5] *BBC Programme, *These Radio Times*, 3 Nov. 1951.
[6] See J. C. Cannell, *In Town Tonight* (1935), pp. 21–22.

1935, but there was a tendency inside the BBC to regard it as a toy and there were disputes both about its control and its use. Two more trucks were bought and both were equipped with Watts recorders, yet they were so huge and unwieldy that they were ultimately used as static channels during the Second World War. L. F. Lewis suggested, more practically, in 1936 that recording apparatus might also be fitted into a lighter touring car, but it was not until September 1938 that a Chrysler was bought for this purpose. It was the war which gave mobile recording the great boost it had never had in time of peace.

In this as in so many other branches of broadcasting, the ordinary listener, when he listened, had no conception of the complexities of organization which lay behind even the lightest of light entertainment. By the very nature of broadcasting, the best results could be obtained only through the willing co-operation—at the programme level—of the producer and the engineer. Lynton Fletcher always saw the importance of this. So did R. T. B. Wynn. Fletcher was not sure, in fact, whether his place should be with programmes or with administration. He thought of the manipulation of technique as 'creative' in itself, a field for experiment as well as a field of service. Wynn shifted attention from the 'big' engineering problems, associated with the Regional Scheme or with Empire broadcasting, to what went on in the studio itself.

That difficulties remained is shown by the history of the last of the systems of recording tried out during the 1930s—the Philips–Miller system. Apparatus for this system was produced in Holland and was first employed by the BBC on a trial basis in October 1936.[1] It was a reliable but expensive film-type recorder system, and it guaranteed better quality than any system previously used.[2] As such it naturally commended itself to the engineers for many types of recording. The Programme Departments, however, were less impressed. They had been asking for more Blattnerphone and Watts disc apparatus and failing to get it, through no fault of the engineers. Now it seemed that, with the more expensive apparatus, they were going to be able to record less than they had recorded before. They clashed with the engineers also on the question of the ease of

[1] *For the beginning of negotiations, Jardine Brown to Meys, 5 Dec. 1935.
[2] *L. W. Hayes to Felix Greene, 29 Jan. 1937.

editing the products of the new system.[1] The result of the difference of opinion, as might have been expected, was a compromise. Philips–Miller apparatus was acquired, but more of
the other apparatus was acquired also. Gielgud collected the
opinions of his colleagues and recommended this compromise
in May 1937.[2]

Techniques helped to shape BBC programmes, but the main
theme of Eric Maschwitz's régime as Director of Variety from
1933 to 1937 was not technique but romance. This was the
'romantic era' in popular entertainment, with a deliberate
emphasis on gaiety, colour, and movement.[3] The mood was
quite different from that of the first BBC shows of the 1920s,
many of them hearty and uninvolved. It was not that simplicity
was discarded—the BBC Year Books speak, indeed, of a reaction
against 'cleverness'—but the simplicity related to techniques,
not to style and tastes.[4] Symbolic of the new period was
Maschwitz's *Balalaika*, written in collaboration with George
Posford and originally entitled *The Gay Hussar*. The story of
what happened to the production of *Balalaika*, as told by Maschwitz, is almost as exciting as the plot itself:[5] so too is the story
of what happened to Variety.

This was the golden age of nostalgic light music, mainly
sweet but sometimes bitter-sweet, as the title of Noël Coward's
highly successful musical play of 1929 expressed it.[6] *Good Night,
Vienna* was revived in 1933 as deliberate 'radio operetta', along
with a number of studio-produced musical comedies. In 1934
Gordon McConnel's production of *The Lilac Domino*—the
music by Charles Cuvillier—and John Watt's version of *Show
Boat*—the great Drury Lane triumph of 1928 with music by
Jerome Kern and libretto by Oscar Hammerstein—were
greatly appreciated. *Bitter Sweet* followed in 1935, as part of the

---

[1] *Note by Fletcher, 9 Feb. 1937.
[2] *Note by Val Gielgud, 26 May 1937. See also Control Board Minutes, 29 June
1937; Bishop to Jardine Brown, 22 Oct. 1937; Jardine Brown to Meys, 26 Oct.
1937. The agreement between the Philips Company and the BBC was signed on
30 Nov. 1938.
[3] *These Radio Times*, BBC Light Programme, 13 Oct. 1951.
[4] *BBC Year Book* (1935), p. 57. See also above, pp. 57–61.
[5] For the fascinating detailed story of this musical play, see *No Chip on My
Shoulder*, ch. vii.
[6] The title was suggested by Alfred Lunt. See *Fifty Years of Vaudeville*, p. 182.

Silver Jubilee Festival, along with a revival of *The Geisha*. *The Student Prince* and *The Vagabond King* (with Bebe Daniels in the leading part) followed in 1936. It says much for Maschwitz's initiative that there was a spate of original BBC musical plays and operettas to vie with such established stage successes. While Gordon McConnel and Henrik Ege were specializing in the difficult art of compressing 150-minute theatre shows into 75 minutes, they and other writers were at the same time producing such brand new BBC shows as *Never Talk to Strangers*, *Three Cornered Hat*, and *Money for Jam* (1936).

Maschwitz did four important things in his tenure of office from 1933 to 1937. First, he started a new BBC Theatre, St. George's Hall, across from Broadcasting House in Langham Place. Second, he pushed towards its logical conclusion the policy of encouraging new performers and new 'runs' or 'series' of shows, of which *Songs From the Shows*, *Music Hall*, *The White Coons*, and *The Kentucky Minstrels* had been early examples. Third, he introduced many new ideas into popular entertainment, from the unscripted Christmas party to the 'symphonic' treatment of dance music. Fourth, he interested the press and the public in what he was doing. For the first time the doings of the BBC became news in the entertainment world. Behind the scenes, Maschwitz was often conscious of almost overwhelming difficulties—the intermittent bans were one, the overwork another—but they were seldom allowed to darken the gaiety and colour of the picture as a whole.

The opening of St. George's Hall in Langham Place on 25 November 1933 was not only a sign that Broadcasting House was too small but that broadcast popular entertainment had reached a position of independence.[1] The theatre had been empty for only a few months since the last performance of Jasper Maskelyne's *White Magic*, and the BBC acquired it after quick and straightforward negotiations. Maschwitz took over a large room above the theatre where he enjoyed what he has described as 'a pleasant sense of escape from the growing formality of existence at Broadcasting House'. The members of the Variety team called each other by their first names, ate and drank together, and 'were friends'.[2]

[1] The first broadcast from St. George's Hall had been given earlier—on 23 Oct. 1933.   [2] *No Chip on My Shoulder*, p. 70.

(a) An Early Outside Broadcasts Hut

(b) A Cup Tie
Corinthians *v.* Newcastle United (1927) with
George Allison commentating

(c) The Boat Race (1928)

8. Outside Broadcasting

(*a*) Jack Payne and the BBC Dance Orchestra (1928)

(*b*) Noël Coward and Henry Hall (1934)

9. The Entertainers

(*a*) Richard Murdoch and Arthur Askey in *Band Waggon* (1938)

(*b*) St. George's Hall (1938)

10. Variety

(a) Microphones used by the BBC (Ribbon, Reisz, and Moving Coil)

(b) Listening Room (1932), re-named Studio Control Cubicle, 1939

(c) The Dramatic Control Panel (1934)

11. Behind the Scenes

There were new faces too—A. W. ('Bill') Hanson, the first producer of *In Town Tonight*, whose unfortunate death in January 1938 robbed broadcasting of a very talented producer;[1] Max Kester, the son of a Yorkshire journalist and cartoonist; Ernest Longstaffe, later of *Palace of Varieties* fame, who had once posted showbills for Karno and had written and produced broadcasts (including the Bee Bee Cabaret) as early as 1926 before becoming a full-time member of the BBC staff in May 1935;[2] and Charles Shadwell, who was appointed Conductor and Music Assistant in the BBC Variety Department in May 1936. Maschwitz recognized the importance of building up a staff, the members of which would be capable of 'writing up a situation or improving artists' material':[3] Shadwell, with his loud and infectious laugh, was certainly to be remarkably effective in bringing the best out of the material which was there, from *Music Hall* to war-time *Garrison Theatre*.

A further new appointment was that of Theatre Organist. In the autumn of 1936 a theatre organ was installed at St. George's Hall, and it was decided to find an experienced permanent organist rather than to employ a number of people on programme contract. The appointment was authorized in June 1936,[4] and Reginald Foort was appointed in November.[5] He broadcast frequently until, in 1938, he followed Jack Payne's example and appeared as an 'act' in music halls, carrying a huge organ round with him. By then his fan mail amounted to 4,000 letters a year. There were other artists appearing in St. George's Hall who turned to the stage after they had made their BBC reputation—even Christopher Stone once appeared on the stage of the Palladium—and it was from St. George's Hall that the weekly *Music Hall* programme was broadcast. Harry S.

[1] *'I like the idea of Hanson, and think we should get him at once', Maschwitz wrote to Eckersley on 10 May 1933. He called Hanson 'an ideal man for a job in which adult good sense, business ability and a flair for production are essential' and said that his appointment was urgently needed if his own appointment 'is to bear fruit'. For Hanson's own story, see *In Town Tonight*, pp. 78–87.

[2] S. A. Moseley, *Who's Who in Broadcasting* (1933), p. 95; *Memorandum on the Variety Department Staff, 17 May 1935.

[3] *Maschwitz, 'Staff Writers for the Variety Department', 13 June 1934.

[4] *Dewar to C. H. Brewer, 29 June 1936.

[5] *BBC Press Release, 20 Oct. 1936, describes the organ. Foort also wrote a BBC pamphlet on the working of the organ, which he described as 'the grandest, most versatile, most satisfying theatre organ in the world'.

Pepper has written, indeed, not of 'the romantic era' but of 'the St. George's Hall era of Variety'.

Maschwitz's second achievement was to discover new performers, including performers from the provinces, and to increase the number of regular 'series' of broadcasts, widening the range to include programmes quite different in scope and style from *Music Hall*. In 1934 alone the new performers included Vic Oliver, Tod Slaughter, Claude Dampier, and Sandy Powell. Other performers who made their reputations with the BBC, as Mabel Constanduros and John Henry had done, were Leonard Henry, Clapham and Dwyer, Ronald Frankau, Elsie and Doris Waters, John Tilley, Les Allen, Gillie Potter, Elizabeth Welch, Olive Groves, Bertha Wilmott, Anona Winn, Tessa Deane, Alexander and Mose, 'Mrs. Feather' (Jeanne de Casalis), Adele Dixon, Arthur Marshall, and Beryl Orde.

'We should do all that we can to discover and groom such stars', Maschwitz wrote in 1936, when he was complaining along the old familiar lines of a shortage of comedians and 'stars'. 'Occasionally', he added, 'they drop like manna out of heaven', like Arthur Marshall and Beryl Orde, but more usually they had to be 'discovered' and 'trained'. With this object in view, he suggested (abortively) an 'act building' department and encouraged the appointment of 'Variety apprentices', young people who made a good impression at auditions and were thought capable of becoming 'first-rate broadcasters'.[1] He also gave his support to a young Canadian producer, Carroll Levis, who in 1937 put before him the idea of programmes of amateur 'discoveries' just when Maschwitz's own ideas for new programmes were running out:

> I wanna be discovered, Mr. Levis,
> Now don't you think that I've got what it takes,
> My family think I'm good, of course, that's understood,
> But somehow I can never get the breaks.

There was some doubt as to whether this song could go on the air, when it had Levis's name in the title and when other songs 'dealing with milk bars, tea, etc. had all been banned'. The song, like the idea, stayed.

---

[1] *Memorandum of 14 Mar. 1935; 'Memorandum on Microphone Talent', 3 Mar. 1936.

In the meantime, while the critics were praising 'the brusque satire of Gillie Potter, the deprecating shyness of John Tilley, the off-hand jokes of Christopher Stone, "Stainless Stephen's" punctilious pronunciation and the never-risky riskiness of A. J. Alan',[1] there had been a quite remarkable spate of new programmes. The first of them was *In Town Tonight* which was first broadcast on 18 November 1933, with its signature tune, Eric Coates's 'Knightsbridge March', chosen by Maschwitz himself. The idea of *In Town Tonight* was a by-product of Maschwitz's experience on the *Radio Times*: the programme was to be a 'shop window for any topical feature that might bob up too late to be included in the *Radio Times*'.[2] For years there had been spaces in the published programmes labelled 'Surprise Item': Maschwitz and Bill Hanson set out in November 1933 to pack the surprise items together in an attractive parcel.

The form of the programme was decided upon only on the morning of the first performance—the 'roar of London's traffic', the flower girl murmuring 'sweet violets', and the 'stentorian shout' of 'stop!' Freddie Grisewood was the first—normally quite unstentorian—shouter.[3] The first programme, like so many of the first programmes of series which eventually became quite exceptional successes, was not a great success. Before long, however, the programme established itself as a popular favourite, bringing to the microphone at the same time each week a great medley of characters who either lived in or were visiting London. A sense of spontaneity was achieved, and Coates's signature tune became as well known as the programme itself.

There seemed to be a danger of success leading to staleness, and in October 1935 the programme was incorporated in a *Saturday Magazine*, one of the earliest weekly magazine programmes. There were so many protests about its disappearance, however, that it was restored in its own right in 1937. 'There is no doubt', the North Regional Programme Director wrote to Hanson in June 1937, 'that *In Town Tonight* is still one of the most popular features, and one hears many regrets in this Region that it should have been stopped.'[4] 'We in Northern Ireland', wrote the Northern Ireland Regional Programme

[1] *The Times*, Broadcasting Number, 14 Aug. 1934.
[2] *No Chip on My Shoulder*, p. 67.
[3] See F. Grisewood, *My Story of the BBC* (1959), pp. 168–70.
[4] *Salt to Hanson, 28 June 1937.

Director, 'are inclined to give extremely sympathetic attention to anything emanating from London and so to take *In Town Tonight* perhaps even more enthusiastically than most of the Regions with the exception of Scotland.'[1] This quixotic remark was, surprisingly enough, corroborated from Glasgow where the Regional Programme Director talked of Scottish listeners to whom 'it is the very elixir of life to be transported on Saturdays to the hub of their heaven'.[2]

Among the other radio series which began between 1933 and 1937 was music from the Café Colette, 'designed to present continental dance music as an alternative to American jazz'[3] —one of the first of several BBC programmes (July 1933) which sought, with music from Walford Hyden, to recreate the atmosphere of Budapest or Paris in a London studio. Others were *Honeymoon in Paris* (1934), a radio operetta by Cecil Lewis and Austen Croom-Johnson; *The Red Sarafan* (1935), with Russian music in a Parisian night-club setting; and, more authentic, a programme of songs by Josephine Baker in October 1933.

Late-night monthly revues, on the lines of those of Noël Coward, were organized by Denis Freeman, with words mainly by Jack Strachey, and brought to the microphone sophisticated West End artists like Nelson Keys, Hermione Gingold, Greta Keller, Eileen Hunter, Elizabeth Welch and—a further French touch—Jean Sablon, borrowed, along with Marion Harris, the crooner, from the Café de Paris. Maschwitz's best-selling song, 'These Foolish Things', also had reminiscences of Paris, with the line 'wild strawberries only seven francs a kilo' sounding far more nostalgic today than 'the Île de France with all the gulls around it'.

Paris and Budapest were close rivals inside Broadcasting House during these years, with Vienna never forgotten. Two foreign writers, Bürger and Walter, produced such combinations of story and music as *Vienna, Holiday Abroad* and *The Story of the Waltz*. While the news bulletins were presenting daily evidence of friction and tension in Europe, the entertainers were offering a quite different image, the Europe not of conflict but of romance, of Ruritania, not Nuremberg.

---

[1] *Sutthery to Hanson, 23 June 1937.
[2] *Scottish Regional Programme Director to Hanson, 22 June 1937.
[3] *No Chip on My Shoulder*, p. 68.

It is interesting that it was towards Europe that the BBC turned—however frivolously—rather than towards the United States. Maschwitz visited the United States on several occasions and according to Maurice Gorham, his successor on the *Radio Times*, they both shared 'the rabid pro-Americanism of the twenties'.[1] There was relatively little direct American influence, however, on British light entertainment as presented by the BBC, despite the dominance of Hollywood in the golden age of the cinema. American artists performed—Eddie Cantor, for instance, and the 'close harmony' Boswell Sisters—and the idea of a 'programme series', pushed much farther by Maschwitz in 1934, owed something to the American idea of 'the So-and-So Hour',[2] yet no attempt was made to copy the comedy-series type of American broadcast, already represented in the early 1930s by 'Amos 'n Andy' and Burns and Allen.

It was in 1929 that Rudy Vallee, sponsored by Fleischmann's Yeast, had extended the dance-band-with-plugs formula in the United States by deliberately introducing 'radio personalities': the same year saw the beginnings of the Amos 'n Andy and Goldberg shows, the latter among the first of the afternoon dramatic serials which were forerunners of the 'soap operas' of the 1930s.[3] By 1934 large numbers of entertainment programmes were being produced in Hollywood, with slick compèring and comedians being allowed to project their personalities through whole programmes rather than contributing 'turns' of strictly limited duration.

It was not until just before the Second World War, however, that such American fashions of light entertainment—influential through the cinema—began to refashion British programmes.[4] Even so, it was a sign of pride that the musical plays chosen for the Silver Jubilee productions in 1935 were all British.[5] Songs were certainly becoming more American long before this. 'The gramophone disc has carried Hollywood's "hits" into many programmes', the *Manchester Guardian* complained in 1930. 'Much of this music is apparently so ephemeral that many of the new numbers given abroad do not live to reach this country.

[1] *Sound and Fury*, p. 38.   [2] *BBC Annual* (1935), p. 59.
[3] L. White, *The American Radio* (1947), pp. 61 ff., 'Love That Soap'.
[4] Oddly enough, it was a transatlantic broadcast from London by Burns and Allen which put them on the stage in America. See *No Chip on My Shoulder*, p. 74.
[5] *BBC Annual* (1936), p. 41.

On the other hand, some tunes which have become popular here have often been heard from the Continent months before they reach us. . . . I have heard the *Broadway Melody* from six different stations in Ireland, Latvia, Germany, Czechoslovakia and France during the last fortnight. For Britain the bloom has worn off it.'[1] In 1934 *The Times* was noting how 'each week the Audition Committee of the Variety Department listens to a dozen crooners offering a fairly accomplished imitation of Bing Crosby, and a dozen impersonators who follow Florence Desmond and Beryl Orde in impersonations of Mae West and Zasu Pitts'.[2] The outstanding BBC crooner of the 1930s was British—Al Bowlly. Singing many of the same songs as Bing Crosby, he had a distinctive style and mood of his own, and he had great popular appeal then and since.

By current standards, even gramophone-record programmes, strictly limited in hours, had a strong British flavour. The American (and continental) reliance on gramophone records as the 'staple diet' of broadcasting was never copied by the BBC. Nor were the gramophone-record companies as sure of the business attractions of radio as they subsequently became. When the BBC turned to the gramophone industry in an effort to break Black's broadcasting ban,[3] at least one gramophone magnate told Roger Eckersley that broadcasting was 'definitely competitive, both to the entertainment industry and to his own business'. He said that he preferred the 'steady sales' which accrued from records of well-known artists whose names had been made apart from broadcasting to the 'jumpy sales' stimulated by broadcasting.[4]

Such pre-Juke Box Jury attitudes record the distance between the 1930s and the 1960s. Already, however, there were signs —at least in retrospect—of the shape of things to come, particularly on the other side of the Atlantic. In the late 1920s various systems of rating popular music and records began to be

[1] *Manchester Guardian*, 19 Sept. 1930.

[2] *The Times*, Broadcasting Number, 14 Aug. 1934.

[3] *Cock, Memorandum of 2 Jan. 1933. 'Private contact should be made with the Gramophone Companies to ascertain to what extent they would support us in including in any future contracts with their artists a clause preventing the latter from signing non-broadcasting contracts.'

[4] *A note by R. H. Eckersley after visiting the H.M.V. Office at Hayes, 26 Jan. 1933.

worked out in the United States,[1] and *Billboard* began a 'Network Song Census' in 1934, the year when the coin record machine went into mass production.[2] By 1939, when millions of dance records were being sold each year in Britain, there were 350,000 coin record machines in the United States.[3] 'A-tisket, A-tasket' sold more than 300,000 copies in 1939, and earlier songs like Mabel Wayne's 'Ramona' and 'Little Man, You've had a Busy Day' became known all over the world.

In 1935 the American radio began its *Hit Parade* programmes, and the ratings given in this series began to be set out a year later in the British *Melody Maker*,[4] which had had its own 'Honours List' (a different conception from the 'Top Ten') in 1928. It was not until 1943, however, that details of 'the Ten Best Sellers in Britain' began to be published weekly. By then a new pattern of 'popular culture' was emerging, although it required very different social circumstances from those of the 1930s to establish the pattern. The producers of entertainment were not as preoccupied with the age gap between different generations of listeners in the 1930s as their successors were to be in the 1950s.

The distance in attitudes is also apparent in the BBC's *Scrapbook* programmes, which were an invention of the 1930s but still retain their appeal today. The first—for 1913—was broadcast in December 1933. The work of Leslie Baily and, in the early days, Charles Brewer, *Scrapbook* programmes, many of them subsequently revived to meet the demands of new generations, have given probably more pleasure than any other long-running series of BBC programmes. Already by November 1934 the *Manchester Guardian* was referring to the *Scrapbook* series 'which Leslie Baily has made famous' and Grace Wyndham Goldie was writing in *The Listener* that statues ought to be erected to Brewer and Baily.[5]

[1] *Variety*, 31 July 1929, listed the three best sellers of the preceding week for each of ten publishers on the West Coast. *Monthly Musical Survey*, 13 Nov. 1929, included details of the six best sellers both in sheet music and records in a number of American cities.

[2] *Billboard*, 30 June 1934; J. L. Davis, *Your All Time Hit Parade* (1957).

[3] Ibid., p. 16. See also R. Gelatt, *The Fabulous Phonograph* (1956), pp. 208 ff.

[4] *The Melody Maker*, 9 May 1936.

[5] *Manchester Guardian*, 11 Nov. 1934; *The Listener*, 14 Nov. 1934. For the early story of *Scrapbook*, see L. Baily and C. H. Brewer, *The BBC Scrapbooks* (1937).

The *Scrapbook* programmes satisfied the Englishman's love of nostalgic reminiscence—as did Leslie Baily's later radio biographies, *Star-gazing*, beginning in October 1936—and at the same time drew on a powerful documentary element which earns them a certain place in the future interpretation of contemporary history. They were based on genuine research, and in Freddie Grisewood, who was narrator for the first two programmes, they were to find the perfect compère. The second and third programmes in the series—in May and November 1934—covered the years 1914 and 1918. 'A night to remember', wrote the *Star* radio correspondent of the first; 'the best broadcast I ever heard' added Archie de Bear in the *Daily Express* of the same day.[1]

To thousands of listeners, as well as to the critics, *Scrapbook* represented the art of sound radio at its best. So too did some of the peak outside broadcasts—the boxing contest between Len Harvey and Jack Petersen in November 1933; the wedding of the Duke of Kent and Princess Marina in November 1934; Maschwitz's own commentary on the Silver Jubilee Ball from the Albert Hall in 1935; the annual British Legion Festival of Empire and Remembrance; and, above all, the Christmas programmes which were devised by Laurence Gilliam.

King George V gave the first of his Christmas broadcasts to both home and Empire listeners in 1932. Reith had suggested such broadcasts to Lord Stamfordham five years before, and at last, in circumstances which Reith has fully described, they found a unique place in the broadcasting year.[2] The King himself was 'very pleased and much moved' by the response to his first broadcast, and his broadcasts almost immediately became an established institution. Much ingenuity and enterprise also went into the arrangements for the programmes leading up to them, with Laurence Gilliam active behind the scenes. Christmas, indeed, was always a broadcasting festival during the inter-war years, not least because it is a family festival. The BBC added to the domestic enjoyment without seeming to intrude. Behind the fun, however, there were elaborate arrangements. In 1933 there was a programme on Christmas Eve in which listeners heard the bells of Bethlehem and carol singing

[1] The *Star*, 10 May 1934; *Daily Express*, 10 May 1934.
[2] J. C. W. Reith, *Into the Wind* (1949), pp. 168–9.

from New York, 'a fine piece of organisation by the programme and engineering staffs'. In 1934 the King's Christmas Day speech was introduced by 'the grand old shepherd of Ilmington'. 'It was a stroke of genius on the part of the producer', wrote Stuart Hibberd, 'to find him and put him in the programme.'[1]

The King's speech was always *sui generis*, but on many other national occasions the BBC was entertaining its audience and doing much more besides. It was holding together 'the great audience' of which Reith was so proud. National pride was, of course, a somewhat uncomplicated emotion, and care was always taken not to damage it. It rang triumphantly through Noël Coward's *Cavalcade* (1931) which was hailed by James Agate, the best-known theatre critic of the day, as a huge success even before the public made it such. Agate also considered Coward to be 'the best comic dramatist since Sheridan' and admired the wit with which he described and criticized many favourite British institutions.

One thing which the BBC did not do during the 1930s was to provide entertainment with a satirical edge. It could tolerate burlesque, although it was never anxious to have itself guyed, as it was guyed in Herbert Farjeon's *Nine Sharp*, with its engaging song 'Thank God for the BBC'. Nor could the Continent be guyed either—for all the whiff of Paris in the air. When Max Kester made suggestions in 1933 that there should be a programme burlesquing continental stations, one BBC official insisted that there should be no references to foreign commercial stations since this would be to draw attention to them. Another official added that it was important to avoid saying anything derogatory about non-commercial continental stations either, because many of them were suffering from severe financial limitations.[2] 'Satire has proved "on the air", as in the theatre, a little too strong meat for British audiences', we read—and believe—in the *BBC Year Book* of 1934.[3]

There was, of course, a persistent search for new means of diversion, and the new ideas in light entertainment which were introduced between 1933 and 1937 included serial thrillers, the first of them Sydney Horler's *The Mystery of the Seven Cafés*

[1] S. Hibberd, *This—is London*, p. 107.
[2] *Programme Board Minutes, 14 Dec. 1933.
[3] *BBC Year Book* (1934), p. 58.

(1935), followed the same year by the introduction of a serial thriller *Strange to Relate* into the *Saturday Magazine*.[1] There were also regular programmes of 'Curiosities'; John Watt's adaptation for radio of Walt Disney's Mickey Mouse features (1936); a 'first night' from a theatre, again with John Watt, this time as a commentator in the foyer; and his *Entertainment Parade* (1936), which set out to present to the public in tabloid form information concerning what was going on in show business, not only in London and the provinces but abroad. Finally there were many experiments in 'symphonic' popular music of the kind that Paul Whiteman was beginning to popularize across the Atlantic. Geraldo's *Romance in Rhythm*, Austen Croom-Johnson's *Soft Lights and Sweet Music*, and Louis Levy's *Music From the Movies* were examples of this genre.

Maschwitz was anxious to break away from the idea that dance music was a 'filler' or a 'routine' programme for the end of a busy day.[2] He also believed at the end of his four years as Director of Variety that there was no longer any need for a BBC Dance Orchestra as such. In a memorandum of February 1937 he pointed out that the situation had changed completely from 1928 when Jack Payne had been appointed. Then there was a dearth of suitable bands. In 1937, however, there was 'an ample supply of dance bands and the facility to create as many as we like': in addition, the coming into existence of the Variety Orchestra had cut down the amount of work that a BBC Dance Orchestra was expected to do. Henry Hall had a 'magnificent record' in his five years at the BBC but the time had come to encourage outside bands, to draw new programme ideas from 'the best brains available in the entertainment world', and to create a separate Dance Music section to translate the ideas into programmes, watch song-plugging, and 'safeguard the interests of publishers, band leaders and listeners'.[3]

Henry Hall had a shrewd idea of the direction of change, as he saw more and more bands appearing on BBC programmes —Ambrose, Sid Bright, Billy Cotton, Roy Fox, Geraldo, Carroll Gibbons, Nat Gonella, Brian Lawrence, Sydney

---

[1] *Saturday Magazine* reverted in autumn 1937 to its old title of *In Town Tonight*.
[2] See above, pp. 86–88.
[3] *Memorandum from the Director of Variety to the Controller of Programmes, 5 Feb. 1937.

Lipton, Joe Loss, Felix Mendelssohn, Jack Payne, Oscar Rabin, Harry Roy, Lew Stone, Maurice Winnick, and 'many others less known'. Some of the bands had had an evening to themselves—Lew Stone, for example, on Tuesdays from 10.30 p.m. to midnight, but in 1937 the policy was to vary hours, 'odd bands at odd hours and fair shares for all'.[1] As suddenly as he entered the BBC, therefore, Hall left it—on 25 September 1937, without any row and characteristically with very little fuss. One of the first and best offers he had was from George Black. He accepted it. On Saturday he was giving his farewell BBC broadcast: on the following Monday he was on the stage of the Hippodrome at Birmingham.

By the time Henry Hall left the BBC Maschwitz had also left, in June 1937, for Metro-Goldwyn-Mayer and the blue skies of Hollywood,[2] and it was John Watt, his successor, who was left to make the arrangements for the new system of 'fair shares' and 'free for all' in dance music. He was assisted by Philip Brown, a band leader from Birmingham, who took charge of dance-music policy. Henry Hall's farewell broadcast on 25 September began with 'Here's to the Next Time' and ended with Gracie Fields singing—as no one else could sing —'You've got to Smile when you Say Goodbye'. Other tunes in the programme included 'It's a Sin to Tell a Lie', 'Red Sails in the Sunset', and 'Let's Put Out the Lights'. There is no better way of evoking a lost moment of time than to listen again to its favourite tunes. 'The regular broadcasts by the BBC Dance Orchestra, under Henry Hall,' the *BBC Year Book* commented prosily, 'will remain a pleasant memory in the minds of many listeners, both in this country and abroad.'[3]

Neither Hall nor Maschwitz was lost to British broadcasting. Hall was to entertain post-Second World War audiences both on sound radio and television. Maschwitz was to return to the BBC in 1958. In his first spell, not the least of his achievements had been to interest the public in what he was doing and to put the BBC in the centre of the entertainment world. The number of light-entertainment programmes had substantially

[1] Henry Hall, *Here's To the Next Time* (1955), p. 148.
[2] *Board of Governors Minutes, 11 May 1937, reports his intending resignation and his replacement by Watt.
[3] *BBC Handbook* (1938), p. 16.

increased—from twenty-nine hours a month in 1933 to forty-four hours a month in 1935, and fifty-nine hours a month in 1936.[1] The fact that the number of staff did not rise *pari passu* with the number of programmes, largely because the right kind of staff could not be recruited, caused frequent organizational difficulties.[2] These, however, were hidden from the public gaze. There were, in fact, considerable increases of staff in 1936—from 43 in February to 56 in November (there had been only 28 in July 1934). By the time Watt took over and there was a further internal reorganization, the department was not under-staffed, although there was no margin in case of emergency, and organization had been effectively rationalized with Charles Brewer as an efficient Assistant Director of Variety.[3]

The 'codes' of the department were also laid down in an interesting mimeographed document for internal circulation entitled *Handbook of Variety Routine* (December 1936). It was compiled by M. M. Dewar, who was Variety Executive from 1935 to 1942, and listed names, titles, procedures, and definitions. It also gave a detailed description (with photograph) of the organ in St. George's Hall, and even had a section on American variety artists. 'Mr. F. W. Alexander will arrange for a special ribbon microphone for American Variety artists who are accustomed to working very close to the microphone.'[4] A further note on microphone technique expanded the point.

After considerable experience with ribbon microphones, it was decided that crooners would not be allowed to come nearer than one foot to a ribbon microphone. This obviously has meant that Producers and Balance Assistants have had more or less to train vocalists, in this new technique, sometimes under great difficulties.

[1] *BBC Handbook* (1936), p. 41; *Memorandum by M. M. Dewar, 5 Dec. 1935; *Memorandum by G. C. Beadle on Variety Department Staff, 30 Dec. 1935.

[2] *For reorganization problems, see below, pp. 449 ff. M. M. Dewar put forward schemes of reorganization to alleviate serious overwork in Nov. 1935, but in Mar. 1936 R. H. Eckersley was writing that 'the increase in work was wholly disproportionate to the increase in staff, the result being that the present staff are being consistently over-worked. The over-work still continues, and Maschwitz is increasingly nervous of breakdowns among his staff.' Eckersley to Graves, 2 Mar. 1936.

[3] *J. Watt to L. Wellington 14 Nov. 1938.

[4] *Handbook of Variety Routine* (1936), p. 46. Dewar's *Day Book* is also a useful source for this History.

On the whole this has been carried out satisfactorily. However, one difficulty has arisen. In cases of American Variety artists, who are accustomed to working very much closer to the microphone, it has been found impossible to get these artists to change their technique for perhaps just one broadcast with the BBC, such artists as the street singer (Arthur Tracey) and Pop-Eye the Sailor (Mr. Costello). The only thing to be done in these cases is to alter the electric circuit, so that the singer may approach the microphone in the usual American way.[1]

The 'usual American way' and the usual British way diverged more in the 1930s than they do today. This does not imply, however, that Maschwitz and Watt did not always emphasize the need for showmanship, or that in the circumstances of their time they were not right to do so. 'If only these lads would think in terms of the microphone and the quiet room where it is listened to instead of the rabble behind the scenes and the applause in front of the stage', Filson Young once exclaimed.[2] The exclamation showed how out of touch he was with the changing mood of the 1930s, although he had always prided himself on responding naturally to changes of mood. Big national occasions like the Radio Exhibition of 1934 or the Silver Jubilee of 1935 were used by Maschwitz and his colleagues to put on special Radiolympia shows and Jubilee Festivals. They helped more than anything else to soften Black's suspicion of allowing his artists to broadcast and they began, sometimes to their own surprise, to force him to consider the claims of artists 'made' by the BBC.

Some of the new shows, produced by John Watt, had definite stage possibilities. Harry S. Pepper, who had written music for many different kinds of shows, produced *Monday Night at Seven* (later *Monday Night at Eight*), a popular light entertainment magazine, which combined music, patter, and detection (Inspector Hornleigh), and gave Mondays a new significance in the listeners' week. On Wednesdays Arthur Askey and Richard ('Stinker') Murdoch entertained a wide public—possibly the widest BBC public that had ever been attracted to light entertainment—in the *Band Waggon* programmes from their imaginary flat in Broadcasting House. Nausea Bagwash, the landlady's

---

[1] *F. W. Alexander to M. M. Dewar, 14 Sept. 1936.
[2] *Filson Young to R. H. Eckersley, 28 Aug. 1933.

daughter, has a permanent place in the mythology of show business, like Suzette Tarri's unlucky spinster and Mrs. Mop in *Itma*. *Band Waggon* was originally booked for thirteen weeks in 1937, longer than any previous British show, and it was planned down to the last detail—sketch, music, 'new voices', and so on. In a search for comedians Watt had gone the round of concert parties and had narrowed the choice to two. He arranged to meet the two in different public houses. He went to the first where Arthur Askey was waiting—and never went on to the second at all. Askey had compèred *February Fill-Dyke*, 'a variety show with a new angle of presentation', in February 1936,[1] but it was after the start of *Band Waggon* that he established himself as a national radio star.[2] Richard Murdoch was brought in separately to complete one of radio's most successful comedy partnerships.

The show as a whole was so successful that other attempts were made to plan entertainment of a similar 'personalized' kind which would have a permanent niche in the listeners' week. The result was *It's That Man Again*, which was worked out at a conference in the Langham Hotel between Ted Kavanagh, the script writer, Francis Worsley, the producer, and Tommy Handley, the inimitable, in June 1939. The idea behind it was not only to capture the large audience of *Band Waggon* but for the first time deliberately to produce British programmes with American-style quick-fire patter. 'Basically, the idea,' Kavanagh has written, 'and it was not a very good one, was to create an English version of the Burns and Allen Show.'[3] It is fascinating that in war-time circumstances the Englishness of the programme was to be its outstanding characteristic.

Itma was the crowning achievement of BBC light entertainment. Already in October 1938, however, it was a sign of changing circumstances that a memorandum was prepared, headed *Notes on the Exploitation of BBC Variety Productions on the Stage*. 'The Corporation has latterly entered, or is about to enter into agreements with outside producers for the stage presentation of certain BBC Variety productions', the memorandum begins. 'These so far include *Palace of Varieties*, *Monday Night*

[1] *John Pudney to Arthur Askey, 6 Feb. 1936.
[2] *Note by A. H. Brown, 14 Jan. 1938.
[3] T. Kavanagh, *Tommy Handley* (1949), p. 96.

at Seven, *Band Waggon* and *Music Hall*, and the outside producer in each case is Jack Hylton (simply because he was first in the field).'[1] There had even been some complaints that *Music Hall* was almost too well suited for the stage. 'There is a growing feeling', Maschwitz wrote in February 1937, 'among listeners as well as among people here, that acts are tending to disregard the microphone and play at the audience.'[2]

An account of the BBC's direct contribution to entertainment during the 1930s would be incomplete if it left out the further development of outside broadcasting, particularly the outside broadcasting of sport, before and after Gerald Cock left Broadcasting House for Television at Alexandra Palace in 1935. His successor, S. J. de Lotbinière, was later to return to this post in the post-war reconstruction of BBC services. There was thus an important connexion between Outside Broadcasts and the development of a separate light entertainment policy, just as there had been an earlier connexion between the *Radio Times* and the beginnings of separately organized light entertainment.

Cock and de Lotbinière covered the whole range of sports, developing the arts of 'running commentary', arts which in the case of cricket, and perhaps even more so in the case of tennis, involved elaborate setting of players in their scene with talk of 'square one' and 'square two' as well as 'square leg'. It was not only big events which were covered. In 1934 the first 'afternoons of Broadcast Sport' were transmitted: they consisted of episodes, with rapid shifts from one sport to another—cricket, tennis, rifle shooting, and speed-boat racing, for example; or football, rugger, hockey, and boxing—'without loss of continuity so as to give the listener a total experience, not confused but blended'.[3]

The breathlessness of the language suggests the novelty of 'the wandering microphone' procedure. In the later 1930s new sports—speedway racing, gliding, darts, pigeon-racing, fencing, clay-pigeon shooting, and table tennis—were added to the agenda. Some of the commentators were experts in their own sports, 'amateurs' of skill and enthusiasm like Lionel Seccombe,

[1] *'Notes on Exploitation', 7 Oct. 1938.
[2] *Maschwitz to Sharman, 9 Feb. 1937.   [3] *BBC Annual* (1935), p. 66.

an ex-heavyweight Blue, on boxing, or Squadron-Leader Helmore who covered air races in the great days of the Schneider Cup: others became public figures. Howard Marshall's masterly handling of the 1934 Test Matches made his voice one of the most familiar in the country: he went on during the 1930s to describe almost every kind of public event. John Snagge, who had joined the BBC straight from Oxford, also found himself 'turning up more and more on every occasion', always in command. There was even talk—at Maschwitz's suggestion—of transferring him to the new post in charge of dance-music programmes, which Philip Brown was to fill. Snagge showed no interest: he was recognized already to be 'an expert on all sporting broadcasts'.[1]

Before the public could listen to sport, there often had to be the same kind of battles behind the scenes with outside interests as there had been in the case of variety and musical comedy. The Football League frequently banned broadcasts of League games: the Football Association was thought to be more helpful. The less popular the sport, the more willing were its sponsors to have it 'advertised' by radio. Cricket, as a solemn national sport, always had a special place. 'I am arranging for an additional membership of the Lancashire and Yorkshire Cricket Clubs to be taken out in the name of the BBC', wrote the North Regional Executive in 1936.[2] There was even more direct participation in sport than this. In December 1936, for example, a BBC car was entered for the motor-racing trial from London to Exeter: the car was not designed to compete but, complete with official pennants, 'to cover the course and to make short cuts where necessary so that we can watch the arrival of competitors at the various controls'.[3]

The author of this note was Richard Dimbleby of the News Department of the BBC. At a later rally which ended at Blackpool in April 1938 he was a co-driver of a BBC car as a competitor with Alan Hess, and the North Region arranged for him to broadcast from the Empress Ballroom in Blackpool Tower.[4] Many new broadcasters, who later established general

[1] *Dewar to Beadle, 11 May 1935; Beadle to Brewer, 16 May 1935.
[2] *H. M. Fitch to A. M. Wells, 12 Feb. 1936.
[3] *Note of 10 Dec. 1936.
[4] *B. D. Freeston to E. H. F. Mills, 12 Apr. 1938; Mills to Freeston, 14 Apr. 1938.

reputations, were introduced to radio audiences through sport. Indeed, throughout the 1930s, there was the same relentless search for talent that there was in the world of show business. The search was nation-wide. One of the first two letters in the surviving BBC file on sports commentating begins: 'Could you, even at this prodigious distance, recommend someone who might be able to cover for us in the National News the All Black versus Ireland Match in Dublin on December 7th?'[1]

Yet supply of more sporting broadcasts never quite kept up with demand. The *Daily Dispatch* understood what not all critics of the BBC understood, that 'it is easier to make a commentator into a temporary expert than a true expert into a commentator',[2] but there were occasional complaints that the BBC's difficulties began not on the field but in the committee room. 'There is a director of everything except sport at Broadcasting House', the *Daily Sketch* exclaimed in 1937. 'As well might a newspaper editor hand over control of his sporting pages to the magazine page editor—or the lift man.'[3]

3. Words and Music

THERE was—and is—no natural frontier within broadcasting between light and serious entertainment. The arrangement of eye-witness accounts of sport was in the hands of the News Department, which was also dealing with issues of life and death. Stanford Robinson, who was Director of Music Productions from 1936 to 1946, was as interested in serious music as he was in *Music Hall*, and was concerned with all types of music from 'little operettas in the Children's Hour' to Bach Cantatas.[4] Leslie Woodgate, who was appointed BBC Chorus Master in 1934, conducted both madrigals and burlesque choruses, and in an interesting letter from Julian Herbage of

---

[1] *R. Murray to McMullan, 23 Oct. 1935.
[2] *Daily Dispatch*, 18 July 1938.
[3] *Daily Sketch*, 25 Jan. 1937.
[4] *Children's Hour Executive to Variety Department Executive, 30 Nov. 1936; Note by Nicolls, 21 Feb. 1940.

the BBC's Music Department to Sir Adrian Boult in June 1936 we read that Sir Henry Wood had suggested that in his absence Woodgate should conduct Constant Lambert's 'Rio Grande' at a Promenade Concert.[1]

In the notes which were prepared to assist Boult before meeting the Ullswater Committee, it was stated that the Music Department of the BBC had in recent years been within the so-called Entertainment Branch, by which it was not meant that he was controlled by the Director of Variety. The term 'entertainment' had been used to distinguish the main Programme Branch from the Branch handling talks, news and instruction.[2] Even at this point on the frontier, there were no clearly marked lines.

The fact that 'entertainment' was not treated as a distinct programme segment by itself reflected Reith's basic approach to programme policy. Listeners were not divided naturally into 'home', 'light', and 'third', nor did 'highbrows' or 'lowbrows', it was felt, want necessarily to be highbrow or lowbrow all the time. Not only might the habitual listener to light music cultivate an interest in 'serious' music, but the habitual listener to 'serious' music might want occasionally at least to listen to light music. The versatility of the artist was a reflection of the 'roundedness' of the listener.

Quite apart from general philosophical questions of this nature, there were certain common problems which affected producers of all kinds, not least the problems (and opportunities) posed by technical factors. Musicians had to concern themselves by the end of the period with the systems of recording at least as much as variety producers: so, too, did talks producers. Unscripted programmes raised difficult questions whether they were political programmes on the one hand or variety programmes on the other; in both cases there were censorship issues lurking behind the love of the formal script. Announcers had to announce all kinds of programme from a religious service to a programme of dance music.

At this point philosophy entered into the discussion again, 'the philosophy of presentation'. What could be more mystical

---

[1] *Herbage to Boult, 22 June 1936.
[2] *Notes for Dr. Boult. See also below, pp. 488–9.

than the following passage from the Announcement Editor in 1936?

The BBC is one Corporation, and can only be thought of by the listener as individual. It has many voices but one mouth. It can speak in many styles, but the variety is due to the difference of subject matter and must not betray any inconsistency of treatment. It is a commonplace that 'announcers sound all alike'. That is a tribute to their training. A announcing a symphony concert should sound like B announcing the next in the series. And C, announcing a concert party, although he should do it in a different style, should remind the listener of A and B, because he is performing the same function. Captain X of the Regiment giving an order *should* and *does* appear to sound like Captain Y giving the same order, although not to a soldier who knows them both, and recognises the separate personalities of each in the identical words.

In language of this kind, which must have left some of the announcers bemused, Byzantium arrived in Broadcasting House. The corollary drawn by the writer was, however, a little more intelligible. 'It is essential that the announcer should announce two concert parties in the same *style—that* is what the BBC thinks of concert parties—but not, however, necessarily in the same words.'[1] The Announcement Editor's views did not represent established doctrine: indeed, they stimulated useful discussion when the initial bemusement disappeared. A simpler pragmatic statement of BBC working policy was that good announcing and presentation were 'whatever was felt to be apt to the particular programme and audience' visualized.

Diversity in unity can be made into a theme of broadcasting. There were, of course, many BBC producers, performers, and even administrators who were highly specialized, particularly by the mid-1930s, and there were always times, even before the mid-1930s, when one kind of expertise did not necessarily seem to lead to another. 'Mr. Sieveking's temporary transfer to Vaudeville was not a success', Maschwitz noted in 1933:[2] this did not imply that Sieveking was not a great success in other BBC activities. There were also occasional signs of jurisdictional jealousy between the different branches of production. 'Before muddle or worse occurs', the Talks Department complained

---

[1] *Memorandum of 13 Nov. 1936.
[2] *E. Maschwitz, Note on Variety Staff, 10 May 1933.

in 1934, 'ought we not to have some definite understanding with Mr. Maschwitz, whose *In Town Tonight* programme seems all too liable to become competitive with the topical talks?'[1]

The story of talks, topical or otherwise, is one of the most complex and fascinating in the history of the BBC. It is a story of ups and downs rather than of continuous progress, of changes in direction as well as changes in organization. Sometimes the Director of Talks, or whatever his official title was, became the most powerful departmental chief in the BBC: at other times 'his kingdom was partitioned, and he himself reduced to a routine administrator'.[2] There were frequent reactions against previous régimes and for a short period in the mid-1930s there was something like an interregnum.

In the autumn of 1926 J. C. Stobart was, in name at least, in overall charge of an empire consisting of talks, news, education, and religion. Lance Sieveking and C. H. G. Strutt shared the work of topical talks and news, the former having the main responsibility for topical talks and the latter for news. Sieveking's main duty was to discover speakers, read and correct their scripts, and advise about new ideas. All new speakers were rehearsed in the studio daily from 5 to 6 o'clock in the same way that comedians or musicians were given auditions. As for the advice on new ideas, 'Mr. Sieveking's work entails a good deal of absence from the office, and on one evening out of three he works late'.[3]

This simple arrangement was changed with the arrival of Hilda Matheson, and in January 1927 the Control Board decided that a separate 'Talks Section' should be formed, quite distinct from education, news, and religion, with Miss Matheson in charge.[4] She remained there until January 1932, leaving a very powerful imprint on the BBC. Before joining the Company, Miss Matheson had been working as secretary to Lady Astor, and in that capacity she had formed a large circle of friends and acquaintances in the worlds of fashion, letters, and politics. Liberal-minded and energetic, she introduced

---

[1] *J. R. Ackerley to Siepmann, 8 Jan. 1934.
[2] R. S. Lambert, *Ariel and All His Quality* (1940), p. 59.
[3] *Note on the Work of the Talks Section, Oct. 1926.
[4] *Control Board Minutes, 18 Jan. 1927; Reith, Diary, 7 Jan. 1927. 'Saw Stobart about the devolution of his department, and he was very nice about it.'

some of the country's best speakers and writers to the BBC and in the course of doing so performed an equally important task, that of introducing the BBC to them. She was, for a time, a genuine Director of the Spoken Word, although she never had the title. 'Under her guidance, it was possible for the younger dons to mention broadcasting at the High Tables of Oxford Colleges without fear of ridicule. The intelligentsia was interested. Society was mildly "intrigued".'[1]

Miss Matheson's contribution was bigger than this, however, despite the fact that her BBC career ended in bitterness and controversy. Since she was genuinely interested in ideas as well as people, she saw that the Talk—it began to get a capital letter—offered a very special opportunity in broadcasting. 'Broadcasting is clearly rediscovering the spoken language, the impermanent but living tongue, as distinct from the permanent but silent print.'[2] Without ever going quite as far as A. Lloyd James, the BBC's indefatigable adviser on 'standard' Spoken English, who complained about 'the tyranny of print', Miss Matheson set herself to extend 'the freedom of the air' in the period after the formal lifting of the ban on controversy in 1928.[3] She welcomed speakers of every kind, and genuinely tried to assist them to express their personalities over the new medium. One of her favourite books was T. H. Pear's *Voice and Personality* (1931) which was one of the few academic studies of the subject. It was based on a series of broadcasts from Manchester, where unique use was made of the microphone in a piece of psychological investigation.

In philosophizing about the 'technique' or 'art' of the talk, therefore, Miss Matheson did not start with the 'essay' or the 'article' in her mind. She started with the broadcasting medium itself. Very quickly she came to the conclusion that the dissemination of ordered ideas and the projection of personality both depended on a formal script. 'Without a carefully prepared and timed talk, how could a speaker be sure of getting all he needed to say in its right proportion, into his fixed space of time?' His words would be listened to in private, so that it would be pointless for him to imagine that he was talking to a public

[1] S. A. Moseley, *Broadcasting In My Time*, p. 35.
[2] H. Matheson, *Broadcasting* (1933), p. 74.
[3] See below, pp. 128–9.

meeting, but the very effect of 'naturalness' would be lost if there were no element of dissimulation in presentation.

Experience almost everywhere has shown that, though a few practised broadcasters, particularly if their speech is an informal accompaniment of music and reading, can speak impromptu with success, most speakers and certainly most novices need a prepared manuscript if they are to avoid tiresome hesitation or equally tiresome verbosity. A technique had, therefore, to be found for the writing, rehearsing and delivery of talks, which would avoid the pitfalls of impromptu speech and yet retain its atmosphere. Speakers, however eminent, welcome rather than resent preliminary discussion of the way in which to approach and present material; they submit with good grace to voice tests to discover points of intonation, rhythm, articulation which may need correction; and they accept with thanks, if tactfully offered, criticisms of a manuscript which retains the form and flavour of an essay or treatise instead of a talk. Many manuscripts submitted require something not unlike translation before they can hope to sound as if they were spoken to a person and not delivered to an assembly.[1]

What Miss Matheson said about the talk influenced all her successors, not least C. A. Siepmann, who succeeded her after a series of much publicized staff disturbances in 1932.[2] It was Siepmann who thought of the talk as resting on a 'double artifice'. What was natural had to become artificial before it would sound natural again.[3] The early members of the Talks Department introduced to broadcasting some of its most brilliant performers—Harold Nicolson, Vernon Bartlett, Ernest Newman, Stephen King-Hall, Raymond Gram Swing, and John Hilton. They were vigilant also in looking for young people who had not established themselves but had great natural gifts, and they had long discussions with 'great men' who could not or for long had said that they would not broadcast, men like Arnold Bennett and H. G. Wells. 'I have always thought it to be pretty devastating', Miss Matheson wrote to Wells in June 1929, 'that an internationalist like yourself—perhaps you are the only real internationalist—shouldn't be making use of the most international means of communication there is.'[4] Her appeal was

[1] *Broadcasting*, pp. 76–77.
[2] See below, pp. 141–2.
[3] See also J. Hilton, 'Talking about Talk' in *This and That* (1938).
[4] *Miss Matheson to H. G. Wells, 14 June 1929.

successful, and Wells was soon extremely interested in discussing the possibilities of broadcasting.

'I remember best the trinity of E. M. Forster, Desmond McCarthy and H. G. Wells,' Lionel Fielden has written, 'who all gave us freely of their time and wise counsels, and would sit round our gas fires at Savoy Hill, talking of the problems and possibilities of broadcasting.'[1] Arnold Bennett occasionally philosophized about broadcasting in print and for a wider public. 'There is no such an entity as the public', he once wrote. 'There are forty publics, and the members of one public are continually changing over to another public according to mood.'[2] For this reason he was an early advocate of 'alternative programmes' and of Reith's philosophy of non-segregation of particular types of programme.

Talk was not only for the great, the kind of people who gave or might have been asked to give the National Lectures which began—following a suggestion of Filson Young—in 1928.[3] It was also for 'ordinary people'. A series on *The Day's Work* in 1930 proved surprisingly popular. 'Most people were keen to hear what the Covent Garden porter, the steeplejack and the postman had to tell.'[4] Cookery talks and garden talks were as much a feature of the work of Miss Matheson and Siepmann as highly controversial talks on political and economic issues, although it was not until 1936 that C. H. Middleton gave the first of his remarkably popular talks on gardening.

Another kind of talk was represented by James Agate, the theatre critic, who boasted in 1932 that he had broadcast 'oftener than anybody else except the announcers'.[5] A friend of Lionel Fielden, he was an excellent broadcaster, lively, bold, and popular even among listeners who had never been to a theatre in their lives.[6] 'The way the subject is presented by Mr. Agate

---

[1] L. Fielden, *The Natural Bent* (1960), p. 105.

[2] A. Bennett, 'Wireless Without Yawns' in *Saturday Post*, 20 Feb. 1927.

[3] *Reith to Filson Young, 24 Apr. 1929. 'In view of the considerable success which has attended the two first National lectures and because of the attention which has been directed to them . . . I want to let you have a line to tell you that we do not forget that this scheme was started as a result of a suggestion by you and has been carried on so far exactly on the lines which you proposed.'

[4] *Broadcasting in My Time*, p. 131.   [5] J. Agate, *Ego* (1935), p. 163.

[6] Agate did his own 'popularity poll' in 1932 when he estimated that '90 per cent. [of his listeners] were either non-theatre goers or very infrequent ones.' *Note of 6 Apr. 1932.

magnifies the "Theatre" into the most *perfect* item in the BBC programmes at the present time', wrote a grateful listener in 1932.[1] Theatre managements were not always quite so grateful. In October 1929 the Society of West End Theatre Managers discussed Agate's review of a play called *The Flying Fool* and held unanimously that it was 'not only prejudicial to the play but also to the interests of all theatres'.[2] Attempts had already been made to prevent him from reviewing plays for which he had not been sent a reviewer's ticket.[3] Until he was rested in 1933 Agate remained a highly controversial broadcaster, often succeeding in provoking his friends as much as his enemies.

The question of controversy was, of course, the central question in the minds of all organizers and producers of BBC talks. In January 1927, at the beginning of the new Corporation, the Secretary of the Post Office had written to Reith stating firmly that in accordance with Clause 4 of the BBC's Licence, the Corporation had to abstain from 'statements expressing the opinion of the Corporation on matters of public policy' and from 'speeches or lectures containing statements on topics of political, religious or industrial controversy'.[4] This thoroughly illiberal approach to broadcasting had always been disputed by Reith,[5] and in January 1928 he asked the Post Office to review the matter 'with the experience of a year's working behind the Corporation'. The Crawford Committee, like the Sykes Committee before it, had recommended cautiously that, 'given guarantees of equality and fair treatment, a moderate amount of controversy should be allowed'.[6] Surely it was now time, Reith argued, for the BBC to be allowed a measure of discretion. 'During the past year well-informed and constructive critics of BBC programmes have deplored the devitalising influence of the absence of controversy. On most problems of immediate interest the service is silent, and if controversial subjects are broached at all it is done in a halting, inconclusive and even

---

[1] *A listener to James Agate, 28 May 1932. Agate sent the letter to Siepmann with the comment, 'I have had a hard struggle with my modesty, which, however, has lost the battle.' (Letter of 31 May 1932.)

[2] *Note of 1 Oct. 1929; B. A. Meyer to Reith, 18 Sept. 1929.

[3] *Walter Payne to Reith, 11 Mar. 1929.

[4] *Sir Evelyn Murray to Reith, 11 Jan. 1927.

[5] See *The Birth of Broadcasting*, especially pp. 269–72 and pp. 380–3.

[6] Cmd. 2599 (1926), *Report of the Broadcasting Committee*, §15.

platitudinous manner. The application of the present policy involves the neglect of many opportunities in forming public opinion in matters of vital importance.'

Critics who have accused Reith, very unfairly, of seeking to avoid controversial broadcasting during the 1930s could not have written a more powerful letter than this. The Governors, he went on, had submitted the request after careful deliberation, viewing it as a 'natural and logical development of the service'. The power would, of course, not be misused: it was essential that it should be directed by a genuine sense of responsibility.[1]

The Post Office could scarcely counter this line of argument had it wished to do so, and on 5 March 1928 the 'ban on controversy' was withdrawn in the light of the 'loyal and punctilious manner' in which the BBC had conformed to the obligations imposed'. Not that there was any rush for freedom. 'His Majesty's Government feels that the time has come when an experiment ought to be made in the direction of greater latitude.' The ban on 'editorializing' remained.[2]

The 'experiment' continued without a break until 1939, with the Postmaster-General repeatedly emphasizing that it was the duty of the Governors and not of himself to interpret the proper scope of controversy. Twice in 1927, before the ban was withdrawn, Sir William Mitchell-Thomson and his deputy, Viscount Wolmer, made it clear that they had no intention of 'directing' the BBC,[3] and once, years later in 1933, when Kingsley Wood was specifically asked in the House of Commons to use his veto power to prohibit talks in a series on India, he replied that he had to trust 'the discretion of the Governors in this matter, who have the responsibility'.[4] There was only one occasion when the ban might have been used in the early 1930s, when the Postmaster-General suggested informally to the BBC that a projected talk by an ex-German U-Boat Commander, Captain Ernst Hashagen, would cause so much offence to the public that it ought to be cancelled. Heavy pressure was placed on the BBC and the talk was, in fact, cancelled by the BBC without the ban being formally used.[5] The decision to cancel was taken by the Board of Governors, with Reith dissenting. Many years

---

[1] *Reith to Murray, 16 Jan. 1928.   [2] *Murray to Reith, 5 Mar. 1928.
[3] *Hansard*, vol. 203, cols. 2004–5; ibid., vol. 212, cols. 598–600.
[4] Ibid., vol. 276, cols. 6–7.   [5] Ibid., vol. 268, cols. 593–4.

later when both Reith and Kingsley Wood were ministers in the same war-time administration, Reith asked Kingsley Wood whether he would in fact have used his veto. 'Not on your life. I would never have done it', was the reply.[1]

Reith has left a full account of the incident as it appeared at the time. Baldwin asked Kingsley Wood to tell him that the Cabinet had unanimously decided that the talk should not be given. 'I had quite an argument with the Postmaster-General,' Reith goes on, 'saying that I thought it was monstrous, and that he would be doing us a good turn by declining to interfere.' He, Whitley, the Chairman of the Governors, and Gainford went round to the Post Office and had a somewhat stormy meeting. 'We could not get out of the P.M.G. what he would do if we refused to cancel, but Whitley made it pretty clear that we were not inclined to do so.' The three BBC representatives then met on their own, with Reith strongly advocating carrying on with the broadcast. He was certain, he said, that Kingsley Wood was bluffing and would not use his veto. The others disagreed. 'I said', Reith ended his account, 'that it was the most important issue that had ever come before us, but I saw that Whitley was inclined to yield, so I said I would stay out of the argument. In fact, I immediately wrote down the reply which the P.M.G. should give to the question in the House that afternoon, that the talk was a serious contribution to the elimination of warfare, but that he had heard from us in the morning that in view of the Lausanne Conference we had decided to cancel it. This is what he said. There was a tremendous downpour of rain as we left the Post Office and this expressed my feelings with regard to the matter.'[2]

Quite apart from the possible threat to the freedom of the BBC from the Post Office, there was always a much more serious threat from public opinion or particular sections of it. Before the ban on controversy was lifted, the *Morning Post* complained that 'the suggestion that prohibition on controversy should be removed opens up a vista of horrible possibilities. The average man or woman, when at leisure with the world, has not the slightest desire to be plunged into disputes on any of these subjects [politics, religion, and industry].'[3] After the ban was

[1] Note by Maurice Farquharson, Apr. 1963.
[2] Reith, Diary, 6 July 1932.   [3] *Morning Post*, 9 Jan. 1928.

lifted, particular broadcasts were always subject to sharp criticism. The *Manchester Guardian* might hail 'the clash of opinions', but *The Times* insisted that 'the balance must be kept' and the *Daily Telegraph* urged that 'much caution will still be re-quisite if the new freedom is to work to the common good'.[1] From March 1928 to November 1929 the BBC had its own 'Con-troversy Committee' which included both Eckersleys, Gladstone Murray, Graves, Stobart, and Miss Matheson. It dealt with all points likely to create difficulty.

Another international incident in 1932 illustrated how easy it was to be provocative. An anonymous speaker on Europe in a New Year's Eve programme mentioned that Poland was spending one-third of its government income on armaments. This statement, true or false, stirred the Polish Ambassador to protest and the Foreign Office to seek to smooth out relations. It then started off a long correspondence in *The Times*, where thirty-one signatories to a most effective letter demanded full independence for the Corporation.[2] The government thought that it was advisable to allow the subject to be aired on the floor of the Commons, and a private-member's motion, backed by the Government Whips, both affirmed the BBC's right to broadcast controversial programmes and urged 'the greatest care in the selection of speakers and subjects'. A Labour amend-ment suggesting the appointment of a Select Committee 'to review the work of recent years and make recommendations' was defeated on straight party grounds, and the private-mem-ber's motion was carried by 203 votes to 27.[3]

Such incidents indicated how difficult it would have been to extend the scope of 'controversial broadcasting' during the 1930s. The difficulties derived in the first instance from the domestic political party system. They began with Budget speeches. These had been severely circumscribed before 1927,[4] but in 1928 Winston Churchill, then Chancellor of the Ex-chequer, was allowed to make a factual statement. 'He delivered a good defence of the Budget, supposed to be non-controversial but it was not', wrote Reith, who accompanied him to Savoy

[1] *Manchester Guardian*, 6 Mar. 1928; *The Times*, 6 Mar. 1928; *Daily Telegraph*, 6 Mar. 1928.
[2] *The Times*, 6 Feb. 1933. The signatories included Rutherford, Keynes, Julian Huxley, F. M. Powicke, W. H. Hadow, and H. A. L. Fisher.
[3] *Hansard*, vol. 274, cols. 1811 ff.   [4] See *The Birth of Broadcasting*, p. 268.

Hill.[1] MacDonald immediately protested on behalf of the Executive of the Labour Party,[2] and in 1929 it was decided inside the BBC not to ask the Chancellor to speak because of the imminent general election. 'Last year the Chancellor's speech could not fail to be, in effect, propaganda . . . though he did it very skilfully. This year its propaganda effect would be doubled.'[3] Snowden broadcast in 1930 and 1931 as Labour Chancellor of the Exchequer, but turned down a request from the BBC in 1931 that his speech should be part of a 'political series'.[4] Neither the Conservative Party nor the Labour Party by itself was prepared to lose the opportunity of political advantage. 'To include the Budget talk in the list of political talks', Snowden's Parliamentary Private Secretary replied, 'would deprive the Government of one broadcast opportunity.'[5]

Snowden's Conservative successor, Neville Chamberlain, took the same line, and this time it was George Lansbury on behalf of the Labour Party who was aggrieved.[6] Chamberlain slightly widened the terms of reference of his reply. 'It would be very undesirable,' his secretary wrote, 'especially in difficult and critical times like these, to make the Budget the subject of a controversial debate on the wireless before an audience which is uninstructed in all the complexities and problems of the financial position at home and abroad. Moreover, the Chancellor of the Exchequer, restricted by the responsibilities of his office, would be at a great disadvantage compared with an opponent who had no such responsibilities.'[7] Chamberlain took up the same position the following year, but a political series centred on the Budget began notwithstanding in 1934, with Chamberlain, Attlee, Herbert Samuel, and J. H. Thomas as the speakers. By 1939 the procedure was generally agreed.

The political rota at general election times often involved the sharpest disagreement. Reith wrote to the leaders of the political parties about the opportunities of political broadcasting in April 1928.[8] The response was encouraging. Baldwin was

[1] Reith, Diary, 25 Apr. 1928.   [2] *MacDonald to Reith, 1 May 1928.
[3] *Miss Matheson to Reith, 20 Mar. 1929.
[4] *Reith to Thomas Kennedy, 25 Feb. 1931.
[5] *Kennedy to Reith, 17 Mar. 1931.   [6] *Reith to Lansbury, 28 Apr. 1933.
[7] *Donald Fergusson to Reith, 27 Apr. 1933. Fergusson also set out the same argument in a memorandum of 27 Mar. 1934.
[8] *Reith to the leaders of the three parties, 19 Apr. 1928.

already an accomplished broadcaster, and MacDonald, then Leader of the Opposition, expressed great interest. 'Lunched with Ramsay MacDonald at the Club', Reith wrote in his diary in February 1929. 'He wanted to talk about political broadcasting, the Labour Party being so dependent on the wireless. I told him we would agree if the three parties agreed among themselves. We might even make arrangements if two of them did. He said the Labour Party were ready to agree to almost anything.'[1]

This statement was too optimistic, and there was much acrimonious debate before MacDonald and J. C. C. Davidson, on behalf of Baldwin, the Prime Minister, reached any kind of agreement. For two Conservative speakers there were to be only one Labour and one Liberal speaker.[2] MacDonald so disliked the arrangement that he remarked somewhat petulantly that 'if they [unspecified] are going to try to manipulate things, the Labour Party will not appear in the scheme at all'.[3] Walter Jerrold in the *Star* was less concerned about the 'double ration' to the Conservative speakers:

'Twill be found when he's finished, his matter is such
That he's talked twice as long and not said half as much.[4]

To complicate matters further, Lloyd George was very annoyed at not being given a date in the same week as Baldwin and MacDonald.[5] He was very alive to the political possibilities of broadcasting at this time, having just made a speech in Parliament asserting that it was 'vital' that broadcasting should be used 'to enable the vast mass of the electorate to know what the issues were' and adding that he 'did not know of any other way by which it could get at them'.[6] Because of divisions between the parties, Reith had had to settle the allocation of party time himself, 'to the equal discontent of all three parties'.[7] There was talk in the papers, however, of the government dictating to the BBC, with the *Daily News* claiming that Baldwin had been 'egged on by Churchill'.[8]

For the first time during this general election the press

[1] Reith, Diary, 13 Feb. 1929.
[2] The agreement was announced in the press on 5 Apr. 1929 in what the *Daily News* called 'curiously ambiguous terms'. The *Manchester Guardian* called it a 'compromise'.   [3] *Sunday Graphic*, 7 Apr. 1929. He was answered by Mrs. Snowden.
[4] *Star*, 7 Apr. 1929.   [5] Ibid., 30 Apr. 1929.   [6] *The Times*, 5 Mar. 1929.
[7] *Into the Wind*, p. 131.   [8] *Daily News*, 5 Apr. 1929.

pointed to the direct influence of broadcasting on politics. The *Manchester Guardian*, for instance, noted that there was one wireless in three houses as against one in six or seven in 1923, and claimed that 'the whole technique of elections must undergo a profound change as a result of the advent of the BBC'. The psychological results were 'not certainly predictable' but it seemed likely that they would be 'good'. Instead of going to a few political meetings devoted to increasing the faith of those whose minds are already made up, the voter will in time become accustomed to following a reasonable debate in which his opponents as well as his own leaders will state their case.'[1] This belief in the 'rationalizing' influence of radio on politics persisted down to 1939 despite what was happening in Nazi Germany. There was a blissful ignorance of hidden persuaders and public relations techniques. 'It is an appeal to the individual reason rather than to the crowd emotion', A. G. Gardiner, the veteran political commentator, wrote in 1931.[2] He was recalling the controversy between free traders and protectionists before 1914 rather than looking ahead to the 1950s and 1960s.

Not everybody welcomed the BBC's willingness to broadcast politics at election times. The *Daily Express* spoke of 'the listener's new ordeal', while the *Daily Sketch* asked bluntly: 'Is Science, which has added so greatly to the horrors of international war to be allowed also to increase the horrors of party politics warfare?'[3] When W. Crawford, the Liberal Member for Wolverhampton West, told the House of Commons that 'each evening a certain amount of politics could be put into the ordinary broadcasting programme', there were loud cries of 'Oh!'[4] The speeches actually given by the politicians in 1929 did not greatly impress the public. Sir Laming Worthington-Evans, the first Conservative speaker, called his experience an 'ordeal' and spoke of the 'terrible microphone': 'he talked like an extract from a political handbook', the *Manchester Guardian* tartly remarked.[5] Arthur Henderson, the first Labour speaker, had a 'heavy father touch', complained the *Star*.[6]

[1] *Manchester Guardian*, 25 Jan. 1929. See also the issue of 16 May 1929 with a leader entitled 'A Mechanised Election'.
[2] A. G. Gardiner, 'The New Style in Elections' in the *Star*, 29 Oct. 1931.
[3] *Daily Express*, 23 Jan. 1929; *Daily Sketch*, 6 Mar. 1929.
[4] *The Times*, 5 Mar. 1929.
[5] *Manchester Guardian*, 3 Apr. 1929.   [6] *Star*, 12 Apr. 1929.

Reith gave an insider's view. The broadcasts confirmed his previous opinions. Chamberlain had prepared nothing. Mac-Donald was far less effective than Snowden. Baldwin was best of all. He had written asking Reith for information about the social classification of the audience, and he wanted to know whether working men listened at home or in clubs and pubs. Reith helped him, as he had helped him before, with his per-oration.[1]

There were few press comments about the effect of broad-casting on the result of the election, which led to the formation of the second Labour government, but by the autumn of 1929 the Conservatives were protesting, like the Labour Party before 1929, against 'too many government speeches'.[2] A different kind of protest came from Winston Churchill, who was increas-ingly estranged from Baldwin. In December 1929 he wrote to Reith saying that he was about to make a 'public offer' to the BBC 'of £100 out of my own pocket for the right to speak for half an hour on Politics. How ashamed you will all be in a few years for having muzzled the broadcast!'[3] Reith replied that not only was the BBC precluded by its Licence from accepting money, but that 'the American plan ... of allowing broadcasting to be available on a cash basis' operated 'irrespective of any consideration of content or balance'.[4] This did not end the argument: indeed, it was to be revived on several occasions before 1939. Churchill wrote that he preferred the American plan to 'the present British methods of debarring public men from access to a public who wish to hear'. He added that the BBC was wrong to seek to regulate its political broadcasts through the political parties. 'I was not aware that parties had a legal basis at all, or that they had been formally brought into your licence.'[5]

The exchange was not unfriendly, and within a few days Reith asked Churchill whether he would be willing to take part in a broadcast discussion, 'preferably of the conversational type', on 'some such subject as the Party system'.[6] Chur-chill by-passed the suggestion with the broad and sweeping

[1] *Into the Wind*, p. 131; Diary, 22 April 1929.   [2] *The Times*, 8 Oct. 1929.
[3] *Winston Churchill to Reith, 29 Dec. 1929.
[4] *Reith to Churchill, 31 Dec. 1929.
[5] *Churchill to Reith, 1 Jan. 1930.   [6] *Reith to Churchill, 8 Jan. 1930.

reply: 'Of course, I am anxious to speak to the public about great questions like Egypt, India, the Navy, the dole, American nationalisation of British industry and so on.' He also stated that he intended to have the whole question of political broadcasting brought up in Parliament.[1] He did not respond to Reith's suggestion that 'the expression of original and provocative points of view . . . can be done more effectively outside the confines of stereotyped party rota'.[2]

As Churchill moved further away from Baldwin, he chafed increasingly at all suggestions of 'stereotyped party rota'. He refused several BBC invitations to broadcast, stating bluntly that he did 'not wish to speak upon the broadcast [*sic*] except on great questions of national policy' or 'for some charitable undertaking'.[3] Lord Beaverbrook was more successful than Churchill in broadcasting on a theme of his own choice in 1930 precisely because he did not raise general questions concerning party control. He took part with Sir William Beveridge in an interesting radio discussion on Free Trade versus Empire Free Trade: 'If he did not comply with all the canons of broadcasting,' the *Manchester Guardian* commented afterwards, 'he achieved the rare distinction of putting his personality across into space.'[4] 'While the other political parties have been earnestly debating . . . how long opponents should be allowed to remain at the microphone,' another newspaper wrote, 'Lord Beaverbrook has cut through the obstacles which bar the way to a proper national broadcasting agreement with the sword of economics.'[5] Beveridge sent the BBC copies of the letters he received after his broadcast talk, 'pretty equally divided between shouts of approval and shrieks of rage'.[6] 'If one was to judge the effect of the broadcast from this correspondence,' Lionel Fielden noted, 'one would say that Beveridge had confused a few of the "middle thinkers" and left the converted where they were. But I suspect that the effect is really much greater upon the mass of "middle thinkers" who don't write.'[7] Unfortunately BBC comments on Lord Beaverbrook's forceful speech do not survive.

[1] *Churchill to Reith, 14 Jan. 1930.
[2] *Reith to Churchill, 20 Mar. 1930.   [3] *Churchill to Reith, 15 Feb. 1931.
[4] *Manchester Guardian*, 29 Aug. 1930.   [5] *Sunday Referee*, 31 Aug. 1930.
[6] *Sir William Beveridge to Miss Matheson, 12 Dec. 1930. This was Beveridge's first broadcast.
[7] *Note by Lionel Fielden, 15 Dec. 1930.

It is interesting to note that Beveridge was 'much more against Baldwin's preference policy than . . . against Beaverbrook's protection policy',[1] and that he willingly refused 'to mention British [political] parties any more than Lord Beaverbrook mentions them'.[2]

The political parties, which so strongly pressed for party control of broadcasting in 1930, were themselves divided by the events of 1931. A number of debates were cancelled because of the pressure of current party politics—including one between Sir Oswald Mosley and Lord Eustace Percy on 'tradition'[3]— and Churchill was refused permission to state his views on India in February. On this occasion letters exchanged between him and J. H. Whitley, the Chairman of the Governors of the BBC, were published in the press. One letter of Churchill's included the tendentious phrase that he wanted the BBC to afford him 'the opportunity of stating the British side of the case'.[4] The press also was divided on political grounds about this bold claim as it was about the whole question of 'access to the microphone'. Questions of freedom shifted all too easily into questions of privilege. Many newspapers pointed out that if Churchill was granted the freedom of the air every one else should be granted it also: the BBC could not possibly allow every one to speak who wished to do so. On the whole the BBC won the press battle. *Time and Tide* noted that 'Mr. Churchill accuses the BBC of having made a lamentable departure from British traditions. It is he who has departed from tradition in endeavouring to embarrass a government dealing with a delicate problem outside the range of home affairs.'[5]

Before the controversy about Churchill had settled, MacDonald stole the limelight. The financial crisis and the formation of the National government during the Parliamentary recess made broadcasting a powerful element in political communication. On the evening of 25 August 1931, just after the

---

[1] *Note by Miss Matheson, 1 Dec. 1930.

[2] *Beveridge to Miss Matheson, 3 Dec. 1930. See also Lord Beveridge, *Power and Influence* (1953), pp. 221–2.

[3] See J. M. Kenworthy, 'Free the BBC' in *Modern Wireless*, Apr. 1931.

[4] *Winston Churchill to J. H. Whitley, 2 July 1931.

[5] *Time and Tide*, 15 Aug. 1932; *The Spectator*, 30 June 1932: 'If it began with Mr. Churchill where could it be depended upon to stop? . . . The line Sir John Reith has taken is absolutely right. Not even Mr. Churchill can be supplied with broadcasting facilities on demand.'

new government had been formed, MacDonald gave a broadcast from all stations in which he appealed for confidence. It was said to have achieved its immediate purpose internationally if not at home. 'Following Mr. Ramsay MacDonald's broadcast speech, the pound sterling rose on all the leading centres', wrote the *Daily Mail*.[1] There were the usual—and, to the historian, devastating—differences of opinion about the essentials of its delivery. 'We heard the Prime Minister last night and sensed his tiredness, his anxiety—and his earnestness', wrote the *Star*: 'admirable in its subject matter, it was admirably delivered', wrote the *Evening Standard*. 'The Prime Minister's voice was strong, clear and dignified. There was no evidence of strain or tiredness.'[2]

The general election of 1931 took place in an atmosphere of far greater political bitterness than the election of 1929, with Labour talking of betrayal and the 'National Government' seeking to rally all good men to the aid of the party. No Labour speaker broadcast in the critical months between August and October 1931, and it was not until the eve of the election that Reith met Glyn, the Prime Minister's Parliamentary Private Secretary and some of his colleagues, and spent about two hours 'discussing what to do about the political speeches'. They said that they did not want Kennedy or Samuel, the representatives at that time of 'National Labour' and 'Liberal National', to take part in the pre-election broadcasts. 'They were all Conservatives', however, Reith noted, and 'I was sure that there would be a racket later'.[3]

As a result of a number of telephone calls—little of this was ever set down on paper—Sir John Simon, a National Liberal, was added to the list. This immediately roused Samuel. 'When Samuel heard that Simon was in as one of the Liberals he went off the deep end.'[4] He did not recognize Simon as a Liberal, although they were members of the same Cabinet. A few days later Arthur Henderson, the leader of the Labour Party, said that the proposed list was quite unacceptable to him. 'There ought to be as many speakers against the Government as for

[1] *Daily Mail*, 27 Aug. 1931; *Financial Times*, 27 Aug. 1931.
[2] *Star*, 26 Aug. 1931; *Evening Standard*, 26 Aug. 1931.
[3] Reith, Diary, 1 Oct. 1931.
[4] Ibid., 3 Oct. 1931.

the Government, and he wanted for his Opposition as many as
for all the others put together.'[1]

In the midst of the troubles Reith took it upon himself to
telephone Lloyd George, who had not been involved in the manœuvres leading up to the formation of the National government.
Lloyd George did, in fact, broadcast on 15 October, claiming that
the election was a 'partisan intrigue under the guise of a patriotic
appeal', and Reith thought that it was a first-class broadcasting
performance. 'I have never met anyone with a more magnetic
personality.'[2] Yet Lloyd George's broadcast, with its 'Bardic
note', did not sway the election result. The most effective and
probably the most savagely controversial broadcasting the BBC
had ever transmitted came from Philip Snowden, who had
moved over with MacDonald, yet still out of sympathy with
him, to join the National government. In his radio talk of 18
October he shocked his old colleagues by referring to Labour
Party policy as 'Bolshevism run mad'. The *Manchester Guardian*
felt that a speech of this kind has 'no persuasive power . . . in the
calm atmosphere' of the home, but there was little doubt that
it both persuaded doubters and, equally important, reinforced
anti-socialist opinion.[3]

Altogether there were nine political speakers in the immediate
pre-election campaign, of whom only one, Baldwin, was Conservative. 'This', Churchill remarked, ignoring the other five
spokesmen of the National government, 'was carrying the
suppression of Conservative opinion beyond the bounds of
reason and fair play.'[4] Baldwin, 'with his feet on our fender',
was as successful as usual,[5] and the Labour Party made poor
use of the facilities offered it. Henderson started well, but moved
along far too fast as 'a fatal urgency got him in its grip'.[6] Clynes
had no understanding of the medium. When Attlee protested
later about the amount of time given to Labour, Kingsley Wood
retorted amid laughter in the House of Commons that if
Labour had been given more time at the election the Labour
Party would have been wiped out completely.[7] No one denied
the influence of wireless in the election, but no one tried to

---

[1] Reith, Diary, 8 Oct. 1931.   [2] Ibid., 15 Oct. 1931.
[3] *Manchester Guardian*, 19 Oct. 1931.   [4] *The Times*, 14 Oct. 1931.
[5] *Manchester Guardian*, 16 Oct. 1931.   [6] Ibid., 24 Oct. 1931.
[7] *The Times*, 12 Dec. 1931. As it was, only 52 Labour candidates were returned.

measure it. 'It is pretty generally agreed that this election was won at the fireside', the *Manchester Guardian* claimed. 'The wireless played a part it never did in any previous election.'[1] 'Local candidates were overshadowed in their own constituencies by the etheric presence of mightier men', wrote Clifford Sharp. 'Electors would sometimes actually leave political meetings for twenty minutes or so to hear Baldwin or MacDonald or Lloyd George, and then return in a spirit perhaps a shade more critical than before of home town oratory.'[2]

At the general election of 1935 the National government won again with a reduced majority—247 against 497—and again there were 'great rows' behind the scenes about the allocation of election talks.[3] This time the Opposition Liberals were the main source of friction. Samuel wanted to include both Lloyd George and Snowden in the Opposition Liberal quota, much to the annoyance of Captain Margesson, the National government's tough Whip. 'Margesson was furious', Sir Stephen Tallents wrote in his Diary, 'and rang up Graves several times, and at length.'[4] Reith refused to take part in the discussion, stating firmly that it was the duty of the political parties, and not of the BBC, to reach an agreement. If Margesson wished to protest, he should protest to the Liberal Whip. Eventually the quota was fixed by the parties themselves at five for the Government, four for the Labour Party, and three for the Opposition Liberals—which was generally felt to be a 'fair deal'. The Labour Party made better use of its opportunity than at the General Election of 1931, and one of its new speakers, Herbert Morrison, was a distinct success.[5] Snowden, who broadcast for the Liberals, despite Margesson's protests, was once again a highly controversial figure. 'His egocentric acidity', wrote the *Evening News*, 'has probed the vitals of every other political leader in turn.'[6]

There was a somewhat more sophisticated approach to the role of broadcasting in 1935 than at previous elections.

---

[1] *Manchester Guardian*, 4 Nov. 1931.
[2] C. Sharp, 'The Recent War on the Air' in *Weekend Review*, 31 Oct. 1931.
[3] Reith, Diary, 25 Oct. 1935.
[4] Sir Stephen Tallents, Diary, 25 Oct. 1935 (Tallents Papers).
[5] *Daily Express*, 9 Nov. 1935; *Manchester Guardian*, 14 Nov. 1935.
[6] *Evening News*, 29 Oct. 1935. The leader was called 'Lone Wolf'. The *Manchester Guardian* ran a contest for its readers based on appreciations of the election speakers. One listener praised Snowden for offering vitriol not syrup (14 Nov. 1935).

The *Daily Express* questioned people as to whether or not they had listened to Morrison and to Baldwin: 29·5 per cent. had listened to the former, it was claimed, 40·9 per cent. to the latter.[1] It was estimated by a second pollster also that about 40 per cent. of the subscribers to wireless-relay systems were listening to the political broadcasts as against a 'normal' audience at that time of 60 to 65 per cent.[2] The greater use of the broadcasting system 'as an instrument of political education' *The Times* maintained, made the result harder to forecast, while the *Daily Express* attributed 'the failure of the official prophets' to forecast such a large majority for the government to the influence of radio.[3] The *New Statesman* looked forward to the next election. The microphone was 'a soul-less non-odoriferous instrument, a one-way traffic affair which does not answer back', but the next election would be a television election. 'The listeners shall see the broadcaster, but he won't see them.'[4]

Prophecies of this kind are obviously of long-term interest, although many political squabbles of this period look petty and unimportant in the light of subsequent history. So too do the squabbles about the BBC's own attitude to 'internal censorship'. Under Hilda Matheson the BBC employed speakers of every persuasion, but this did not save it from charges of 'left-wing bias'. Under Siepmann the same charges were frequently repeated, and the Corporation found it desirable to seek 'right-wing speakers' who would offset criticism. To many people outside the BBC the explanation of what was happening inside the organization was political. Miss Matheson, it was suggested, had to leave because of political opposition to her. Siepmann's difficulties arose, others suggested, for exactly the same reason.

In fact, the difficulties centred as much on personalities as on principles, and there is no evidence to suggest that either Miss Matheson or Siepmann used the BBC to push one particular point of view or even to over-represent it. The circumstances leading up to Miss Matheson's resignation were, indeed, peculiarly complicated and were concerned as much as anything else with her administrative relations with Siepmann.

[1] *Daily Express*, 9 Nov. 1935, 12 Nov. 1935.   [2] *Daily Telegraph*, 31 Oct. 1935.
[3] *The Times*, 16 Nov. 1935; *Daily Express*, 16 Nov. 1935.
[4] *New Statesman*, 9 Nov. 1935.

There was a great deal of mutual scrutiny of motives in 1929 and 1930, and as Hilda Matheson lost her monopoly of the Spoken Word, there was also a good deal of bad temper and jealousy. She proved testy and difficult to co-operate with, and recriminations multiplied on both sides. This was the second of the BBC's difficulties with officers in positions of responsibility, the first being the resignation for domestic reasons of the Chief Engineer, Peter Eckersley, in 1929.[1] In both cases the press took up the stories, concentrating on issues which were general and leaving out many of the relevant particularities.[2]

Siepmann, who succeeded Hilda Matheson, had joined the BBC in the autumn of 1927 on the recommendation of Sir George Gater. He was a lively, enterprising, and ambitious young man, who saw the opportunities of broadcasting in much the same terms as Hilda Matheson. His first job in the BBC was that of deputy to R. S. Lambert in the Adult Education Section, which hived off from Stobart's empire early in 1927,[3] and when Lambert became editor of *The Listener* in October 1929, Siepmann succeeded him. He worked extremely closely with Hilda Matheson and in July 1929 it was decided to amalgamate the Adult Education Section with the Talks Department.[4] The change took place in December. 'Mr. Siepmann and his Assistant will transfer from Cecil Chambers to Savoy Hill', the Internal Memorandum stated. 'He takes seniority and general responsibility next Miss Matheson but to some extent on a colleagueship basis, having direct responsibility on matters affecting the Central Council for Adult Education.[5] The term "Adult Education" disappears internally.'[6]

The language of this memorandum was more vague in its references to the future of Charles Siepmann than it was to the future of the term 'adult education'. Nor was it immediately obvious what lay behind a further memorandum of February 1931. 'In view of the development of Talks Department's activities and in order to demarcate responsibilities more precisely as between the Corporation and the Central Council for Broad-

[1] See below, p. 543.
[2] See, for example, the *News Chronicle*, 2 Dec. 1931.
[3] See below, p. 222.
[4] *Control Board Minutes, 16 July 1929.
[5] *Internal Memorandum, no. 125, 5 Dec. 1929.
[6] For the organization of adult education, see below, pp. 217 ff.

cast Adult Education, Miss Matheson will in future act (and be known) as Director of General Talks and Mr. Siepmann as Director of Adult Education Talks. These will be distinct departments, but with a single executive (Mr. Rendall).'[1] This arrangement did not work well, and when suggestions were made that there should be further reorganization, Miss Matheson sent in her resignation on 12 October 1931.

Siepmann formally replaced her as Director of Talks in January 1932. Yet it was not a straight replacement. Some of Reith's critics have seen the Director-General's hand behind 'the advancement of Siepmann'.[2] In fact, he appointed him to the post previously occupied by Miss Matheson only after very careful thought and prolonged discussion both with Siepmann himself and with the Chairman of Governors. He was very glad indeed, however, to see Miss Matheson go.

There was rumour of other members of the Talks Branch resigning in support of Miss Matheson,[3] but this very quickly fizzled out. J. M. Rose-Troup took over as Assistant Director (and Executive); Fielden, who had been very close to Miss Matheson, was placed in charge of General Talks; and Rendall took over Adult Education Talks and became Secretary of the Central Council for Broadcast Adult Education.[4] Under Siepmann's general direction, the reorganized Talks Branch settled down to plan some of the liveliest talks in the BBC's history.

An excellent series called *Whither Britain?*, for example, was broadcast in 1934 (with Wells, Bevin, Shaw, and Lloyd George among the speakers) and this was followed later in the year by a series on *The Causes of War* (with, among others, Lord Beaverbrook, Norman Angell, Major Douglas—of Social Credit fame —and Aldous Huxley). A few months earlier, in the spring of 1933, two of the best of BBC talkers were on the air. Professor John Hilton gave his first series on industrial relations—his talks evoke the mood of the 1930s almost as strongly as the popular songs of the period—and J. B. Priestley, whose war-time broadcasts still recall a quite different mood, offered a personal comment on current events called *I'll Tell You Everything*. Alistair

[1] *BBC Internal Memorandum, no. 149, 25 Feb. 1931.
[2] *Ariel and All His Quality*, pp. 72–73; *The Natural Bent*, pp. 116–18.
[3] *The Natural Bent*, p. 117.
[4] *BBC Internal Memorandum, no. 174, 8 Jan. 1932.

Cooke, who was also to become one of the best of all broadcasters, began his radio career in 1934 as a cinema critic. His
early correspondence with the BBC is enlivened by a telegram
of 1936 which reads 'Script today would have to be about two
good books and game of ice hockey, for in 23 general releases
and 6 new films nowhere to go for a laugh or a cry.'[1] Despite
candid comments like this, Cooke avoided the sort of friction
with film interests which Agate continued to provoke with the
theatre. He was already hailed in 1936 as 'a really good broadcasting personality'.[2] His was a voice of the future. Meanwhile
the National Lectures, which had been inaugurated by Robert
Bridges, the Poet Laureate and the first poet to write on broadcasting, went their somewhat sombre way, with occasional
peaks of retrospective drama like Lord Rutherford's lecture in
October 1933 on *The Transmutation of the Atom*.[3]

The record is impressive, but the way of the Talks Branch
was never smooth. There was trouble both about personalities
and about 'message'. Churchill's difficulties, for example, did
not end in 1931. Having pressed hard to broadcast on the world
economic crisis in 1932,[4] the imminence of the Lausanne Conference was given as a reason for 'feeling' that a talk at that time
would not be 'appropriate'.[5] He took part in the *Whither
Britain?* series, however—with 'a broad latitude' to speak on
what he wished[6]—and in the later series on *The Causes of War*;
and in 1935 he gave his long-postponed talk on India. Whitley
told him in October 1933 in the most friendly fashion that the
reason he had not been asked to broadcast earlier on India was
because the Parliamentary Advisory Committee of the BBC had
recommended against it. There was a small inter-party consultative committee to advise on political talks, the idea of which
had been suggested by MacDonald in September 1932.[7]
This was implemented almost immediately, and the previous
elaborate arrangement with party Whips was abolished except
at election times. A small committee of five—Lord Rankeillour,

[1] *Telegram to Malcolm Brereton, 17 Jan. 1936.
[2] *J. Rose-Troup to C. G. Graves, 15 Jan. 1936.
[3] For a list of talks between 1930 and 1935, see *BBC Annual* (1935), pp. 28–33.
[4] *Winston Churchill to Reith, 28 Mar. 1932, 14 Apr. 1932.
[5] *Reith to Churchill, 27 May 1932.
[6] *Churchill to Dawnay, 6 Nov. 1933.
[7] *Into the Wind*, p. 162.

Lord Gorell, John Buchan, Major Milner, and Ian Macpherson
—was set up to meet at the BBC's request two or three times a
year.[1] The scheme did not work very well, however, since
Lansbury did not approve of Major Milner serving, and Milner
never attended.

The existence of this committee made it difficult for speakers,
like Churchill, who were not on good terms with their parties,
to broadcast on major political questions. 'Surely', Churchill,
Lloyd George, and Austen Chamberlain complained in 1933,
'it introduces an entirely new principle of discrimination in
British public life—namely the elimination and silencing of any
members of Parliament who are not nominated by the party
leaders or the party whips.'[2] Snowden, who had been given the
opportunity by the Liberal Party of making his voice heard at
a critical time in 1935, joined in the protest on the ground that
it 'crushes out all independent political views'.[3] The parties continued to exercise direct or indirect influence, however, even after
the eclipse of the Parliamentary Advisory Committee, and the
public heard men like Churchill only rarely. This was a national
loss. Churchill, who turned down a number of requests to
broadcast on what he thought were subjects of little national
importance, spoke in 1937 'about the Navy in its relation to the
Empire'.[4] 'I should like to dwell', he told the BBC, 'on peace
and freedom, tolerance, Parliament and law, as well as upon the
Navy which renders our existence and mission possible.'[5] He
also broadcast on the Mediterranean in October 1938, when he
told a BBC official that he still felt himself to be 'muzzled'.[6]

It is necessary to add that the BBC was influenced in its
political broadcasts policy not only by the parties but by the
pressure of public opinion. There was always a powerful current
of opinion which resented the expression of all 'strong' political
statements and accused the BBC of bias in one direction or
another. Churchill was identified with a 'strong' right-wing
position before he turned increasingly to the international scene

---

[1] Ibid., p. 172. *Control Board Minutes, 27 Sept. 1932.
[2] *Winston Churchill, D. Lloyd George, and Sir Austen Chamberlain to J. H.
Whitley, 25 Aug. 1933.
[3] *The Times*, 12 Sept. 1933.
[4] *Churchill to Reith, 5 Mar. 1937.
[5] *Churchill to the Programme Contracts Executive, 24 Mar. 1937.
[6] *Note by Guy Burgess, 4 Oct. 1938.

in the 1930s, and having roused left-wing opinion during the General Strike—which left memories inside the BBC—he roused moderate Conservative opinion during the Indian discussions. After he had given his talk in the 1934 *Causes of War* series there were complaints that he had delivered a 'gratuitous attack on Germany', and one writer said that it was 'in need of far more censorship than Professor Haldane's', a talk on the extreme left.[1] The mood of the 1930s was not congenial to the forthright communication of Churchillian themes, and the BBC did not seek to dispel it.

It had difficulties also, of a quite different order, with Vernon Bartlett, the BBC's 'foreign correspondent' who broadcast regularly (on programme contract) on foreign affairs from London and the European capitals from 1932 onwards. For five years before that he had given a weekly talk entitled *The Way of the World*. Bartlett was an excellent broadcaster but he ran into many difficulties, particularly when articles he wrote in the press were set alongside his broadcasts. A talk which he gave on Nazi Germany in October 1933 provoked a letter from Ramsay MacDonald, who stated bluntly that 'a propaganda in favour of Germany is certainly the most dangerous thing that can be started at present'.[2] A later talk by Bartlett on Germany's withdrawal from the League of Nations, which was also held by his critics to be pro-German, provoked a burst of public protest—along with a far greater burst of appreciative praise. Questions were asked in the House of Commons about this broadcast,[3] and there was serious strain in the BBC's relations with the Foreign Office. Sir John Simon, the Foreign Secretary, had always hinted that the BBC made crises more critical, and Sir Robert Vansittart backed him up. After abortive discussions on the scope of future broadcasts, Bartlett left the BBC for the *News Chronicle*. Yet he understood the BBC's point of view and frequently broadcast after this, as did other speakers who had temporary difficulties with the Corporation. He later became an Independent Progressive Member of Parliament for Bridgwater in 1938. Reviewing his experience as a commentator on

---

[1] *Note by S. J. de Lotbinière, 20 Nov. 1934.
[2] *J. R. MacDonald to J. H. Whitley, 16 Oct. 1935.
[3] *Hansard*, vol. 285, col. 1577. See an article on this and allied subjects by Mrs. Hamilton, a BBC Governor, in *Harper's Magazine*, Dec. 1935.

foreign affairs he concluded that 'no one person should be given a position of such authority and responsibility'.[1]

If interpretations of Nazi Germany posed problems, so did interpretations of the Soviet Union. Vansittart complained, indeed, in 1937 that a talk by John Hilton on Russia was misleading and dangerous, and urged the BBC 'to keep off Communism and Nazi-ism and Fascism for the next year or so'.[2]

In August 1934 a new General Talks Department had been formed in the BBC by the amalgamation of the old General Talks Department and the Adult Education Department. The Head of the Department under Siepmann as Director of Talks was G. N. Pocock, and there were four General Assistants (including Felix Greene and J. S. A. Salt) and two part-time assistants, one of whom was Mrs. Mary Adams, the highly intelligent wife of the highly independent Conservative Member of Parliament, Vyvyan Adams. Fielden was 'promoted' to the post of special assistant to Siepmann, 'with the duties of providing ideas for Talks programmes, producing special Talks features and stimulating and criticising the content and execution of Talks throughout the Branch'.[3] Within a year, on Reith's recommendation, Fielden was on his way from Broadcasting House to India to take charge of broadcasting there.

The new man inside the BBC who made the reorganization necessary was Professor John Coatman, former Professor of Imperial Economic Relations at the London School of Economics, who was deliberately brought in as 'right wing offset' to 'balance' the direction of talks and news. Reith had decided to divorce 'News and Topicality' from 'Talks' in May 1934, the first open sign that Siepmann's empire was about to disintegrate.[4] Coatman was not the first man to be thought of in relation to the 'News' job, but he was strongly supported by Norman and Dawnay. His arrival almost immediately caused strains and difficulties with Siepmann. Not only did the two men have different views, but Coatman did not behave as a subordinate. He insisted on his own independence as a maker of policy. As the strains between him and Siepmann intensified Reith became increasingly concerned not only about Coatman's but about Siepmann's behaviour. There was ominous talk—inside and outside committee rooms—of parallels with the last days of Miss Matheson in 1931. The climax came in June 1935 when Siepmann was moved from his post as Director of Talks to the new post of Director of Regional Relations. The Talks Department then passed into the hands of Rose-Troup.

Rose-Troup's tenure of office was little more than an inter-regnum when contending forces struggled against each other. Indeed, he himself accepted the post only on condition that it would be temporary. Norman Luker, who had joined the Talks Department in 1934—and was eventually to become Head of Talks—has called it 'a period of anarchy'.[1] It ended with the appointment in February 1936 of Sir Richard Roy Maconachie as Director of Talks. Maconachie had served as British Minister at Kabul from 1930 to 1936 and had established an Indian reputation as a 'master of the pen'. His appointment to the BBC was naturally seen as a 'swing to the right', but it was something more than this. Convinced of the significance of Talks and News inside the BBC's organization, he battled hard (and sometimes irascibly) in the interests of his department. He had a genuine interest in promoting the work of young men, and he soon won their confidence by allowing them both security and freedom. John Green, who was a young man in 1937 and eventually was to be one of Maconachie's successors, has written of him:

He came to the BBC at a period of unusual frustration and threatened resignations, when the cult of the temperamental producer was slowly yielding to more professional and perhaps prosaic concepts. A virtual anarchy (rather topical at that time because of the Spanish Civil War) was in operation when the Talks Department was summoned to the Board Room to what was thought to be at worst dismissal, at least another perplexing reorganization. It was Sir Cecil Graves who merely announced that the Governors had appointed 'a Sir Richard Maconachie to be Director of Talks', and added most laconically as he left the room 'he is a most distinguished public servant whom I am sure you will all like'. I well remember

[1] Note by N. Luker, 7 Dec. 1962.

the only lifebelt that could be grasped in that cold sea was the
Governors' solitary *Who's Who*. When one of those present had read
aloud the Kiplingesque dossier of deeds wrought on the Indian
Frontier the situation seemed more unusual than ever. Ten years
later the only exceptionable word was 'like' because the whole body
of young idealists and intellectuals would unanimously have preferred 'love'.[1]

The tribute rings true, even though in retrospect the choice
of a man with Maconachie's background must still be considered as a further retreat into caution. In the last two years of
the peace there were few series of talks which compared in
excitement with those of the earlier 1930s, and controversy
itself began to seem somewhat *vieux jeu*. The most interesting
reaction inside the BBC was technical rather than political.
Both from 'left' and 'right' there was a demand for new techniques in the broadcasting of the spoken word. The approach
of Hilda Matheson and Siepmann seemed to be out of date,
particularly in its emphasis on the formal script and the single
speaker. Could not the BBC learn from Mass Observation? Did
it have to rely on an élite? Could not more use be made of
speakers in the regions, speakers who would not naturally use
the standard BBC English with which the Talk was associated?
Was it not necessary to break with 'intellectualism', with 'the
Platonism of the founders'?

Against this background, new kinds of programmes began
to be transmitted, or rather ideas associated with older programmes were given a new airing. *Conversations in the Train*
(1932) had associated conversation with 'appropriate sound
effects': the idea was Hilda Matheson's,[2] but whereas she wanted
to use first-class speakers, like E. M. Forster or Roger Fry, by
1935 professional actors—of the calibre of Gladys Young, Mabel
Constanduros, Carleton Hobbs, and Charles Mason—were
'performing' in scripts written by outsiders. The change of mood
inside the BBC is well illustrated in a note by Felix Felton in
1938: 'I suggest that *Conversations in the Train* should be taken
over by us under the new title *Casual Conversations*. This would
have the advantage (*a*) of being a new title though reminiscent
of the other and (*b*) of suggesting that the series will, in our

---

[1] See *The Times*, 25 Jan. 1962.
[2] *H. Matheson to R. H. Eckersley, passed to Reith, 4 Dec. 1931.

hands, deal with private and human problems rather than ones as cosmic as "fixed Easter" or the metric system.'[1]

In 1935 a series of unrehearsed debates was arranged by Mrs. Adams—there had already been many of these since 1927[2]—on Saturday evenings. The two speakers and their chairman met only once, at most, before the debate, and when Bertrand Russell and G. K. Chesterton debated the motion 'that parents are unfitted by nature to bring up their own children', no preliminary meeting was held until 'a light supper in the Green Room' immediately before the broadcast.[3] Fear of silence seems to have worried producers as much as fear of the uncensored, though surely not in the case of Russell and Chesterton. There was certainly little fear of sharp confrontations of opposing points of view. A recorded debate in December 1936 was described by Graves to Rose-Troup as 'too obviously rehearsed and lacking in interest because the divergence of views of the three speakers was not sufficiently divergent'.[4]

The BBC's files on the debates contain many items of historical interest. In late 1936 and early 1937, for example, to take one short spell alone, Roger Wilson was arranging a series called *This Planning Business* with Professor Arnold Plant defending *laissez-faire*, John Strachey attacking it, and Harold Macmillan taking 'a middle line';[5] Graves was saying that it was time to give Crossman 'a rest' as a Labour speaker, but that he had not heard of Gaitskell;[6] and C. V. Salmon, the producer, after arranging a discussion on 'The Younger Generation', was asking, with genuine solicitude, 'I understand that Cloudesley Brereton always has a first-class railway voucher on these

[1] *Note by Felix Felton, 9 June 1938.
[2] *Miss Matheson wrote to Reith on 1 Feb. 1927, 'I should very much like permission to experiment with one unwritten debate', to which he replied (2 Feb. 1927), 'By all means have an unwritten debate provided you can be certain that things will not be said which will subsequently get us into trouble.' Such debates were subsequently arranged, and Miss Matheson was well aware of the technical problems they posed. 'We shall never get ideal conversational stuff in a completely natural and yet completely audible tone until . . . the whole room is equivalent to a microphone. The present arrangements, though an improvement in some ways on the past, are still too like Heath Robinson cartoons.' (Miss Matheson to W. E. G. Murray, 27 Mar. 1930.)
[3] *Mrs. Adams to Rose-Troup, 13 Mar. 1936.
[4] *Graves to Rose-Troup, 7 Dec. 1936.
[5] *Wilson to Salmon, 25 Feb. 1937.
[6] *Graves to Rose-Troup, 18 Dec. 1936.

occasions. Do you think that C. P. Snow ought to have one as well?'[1]

It is of importance to note that among the significant broadcasting developments of the years just before the war, developments in the Regions were as interesting—and in some cases more interesting—than developments at the centre. It was in Manchester, Birmingham, and Bristol that changes in talks policy were most clear and most striking.[2] Agricultural talks from the Midlands and West Region, 'Midland Parliament' and 'Northern Cockpit' programmes from the Midlands and North,[3] and, above all, two series of programmes from the North, planned by Donald Boyd and Roger Wilson, broke entirely new ground. In 1937 Wilson had paid a visit to the United States to study 'serious broadcasting', and in the course of his trip he made acquaintance with the Chicago Round Table programmes, a serious unscripted discussion series sponsored by the University. With the help of Boyd he determined on his return 'to use the idea better' than the Americans had done, in the North Region. *Why Do You Believe That?* was the first of the two series of programmes he devised. In it J. H. Sprott of Nottingham University conducted a Socratic dialogue with three 'partners in discussion', one of them a steelworker from Scunthorpe. This programme series ran into difficulties with Iremonger, the BBC's Director of Religion, who listened zealously to all programmes on 'moral themes', not only on Sundays.[4] In the second series of programmes, *Public Enquiry*, an audience of 200 people in Manchester listened to two speakers of opposing views discussing issues in local government. Questions were asked from the audience who genuinely participated in the broadcast. One of the technical difficulties, which Miss Matheson had noted, was that in the absence of an omnidirectional microphone, microphones had to be placed everywhere in the hall. This programme was so successful, however, that it was due to be included in the National Programme in the autumn of 1939. War, of course, intervened.

The Regions always had the ambition of having their programmes carried on the National Programme for reasons both of finance and prestige. They had the advantage over London,

[1] *Salmon to the Talks Executive, 28 May 1937.   [2] See also below, p. 330.
[3] See below, p. 338.   [4] See below, p. 246.

however, of being able to deploy the operational resources of the whole regional staff and not just a section of it. A series from the North, called *Burbleton* after the name of an imaginary borough with a mayor called Alderman Wool, had a script written by T. Thompson, the Lancashire short-story writer. Its realism was well enough established for a Staffordshire town clerk to write to the Burbletown Town Planning Officer to ask for his advice and for a Cheshire town councillor to accuse the BBC of having copied a speech he had just delivered to his own council.[1]

It is interesting to speculate what would have happened to this genre of broadcast had not war intervened. As it was, one of the great successes of Howard Thomas's war-time Brains Trusts had made his début in 1935 in an interesting unscripted series, *Men Talking*. 'At last we have found the right man for the *Men Talking* series,' Stuart Hibberd wrote in his diary, 'a Commander Campbell, R.N.R., a man with a good broadcasting voice and a collection of sailor's yarns which must be unrivalled —spun not by the yard, but by the mile.'[2]

The story of Talks is related at almost every point to the story of News. In December 1929 the News Section had been separated from the Talks Department and placed under the direct control of the Assistant Director of Programmes,[3] but in February 1932, after Miss Matheson had left, the News Section was brought back within the aegis of the Talks Branch and thereby under the control of Siepmann.[4] When Professor Coatman joined the BBC as Senior News Editor in August 1934, the News Section became a department again, and a few months later it became quite independent of the Director of Talks.[5] It remained separate and distinct, reporting direct to the Controller of Programmes, until May 1940.

More interesting than these formal details of organization are the facts concerning the timing and presentation of news, the enormous spread of activities, and the relations in the back-

[1] Note by Donald Boyd, Dec. 1962.
[2] *This—is London*, p. 119.
[3] *BBC Internal Memorandum, no. 125, 5 Dec. 1929.
[4] *BBC Internal Memorandum, no. 149, 25 Feb. 1931.
[5] *BBC Internal Memorandum, no. 277, 27 Aug. 1934; BBC Internal Memorandum, 1 Apr. 1935.

ground with the powerful news agencies. Between 1927 and 1939 the BBC established its reputation as the most honest purveyor of news in the world: it was a reputation which was to stand it in good stead when war broke out. Yet there was a remarkable contrast between the beginning and the end of the period. It was only in January and February 1927 that Reith, bargaining with great skill, reached agreement with the press and the four main news agencies allowing the BBC to broadcast its first news bulletin at 6.30 p.m. (instead of 7 p.m.) and to transmit a strictly limited number of 'eye witness descriptions'. Even then the Newspaper Proprietors' Association, the Newspaper Society, Reuters Ltd., the Press Association, the Exchange Telegraph Company, and the Central News—the parties to the agreement—severely restricted BBC activities. The BBC had to promise to take its news bulletins exclusively from the four press news agencies and not to give its listeners more racing or sporting information than it was giving them at the end of 1926.[1] Although the term 'copyright reserved' could be used in bulletins instead of the older ritualistic formula of obligation, the longer acknowledgement had to be made once a week. Reith's skill in reaching this agreement was greatly appreciated by his colleagues. C. F. Atkinson, who was present at the final meeting with the news agencies, rushed in jubilation to Carpendale's room afterwards and said that the Director-General by his conduct of the negotiations had earned a year's salary in little over an hour.

The BBC felt that it had gained an immense amount by the new agreement, limited though it was. Its first 6.30 news bulletin was given on 3 January 1927 and its first running commentaries in the same month. Geoffrey Strutt, who was in charge of the section, had prepared a most interesting memorandum on its future in September 1926. He lamented the inability of the BBC 'to use the peculiar quality of our medium for describing events as they happen', urged that there should be more running commentaries, and emphasized above all else the need for 'accuracy' in news bulletins. In the long run the members of the public would appreciate accuracy, even though

[1] *Arrangement made between the BBC and Various Press Organisations, 22 Feb. 1927. Agreement about payment to the news agencies was reached in Sept. 1927, when a fixed annual payment was substituted for a sliding scale.

they would lack the 'sensationalism' of the press. It would be enough for people to say, 'if it came through the BBC, it is so'.[1]

There were only two sub-editors working in the News Section in January 1927 and at the end of the year still only three. Their work, which did not, of course, include outside broadcasts,[2] seems to have been limited in scope to checking the content of news rather than sub-editing it. It was not until February 1930 that the BBC put out the first news bulletin to be fully edited at Savoy Hill. By then there had been new agreements with the press and the agencies, and the first evening news bulletin was given at 6 p.m. instead of 6.30.

All issues relating to the news had to be thrashed out at a meeting of a joint committee of press and BBC, presided over by Lord Riddell, who had been actively engaged in all discussions between the press and the BBC since 1922. He was still talking in 1927 of the BBC 'damaging the Press',[3] and even three years later Reith was complaining openly of the committee's 'obstructive attitude'.[4] In September 1928, however, the earlier news bulletins were permitted and an increase in the number of 'running commentaries' was allowed,[5] while in 1930 direct tape machines were installed at Savoy Hill and the BBC's editorial staff was doubled so as to provide two editors and two sub-editors, working in two shifts.[6]

'Special efforts were made' in 1930, we are told, 'to improve the presentation of news, so that items should be brief and simply worded. A very definite standard of quality was aimed at, and when news of that quality was lacking, no padding was employed. When there was not sufficient news judged worthy of being broadcast, no attempt was made to fill the gap, and the announcer simply said "there is no news tonight".'[7] In this un-ostentatious way the BBC sharply distinguished itself from the newspapers. When news did come in, as it usually did, little attempt was made to supplement agency messages. News was

[1] *G. H. G. Strutt, Memorandum on the BBC's News Service, 29 Sept. 1926.
[2] See above, p. 80.
[3] Reith, Diary, 3 July 1927.   [4] Ibid., 26 Nov. 1930.
[5] *Arrangement made between the BBC and Various Press Organisations, 18 Sept. 1928.
[6] *News Service, 'Review of the Year 1930', 4 Jan. 1931. Agreement had been reached with Exchange Telegraph in Feb. 1927 to instal one tape machine at Savoy Hill.
[7] *'Review of the Year 1930.'

collected as it came off the tape machines and was written up in 'items' for broadcasting purposes.

In November 1932 a greater measure of freedom of a more positive kind was secured. At a meeting of the joint committee the BBC secured consent to put out at any time news of unforeseen events of special importance. The discussion on this occasion showed that the balance of power between BBC and press had begun to tilt in favour of the BBC. When press representatives objected to the BBC broadcasting Test Match scores from the tape, Reith retaliated by 'indicating that if they were obstructive we might decline to prohibit the re-diffusion of important running commentaries, particularly of sporting events, which they have always been bothered about'.[1]

The most interesting experiment before the News Department was founded in 1934 under Coatman was the 'news reel', first introduced in the summer of 1933. The idea came from John Watt and the first broadcast of 1 July 1933 was described as 'frankly experimental'. News and comment were welded into a continuous fifty-minute programme, with switch-overs to Manchester and Paris, gramophone and Blattnerphone excerpts, including Derek McCulloch talking about the anniversary of the Battle of the Somme, and a record of a lawn-tennis commentary earlier in the day. Listeners' comments were mixed. One correspondent said that he wanted the news 'as short as possible, at the regular time, and then I want to get on with my Bridge'. 'It compelled me to listen,' wrote another, 'and by 9.15 my yearning for cricket scores had vanished.'[2] 'The news reel', wrote *The Times*, 'exploited the element of surprise, and conception of news as something more than facts. News in this wider sense is facts present, plus facts past, plus human reactions, and the experiment showed something of what may be done in presenting such news for the ear alone.'[3]

News Reel was, in fact, too expensive to survive in the conditions of 1933. There was not a big enough staff or a staff of the right kind, and recordings were still thought to be an expensive luxury rather than a necessary item of equipment. The programme was taken off the air in December 1933. A few months later, under Coatman, the size of the News staff was greatly

[1] Reith, Diary, 16 Nov. 1932.   [2] *Radio Times*, Nov. 1933.
[3] *The Times*, Broadcasting Number, 14 Aug. 1934.

increased and a separate News Section was started inside the
Empire and Foreign Services Branch. J. C. S. McGregor was
transferred as Empire News Editor, and the two units worked
quite separately. By 1940 the Empire News Section had grown
into a huge Overseas News Department, serving not only
English-speaking audiences in the Empire but foreigners in all
parts of the world.[1] This was one of the most remarkable trans-
formations in the history of the BBC. Yet both branches were
of the same tree and shared the same approach to news, and in
1934 it was Coatman's department which seemed the more
important.

Coatman made it abundantly clear to all the newcomers to
the News Department that his intention was to create a service
on new, professional lines which would be responsible through
the Chief News Editor to Dawnay. Two professional journalists
were appointed to Coatman's staff—R. T. Clark, the Foreign
News Editor, who was a veteran of the *Daily Telegraph* and the
Manchester Guardian, and Kenneth Adam, Home News Editor,
who went to the BBC direct from the *Manchester Guardian*. They
were supported as sub-editors by F. D. Walker and Michael
Balkwill. Coatman left the actual compilation of news bulletins
to his staff, but his personality and methods quickly made him a
power inside Broadcasting House. His appointment had been
as controversial as that of Maconachie was to be: the *News
Chronicle*, for example, referring to his earlier career in India,
hailed it with the headline, 'Strange Appointment at the BBC:
Ex-Police Official is News Editor'.[2] His colleagues do not
think of him in this context. 'He was an old-fashioned radical',
Kenneth Adam has written, 'whose two personal enthusiasms
were the Empire and cricket. He had a spendid contempt for
protocol and formality, and his special delight was to return to
the fifth floor of Broadcasting House late in the evening, often
after an official dinner, and sweep the whole staff, including
secretaries, off to a nearby public house for sausages and bitter.'[3]

In extending the scope of the news service Coatman had the
active support of Reith, who was keenly interested in the BBC's
presentation of news and often rang up at the end of a bulletin
to commend or to criticize the manner in which a particular

[1] See below, p. 408.   [2] *News Chronicle*, 15 Aug. 1934.
[3] *Note by Kenneth Adam on the News Department, June 1963.

news item had been treated. When there were press or agency protests about the increase in coverage, Reith himself was the BBC's chief advocate. Two of the signs of change were the opening of a News Library, with A. V. Batchelor from *The Times* in charge and Elizabeth Barker, daughter of Sir Ernest, as his assistant, and the beginnings of independent BBC reporting. Vernon Bartlett had never been able to secure from the BBC the same kind of terms as a foreign correspondent would secure from a newspaper, even though he believed the BBC 'to be so much more influential than any newspaper'.[1] Ralph Murray, who was placed in charge of 'News Talks' after J. R. Ackerley was appointed Literary Editor of *The Listener* in 1935, felt no such insecurity. He proved to be both an organizer and a performer of high quality, and his lucid descriptions of the League of Nations and the Geneva scene were either recorded or fed directly into news bulletins. The Foreign Office was later to claim him as an ambassador. In the meantime, Kenneth Adam was active on the home front, covering such varied events as the lying-in-state of George V, a speech of Lloyd George at the Trades Union Club, the Spring Show at the Old Horticultural Hall, and a new Shaw play at the Malvern Festival.

Not all the initiatives of the News Department developed without hitch. A dramatic presentation of the news of a twenty-four-hour revolution in Barcelona, with a team of announcers representing 'the Voice of Barcelona', 'the Voice of Madrid', and 'the Voice of the Outside World', was described in some sections of the press as 'the occasion of a public sense of outrage'. Members of Parliament even tried to ask questions about it in the House of Commons. Coatman stood foursquare behind his erring editors, and Reith's rebuke was mild even though the participants in the programme had committed the additional sin of over-running their time. This was the first time, though not the last, that the BBC News made news. The initiative was warmly welcomed in some circles. An editorial in *Popular Wireless*, for example, noted in August 1935 that 'the vast improvement in the News Service lately cannot have escaped any one's notice. A number of most interesting stories have been collected and nicely written up. There have also been a number of summaries of official reports which have been extremely inter-

[1] *Vernon Bartlett to R. H. Eckersley, 15 Jan. 1932.

esting. Even the warnings have been delicately proclaimed. One likes to hear experts and men on the spot, too, in the News Bulletins. They give the bulletins the right authoritative touch.'[1]

It is possible to exaggerate the extent of change before 1939. Vernon Bartlett's dream of 'a panel' of foreign correspondents and speakers on foreign affairs was not realized,[2] nor was there a spoken counterpart of the current television programme, *Panorama*. In March 1937, however, a new fillip was given to 'on the spot' reporting of news during the Fen floods, and the mobile van was kept very busy. Recordings were also used at the time of the *Thetis* disaster, and before war broke out some of the younger members of the BBC staff were beginning to talk of a new sub-section of the News Department to be called 'actualities'.[3]

Instead, listeners were offered more news at fixed times. Six o'clock was still the time of the first news, and the 9 o'clock news had not yet become a national institution. In the early spring of 1936 a short news summary was provided at 11.30 p.m. for the benefit of late home-comers, and later in the same year the number of news bulletins and summaries was increased and the length of the two main bulletins reduced from thirty to twenty minutes. Two other points were made at the time of these changes. First, listeners were told that practically all topical talks would be relegated to one fixed period—from 10.15 to 10.25 p.m.—so as to avoid holding up the news. Second, they were promised more news about sport. 'Sports experts have been added to the News staff, with the object of making the sports service as efficient and as comprehensive as is possible in the time available.'[4]

It is interesting to note reactions to these developments. Six o'clock and 9 o'clock became hallowed times, particularly 9 o'clock, yet 6 o'clock had its critics inside the BBC. 'Six o'clock is too early for the majority of our listeners', Rose-Troup told Siepmann in 1932. 'On the other hand we have always been fighting the newspaper proprietors for an earlier news timing.'[5] Nine o'clock did not establish itself until October 1938, after several experiments in timing had been tried—9.30, 9.40, and

[1] *Popular Wireless*, Aug. 1935.
[2] See V. Bartlett, *This is My Life* (1937), ch. xi.
[3] *L. F. Lewis, 'Report on Mobile Recording, 1935–1941'.
[4] *BBC Annual* (1937), p. 43.
[5] *Rose-Troup to Siepmann, 14 Apr. 1932.

10 o'clock. More sport produced on the whole favourable re-actions, with one section pressing for even more. In 1932 the *Manchester Guardian* directed attention to the fact that the BBC had broadcast three-and-a-quarter hours of sporting running commentaries the previous Saturday: 'this is the first occasion a programme so ambitious has been undertaken'.[1] Gerald Cock, the *Daily Mirror* pointed out, had been responsible for this 'enter-tainment medley which was one of the best'.[2] Yet five years later, after the further extension of sports broadcasts, the news-papers were still asking for more.[3] There were a few comments on the other side. 'We confess our astonishment', the *Children's Newspaper* editorialized in 1935, 'that the BBC Announcer should think it well, at a time when grave issues are in the balance, to begin his news items with a long account of a horse race. Not content with giving the result of the race, he even told us who trained the winning horse.'[4]

While the public was being shocked, amused, or just informed, there were difficult negotiations behind the scenes which led to a new agreement being signed with the Newspaper Proprietors' Association and the Newspaper Society in March 1938.[5] In this agreement the press agencies were for the first time left out. By the new agreement, which applied to home-service broad-casting only, the BBC confirmed its previous policy of broad-casting news bulletins only between the hours of 6 p.m. and 2 a.m., promised not to broadcast betting news, and agreed, as it had done in 1927 and earlier, not to broadcast paid adver-tising matter. Apart from these three strictly limited restrictions, it was left free to do as it pleased—completely free, for example, in relation to outside broadcasting policy. The agreement was signed on behalf of the BBC neither by the Director-General nor by the Controller of Programmes but by Sir Stephen Tal-lents, the Controller of Public Relations.[6] This was a sign that relations with the press had now become a matter of public rela-tions only and no longer a serious restraint on programme policy.

[1] *Manchester Guardian*, 27 June 1932.
[2] *Daily Mirror*, 27 June 1932.   [3] See above, p. 121.
[4] *Children's Newspaper*, Apr. 1935.
[5] *The BBC sent the press interests formal notice that it intended to terminate the older agreement on 30 Nov. 1937.
[6] *Arrangement made between the BBC and Various Press Organisations, 24 Mar. 1938.

One of the most complex questions in the BBC's relations with the press agencies was whether or not the Corporation should make use of the British United Press, which was not a member of the consortium and to which they were bitterly opposed.[1] As early as 1931 Gladstone Murray had had talks with the Chairman of British United Press,[2] but it was not until September 1939 that agreement was reached.[3] Negotiations with some of the other agencies were proceeding 'in the open market' when war broke out.

'This is an Age of News', Sir Stephen Tallents told the Institute of Journalists in October 1937 in a talk entitled 'Fleet Street and Portland Place'. 'All over the world they seem to be turning from fiction to reality.'[4] Although the appetite for news was to grow sharper still during the Second World War, there certainly seems to have been a greater appetite for news during the 1930s than there was for drama. 'Almost all of us have, consciously or sub-consciously, a strong sense of the dramatic', R. E. Jeffrey, the BBC's first 'Productions Director', had written, highly rhetorically, in 1924; 'the hidden books of our lives are, for the best part, made up of pages full of dramatic incident. We have all been thrilled by joy, fear, agony, love, hate, inspiration, anger, passion, and other emotions. Strict training and temperamental reluctance to allow these feelings to take possession of us, has, perhaps, caused us to exercise restraint which has permitted these soul-moving moments to be rigorously suppressed.'[5] This was heavily dated by 1934, if it was anything else in 1924. Even at best, it sounds more like a prelude to *This Is Your Life* than to serious drama.

Val Gielgud took over from Jeffrey on 1 January 1929. His empire included variety as well as drama, but it was drama

[1] *The position on the eve of the termination of the agreement is fully summarized in an important paper by Nicolls, 'The Present Position in Regard to Restrictions on the Broadcasting of News and the Cost of the Service supplied by the News Agencies', 7 Sept. 1937.

[2] *Notes on meeting between Murray and C. F. Crandall, 19 May 1931; see also Reith to Crandall, 13 Apr. 1934, saying that the BBC would have to abide by its Press Agreement; Control Board Minutes, 29 Sept. 1936, reporting favourably on the value of the B.U.P. service; Control Board Minutes, 13 Apr. 1937, for the start of negotiations.

[3] *Control Board Minutes, 1 Sept. 1939.

[4] Sir Stephen Tallents, 'Fleet Street and Portland Place', 12 Oct. 1937.

[5] *R. E. Jeffrey, 'Wireless Drama', 1924.

which interested him most.[1] His main helper was Howard Rose, who had joined the BBC staff as a producer in 1925, having already acted in broadcast Shakespeare. From the start, Gielgud was given a very free hand. He was responsible not only for the production of plays in the studio, but for the choice of plays, in short for the whole of dramatic policy. 'Apart from having to observe the amber warning lights at the cross roads of Sex, Religion and Politics,' he has written, 'I could drive straight ahead with reasonable confidence of security.'[2] The proviso was an important one, more important, indeed, than the statement, yet it was an almost inevitable proviso in the Britain of the 1920s and 1930s. Not only does current drama reveal an age, through its attempt to escape as much as through its involvement, but the choice of the drama of previous generations is almost equally revealing.

In the ten years after 1929, the BBC broadcast a very wide repertoire of plays. In 1934, for example, five Shakespeare plays were broadcast, along with two Chekhov plays and two plays by Ibsen. At the same time six plays were specially written for broadcasting and five novels were adapted for radio, including *Oliver Twist*, *Wuthering Heights*, and *The Man Who Could Work Miracles*. Gielgud was part-author of one of the plays, and Laurence Gilliam, who was one of the pioneers of the 'feature', adapted *The Man Who Could Work Miracles* in co-operation with the author, H. G. Wells.

Some plays had to be ruled out on obvious grounds—classical plays dealing with exchange of identity, for instance (perfect for television), or multiplicity of disguises, and some of the most popular current plays of the 1930s, like the Ben Travers farces, which relied on comic situation (visibly communicated) rather than on dialogue. Other plays might tend to be ruled out, if their 'predecessors' had bored the great audience rather than entertained it. A series called *Twelve Great Plays* in 1928 was animated by the worthiest intentions, but its reception made it difficult for several years for Gielgud to persuade his 'elders and betters in the programme field to let me tackle anything in the nature of classical plays except Shakespeare'.[3]

[1] See above, p. 89.   [2] V. Gielgud, *British Radio Drama, 1922–1956*, p. 36.
[3] *Gielgud, 'Considerations Relevant to Broadcasting Drama based upon Experience in the Years 1929 to 1948'.

One freedom Gielgud greatly prized was that of being able to select plays both short and long, a freedom which he said American commercial broadcasting never permitted. He was opposed to the 'tyranny of the stop watch', and in the conditions of the 1930s found it less difficult to defend this policy than it was to be later. During the early months of the Second World War, for instance, all plays had to be cut short to fit into the single programme.[1]

The balance of different kinds of play did not change much in subsequent years from that of 1934, although listener-research suggested that there was a greater popular interest in radio drama than had earlier seemed likely,[2] and Gielgud himself had noted after a visit to Sweden in 1934 that 'it was something of a reproach to us that a comparatively small organisation such as the Swedish Broadcasting Committee can handle twice as many plays as we do—with extremely inferior accommodation'.[3]

One way of increasing output which Gielgud always resisted was that of encouraging a bigger spate of productions from the Regions. From the very beginnings of the Regional Scheme, he had feared that regional drama would not reach 'a high standard',[4] and he continued throughout the 1930s to criticize regions for seeking to achieve results beyond their reach.[5] He even attempted, against the trend of the times, to increase centralized control of Drama from London.[6] The Regions went ahead, however, in spite of his criticisms, partly by producing plays of the type that Gielgud welcomed—those which set out 'to reflect and promote the cultural and social life of the area'[7]— and partly by producing plays which London was not putting on.[8] His objection was not to West Region performances of

[1] *BBC Handbook* (1940), p. 22.
[2] See below, pp. 272–3.
[3] *Gielgud to Maschwitz, 19 Jan. 1934.
[4] *Gielgud to R. H. Eckersley, 22 Aug. 1929; 8 Oct. 1929.
[5] *A most interesting 'Memorandum on Regional Dramatic Policy' setting out the opposite point of view, was written by Cyril Wood in Bristol in Sept. 1935.
[6] *'Memorandum from Director of Drama to Controller (Programmes)', 8 May 1936. For the trend, see below p. 334.
[7] *H. J. Dunkerley to Gielgud, 26 May 1936.
[8] *For regional opposition to Gielgud's views, see Siepmann to Gielgud, 3 June 1936. 'There is unanimous opposition to D.D's proposal for centralised control. This is thought to undermine the authority of Regional Programme Directors. There is also a general feeling that D.D. neither appreciates nor sympathises with

Eden Philpotts or J. R. Gregson's productions from the North of England, but to plays of universal interest with a lower standard of production, so he thought, than that insisted upon in London.

There were some Regional Directors who agreed with him. G. L. Marshall wrote from Belfast, for example, in February 1939 that he regretted to see staff in the Regions 'making names for themselves by the writing or production of notable programmes which find their place in the National wave length' while people writing or producing genuine regional programmes, 'first and foremost for the Region', should receive no acknowledgement. 'I find my Programme Director becoming a salesman for the Region,' he complained, 'going up to London every quarter and doing his best to sell a number of programmes to Head office.' 'Only rarely', he concluded, 'should a programme be produced which is foreign to the localised needs of listeners, and that because, fortuitously, some member of the Regional staff happens to be the best man in the whole Corporation to deal with the subject.'[1]

Gielgud always maintained this, although his insistence on 'standards' never reflected unwillingness to encourage experiment. The very reverse, indeed, was true. In 1937, therefore, while maintaining the balance of London productions, he introduced an 'Experimental Hour', modelled on the 'Workshop' of the Columbia Broadcasting System of America. The new programme was designed to give producers an opportunity to try out new techniques, and was put on late at night since it was realized that the plays 'might not be to the taste of a large public'.[2] The first production in the series was *The Fall of the City*, a verse play by the American poet, Archibald McLeish. It was followed by *Words Upon the Window Pane* by W. B. Yeats, and a scene from *Twelfth Night*, presented first in modern English and then in Elizabethan pronunciation. The series failed to survive not because the public was uninterested—the audience was again bigger and more enthusiastic than had been anticipated—but because 'worthy material' could not be found in sufficiently large quantities.

that aspect of dramatic policy which refers to (*a*) encouragement of local players and (*b*) the representation of Regional dramatic work by writers past and present.'
[1] *Marshall to Nicolls, 21 Feb. 1939.   [2] *BBC Handbook* (1938), p. 15.

It was difficult either to choose broadcast plays or to produce them without having some 'theory'. Were stage plays really adaptable for radio, particularly current plays, unknown to the millions of the 'great audience'? Were not 'plays of ideas' particularly well suited to the medium, plays like those of Shaw or Wilde which cascaded words and poured out paradox? Was there not a special place for plays of suspense and mystery? Did not the radio play break down the barriers of costume, grease paint, stage, footlights, and orchestra stalls? 'The story arrived, in the simplest domestic circumstances, told by voices un-adorned.' Was it not essential, therefore, to break down the final illusions associated with the theatre—those resting on the announcement of the names of the actors?

Gielgud tried out the last theory and ruled, when he first took over, that cast lists of plays should not be published in the *Radio Times*. Before he had had time to test his theory, however, there was such a furore, both from actors and the press, that it had to be set on one side.[1] Intellectuals made much of the 'ideas' theory, if only because it offered them a more ample diet of intellectual plays, and Gielgud went part of the way with them. 'The play of discussion is probably far nearer to what may be called, for lack of a better expression, "Pure Radio", than any play of action can be.'[2] Ordinary listeners agreed with R. E. Jeffrey that there was much to be said for the 'mystery and suspense' theory, and certainly there were few more effective radio plays than Patrick Hamilton's *Rope*, first broadcast in January 1932. Filson Young emphasized the relevance of the first theory. 'One of the great properties of radio drama is the intimacy of its appeal to the listener. Of all material for broad-casting, it seems to me to benefit best from being heard in dark-ness.'[3] This 'intimacy' was impossible in the theatre, and all 'theatrical' influences had to be cast on one side in the produc-tion of radio drama. How many families actually listened in darkness was the kind of question Filson Young never asked.

There were two other approaches to radio drama—the first imaginative rather than theoretical, the second supremely prac-tical. The first was represented by Lance Sieveking, the second

[1] *British Radio Drama*, pp. 40–41.
[2] See V. Gielgud, *How to Write Broadcast Plays* (1932).
[3] *Shall I Listen?*, p. 137.

by L. du Garde Peach. Sieveking had been a leading figure in the small Research Section of the BBC, founded in 1928, and had had E. A. F. Harding, E. J. King-Bull, and Mary Hope Allen as colleagues.[1] It was to this Section that Jeffrey was transferred before he left the BBC. The Section was not concerned solely with drama, but it interested itself from the start in new dramatic techniques, particularly the techniques associated with the 'mixing-and-controlling unit', later called by Sieveking 'the Dramatic Control Panel'.[2]

This panel was used with great enterprise and imagination by Sieveking in *Kaleidoscope I*, 'A Rhythm representing the Life of Man From the Cradle to the Grave', which some critics hailed as 'real wireless drama at last'.[3] Words, effects, and music were blended together with the technical assistance of the panel, and Sieveking was very cross with Tyrone Guthrie for referring to it in his preface to *Squirrel's Cage and Two Other Microphone Plays* as a 'device known as a mixing-panel', 'in the bald sort of way one might mention that there was a telephone installed'.[4] Sieveking was very cross, also, with Gielgud, with whom he said he was in total disagreement on the subject of radio plays. He wanted radio plays—both in their writing and their production—to exploit every opportunity of the medium, and to be consciously modern at all times. Drawing on yet another art, he quoted with approval Renoir's dictum, 'on doit faire la peinture de son temps'.[5]

L. du Garde Peach, who wrote more radio plays than any other playwright, was, above all else, a craftsman, and he knew how to appeal to the greatest possible audience for radio drama. His *Ingredient X* (1929), *Path of Glory* (1931), and *The Marie Céleste* (1931) were early successes which won him wide acclaim. Of the performance of the first-named, a writer in the *BBC Year Book* said that 'technical production reached what is probably its highest level in the history of broadcast drama, and an author was found with an almost uncanny sense of the appropriate balance of writing for the microphone'.[6] Du Garde

[1] Sieveking was given control of this Section under Roger Eckersley's overall direction in July 1928.
[2] See above, pp. 59–60.
[3] See L. Sieveking, *The Stuff of Radio* (1934), p. 24.
[4] Ibid., p. 52. [5] Ibid., p. 62.
[6] *BBC Year Book* (1930), p. 77.

Peach went on experimenting, at many levels, but his basic approach was essentially simple, perhaps misleadingly simple. 'A stage-play need not be about anything in particular as long as it tells a story, but a good radio-play must have an idea behind it. Where there is nothing to look at, there must be something to think about.'[1]

Gielgud made ample use of the work of both du Garde Peach and Sieveking, although the Research Section was very quickly swallowed up in the bigger Drama organization.[2] With the move from Savoy Hill to Broadcasting House, facilities for producing drama greatly improved—not always, however, a guarantee of quality—and a whole 'suite' of rooms was reserved for Drama inside the tower on the sixth and seventh floors. There were five speech studios, an effects studio and a gramophone studio. Quick intercommunication between the studios made multi-studio productions possible. The two Dramatic Control Panels gave greater scope for experiments than the one at Savoy Hill. The producer could handle his play at a distance by loudspeaker and by microphone, judging the performance as listeners would judge it through his ears alone. He could manipulate the Dramatic Control Panel to control all effects without stirring from one room.

When R. E. Jeffrey had tentatively suggested in 1926 that 'an outside Drama studio (or whatever in future it may be named) will elevate our work to a dignity it will never otherwise possess',[3] he had not had this kind of studio in mind. Nor had Nicolls, when he opposed Jeffrey's idea on the grounds that it 'involved the abandonment of all idea of a separate broadcast technique and a lead back to the theatre'.[4] The whole object of the new dramatic studio was to differentiate it from a theatre. Yet not all producers—or actors—liked the new arrangement, which involved prolonged rehearsals. They felt that they were isolated from each other—the producer in his box, the actors

[1] Quoted in *The Stuff of Radio*, p. 54.
[2] See above, pp. 89 ff.
[3] *R. E. Jeffrey, 'The Drama Studio', undated memorandum.
[4] *B. E. Nicolls, 'The Drama Studio', 13 Apr. 1927. 'Frankly I think our experiments might begin at home,' he added, 'e.g. by eliminating obtrusive declamation. On the artistic side I do not candidly think that we have been conspicuous in the past for artistic choice or artistic production of plays, and I do not see how transferring our attentions to a small theatre, in order to secure a visible audience, will help matters.'

'on the floor'. Directions by microphone were not always as effective as directions from the floor. And some producers—and playwrights—distrusted the Dramatic Control Panel itself and preferred to leave its operation to engineers. This to Sieveking was the final betrayal.

Differences of opinion on basic problems of production are fairly common in the theatre, and there is little doubt that the *avant-garde* of the 1930s was distinguished from the rest by its willingness to experiment with the Dramatic Control Panel. As Gielgud has written, however, a price had to be paid for their enthusiasm. 'Plays were written—and produced on the air—less for their merits in terms of drama than because they offered opportunities for the simultaneous use of more and more studios, more and more ingenious electrical devices. Producers concentrated more upon knobs and switches than upon actors and acting. The radio play had so far always been among "minority" programme items. At this particular stage it tended to grow progressively and self-consciously minority.'[1]

Thirty years later, the experimentalism itself seems somewhat dated. Although it is easy to understand the excitement it generated, it was far less creative than experimentalism in poetry, which was being reshaped during the 1930s under the influence of socially conscious poets, men who were interested not only in language but in content. Much the most interesting of the new dramatic techniques was the development not of the play but of the feature. At its best it was the outstanding artistic achievement of sound radio, able to accomplish far more in its own medium than another of the comparable artistic achievements of the 1930s, the documentary film.

There were great difficulties at first in defining what a 'feature' was. At one end of the scale was Laurence Gilliam's Christmas Programme, designed for a 'mass audience' and incorporating the King's speech among all the other varied materials. At the other end of the scale was the 'literary pro-gramme', blending words and music, and designed for, as well as listened to, by a minority audience of the kind that now listens to the Third Programme. Features like *Erasmus* and *Coleridge* belonged to this tradition. So did G. K. Chesterton's *Lepanto* backed by Tchaikovsky's Fourth Symphony. Other

[1] *British Radio Drama*, pp. 60–61.

features, which attracted varying sizes of audience, included
'small-scale actualities', like *Gale Warning*, *Fog*, and *Trinity
House*; 'large-scale actualities', like *Scotland Yard* or *Underground*;
commemorative programmes, like *Gallipoli*, *Scott in the Antarctic*,
or Arthur Bryant's *The Thin Red Line*; and 'specialist programmes', like the series of *Famous Trials* or of episodes from
history, such as D. G. Bridson's outstanding *March of the '45*.
Some of these features overlapped with Talks, some with News,
some with Outside Broadcasts, some with Drama. Laurence
Gilliam drew a distinction between Features and Drama which
would have appealed to Tallents when he delivered his talk to
the journalists. Features dealt with fact, Drama dealt with
fiction. Where fact ended and fiction began was never clear, as
Auden pointed out, even in—or perhaps particularly in—the
newspapers of the day.

Although Drama and Features drew on the same group of
actors and employed similar techniques, there was obviously
a case for organizing them separately inside the BBC, and
Gielgud, who had lost Variety—without regrets—to Maschwitz in 1933—delegated Features to Gilliam in May 1936. The
Drama Department was then split up into three sections, all
under Gielgud's overall direction; the first, Drama (with
Howard Rose in charge, assisted by Sieveking, Creswell, and
Miss Burnham); the second, Features (with Gilliam in charge,
assisted by Felton, Whitworth, and Miss Allen);[1] and the third,
Children's Hour, which had been attached to the Drama
Department as an independent programme section in July
1935.[2] A few months later the title of the whole department
was changed to Features and Drama, and, as if to show how
open its frontiers were, Moray McLaren was transferred from the
Talks Department as Assistant Director.[3] Gilliam had joined
Gielgud's staff in October 1933 from the *Radio Times*, another
instance of the influence of that *milieu* on the development of
broadcasting.[4] Among the outstanding Features writers, E. A. F.
Harding, who had produced his *Imperial Communications* as
early as 1929, had gone on to be Head of Programmes for the

---

[1] *BBC Internal Instruction, no. 350, 7 May 1936.
[2] *BBC Internal Instruction, no. 308, 12 July 1935. Children's Hour became
'independent' again nearly three years later. *Memorandum by D. H. Clarke,
31 Mar. 1938.   [3] *BBC Internal Instruction, no. 361, 13 Aug. 1936.
[4] For other instances, see above, pp. 89, 91.

North Region, where 'he had a hand in the discovery of Geoffrey Bridson, of Francis Dillon, and of Cecil McGivern, all to become outstanding radio personalities'.[1] Again it was a sign of BBC flexibility that he became the BBC's first Chief Instructor in the Staff Training Department.[2]

The last development in Drama before 1939 and the one that again pointed the way forward to the world after the war was the development of the dramatic serial programme, not along American soap-opera lines[3] but as a genuine 'middlebrow' form of entertainment, seldom sinking lower, sometimes rising higher. In 1938—immediately following the 'Experimental Hour'—Dumas's *The Three Musketeers* was produced in twelve parts, with Terence de Marney in the lead. It was an immediate success and served as the forerunner of a large number of BBC serials—stories by Dickens, Scott, Trollope, and Thackeray being among the number. Many listeners must have gone back to read the novels after hearing the serials. In a lighter vein, the detective serial *Send for Paul Temple* was also broadcast for the first time in 1938 from the Birmingham studio with Martyn C. Webster as producer. Unashamedly popular, the Paul Temple series was to be exceptionally entertaining, making use, in its own way, of unique facets of radio and exploiting an element of suspense at the end of each instalment.

The gap between Paul Temple and the serious music of the 1920s and 1930s seems very wide. The days when the 'signature tunes' or theme songs of popular dramatic programmes were to take their place in the 'hit parade' had not dawned in 1939, and despite the linking activities of Stanford Robinson or Leslie Woodgate, there were doubtless many people who felt, like Sieveking, that Music and Drama belonged to different spheres. 'There is no such thing as radio music', Sieveking wrote. 'Composers go on composing music just as if wireless had not been invented, and the music of all periods is played before microphones in exactly the same way as it has always been played. It does not have to be "adapted". Imagine reading in a programme *Concerto No. 2 in C. Minor, for pianoforte and orchestra (Op. 18), Rachmaninoff. Adapted for Broadcasting by John Robertson.*'[4]

[1] *British Radio Drama*, p. 51.   [2] See below, p. 515.
[3] See above, p. 109.   [4] *The Stuff of Radio*, p. 24.

Sieveking did not foresee the elaborate and expensive individual orchestrations which were so popular with light musicians, particularly dance orchestras, in the 1930s. Nor did his absolute contrasts leave a place for the remarkable parallels between the organizing of Music and the organizing of Drama. In both cases there were two main problems—selection and performance. In the case of selection, one of the most interesting choices was that between 'traditional' and 'contemporary' work, a choice made more interesting—and also more difficult—by the resistance of large sections of the British musical public to 'modern music'. There was also a tendency to prefer 'the worst music of the best composers to the best music of the worst composers'.[1]

There were also very similar problems in Music and Drama arising out of the relationship between Centre and Regions. How much music should be transmitted regionally, and what kind of music should it be? What should be the relationship between the 'amateur' and the 'professional'? As in the case of Drama, there were powerful regional pressures during the late 1930s, when some of the orchestras which had been disbanded in the early years of 'centralization' came back to life. The Northern and Midland Orchestras, for example, were formed in 1934, and worked in close touch with the Hallé and the City of Birmingham Orchestras. In 1935 the BBC Scottish Orchestra and the BBC Welsh Orchestra were formed.

Two men directed the BBC's music policy in London during the period from 1927 to 1939. The first was Percy Pitt, who had joined the BBC in May 1923 as part-time Music Adviser and left it as Director of Music in December 1929. The second was Adrian Boult, who became Permanent Conductor and Director of Music in 1930. During Pitt's tenure of office the 'foundations of music'—to use the title of one of his favourite series—were laid. The 'panorama of music' which he presented in 1928 included Handel harpsichord pieces and Wolf songs in the *Foundations* series; chamber music by young composers, like Alan Bush; a recital by Bartok of his own work and Hindemith playing his own violin concerto; twenty symphony concerts, including Beecham conducting his beloved Delius, and Stravinsky conducting the music of two of his own ballets; twelve

[1] 'A Listener', 'The BBC and Music' in the *Political Quarterly*, Oct.–Dec. 1935.

'grand' operas, among them Debussy's *Pelléas et Mélisande*; and a set of Schubert centenary programmes. It is scarcely surprising that Ernest Newman, one of the foremost music critics of his day, stated that the coming of wireless had placed 'the musical destiny of this country in the hands of the BBC'.[1]

Boult not only saw the Music Department grow to one of the most important in the BBC, but he built up the BBC Symphony Orchestra to be one of the great orchestras of the world. This was a general verdict, and it was eloquently expressed by Toscanini, who conducted four BBC symphony concerts in 1935, two in 1937, and six in 1938. 'You have done with the BBC Orchestra in three years', he told Boult, 'what took me with the New York Philharmonic Orchestra five years', and 'you have made it into one of the finest orchestras in the world'. The Toscanini concerts, which were arranged by Owen Mase, created immense interest. Over 17,000 letters of application were received for the 1937 concert at Queen's Hall and a ballot had to be held to decide who should receive a ticket. 'Our chief difficulty', the manager of Queen's Hall wrote, 'was the enormous public interest in Toscanini.'[2]

Neither Pitt nor Boult would wish to take all the credit for the formulation and success of the BBC's music policy or the quality of its performance. Music rests on co-operation, both for its performance and for its planning. The BBC Symphony Orchestra, along with other BBC orchestras, was able to get a fine complement of musicians from the start, men like Arthur Catterall, the first leader, Lauri Kennedy, the Australian cellist, Frederick Thurston, the clarinettist, and Aubrey Brain, the horn player. There were also men behind the scenes. Before Boult took over in 1930, Julian Herbage and Edward Clark, working in the Music Department, had devised a scheme of 'Comprehensive Orchestral Organization' and had made most of the contacts which were necessary to make the scheme effective. Edward Clark, who left the BBC in 1936, should have a key place in any history of twentieth-century British music. It was he who knew everything that was going on in the world of contemporary music—particularly in Europe—and everybody who was engaged in it. The BBC was involved from the 1920s

[1] *Sunday Times*, 15 Nov. 1933.
[2] B. Geissner, *The Baton and the Jackboot* (1944), p. 301.

onwards in the hazardous enterprise of introducing to the British listener Schönberg and Webern as well as Bartok and Stravinsky.[1] In music it was always among the *avant-garde*, and Clark knew just where the *avant-garde* was to be found. Other active figures in the organization of music at various times were Kenneth Wright, formerly Station Director at Manchester; R. J. F. Howgill; Owen Mase, who joined the BBC as an accompanist in 1927 and became Music Executive in 1930; Aylmer Buesst, who joined the BBC as Assistant Music Director in 1933 and remained there until 1935; and R. S. Thatcher, later Head of the Royal Academy of Music, who became Deputy Director of Music in 1937. Thatcher's gifts were completely different from those of Clark, but they fitted him to tidy up administration and to free Boult for more creative work. Howgill, who was to become Controller (Music) in 1952, was in charge of many of the negotiations with outside musical interests in Programme Administration, of which he became Director in 1938.

The BBC had to operate in the ranks as well as in the vanguard of the musical world. In 1927, which began with one of the most memorable concerts yet broadcast, one entirely devoted to Berlioz, the BBC saved the Promenade Concerts from disappearance. After the death of Robert Newman, who had founded the concerts along with Sir Henry Wood in 1895, the 'Proms' were given up as lost. Then a cartoon appeared in *Punch* showing Sir Henry Wood walking out of the Queen's Hall, where the 'Proms' had always been given, with posters in the background announcing 'No More Proms' and Beethoven's ghost saying to Wood, 'This is indeed tragic, but I cannot believe that this rich city will fail to find us a permanent home.' The BBC came to the rescue, with Reith himself taking the main part in the complex negotiations by which the BBC maintained the 'Proms' in being without a break. He had to negotiate with William Boosey, the managing director of the Queen's Hall, who had given evidence before the Crawford Committee that broadcasting would ruin the concert world.[2] Boosey had

---

[1] Schönberg conducted his *Gurrelieder* on 27 Jan. 1928. A London critic, not unrepresentative, wrote that it was 'a remarkable work (caviare to the general), that we shall, I suppose, never hear again'. Quoted in *This—is London*, which provides an admirable running commentary on BBC music, p. 35.

[2] See *The Birth of Broadcasting*, pp. 276-7.

somewhat grudgingly come to the conclusion that 'it would be more profitable to let the Queen's Hall direct to the powers that govern broadcasting . . . rather than to embark on a competition which was really a competition with the Government itself'.[1]

This was to misread both the constitution of the BBC and the changes in public interest in music which were to spring from BBC policy. Reith himself was very happy about the new arrangement. 'Today I fixed up a contract with Sir Henry Wood', he wrote on 13 April. 'To hear Wagner at the Proms,' he wrote on 5 September, 'seeing Sir Henry Wood in the interval. He [Wood] was delighted with everything, and said it was the most successful Season he had had.'[2] At the first concert under the new régime Wood conducted Elgar's *Cockaigne* Overture, and told a friend that he was so elated he had never conducted with greater spirit. He also said how wonderful it was to be free at last from 'the everlasting box-office problem'.[3] With equal zest he took part in a series of eight popular symphony concerts ('at Woolworths' prices') held at the People's Palace in Mile End Road. Other conductors included Percy Pitt, Geoffrey Toye, and Sir Edward Elgar.

Sir Thomas Beecham had made his broadcasting début in March 1925 with the Hallé Orchestra from Manchester, and there had been suggestions even earlier that he should be associated with a series of subscription concerts.[4] He soon emerged, however, as we have seen, as an irascible critic of broadcasting, and it was thought to be something of a triumph in 1928 when Sir Landon Ronald of the BBC's Musical Advisory Committee wrote to Roger Eckersley that 'I have really at last entirely broken down Beecham's opposition to broadcasting.'[5] There were long negotiations, indeed, in 1928, 1929, and 1930 about the formation under Beecham of a new National Orchestra, to be given financial support from the BBC, and at one stage Beecham thought that the enterprise seemed 'fairly

[1] See W. Boosey, *Fifty Years of Music* (1931), p. 178; R. Elkin, *Queens Hall, 1893–1941* (1944), p. 33. The negotiations with Boosey were successfully concluded in May 1927.

[2] Reith, Diary, 13 Apr., 5 Sept. 1927.

[3] *W. W. Thompson in the BBC Programme *Scrapbook*, 18 Jan. 1948.

[4] *Board of the British Broadcasting Company Ltd., Minutes. This was at the very dawn of broadcasting, and the suggestion was made by Godfrey Isaacs.

[5] *Sir Landon Ronald to R. H. Eckersley, 13 Mar. 1928.

straight sailing'.[1] The orchestra, both the BBC and Beecham hoped, would be called the Royal Philharmonic Orchestra, if the Royal Philharmonic Society approved.[2] The players would be under contract at fees ranging from £500 a year for the rank-and-file to £1,200 a year for principals, and the deputy system, which had for long been the bane of British orchestral music,[3] would be abolished. The orchestra would give over a hundred concerts a year at the Queen's Hall, the Royal Albert Hall, and in the provinces, and would take part in opera seasons at Covent Garden.[4]

Negotiations finally broke down in January 1930,[5] by which time the BBC was losing a considerable amount of money on a trial series of symphony concerts which it had hoped it would be able to share with other musical organizations (and Beecham).[6] The Royal Philharmonic Society and the BBC went their own ways, with the Secretary of the Society hoping that 'some day, perhaps we may yet be able to work together';[7] and Beecham remained an angry judge of everything the BBC tried to do. Among the casualties of the abortive scheme was a new National Concert Hall: the site of All Soul's, Langham Place, was talked of at one time as a serious possibility[8] (before the days of Broadcasting House). Beecham went on to form the London Philharmonic Orchestra in 1932.

The failure of the negotiations of the late 1920s left the BBC to create a new independent orchestra of its own. The reconstitution of the London Symphony Orchestra in 1929 did not interfere with the building up of the BBC Symphony Orchestra:[9] indeed some members of the L.S.O. joined the BBC which, like

[1] *Sir Thomas Beecham to R. H. Eckersley, 19 June 1928.
[2] *Eckersley to Beecham, 27 Dec. 1928.
[3] For the system, see T. Russell, *Philharmonic* (1942), pp. 28 ff.
[4] See C. Reid, *Thomas Beecham, An Independent Biography* (1961), p. 196; H. Foss and N. Goodwin, *London Symphony* (1954), p. 122.
[5] *They broke down with an exchange of legal letters. W. R. Bennett and Co. to Steadman, Van Praagh, and Gaylor, 31 Dec. 1929; Steadman, Van Praagh, and Gaylor, to W. R. Bennett and Co., 22 Jan. 1930.
[6] *R. H. Eckersley to Beecham, 15 July 1930.
[7] *Cooper, the Secretary of the Royal Philharmonic Society, to R. H. Eckersley, 21 Mar. 1930.
[8] *Reith to R. H. Eckersley, 18 Mar. 1929. A site in Russell Square was talked of as another possibility, with the advantage of offering more space. (Eckersley to Goldsmith, 7 Oct. 1929.)
[9] *London Symphony*, p. 123; *R. H. Eckersley to Reith, 16 Mar. 1929.

Beecham's projected orchestra, abandoned the deputy system.[1] The members of the orchestra, Beecham admitted, were 'the best known instrumentalists of Great Britain'.[2] By the summer of 1930, 114 players had been chosen, an Orchestral Manager and a Concert Manager had been appointed, and Boult, who welcomed his new opportunity, was in excellent spirits. The first appearance of the new orchestra was at the Queen's Hall in October 1930. It was a great success and by 1935, when the orchestra made its first continental tour—to Brussels—it had established an international reputation. There was a further tour to Paris, Zurich, Vienna, and Budapest in 1936.[3]

The orchestra always attracted good players, and when replacements had to be made, like that of Paul Beard (from Beecham's London Philharmonic Orchestra) for Catterall in 1936, they always guaranteed the highest standard. Yet there remained the problem of finding adequate accommodation. The orchestra could not always use either the Queen's Hall or the Royal Albert Hall, and before the move to Broadcasting House the biggest studio at Savoy Hill was far too small for rehearsals or performances by the larger sections. After a long search, an empty and dingy warehouse just across Waterloo Bridge, on the south side of the river, was taken over and known as No. 10. In 1934 a large property was acquired at Maida Vale, an old skating-rink, and it was from a studio there that many of the BBC's concerts were conducted. The redecoration, reseating and re-equipment of the Queen's Hall in 1937 suggests that the attempt to find another concert hall had been abandoned. The newly equipped hall had only two full seasons, however, before it was destroyed in the 'blitz' of 1940.

Broadcasting House, of course, provided subsidiary facilities, particularly for sections of the Symphony Orchestra and for the cluster of new orchestras and ensembles which the BBC brought into existence during the early 1930s—the Theatre Orchestra (1931),[4] for example, the BBC Chorus and the BBC Singers,

[1] *Control Board Minutes, 29 Jan. 1930. Sir Hamilton Harty of the Hallé Orchestra, who complained that the BBC was stealing players, had the worst of the argument. He lost two.   [2] N. Cardus, *Sir Thomas Beecham* (1961), p. 64.

[3] British music (Walton, Vaughan Williams, Elgar, and Bax) was chosen as part of the repertoire.

[4] This orchestra was transferred from the Music Department to the new Variety Department in June 1933.

and, most nostalgic of all, the Gersholm Parkington Quintet, which was employed on an *ad hoc* contract basis. The high quality of performance of some of the smaller ensembles is difficult to recapture in print. So too is the mood. The Gersholm Parkington Quintet was engaged to broadcast light music on every possible kind of social occasion—for example, between the announcements of the general election results in 1935. The BBC Chorus, formed in 1928, consisted of 260 amateurs, and it was a condition of membership that candidates for the chorus should also be members of another practising choral society. It changed its name to the BBC Choral Society in 1934. The Wireless Chorus, by contrast, was a body of 40 professionals of whom any combination from 9 to 40 would be called on as required: its nucleus was the group of BBC Singers, who were employed on full-time contracts.

The Concert Hall in Broadcasting House was on the lower ground floor, and the eighth floor was reserved at first for the BBC's Military Band, which had been formed in August 1927 under the conductorship of Lieut. B. Walton O'Donnell, formerly Director of Music of the Royal Marines at Portsmouth. Relations between the Symphony Orchestra and the Military Band were always good. Filson Young once complained, indeed, that the same pieces were too often broadcast within a short space of time by the band and the orchestra.[1] When B. Walton O'Donnell left Broadcasting House for Northern Ireland in 1937 he was succeeded by his brother, Major P. S. G. O'Donnell, also a former Director of Music of the Royal Marines, at Plymouth.

The last feature of musical interest in Broadcasting House was the organ in the Concert Hall which was opened on 16 June 1933, before a distinguished audience, by Sir Walter Alcock, G. Thalben Ball, and G. D. Cunningham. The presence of the organ made possible new combinations, like one described by Stuart Hibberd in 1936—*Melodies of Christendom*, arranged by Sir Walford Davies, the great pioneer of radio music, with Dr. Thalben Ball at the organ. 'It was a splendid Sunday night programme', Stuart Hibberd wrote, 'which ended with some of the St. Matthew Passion music by Bach, finely sung by the BBC Singers. Such was Sir Walford's passionate desire to

[1] *Filson Young to R. H. Eckersley, 19 Aug. 1933.

achieve as near perfection as possible, that even this performance did not satisfy him, and as he said good night he added, "And I do wish it had been better".[1]

Emphasis on quality was always a hallmark of the BBC's approach to music, even when the quality of both microphones and wireless reception, as in Pitt's early years, was notoriously bad. It once led to one of the few disagreements between Reith and Boult—as to whether a Bach motet should be broadcast when Boult thought its level of performance was not up to standard. 'I was quite certain that there would be far less prejudice to the Corporation through an inferior performance than there would have been through cancellation', wrote Reith.[2] Another BBC emphasis, also associated with Sir Walford Davies, was on musical education. This was not always popular either inside or outside the BBC, some critics accusing the Corporation of rating musical culture higher than other forms of culture.

The desire to ground listeners in this culture lay behind Filson Young's notion of the *Foundations of Music* series which began on 3 January 1927. 'Any one who chooses to . . . switch on the loud speaker will be sure of hearing ten minutes of pure music . . . music about which the most extreme schools are in agreement . . . and which constitutes the foundation from which the whole of modern music is derived and on which it rests.'[3] At first the music, like Gielgud's actors, was anonymous, speaking for itself. The identification of the particular pieces in the *Foundations* series began at the same time as the first broadcast of the Bach Cantatas on Sunday, 20 May 1928. These programmes were felt to constitute perfect listening for Sundays, unlike some of the works of the great dramatists, like Ibsen, which ran into difficulties with the Director of Religion. 'May I state in half a dozen sentences my reasons for doubting whether *A Doll's House* should be broadcast on a Sunday?' Iremonger had begun a memorandum to Graves in 1936.[4]

As far as opera was concerned, most of the difficulties which the BBC faced related not to content but to organization. 'Grand Opera is a curious business', Victor Cazalet once told Ogilvie, Reith's successor. 'As the season approaches almost every one

[1] *This—is London*, pp. 128–9.   [2] Reith, Diary, 2 May 1932.
[3] *Radio Times*, 31 Dec. 1926.   [4] *Iremonger to Graves, 8 Oct. 1936.

connected with it assumes some small part of the temperament of a *prima donna*.'[1] Ogilvie knew little about opera at that time: Reith had learned an immense amount. If the negotiations leading up to the formation of the orchestra were complex, the negotiations relating to opera—in which Reith again took a prominent part—were even more so. In both sets of negotiations Beecham was directly involved, and another of the main figures in the opera story was Mrs. Snowden, one of the most controversial Governors of the BBC.[2] Keenly interested in opera, she was also the wife of the Chancellor of the Exchequer. This gave her both cultural and political standing.

The first BBC agreement with opera interests was made in 1926, when it was allowed to broadcast three acts a fortnight from the International Grand Opera season at Covent Garden in return for lending Percy Pitt as Conductor and Director of Music.[3] Pitt had been Musical Director of the British National Opera Company before joining the BBC, and this seemed an eminently sensible arrangement. There were many difficulties in practice, however, particularly about finance, and the listener who happily heard *Der Rosenkavalier* in May 1927 or the twenty excerpts from Covent Garden in 1928 was fortunate that he did not know how much strain there had been. Sometimes, however, he was informed about at least one kind of difficulty. In 1929 a broadcast of *Die Valkyrie* had to be cancelled because Florence Austral would not allow herself to be broadcast. A similar cancellation had to be made in 1930, this time with *Tosca*, because Gigli would not broadcast.

The extent of the financial difficulties was revealed in December 1926 at the first meeting of a small BBC Advisory Committee on Opera. The meeting was held at Savoy Hill, with Sir Hugh Allen in the chair, and Reith outlined problems which were to preoccupy him for the next six years. 'The British National Opera Company, of whose performances the BBC had made considerable use, had relied to an increasing extent on payment from the BBC to save it from financial failure, and it was now

[1] *Victor Cazalet to F. W. Ogilvie, 12 Dec. 1938.
[2] See below, pp. 425–8.
[3] *For the implementation of the same scheme in 1927, see Eustace Blois to Reith, 21 Feb. 1927; Reith to Eustace Blois, 26 Feb. 1927; Control Board Minutes, 8 Mar. 1927. The first broadcast from Covent Garden had been given on 8 Jan. 1923.

asking the BBC to subsidise it to an extent which made it imperative that the whole question be reviewed. The BBC had also been approached by the Carl Rosa Company and by others, so that it was essential to have a new study of the whole question.' Speaking immediately after Reith, Allen said that 'the co-operation of the BBC might be the one remaining opportunity of establishing Opera on a sound basis in this country'.[1]

The British National Opera Company ceased to function in 1928, when it was heavily in debt.[2] One year before its collapse the BBC was approached by H. V. Higgins, the chairman of the Grand Opera Syndicate, about the possibility of a direct link-up with Covent Garden.[3] The plan failed, however, not least because of Higgins's tactlessness. 'I was under the impression', he told Reith, whom he insisted on addressing as Sir James Reith, 'that you had recognised that unless somebody assisted Opera in some form or other, there would cease to be any Opera worthy of the name in this country, but it appears that the whole idea was to obtain from various operatic and musical institutions assistance for the Broadcasting Company [*sic*] to enable them to add to their entertainment on terms greatly advantageous to themselves.'[4]

Negotiations were resumed in 1930 when F. A. Szarvasy, a Hungarian financier, working with Colonel Eustace Blois, approached the BBC to help form a new Covent Garden Opera Syndicate. After long negotiations between the Syndicate, the BBC, the Gramophone Company, and the Treasury, agreement was reached in the autumn of 1930. A new company was formed —Covent Garden Opera Syndicate (1930) Ltd.—with Szarvasy as chairman and the BBC as a shareholder.[5] The Corporation also guaranteed Covent Garden a large regular income of £25,000 each year for five years.[6] The novelty of the arrangement was not so much that the BBC took a controlling interest in the shares of the Syndicate as that the Treasury (with Snow-

[1] *Advisory Committee on Opera, Minutes, 13 Dec. 1926.
[2] H. Rosenthal, *Two Centuries of Opera at Covent Garden* (1958), p. 621.
[3] *H. V. Higgins to Reith, 18 June 1927.
[4] *Higgins to Reith, 1 Apr. 1927.
[5] *Draft Agreement, 'Opera in Great Britain, A New Basis', 13 Nov. 1930; Reith to F. A. Szarvasy, 13 Nov. 1930. The BBC held 84 shares, Szarvasy 7, and the Gramophone Company 7. The Agreement was not completed until the end of the year.
[6] *Control Board Minutes, 9 July 1930.

den as Chancellor of the Exchequer) under-wrote the agreement
and offered to contribute a subsidy of £5,000 for 1930 and
£7,500 a year for the subsequent five years from January 1931
onwards.[1] The Treasury offer was set out in a Supplemental
Agreement between the BBC and the Post Office, signed on
behalf of the Post Office by Attlee. It was the first earmarked
subsidy the BBC had ever arranged. And it was granted in face
of considerable political and press opposition just before the
beginning of the great financial and political storm of 1931.
'There are better ways of spending £17,500 than in subsidising
a form of art which is not characteristic of the British people',
wrote the *Daily Express*.[2]

Reith sat on the Opera Board, which met regularly. It caused
him endless worry,[3] although he frequently stressed to Szarvasy
that 'we are partners with you in this enterprise'.[4] Part of the
worry centred on Beecham, whose erratic plans were always
difficult to co-ordinate with the plans of others. His Imperial
League of Opera, founded in 1927 to mobilize opera lovers
throughout the country, was extremely difficult to encompass
within a national arrangement;[5] and negotiations started, were
broken off, and restarted on many occasions. Beecham's flam-
boyance—artistic genius coupled with financial wildness—
never made matters easy. In July 1931, for example, he was
talking at a private lunch party at Claridge's as if he were
addressing a public meeting.[6]

Another part of the worry in 1931 centred on finance. Covent
Garden lost £8,000 more than had been anticipated in the
season of that year,[7] and in May 1932 the Carl Rosa Company
had to be helped to pay salaries due at the end of the week.[8]

---

[1] The BBC had tested the Treasury and the Post Office on this subject long
before 1930, although Mitchell-Thomson denied in the House of Commons in
March 1927 that he had been approached on the question of a subsidy. *Hansard*,
vol. 203, col. 228. Mitchell-Thomson was answering Colonel Day.

[2] Cmd. 3884 (1931), *Supplemental Agreement Between H.M. Postmaster-General and
the BBC*, June 1931. For the opposition, see the *Daily Express*, 2 Nov. 1932.

[3] He wrote, for example, in his diary on 18 Mar. 1932, 'Opera Board in the
afternoon, as wearying as ever.' On 5 Apr. he was talking about 'everlasting opera
troubles'.

[4] *Reith to F. A. Szarvasy, 29 June 1931.

[5] See C. Reid, *Thomas Beecham, An Independent Biography* (1961), pp. 192–3.

[6] Reith, Diary, 16 July 1931.

[7] Ibid., 1 Oct. 1931.

[8] *Control Board Minutes, 31 May 1932; 14 June 1932.

Szarvasy blamed the musical difficulties of the year on 'the great National Crisis, the abandonment of the gold standard, the formation of the National Government and the General Election',[1] and these difficulties were used by the newly formed National Government to get out of the subsidy in 1932.[2] Reith felt that there had been a breach of faith—'the Corporation did not press the Treasury to enter into the arrangement, and we can hardly imagine that an obligation of the Treasury's would be dishonoured and the Corporation left to discharge it'[3]—while Lady Snowden said that her husband had expressed 'horror' at the idea of abandoning the subsidy.[4] The subsidy was 'suspended' in 1933, however, and the BBC was left again to fend for itself. It promised 'to undertake to assist opera generally in 1933 to such an extent as can be proved to its satisfaction to be desirable'.[5]

Opera interests by no means always agreed that what the BBC thought was desirable was suitable for them. More usually, indeed, they failed to agree about anything. Reith did his best, however, to persuade the various opera interests to work together amicably, and it was largely as a result of his efforts that in October 1932 a new organization called the National Opera Council was set up. It followed an agreement between the Covent Garden Opera Syndicate, which was enlarged (Beecham joined its Board), the Imperial League of Opera, the Sadler's Wells Theatre, the Old Vic Theatre, the Carl Rosa Opera Company, and the BBC. Reith left the world of opera at this stage, after lunching with Beecham on 27 October. 'I have been exceedingly bored by all these long, periodic discussions', he wrote in his diary. 'They are on the straight road now, although there are still plenty of difficulties to overcome for proper collaboration among the various concerns.'[6]

British opera was not, in fact, on the straight road, although the BBC did its best to continue to support it. There were difficulties about the formation of the new company to replace the 1930 Syndicate, and further difficulties between Geoffrey Toye, who became manager of Covent Garden under the new

[1] *F. A. Szarvasy to Reith, 24 Oct. 1931.
[2] *Reith to Sir Evelyn Murray, 23 Mar. 1932.
[3] *Reith to Murray, 5 Apr. 1932.
[4] *Lady Snowden to Reith, 24 July 1932.
[5] *Note by Reith, 28 Oct. 1932.   [6] Reith, Diary, 27 Oct. 1932.

scheme, and Beecham, his sponsor. There was continuous pressure on the BBC to maintain or to subsidize not only Covent Garden but most of the other opera interests, with J. H. Thomas, a most unlikely go-between, entering into negotiations in 1934. In fact, the BBC gave considerable financial help not only to Covent Garden but to Sadler's Wells and Carl Rosa,[1] and it broadcast opera from Glyndebourne as early as 1935. Indeed, it broadcast more opera than most of its listeners liked. Thirteen broadcasts, for example, were relayed from Covent Garden in 1932 and thirteen from Sadler's Wells and the Old Vic—along with Sir Henry Lytton's farewell performance in *The Mikado* from the Savoy Theatre. By 1937 there were twenty performances from Covent Garden, nine from Sadler's Wells, and five from Glyndebourne—besides a number of Carl Rosa broadcasts from the provinces.[2]

In the meantime, studio opera had been revived after a long lapse. Boult had been pressing for more studio opera for several years, and there was considerable enthusiasm within the BBC. It had been hoped at first that an Opera Section could be created in the Music Department and that Stanford Robinson, after a period of sabbatical leave studying opera on the Continent, would then take over with a full Opera Orchestra.[3] For financial reasons, however, the scheme had to be delayed and modified,[4] and when the new Section was formed it was known as 'Music Productions', with no special orchestra but with Stanford Robinson as Director and Conductor and Gordon McConnel as Producer.[5] The first full opera was presented in January 1938. Massenet's *Manon* was specially chosen for the occasion, since it did not demand such complicated microphone arrangements as other operas would have done.[6] It was followed later in the year by Gounod's *Faust*, Smetana's *Bartered Bride*, and Vaughan Williams's *Hugh the Drover*. English librettos were used throughout.

Many of these ventures met with scant support from the Music Advisory Committee, and Beecham continued until 1939

1   *An important Opera Advisory Committee Report was prepared in 1936.
2   Cmd. 4051 (1934) *BBC Seventh Annual Report*, p. 3; Cmd. 5951 (1939), p. 5.
3   *The Times*, 23 Apr. 1936.
4   *Notes of a Meeting in Controller (A)'s Room, 2 Apr. 1936.
5   *BBC Internal Memorandum, 1 Sept. 1937.
6   *BBC Press Release, Dec. 1937.

to press the BBC from outside to give more financial help to Covent Garden. 'There is one simple way', he told Ogilvie in 1939, 'in which your organisation could be of service, not only to us but to the public, and that is by exercising to a fuller extent than last year your right to broadcast our performances.'[1] Ogilvie replied simply, referring to 'the sad fact that lovers of opera and serious music constitute only a small proportion of the listening public. We have in consequence many other demands on our programme space in meeting the needs of the majority.'[2]

The BBC's efforts to promote music seldom met with the full support they deserved. Its own Music Advisory Committee, of which Sir Hugh Allen, Sir John McEwen, and Sir Landon Ronald were all members, was vigorously—and rightly— criticized by Boult in his evidence before the Ullswater Committee for its narrow-mindedness and lack of imagination.[3] 'In so far as the advice of the Committee is directed to the good of the broadcasting service, that advice is followed where possible, but more often than not the members occupy their time at the meetings trying to bully the Corporation into adopting courses of action which they think would be to the benefit of the music profession, but without due regard for the Corporation's programme standards or for the interests of the listening public.'[4] Sir Landon Ronald, a prominent member of the committee, was never alive to the opportunity as Boult saw it. 'Regarding the BBC', he wrote with excessive caution in the 1930s, 'I think that if they do a certain amount of damage to professional music teachers and small choral societies they make up for it by giving hundreds of singers and instrumentalists engagements they would never have got ten years ago, and that the way they are spreading the love and knowledge of great music through the land must atone for certain sins they are accused of committing —personally I should say it was a question of fifty-fifty.'[5] There was, indeed, a basic 'protectionism' about the committee, which reflected the 'protectionism' in British music as

---

[1] *Sir Thomas Beecham to F. W. Ogilvie, 22 Mar. 1939.
[2] *Ogilvie to Beecham, 27 Mar. 1939.
[3] For the Committee, see below, pp. 476–504.
[4] *Memorandum to the Ullswater Committee by Sir Adrian Boult, p. 1.
[5] Landon Ronald, *Myself and Others* (1931), p. 206.

a whole—the suspicion of new works, the distrust of foreign artists, the reliance on the known and the tried, and the low level of criticism. The BBC did its best to change attitudes and to direct tastes, but it was not helped in its battle against 'philistinism' by the conservatism of some of its avowed advisors and the bitter arguments between them. Boult saw the chance and took it.

As Music Director of the Corporation [he concluded his Memorandum to Ullswater], it is a little difficult for me to give an opinion on the Corporation's contribution to the musical life of this country, but as the majority of those who have so far given evidence before the Committee have shown no appreciation of the value of the Corporation's work in this field, I feel it incumbent upon me to do so. Five years ago, prior to the formation of the Corporation's Symphony Orchestra, the reputation of British music and British musicianship abroad was extremely low. Our capital city contained but one orchestra, and that an inferior one. One of our provincial orchestras—the Hallé—was the best that this country could boast. The formation of the Corporation's Symphony Orchestra was the turning point. Symphonic musicians for the first time were offered whole-time contracts under reasonable and humane conditions. They for their part were prohibited from accepting outside engagements and appointing deputies in their place, an evil system which had become traditional in this country. With this fine Orchestra working under admirable conditions, the Corporation was clearly capable of reaching a standard hitherto undreamt of in this country.

In this forthright statement, Boult left out the listeners. Wood, who knew so much of British traditions and their limitations, knew just where he thought the BBC was managing to fit them in. It was making them understand music and enjoy music at the same time. 'With the whole-hearted support of the wonderful medium of broadcasting,' he once exclaimed, 'I feel that I am at last on the threshold of realising my life-long ambition of truly democratising the message of music and making its beneficent effect universal. . . . I am quite convinced that not only in music, but generally, the medium of broadcasting, as utilized and developed in this country, is one of the few elements ordinarily associated with the progress of civilisation which I can heartily endorse.'[1]

[1] Quoted in B. Maine, *The BBC and Its Audience* (1939), pp. 47–48.

4. Education

IN the cause of 'the progress of civilization' the crude distinction between 'entertainment' and 'education' was never acceptable to the BBC. 'When a critic complains that there is too much education and too little entertainment in broadcast programmes,' Reith asked in 1931, 'where does he draw the line? Is it to the left or the right of Sir Walford Davies, Sir James Jeans and the like? Mr. Harold Nicolson will pass as entertainment without much opposition, but what about Mr. Vernon Bartlett's weekly summary of foreign affairs?'[1]

The distinction which Reith himself drew was between the educational effect of programmes specifically designed as 'educational' and the educative influence, potential or actual, of the whole range of the BBC's activities. Education was inevitably associated 'with hard benches in schools and colleges and universities, with the cramming of a certain amount of knowledge in order that certain tests may be passed. I wish someone would invent another word to describe the sort of education which makes life so much more interesting and enjoyable than it otherwise would be.'[2]

Filson Young, also, wrote about the public response to the two words 'entertainment' and 'education'. 'One of these words appeals to everybody: the other, except for associations of people who prefer administering doses to taking them themselves, is a word of somewhat repellent association. . . . There is a gaiety about the word "entertainment" which sets the eyes sparkling and the blood singing; but about the word "education" there is a sleek oppressiveness; it suggests a process rather than an occasion; [and] . . . long after, perhaps, we have found that in the over-pursuit of entertainment it is apt to turn to ashes in our grasp, nevertheless the two words continue to represent two definite things: an attractive thing and a dull thing.'[3]

Dull or gay, education had a very early place in the BBC's scheme of priorities. Almost from the beginnings of broadcasting

[1] J. C. W. Reith, 'Education by Broadcast' in *Today and Tomorrow*, 26 Feb. 1931. For an earlier expression of this view, see *Broadcast Over Britain*, p. 147.
[2] *The Listener*, 30 Apr. 1930.
[3] *Shall I Listen?*, pp. 110–11.

there had been interest in specific educational broadcasts both for children and adults; and Reith believed also in the 'great educative work' which the BBC could carry out more generally.[1] The two conceptions of how the BBC could help 'education'— through direct educational broadcasts and through 'educative' programmes—were, of course, related to each other. They had more than one root. The deepest root stretched deep into the culture of Scotland, which nurtured not only Reith, but the most powerful personality in the history of schools broadcasting, Mary Somerville, whose father had been chairman of a School Board in Scotland.

Other roots were hidden in new soil. There had been a widespread feeling during and after the First World War that the country had failed 'to conceive the full meaning and purpose of national education as a whole'; there was also concern to create a more 'educated democracy'. The mood was well expressed in such documents as the 1919 *Report on Adult Education* and the 1921 *Report on the Teaching of English in England*. It was not a coincidence that H. A. L. Fisher, who had devised the great Education Act of 1918, was a Governor of the BBC from 1935 to 1939, nor that Sir Henry Hadow, who was chairman of the Board of Education Committee which produced one of the most striking official educational documents of the inter-war years, *The Education of the Adolescent* (1926), should also have been chairman of the BBC Committee which produced the report *New Ventures in Broadcasting* in March 1928. Reith maintained with justice that this report might equally have been entitled 'New Ventures in Education'.

The two conceptions of how the BBC could most effectively serve education are best thought of as associated approaches to the task of speeding up educational advance. Hadow had talked of that advance in his *Education of the Adolescent* as the development of 'a broad, general and humane education under the stimulus of practical work and realistic studies'. He was as much concerned with the cultivation of the quality of imagination as with the acquisition of knowledge. Mary Somerville believed that broadcasting could fire the imagination more quickly than any other educational agency. The first broadcaster she heard was Sir Walford Davies speaking

[1] See *The Birth of Broadcasting*, p. 138.

on music one evening in the spring of 1924, and she heard it in a country schoolmistress's parlour along with the schoolmistress and three pupils. 'It was not a broadcast to schools', she wrote later. 'No matter, he was teaching, and he was making music, and the impact of his personality, and of his music, was tremendous. Things happened in all of us, in the children, in their music-loving teacher and in me.'[1]

While at Oxford, Mary Somerville had dreamed of taking part in what the *Report on the Teaching of English in England* called 'the diffusion of knowledge' by 'a fraternity of itinerant preachers'. The knowledge was not to be departmentalized within subject boundaries but unified through experience. Broadcasting provided her with a possible means of realizing her dreams. Many of the other early recruits to the BBC, as we have seen, joined it because they felt that they could contribute to the realization of a high purpose.[2] Education in the broadest sense was associated with that purpose: it was not dull, but exciting. 'There was the same feeling of dedication and hope which had characterised the League of Nations in its earliest days.'[3]

Such a feeling does not necessarily produce practical results: it often peters out in frustration and disillusionment. In the BBC itself the excitement of the young was encouraged by J. C. Stobart, the older man whom Reith had brought in from the Board of Education in the summer of 1924 and who remained in the BBC, giving it loyal and devoted service, until his death in 1933. Stobart was a keen classical scholar and wrote two books which still command a wide public, *The Glory that was Greece* and *The Grandeur that was Rome*. He had all the limitations of a classical education and, for all his great culture, understood little either of the changing social background of Britain in the 1920s or of the techniques of radio. Yet he had great vision, made his own mark as a broadcaster, with his famous 'Grand Goodnight'—it ended the year's broadcasting in 1927—and laid enduring foundations for the more specialized activities of others.

[1] M. Somerville, 'How School Broadcasting Grew Up' in R. Palmer, *School Broadcasting in Britain* (1947), p. 9.

[2] See above, p. 13.

[3] L. Fielden, *The Natural Bent* (1960), p. 103.

One of his critics has paid tribute to his 'many attractive qualities and sound virtues'. 'He was the first educator of any standing to respond to the call of the new medium, broadcasting, when it was still in its infancy, and regarded by most intellectuals as a new toy. Some vision had entered Stobart's mind of what broadcasting might achieve in the cultural life of the community; and so he had left the sheltered life of a Board of Education inspector, and had embarked, fairly late in life, on a new career at the BBC.'[1] At least one of his early memoranda is very boldly conceived. He outlined a plan for a 'Wireless University', breaking away from existing university traditions, providing courses lasting for two years, some taught wholly, some partially, by radio. The courses would be free for all: 'no one need be prevented from learning science by inability to pass in Latin'. Stobart described his plan as 'a Wellsian sketch of possibilities', but he passed it on to Reith for critical observations.[2] Reith thought it greatly to his credit, but when adult education was developed, it was not quite on this scale.

Between 1927 and 1931 many different branches of BBC activity separated themselves out from Stobart's office—talks, news, and publications as well as schools and adult educational broadcasting.[3] Stobart struggled manfully to establish schools broadcasting and made an excellent impression in many circles, but there were limits to his success. He never found it easy, for example, to win the confidence of teachers or children. 'He doesn't know one end of a child from another', one of his colleagues, Frank Roscoe, a former pupil-teacher, once remarked.[4] Another limit to success was set by ill health. Stobart was seriously ill during the late 1920s, and much of the work that would normally have fallen to him—work of the kind which had fallen to him before 1927—passed into other people's hands.[5] The other people, Hilda Matheson, Siepmann, Mary Somerville, and Fielden, among others, were the key figures in

[1] R. S. Lambert, *Ariel and All His Quality* (1940), pp. 49–50.
[2] *J. C. Stobart, 'The Wireless University', 8 Oct. 1926.
[3] For the organizational changes consequent upon this division of labour, see above, p. 124 and below, pp. 441–2.
[4] Note by Miss Somerville, Nov. 1962.
[5] For Stobart's work before 1927, see *The Birth of Broadcasting*, pp. 201, 242, 253–4.

the development of the serious side of sound radio in its greatest
phase of expansion.

Between 1927 and 1939 a most successful system of schools
broadcasting was devised by the BBC which soon became the
envy of educationists in every other country. The system was
supremely practical both in its approach and in its organization.
In 1927, at a generous estimate, 3,000 schools were listening
to the BBC's schools broadcasts in England and Wales, as
against 220 in late 1924: at the outbreak of war in 1939 the
figure had risen to 9,953. In 1939 thirty-nine school programmes a week were being transmitted.

Even more important than such statistics was the impact of
the BBC on the quality of effort and imagination inside the
schools. It played a key role in a still unfinished 'silent revolution', in part a revolution of educational provision and technology—books, pianos, projectors, and materials for art and
crafts as well as wireless sets—in part a revolution of educational
aspiration and ambition, associated with the widening of curri-
cula, the use of experimental teaching methods, and the relaxation of purely external discipline.

H. A. L. Fisher talked to Mary Somerville of 'streams of
water irrigating thirsty lands', but he warned her against using
language of this kind too freely even in her dealings with educationists.[1] She would have to get on with the job, he advised
her, without talking too much about the dreams that inspired
her. He was right. The same kind of warning had been given
by an earlier educationist, Michael Sadler, who told his
colleagues that the loftiest sentiments of John Ruskin would
hardly be 'persuasive' if made to the members of a City Education Committee, assembled at a meeting with the usual
agenda.[2]

It certainly took time and patience to set schools broadcasting
on the right course, and many problems arising out of the
relationships between the BBC and other educational bodies,
including the Board of Education, still remained unsolved in
1939. It was necessary throughout the whole period of growth
to convert the missionary zeal 'to do good' into a practical

[1] Note by Miss Somerville, Nov. 1962.
[2] Quoted in G. A. N. Lowndes, *The Silent Revolution* (1937), p. 108.

grasp of such diverse subjects as the administrative network of British education, the art of the teacher, the properties of sound radio as a medium, and the place of the child both in his 'listening situation' and in his society. The schools broadcasting department of the BBC had been forced to concern itself directly with the sociology of its listening public in the schools before the BBC as a whole examined the sociology of its listening public in their homes.[1]

The great turning-point in the early story was a report on schools broadcasting in Kent which was completed in May 1928. Two years earlier, with the aid of a grant from the Carnegie Trust, an experiment in schools broadcasting had begun in the Kent schools organized by the BBC and the Kent local education authority working in close co-operation.[2] Reith had suggested informally to Colonel Mitchell of the Carnegie Trust early in 1926 that 'it was time the Carnegie people took an interest in our educational activities':[3] the Trust, in consequence, made a grant of £300, a small sum which has subsequently paid enormous dividends. It was used entirely to buy 'good receiving sets' for a limited number of Kent schools.

Kent was chosen for the experiment for four reasons. It was close to London; its energetic Director of Education, E. Salter Davies, was a Carnegie trustee and was also keenly interested in wireless; doubtless in consequence, the authority already had within its boundaries a relatively large number of listening schools; and, not least, the county of Kent had a varied economy with parents of schoolchildren living in widely differing social circumstances. Furthermore, the Kent Advisory Committee of Teachers approved of the experiment and offered to take part in it on 23 June 1926.

The experiment began in the Easter term of 1927 and continued until the end of the year. Careful study was made of the various Kent schools listening to BBC broadcasts. There were 20 urban and 52 rural or semi-rural schools in all, 12 of the 72 schools having less than 80 pupils and 14 having more than

---

[1] See below, pp. 256 ff.
[2] See *The Birth of Broadcasting*, p. 262.
[3] *Reith to E. R. Appleton and D. Cleghorn Thomson, copy to Stobart, 18 Oct. 1926.

250 pupils. Both children's and teachers' opinions were collected from observers in the schools, from questionnaires, and from comments made at teachers' conferences.

The Report concluded that broadcast lessons effectively imparted a knowledge of facts, stimulated interest in ways which could be definitely observed, created impressions as durable as those produced by ordinary classroom lessons, and were particularly interesting to clever children. In addition, they supplied views and information which teachers by themselves could not have supplied, gave teachers new ideas for lessons, and interested some hitherto indifferent parents in the work that their children did at school.

'All courses', the Report added, 'were not uniformly successful. Much remains to be done to ensure better co-operation between lecturers, teachers and pupils, and further investigation is needed in many directions.' While the experiment was in progress, much had changed. 'There were improvements in the method and content of the lectures, in the degree of co-operation between teacher and lecturer, in the efficient maintenance of the wireless apparatus, and in the actual method of the enquiry. . . . Some schools dropped out, others came in late.'

It was generally agreed that at the transmitting end broadcasters had to be 'expert', to have a good delivery, and to possess some of the qualities of the classroom teacher. They also had to be prepared to study the special problems of wireless teaching. There was no reason, indeed, why wireless programmes should consist simply of straight lectures, which involved strain in listening without visual relief; 'talks might be modified by the abandonment of the straight lecture in favour of a system of closer collaboration between the lecturer and the teacher'.

The general conclusions were stated in such a way that they might at the same time reduce suspicion and kindle interest. There was no question of broadcasting superseding the teacher. On the other hand, the teacher could not afford to ignore 'the new instrument which science has placed in his hands'. 'The need at this moment is for sober and careful investigation by men and women who have "the forward view". . . . Another great instrument of culture and recreation—the cinema—has been allowed to be exploited for commercial purposes without control. It would be a tragedy if the development of wireless were allowed to follow the same line.'[1]

As important as the conclusions of the Kent inquiry were two features of the way in which it was conducted. First, it had depended upon close co-operation between the BBC and a lively local educational authority. Such co-operation was a good example to set to other and less keen—or even hostile—local authorities. Second, it taught BBC officials a great deal that they did not know. They had been taken to a new region 'on the other side of the microphone'. The engineers learned much too, for one of the greatest obstacles in the way of co-operation between the educational authorities and the BBC was bad reception of programmes.

There was much general hostility also in educational circles to the novel idea of enlisting wireless in the classroom. The earliest surviving BBC document relating to schools broadcasting is a copy of a letter written by A. R. Burrows to the Director of Education of the London County Council in November 1923. 'We recognise that the London County Council is a great educational authority', Burrows wrote, 'and we think it desirable that we should endeavour to ascertain the views of that body in order that we may co-operate with it, as far as is possible, in any educational work that we may undertake.'[2] The London County Council expressed no desire to co-operate. It remained aloof and suspicious, partly on the grounds that receiving apparatus was often inadequate to permit intelligent group-listening in schools, partly because it feared interference with the freedom of the teacher to plan his lessons as he wished, and partly because the material used in broadcasts was said to be (in the vaguest terms) 'not suitable'.[3]

[1] Carnegie Trust, *Educational Broadcasting, The Report of a Special Investigation in the County of Kent during the year 1927*.

[2] *A. R. Burrows to the Director of Education of the London County Council, 21 Nov. 1923. 'It appears probable', Burrows began, 'that very material assistance could be afforded to the scholastic profession by the broadcasting of lectures and instructive talks to schools, and we are anxious that the vast potentialities of broadcasting shall be directed to useful channels as well as to those of pure amusement.'

[3] For difficulties of reception, see below, p. 202. *That the L.C.C.'s early fears about poor reception were not without foundation is shown by the complete failure of receiving apparatus at an address and demonstration given by Burrows before an audience of about 300 inspectors and teachers at University College, London,

Underlying these rationalizations was the same kind of conservative attitude to broadcasting which had always been shown
by St. Paul's Cathedral and sections of the press.[1] The only
concession the L.C.C. would make was that pupils in elementary schools could listen to broadcasts during the last half-hour
on Friday afternoons, from 4 p.m. to 4.30—and from January
1925 onwards such broadcasts were arranged.[2] There were
further relaxations in 1926 and, with the Kent experiment in
mind, experiments were carried out in London in 1927.[3] As an
expression of a change in attitudes, the L.C.C. gave permission
in 1927 for schools to listen to the ordinary Friday BBC schools
programmes provided that the lessons were 'integrated into the
school curriculum' and that the receiving apparatus used was
passed as adequate by BBC engineers. In July 1928 it went
further and decided that schools could take any lessons approved
by the Education Officer.

The L.C.C. had been one of the most prominent local education authorities to doubt the value of schools broadcasting:
many other authorities were cautious also. So too were some
teachers, who strained every argument to show how 'useless'
wireless was.[4] The success of the Kent experiment helped to
convert them. The very idea of treating broadcasting as a controlled 'experiment' seems to have had value in itself, not only
for Charitable Foundations and Directors of Education but for
teachers and pupils. 'It has been found that a good way to
introduce schools broadcasting into a large school', wrote the
headmaster of West Leeds High School late in 1928, 'is to appeal

in Jan. 1924. A later demonstration by J. C. Stobart in County Hall in November 1924, however, was attended by 150 teachers and 'immensely impressed the
audience and aroused their interest'.

[1] For examples of this conservative attitude, see *The Birth of Broadcasting*,
pp. 262–7, 274–5.

[2] *On 17 Dec. 1924 the Education Committee of the L.C.C. considered a report
on the broadcast lessons arranged since March 1924 and reached a generally
unfavourable verdict.

[3] In March 1926 Central Schools where French was taught were allowed to listen
to a new series of BBC French talks, and permission was given to the schools to
listen to a series of orchestral concerts, the first of which had been broadcast on
25 Sept. 1925 from the People's Palace. The French talks were criticized by an
L.C.C. inspector on the grounds that they taught idiomatic French rather than the
use of the pluperfect.

[4] There had been a sustained attack on broadcast education by 'A Teacher'
in *The Times* (30 Oct. 1926) in an article called 'Do Schools Need Wireless?'
It provoked a reply from Stobart and a number of other letters.

to the school, staff and boys to enter into the experiment; to ask for suggestions and criticisms; to allow the wireless lessons to justify themselves.'[1]

The second feature of the Kent experiment which was of critical long-term importance was its influence on people inside the BBC. 'The BBC itself learned much from interim reports and conferences', it was stated baldly in the *BBC Handbook* for 1928. 'There was a revision of studio methods. The lecture was made more like a lesson, in which response was expected, the classroom teachers were shown what part they were expected to play, and valuable reinforcement was given by means of printed pamphlets.'[2]

Behind these phrases was a fascinating personal crisis. At Easter 1927 Mary Somerville went with Stobart to a conference at Stratford-on-Avon. There she learned from Salter Davies that 'the Kent experiment was not going well'. Problems multiplied in the summer of 1927 when Stobart was ill, and Mary Somerville was given full powers by Reith to develop what came to be called 'listening-end work'. She was given authority to go around the Kent schools, collecting the comments of teachers and children and seeing for herself what actually happened in the classroom. To enable her to do this, an extra appointment was made at Savoy Hill in September 1927, and she was relieved thereby of some of her central administrative duties. Shortage of staff had hitherto been one of the reasons for limited ventures inside the schools: another had been Stobart's initial suspicion of Mary Somerville 'putting her nose inside a school'.[3]

Miss Somerville revelled in her new opportunity, even though, as she later admitted, it involved much eating of humble pie. 'I found poor patient children sitting in rooms being bored. Back I came at the gallop and did something about it. . . . It wasn't that the programmes were bad. They were of the highest standards, and some, for instance, Walford Davies, could be rated good radio. But they were *not* produced or given by people who knew children in their bones. By the

[1] T. Curzon, 'School Broadcasting from the Schoolmaster's Point of View' in the *BBC Handbook* (1929), pp. 231–3.
[2] Ibid., p. 113.
[3] Mary Somerville, Speech at Governors' Dinner, 20 Dec. 1955.

autumn of that year—well, things were different. Programme assistants *and* broadcasters were led by the ear into the schools. Schools broadcasting as we know it now had begun.'[1] By the end of the year 'a sufficient number of Kent teachers confirmed our faith in the educational possibilities of our medium. We had come very near to failure, but we had at least begun to learn to work as pioneers in radio education. We were to go on broadcasting but with a difference.'[2]

The study of broadcasting from the receiving end rather than from the transmitting end revolutionized the use of the medium as an educational instrument. One of the first developments was an extension of the publication of illustrated pamphlets, and 233,000 pamphlets were issued to schools in 1927.[3] The first BBC schools pamphlet—Sir Walford Davies's *Melody Book No. 1* —had been issued in September 1926.[4] A second development was a more systematic study of the language used in the broadcasts. Mary Somerville quickly realized that many of the criticisms made by teachers were fair—that broadcasts included unintelligible words and unfamiliar metaphors. Thereafter there was a progressive development of broadcasting technique in the light of what was happening at the receiving end. Even Sir Walford Davies's style of broadcasting was affected when he was given an observer in a Kent school whom he affectionately called his 'watchdog'.[5]

New broadcasters, some of whom were to make the best possible use of 'story telling' in school broadcasts, were offered a warm response by children, who began to feel that their broadcasts were 'just right'. Rhoda Power was outstanding among the very first of the new team. Her *Boys and Girls of Other Days* was a genuinely pioneer series, the first of many. Stobart had argued that wireless lessons 'must always partake of the nature of a lecture' and that this would inevitably mean that they would play a subordinate part in the education of the

---

[1] Mary Somerville, Rough Notes for a Co-ordinating Committee Discussion, Oct. 1954.

[2] Mary Somerville's Introduction to Palmer, *School Broadcasting in Britain*, p. 12.

[3] *BBC Annual Report* (1927), p. 6.

[4] The early broadcast lessons had sometimes been accompanied by blackboard notes, maps, diagrams, and bibliographies, which were issued from Savoy Hill and could be obtained free on application. The *Radio Times* was also used for illustrating and following up talks from the autumn of 1924.

[5] Palmer, *School Broadcasting in Britain*, p. 12.

very young.[1] Rhoda Power proved just how wrong he was. With new techniques there was the prospect of making a wider appeal to children of all ages. There was also the prospect of a genuinely close relationship with teachers, since it had now become clear that teachers and broadcasters were not competitors but associates. They supplemented each other not only in the classroom work related to broadcasts, but in formulating ideas for future programmes and in discussing the best way of 'putting across' material. One of the suggestions of the Kent Report was that permanent machinery was needed 'to secure continuous contact between the BBC on the one hand and, on the other, the Board of Education, the Local Education Authorities and the whole body of teachers'.[2]

This suggestion, which had also been put forward by the Hadow Committee earlier in 1928, was implemented in February 1929 when the BBC set up the Central Council for School Broadcasting. The new body was constituted on a representative basis with a dependent committee for Scotland. The Council took the place of the National Advisory Committee on Education, which had first met in October 1923 and met for the seventh and last time in June 1928.[3] The constitution and membership of the new Council were hammered out by a small 'interim committee' which had Salter Davies as its chairman: it also included Sir Walford Davies, Frank Roscoe, G. H. Gater of the London County Council, and G. T. Hankin, a Board of Education Inspector. All these men were to play an important part in the future of schools broadcasting. Gater, along with two other members of the interim committee, provided a link with the old National Advisory Committee on which they had served.

Before the first meeting of the new Council, H. A. L. Fisher was chosen as chairman ('no one more suitable could we think be found'[4]) with Roscoe as vice-chairman and chairman of the Executive Committee which was to meet once a month. The composition of the Council was representative: it included nominees of the Board of Education, the local education

---

[1] *J. C. Stobart, Lecture to the Grantham Education Society, 15 Mar. 1927.
[2] *Educational Broadcasting* (1928), p. 8.
[3] For the history of the National Advisory Committee, see *The Birth of Broadcasting*, p. 242.   [4] *Reith to H. A. L. Fisher, 17 Dec. 1928.

authorities, and teachers' associations and unions as well as
a number of independent members. Among the 'independents'
was W. W. Vaughan, the headmaster of Rugby, who was later
to be an active and distinguished chairman of the Council.
From many of these people—notably Roscoe, Hankin, and
Vaughan—Mary Somerville was to receive the most valuable
encouragement and assistance.

Whatever may be said in general terms of the influence of
committees on the creative arts of broadcasting, in the case of
schools broadcasting machinery and committees did not kill
'the vision of exploration, delight and understanding' which had
inspired Mary Somerville and her colleagues. They rather
helped to bring the vision to fulfilment.[1]
From the point of view of programme building, the most
important work after 1929 was done not by the Council itself
but by its network of Programme Sub-Committees, each of
which was charged with the task of determining what special
contribution broadcasting could make to the development of
a particular subject in the schools curriculum. At its first meetings in 1929 the Council appointed sub-committees to deal with
geography, history, modern languages, English literature,
music, special secondary-school courses, and an experimental
course in science. The majority of members of these sub-committees were teachers using the broadcast courses in their
schools. The other members included specialists in the subjects
concerned, representatives of the Executive Committee of the
Council, and officials of the BBC. These sub-committees helped
to draft the first new schools syllabus which covered the
academic year from September 1929 to June 1930.
It was a national syllabus which was used fully or in part by
5,000 schools: 2,356 schools listened regularly in 1929–30, an
increase of 912 on the previous year.[2] Over 560,000 pamphlets
were distributed. The extension of the work nationally and the
imposition of higher standards implied the end of local broadcasts to schools which had been given since the early days of
the Company. Many of these had been of an undoubtedly
low standard and did not reflect the growing interest in the

[1] K. V. Bailey, *The Listening Schools* (1957), p. 25.
[2] *BBC Annual Report* (1929), p. 9.

possibilities of sound radio as a unique educational medium. At the same time the system of receiving and correcting written work from schools and awarding prizes to schoolchildren on a competitive basis—a system which had been favoured by Stobart—came to an end. The last prizes were distributed by the Duchess of Atholl in July 1930.

In the early days of the Council the sub-committees were able to take a very active part in the planning of courses. They advised the Council on the commissioning of series—and even on speakers—and they edited educational pamphlets. Under their influence many new ventures were begun. In 1931, for example, a new kind of history course was introduced called *Tracing History Backwards*: it was an attempt to deepen knowledge of current problems by examining them in historical perspective. Another course, *King's English*, devised by Lloyd James, was designed, with the help of experiment, to test the effects of a broadcasting series on children's pronunciation. A year later current affairs talks on such controversial problems as unemployment, the means test, and the Irish question were given with great success. Raymond Gram Swing was brought in to explain the American point of view on the 'repayment of the American debt', and 'unfinished debates' were arranged with two seven-minute broadcast speeches from mover and opposer and the schools continuing the debate for themselves. Three years later, despite all the denominational difficulties, attempts were made to start experimental courses on Bible study and religious knowledge.

From the point of view of the BBC the great merit of developing new schemes through the sub-committees was that it brought producers into close touch with teachers: BBC programme assistants were the acting secretaries of the sub-committees. 'For every broadcast course', it was stated in 1932, 'there is provided an interplay of the ideas of five or six persons, each possessing some special qualification of scholarship, broadcasting technique or practical knowledge of the schools.'[1] At a time when it was far from easy to recruit good programme assistants with teaching experience—if only because of pensions problems—this interplay was necessary.

---

[1] *Some Problems of School Broadcasting, Reviewed by the Central Council for School Broadcasting after Three Years' Experience* (1932), p. 4.

The *Annual Report* of the BBC for 1930 stated simply that 'the machinery set up by the Central Council for School Broadcasting worked smoothly'.[1] Between 1930 and 1935, however, as the number of schools broadcasts greatly increased, particularly from 1933 onwards, there were signs of serious congestion in the BBC's annual timetable. The full-time BBC officials were being seriously overworked as a result of a superabundance of programme sub-committees meeting in the early part of the year, and complaints of 'unwieldiness of machinery' began to arise.[2] In the year 1934–5 over seventy Central Council Committee meetings were held at Broadcasting House and 7,000 sheets of foolscap were duplicated for circulation.[3]

Much of the foolscap concerned the sub-committees, which might be dealing not with one or two but with several courses, and it began to be difficult to justify the amount of time taken up at least by the more ineffective of them. Some of the sub-committees, if not ineffective, were inactive in suggesting new ideas. 'Broadcast lessons should present the opinions of those who are at the head of the main body of educational doctrine,' G. T. Hankin, one of the liveliest members of Council and sub-committees had written in 1931, 'not of the Advance Guard, still less of the Forlorn Hope.'[4] If the sub-committees began to lag behind, the results were serious. They became vested interests, out of touch with new thought. Teachers' opinions on the merits of programmes were not unanimous, and a sub-committee had to have definite standing if it was to pursue a forward-looking policy.[5]

By 1935 there were further arguments for reform of procedure. First, listening-end work still needed further development. 'Work at the transmitting end had naturally developed in advance of work at the listening end', Reith commented in 1932. 'The machinery for ensuring that the Council should control the educational content of the programmes and pamphlets was

[1] *BBC Annual Report* (1930), p. 8.
[2] *Mary Somerville to Schools Executive, 19 Nov. 1935.
[3] *Revision of Central Council Machinery: Memorandum on Behalf of the BBC, Feb. 1936.
[4] *Memorandum by G. T. Hankin on 'The Educational Problems of School Broadcasting', 30 Dec. 1931.
[5] For differences of opinion between teachers, see *The Evidence Regarding Broadcast Geography Lessons* (1932) which shows how uncertain was the guidance offered by random collections of teachers' opinions.

apparently satisfactory, but the Council's policy with regard to listening-end work was not so clear.'[1] A full-time 'listening-end officer' was, in fact, appointed in 1932, but he was concerned with adult education as well as school education.[2]

Second, the sub-committees thought essentially in terms of 'subjects'. If the BBC was to do what its educational officers had always wished, to link subjects and to explore the boundaries between them, a different kind of machinery was necessary. Hankin was one of the men within the inner councils of schools broadcasting who, from the start, refused to be bound by narrow, categories. He was a good historian, the chairman of the History Sub-Committee, but he wanted to see history linked with geography, economics, literature and, above all, with current affairs.

Third, there was perhaps not quite the same need as there had been in 1929 for large numbers of teacher representatives at the programme level since a corps of experienced educational broadcasters—both writers of scripts and performers—was beginning to be built up. Among them were broadcasters of great distinction, like Rhoda Power, Stephen King-Hall, and Professor Winifred Cullis, people of great creative ability who found a natural outlet for their educational vocation in teaching through the medium of sound radio. The background of the schools broadcasters varied considerably. Out of thirty-two speakers between 1928 and 1932, seven were schoolteachers, two training-college lecturers, seven university lecturers, and sixteen outside specialists.[3]

Whatever their background, the speakers had to devote a good deal of time to 'acquiring a good technique of broadcasting'. Mary Somerville had once been reproved by Stobart for having the impertinence to write to a distinguished Professor of Literature at Oxford requesting him to rewrite a script. Such a reproof would have seemed absurd during the early 1930s when scholars and specialists with an international reputation were expected to rehearse for long spells, to visit schools to discover the reaction to their performances, and even to listen to recordings of their voices on Blattnerphone in order to eliminate 'future mistakes'.

[1] *Comments by Reith on the pamphlet *Some Problems of School Broadcasting*.
[2] *Memorandum, 'Work at the Listening End', 17 Aug. 1932.
[3] *Some Problems of School Broadcasting*, p. 11.

(*a*) Toscanini
conducting the
BBC Symphony
Orchestra in the
Queen's Hall
(1935)

(*b*) The BBC
Symphony
Orchestra
conducted by
Sir Adrian
Boult
(1939)

12. Music

13. The Midland Parliament (1934) discussing 'The Sack at 18'

14. Gardening from Alexandra Palace (1937), with C. H. Middleton (centre)

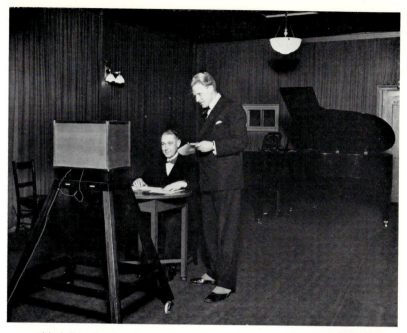

(*a*) A French Lesson from Savoy Hill. M. Stéphan and Stuart Hibberd

(*b*) Pupils at Wembley School listening to a Broadcast (1933)

15. Education by Radio

A SOP TO CERBERUS:
OR, THE DOGS' CHANCE.

16. Political Broadcasting. Cartoon from *Punch*,
16 Aug. 1933

CALIBAN'S CABINET (1)   *Minister of Propaganda*

17. Sir Richard Maconachie (1938)

18. R. W. P. Cockburn with the
longest listener's letter ever received
by the BBC (1938)

Quite apart from forces making for change and development within the schools broadcasting system between 1929 and 1935, two main sets of difficulties continued to put obstacles in the way of spectacular growth. The first set of difficulties concerned finance and the second inadequate facilities in the schools for good wireless reception.

Finance had always been a problem, and both Stobart and Mary Somerville had worked with very slender resources. Reith hoped, indeed, that the Board of Education itself might pay a contribution towards schools broadcasting or 'pass a strong recommendation to the Post Office, from whom our revenue comes, endorsing the value of the educational work we are doing—particularly the work at the listening-end, which is outside our proper responsibilities'.[1]

A spokesman of the Board replied tersely in 1930 that 'it does not seem to be practicable to consider the finance of your educational activities separately from the whole question of your financial relations with the Exchequer'.[2] The BBC, therefore, was left to finance both programmes and listening-end work from its own resources. It is difficult from surviving financial returns to say exactly how much was spent on educational activities each year. Indeed, the Central Council for School Broadcasting itself complained on at least one occasion that it had inadequate information about the financial side of its work.

Three points are clear about the course of events between 1929 and 1935. First, schools broadcasting suffered from the general inability of the community to take education sufficiently seriously. The *élan* of the last months of the First World War and the period immediately following the war had gone, and Hadow's Report on the Primary School in 1931 and Spens's Report on Secondary Education in 1938 were at best declarations of faith rather than blueprints of immediately applicable policy. Second, the financial crisis of 1931, which led the Corporation voluntarily to relinquish a portion of its income to the government, slowed down the development of schools

[1] *Memorandum by Reith on 'The BBC and Education', June 1930; Reith to E. H. Pelham, 23 June 1930; Pelham to Reith, 13 Oct. 1930; Reith to Pelham, 14 Oct. 1930.
[2] *Pelham to Reith, 1 Nov. 1930.

broadcasting.[1] Third, financial considerations influenced a basic revision of the constitution and organization of the Central Council which took place in 1935.[2]

Difficulties with reception were noted from the very earliest days of schools broadcasting. Complaints came in from several schools and Directors of Education about bad reception ruining interesting programmes. 'Collective listening' was a hazardous activity. In April 1924 the first Education Engineer, R. W. Blackwell, was appointed to the BBC staff and a few months later, in September 1924, the Chief Engineer, Peter Eckersley, sent round the first list of technical instructions to schools. In 1925 Blackwell was seconded full-time to the Schools Service, and on leaving the BBC at the end of 1926 was replaced by H. L. Fletcher. By January 1927 there were four full-time engineers in what was called the Education Sub-Section of the Engineering Department. In April 1927 there were eight; at the end of the year—with the Kent experiment in full progress —twelve; and by the spring of 1928, fourteen. 'In those early days,' one of the engineers has written, 'probably the greatest menace to the success of educational broadcasting was bad reception. And the BBC tried to impress on teachers what good reception was really like by giving simple demonstrations of broadcast talks on suitable apparatus.'[3] Among the engineers who went down to Kent was Harold Bishop, who, after Ashbridge, was to be Director of Engineering of the BBC.

The change from business-sponsored Company to public Corporation enabled the BBC to carry out its work of advice and technical assistance rather more easily than it might otherwise have done, but there were still some difficulties because of the fear of appearing to support one firm in the radio trade rather than another. 'We are an association of manufacturers', Reith had written in the days of the Company, 'and in addition to impartiality, the trade expects us to encourage the sale of complete sets or anyhow not to discourage it. The whole situation,

---

[1] *BBC Annual Report* (1931), p. 10. The Report for the following year noted, however (p. 10), that 'school broadcasting suffered less than might have been expected from the financial crisis'.

[2] See below, pp. 208–9.

[3] *Unpublished BBC Notes on the History of School Broadcasting; cf. *Notes of A. R. Burrows, 6 June 1924: 'Educational broadcasting is only successful when the reception is really faultless.'

owing to our constitution, is one of critical delicacy, and only the serious prejudice accruing through the use of inferior apparatus justifies our offer of help in the matter.'[1] Even when the constitution had changed, the 'delicacy' lingered. It was difficult for the BBC to advise the use of one particular wireless model for schools. 'We must still be circumspect,' Reith told Mitchell, the secretary of the Carnegie Trust, 'not to appear to be contrary to the interests of the trade in general or to favour any particular manufacturer or group of manufacturers.'[2]

Fortunately, the radio trade itself understood the dilemma in which the BBC found itself, and did nothing to impede the extension of the market for wireless sets to schools and local education authorities. It was as well aware as Mitchell that 'bad reception could kill the whole thing'.[3] In 1930 the chairman of the Radio Manufacturers' Association attended a meeting of the newly formed Technical Sub-Committee of the Central Council and presented a resolution adopted by his association, pledging willingness 'to co-operate to secure good broadcast reception in schools'.[4]

The Technical Sub-Committee had been known at first as the Reception Committee. It started its work by circularizing Directors of Education about general factors influencing reception conditions, and went on to make detailed inquiries into conditions in a number of areas as widely scattered as Buckinghamshire and Fife, Blackburn and Reigate. Late in 1930 it co-operated with the Department of Scientific and Industrial Research in a scheme to test sets submitted by manufacturers against standards determined by the sub-committee. The Central Council passed on detailed information collected by the sub-committee to interested authorities, thus absolving the BBC itself from recommending specific makes of sets.

A method of judging listening conditions in schools without being forced to pay visits to them was also devised in 1930. A series of twenty-five words, each containing three fundamental speech sounds, was listed and broadcast daily. The sounds were

[1] *Reith to the Station Directors, 22 July 1925.
[2] *Reith to Mitchell, 3 Nov. 1926. He was anticipating the change of constitution.
[3] *Mitchell to Reith, 5 Nov. 1926. 'Last night,' he added, 'I had the greatest difficulty in getting even Daventry successfully, and finally I got it with one of the dials at a quite unusual number.'
[4] *Meeting of the Technical Sub-Committee, 4 July 1930.

recorded by children in schools and the results compared with returns made by certain selected schools where the reception conditions were known. The comparison of results enabled schools to tell whether or not their reception conditions were good enough to justify their making regular use of broadcast lessons. Advice on these tests was given by Dr. Cyril Burt, the psychologist; and an Investigation Committee, with O. F. Brown of D.S.I.R. in the chair and Harold Bishop and Lloyd James among its members, supervised the scheme.

Reports from individual schools often give a vivid picture of working conditions in schools in 1931 and 1932. 'The head-master has frequently used his own set for school purposes, and intends to instal a school set shortly.' 'The existing set is obsolete and not in use. The headmaster is enthusiastic, but does not consider that a set could be of very much value to the school at present. In the event of an increase in the number of children in the school and the installation of electric light, he would certainly endeavour to instal a set.' 'The headmistress has collected £20, but the governors have refused their permission for a set to be installed on the grounds that the number of children who would benefit is very small.'

In collecting such reports and in commenting on the kind of apparatus which schools used, the Education Engineers were placed in a strategic, if somewhat anomalous, position. Their advice was indispensable, but it was not easy to say where engineering problems ended and where educational problems began. 'Education engineers are not expected to express opinions on questions relating to the treatment of subject matter either in the studio or in the classroom,' a memorandum of 1928 stated, 'nor is it thought desirable that they should do so, but some knowledge of the nature of the lessons broadcast is essential if these visiting representatives are to be able to convey the right impression of the BBC's policy to schools as well as convey the nature of the teachers' difficulties to Head Office'.[1] Apparently doubts about the status of the engineers remained, and in January 1930 Carpendale had to settle the matter at the highest level. 'The section was an integral part of the Engineering Branch and under the direct control of the Assistant Chief

---

[1] *'Report on the Range, Scope and Effects of the Work of Education Engineers, Nov. 1926 to Dec. 1928.'

Engineer. Education Engineers were to take their instructions from the Senior Education Engineer, who works in accordance with the requirements of the Secretaries of the Central Councils for School Broadcasting and Adult Education.'[1]

One of the most popular ways of persuading would-be listeners that receiving problems were not insuperable, and one in which both engineers and broadcasters played a big part, was the staging of demonstrations not only in individual schools but at large national conferences like the annual meetings of the British Association. A thousand people were present at a British Association demonstration at Leeds in 1927, and at the 1928 meeting of the Association in Glasgow a model studio was constructed, and Stobart and Salter Davies spoke to large audiences about the Kent experiment. In one of his speeches at Glasgow Stobart told his audience that he had been wakened that morning in a sleeper at the Central Station by a railway worker whistling Tchaikovsky's No. 1 Piano Concerto. He said that 'this disturbance' proved the value of broadcasting—not to the railway worker but to himself, for he had profited to the extent of being able to recognize what the railway worker was whistling.[2]

By 1935, when important changes were made in the constitution of the Central Council for School Broadcasting, reception difficulties had been greatly reduced and emphasis was passing naturally to the bigger question of how to finance the provision of wireless sets in those schools which were still without them.[3] The chairman of the Central Council between 1932 and 1935 was Lord Eustace Percy. Succeeding Fisher, Percy brought to bear on the work of the Council a wide experience of different aspects of education. He had been President of the Board of Education from 1924 to 1929,[4] and as chairman of the Council he made it one of his chief tasks to plead the case for large-scale public provision of wireless sets in schools.

[1] *Memorandum of the Assistant Controller, Jan. 1930.
[2] Note by Reith, June 1963.
[3] The difficulties by no means completely disappeared. 'There is no doubt that reception leaves much to be desired', a number of H.M.I.s reported in January 1937. They added that 'it may be worth noting that no significant correlation could be discovered between the make of the receiving set and the quality of the reception'. *Board of Education, *Use of Broadcasting in Secondary Schools*, Jan. 1937.
[4] See Lord Percy, *Some Memories* (1958), ch. vi.

There is an illuminating note in the BBC Archives headed 'The Estimated Cost of Supplying all Public Elementary Schools in England and Wales with Receiving Apparatus suitable for School Broadcast Reception'. It was drawn up, at Mary Somerville's request, by an official in the Board of Education.[1] Assuming that the retail price of the appropriate receivers was between £10 and £15 and that a large order could bring the price down to as little as £8, the cost of installing receivers in senior schools, 'unreorganised departments', junior schools, and infant schools in England and Wales would have been £420,000.[2]

Percy referred to this figure in the draft of his Report on the work of the Council for 1935, stating that the BBC might set aside this sum. Although one senior official of the BBC described it as 'a fantastic suggestion', Reith was sympathetic and commented that it might be possible to raise the necessary sum from the portion of the 10s. licence which the Treasury had hitherto retained.[3] Mary Somerville maintained that 'the position outside' at the time was such as would justify the BBC 'thinking "big"'. 'Mr. Ramsbotham [the President of the Board of Education]', she added, 'has been publicly declaring the need for schools to have wireless receiving sets and projectors and has persistently been refusing to be squashed by the officials at the Board and Treasury in his determination to get the necessary funds.' Her financial proposal was different from that of Percy. 'What I have in mind', she went on, 'is that a block grant might be made to the Board of Education by the government from the Wireless Licence Revenue and the Cinema Entertainment Tax respectively to be devoted to the annual equipment of a certain proportion of schools throughout the country.'[4]

These sanguine hopes were not realized, and the most that the BBC could do in 1935 was to salute those local authorities who were prepared to embark upon ambitious plans of wireless installation. One of the earliest authorities to enter the field was

[1] *P. Wilson to Mary Somerville, 18 Apr. 1935.

[2] This figure assumed that two sets would be required for senior schools with between 250 and 350 pupils and three sets for such schools with more than 350 pupils. In other cases, one set only would be required, with the exception of junior schools with more than 350 pupils which would be allotted two.

[3] *Siepmann to Reith, undated note; Reith to Siepmann, undated note.

[4] *Mary Somerville to Siepmann, 7 Mar. 1935.

Ayrshire, which celebrated the Royal Jubilee by providing each of its schools with a wireless set. Edinburgh granted £300 a year towards such installations in 1935 and Hertfordshire £450, although the Education Committee's proposals in Hertford-shire met with resistance from the Finance Committee. Interest was quickened in the fate of such schemes in 1938, and many local authorities, some stimulated by teachers, agreed to pay, if not for equipment, at least for licences and a supply of pamph-lets.

This pressure on the part of teachers was greatly welcomed inside the BBC.[1] The Manchester Teachers' Consultative Com-mittee, for example, published a report in 1935 which the BBC felt was 'decidedly favourable'. A resolution of the Oxford Schools Management Sub-Committee was also noted with pleasure: 'the practice has grown up whereby half the purchase price of various mechanical aids to learning is provided out of school funds and half by the Education Committee. This was suited to a period of experiment, but the value of these aids is now clearly proved. The sub-committee are of the opinion that if these aids are recognised as necessary, the whole cost should be borne by the Committee.' It is fair to add that the Oxford Committee associated percussion bands (for infants' schools only) with wireless sets as 'necessary aids to learning'.[2]

The London County Council was once again suspicious of precipitate action. 'The L.C.C. has decided to institute an enquiry by its Inspectorate into the use of broadcasting in L.C.C. schools', it was reported in 1935. 'A preliminary conference was held with the Inspectorate on October 25th. This revealed a disappointing ignorance on the part of the Inspectorate both as to the policy of the BBC, the work of the Council, and the amount of broadcasting actually being used in the schools.'[3]

What was particularly pleasing about the Oxford resolution, which was followed up by effective implementation, was its clear statement that 'the period of experiment' in schools broad-casting was now over. This was the theme of the last report of

[1] *Cameron to F. Mander, the Secretary of the N.U.T., 14 Dec. 1936.
[2] *City of Oxford, Minutes of School Management Sub-Committee, 12 Dec. 1934.
[3] *BBC Note on Action taken by Local Education Authorities, Nov. 1935.

the Central Council before Percy retired. 'We find that the time has come definitely to record our opinion that School Broadcasting has established itself as an educational influence of considerable importance, and to claim that it should be regarded as an asset of great potential value to the public service of education.'[1]

The Council went on to draw conclusions. Hitherto, it said, its policy had not been to 'force the pace of development'. It now believed that expansion should definitely be planned. As many as 1,271 schools were listening to travel talks, the most popular item of fare, 1,002 to music programmes, 973 to British history (significantly, as against only 555 to world history),[2] and 934 to nature study. A new subject like regional geography could secure an immediate following in 600 schools without there being any decrease in the number of schools listening to travel talks. 'We have so far presented the programme', the Report added, 'under the customary subject divisions in order to facilitate the incorporation of the broadcast talks in the school timetable, but the material of the broadcasts in most cases is by no means confined within the limits of any one subject and we believe that broadcasting is particularly fitted to break down any unnecessary barriers between the subjects of the curriculum.'[3]

The reorganization of the constitution of the Council—for the various reasons which have been outlined—began with the appointment by the Executive Committee in February 1935 of an *ad hoc* committee to make recommendations about a simplification of machinery. This small committee recommended that while the Council should continue to be of roughly the same size and composition, the Executive Committee should be divided into two—one section dealing with education and the other with finance and general purposes—and 'greater expedition in the conduct of business of the sub-committees should be achieved'.

---

[1] *Report to the BBC on the Present Position of School Broadcasting*, 19 Jan. 1935.

[2] H. G. Wells later criticized (in May 1938) what he called the exaggerated emphasis on British history. By then, however, 3,739 schools (age level 9–11) were taking courses in world history as against 3,531 in British history (age level 11–14). *Hankin wrote to Steele, 30 June 1938, 'I think we might send H. G. Wells a copy of our next year's programme and ask his opinion. The letter would have to explain why we stick to British history.' Hankin did not explain why.

[3] *Report to the BBC on the Present Position of School Broadcasting*, p. 2.

These proposals were accepted—with the exception of that relating to the division of the Executive Committee—on 11 June 1935. A more important change followed. Mary Somerville, with the support of Percy and his successor Vaughan, suggested to Reith that there should be a division of interest and labour between the Council and the BBC. She had been ill in the autumn and winter of 1934–5 and had come to the proper conclusion that too much work was falling on the shoulders of the few people inside the BBC who were fully concerned with school broadcasting. She herself wished to concentrate on work inside the BBC, and put forward a new scheme for divided responsibility, with the Central Council becoming a public body with its own secretary and a substantial degree of autonomy. Her scheme recognized that there was a 'duality of function' between programme builders inside the BBC and people inside 'the world of education'. The Head of the Schools Department inside the BBC should be placed in a position where she could 'direct the production of the school programme and its related services, giving that attention to the details of presentation and development of microphone technique which has for some time been impracticable'. In future she should attend the Council as 'the accredited officer of the BBC responsible for interpreting to the Council such considerations as relate to the over-riding powers retained by the BBC vis-à-vis the Council'. On the other side, the work of the Council would 'attract more attention and carry greater weight' in the world of education if it was represented by officers who were recognized as 'responsible servants of an independent educational body'.[1]

Miss Somerville went to great pains to set out details of her scheme in diagrammatic form (see p. 210).

Reith, however, needed no persuading. He wrote later that he had always been in favour of giving the Council as much autonomy as possible 'since the BBC is not a recognised educational instrument'.[2] He welcomed Mary Somerville's proposals, therefore, and gave them his full support. So too did the Ullswater Committee.[3] When A. C. Cameron, the Director of Education for Oxford and a Governor of the British Film Institute, was

[1] *Mary Somerville, undated Memorandum on Proposed Staff Adjustments relative to the Schools Department.
[2] *Reith to Graves, 21 Apr. 1938.   [3] Cmd. 5091 (1936), §102.

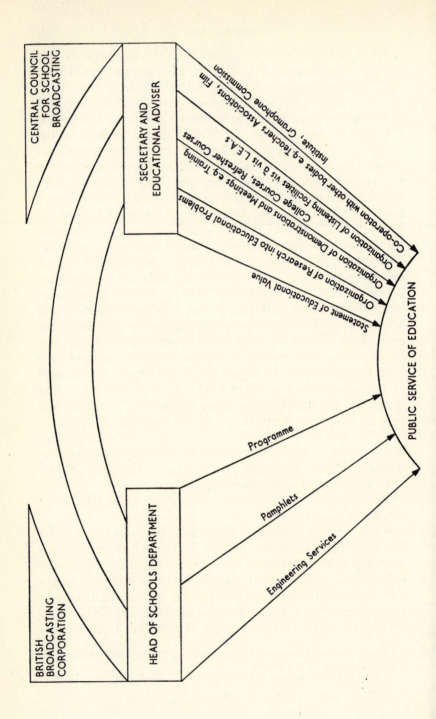

CENTRAL COUNCIL FOR SCHOOL BROADCASTING

SECRETARY AND EDUCATIONAL ADVISER

Co-operation with other bodies e.g Teachers Associations, Film Institute , Gramophone Commission

Organization of Listening facilities vis à vis L.E.A.s

College Courses, Refresher Courses

Organization of Demonstrations and Meetings e.g. Training

Organization of Research into Educational Problems

Statement of Educational Value

PUBLIC SERVICE OF EDUCATION

Programme

Pamphlets

Engineering Services

HEAD OF SCHOOLS DEPARTMENT

BRITISH BROADCASTING CORPORATION

appointed Secretary of the Council, Reith noted in his diary, 'I have always wished the Council to be more independent of the BBC, and this looks like getting down to it.'[1]

The new Council was to have 'full responsibility for a certain field of work'. 'The Corporation has no desire in future', it was stated, 'to interfere in any question of the management of the Council or in the detail or policy of its arrangements for activities at the listening end.'[2] To secure the Council's independence of action, separate funds were to be placed at its disposal.[3] Mary Somerville hoped that these would be made available in the form of a block grant.[4] Instead, they were based, as before 1935, on annual estimates. The first grant was from April 1936. To emphasize the independence of the Council, Cameron's offices were sited in a house in Portland Place which at first was quite unconnected with Broadcasting House.

Cameron took over his duties on 1 November 1935. He emphasized that his task was 'to strengthen the links between producer and consumer'. With this purpose in view, he was given subordinate officials to assist him at the listening end. They included R. C. Steele, a Cambridge graduate, who had been an Inspector of Schools since 1933. Steele was a most effective adviser on educational policy. Cameron himself was less interested in the 'technique of broadcasting' than Mary Somerville, but he was popular with teachers and administrators, and an effective spokesman of the general educational policy of the BBC. 'Broadcasting is not just a convenient mechanical aid to teaching in the classroom, like the gramophone or the magic lantern', he told the press soon after his appointment. 'First and foremost, it brings to the school the personality of the expert. The broadcast talk does not brush the teacher aside: it offers what the best teachers are constantly seeking, a link between the school and life outside, between the classroom and the home. . . . We are concerned to secure not the introduction of something called "School Broadcasting", distinct from programmes which the ordinary listener enjoys, but that every school is equipped with a set that will enable it to

[1] Reith, Diary, 6 June 1935.
[2] *Revision of Central Council Machinery: Memorandum on Behalf of the BBC, Feb. 1936.
[3] *Director-General's Meeting, Minutes, 21 May 1935.
[4] *Minutes of the Central Council, 11 Mar. 1935.

receive any talk, whether in the school programme or not, which will enable the pupil to become a more discerning citizen.'[1]

The newly constituted Council very quickly established close relations with the Board of Education and the local authorities. It was perhaps less successful in carrying out the kind of research into educational problems which Mary Somerville believed to be essential to the future development of sound radio. Before her illness in 1934 she had made arrangements to send out a series of questions to schools on their reaction to particular programmes. The inquiry was made by Miss Ussher, and was not officially supported by the Board of Education.[2] A further inquiry was carried out on an even bigger scale in 1935, when over 1,700 replies from 2,500 listening schools were analysed carefully by Dr. Perrie Williams to discover what the children enjoyed and what they found 'stodgy' and what the teachers liked and what they found 'useless'. Dr. Perrie Williams suggested that equal attention should be paid to the planning of junior and senior courses and that the BBC should move still further from the classroom and explore the world outside the schools.

The Board of Education itself began to take an increasing interest in detailed investigation after 1935. It moved very slowly, E. G. Savage telling Cameron in January 1936 that he was 'rather ashamed' at the delay inside his own organization.[3] 'Our projected programme is that we should select two or three courses, or at the most four,' he explained to Cameron, 'and have them followed lesson by lesson, possibly throughout the whole of the course in the schools where reception is good.' There was to be no wasting of Inspectors' time. 'We are particularly anxious not to have any wasted visits in places where reception is likely to be defective.'

Following this initiative, which was limited to elementary schools, a number of Inspectors of Schools reported in 1936 on

---

[1] *BBC Press Release, 31 Oct. 1935.
[2] *Analysis of School Report Forms, 11 Nov. 1935.
[3] *Savage to Cameron, 10 Jan. 1936. Cf. a letter from A. G. Philip of the Board to Reith, 28 June 1935: 'I have never really had any doubt about the ultimate triumph of broadcasting in the schools, but perhaps my experience of the educational machine has given me the habit of expecting new things to advance sedately, even such startling magic as broadcasting.'

teachers' and children's reactions to a number of BBC courses in history and geography. In general, they concluded that 'the broadcast talks had been well worth while': they had stimulated interest, 'in particular by means of the dramatic interludes which by skilful use of sound produce mental pictures in a way in which no individual teacher, however gifted, can hope to do'. Yet they went on to make specific criticisms not only of the difficult language of some of the broadcasts but of the attempt to put across difficult ideas to children who were incapable of grasping them. One cautious Inspector could not resist adding, 'how much enjoyment is still due to novelty and how much to real interest is difficult to gauge'. Another Inspector wisely pointed out that 'the wireless lesson is not a soft option which relieves the teacher of his responsibility. It is an exceedingly difficult form of lesson needing much thought.'[1] The Inspectors' views were supplemented by information from local BBC officials. 'This is a fairly ordinary school of the older type', one Lancashire official wrote bluntly. 'I do not think that the Head-master is much out of the ordinary either.'[2]

Inspectors' reports were followed up by discussions inside the Programme Sub-Committees which had been left with less initiative after 1935 than they had enjoyed before. They no longer had programme assistants as secretaries, and they were less directly involved in detailed programme planning. Yet many interesting discussions took place inside them. In the History Sub-Committee, for instance, Hankin pressed some of the same points that had been made in Board of Education reports. 'It is a great mental strain for children of thirteen to listen to connected thought for twenty minutes. . . . If one gets across three big ideas it is a good day's work.'[3] Hankin also added many points of his own. He was a shrewd observer of the social conditions in which broadcast lessons were received, and warned his colleagues on more than one occasion about putting across 'a middle-class point of view'.[4] He also knew a good deal about his colleagues. When Cameron proposed adding an Inspector of Schools to the History Sub-Committee in 1938,

[1] *Digest of Reports by H.M. Inspectors on Broadcast Lessons Listened to in the Summer Term*, 1936.
[2] *Notes appended to the Reports by the North Regional staff of the BBC.
[3] *Hankin to Miss Gibbs, 10 Nov. 1938.
[4] See above, p. 41.

Hankin replied, 'By all means get an H.M.I. for the History Committee. It will do him good, whoever he is.'[1]

In 1937 and 1938 the Board of Education produced reports, through its Consultative Committee, on the use of broadcasting both in elementary and secondary schools. These reports were received by the Council in March 1938. Reception conditions were shown to be still unsatisfactory in some schools and the Education Engineers were asked to investigate why this was so. Little that was new was said in the Report on Elementary Education: on Secondary Education, however, where the Central Council for School Broadcasting was making a new drive, the Inspectors raised some new issues, not always winning the assent of the BBC. 'There can be little doubt', one Inspector had said, 'that this form has been wasting its time, for the course is of practically no value for revision purposes for School Certificate.' The BBC did not retaliate by asking why this should have been the test.

A certain narrowness of outlook pervades the reports, and there seem to have been serious misconceptions about schools broadcasting, including a fear lest it would make children passive and 'standardize or stereotype methods'. A main general point of the Inspectors was that although pupils liked broadcasts, 'they did not know how to listen'. They talked in vague terms of 'the restiveness incidental to a new educational experience', but they did not suggest how the art of listening could be developed. Both these points had been dealt with more convincingly by Hankin in a note which he prepared as an appendix to the BBC's evidence before the Board of Education's Consultative Committee met. 'Some teachers may be tempted to use examinations as a convenient excuse for avoiding the strain of thinking out the use of new methods and new devices and for avoiding also the risk of failures that may affect their future success in their profession. . . . It is true that many adults lack concentration and cannot listen seriously to broadcasting. That is only a proof that they have not been trained to do so. It does not affect the argument that intelligent purposive listening can be a valuable part of the educational process.'[2]

Hankin dared to judge quite freely and with all the zest of

[1] *Hankin to Cameron, 15 June 1938.
[2] *Hankin to Cameron, 29 Sept. 1936.

an independent critic. The Consultative Committee was much more cautious. It did not, for example, make much of the fact, as the BBC put it, 'that many teachers seem to have missed valuable opportunities of using the broadcast as a second expert opinion for purposes of comparison and to train the pupils' critical faculties'.[1] The liveliest ideas came from the Central Council itself. The pressure of School Certificate and Higher School Certificate examinations was apparently felt in 1938 not only by pupils and teachers but by officials of the Board of Education. When Steele sent in the sets of comments which the Council made on the Board's Report, he received the reply from F. R. G. Duckworth that 'I am afraid the pressure of the Higher School Certificate Examination will prevent me from really clamping down to it for the next few weeks.'[2]

There was a great deal of correspondence between the Council and the Board of Education in 1938 and 1939, concerned with conferences, courses, and technical problems, including the best place to install school wireless sets. The closer involvement between Council and Board was what Cameron wanted. It is revealed in such matters as the Board objecting to a course on physical education in Scotland because neither it nor its Inspectors had been consulted first—and later providing massive help with the broadcasts.[3] In the same spirit the Council asked for, and received, approval to be added to the list of bodies who were circulated with the 'ordinary communications' which the Board of Education made to local education authorities.[4] In June 1938 the Board requested the Council's permission to include broadcasting statistics in a bulletin which it prepared and circulated to Inspectors and other officers.[5] One of the Board's Inspectors even took the initiative in proposing a series

[1] *Comments of the Central Council on the Report of the Board of Education on the Use of Broadcasting in Secondary Schools*, Mar. 1938. Not all teachers failed to respond. *The Principal of the Municipal College at Smethwick wrote a long report to Cameron on 16 Sept. 1936, which included the sentence: 'I believe the greatest gain is obtained from the broadcast lessons by the teacher. Although he sometimes thinks the lessons a nuisance and an interference with routine, yet he gets jerked out of a rut and is generally stimulated to think more of his job.'
[2] *F. R. G. Duckworth to R. C. Steele, 22 Mar. 1938.
[3] *S. H. Wood to Cameron, 11 April 1938.
[4] *W. R. Reid to S. H. Wood, 13 May 1938; *Wood to Reid, 19 May 1938.
[5] *Wood to Reid, 1 June 1938.

of broadcasts for junior schools and sixth forms.[1] The idea was carefully considered but turned down, with the note that the Council would be very glad to hear at any time 'any further suggestions you or your colleagues may care to put forward'.[2] Another venture that failed was the attempt to install an 'effective' wireless set in the Board of Education itself. 'For the present, we will manage without', W. R. Richardson of the Department of Intelligence and Public Relations of the Board told Cameron in November 1938.[3]

This correspondence was in the background in 1937, 1938, and 1939. In the public foreground was the great increase in the number and range of schools broadcasts during the last three years of peace. By 1937 there were twenty-seven broadcast courses in England and Wales—one for Infants, six for Juniors, three for Juniors and Seniors, eleven for Seniors, and six for Secondary Schools. Two of the weekly talks were given in Welsh. In Scotland also there were as many as twenty-six series. The programmes for young children, notably Ann Driver's highly successful *Music and Movement for Very Young Children* series, which was first broadcast in 1934, were particularly interesting in that the pioneers of schools broadcasting had thought that only older children would be able to benefit from the work of the BBC. Following Dr. Perrie Williams's recommendations, the Junior and Senior programmes became increasingly distinctive, and more use was made of outside broadcasts. The replacement of *Districts of England*, a series of talks for rural schools, by *Our Village*, a dramatized series popular both in village and city, was a sign that Hadow's ideas had begun to change schools broadcasting itself.[4] R. C. Steele claimed without exaggeration that 'the outside world has begun to have access to every class room in a way that could not have been imagined twenty years ago'.[5]

There had, indeed, been many changes since the earliest days. 'I always say that educational advance has traditionally gone in this country in three stages', Cameron wrote in 1938.

---

[1] *R. H. Barrow to Cameron, 8 Oct. 1938.
[2] *Cameron to Barrow, 15 Dec. 1938.
[3] *W. R. Richardson to Cameron, 17 Nov. 1938.
[4] *The Listening Schools*, p. 46.
[5] Quoted in *The Listening Schools* from an article by Steele in the *Year Book of Education* (1938).

'First Stage: pioneers' experiments. Second Stage: responsible teaching opinion generally becomes convinced that the value of the new medium or whatever it is may be proved and begins to demand its official adoption. Third Stage: the local education authorities accept their recommendation. With School Broadcasting it seems to me that we are now well into the third stage.'[1]

In 1938 there was an increase of over 1,600 elementary schools using wireless lessons, and the number of secondary schools had reached the figure of 891.[2] This increase, which was carried still further in 1939, had taken place despite internal pressures within the BBC for 'consolidation' on the grounds that there was inadequate studio space, that the Schools Department was housed at some distance from the studios and, above all, the old complaint, that there was not enough money.[3]

The shortage of money was felt even more acutely in 1937, 1938, and 1939 by the Adult Education Section of the BBC, a section which had been brought into very close relation both with the Central Council for School Broadcasting and the Board of Education after the rearrangement of the Council in 1935. 'The foundations of listening to adult talks may be laid during school days', Cameron wrote in 1936.[4] 'The BBC has afforded every opportunity during the past year to the Council's Staff', an official report of the same year noted, 'for getting into touch with what is happening on the Adult Education side and of working in co-operation with those concerned therewith.'[5] The six Regional Education Officers of the BBC in 1939 were engaged both in the organization of schools broadcasting and of adult education, but it had already been decided that the 'listening-end work' in adult education should cease to be a financial obligation of the BBC in 1940. Parliamentary discussions took place in 1937 as to the possibility of transferring the cost of listening-end work in schools education also.

Reith had sounded the Board of Education on this point as early as 1930.[6] In June 1937 he asked Nicolls 'to start the ball rolling again'.[7] 'The whole issue' was, as Graves put it, 'whether

[1] *Cameron to H. H. Cartwright, 13 Apr. 1938.
[2] *W. R. Reid to the Board of Education, 31 May 1938.
[3] *Mary Somerville to Reith, 9 Apr. 1937.
[4] *BBC Press Release, 17 June 1936.
[5] *A. C. Cameron, Policy Revision, 4 Nov. 1936.
[6] See above, p. 20. [7] *Note by Nicolls, 23 Sept. 1937.

it is agreed by the Board of Education that School Broadcasting is now so firmly established that we have done all the listening-end work which we legitimately should, and that it is now some-one else's duty to carry on this work, which is now an important feature of our national educational system.'[1] The Board of Education was never formally sounded, for it was the advice of Sir Henry Richards, a nominated member of the Board on the Central Council, that the Board would be unlikely 'to be pre-pared at present to take any positive action' if the BBC's educa-tional services at the listening end were discontinued. Most of the people inside the Board would 'probably be indifferent to it'.[2] For all the progress that had been made, Reith never realized his hope that what the BBC had started, the com-munity would fully take up.

The BBC's efforts in adult education were less successful than schools broadcasting, although for a time they produced what looked like spectacular results. R. S. Lambert, who was in charge of the first work, wrote in 1927 to members of the Workers' Educational Association, which he had served as a tutor: 'The W.E.A. has long experience and knowledge of what is wanted educationally: the BBC has an instrument of un-paralleled range and power for reaching the mass of the people.'[3] There was vision, therefore, in adult education as in schools broadcasting.

The efforts took practical form, like the first large-scale experiments in schools broadcasting, after the publication of Hadow's *New Ventures in Broadcasting* in 1928. Much earlier, however, a conference had been held at King's College, London, to discuss adult educational talks, and Stobart had told a repre-sentative group of adult educationists that 'the BBC took this side of its work very seriously'.[4] Adult educational talks had been broadcast first in the autumn of 1924, and in April 1927 Lambert had joined the BBC specifically to arrange such pro-grammes. There is a familiar ring in a comment made by Reith

---

[1] *Note by Graves, 23 Sept. 1937.

[2] *Report on an Interview between Rose-Troup and Sir Henry Richards, 2 Dec. 1937.

[3] R. S. Lambert, 'Broadcasting This Winter' in *Highway*, Oct. 1927.

[4] *Minutes of a Conference on Broadcasting in Relation to Adult Education, held at King's College, London, 18 July 1924.

in October 1926 that development of this work awaited the development of 'alternative programmes',[1] but Lambert's appointment coincided with a burst of activity. A series of early evening talks in 1927 was envisaged as the first attempt to organize weekly adult educational programmes as part of a continuing process, and the first 'aid to study' pamphlet, *One Hundred Years of Working Class Progress*, was published in May 1927. At one of many adult-education demonstrations that year the two main speakers were Reith and Harold J. Laski.

The Hadow Report provided a kind of charter for people who were already interested in the possibilities of broadcast adult education. It maintained that broadcast adult education could supplement existing work in adult education without supplanting the voluntary or public agencies which were already in the field. Among its main recommendations were the setting up of 'listening groups', formal or informal, to discuss BBC adult educational programmes, the launching of a 'weekly educational journal', and the creation of a representative Central Council for Adult Education, supported by Area Councils representing local opinion and local organizations.

As in the case of schools broadcasting, an 'interim committee' hammered out the constitution of the new council. It had an impressive membership, including G. H. Gater, who provided a link with the Schools Broadcasting Interim Committee, G. D. H. Cole, Oliver Stanley, Miss Hadow, and Miss Haldane; T. H. Searls represented the British Institute of Adult Education, and the chairman was Lord Justice Sankey. J. W. Brown of the Institute and Lambert were the joint secretaries. Before the Council was brought into existence in November 1928 (with more than forty members and with Siepmann as secretary), the projected educational periodical *The Listener* was already in its first stage of planning and Lambert had been appointed its first editor.[2] Specialist Education Officers were also being appointed in the Regions to undertake both adult educational and schools broadcasting work.

There were many parallels between the organizational pattern for adult education and that for schools broadcasting. The Council was given a small initial grant from the BBC and a

---

[1] *Managing Director's Report to the Board Meeting, 21 Oct. 1926.
[2] For the stormy launching of *The Listener*, see below, pp. 286 ff.

research benefaction of £2,200 from the Carnegie Trust for the encouragement of 'follow-up' work. It had an Executive Committee, with Gater as its first chairman and Cole as its first vice-chairman, a Finance and General Purposes Committee, and a Programmes and Publications Sub-Committee. When Sankey resigned as chairman of the Council on becoming Lord Chancellor in the second Labour Government, William Temple, then Archbishop of York, took his place.

This was a remarkable start, and there were many early successes to report in the organization of 'listening groups'. The first training course was held for group leaders at the University College, Hull, in April 1929, and in the autumn of that year the first comprehensive syllabus was drawn up with the help of members of the new Council.[1] By the winter of 1930–1 there were over a thousand listening groups in existence—200 in the North of England alone—and the first National Conference of Group Leaders was held at the London School of Economics in January 1931. One of the groups had an attendance on one occasion of 123, and Sir William Beveridge found it worth while to go up to Liverpool after giving a series of broadcast talks on unemployment to discuss the series with the Liverpool group.[2] 'Quite apart from the listening groups,' the W.E.A.'s journal commented in 1931, 'the BBC is doing a very important educational service, the full results of which cannot yet be seen. All concerned with adult education should remember that a new ally has suddenly come into the field.'[3]

The ethos of the expansion is reflected in a sentence in the *BBC Year Book* for 1932. 'Russia has a Five-Year Plan; so also has the Central Council for Broadcast Adult Education.' It was careful to add, however, *pace* G. D. H. Cole, that it was 'a plan with a difference, for it is an attempt to foster a natural growth, and not to force the pace unduly'.[4] There was most excitement about expansion in 1931 and 1932, when perhaps the best-remembered series of BBC adult educational programmes was broadcast under the title *The Changing World*. The series ran for six months, and each of the programmes lasted for half an hour

---

[1] For the adult educational background in 1929, see Paper 9 of the Adult Education Committee of the Board of Education, which had been set up in 1921, *Pioneer Work and other Developments in Adult Education* (1929).

[2] *BBC Year Book* (1932), p. 156. For the talks, see above, pp. 41–42.

[3] *Highway*, Oct. 1931.   [4] *BBC Year Book* (1932), p. 175.

instead of the usual twenty minutes. Five special pamphlets were published, along with a 'master pamphlet', *Discussion Groups and How to Run Them*. This pamphlet was also published in Braille. Along with a Board of Education pamphlet, *Adult Education Wireless Listening Groups*, published in 1933, the literature surrounding *The Changing World* transports the reader back into the excitements of the brief hey-day of wireless adult education.[1] It also recalls the extent of prejudice. Reith himself remembers being told by a crusty old diehard in a club that the BBC was 'of course, left wing', and on asking why being given the simple reply, 'Well, look at the title of the series that is on now—"The Changing World".'

The excitement did not last as long as the prejudice, although much useful local work continued to be accomplished. There were many reasons both for the failure to expand and for the ultimate decline. First, the great successes in the field of schools broadcasting diverted more and more professional BBC effort in the provinces towards schools broadcasting rather than adult education. It has always been difficult to maintain momentum in adult education: peaks are followed by troughs in a way that is never true of compulsory child education. For every wave of excitement there is a surfeit of grey routine. Even the waves often look like ripples as they move into history.

Second, whereas the success of schools broadcasting depended above all else on co-operation with teachers and local-educational authorities, the success of adult educational broadcasting depended upon reaching agreement with a number of rival bodies, some extremely cautious, all dominated by their own traditions. The relationship between 'expert' tutor and formal class was a powerful one, particularly when the expert thought of himself as a member of the group and the formal class had social cohesion as well as educational purpose. 'The BBC study group cannot take the place of sustained class work', it was often felt, 'but it may meet the needs of many who at present are not attracted by the offer of formal classes.'[2] This was a reasonable attitude, but it could all too easily be twisted into protectionism, with all the emphasis being placed not on the

---

[1] H.M.S.O., *Adult Education Wireless Listening Groups* (Pamphlet 92, Mar. 1933). See also *The Listener*, 22 Mar. 1933.

[2] W.E.A. Yorkshire North District, *Sixteenth Annual Report* (1930).

size of the potential audience but on competition between the BBC and the voluntary body in relation to the existing audience. The 'listening group' could be branded as 'superficial' and 'ill equipped' and the dream of a greatly expanded adult-education movement could be made to end all too soon. 'Many keen members of the broadcast audience prefer individual listening in their homes to class work', wrote one spokesman of adult education, R. Peers, in 1934. 'Immediately we cannot expect to receive flocks of new students from this source.'[1] Co-operation between the BBC and other adult education bodies, therefore, was never as real as it might have been. To a few of the bodies the BBC appeared almost as an interloper: to others it failed to communicate the sense of unprecedented opportunity which had fired the Hadow Committee. The most effective co-operation was in the training of listening-group leaders which was only possible with the assistance of the extra-mural departments of universities and the Workers' Educational Association.

Third, there were organizational difficulties in the BBC's own structure, both at the top and the bottom. The place of adult education in the BBC's central organization was never secure. In February 1931 it hived off from the Talks Department and became a separate department under the direction of Siepmann; in February 1932 it became a department of a new Talks Branch when Siepmann replaced Hilda Matheson as Director of Talks; in September 1934 it was fully merged in the Talks Branch, losing its departmental identity. Behind these vicissitudes there were not only personal differences but deeper uncertainties about what exactly was the relationship between talks and organized adult education.[2] At the base of the pyramid there was no local organization equivalent to that of the W.E.A. branch, and in the middle it proved impossible to put into practice the Hadow Committee's project of Area Councils. Under the original scheme, fourteen Area Councils were to be set up: only four, however, came into existence. The first was in the West Midlands, and this was followed by a North-Western Council, a Western Council, and a Council for Yorkshire. The rest of the country was left blank. In Scotland only Lanark and Dumfries had a committee organization, and there was no committee for Wales.

[1] R. Peers, *Adult Education in Practice* (1934), p. 86.   [2] See above, pp. 141–3.

By the time the first 'Five-Year Plan' was due to expire, there was no thought of a second. In the nine months before the life of the first Central Council came to an end—in July 1934—there was much talk, instead, of 'streamlining' and 'rationalization'. It was decided first in April 1934, in the light of the findings of Dawnay's Programme Revision Committee, that the adult-education periods should be cut from five to three a week.[1] It was decided later that the Central Council should be dissolved and replaced by a smaller Central Advisory Committee for Broadcast Education with no executive powers. The Area Councils were to be reorganized and their number reduced to seven. Both the Central Committee and the Area Councils were no longer to include representatives of other bodies: instead, they were to consist of nominated members, or in the case of the Central Committee, representatives of the Areas. In the background of these proposals was a powerful financial motive. The BBC made it as clear as it could that it could not regard as 'permanent' its administrative and financial responsibility for 'listening-end work' in adult education. The new system of Area Councils was to be 'the basic machinery for the development of broadcast Adult Education', but the BBC hoped that it would soon be able, 'through their advice and assistance to transfer, in due course, its financial and administrative responsibility in respect of all listening-end work to some other body or bodies'.[2]

The Central Advisory Committee came into existence in December 1934 and disappeared at the end of two years. By then the break had already been made, and the changes of 1937 merely ratified it. On 1 January 1937 listening-end work passed into the hands of an autonomous organization based on the Area Councils and loosely linked through a Central Co-ordinating Committee. The chairman of the Central Committee was Principal J. H. Nicholson of Hull University College and its secretary was A. C. Cameron. The transmission-end was organized on quite a new basis with a Talks Advisory Committee, chaired by Sir Walter Moberly, to consider all talks, including adult education. There was no doubt about the shift of policy— away from the adult education audience to the general audience.

[1] See above, p. 48.
[2] *BBC Press Release, 14 Dec. 1934.

Before the new bodies met, an internal memorandum announcing three weekly series of talks suitable for discussion groups emphasized that 'it must be understood that these series form part of the Corporation's general talks programme and that, coming at important listening periods, they must be of interest to a wider audience than is likely to listen in groups'.[1]

The BBC provided the executive offices and the office space for the Area Councils and the Central Co-ordinating Committee; it also gave an annual grant, which it insisted would expire in 1940. The Central Co-ordinating Committee was once more constituted on a representative basis, however, and under Nicholson's chairmanship it managed to win a considerable measure of support from other bodies in adult education. It had its own Programme Sub-Committee, under the chairmanship of Sir Francis Acland, and it made suggestions to the BBC for series of talks suitable for listening groups. Cameron saw its role as providing for what he called, 'without disrespect', 'the second eleven' of adult education, those who 'took what they were doing seriously but hesitated to incur the obligations of formal adult education'. In the first eleven he put the W.E.A. and the extra-mural departments.[2] That there was still a demand for group listening was shown by the statistics for the winter of 1937–8. Altogether 1,393 groups were recorded as having listened to one or more series of talks.[3] Among the groups were day-time classes of unemployed, for whom special financial provision had been made. 'There is no specific pattern for a group', Cameron wrote in 1937; 'they may range from the most informal gatherings of two or three friends round the fireside of one of them to grant-earning classes formally run by Local Education Authorities under an instructor paid by them.'[4]

Cameron offered these facts and opinions to the General Advisory Committee of the BBC, which discussed 'group listening' for the last time on 15 June 1938. It was an interesting, if academic, discussion, for the Chairman of Governors, R. C. Norman, made it clear that the BBC would not in any circum-

---

[1] *Memorandum regarding the Future Organization of the Group Listening Movement, Oct. 1936.

[2] *A. C. Cameron, *Report to the General Advisory Council of the BBC*, May 1938.

[3] *Ibid.

[4] A. C. Cameron, 'Broadcasting and Adult Education' in *Highway*, Nov. 1937.

stances contemplate an extension of its financial assistance 'at the listening end' beyond 1940. The General Advisory Committee, which included two people who had sat on the original Hadow Committee of 1926, paid tribute to the work which had been done, and a number of speakers urged that it should continue. Among them were Sir Walter Citrine, who said he believed that television would provide an impetus to group discussion in the future, and Sir William Beveridge, who expressed doubt concerning the BBC's decision that the finance and organization of listening groups fell outside its permanent province. 'Distribution and consumption were at least as important as production, and it was necessary for the BBC not only to provide the best possible programmes and engineering arrangements but also to get the broadcasts right into the minds of the listeners.' Moreover, in an age of international tension there was need to reinforce democracy at the grass roots. The resistance of the British people to propaganda depended upon the informal discussion of matters of general interest in the public house and elsewhere. 'The BBC ought to do everything in its power to encourage the spirit of local leadership which prompted men with a little more intelligence than their fellows to initiate discussion and criticism.'

More interesting even than these general comments was the speech of a Mr. Etherington, a listening-group leader. He described how his group had been in existence for seven years in a tiny Yorkshire village, with a population of 300, where previously there had been no adult education of any kind. Practically without exception the people had had no education other than the elementary school, and many of the older ones had left school at the age of twelve or thirteen. 'Yet nearly all of them have a much higher measure of intelligence than is generally supposed and such people are very keen to do something in the nature of mental recreation or further education if the right means can be found.' They had organized a most successful group, first in the village school, then, when the seats proved too hard, in the school-house. Their formal meetings were supplemented by further informal meetings 'in the village brickyard or near the railway line'. The most important effect of the group, however, had been that 'after a year or two, whenever there was anything in the village which wanted doing, whether it was raising money for a playing field, or running Coronation celebrations or badgering the District Council into giving us a water supply, it was the members of my group who were the people willing to take responsibility and to start things going'.[1]

This was the authentic voice of adult education. But Norman had to return to his brief. The BBC had undertaken a pioneer experiment in adult education. It was not itself an adult-education authority, and it did not wish to interfere with local education authorities. The BBC was getting near to receiving the full 100 per cent. of licence revenue from the government and there were many urgent claims, including those of television, on that income. Broadcast talks for groups would continue: the groups must learn, however, to fend for themselves.

By the time that 1940 came, many members of the pre-war groups were already in the Forces, and once the issues were raised again seriously inside the BBC, television could not be left out of the reckoning. That the work of adult education itself involved complex psychological and social issues was never in doubt. Nor was it in doubt that there was an undercurrent of resistance. 'We can imagine no more unsuitable medium for adult education than a state-owned service which enters the homes of people of every age, sex, religion, political colour, standard of intelligence, and rank in society', the *Glasgow Evening Citizen* had declared comprehensively in 1927.[2]

The term 'adult education' was used as sparingly as possible by the BBC between 1927 and 1939. There was also a growing feeling that it should not monopolize 'peak hours'. As the Wireless Organizations Advisory Committee put it in a resolution of April 1927 at the very beginning of the period: 'While every encouragement should be given to the use of broadcasting for adult education, no additional matter of this nature should be introduced into the programmes after 7 p.m.'[3] The *Daily Mirror* went further. 'The indulgent listener is middle-aged. Around him fuming impatiently sit all the younger members of his family. They want to be amused. They do not want to be educated.'[4]

[1] *General Advisory Council, *Précis of Discussion*, 15 June 1938.
[2] *Glasgow Evening Citizen*, 12 Jan. 1927.
[3] *Letter of the Wireless Organizations Advisory Committee to Miss H. Matheson, 3 May 1927.   [4] *Daily Mirror*, 10 Jan. 1927.

5. Religion

I F there was a danger of adult education impinging on the peak hours of evening listening, there was an ever-present threat to 'entertainment' during the Sunday peak hours, when religion set the mood of broadcasting and shaped the pattern of programmes. 'We began by assuming that we are living in a Christian land', Stobart wrote a few months before the Corporation was founded, 'and that services were to be Christian and Catholic in the broadest sense.'[1] Sunday was a special day set apart from the rest of the week. If the radio could not be silent, it should not pollute the air with programmes which would offend the Christian. There was more controversy about this aspect of BBC policy during the 1930s than about anything else. To the critics there was a 'disdainful flouting of millions of listeners': 'this day of all days should be for "peak" listening and should include the worthiest efforts of the best programme builders'.[2] To the BBC Sunday was the day of all days in a different sense.

The controversy was sharpened by the fact that it was publicly known that Reith himself was personally behind the policy, that he had initiated it, and that he defended it against all inside as well as outside challenge. One English bishop went so far as to claim that the BBC's attitude to religion was 'entirely due to the faith of one man',[3] and Reith himself told the Archbishop of York that he was 'more anxious about the general religious policy of the BBC in matters great and small than about anything else'.[4]

In January 1927 almost all the religious broadcasting transmitted by the BBC took place on Sundays, and there was no broadcasting at all on that day until half-past three in the afternoon. Religious policy was discussed in detail by a Central Religious Advisory Committee which had first met, under the chairmanship of Dr. Garbett, then Bishop of Southwark, in

[1] *Methodist Times*, 25 Feb. 1926.
[2] S. A. Moseley, *Broadcasting In My Time*, pp. 161, 167.
[3] Dr. C. S. Woodward, the Bishop of Bristol and Chairman of the West Regional Religious Advisory Committee in the *Western Daily Press*, 29 July 1935.
[4] *Reith to the Archbishop of York, 20 June 1930.

May 1923: the fact that this was the first of the BBC's Advisory Committees reveals the basic priority given to religious broadcasting.[1] In the provinces there was a network of religious advisory committees guiding each Station Director in the organization of Sunday religious services—with an understanding, dating from June 1925, that no services should be broadcast at the times of ordinary church and chapel services.[2] 'With the exception of those somewhat infrequent occasions when an ordinary service is broadcast in full from a cathedral or church, the wireless religious services are held outside the regular church hours.'[3] Every second Sunday in the month there was an undenominational, national service from St. Martin-in-the-Fields.

It was from St. Martin's that the Rev. H. R. L. (Dick) Sheppard preached in a style that made Christianity live for the ordinary listener. His was the kind of Christianity which Reith wanted the BBC to expound—'thorough-going, optimistic and manly', unconcerned with the 'narrow interpretation of dogma' and centred on 'the application of the teaching of Christ to everyday life'.[4] Of Sheppard's preaching Reith was to write, 'it was the work of a man who understood profoundly the needs and sorrows and fears of humanity. The subtle mingling of humour and sharp visual imagery and sincerity had an aptness and reality which more complex sermons would have lacked entirely.' Above all, Sheppard, as a perfect broadcaster, could appeal direct to the individual listener, as if he were talking not to a vast audience but to each member of it alone.[5]

Other preachers broadcast from other churches and chapels on the fourth Sunday of the month, and on the third Sunday of the month there was a Children's Service. Once a week there was a Sunday Bible reading, and once a month there was a Sunday missionary talk. The other regular features were the Week's Good Cause which followed the evening service and the Epilogue which brought the day's programmes to a close 'with its quiet suggestions through hymn and reading'.[6] On weekdays

[1] See *The Birth of Broadcasting*, pp. 241–2.
[2] Ibid., p. 274.
[3] *BBC Handbook* (1928), p. 131.
[4] Ibid.
[5] H. Marshall and others, *Dick Sheppard by His Friends* (1938), p. 81.
[6] *BBC Handbook* (1928), p. 133.

the only religious service was a weekly Evensong from Westminster Abbey on Thursday afternoons 'for the special benefit
of the sick'.

There were three most important developments between 1927
and 1933, when as part of the reorganization scheme[1] the Rev.
F. A. Iremonger was appointed Religious Director of the BBC.
The first was the introduction of the daily service; the second,
an increase in the scope and volume of religious broadcasting
on Sundays; and the third, a growing gap between Sunday
programmes (and hours) and those of the rest of the week.

The daily service was the product not of BBC initiative but of
private pressure. In June 1926 Reith received a letter from an
unknown correspondent, Miss K. M. Cordeux of The Cottage,
Bushey Grove Road, Watford. It was headed 'Sunday evening'.
'Are letters still arriving for more Services to be broadcast?' she
asked Reith. 'I am assured that lots of people have written to
you and names still come to me. I hope, however, to get many
more. It would be such a pleasure to me if I might meet you
some day. If I were in town could you spare me time?' Reith's
secretary replied: 'Mr. Reith has received your letter of the 11th
and asked me to reply as he is so exceedingly busy. Unfortunately he has an unusual amount of detailed work on his hands
just at present. . . . He suggests, however, that you should come
up here and meet Mr. J. C. Stobart, who handles all matters
concerned with our Services and Religious Addresses.'[2]

This might have been the beginning of one of a thousand
brief exchanges of letters in the BBC. Instead, it drew the BBC
—and Miss Cordeux—into a prolonged and quite exceptional
correspondence, which was conducted on the side of the BBC
by almost every important official and on Miss Cordeux's side
with an extraordinary combination of simplicity and force. Miss
Cordeux had already sent a letter to the *Radio Times*, which was
printed in the May issue which never reached the public because
of the General Strike. In it she had appealed for a daily service
each evening for the benefit chiefly of invalids and hospital
patients, and her letter had been given an editorial postscript.

---

[1] See above, p. 25; below, p. 242.
[2] *K. M. Cordeux to Reith, 11 July 1926; Miss Stanley to Miss Cordeux, 13
July 1926.

At Reith's suggestion, the letter was reprinted in the *Radio Times*, but did not appear until November 1927. 'A large number of those who listen-in long to hear something daily of God and his love', she began. 'Already five thousand signatures and letters have been received by the writer testifying to this. . . . We hope that the time may now have come for such urgent need to be met. Few, if any, listeners will grudge say twenty minutes out of eight and a half hours a day, to bring peace and consolation to the sick, the lonely and the sad.'[1]

Miss Cordeux was thinking of an Evensong service after the end of Children's Hour, but this proposal was not very welcome to the programme planners. When talk of 'alternative programmes' suggested that it would soon be easier to meet the demands for new kinds of programmes, Miss Cordeux shrewdly wrote again asking at least for a trial run.[2] Stobart told Miss Cordeux that it was necessary 'to proceed gradually in this matter': in private, he said that while 'one cannot but admire the pertinacity of Miss Cordeux, I find it hard to gauge the strength of this demand. Apart from Catholics (Roman and Anglo) the number of those who attend a daily service must be infinitesimal. It is this and the fear of making unreasonable demands upon programme time that has held me back. I wonder whether a Morning Service might meet the demand.'[3]

It was the idea of the Morning Service which won—only after experimental transmissions had begun from 5XX (Daventry) on 2 January 1928. The hour of 10.15 was free, and after the first broadcast listeners were asked to say whether they thought the idea and the time were satisfactory. Within two weeks 7,000 letters of appreciation had been received and very few complaints or criticisms. 'I have just been listening to that lovely little Service from Daventry', Miss Cordeux wrote at once, 'and joining in it with all my soul. It was so beautiful and reverent as it came through—and one feels that it may be the small beginning of so much.' This time Stobart did not hesitate. 'I think you may take it that henceforward the Daily Service is an established feature of our programmes.'[4]

[1] *Radio Times*, 11 Nov. 1927.
[2] *K. M. Cordeux to Reith, 1 Feb. 1927.
[3] *Stobart to Miss Cordeux, 5 Aug. 1926; Stobart to Reith, 23 Sept. 1927.
[4] *K. M. Cordeux to Stobart, 2 Jan. 1928; Stobart to Miss Cordeux, 3 Jan. 1928.

SUFFERERS and OTHERS "LISTENING-IN."

How many are there who "listen-in" who long to hear something daily of God and His love?

We are told of the great numbers of wireless sets installed in hospitals and nursing homes, and we rejoice. But do those who so generously bring these gifts within reach of the pillows of the sick, realise the feelings and thoughts of those who lie there suffering?

Life is a very real affair, and often so terribly grim to a large proportion of them (as well as to many others among the vast audience) that secular music—however sweet and inspiring some of it may be—and variety-turns, talks and suchlike—however desirable and helpful as instruction or pastime, fail altogether to satisfy the desperate need of something deeper, whereon the soul may rest.

Surely the time has come for such need to be met, even though a section of listeners incline to raise objections on the ground that they personally would be bored. And, after all, we know that these are really warm-hearted people who will, for the most part, cheerfully consent to give up half-an-hour a day—say just after the children's hour—when invalids are ready to settle down for the night.

Indeed, since there is such wonderful opportunity of bringing peace and hope to those who are sick or sad, dare we, *dare any of us*, any longer withhold them?

Almost every day there are some amongst those who "listen-in" who listen for the last time before passing on into eternity.

Will all listeners who are in sympathy with this suggestion please sign the appeal? When complete to be posted to

K. M. C.,

THE COTTAGE,

WATFORD.

We greatly appreciate the Sunday evening Wireless Services, and the Evensong relayed weekly from Westminster Abbey; but all the more because these are precious to so many do we plead earnestly for a *daily* consecrated half-hour.

We believe that we shall get this. Already nearly five thousand letters and signatures have been received. Many of them of a most touching nature, from blind, bedridden and aged folk. Bishops, clergy, ministers of all denominations, doctors, sisters and nurses have united to encourage us to press on.

Please send a long list of signatures without delay, remembering that each *one* counts.

[P.T.O. FOR SIGNATURES.

19. Miss Cordeux's Printed Appeal, 1926

Within a month, Miss Cordeux was asking for daily Evensong too. 'Now that the dear little Morning Service seems to have taken good root and be thriving shall I ask for another quarter of an hour daily as Evensong?' Again Stobart was cautious. 'I do not think it would be wise to ask for more at present, or indeed until we can offer alternative programmes to the majority of listeners. The Morning Service might have had a rather different reception if it had cut across anything to which the entertainment public were accustomed and attached.'[1] Miss Cordeux was not put off. She went on collecting more signatures and bided her time until it was announced that alternative programmes were on the way. 'I feel rather like Oliver asking for more', she wrote in November 1929, but her feelings did not stop her from asking.[2]

She did not get what she wanted even when alternative programmes were generally introduced under the Regional Scheme. 'I don't think alternative programmes make any difference at all', Graves told Stobart in November 1929, 'as D.P's [Roger Eckersley's] feeling is not dictated so much [sic] on the question of available time as on the undesirability in his opinion of putting in any more regular religious work. He feels that we have reached a point beyond which it would be unwise to go.'[3] It is interesting to have this comment on Eckersley's views, for in his autobiography he recalls that he was never 'altogether at one with the Corporation's religious policy in those distant days'. He wanted alternatives to the religious service, longer programme hours, less rigid taboos on what was broadcast, and 'no yielding to the views of "a vociferous (Sabbatarian) minority"'.[4] He said later that if his inclinations had been followed, the BBC would never have lost large numbers of listeners to the foreign commercial stations.[5]

Miss Cordeux never got her daily Evensong. Stobart replied dutifully that 'we might easily make a grave mistake if we overdid the religious element in our broadcasting policy'.[6] The same

[1] *K. M. Cordeux to Stobart, 27 Jan. 1928; Stobart to Miss Cordeux, 31 Jan. 1928.
[2] *K. M. Cordeux to Reith, 6 Nov. 1929.
[3] *Graves to Stobart, 26 Nov. 1929.
[4] *R. H. Eckersley, The BBC and All That (1946), pp. 163–4.
[5] See below, pp. 363–4.
[6] *Stobart to Miss Cordeux, 27 Dec. 1929.

reply was given by successive BBC officials, ending with Ire-monger. Beadle told her in May 1933 that there was not 'the slightest chance of the request being granted', however many signatures she collected: 'it is probable that a larger number of signatures could be obtained to an appeal for an increase in various types of entertainment'.[1] 'I am very much afraid that it is impossible for us to fall in with your suggestions', said Ire-monger, without giving any reasons at all.[2] Finally, Reith looked behind the voluminous correspondence to the tenacious lady who had started it all. 'Are we irrevocably opposed', he asked in 1935, 'to an evening five minutes of the sort she wishes?'[3] 'Yes,' said Dawnay, 'I am afraid that this decision will cause you much disappointment, but it was reached only after we had thoroughly weighed the claims of our listeners as a whole and the general make-up of our daily programmes.'[4]

If daily Evensong was not conceded, the Morning Service went from strength to strength. From 12 January 1928 onwards it was broadcast from London 2LO as well as Daventry, and from December 1929 onwards from all BBC stations. The service, which lasted for a quarter of an hour, was anonymously conducted and usually consisted of a hymn, a few prayers, a psalm, a Bible reading, another prayer, and a closing hymn. On Wednesdays and Saturdays, when the BBC Singers were not available, there was no choir and the psalms were read. The early services were all conducted by the Rev. Hugh Johnston of St. Martin-in-the-Fields, who has described the form and content which he deliberately tried to vary.[5] From January 1932 onwards he was no longer solely responsible, and Iremonger took it under his personal control after his appointment as Religious Director in 1933.

The service seemed to offer what Sydney Moseley called 'a simple message of cheerful, religious comfort, not narrowed or crippled by denominational prejudice or inhibition'.[6] Another more 'highbrow' writer chose very similar words. The Morning Service along with the Epilogue were 'definitely new both in conception and in method', he suggested. 'They are,

[1] *G. C. Beadle to Miss Cordeux, 29 May 1933.
[2] *F. A. Iremonger to Miss Cordeux, 18 Dec. 1933.
[3] *Reith to Dawnay, 5 Apr. 1935.   [4] *Dawnay to Reith, 24 Apr. 1935.
[5] See H. Johnston, *When Two or Three* (1932).
[6] *Broadcasting In My Time*, p. 169.

in essence, a presentation of a crystallised Christian thought, each day and each week, altogether removed from the customary excrescences of creed, verbiage and circumlocution.'[1]

Some indication of the popularity of the service is given by the fact that it inspired more correspondence from listeners than any other BBC programme. When the prayers used in the service were published in 1936, over 80,000 copies were sold within less than three months.[2] The service was certainly unique of its kind in the world.

The increase in the scope and volume of religious broadcasting on Sundays followed naturally from the increase in programme hours and the growing willingness to develop outside broadcasting. Although a new religious studio was designed for the new Broadcasting House by Edward Maufe, the architect of Guildford Cathedral, by 1933 there were far more outside broadcast services than services from the studio.[3] The main reason for this was the preference of listeners. They made it plain in the press and in letters to the BBC that they liked to feel 'the atmosphere of an actual church' and to know that they were linked with a genuine congregation. A subsidiary reason was that more churches were anxious to have their services broadcast as early suspicions both of broadcasting and of the BBC disappeared. The churches soon found that broadcasting actually increased the size of their congregations. Thus, at Chichester, the Dean reported that many inhabitants of the small town attended the cathedral for the first time when the service was broadcast. In Edinburgh the Minister of St. Cuthbert's hesitated for a long time before consenting to put on a broadcast service at 8 o'clock instead of the traditional 6.30. When the service took place, the church was crowded to the doors. At St. Martin-in-the-Fields it was found difficult to persuade the 6.30 congregation to leave the church before the 8 o'clock broadcast service began, and many people sat through both services.[4] During the 1920s the BBC established close and

---

[1] E. H. Robinson, *Broadcasting and A Changing Civilisation* (1935), p. 101.

[2] *New Every Morning* (1936).

[3] For the design of the studio, see *Broadcasting House Souvenir Book* (1932); *BBC Year Book* (1932), p. 70; *The Listener*, 18 Apr. 1932 (for the first service broadcast from the studio).

[4] *'Notes on Religious Broadcasting' (July 1930), p. 13.

continuous relations with a number of churches and cathedrals. Canterbury Cathedral, York Minster, Manchester Cathedral, St. George's Chapel, Windsor, and Liverpool Cathedral, for example, were all permanently wired for periodical religious broadcasts.

The danger in the extension of outside broadcasting, even to the cathedrals, was that 'the standard of religious addresses' might fall as 'the net was cast wide'.[1] This had sometimes been felt to be the case when the local stations had been quite free to plan their own religious broadcasts. In an effort to raise standards by controlling the procedures, the BBC issued a brochure, *Hints to Sunday Speakers*, in 1928. 'The address, which should in all cases be read,' it began, 'is limited to ten minutes, and must avoid sectarian propaganda or provocative argument. It is intended primarily to be of a practical nature, of such a kind as may prove helpful to all listeners.' Manuscripts had to be sent to the BBC ten days before the broadcast. 'You are asked to remember', speakers were told, 'that your vast audience is not a crowd or a congregation but various individuals to whom you are speaking in the intimacy of their homes.' They were also to remember that listeners were apt to stop listening at will and 'thousands of them will "switch off" their sets if the opening is unattractive'.

These directions must have cramped the style of those preachers who trusted to the power of the spirit to guide their words. In fact, it is recounted that after one famous Edinburgh preacher had been told that he had to write out his sermon ten days before broadcasting, he replied to the BBC, 'I have never done this before and I am not starting now'.[2] Extemporary prayer caused difficulties also—notably 'preaching prayer' of the type expressed in a Scottish prayer beginning 'Paradoxical as it may seem, O Lord'.[3] There is no evidence, however, that broadcasting destroyed pulpit eloquence. It favoured direct sermons, but it raised the standard of exposition and made for economy and relevance.

A second element of control was the development of a 'rota system', linking the National and Regional programmes. On

---

[1] *Reith to Eckersley, 2 Sept. 1926, quoting a Canon of Westminster Abbey.
[2] Quoted by M. Dinwiddie in the BBC Programme *The Scattered Seed*, broadcast on 30 Dec. 1962.   [3] Ibid.

the first Sunday of the month in 1931 a London studio service was given on the National programme with 'an eminent preacher': there was no regional alternative from London, but contrasting regional services could be arranged by Regional Directors if they wished. On the second Sunday of the month St. Martin-in-the-Fields had sole command of all BBC stations. On the third Sunday there were contrasting denominational services on the National and Regional programmes. On the fourth Sunday on all stations a service was broadcast simultaneously, 'usually of the Cathedral type', and on the fifth Sunday, when there was a fifth Sunday, there was a studio service on the National programme for 'such bodies as the Brotherhood Movement, the Salvation Army and the Quakers', with regional contrasts from the provinces. Even this intricate system did not always guarantee contrast. On 15 June 1930, by a coincidence, three of the principal stations in the country chose a Roman Catholic service.

The denominational range was wide, including, in the early days, at least one Unitarian, Dr. Gow, and a number of Moravians, but there were no broadcasts from Christian Scientists or Christadelphians. Membership of the Free Church Council became something of a test of Nonconformist claims. At the opposite end of the religious spectrum, Catholic broadcasts never included the broadcasting of Mass, even though some continental radio stations broadcast Mass regularly. In the middle of the spectrum, an attempt was made to 'represent' the various types of Anglican churchmanship, although there seems to have been a predominance of 'Broad Churchmen' and of clergymen who had served with the Forces during the First World War.

Successive *BBC Handbooks* sought to define what was often extremely elusive, the attempt to place broadcasting within 'the mainstream of the Christian tradition'. In 1932, for example, the *Handbook* reaffirmed that 'broadcast services are not the occasion for sectarian propaganda. All denominations alike welcome the opportunity of the great audience which wireless affords them and are content to preach the gospel of Christ on its universal terms of love and charity to all men, to dwell rather on that which unites than on that which divides.'[1] A further

---

[1] *BBC Year Book* (1932), p. 216.

statement in 1935, after Iremonger had been in charge of religious policy for nearly two years, was even fuller. The BBC's policy

has been—and is—in range, to 'tolerate the tolerable'; in method, to be continually mindful of the almost endless variation in the spiritual and intellectual attainment of a wireless audience; and, in message, to stress the fundamental truths of personal and corporate religion. Merely to state these ideals is to expose the difficulty of fulfilling them; in practice, they mean that facilities for broadcasting are given to ministers of all important denominations that can be said to be in the mainstream of the Christian tradition; that no attempt is made to satisfy the need of every kind of listener in the same broadcast; and that, while nothing could be less effective than a religious 'lowest common denominator', it has been found possible to disseminate a spiritual 'highest common factor' from which the listener can profit and of which no church need be ashamed.[1]

Decisions about 'range' and 'balance' and 'the mainstream of the Christian tradition' were taken by the Central Religious Advisory Committee, which by 1931 had fourteen members, representative of the main denominations. Garbett was still chairman, and his colleagues included five Anglicans, five Free Church members, two Roman Catholics, one of whom was Father C. C. Martindale, S.J., and the Rev. H. R. L. Sheppard as a 'supernumerary'. None of the members was a layman. There were also five Regional Advisory Committees, including a Scottish Committee presided over by the Rev. Professor Archibald Main, and to assist in the co-ordination of the national system three representatives of the Regional Committees sat on the Central Committee. Reith always attended meetings of the Central Committee along with other representatives of the BBC.

It was the task of this committee to ensure that the allocation of services and speakers among different denominations was 'fair'. This task, which might have been difficult, was successfully accomplished with little strain. It was not thought of as an arithmetical exercise or a scheme based on proportional representation. Almost all the decisions of the committee were unanimous, and the spirit of its meetings seems to have been genuinely ecumenical. It is probable, indeed, that radio—along

[1] *BBC Annual* (1935), pp. 66–67.

with other instruments of mass communication—has favoured
ecumenical influences inside the churches by making it possible
—and necessary—for preachers of one denomination to address
members of another and by requiring spokesmen of different
denominations to serve as colleagues on committees like the
C.R.A.C.

BBC policy favoured ecumenical influences in a more specific
way. Reith was anxious that emphasis should be placed on the
points where Christians agreed and not where they disagreed.
He achieved his wish. Thus, when the ban on controversy was
lifted in 1928, the C.R.A.C. issued a public statement that 'the
removal of the ban on controversy in regard to religion creates
a new position for the BBC in theory rather than in practice.
The responsibility remains with the BBC to see that nothing is
broadcast that is likely to provoke or offend large numbers of
their Christian audience. It can still be assumed that the policy
of religious broadcasting has the support of the vast majority.
This policy excludes sectarian propaganda or contentious argument. The Religious Advisory Committee will still guide in the
choice of speakers and in other questions of procedure in the
sphere of religious activities.'[1]

There were criticisms that Christianity without controversy
lacked 'bite' and 'depth' and that emphasis upon the more
cheerful aspects of the Christian message robbed Christianity of
much of its subtlety. The Roman Catholic Archbishop of Liverpool and the Bishop of Salford argued in 1928, for instance, that
'emasculated Christianity' should be replaced by the broadcast
of 'very definite doctrines so long as this is done without denun-
ciation of other creeds'.[2] Such thoughts were also in the mind of
Canon E. G. Selwyn when he moved in the Lower House of
the Convocation of Canterbury in 1930 that a committee should
be set up to report on 'the religious value of broadcast services
and their bearing on public worship'. More intellectual Christian teaching over the radio was required, he argued, with
greater precision of statement. Listeners were becoming tired of
constantly being told to be better Christians.[3] Selwyn's resolution was carried, and a committee was appointed under the

---

[1] For the lifting of the ban, see above, p. 129. *BBC Press Release, Mar. 1928.
[2] *Summary of the Views of the Archbishop of Liverpool and the Bishop of
Salford, 3 Apr. 1928.   [3] *The Times*, 14 Feb. 1930.

chairmanship of the Bishop of Ely, Dr. White-Thomson. Its
Report was very favourable both to broadcasting and to the
BBC in particular, and the two Houses of Convocation passed
'emphatic resolutions' in January 1931 recording 'grateful
appreciation of the service rendered to the cause of religion by
the BBC'.[1] The Report stated that the effect of religious broadcasting had been exceedingly valuable since it had brought
'religion once again into the market place'. It added, however,
that 'more definite instruction should be given as to what
a Christian ought to know and believe and do for his soul's
health'.[2]

Both the BBC and the C.R.A.C. were sensitive to the dangers
of emasculated versions of Christianity. They had never tried to
deny that 'people whose only religious contact is through listening miss some of the most essential influences of religion'.[3] As
early as 1929 and 1930 they had arranged series of talks on such
subjects as 'The Psychology of Religion', 'Politics and Society
in the Old Testament', and 'The Beginnings of Christian
Theology'. They had also contemplated religious 'features'—
with a mild disagreement between Stobart and the 'Research
Section' as to who should plan them.[4] The most ambitious series
of talks planned in the early 1930s was *God and the World Through
Christian Eyes*, broadcast in 1933.[5] Stobart made it clear to the press
that they would not seek to soothe rather than to search. 'Until
recently we expected preachers not to be controversial. The
word we should use nowadays is not "controversial" but "offen-
sive" or "injurious". We want to avoid anything that may offend
the feelings of another Christian.'[6] The dangers of radio as
a medium of religious broadcasting, as well as its opportunities,
were frankly faced in the BBC's own *Year Book* for 1933. 'Any

---

[1]   *The Times*, 24 Jan. 1931; Reith, Diary, 23 Jan. 1931.
[2]   Report of a Joint Committee of the Convocation of Canterbury, *The Religious
Value of Broadcast Services and their Bearing on Public Worship* (1931). Canon Selwyn
was on the Committee which also included Canon Gray Rogers and the Rev.
W. P. G. McCormick ('Pat' McCormick), who succeeded Sheppard at St. Martin-
in-the-Fields. (See R. J. Northcott, *Pat McCormick* (1941).)
[3]   BBC statement quoted in the Report of the Joint Committee, p. 3.
[4]   *The disagreement was stated in a number of memoranda of July 1929.
[5]   *BBC Press Release, 6 Oct. 1932. The lectures lasted for half an hour and were
followed by prayers and hymns. 'The purpose is to give a connected and definite
exposition of the basic principles of the Christian religion for the benefit of thinking
men and women.'
[6]   *Morning Post*, 28 Oct. 1932.

clergyman's advice necessarily loses that quality of point, vigour and strength when it has to be broadened to meet the spiritual needs of unknown millions.'[1]

Criticisms from religious bodies never ceased during the 1930s. 'England is already suffering from a mild form of Christianity which prevents her from catching the real thing', the Bishop of Southampton complained in 1935; 'I fear that wireless services give inoculation of the mildest form of Christianity yet discovered.'[2] A Roman Catholic Radio Guild was founded in the same year to press for more Roman Catholic services of a more proselytizing kind, and its sponsors even argued that there should be a separate Catholic radio station.[3] Militant Protestants felt that Roman Catholics had too much time on the air. There was a storm of anti-Papal feeling in 1930 when a Roman Catholic preacher prayed 'for our separated brethren'—the prayer was not used in Roman Catholic services after this date —and whenever Roman Catholic celebrations were broadcast, there was always a vocal and hostile response from some listeners. Services from St. Martin-in-the-Fields were frequently attacked from many sides for their 'colourless undenominationalism' and even for their 'monopoly', and in March 1936 the C.R.A.C. itself agreed that outside speakers should broadcast in the St. Martin's services.

There were quite different currents of criticism also. The strongest-moving was that from the 'left'. Certain sects were being kept from the microphone altogether—Fundamentalists along with Free-thinkers, the first because of their doctrines, the second because of their lack of them. Unitarians also, despite Reith's personal interest in their views,[4] were usually excluded on the grounds that their views did not fall within 'the mainstream of the Christian tradition'.[5] Other sects which were always excluded were Christian Scientists, Spiritualists, and Mormons—Reith had a number of private complaints about their exclusion—and there was no broadcasting of worship from Jewish synagogues. Although the National Secular Society con-

---

[1] *BBC Year Book* (1933), p. 188.
[2] *Manchester Guardian*, 7 Oct. 1935.
[3] *Catholic Times*, 1 Mar. 1935.   [4] See *Into the Wind*, pp. 194–5.
[5] *There were, in fact, eleven Unitarian services on different wavelengths between 1934 and 1939. See 'Memorandum on the Allotment of Religious Services to the Churches', 5 May 1939.

sistently attacked the BBC's religious policy on rationalist grounds, there was sometimes a more comprehensive note of protest. 'Surely it would be the sound democratic method in a country which is officially Christian to yield space generously from time to time to the reasoned expression of opposing arguments, and to allow free thinkers and adherents of the less populated sects at any rate a hearing now and then. There is something timid, high handed and medieval about the scant consideration given by our radio authority to the unorthodox in religion as well as in politics.'[1]

The BBC did not accept the notion of 'open access' to the microphone for all religious or humanist groups, any more than it accepted the notion of open access for Churchill. Nor did it consider that in a society where there were multiple means of expression its own attitude was 'undemocratic'. It wanted the conduct of its religious services to command the assent of the great majority of its listeners. Some of its services undoubtedly accomplished this. During the dark days of October 1931, for example, the Rev. W. H. Elliott, at Reith's personal suggestion, began a weekly series of broadcasts from St. Michael's, Chester Square, which continued each week until 1936 and created unprecedented interest.[2] When there was the first break in the broadcasts in August and September 1932 to allow Canon Elliott to take a holiday, over 11,000 people wrote to the BBC urging a resumption of the series. When Canon Elliott founded a Guild of Prayer in 1936, it soon had a quarter of a million listeners enrolled in its ranks, and his fifth anniversary service later in the year was attended by 7,000 people. Elliott's personal success created the same kind of problems as the success of individual broadcasters in other fields of radio—the danger of becoming stale or of 'stereotyping' response—and although he

[1] D. C. Thomson, *Radio is Changing Us* (1937), p. 105. For Rationalist criticisms, see *The Free-thinker*; also 'Clericus', *BBC Religion* (Rationalist Press Association, 1942).

[2] For the first broadcast, see *BBC Press Release, 25 Sept. 1931. Elliott had broadcast frequently before 1931, and Sydney Moseley described him as 'one of the pioneers of church broadcasting, having started with his distinguished sermons from Folkestone'. *Who's Who in Broadcasting* (1933), p. 55. It was partly due to Elliott's good offices that the opposition to broadcasting of the Chapter of St. Paul's Cathedral was broken in 1930. The first service broadcast from St. Paul's was on 25 June 1930. Evensong was broadcast for the first time—this time at the request of the Dean and Chapter—on 27 July 1930.

remained a popular and most effective broadcaster after 1936, his appearances at the microphone became less frequent.

From 1927 to 1933 the Central Religious Advisory Committee was the only 'expert' authority to which the BBC could turn. In June 1933, however, the general reorganization took place, and the Rev. F. A. Iremonger was appointed Religious Director. He began his duties on 17 July. Long before the Corporation was founded Reith had thought of such an appointment, and there had even been talk of it in wider circles. 'I considered about a year ago', Reith wrote to Gladstone Murray in February 1926, 'whether it would not be desirable to have religious matters handled more definitely. In fact, would it not be desirable to have a specialist. You might discuss the matter with Mr. Stobart and he can have a talk with me about it later. It is a line of activity of sufficient importance to warrant undoubtedly proper handling.'[1] In the wider circles, where the matter was discussed, the name of Sheppard was frequently raised.[2] It was not until 1933, however, that the decision was taken.

Iremonger had wide ecclesiastical experience. Ordained in 1905, he had spent eleven years in the East End of London, first at Poplar and Blackwall, then as Head of Oxford House in Bethnal Green, and finally as Vicar of St. James the Great, Bethnal Green. From 1923 to 1927 he had been editor of *The Guardian*, and from 1927 he had served as Vicar of Vernham Dean, Andover. He had been appointed Chaplain to the King in 1927 and Honorary Chaplain to the Archbishop of York a year later.[3] He had also written a book, *Men and Movements in the Church*. He was recommended independently to Reith by the Bishops of Winchester and of Chichester, by the Chaplain to the Archbishop of Canterbury, and by the proprietor of *The Guardian*.

When Reith talked to Iremonger about his appointment he promised him the utmost help, without seeking to hide the fact that Iremonger would 'have a most harrowing time and would have to work at a rate which would be quite new to him'. Reith had no doubts that Iremonger would be co-operative or forceful

[1] *Reith to W. E. G. Murray, 5 Feb. 1926.
[2] See E. Roberts, *H. R. L. Sheppard, Life and Letters* (1942).
[3] *BBC Press Release, 28 May 1933.

as the occasion demanded, and that he would be capable not only of dealing specifically with religious broadcasting, but of playing an active part in more general discussions, for example, about the shape of Sunday programmes. 'I watched his work pretty closely all through the years', Reith recalls. 'Iremonger used to tell people he always sat very much on the edge of his chair on Monday mornings waiting for the three short rings on the telephone which meant that I was on the other end, with comments about the day's work. I never had the shadow of disagreement with him, except that he did not like old-fashioned hymns like "Rock of Ages" and I did. He did magnificent work for the BBC.'[1]

As a leading member of the staff of the BBC, Iremonger pursued the basic 'ecumenical' policy which Reith had demanded. A convinced Anglican himself, he was always fair to other denominations. He was also unobtrusively secure within the BBC hierarchy. It was Roger Eckersley who wrote of him that he was 'a fearless, outspoken and utterly kindly person who stood no nonsense and proceeded to put his ideas ruthlessly into action'.[2] Finally, he became a good broadcaster. Reith found him a 'thoroughly bad Bible reader' in 1933 with 'a typically parsonic' voice,[3] but before long his conduct of the Daily Service was greatly appreciated by large numbers of listeners. At the Coronation of 1937 he was the main religious broadcaster, and Stuart Hibberd bracketed him with the King, the Queen, and the Archbishop of Canterbury as the successes of the occasion.[4]

Iremonger left the BBC in April 1939 to become Dean of Lichfield, and was succeeded as Director of Religious Broadcasting, a new title, by an ex-missionary, Dr. J. W. Welch, Head of St. John's Training College, York. The ecumenical emphasis remained. 'Broadcast services make an obvious contribution to the unity of the Churches', Welch wrote soon after his appointment. 'The religious services of all denominations are heard by all; each denomination learns from the others. Listeners feel that they are sharing in a Christian, not merely a denominational service; suspicions and misunderstandings are removed;

[1] Note by Reith, June 1963.   [2] *The BBC and All That*, p. 100.
[3] Reith, Diary, 22 May 1933.
[4] S. Hibberd, *This—is London* (1950), p. 146.

divisions due to accidents of history, now meaningless, disappear, and there is a growing sense that, though some differences are great, yet the things we have in common are far greater.'[1] Such language is far more common in the 1960s than it was in the 1930s.

Iremonger was given a deputy, the Rev. J. E. Fenn, a Presbyterian, just before he left the BBC, but there was no BBC clergyman outside London until July 1939, when the Rev. C. V. Taylor, an Anglican, was appointed to supervise religious broadcasting in the West and Midland Regions. There was a 'Religious Executive', however, D. P. Wolferstan. Religion had no place in pre-war television, and when Gerald Cock once suggested religious television the Dean of Liverpool commented that the very idea of television 'close-ups' of preachers made him laugh.[2] The use of sound radio for religious services for the Empire raised no such uncertainties. On the second Sunday of every month, from June 1935 onwards, Empire services were given from St. Paul's—the first preacher was the Dean, Dr. W. R. Matthews—and relatives of people living in the Empire were invited to take part.

The pattern of home religious broadcasting was extended rather than modified after 1933, in what have been described as 'the years of consolidation'.[3] One new service on Sunday mornings was introduced in October 1935.[4] The proposal had first been mooted almost a year earlier and Iremonger had said then that he favoured both outside broadcasts and studio services, preferably beginning at 9.30 a.m.[5] Reith had put the idea in Iremonger's mind, and thought such services would be '*very* useful'.[6] The initial delay in implementing it was caused not by difficulties of programming but by objections from the engineers. 'Hitherto we have regarded Sunday morning as a very valuable time for maintenance and special tests', Harold Bishop reported in December 1934, adding that if the morning

[1] *BBC Handbook* (1940), p. 66.

[2] *The Dean of Liverpool to Iremonger, 1 June 1935. He found Cock 'a delightful man'.

[3] *Memorandum on 'Religious Broadcasting: History and Current Practice', Feb. 1943.

[4] *BBC Press Release, 6 June 1935.

[5] *Iremonger to Reith, 22 Nov. 1934.   [6] *Note by Reith, 23 Nov. 1934.

religious service was introduced, there would have to be a further increase of engineering staff.[1]

While the question of trying to proceed without additional staff was being considered, more problems arose. A quest started for speakers, with one of the first names to come in being that of Leslie Weatherhead, then in Leeds.[2] Nicolls remarked that although Iremonger did not approve of the idea of 'a second St. Martin's', 'the best solution from an administrative point of view' would be if 'a regular service could be established from one church'.[3] Other officers of the BBC shared Iremonger's preference for services from various churches, however, and it was left to the Central Council to fix on the time—9.30—and to discuss the allotment of services.[4] There were difficulties about this also, or rather about the type of services which the different denominations might plan. Some Anglicans thought that it would be 'a sheer disaster' if Morning Prayer or a 'mixed service' should be broadcast at that time of day and advocated Sung Eucharist: others, including the Archbishop of York, held that 'there was something false in principle about the broadcast of the Eucharist'.[5]

Finally, yet another problem arose. 'I urge strongly the desirability of holding up the beginning of this new programme service until October', Wellington wrote to Iremonger in March. 'June is the time of year when we are cutting down our activities, not embarking on new ones. . . . Will you bring the matter up for discussion at Programme Board, so that we may underline the necessity to stand firm when we are asked to fill up the period between the end of the morning service and the beginning of regular programmes at 12.30? You will remember our experience with the weekday morning service and the pressure which was immediately put upon us to fill that gap.'[6]

The interval between the inception of an idea—put forward by Reith—and its realization was ominously long and showed just how complex the planning procedure of the Corporation

[1] *H. Bishop to Dawnay, 3 Dec. 1934.
[2] *E. G. D. Liveing to Iremonger, 24 Jan. 1935.
[3] *Note by Nicolls, 6 Feb. 1935.
[4] *Central Religious Advisory Committee, Minutes, March 1935.
[5] *For the two points of view, see letters from the Dean of Rochester to Iremonger, 11 June 1935, and the Archbishop of York to Iremonger, 13 June 1935.
[6] *Wellington to Iremonger, 13 Mar. 1935.

had become. Once started, however, the Sunday morning services became an established fixture. 'They evidently fulfil a need, and the hour at which they are given appears to be suitable', the BBC stated in March 1936.[1] They also gave a symmetry to Sunday broadcasting, which now began with a service and ended with an Epilogue.[2]

There were other interesting developments during the late 1930s—an extension of the series of religious talks; new experiments with religious 'features'; and the introduction of greater variety into children's religious broadcasts. Among the series of talks broadcast in the late 1930s were *The Way to God* (1934/5), with Canon Raven, Father Martindale, the Rev. J. S. Whale (a Congregationalist), Dr. G. F. McLeod of the Church of Scotland, and the Rev. W. R. Matthews seeking to appeal to the 'will and the heart' as well as the intellect;[3] *Christian Living* by Donald Soper; and Dr. Whale's *Explaining the Christian Way* (1938). Iremonger hoped that the standard of these talks would provide an example not only for listeners but for preachers at the Sunday evening services. In February 1937 he said that he was 'very uneasy' about these services, some of which 'were worthy neither of the Churches nor of the BBC'. It was not merely that the preaching was often poor, but that the preaching was frequently the worst feature. The example of the Talks Department should be followed and an effort made to secure 'the best possible'. 'The subject of the Talks may be such as will appeal to few or to many, but if the Talks are to be popular, the Director of Talks will spare no effort to make them "good popular", which is as easy to recognise as "bad popular" and shows it up as nothing else can.'[4]

Religious features drew the religious broadcasters into a different set of production problems. Filson Young had been fascinated by these in the late 1920s, and his arrangements of the Nativity Play from the church of St. Hilary in Cornwall were designed to stress the symbolic and the universal rather than the didactic and the contemporary.[5] The Vicar of St. Hilary's, the

---

[1] *BBC Press Release, Mar. 1936.

[2] *Of the first 26 morning services, 14 were Anglican, 4 Methodist, 2 Church of Scotland, 2 Roman Catholic, 2 Baptist, and 2 Congregationalist.

[3] See *The Church of England Newspaper*, 7 Sept. 1934.

[4] *F. A. Iremonger, Memorandum on Broadcast Religious Services, 25 Feb. 1937.   [5] See *Shall I Listen?*, ch. xi, 'Voices from the West'.

Rev. Bernard Walke, wrote the plays which were broadcast regularly from 1926 to 1934. From inside the studio the most ambitious religious dramatic broadcast attempted to that date was transmitted on Christmas Day 1935. It was a programme devised by R. Ellis Roberts and produced by Robin Whitworth, and its title was *Unto Us*. Music was under the direction of Sir Walford Davies, who also produced a popular Sunday evening series, *Melodies of Christendom*. *Unto Us* was followed by further programmes of the same kind on Maundy Thursday 1936 and All Saints' Day, and repeated at Christmas 1936. And in 1938 Dorothy Sayers, who was to write the remarkable war-time play cycle *The Man Born to be King* (1942), was first commissioned by the BBC to write a nativity play, *He That Should Come*.[1] T. S. Eliot's *Murder in the Cathedral* had been broadcast in January 1936.

Children's programmes had often had a 'feature' element in them, even in 1924 and 1925 when there was a Sunday Children's Hour arranged by each station in turn. Special children's services were broadcast each month from 19 September 1926 onwards, and in February 1930 the first of E. R. Appleton's *Joan and Betty's Bible Story* programmes was transmitted.[2] In the same year Dr. Basil Yeaxlee, Principal of the West Hill Training College, Birmingham, formed a group of the Council of Christian Education to suggest suitable programmes for children to listen to on Sunday afternoons, and from their discussions a kind of rota system emerged, on similar lines to those of the church services rota. The Committee of Convocation in 1931 paid special tribute to these programmes which it believed reached families untouched by the Sunday Schools.[3] Along with the sick, the aged, and the infirm, it suggested, children had been specially provided for by the BBC. Experiments continued, and from October 1936 onwards Geoffrey Dearmer produced interesting programmes on the lives of famous Christians. He was assisted in this work by Lance Sieveking. BBC policy was to leave the contents of the Sunday half-hour for the children 'as elastic as possible'.[4]

[1] *BBC Handbook* (1939), p. 22.
[2] Appleton had also been responsible for 'The Silent Fellowship' broadcasts from Cardiff which were discontinued in 1935.
[3] *The Religious Value of Broadcast Services*, p. 5.
[4] *Central Religious Advisory Committee, Progress Report, 1 Oct. 1936.

Not everything went smoothly, however, during the 1930s. In 1936, for instance, the question of censorship of religious addresses came to the forefront again. Eight years before, Roman Catholic preachers had been allowed to submit their sermon manuscripts to their own Roman Catholic colleagues on the Central or Regional Advisory Committees.[1] The subject was raised again in 1936 when a provocative statement in a sermon by Father Valentine Elwes led to a storm of disapproval. At a meeting of the Central Religious Advisory Committee in March 1936 it was agreed that in future all sermons by Roman Catholic preachers, whether from a church or from the studio, should be sent in the first place to the Director of Religion— there had been no such post in 1928—and then, if necessary, sent on to Father Martindale.[2]

The change of procedure created no difficulties, and the major preoccupation of the Central Religious Advisory Committee during the years before the Second World War was not the relationship between different religious denominations but the increasing pressure for a 'secular' Sunday. Quite apart from outside pressure, there were people inside the BBC who objected to the Sunday 'code' as it had been formulated in the 1920s and early 1930s and argued forcefully that 'if we took "the better the day, the better the deed" as our motto and put the *best* contemporary light stuff in on Sundays—thus excluding the banal and the vulgar—we might evolve a new and enlightened definition of Sabbatarianism'.[3] The Committee left the formulation of policy to the BBC, 'noting' in March 1938, for instance, that the proportion of British listeners to continental radio stations was increasing substantially and that the BBC was proposing to fill in with 'light programmes' the hitherto silent hours between 10.45 a.m. on Sunday mornings and 12.30 p.m. On the motion of Dr. Scott Lidgett, seconded by Canon Rogers, the Committee decided that it wished to express no view and to leave the decision in the BBC's hands.[4] This interesting decision was a sign of trust in the BBC, not a gesture of neutrality.

Sunday morning programmes were extended, and there was

[1] *Memorandum on Religious Broadcasting, 1930.
[2] *Central Religious Advisory Committee, Minutes, 5 Mar. 1936.
[3] A. P. Ryan to S. Tallents, 10 Sept. 1936 (Tallents Papers).
[4] *Central Religious Advisory Committee, Minutes, 3 Mar. 1938. For Sunday programmes, see also above, pp. 52–55.

talk of a further extension in 1939 when the Committee met for the last time before the outbreak of war. The BBC proposed to move Sunday evening services in the Regional programmes to 5.30 p.m. and to broadcast a secular programme—in keeping with BBC standards—as an alternative to the religious services. In the discussion which followed an account given by Nicolls, who was then Controller of Programmes, of the reasons for the proposed changes, most members of the Committee maintained that there was no real evidence of a desire for change among listeners. Doubt was also expressed as to whether the BBC's 'secular programme' would be of the type which would succeed in winning listeners away from Radio Luxembourg and Radio Normandie. Again it was Dr. Scott Lidgett and Canon Rogers who took the initiative.[1] A proposal by Rogers, seconded by Lidgett, that 'the present arrangement should continue' was carried *nem. con.*, and it was not until the introduction of the Forces Programme in 1940 that a secular alternative was introduced. On its own initiative, however, the BBC had admitted cinema organ recitals into Sunday programmes[2] and had collected new evidence from its listeners' panel about the size of the public listening to foreign radio stations on Sundays.[3] Although for the whole of the period covered in this volume, the BBC's Sunday policy was preserved intact, there were many signs in 1939 that the position would not be maintained in the future. There was a suggestion, indeed, that the Archbishop of York should give a talk on 'The Meaning of Sunday' and follow this up by discussing the subject on the air with a group of listeners.[4] This was to point forward to a quite different phase in the history of religious broadcasting.

[1] Central Religious Advisory Committee, Minutes, 2 Mar. 1939.
[2] *Programme Committee, Minutes, 9 Mar. 1939; S. G. Williams to C. Max-Muller, 10 Mar. 1939.
[3] *General Listening Barometer, Interim Report, No. 10, 8 Feb. 1939. See also below, p. 364.
[4] *Report of Informal Conference on Sunday Broadcasting, 20 June 1939. See also below, pp. 654-5.

III

AUDIENCES: AT HOME AND ABROAD

I have now been a regular listener for ten
years, that is from the age of twelve, and I
should like to take this opportunity of thank-
ing the BBC for the part that it has played in
my education, pleasures and formation of my
tastes and opinions.

LETTER FROM A BRITISH LISTENER, 1938

My grandmother was born in New Zealand
before the arrival of the first four immigrant
ships from England in Lyttleton Harbour.
I am a staunch Englishman at heart as well,
and anything British appeals very strongly to
me. . . . My wife and I never fail to get a thrill
when we hear 'This is London calling you'.

LETTER FROM A NEW ZEALAND LISTENER, 1936

1. Home Listeners

By the mid-1930s listeners to BBC programmes constituted a representative cross-section of the British public. There were 2,178,259 licence-holders in Britain when the Corporation was founded. By the outbreak of the Second World War in September 1939 there were 9,082,666. The figures climbed steeply even in years of economic depression. Between March 1929 and March 1933, for instance, the number of licence-holders doubled. The biggest percentage increase in a single year was in the gloomy months from March 1930 to March 1931. In the following year also there was an increase of over 20 per cent. in the number of licences. By 1935 98 per cent. of the population could listen—on a cheap wireless set—to one BBC programme, and 85 per cent. could choose between two. There were seventy-three licences for every hundred households in the United Kingdom by September 1939.

We know little of the social composition of this 'great audience', as it came to be called, but it clearly included people from all sections of the community—among them the poorest, that large segment of the population, estimated at between 15 and 30 per cent., who were in chronic poverty or near it before the Second World War. The wireless 'enthusiasts' of the 1920s, the men who revelled in the art and craft of radio, became submerged in the growing ranks of the 'listeners'. More and more people felt that it was 'necessary' to buy a wireless set, and the price of sets in a competitive market fell sharply enough between 1931 and 1937 to cause anxiety to a section of the manufacturers. In 1938, for instance, 'a sharp downward trend' in retail prices was said to have caused alarm 'until it was checked'. When Philco introduced 'People's Sets' at Radiolympia in 1936, selling retail at five and six guineas, there was prolonged discussion in the radio trade about discounts and selling terms. A *Trader* analysis of the market in 1937 showed that over 600 current models were being produced.

Many of the sets, including the fashionable 'Radio Grams', were being bought by hire purchase: exact figures are not known, but the hire-purchase trade multiplied twentyfold in the golden age of wireless, and the first Hire Purchase Bill went through Parliament in 1938.[1] About 4,200,000 of the 9,082,666 wireless licences in the autumn

20. An early Radio Gramophone, 1929

of 1939 had been taken out by people with incomes of between £2. 10s. and £4 a week and 2,000,000 licences by people with an even smaller income. This last group included a large proportion of big families, but it also included large numbers of persons living alone, old-age pensioners particularly, to whom, along with the blind, the wireless set meant more perhaps than to any other section of the community.[2]

Britain came next after the United States both at the beginning and at the end of the period in the ranking order of countries with large numbers of wireless sets; and in terms of numbers of sets per hundred of the population, only Denmark and Sweden in Europe and New Zealand and the United States outside Europe were more 'radio minded'.[3] The same kind of pattern was to be repeated in the history of television, although the post-war television audience grew much faster after the first five years than the wireless audience had done.[4]

The density of distribution of wireless licences on the eve of

[1] For the fortunes of the radio trade, see the useful summary in *The Wireless and Electrical Trader*, 25 Mar. 1944. For the social side of hire purchase, see also J. Hilton, *Rich Man, Poor Man* (1944), a published edition of the Halley Stewart Lectures delivered in 1938.

[2] R. J. E. Silvey, 'The Listening Public' in the *BBC Handbook* (1940), pp. 76–79.

[3] Ibid., p. 10.

[4] B. Paulu, *British Broadcasting in Transition* (1961), p. 175; R. J. E. Silvey, 'Viewers, Viewing and Leisure' in the *BBC Quarterly*, Spring 1952, pp. 31–40.

the war was greatest in the Midlands and West of England, where eight families out of ten held licences. There was almost complete wireless coverage, however, largely as a result of the deliberate policy of the BBC to 'spread the service'. Even in the most remote parts of Britain—Northern Scotland, for example —there were over 14,000 licences distributed among less than 40,000 families living in the area. It was perhaps in the most remote parts of the country, as in the socially least privileged sections of the population, that there was most deep-felt appreciation of the 'solace' of wireless. 'The farther you get

21. Wireless Set, 1937. Model in cost range 8 gns.
to 16½ gns.

from London, the more broadcasting seems to mean.'[1] In the towns and great cities broadcasting was accepted casually and easily as an unobtrusive element in daily life.

Wireless provided everywhere a new shape not only for the day but for the week. 'Our eye is much more on the clock so that we can get the programmes we specially want to hear', wrote the Scottish Regional Director of the BBC in 1936. 'We have become more time-conscious since the introduction of broadcasting.'[2] Among the first points which were fixed in the week were the News Bulletins, the Weather Forecasts, and the Children's Hour. Later, as we have seen, religious services followed, and later still entertainment programmes, like *Music Hall*, *In Town Tonight*, and *Band Waggon*.[3] So accepted did the

[1] Filson Young, *Shall I Listen?* (1933), p. 184.
[2] M. Dinwiddie, 'The Influence of Broadcasting on Modern Life' in the *Transactions of the Royal Philosophical Society*, Glasgow, 1936.
[3] See above, pp. 104 ff., 117.

idea of such fixed points become that there was sharp public resistance to any change. When Eric Maschwitz, for example, once cut out the regular late-night dance music and substituted a dance-band feature-programme, 'the public gave the BBC hell' and late-night dance music came back to stay.[1]

The programme builders were well aware of the general problem. 'Argument is always circling round the question of fixed points', it was stated in 1933. 'Too many of them are apt to keep programmes and listeners in a rut: they may make it difficult to fit in unusual programmes of unusual length. . . . To combine convenient regularity with stimulating irregularity is one of the major problems of programme building.'[2]

Also involved in the process of programme building was the assessment of the size of 'potential audience'. It was recognized in the 1930s that 'peak times' of listening were from 8 to 9.30 in the evening, and it was generally assumed, although not tested until 1937 and 1938, that Saturday night yielded a maximum audience for entertainment. At the end of the period it was estimated that by 10.30 in the evening half the listening public had switched off their sets for the night and that after 11 o'clock only one listener in five was actually listening. 'After midnight only a small fraction remained.'[3]

Interest in listeners' habits—and in the social composition of the 'great audience'—was slow to develop.[4] At first, there was more interest in the quality of reception and the anti-social behaviour of 'oscillators' who spoiled other listeners' evenings. As early as 1930, however, both Gielgud and Siepmann, the one concerned with entertainment, the other with education, stressed the necessity for some sort of systematic research into the social psychology of regular listening. The members of the Central Council for Broadcast Adult Education had been pressing for the appointment of a 'salaried investigator' even before that. They wanted a man who would find out 'the most suitable times for broadcast talks for different sections of the listening public, general preferences for subjects, the extent of continuity of listening, the most suitable length of talks, the

---

[1] J. Payne, *Signature Tune* (1947), p. 35.
[2] H. Matheson, *Broadcasting* (1933), pp. 49–50. See also above, p. 49.
[3] *BBC Handbook* (1940), p. 77.   [4] See above, pp. 67 ff.

psychological effect of microphone personality, and the extent
to which broadcast talks lead to a follow-up of any kind, e.g.
reading'.[1] This was an over-ambitious list of objectives, and it is
difficult to imagine what kind of man would have been qualified to pursue them. It was natural, however, that adult educationists should seek information about their audience before

Frigidity on the 9.15.   A suspected oscillator in doubtful social popularity.

22. Anti-Social Behaviour: A Bateman Cartoon

they planned programmes: after all, similar 'listening-end' work
had been thought to be indispensable in the Kent experiment
in schools broadcasting.[2]

    Whereas in the United States listener research began as a
branch of market research—in an endeavour to give the listener
'what he wants'[3]—in Britain the first pressures came from people
who wanted to develop educational programmes. A number of
proposals were put forward in 1929, 1930, and 1931, when
Caradog Jones, Mrs. Webb, Professor Bowley, and Professor
Saunders Lewis were consulted; and at least one local survey
of listening habits was made by H. C. Shearman, then a

[1] *Central Council for Broadcast Adult Education, Executive Committee,
Memorandum on Survey of Listening Public, Sept. 1929.
  [2] See above, p. 191.
  [3] See above, p. 46.

C 1995   S

W.E.A. tutor, of six villages in north and mid-Bedfordshire.[1] More ambitious schemes were dropped, however, mainly on grounds of finance.[2] One early project, based on answers to 115 questions from a sample of 10,000 listeners, was dismissed as good material to hand over to John Watt for a variety sketch.[3] For long it was true that the schools occupied 'the unique position of being the only section of wireless listeners able by means of thorough questioning to influence the choice of its programmes'.[4]

Reith himself was uneasy about the possible implications of listener research—particularly about the value judgements underlying the demand for it[5]—but as the 'great audience' grew in size and the number of BBC programmes increased, pressure for more listener research from inside the organization was considerable. 'It becomes important not only for sectional interests . . . but also to adapt the service in matters of timing to social requirements related to the hours of leisure', a BBC official put it in 1932. 'Much, of course, has been achieved and can still be achieved by a process of trial and error, but one is left in the isolation of headquarters with the uneasy sense that the service is still inadequate to the potential demand.'[6]

Those people inside the BBC who were concerned not with sectional interests but with the tastes and preferences of the large majority were not silent in this domestic argument. An undated memorandum from the Outside Broadcast Department, for example, asked for information about the relative

[1] *C.C.B.A.E. Executive Committee, Minutes, 13 Dec. 1930; Siepmann to R. H. Eckersley, 17 July 1930.

[2] *C.C.B.A.E. Executive Committee, Minutes, 15 Jan. 1930, for an abortive proposal to prepare 'a statistical survey of the needs and tastes of listeners in isolated areas'. The Eighth Report of the Executive Committee of the C.C.B.A.E. outlined a proposal for a statistical survey, covering the whole field of broadcasting, which had been prepared with the collaboration of Professor Bowley. It had been turned down by the Director-General and Governors on the grounds that it was too elaborate and expensive. Alternative proposals made by the Corporation also lapsed in 1932. They are set out in the *BBC Year Book* (1932), pp. 161-3. For the Corporation's negative attitude, Board Meeting Minutes, 14 Jan. 1931.

[3] *Atkinson to Carpendale, 24 July 1930.

[4] *BBC Press Release, 22 Nov. 1935. The number of teachers' reports increased from 600 in 1932 to 8,788 in 1936. Undated Note by Sir Stephen Tallents on Listener Research.

[5] See above, pp. 55 ff.

[6] *BBC Year Book* (1932), 'A Survey of Listeners', p. 162.

appeal of running commentaries and eye-witness accounts
given after the event. Among the other questions it raised were:
'Do listeners prefer operas relayed from the stage to those
arranged for broadcasting specially by ourselves?', 'Do listeners
prefer what may roughly be described as the tone, or effect
of a concert relayed from outside, to one in the dampened
atmosphere of studios?', 'Does the listener prefer short excerpts
from operas and musical comedies rather than the whole performance lasting up to two hours?', and 'In religious broadcasts, what is the relative popularity of outside Church Services
compared with those in the studio?'[1]

Many of these questions were answered weekly in the correspondence columns of the *Radio Times* and in letters from
listeners received in the Programme Correspondence Section.[2]
To Gielgud and Siepmann, however, this flow of information
and views was quite inadequate and—even more important—
quite unrepresentative. 'I cannot help feeling more and more
strongly that we are fundamentally ignorant as to how our
various programmes are received, and what is their relative
popularity', Gielgud complained after a meeting of the Programme Board in May 1930. 'It must be a source of considerable
disquiet to many people besides myself to think that it is quite
possible that a very great deal of our money and time and effort
may be expended on broadcasting into a void.'[3]

Graves, who was Assistant Director of Programmes in 1930,
supported Gielgud's views: indeed he had asked Gielgud to
prepare his memorandum on the subject.[4] Neither he nor
Gielgud, however, had much trust in questionnaires as guides
to listeners' habits and preferences: they were more interested
at the time in comprehensive foreign surveys of listening habits,
particularly a German inquiry, complete with Hollerith
machines, in the Berlin region in 1928–9; a plebiscite arranged
by the Danish Post Office; and the Starch Report, an American

[1] *Survey of Listeners' Views from the Point of View of Outside Broadcasts.*
[2] See above, pp. 67 ff.
[3] *Programme Board Minutes, 9 May 1930; Memorandum by V. Gielgud,
12 May 1930, 'Listeners' Reactions to Programmes'.
[4] *Graves to R. H. Eckersley, 15 May 1930. Eckersley wrote a note in pencil to
Siepmann at the end of this memorandum: 'Before I take this any further I would
be glad to know what you have in mind from your angle as to an exploration of
this kind.' Eckersley later approved in an undated pencilled note.

test made by the sampling method.[1] The results of these foreign inquiries were summarized by C. F. Atkinson, and Siepmann gave his support to the idea of systematic British inquiry, sharing Gielgud and Atkinson's view that 'some alteration in our present system of measuring the reaction of the public is required'. He said that he had no faith in the soundness of the conclusions reached from the perusal of listeners' correspondence, but he urged that an inquiry should be not so much statistical—counting heads—as sociological—finding out more about 'types and tastes among the various classes of society and in the various parts of England'. By itself, he added, a single inquiry would not be enough: there should rather be a regular 'intelligence service' with BBC officers scattered throughout the regions.[2]

Something of the difficulty surrounding such projects is brought out in a difference of opinion, or at least of language, between Gielgud and Siepmann in their memoranda of 1930. Behind the difference were other people's fundamental differences of approach. Gielgud said that he had been surprised by a remark made by Stobart in the Programme Board that 'broadcasting is not and should not be democratic'. 'It seems to me,' Gielgud confessed, 'that there is no other entertainment in the world which is so much at the mercy of every single member of its audience as is broadcasting.' Siepmann replied in language very similar to that of Reith. 'I do not share Gielgud's view on the democratic issue. However complete and effective any survey we launch might be, I should still be convinced that our policy and programme building should be based first and last upon our own conviction as to what should and should not be broadcast. As far as meeting public demand is concerned, I believe that the right way is to provide for a more conscious differentiation of objective within our daily programme.'[3]

---

[1] *Memorandum by C. F. Atkinson, 15 May 1930. David Starch's report on 'the entire United States' with a special survey of the Pacific Coast was made for the National Broadcasting Company; 18,000 families were personally questioned by investigators. Atkinson prepared a further paper called 'Notes as to Statistical Surveys carried out in Germany, Denmark and U.S.A.' He noted that there had been strong American opposition to questions in the 1931 census as to whether the form-filler owned a radio. The object of this, the critics explained, was to provide 'the Owen Young interests' with 'talking points in their efforts to sell programme time to advertisers'.   [2] *Memorandum by C. A. Siepmann, 26 May 1930.
[3] *Ibid.; Gielgud's memorandum of 12 May 1930.

In the background of these discussions, Reith was an interested observer. He was prepared to join Siepmann in consulting Seebohm Rowntree in June 1930 about the most effective techniques of research, but he believed that, however much Siepmann might distinguish between objectives, the introduction of regular listener research would inevitably have the effect of influencing, even of dictating, programme policy: in the distance he feared the shadowy shape of programme planning based on programme rating, on what Clancy Sigal was to call 'the tyranny of Tam'.[1] Stobart's approach was more old-fashioned and prejudiced. 'As I hold very strongly that the ordinary listener does not know what he likes, and is tolerably well satisfied, as shown by correspondence and licence figures, with the mixed fare now offered, I cannot escape feeling that any money, time or trouble spent upon elaborate enquiries into his tastes and preferences would be wasted.'[2]

Apparently this view was shared by some even of the younger people inside the BBC. 'The real degradation of the BBC started', Lionel Fielden has written, 'with the invention of the hellish department which is called "Listener Research". That Abominable Statistic is supposed to show "what listeners *like*" —and, of course, what they like is the red-nosed comedian and the Wurlitzer organ.'[3]

Such forthright language evades most of the issues. Listener research, when it came, did not, in its early phases, dictate programme policy. The attempt to know more about the public is not the same as 'pandering' to every demand 'from below'. Given the increase in the size of the audience and the 'output'

---

[1] *Reith to Graves, 12 June 1930. C. Sigal, 'The Tyranny of Tam' in the *New Statesman*, 20 Oct. 1961. Rowntree suggested an inquiry based on the detailed investigation of one street in London.

[2] *Stobart to Siepmann, 29 May 1930. He attached a passage from a newspaper: 'A questionnaire, about 42 feet long, and containing 1,630 questions was sent to all collective farms in its district by the Seed Trust of Omsk. The government quickly annulled the document and punished the responsible officials.' Cf. Alan Howland's reply to a request to embark upon a survey of children's attitudes to Children's Hour: 'I do not think any useful purpose could be served by my submitting a questionnaire with regard to the Children's Hour. We already hold two "Request Weeks" every year, and are in close touch with Children's Hour listeners. Any further enquiries, I fear, would only serve to confuse the issue.' *Howland to Graves, 30 June 1930. The Children's Hour request weeks were well advertised in advance and elicited up to 8,000 replies (*Note by D. McCulloch, 31 Dec. 1935).

[3] L. Fielden, *The Natural Bent* (1960), p. 109.

of programmes, more careful attention to the problems described by both Gielgud and Siepmann was ultimately necessary. In a segmented and stratified society, also, there were few instinctive ways of knowing what people of different ages and of different social groups really believed and felt. The obvious preference of a large number of BBC listeners for the continental commercial programmes added a sense of urgency to the quest for information, yet at the same time made those people who were afraid of research reluctant to have their worst fears confirmed.[1] In national perspective the reluctance to find out about the listening habits of listeners was one aspect of the general unwillingness of Englishmen in the 1930s to take full stock of their position. Hilda Matheson rightly complained in 1935 that more attention was being paid to social change in primitive societies than to the social effects of radio in Britain.[2]

Yet although Miss Matheson sympathized with the demand for organized listener research, she also appreciated the intense sociological interest of the unsolicited listeners' letters.[3] 'The majority of such correspondents are very ordinary people, including "the cabman's wife in Wigan" and dozens of that type, not the sort who writes to the papers: they cover literally every walk of life. I have seen in this way some of the most interesting letters I have ever seen in my life, and a personal scrutiny of them and of others has been of real help to us.'[4] The Programme Correspondence Section continued in existence throughout the 1930s: although its conclusions were often impugned, it played an essential part in the BBC's system of public relations. 'I don't believe that correspondence is valueless, that it should be disregarded with impunity, or that it is written mainly by cranks', R. W. P. Cockburn exclaimed in June 1936.[5] Like Hilda Matheson, however, he did not object to 'useful developments' in listener research.

No definite decision about the launching of research was taken in the light of the discussions of 1930, and after a long delay the matter was raised again by Gielgud in November 1933.

[1] See above, pp. 54–55.
[2] H. Matheson, 'Listener Research in Broadcasting' in the *Sociological Review*, vol. xxvii (1935), pp. 408–22.
[3] See above, p. 68.
[4] *H. Matheson to Graves, 28 May 1930.
[5] *R. W. P. Cockburn to M. G. Farquharson, 10 June 1936.

Press criticism, he said, was trivial or biased. Letters received, *pace* Hilda Matheson and Cockburn, were written for the most part by 'ego-maniacs, cranks, axe-grinders or the incorrigibly idle who can find nothing better to do'. Once more he pleaded that the BBC should pay more attention to 'listeners' real reactions to our work'. 'What does the listener—whether at Wigan, Chipping Sodbury, Stow-on-the-Wold or in the Western Isles —really feel about the broadcasting programme in which his interest is apparently not subservient to that of audiences in the Queen's Hall or St. George's Hall?' He (Gielgud) was still just as much 'in the dark', he went on, as he ever had been. 'It is, in fact, only when I occasionally give a lecture in public that I begin to have the slightest idea as to what listeners think of our dramatic work.'[1]

Lindsay Wellington agreed with Gielgud that the desire for a 'barometer of public opinion' was 'inevitable and proper', but doubted whether it could ever be gratified. There was too much 'guessing' about listeners' reactions, but the trouble with Gielgud's ideas was that they were 'Utopian'. 'We have so many publics (and no Public) that I doubt the existence of "the average listener" unless he is so low a common denominator of licence payers that we could not possibly arrange broadcasting to implement his wishes.'[2]

It was perhaps to meet Wellington's objections that in March 1934 Gielgud made a very particular and very precise appeal to listeners to let him know by letter what they thought of radio plays. 'Write to us and say, as candidly, as clearly and as categorically as you can what you feel about the whole question. Are there too many plays broadcast? Are there too few? Do you hear the sort of plays you like to hear? . . . To some extent, our future dramatic policy will depend upon the result of this appeal.'[3] Over 12,000 letters were received in response to this direct request.[4]

Suggestions that there should be a listeners' panel to collect views on the work of other BBC departments were turned down, however, as was a proposal for 'intensive research' put forward

---

[1] *Gielgud to R. H. Eckersley, 18 Nov. 1933.

[2] *Wellington to R. H. Eckersley, 21 Nov. 1933.

[3] *V. Gielgud, Broadcast Appeal, 8, 9 Mar. 1934.

[4] *Gielgud to Dawnay, 17 Apr. 1934. Of the 12,726 letters, only 323 were in general 'critically adverse'.

by Maurice Gorham, the editor of the *Radio Times*, and Professor T. H. Pear.[1] By March 1935 Atkinson was returning patiently to ideas which he had first expressed five years before. 'Analysis of listeners', he reported, 'is not the same thing as analysis of listeners' (real or supposed) programme preferences.' The main object of a new inquiry would be to find out *who* the listener was and *when* he listened to this and that sort of material —in other words, to establish an electoral register, not to carry out a plebiscite.

In 1930 Atkinson had referred to evidence collected in the Germany of the Weimar Republic: in 1935 he had more powerful German ammunition at his disposal. *The Times* had recently concluded that 'the phenomenal success of Nazi broadcasting in 1935' as compared with 'the relative failure of its first crude efforts' in 1933 and 1934 was due to the fact that 'the most elaborate measures' had been taken '(*a*) to get a picture of the community and (*b*) to engage its interest'. The same, Atkinson added, was true of Russia.[2] Atkinson restated his case in August 1935—this time with references to the highly controversial experience of the British Peace Ballot as well as to Nazi broadcasting.[3] He pointed out also that in the task of compiling the *BBC Annual* he had heard from a lot of people inside the BBC that they wanted far more information about listeners.

Yet once again the whole question of organizing a general scheme of research was shelved. At the Director-General's meeting in August 1935 it was decided to leave over decisions until Sir Stephen Tallents, who had just been appointed Controller of Public Relations, had surveyed the position for himself.[4]

[1] *Memorandum by M. Gorham, 'What Listeners Like: Intensive Research', 20 Aug. 1934. For Gorham's considered views on listener research, see *Sound and Fury* (1948), pp. 58–60. For other proposals by J. S. A. Salt, see a note on a Talks Listening Panel, 12 Nov. 1934. Rose-Troup was not impressed: 'Mr. Salt's suggestion, which at first sight looks attractive, is one which comes forward with a fair amount of regularity from newcomers to our organisation. It is a scheme which has been turned down with equal regularity.' Rose-Troup to Pocock, 14 Nov. 1934.

[2] *The Times*, 15 Feb. 1935; *Memorandum by C. F. Atkinson, 'Listener Analysis', 1 Mar. 1935.

[3] *Memorandum by C. F. Atkinson, 'Listener Survey', 2 Aug. 1935.

[4] *The D.G.'s meeting took place on 13 Aug. 1935: at this period D.G.'s meetings had taken the place of the Control Board meetings. See below, p. 435. For Tallents, see above, p. 19 and below, p. 448. *See also a note by Graves, 14 Aug. 1935: 'I feel this subject is definitely one that might be handed to Tallents to chew over', with an addendum by Carpendale: 'Keep for Sir Stephen Tallents's arrival.'

Nicolls put the position as it was before Tallents's arrival with great succinctness and force. All the old objections remained. To add to them, there was 'the main objection' of them all. A large-scale inquiry would not even tell the BBC much that it did not already know. 'For instance, the ballot would tell us that large numbers of people like dance music, other large numbers have high tea at six and listen to the early evening programmes and then go to bed early, etc. If any surprising information came out of the plebiscite [the term lingered], we would not accept it, except in the case where the plebiscite was an absolutely complete one of every licence holder: otherwise we would say that it was a freak result. I do not say that such a survey would not be valuable, either on policy grounds, i.e. as a stunt, or for the effect it might have on staff who were closely in touch with the conducting of it, but I think that the least valuable result would be the actual information received.'[1]

Tallents had the reputation of being interested in 'stunts'— in widespread press publicity, exhibitions, 'and so forth'. Yet as the *New Statesman* remarked, he was also 'a cultured and progressive man' who could be relied upon 'to "sell" an idea with the minimum of vulgarity'.[2] Some of the press comments on his appointment linked it directly to the need for listener research. 'At present the BBC has to depend mainly for its contacts with the public on the letters it gets from all those who listen to its entertainment. Letters are a better contact than none at all, but after all, the man or woman who, having heard a programme he likes or dislikes, sits down and writes to the BBC to say what he thinks and why is rather an exceptional than a representative member of the audience. Ought there not to be some genuinely representative body like the Committee of Businessmen which I believe is occasionally consulted by the Post Office? [Tallents had been in charge of public relations at the Post Office.] You want a Consumers' Council, so to say, to guide the policy of the BBC programmes.'[3]

This was just what Reith did not want. Nor did a large section

[1] *Memorandum by B. E. Nicolls, 'Listener Survey', 14 Aug. 1935.

[2] *New Statesman*, 13 July 1935. It added, 'Sir Stephen Tallents has . . . something of a philosophy of publicity—he believes in the possibility of making democracy function through the work of the sympathetic interpreter of chaotic group opinion.'

[3] *Daily Sketch*, 10 July 1935. Some newspapers had been running 'radio popularity ballots' of their own. See above, p. 70.

of the programme builders within the BBC want it. They might demand more sociological information or better public relations, but they did not want to rest programme policy on declared public preferences. Many sections of the press supported this fundamental approach. 'The BBC ought never to be too anxious to please the public at all costs. . . . The promoter of entertainment who tries slavishly to follow public taste is always left behind and it is the promoter with the courage and the insight to lead the public tactfully towards new satisfactions who is rewarded in the end. Sir John Reith has done a great deal to enlarge British conceptions of entertainment, and at the same time he has striven valiantly to expose the fallacy of the tradition that education must always be dull. There does not seem, therefore, to be any urgent need for the BBC to revise drastically its own policy or its attitude to the public.'[1]

Tallents, however, went forward on his own lines. In private letters and in public speeches alike, he urged the need for 'substantial' listener research. Describing his post to his son in a letter probably written early in 1936, he said that he was working out a scheme for 'what we call listener research'. 'We want to know more than we do about the habits and tastes of listeners in different parts of the country and at different times of the year. . . . As to people's habits, there is a lot of information to be got indirectly from indirect sources such as gas and electric light companies—and even water companies, for the water engineer at Portsmouth has just sent us a graph showing how every one ceased to use water for cooking, washing etc. while the broadcast of the King's Funeral was on.'[2] With the help of his friend and colleague, A. P. Ryan, who had worked with him at the Empire Marketing Board, he went through all the old files on listener research which had accumulated since the Kent experiment of 1926, preparing his own résumé as he went along.[3] He also consulted the heads of departments, not all of whom were able or willing to give him much assistance.[4] The

[1] *Yorkshire Post*, 10 July 1935.
[2] Undated Note by Tallents to his son, probably written in Feb. 1936 (Tallents Papers).
[3] *Sir Stephen Tallents, 'Past and Present Practices in Listener Research', undated.
[4] *Rose-Troup, then Director of Talks, replied, for example: 'I doubt whether any one can say that anything in the nature of Listener Research in the current meaning of the phrase has ever been undertaken.' Memorandum of 20 Dec. 1935.

material he collected provided the basis for a paper which was submitted to the General Advisory Council of the BBC in January 1936.[1]

This interesting paper distinguished between four different kinds of research—research into listeners' habits, of the sort that had always been advocated; research into the efficiency of the different broadcasting techniques (Mary Somerville insisted on this);[2] research into listeners' preferences; and research into 'reactions of a type which are of more direct interest to the psychologist or sociologist than to the BBC'—for example, whether the coming of wireless tended to strengthen family life. The last kind of research was suggested by Professor T. H. Pear, who had long been advocating this line of inquiry and who was one of the few people who had pronounced upon the subject in public.

The clear distinction between the third kind of research —analysis of listeners' preferences—and the other three was particularly useful since there had been for so long so many blurring misunderstandings of the difference. Tallents was at pains to insist, indeed, that 'the surrender of programme policy to a plebiscite would undermine the responsibilities imposed on the BBC by its Charter'. In his conclusion he also made the important point, first enunciated by Atkinson, that listener research required expert and specialized management unless money and effort were to be wasted and work duplicated.

At the General Advisory Council of 13 January 1936 Tallents's distinctions and suggestions were discussed in an 'exploratory' fashion.[3] From the chair, William Temple, then Archbishop of York, stated that in his view it would be unfortunate if a great deal of money were spent in elaborate research: data was needed, but there were inexpensive means of getting 'representative and authoritative opinions'. Sir Arthur Salter and Professor Ernest Barker supported this view also, the former adding, like Reith, that he distrusted all large-scale methods, large masses of correspondence, and even the simplest and most carefully drawn up questionnaires. Principal J. H. Nicholson,

---

[1] *BBC General Advisory Council, 'Listener Research', Jan. 1936.
[2] *Undated Note for Tallents on 'Enquiries Already Undertaken'.
[3] *General Advisory Council, Precis of Discussion of 13 Jan. 1936. For the role of the General Advisory Council, see below, pp. 470 ff.

who was so directly involved in the BBC's plans for adult education, warmly supported Tallents's memorandum, noting that the organized listener groups could play an active part in any plan of research: they were 'a special constituency of regular listeners with an importance out of proportion to their numbers'.[1]

With this discussion in mind, it is scarcely surprising that the first steps taken to discover listeners' reactions were of the most modest kind. Reith himself wrote to Salter after the meeting agreeing with his view and going on to add that if anything was to be done with respect to listeners' habits, 'I do not think that it need be very much, and certainly nothing formal'. The General Advisory Council itself might make soundings: small panels of listeners—they were later called 'glow worms'—should be seen by members of the Council or by Governors, and should be encouraged to put forward new ideas for broadcasts.[2]

There is no evidence that such panels ever met. Regional questionnaires were sent out, however, in some parts of the country—a Scottish questionnaire, for example, sent to 114 'known listeners', 99 of whom had written to the BBC about programmes and 15 to 'personal friends' of George Burnett in Edinburgh. Cardiff suggested a Welsh questionnaire addressed not to people who had written in about programmes—'after all,' a regional representative noted, 'they are people of a rather unusual mentality'—but to people who would write to the BBC asking for questionnaire forms after an appeal had been made over the air.[3] This idea was turned down by Tallents on the grounds that 'any such job wants doing more carefully and on a properly thought out plan'.[4]

Among the other modest proposals which were put into practice at this time was a series of talks to listener groups and women's meetings. Tallents himself addressed a large-scale Women's Conference in April 1936. The BBC, he told his hearers, wanted to take listeners into its confidence and to learn from them. 'This was not altogether easy, when its audience

[1] For Nicholson and the Listener Groups, see above, pp. 223 ff.
[2] *Unsigned Memorandum of 14 Jan. 1936; Note on a meeting with Salter on 15 Jan. 1936.
[3] *Results of Questionnaire sent to Listeners, Jan. 1936; Note from Miss N. G. Jenkins to Tallents, 20 Feb. 1936.
[4] *Note by Tallents, 25 Feb. 1936.

had grown to be the whole Nation.'[1] In an article in *John Bull* in December 1935 he had written that there was no subject on which the BBC spent as much anxious study as the problem of meeting 'the infinitely various needs of its vast listening audience'. 'It is a study which should last as long as broadcasting endures.'[2]

In a memorandum of March 1936, addressed to Carpendale, Tallents stated that he had got a clearer idea of what a 'listener research' organization could and should do. Reith had eventually agreed to his experimenting on a limited scale with such research, and Tallents began to set out the terms of his analysis. Research concerning listeners' habits demanded expert treatment from psychologists and sociologists: research concerning listeners' tastes depended upon the building up of a 'sensitive network of selected listeners throughout the country from whom we can get reports on particular points . . . (a small gratuity, such as a free copy of *The Listener* might be offered to these super glow worms)'; research concerning listeners' sets required the co-operation of the radio trade. The third kind of research was still important in relation to the other two. 'Information about the capacity of sets in constant use is very important to programme building, and even to regional structure.'[3]

Tallents suggested that a special BBC officer should be appointed to deal with all research problems, and this proposal was accepted by the Control Board on 10 March 1936.[4] Carpendale suggested the appointment of Atkinson who had written so many memoranda about research: in fact C. V. Salmon was chosen.[5] Associated with him was a small 'Listener Research Group', which included Tallents, Maurice Farquharson, with whom Salmon had been working, Ryan, Siepmann, and Atkinson.[6] Tallents tried to enrol F. W. Fox of the Post Office's research department as a member of this group, but Sir Donald Banks of the Post Office said that he was so busy that he could not take on any additional work.[7]

---

[1] *Report on the Women's Conference, 24 Apr. 1936.

[2] *John Bull*, 14 Dec. 1935. Reith congratulated Tallents on this article.

[3] *Tallents to Carpendale, 6 Mar. 1936.

[4] *Control Board Minutes, 10 Mar. 1936. The Board said that 'this assistant should be drawn from existing staff if possible'. 'Research was to be selective, specialized and more or less informal.'

[5] *Note appended to Tallents's letter of 6 Mar. 1936.

[6] *Control Board Minutes, 28 Apr. 1936.

[7] *Tallents to Sir Donald Banks, 15 Apr. 1936; Banks to Tallents, 23 Apr. 1936.

The first meeting of the group, planned for May 1936, does not appear ever to have been held, and a few months later R. J. E. Silvey of the London Press Exchange was appointed

"TUNER'S" Questionnaire

....

What kind of Programme do YOU like on the Wireless?

———— •••• ————

"Tuner," "The Yorkshire Observer" wireless critic, asks you to indicate the type of programme you like best on the voting form printed inside this circular.

Will you kindly fill it up and hand it to our representative when he calls for it in the course of the next few days?

23. A Newspaper Poll

from outside the BBC to assist Tallents with listener research. He had been with the London Press Exchange since 1929 and was part author of the book *The Home Market*. It was Silvey who was to build up through the years a highly organized system of listener research.[1] His appointment coincided with an increase in outside interest. A number of newspapers organized listening polls; Professor Pear gathered together a group of psychologists to discuss 'twenty-five problems suitable for listener research investigation'; across the Atlantic there was talk of the invention at the Massachusetts Institute of Technology of a new 'radio meter' to test the preferences of radio audiences; in the British radio trade there were proposals for a Radio Development Association to conduct advertising and market research; and in March 1936 the Institute of Incorporated Practitioners in Advertising had prepared a survey of the radio listening habits of the public, based on 20,000 interviews.

Evidence of this kind was carefully scrutinized inside the BBC, although one continuing sceptic said that the Institute's document was 'not worth the paper it is printed on as the sampling is only 20,000'.[2] As for the radio meter, it was based on a quantitative fallacy, which could ruin programme building. What was thought to be more useful evidence concerned the use of audience research by competing or complementary media. It was noted with interest that there were sharp seasonal fluctuations in cinema audiences, and that the *Spectator* had sent out a questionnaire inviting its readers to criticize its content and format and to make suggestions for the future.[3]

When Silvey began working for the BBC, available evidence from outside, trustworthy or untrustworthy, suggested that 'average listening' was about four hours a day; that about a third of the listeners listened for as much as $37\frac{1}{2}$ hours a week; that over three-quarters of the listeners spent one-sixth of their listening time hearing light music; that a half listened to all studio variety programmes; that variety or theatre relays were by far the favourite programmes; that four out of ten listeners never listened to an educational talk and two out of ten never listened to a talk of any kind; that 16 per cent. of listeners never

[1] *General Advisory Council, Report for Sept. 1936; BBC Press Release, 18 Sept. 1936.
[2] *Memorandum from R. Judson, 16 Mar. 1933. Judson was Advertisement Manager of the BBC. Also *Note by Tallents on Pear's projects, 5 June 1936; *New York Herald Tribune*, 16 Mar. 1936; *Broadcaster's Review*, 16 Apr. 1936.
[3] *Note on S. Rowson's *Statistical Survey of the Cinema Industry in Great Britain in 1934*; Note by Tallents on a *Spectator* dinner, 2 Mar. 1936 (Tallents Papers).

listened to religious services; that the best listening hour was from 8 p.m. to 9 p.m.; that programmes 'tailed off' after 9 o'clock; that large numbers of listeners did not listen after 10 o'clock; and that two-thirds of listeners never listened after 11 o'clock.[1]

Drawing on evidence collected from the seven chief relay exchanges, Garry Allighan, a radio journalist, concluded that the highest recorded audience (91 per cent.) was for the King's Christmas talk, that *Music Hall* attracted 60 per cent. of listeners, and that even the *Foundations of Music*, frequently attacked by 'lowbrows', had a rating of 15 per cent. Allighan also noted that on Sundays the percentage of relay listeners listening to BBC programmes varied from as low a figure as 10 per cent. to 35 per cent. and that the percentage listening to continental programmes reached as high a figure as 80 per cent., depending on the BBC alternative. Only on exceptional occasions did more than 35 per cent. listen to the BBC.[2] These figures were not quite borne out by the Advertising Institute's survey, which estimated a maximum Radio Luxembourg audience of 45·7 per cent. on Sundays.

The Institute tried to break down the public in terms of social class. Interest in commercial radio programmes was greatest in Class C of the population, those with chief wage-earners receiving £5 a week or less. The programme preferences of this class were markedly different from Class A, where the chief income receiver was in receipt of an income of £600 a year and upwards. In Class C 82·5 per cent. of the sample put variety as their favourite type of programme: in Class A 65·5 per cent. The figures for serious talks were 19·5 per cent. and 37·1 per cent.

Silvey's own researches began in the spring of 1937 with a series of inquiries into 'particular' audiences. The first to be chosen was the audience for drama and features: 350 listeners, whose only qualification was a known interest in this work—they were not expected to have technical knowledge—were asked to co-operate by completing questionnaires about each play or feature programme which they heard over a period of

---

[1] These estimates are based on the newspaper reports and other reports cited above.

[2] *Garry Allighan, Note of 11 Dec. 1935.

four months. This unpaid panel was composed of 'men and women of all ages, drawn from all parts of the country, and included civil servants, miners, shop assistants, teachers, working-class housewives, and unemployed workers'.[1]

Its conclusions were that plays were often not easy to follow, that plays specially written for radio had not on the whole been very satisfactory, that background music was often too loud, that effects were often too insistent, that the construction of features was less successful than the choice of subjects, and that too many narrators spoiled the broth.[2]

Grace Wyndham Goldie, then *The Listener*'s drama critic, rightly pointed out that almost all the conclusions of this 'vast, imposing and long awaited Report' had been set out week by week in her own personal column in *The Listener*. The importance of the Report, she said, was that it had been drafted not by an individual but by 'a panel of four hundred representative listeners'.[3] The appeal to the representative listener was the new development. Apparently the response of listeners was considered so encouraging that it was decided that the 'panel' method, about which so much had been written earlier, was a technique applicable to all programmes 'where the ordinary listener would be capable of some degree of analysis of his reactions'. The comments which had been received in the drama survey were thought of (*pace* Grace Wyndham Goldie) as providing 'a photograph of a cross section of listeners and not a collection of critical opinions'. They were considered sufficiently illuminating, however, to suggest 'possible fruitful application to the work of other programme departments'.[4]

Later in 1937, therefore, the panel method of evaluation was applied to a series of talks about the cinema and a series of 'serious' talks called *Clear Thinking*. The first of these inquiries, which attracted a thousand listeners 'at one of the worst times of the year', gave an indication of what listeners wanted from talks about current films: the second—also with a thousand listeners—of the qualities they expected to find in a good broadcaster.

[1] 'Testing Listeners' Tastes' in *The Listener*, 21 July 1937.
[2] *Listeners' Views on Radio Plays, Report of an Enquiry.
[3] Grace Wyndham Goldie, 'What About It?' in *The Listener*, 21 July 1937.
[4] *Note by Silvey, 'Drama Reports Scheme', 14 Apr. 1937; Note by Tallents, 17 June 1937.

In addition, listener research of a simpler kind was applied to the timing of Mr. Middleton's gardening programmes. The question was whether his talks should be on Fridays at 7.10 or on Sundays at 2, and Middleton broadcast a message to his listeners asking them to let the BBC know by postcard which time they preferred. 'There does not seem a better way of finding out what your wishes are, whether you regard me as a stimulation for the weekend's gardening or to send you off to sleep after Sunday lunch. The BBC want to please you and I am quite prepared to do what I'm told as far as I can and to give you what you want.'[1] Seven thousand and nine listeners preferred Sunday, 2,950 Friday: 66 stalwart Middletonians answered 'for either or any time'.[2]

The question inevitably arose as to whether this simple plebiscite method could be applied substantially to other problems of timing, for example, the timing of Saturday's *Music Hall*. Silvey had his doubts. He raised the basic statistical point that if such invited postcards were to be taken as guides to public attitudes, the invited response had to be 'a microcosm of the whole'. Were there, in fact, any forces at work which would prevent the response from being representative? One, he suggested innocuously enough, might be a greater readiness to send in a postcard among those who either wished or resisted a change than among those who did not mind whether there was a change or not. 'Suppose the gardening talks public is half a million strong. Then for our vote to be valid 150,000 of them must prefer Friday and 350,000 must prefer Sunday.' But suppose that 400,000 listeners did not mind on which day the talks were broadcast. 'So long as the possibility remains open that listeners who are indifferent to a given point do not respond *at the same rate* as those who are more readily affected by the issue, grave doubt is bound to be cast upon the statistical validity of samples elicited by appeals from the microphone.'[3]

By sounding such a note, Silvey directed attention towards possibilities of random sampling, of 'investigation on scientific lines'. Distrust of this method was strong among social investigators of the reputation of Seebohm Rowntree—one of the

[1] *Broadcast of 25 June 1937.
[2] *Note by Ryan, 'The Middleton Poll', 7 July 1937.
[3] *Note by Silvey, 13 July 1937.

people the BBC consulted.[1] Silvey, however, had begun to move along the road which the BBC has subsequently followed. Reith congratulated him on the success of his first experiments[2] and talks began with other departments in the BBC, not only about 'panel' methods, but about the invention of a 'listening barometer'.

The first reference to the need for a random sample scheme based on 30,000 out of 12,000,000 *homes* was made in a memorandum by Silvey in July 1937. Reactions would be tested four or five times a year, and questions would be as simple as possible. 'It should not be impossible in these days of football pools', Silvey noted, 'to design a form which should frighten off only a tiny minority.' A sample of 30,000 would include about 9,000 persons under the age of fourteen; and one-third of the homes could be without sets. Silvey specifically referred to differences of age in determining 'representativeness' but did not refer to differences of class.[3]

Such points about the 'representativeness' of samples were made in a different context by Maconachie, the Director of Talks. He rightly expressed doubt about the representativeness of the 'panel' reactions of the organized Listening Groups. The BBC's Education Officers had 'tried very hard to persuade me, so far without success, that the Group Listener was exactly the same in nature as the general listener and that, therefore, the group listener's verdict on talks was a good indication of the general listeners' reaction. It seemed to me, on the other hand, that the very fact that one person would take the trouble to change and wash at the end of the day in order to listen to talks indicated the essential difference between him and the man who merely sat by his own fireside and switched on to a talk by chance.'[4]

The next development was an experiment carried out in connexion not with talks but with light-entertainment programmes. It was concerned neither with random sampling nor with what Maurice Farquharson called 'the searchlight scheme'

[1] See A. Briggs, *Seebohm Rowntree* (1961), ch. v.
[2] *Handwritten note to Tallents of 8 July 1937.
[3] *Silvey to Tallents, 15 July 1937, following a conversation of 7 July; Memorandum by Silvey, 'Proposals for Machinery for Sampling Listener Opinion'.
[4] *Note by Maconachie for Talks Meeting, 12 July 1937.

—a plan to study listeners' habits and tastes by indirect means, 'asking those who were in a position to know the habits and tastes of their fellows'.[1] It pointed forward, however, to the most familiar of all post-war techniques of listener research—programme rating. It was known already from outside surveys and listeners' letters that these programmes appealed to the widest public, and an attempt was made to secure a measure of listeners' opinions comparable with box-office information available to a theatre manager.[2] Two thousand listeners were chosen at random from 47,000 who volunteered to help in response to a broadcast appeal by John Watt on 18 September 1937 immediately after Saturday *Music Hall*.[3] The 2,000 were sent week by week 'log sheets' which set out the forthcoming week's light-entertainment programmes and were asked to indicate to which of the programmes they listened and how much of each programme they heard. Alongside this group a control group was organized to ensure 'the representativeness of the sample'.

There were some doubts about the 'representativeness' of the 2,000. First, they had all been picked out from the Saturday *Music Hall* audience. Second, they had all been supplied with very convenient programme summaries in the form of their log sheets. Third, there was a danger that, as volunteers, they would listen to wireless programmes more frequently than they would normally have done under a mistaken obligation to the BBC to do so. The control group was designed to act as a check on such possible disturbing factors. It consisted of 1,000 members of the general listening public chosen by and interviewed in the presence of 'agents'. They were not given log sheets and they were distributed throughout the regions according to the numerical strength of the regional listening public. They were interviewed in only one week out of four throughout the research experiment. No criterion was applied to membership of the group except that it would consist of people who liked to listen to variety programmes. It was 'hoped' but not insisted upon that 'men and women would be approximately equal in numbers in the final figures and that the average

---

[1] *Memorandum by Silvey of 15 July 1937.
[2] *Silvey to Farquharson, 12 July 1937.
[3] The original idea had been to have 1,000.

THE BRITISH BROADCASTING CORPORATION

Where alternative answers are given please put a X against the one you agree with.

.1. Would you personally like more or less of the
following **types** of programme?

		Too Much	The Right Amount	Not Enough
(a) Straight Variety	(*Examples: Music Hall, Palace of Varieties*)	......	......	......
(b) Serials	(*Examples: Inspector Hornleigh, The Plums, Mr. Muddlecombe, J.P.*)	......	......	......
(c) "Interest" programmes	(*Examples: Scrapbook, Star-gazing*)	......	......	......
(d) Comedy Shows	(*Examples: Radio Pie, Flying High, Kentucky Minstrels*)	......	......	......
(e) Concert Parties	(*Examples: White Coons, Fol-de-rols*)	......	......	......
(f) Musical Comedy	(*Examples: Arlette, Hit the Deck, Money for Jam*)	......	......	......
(g) American & foreign relays	(*Examples: Broadway Matinee, Five Hours Back*)	......	......	......
(h) Dance Music		......	......	......
(i) Reginald Foort at the B.B.C. Theatre Organ		......	......	......
(j) Other Cinema Organs		......	......	......

2. Do you dance to broadcast dance music?   Often.... Seldom.... Never......

3. Which of these times do you prefer for Saturday night Music Hall?
8.0 - 9.0 ...... 9.20 - 10.20 ......
Is it usually quite impossible for you to hear this programme
unless it is on at the time you have marked?   Yes....No......

4. If a specially good programme were put on regularly at
6.30 p.m. on Fridays, could you hear it?   Yes....No......
Would 6.30 p.m. on any of the following days be
more convenient to you?   Monday...... Tuesday..... Wednesday.... Thursday......

5. About what time in the evening do you usually stop listening
(a) on weekdays (not Saturday)?....................(b) On Saturdays?....................

6. Do you listen regularly to foreign stations
(a) on weekdays? Yes.....No...... (b) on Sundays? Yes.....No......

7. Between what hours, approximately, do you usually listen to foreign stations
(a) on weekdays?..................
(b) on Sundays? ....

8. Which foreign stations do you usually listen to
(a) on weekdays?..................
(b) on Sundays? ....

*If there is anything else you would like to say about our light entertainment programmes, please
write it on the back of this form.*

Name..................................   Address...

....

24. A Programme Questionnaire, 1937

listener included would be at somewhere [*sic*] about the £4 a week level'.[1]

Unlike post-war rating techniques, the listening barometer was designed to show not the total audience appeal of particular programmes but 'the relative sizes of audiences to different types of output from a given department'. The demand for music was not to be judged by the demand for light entertainment. 'A Variety Listening Barometer would be kept quite separate from an Outside Broadcasts Listening Barometer or a Music Listening Barometer.'[2] The old determination not to relate directly the distribution of particular kinds of programmes to listeners' tastes remained.

It is doubtful whether Reith would have approved of an analogy drawn by Silvey between the work of the BBC and a department store[3]—or even of references to 'market research now being used by many of the greatest industries in the country'[4]—but he would have had every sympathy with a comment in the *Observer* that a possible danger in a philosophy of listener research was that of 'seeking to give the public what it wants when it has no idea of what it wants—until it hears it'.[5] Another analogy which Silvey employed had unmistakable Reithian undertones. 'Think of broadcasting as a ship. Its final destination is determined by considerations of policy. The course it takes is affected by many factors, including its available fuel and the likelihood of the presence of icefields. But the task of the helmsman will be made infinitely easier by good charts. It is the job of Listener Research to prepare those charts.'[6]

By the autumn of 1938 the information files of the BBC Listener Research Department were beginning to get fatter and the number of times when Silvey had to say that there were no facts available about listener reactions was getting less fre-

1 *Memorandum, 'Variety Department Control Group', 19 Oct. 1937. Silvey to Regional Directors, 14 Sept. 1937: 'The plan for this control group has not been worked out in detail.'

2 *Proposals for Variety Listening Barometer, 24 Aug. 1937.

3 *Silvey, Suggested Outline for a Talk on Listener Research, 13 Oct. 1937.

4 *Silvey, Outline of Address to Press Conference, 26 Oct. 1937.

5 *Note from Farquharson on a comment in the previous edition of the *Observer*, 2 Nov. 1937.

6 R. J. Silvey, 'What is Listener Research?' in *Ariel*, June 1938. For Reith's captain and ship metaphor, see *Broadcast over Britain* (1924), p. 23; *The Birth of Broadcasting*, pp. 4, 69.

quent.[1] The first random sample had been taken in January 1938—with the co-operation of the Post Office[2]—and there had been 'searchlight enquiries', including one into the popularity of Children's Hour. Outside research had not diminished in volume or scope as a result of the BBC's own enterprise. Research into listeners' habits was being carried out, for example, in Glasgow and Liverpool Universities.[3] The pattern of listening from one time of the year to another and from one part of the country to another was becoming clearer than it had been before. Other points of division—for example by class, by age and sex or by occupation and specialized interest—were beginning to be examined,[4] and information was collected about listening to foreign stations. 'Middle-class log-keepers exercise a wider range of choice and listen to more non-commercial than commercial stations. The average working-class log-keeper, on the other hand, listens regularly on Sundays to twice as many commercial as non-commercial stations.'[5]

It is difficult to tell, however, how far all this activity influenced the pattern of BBC work in 1937 and 1938. W. A. Robson had complained in 1936 that the BBC had 'only the vaguest and most remote contact with the world of listeners. It does not really know who they are, to what they listen and what their views are.'[6] The Corporation knew far more in 1938 and 1939, but the research work itself was admittedly experimental, lively but incomplete, and in places insecurely based. Moreover, the communication of research conclusions within the organization took time and effort.[7] Policy-making still rested on many other criteria, and most people believed that it should continue to do so. An element in the story, of course—and it was always freely admitted—was the cultivation of good public relations.

[1] 'What is Listener Research?'

[2] *Report on Conversation between Farquharson and Welch of the General Post Office, 3 Sept. 1937.

[3] *Note of 4 Aug. 1937.

[4] *Outline of Proposed Searchlight Scheme, 20 July 1938; Silvey to the North Regional Director, 9 Sept. 1938.

[5] *General Listening Barometer, Interim report No. 1C, 8 Feb. 1939.

[6] W. A. Robson, *Public Enterprise* (1937), p. 100.

[7] For Silvey's brief account of what he calls 'the years of experiment' before 1941, see his important paper 'Methods of Listener Research Employed by the British Broadcasting Corporation' in the *Journal of the Royal Statistical Society*, vol. 107 (1944).

In this connexion imitation was perhaps the best form of flattery. 'Please note that the *Daily Mirror* is starting a listener research scheme', Ryan wrote to Tallents in July 1937.[1] 'Listen in to . . . Yourself', the *Daily Mirror* told its readers. 'Our idea is to select a corps of critics representative of all shades of opinion. . . . My last words to the BBC', the author added, 'are . . . "Look Out!"'[2]

2. Spoken and Written

BY 1937, when the *Daily Mirror* threatened to compete with the BBC, the Corporation was itself running a thriving publications business which was the envy of many other publishers. It had been established in face of great distrust and opposition and it served two invaluable purposes—first, that of providing a forum for radio, through the publication of programmes and the printing of outstanding talks; and second, that of augmenting the Corporation's frequently inadequate revenue. It was so successful in achieving both these purposes that the Corporation was involved in frequent quarrels with the press.

The three main BBC publications had different objects and different histories. The *Radio Times*, founded in 1923, gave all the details of programmes, details which the press had once refused to print.[3] It also provided notes about programmes and performers, space for listeners' letters, and technical articles about radio. Because of its large circulation, it was a perfect advertisers' medium. *World Radio*, formerly the *Radio Supplement*, was founded in 1925, over objections from the trade press, to contain foreign programmes and technical articles, and it was expanded in 1932 to meet the special needs of Empire broadcasting. *The Listener* was the most contentious of the trio. Born in contention in January 1929, it has survived to become one of the most respected weekly journals. The greater part of its contents has consisted entirely of broadcast material: this,

---

1 *Ryan to Tallents, 20 July 1937.
2 *Daily Mirror*, 20 July 1937.
3 See *The Birth of Broadcasting*, pp. 295 ff.

indeed, was a condition of the periodical coming into existence at all.

The table given below sets out the comparative circulation figures for the three journals, and the combined net profits which were passed over to the Corporation. It shows that while the circulation of the *Radio Times* climbed sharply, it did not quite keep pace with the increase in the number of listeners; that *World Radio* reached an early peak and thereafter slipped and fell—it went out of existence in 1939; and that the circulation of *The Listener* moved steadily along a plateau from 1934 to 1939: the 'intelligent listener' public to which it appealed was obviously strictly limited. In the cases both of the *Radio Times* and *The Listener*, however, the figures should perhaps be compared with post-war figures if they are to be set in proper perspective. By 1950 the average weekly circulation of the *Radio Times* had passed the 8,000,000 mark, and the average weekly circulation of *The Listener* was up to nearly 150,000. Clearly the written word was not losing its appeal.

BBC PUBLICATIONS

Year	Average weekly net sales			Total net profits accruing
	Radio Times	World Radio	The Listener	
1927	851,657	60,308	..	..
1928	977,589	95,962	..	
1929	1,147,571	121,234	27,773	..
1930	1,334,063	153,595	33,803	£160,209
1931	1,575,151	181,513	37,586	£237,834
1932	1,825,951	157,545	38,087	£322,285
1933	1,962,047	125,485	42,627	£391,823
1934	2,155,371	122,802	50,670	£347,706
1935	2,456,764	113,516	52,379	£421,576
1936	2,628,757	102,530	50,626	£442,009
1937	2,821,597	105,752	48,180	£480,527
1938	2,880,747	97,419	50,478	£365,567
1939	2,588,433	76,464	49,692	..

The figures for net profits also include net profits from other BBC publications—pamphlets, reports, and so on—some of which have already been mentioned and none of which was ever published in order to make a profit. The first book published by the BBC was a slim souvenir volume, *Shakespeare's*

Heroines, which appeared in September 1926 and was issued in conjunction with a series of Sunday afternoon broadcasts by well-known actresses and actors: it was published and distributed as a contribution towards the Shakespeare Memorial Theatre Fund. This was an exceptional enterprise. The BBC's general policy was never to issue any book which could equally well be produced by an outside publisher.

The history of the *Radio Times* was reasonably straightforward during this period. It had only three editors—Walter Fuller, who died suddenly in 1927, Eric Maschwitz, who remained in the post until 1933, and Maurice Gorham, who stayed on until 1941. They were all remarkable men, keenly interested in life as well as in all aspects of radio. Their liveliness prevented the *Radio Times* from ever becoming a mere programme sheet. There was, indeed, a kind of philosophy behind the *Radio Times,* certainly in its early years. Its slogan was 'Plan Your Listening in Advance', and it secured a reasonable response from listeners. Whereas American and continental listeners, for different reasons, were liable to take radio as it came— 'on tap'—British listeners were encouraged by the *Radio Times* itself to be 'discriminating'. Filson Young, for example, hammered home the message week after week for many years in his 'The World We Listen In'; and other 'features'—'Both Sides of the Microphone' and 'What the Other Listener Thinks' —were designed to make for more intelligent and critical listening. A. A. Thomson's 'Strolling Commentaries', which started as a purely comic column in 1934, quickly became what Gorham called 'a very useful form of readable popular propaganda for BBC programmes, and is in fact to a considerable extent doing the work that "The World We Listen In" should really do'.[1]

Two interesting documents survive setting out the views of Maschwitz and Gorham on their job as editors of this most successful paper. In January 1928 Maschwitz stated that the paper had three main objects. First and foremost, it was a programme, and whilst it had the advantage over programmes printed in the newspapers, it had, to some extent at least, to compete with them. The policy of 'getting the most out of the

[1] *Gorham to W. E. G. Murray, 12 Oct. 1934.

programmes' had started with Fuller and had been pushed
further in the light of experience. There was more annotation,
more economy in language, and more intelligent use of pictorial aids to give 'some real hint of the brain and character
behind the voice'. Listeners had shown that they did not like
caricature: 'humorous distortion of their favourite broadcasters
always arouses their resentment'. They had shown too that
they were insufficiently sophisticated to appreciate 'the modern
style of illustrative design'. They had a tremendous unappeased
desire to have more running commentaries and eye-witness
accounts of sporting events. It is easy to see from Maschwitz's
development of these themes why the *Radio Times* was a centre
of ideas about programmes during the 1920s and 1930s and not
simply a recording agency for the programmes which had
already been planned.

The second purpose of the *Radio Times*, Maschwitz went on,
was to serve as 'the Listeners' Magazine'. This meant that it
had to have editorial matter, with a minimum requirement,
however great the demand for advertising space, of seven pages.
This matter should consist first of general or leading articles,
not articles by 'great men' published for reasons of prestige
but genuine contributions to the critical appreciation of radio.
'Broadcasting has, one feels, since the day when its sheer
mechanical novelty wore off, suffered from disregard as an Art.
There is not growing up round the Art of Broadcasting that
strife and contention, that nucleus of critical writing, which has
grown up round the other Arts. There is, indeed, a tendency to
look upon it not as an Art but as a bastard form of the other
Arts. Listeners do not give it the same critical attention they
award the Drama and the Cinema, for example. The reason for
this may be that Broadcasting is too "easy" to listen to or that
there is a general unexpressed impression that it is second best.'
Alongside articles designed to promote a more critical appreciation of particular programmes, there should also be articles
setting out 'the various major changes in the policy and service
of the Corporation'.

Maschwitz said that he had ruled out the reprinting of talks,
for which there had been a great demand, on the grounds that
unless they were almost all to be reprinted, the listener would
become even more disappointed than he was with none. He

was prepared to change his mind on this point, however, and he thought that it was a good idea always to print a note, 'Points from Talks'. Articles on music he particularly welcomed, and he intended to make the most both of 'Listeners' Letters' and of the gossip pages of the paper, which he knew were very widely read. 'Whether regrettable or not, the reader today likes his facts served up in this particular form, and many news-papers today owe a great percentage of their circulation figures to a well-edited gossip page.' He ended his document with a most effective peroration. 'My ambition for the *Radio Times* is no purely journalistic or commercial one (my own belief in, and enthusiasm for, Broadcasting would never permit this) but I should be doing less than my duty by the paper if I did not wish both its circulation and its revenue to be as great as possible.'[1]

Circulation had in fact trebled by the time Gorham wrote his 'manifesto' in 1934. Guy Rice, who had been Secretary of the old British Broadcasting Company, was still Business Manager, but there had been several changes, as enterprising young men like Laurence Gilliam made their way to other branches of the BBC. The biggest change of all was that with the launching of *The Listener* some of the purposes that Maschwitz had underlined now belonged more properly to the new paper than to the old. 'There is no attempt to make the paper a literary weekly', Gorham began, therefore, in 1934, 'com-peting on the ground of literary contents with the old-fashioned literary weeklies (the circulations of which, incidentally, gener-ally range between ten thousand and fifty thousand copies).'

'The present policy', he went on, 'is based on the belief that what readers of the *Radio Times* want [the emphasis is interest-ing] is every kind of information that can help them to appre-ciate broadcast programmes. This does not preclude occasional humorous articles, nor occasional articles on the wider aspects of broadcasting; but it does mean that the standard feature of the paper is no longer the page essay, which I have seen described in a letter of introduction given to a contributor (before my time) as "needing to have only the remotest connec-tion with broadcasting".'

Gorham welcomed the recent relaxation of the 'anonymity

[1] *E. Maschwitz, 'Radio Times, Editorial Policy', 16 Jan. 1928.

rule' on the grounds that listeners liked to feel that they were listening to 'real people'. He intended, he said, to start a new feature called 'People You Hear and People You Don't Hear', giving a piece of personal matter about a well-known broadcaster alongside material about a 'man behind the scenes' who was never heard on the air. He admitted that the trouble inside the BBC was that the people the *Radio Times* most wanted to publicize were often those who were most difficult to approach.

The programme section was, he thought, quite satisfactory, although some Programme Departments sent him material late so that he could not make the best use of it or did not tell him which they thought would be the really important programmes to feature. The brighter the programme pages, the better would be the circulation. As things stood, there were marked seasonal fluctuations, aggravated in 1934, he claimed, by the extremely unpopular attempt of the BBC to introduce a twenty-four-hour clock. 'The paper picked up well after the summer slump [when incidentally there was always a marked fall in the sale of radio receivers]—the Tenth Anniversary Number created a certain amount of friendly interest, and the Christmas Number was a notable peak.' There had also been a rise in January, when a new make-up was introduced. Summing up, he concluded that 'the paper is healthy and ready to develop in scope as well as in circulation'.

The two-fold function of the *Radio Times* is, I take it [he concluded in his peroration], to achieve the largest possible circulation and to give the most helpful kind of service ancillary to broadcasting. For both these purposes, it is essential to consider the really average listener; the person we have been accustomed to personify, in the office, as 'the cabman's wife'. This really average listener will probably buy the paper primarily for the programme pages; that is why they will always remain the backbone of the paper. . . . [Yet] to make such listeners read as much as possible of the *Radio Times*, and to make what they read there help them to understand and appreciate their broadcast programmes is our obvious goal. To attain it, it is necessary to avoid being highbrow but not necessary to be cheap.[1]

Broadly speaking, this remained the policy of the *Radio Times* throughout Gorham's long tenure of office. And it is interesting

[1] *M. Gorham, 'The Radio Times', 1 June 1934.

to note what an able staff he managed to build up, given these objectives. As a former Art Editor, it was natural that he should pay particular attention to illustrations and covers, and there were, indeed, many fascinating achievements, particularly Special Numbers, which remain interesting relics of the art of the 1930s. Every school of artist was represented from Frank Brangwyn to Austin Cooper, and there were two particularly good colour covers in 1937, one for the Coronation by H. W. Nevinson and one for a Woman's Number by Rex Whistler. Until 1935 *Radio Times* drawings were done mainly by Arthur Watts, who had made his name with drawings in *Punch*, and after his death in an aeroplane crash a very different kind of artist was engaged, Bob Sherriffs, who remained in the post until 1940. Watts and Sherriffs used to illustrate each week Gorham's own column, 'Both Sides of the Microphone'.

An equally remarkable group of writers on music was also assembled. They included Ralph Hill, who later became music editor of the *Daily Mail*, and Gerald Abraham, who later became Professor of Music at Liverpool University. The Music Editor was Felix Goodwin. Another field in which Gorham was particularly interested was television. He appreciated very quickly the potentialities of a medium which he was later to control, and employed as television writer Harold Rathbone, a great enthusiast also, who was killed during the Second World War.[1]

If Gorham was interested in the 'average' listener—a somewhat dangerous concept—R. S. Lambert, the highly talented editor of *The Listener*, was interested in the serious student. The idea of a magazine which would back up the then dubious authority of the spoken word with the sacred authority of the written word was first mooted by the Hadow Committee.[2] A journal, it was felt, would supplement pamphlets and assist 'follow-up'. Many memoranda were written, however, before it was finally decided to plump for a 'popular two-penny' rather than a 'stately sixpenny', and there was even an argument about whether the title *The Listener* was appropriate.

---

[1] For these and other details, see M. Gorham, *Sound and Fury* (1948), especially chapter vi.
[2] See above, p. 186.

Nicolls, who was then General Editor of Publications, played an active part in these discussions, and Lambert set to work in the autumn of 1928 to produce the first 'dummy' numbers.[1]

There was immediate opposition from almost every quarter. The publishing interests accused the BBC of entering a field which was not its own, while the existing weeklies raged against unfair competition. Lord Riddell and Sir James Owen, in particular, were so incensed that they decided to appeal direct to the Prime Minister. Never could there have been a bigger row about the launching of an innocent non-political journal.

The *Financial News* led the first attack, which was followed up with vigour by the *New Statesman*. 'It is without doubt a profit-making proposition,' the *Financial News* complained, 'and is an illegitimate stretching of official activity.'[2] 'The project is thoroughly objectionable, ought never to have been authorised, and ought, even at the eleventh hour, to be abandoned', editorialized the *New Statesman*.[3] The flood of criticism carried with it some of the popular dailies, but it was the *New Statesman* which enjoyed itself most. 'That the BBC should seek to invade the press with a view to influencing the public through its eyes as well as its ears seems to us to a wholly intolerable and indefensible proposition. . . . Are we presently to have a BBC *Times* and a BBC *Daily Mail*?'[4]

The *Spectator* came to the defence of the BBC. 'A few of the extreme champions of private trade seem to us to have exaggerated their grievance.' It did not claim that the BBC was wrong to move over from the spoken word to the written word —oddly enough, in this context, G. D. H. Cole had been its biggest advocate—but it urged it to be cautious in its advertising policy. 'The BBC has performed a great service in bringing backward minds all over the country to a dawning recognition of what is good and what is bad in the spoken word.' Could not the same service be performed now with the written word as well? 'There is one way in which the BBC could take all the sting out of its proposed enterprise, and that is by refraining from competing with existing papers for the custom of advertisers.'[5] It is difficult not to see in the background of both gentle

[1] *BBC Press Release, 3 Jan. 1929.   [2] *Financial News*, 7 Dec. 1928.
[3] *New Statesman*, 28 Dec. 1928.
[4] Ibid.   [5] *Spectator*, 12 Jan. 1929.

remarks of this kind and the fierce remarks of the *New Statesman* the fear of a minority counterpart to the majority *Radio Times*.

From the literary cavalry of the *New Statesman* and the *Spectator*, the battle moved to the big battalions in December 1928, when the formidable quartet with whom the BBC had had so many dealings—the Newspaper Proprietors' Association, the Newspaper Society, the Periodical Trade Press, and the Weekly Newspaper Proprietors' Association—appealed direct to the Postmaster-General. They asked him to receive a deputation of protest against the proposed publication of *The Listener* on the grounds that it was 'an undesirable incursion by the Corporation into the newspaper and magazine publishing business' and that the BBC was taking unfair advantage of its Charter.

The Postmaster-General refused to receive the deputation so, nothing daunted, the Big Four then directed their attention at the Prime Minister himself. They wrote a letter on 3 January claiming that 'the BBC was diverting trade from legitimate trade channels', and persuaded the Prime Minister to receive the deputation. The Newspaper Proprietors' Association sought to strengthen its argument, which was very fully backed by most other press interests, by pointing out that it represented from two to three hundred million pounds of capital. 'It is curious', Lambert noted laconically, 'that a Socialist weekly should have been the means of setting in motion such a gigantic block of capitalist power, and that the leading Socialist daily should not have dissociated itself in any way from this claim on behalf of the sanctity of private enterprise.'[1] Gladstone Murray, however, had a more shrewd idea of what was happening. When the attack reached its height 'on all vulnerable points', he saw behind it the influence of Lord Riddell as a kind of *agent provocateur*. 'If the Corporation remains steady,' he went on, 'all will be well.'[2]

Reith was abroad in Switzerland when the attack was raging, and he returned to England in a thoroughly bellicose mood himself. He had been the most powerful advocate of a serious BBC journal, and he was determined not to allow Lord Riddell and Sir James Owen to manœuvre with the Board of Governors to stop the BBC from doing what he wanted. 'Apparently every

---

[1] *Ariel and All His Quality*, p. 102.
[2] *W. E. G. Murray, Notes of 7 Jan. 1929.

newspaper in the country is trying to prevent our publishing it',
he wrote on 7 January 1929. 'I was not the least bit worried if
only the damn silly Governors would keep out of it.'[1] As soon
as he got back, he went to see the Prime Minister himself,
suggesting plainly that Baldwin should tell Riddell's committee
to see what it could do with the BBC before bothering him.[2]
The next day Riddell telephoned Reith and fixed up a meeting.
Reith had been expecting a committee of three or four people.
There were, in fact, thirteen or fourteen. 'They had even
mobilised the printers.' Reith himself was alone—'deliberately
so'. He told Lord Riddell, Sir James Owen, J. J. Astor, and the
other press representatives to their faces that they had been
unwise not to consult the BBC before appealing to the Prime
Minister. Reith created a remarkable impression. 'Riddell drove
me back to Savoy Hill; he said he thought I would be Prime
Minister one day.'

After meeting the press representatives, Reith went back to the
Board of Governors carrying a short statement, with which they
agreed. He then met the press committee again—by himself
—and within an hour got them to accept his statement in place
of a long and, to Reith, unacceptable memorandum by Riddell.
The press delegation was then received by the Governors, that
part of the proceedings lasting for ten minutes. The result was
a settlement which was very favourable to the BBC, and Baldwin sent for Reith to tell him how pleased he was about the
way things had worked out. The BBC had got its serious journal, much to the delight not only of Reith but of Lord Justice
Sankey and the members of the Adult Education Council. The
Corporation made it clear, however, that it did not want to
publish much material in *The Listener* other than broadcast
talks, and that there would be no difficulty in a figure of 10 per
cent. as the maximum for other kinds of material. This was
put on record, and the BBC also promised not to accept for *The
Listener* more advertisements than were 'strictly necessary'. With
the agreement signed, the first number of *The Listener* came out
as planned on 16 January.

The restraint on advertising helped *The Listener*, and the

[1] Reith, Diary, 7 Jan. 1929.
[2] *Into the Wind*, p. 129. The account which follows draws heavily on this source,
pp. 129 ff.

10 per cent. quota was conceived of so flexibly that it proved no barrier to Lambert's plans for the new journal. The noise of battle very quickly subsided, and *The Listener* took its proper place among British weeklies. Lambert wrote a most interesting memorandum on his plans in July 1930. 'There need be no despondency about the circulation', he began, 'although there might be room for a feeling of depression about the size of the intelligent reading public in this country.' Of the alternate ways of treating the periodical, the first as a narrowly educational paper, the second as 'a vehicle of general culture', Lambert unhesitatingly preferred the second. He felt, however, that the periodical had three weaknesses. It lacked editorial personality, it had a certain monotony and 'lack of elasticity' arising from 'the printing of so many serial talks', and it did not contain enough book reviews. The first defect could be remedied in time although remedies would all fall short of giving the editor the full independence of, say, the editor of the *New Statesman*; and the second and third needed immediate attention. Nicolls also was quite sure that 'from every point of view it would be a mistake to lower the "brow" of the paper'.[1]

The 'brow' was not lowered, and *The Listener* soon became renowned not only for the quality of its book reviews but for the variety of its intellectual fare. The issues for July 1930, the month when Lambert was preparing his memorandum, included articles by Sir John Simon on 'The Future of Indian Government', Ivor Brown on 'The Game of Cricket', Solly Zuckerman on 'Monkeys and Men', Leonard Woolley on 'Treasures of the Grave', Sir Henry Hadow on 'The Universities and Industry', and Beatrice Webb on 'Taking the Strain off Parliament'. There was also a supplement on 'Race and Labour' by the anthropologist, Bronislaw Malinowski. New novels were reviewed by V. Sackville-West, Harold Nicolson wrote on 'People and Things', Lambert had an editorial on television called 'Looking-In?', and there was an advertisement for Beecham's Imperial League of Opera.

Advertisements and correspondence are almost as interesting to the historian as the articles and reviews. The reviews, however, were of high quality, since Janet Adam Smith and J. R. Ackerley, who succeeded her as review editor, were people of

[1] *Note of 1 July 1930.

sensitivity and style who brought to the periodical a wealth of experienced writers, including poets and novelists. From time to time new features were introduced, including 'News Reel' in 1935—this brought welcome congratulations from the Advertising Manager[1]—and the photographs of the late 1930s were of a high quality which has never since been excelled. Radio criticism began with Grace Wyndham Goldie's appointment as radio drama critic in April 1935. It followed talks between Lambert and Gielgud, the latter being 'enthusiastic for the idea'.[2] Mrs. Wyndham Goldie's eminent suitability for the appointment is shown in the first article she wrote, in which she stressed that there could be no effective radio criticism 'based on ignorance of the conditions of work'. 'The physical limitations imposed upon any art by the material through which it works determines its form, and it is impossible to criticise without knowing what they are.'[3] This was a good start to radio's deliberate self-criticism. There followed in March 1938 the regular feature 'Critic on the Hearth, Comments of a Casual Listener'.[4] As for the main staple of *The Listener*, the broadcast talks, they imparted to it, as Lambert remarked, something of the quality of an anthology. The paper had 'a subtle quality, rather akin to the flavour of fine wines, which many palates cannot appreciate'.[5]

The publication of talks raised, of course, far more profound questions about the relationship between the written and the spoken word. Miss Matheson and Siepmann were at pains to treat the Talk as a separate art form: they did not care whether it read well or not, if it sounded right.[6] This made them distrust editorial tidying up in *The Listener* office. They wanted something nearer to a *Hansard* of talks than Lambert was willing to concede. The result was an undercurrent of controversy which was made no easier when the unscripted talk and discussion began to come into their own and posed even more problems for the editor of *The Listener*.[7] Lambert complained also that

[1] *Judson to R. S. Lambert, 5 Nov. 1935.
[2] *Lambert to W. E. G. Murray, 18 Apr. 1935.
[3] G. Wyndham Goldie, 'At the Broadcast Play' in *The Listener*, 22 May 1935.
[4] *The Listener*, 23 Mar. 1938.
[5] *Ariel and All His Quality*, p. 116.
[6] See above, pp. 125–6.
[7] *R. S. Lambert, 'Editing *The Listener*', 2 Feb. 1938.

in 1936 talks lacked 'outstanding names and arresting subjects' and failed to provide 'journalistic attraction'.[1] He remained editor until January 1939, surviving the furore of the Mongoose Case.[2] Eventually he retired of his own choice when he felt that he wanted a new kind of work.

Lambert was essentially an individualist, interested in the 'circle' which broadcasting was creating, the writers, poets, novelists, and artists who in some sense were being drawn towards the 'Establishment' of the BBC. It is revealing to note that in his book *Ariel and All His Quality* he makes no judgements about listener research, which was one of Maurice Gorham's favourite preoccupations as editor of the *Radio Times*. Gorham was interested, above all else, in listeners: Lambert in *the* listener. Yet both men were, after all, a part of the circle themselves, critics of Reith yet directly associated with the projection of the BBC's philosophy of broadcasting. From time to time Lambert wrote editorials on British broadcasting in international perspective. In 1934, for example, he compared criticisms of British radio with criticisms of American radio, noting that there was 'a close connection between the kind of organisation built up and the kind of programme which is offered to the listener'.[3]

Outside the London circle, far from the 'Bloomsbury Circle' which H. A. L. Fisher quite erroneously felt was exerting too much influence in the counsels of *The Listener*,[4] were the broadcasting circles of the regions. What broadcasting was doing or not doing there raised a quite different set of questions, some of them, however, of an equally controversial character.

[1] R. S. Lambert to S. Tallents, 20 July 1936 (Tallents Papers).
[2] See below, pp. 472–3.
[3] *The Listener*, 3 Jan. 1934. Lambert pinned this editorial on a talk by Ernest Barker on 'The Constitution of the BBC' and an American book by H. Hettinger called *A Decade of Radio Advertising*. He also quoted a *Literary Digest* straw vote of American readers' radio dislikes. They included 'trashy, coy, cute, patronising, wise-cracking announcers', 'thrillers bad for children', and 'children trying to sing sex songs'.
[4] *Note by Sir Stephen Tallents on a conversation with H. A. L. Fisher, 10 Nov. 1937.

3. Regional Broadcasting

ONE aspect of increased social inquiry in the late 1930s was unprecedented interest in the life of the regions. 'BBC staff resources are very small whether for establishing comprehensive public relations throughout the country or for tapping local programme resources,' Tallents wrote in August 1937. 'This suggests that each Region should be surveyed on a plan, and that the results should be systematically recorded, and made available to the different departments of the Regional staff.'[1]

This interest marked a new phase in the story of regional broadcasting, one of the most important of the BBC's inter-war ventures. In 1935 Charles Siepmann, on leaving the Talks Department, had been appointed Director of Regional Relations. He produced a fascinating *Report on Regions* in January 1936, in which for the first time an official of the BBC fully explored the social and cultural aspects of regional broadcasting. 'After nearly ten years of concentrated work in London,' he began, 'I could not fail to be impressed by contrasts in the conditions and attitudes of mind which obtain outside London . . . [yet everywhere] I found a common pre-occupation with the dangers resulting from the increasing tendency for administrative, cultural and industrial concentration in the London area.'[2] These comments raised issues which had deep roots and which spread over into many other activities besides broadcasting.

The origins of the BBC's 'Regional Scheme' belong to a much earlier period, and concern different personalities and problems. They are related to an engineering background—to questions concerning the need for 'more extensive broadcasting', which had been raised before the Company was converted into a Corporation.[3] Given that a limited number of wavelengths were available for the development of British broadcasting, how were the wavelengths best to be used in the interests of a

[1] *Tallents to all Regional Directors, 17 Aug. 1937. At a meeting of 8 Oct. 1937, at which Reith was present, all the Regional Programme Directors expressed their interest in Listener Research. (Note by Tallents, 13 Oct. 1937.)

[2] *C. A. Siepmann, *Report on Regions*, Jan. 1936, p. 2.

[3] See *The Birth of Broadcasting*, esp. pp. 213-27.

growing radio public? The original Regional Scheme was a plan for building five high-powered twin-wave stations—the strength of transmission on each wavelength being more or less the same—to supersede the older system of nine main transmitting stations and eleven subsidiary relay stations of low power.[1]

The nine main transmitting stations had been located in London, Manchester, Birmingham, Newcastle, Cardiff, Glasgow, Aberdeen, Bournemouth, and Belfast,[2] and the eleven relay stations were in or near Sheffield, Plymouth, Edinburgh, Liverpool, Leeds, Bradford, Hull, Nottingham, Dundee, Stoke-on-Trent, and Swansea. The 'relay station' policy had been effective in increasing coverage at a time when the BBC wished to increase licence revenue yet could not employ large amounts of capital. It was impossible to extend it, however, partly 'because the nations of Europe were rapidly building up similar systems and interference between stations even within their proper service areas was growing acute', partly because the scheme did not meet the needs of listeners outside the densely populated urban areas.[3]

In place of the local network, therefore, it was suggested by Peter Eckersley that there should be a number of 'Regional stations', serving the needs not only of townsfolk but of country dwellers. The building of Daventry, a genuinely pioneer experiment in long-wave high-power broadcasting, permitted 'the experimental beginnings of a Regional Scheme'. Reliance on relay stations had 'consolidated the Company's resources and made Daventry possible'.[4] The opening of the new station, the biggest broadcasting station in the world, in July 1925 ensured that 94 per cent. of the population of Britain could enjoy practically uninterrupted reception of a 'National' (5XX) programme.[5] As the Regional Scheme evolved, each of the five

---

[1] For the development of this pre-regional system, see *The Birth of Broadcasting*, pp. 215 ff.

[2] The scheme of building British broadcasting around these station points had been put forward before the Company came into existence. Bournemouth was substituted for Plymouth, however, and Belfast added to the list after Eckersley's appointment. See *P. P. Eckersley, *Regional Scheme Report*, 20 June 1927. This was an important document of sixty pages.

[3] Ibid.   [4] *BBC Handbook* (1928), 'The Regional Scheme', p. 60.

[5] The predecessor of 5XX was an experimental long-wave station at the Marconi works at Chelmsford. It began to function in July 1924. See *The Birth of Broadcasting*, pp. 223–4.

new high-power twin-wave transmitters was designed to transmit two programmes—the first its own, and the second the
'National' programme, originating in London and transmitted from Daventry.

Before Daventry was opened Peter Eckersley, the Chief
Engineer of the BBC, had already conceived of regional broadcasting. The idea came to him, he has written, in 1924.[1] At
that time it was a particularly bold and imaginative idea, for
there were only a million licence-holders in the whole country.
His purpose was not to tap reserves of local talent in Britain,
the programme builder's notion,[2] or to seek to give provincial
culture a new place in the Britain of the future.[3] What he
wished to do was far more simple—to make a start, through
regional broadcasting, on the necessary task of giving listeners
in all parts of the country the chance of listening to 'alternative
programmes'.

He began by stating the problem in technical terms. 'There
is an analogy which, if a little far-fetched, is nonetheless essentially sound. The problem of broadcasting distribution is not
unlike that of trying to illuminate a square or market place
with red and blue light so that two colours (red and blue) can
be seen and appreciated everywhere. There are two problems
(a) to keep the actual illumination constant over the area; (b)
never to have a preponderance of either red or blue. Problem
(a) is best solved by having the greatest number of lamps
practically possible and problem (b) is solved by making pairs
of lamps so that one colour can never dominate.'[4]

Because of the shortage of wavelengths not only in Britain
but in Europe, a shortage which had become so acute that it
had speeded up the formation of the International Broadcasting
Union to 'regulate the ether',[5] the most that could be offered to
the majority of British listeners was a choice of two programmes.

[1] See ibid., pp. 396–7. See also P. P. Eckersley, *The Power Behind the Microphone*
(1941), esp. ch. vii, 'The Regional Scheme'; *Radio Times*, 7 Mar. 1930.
[2] See above, pp. 26 ff.
[3] See, for example, *BBC Annual* (1936) which spoke of the effort of the BBC 'to
employ and foster the characteristic resources of each part of the country' (p. 26).
[4] *The Regional Scheme Report*, 20 June 1927.
[5] *The Birth of Broadcasting*, pp. 315 ff., discusses the origin of the IBU, described
there under its French name, the Union Internationale de Radiophonie. See also
below, pp. 339 ff.

'Two', Eckersley rightly thought, 'were at any rate better than one.'[1] 'One man's meat is another man's poison, and without the possibility of alternative programmes a great deal of irritation is caused to listeners because of continual compromise.'[2] Eckersley hoped that alternative programmes would 'contrast' with each other. 'What are we going to do to ensure a real contrast?' he asked. 'What can be contrasted? Talk and Music? But suppose Sir Oliver Lodge (who is popular because he is fallacious) and Melba singing in *Bohème* occur simultaneously, the listener is faced with *embarras de richesse*.'[3]

Although the distinction between 'Home' and 'Light' was not anticipated at this juncture, there was talk inside the BBC of 'highbrow' and 'lowbrow', and Eckersley himself realized clearly that one way of ensuring 'contrast' would be to use one BBC programme to make a special appeal to minorities and the other to cater for the wants of the majority. He drew a distinction between 'universal' and 'speciality' programmes, claiming that each had its place. Yet he was more interested in the fundamental point of choice than in the details of what was to be chosen.

Reith was equally determined that listeners should have the right to choose. When a number of BBC officials suggested that there was no need for alternative programmes, Reith pressed the case for extending choice as well as 'spreading the service'. He agreed with Eckersley that a 'loss of interest in the service as well as loss of pride of place in world broadcasting' would occur if the Regional Scheme or something like it were not put into operation.[4]

The matter was first discussed by the Board of the old Company in February 1925, when Reith told the other members 'that there was an increasing demand by the public to hear

---

[1] For the shortage of wavelengths, see *The Birth of Broadcasting*, pp. 308 ff.; *The Power Behind the Microphone*, p. 116; *Report on the Proposed Regional Scheme by the Chief Engineer*, 1929, p. 3. 'Continental stations increased rapidly in number and, with the limited number of channels available, caused mutual interferences. . . . After a study of the international situation . . . it became obvious that broadcasting, in whatever country, should be based on the use of fewer transmitting stations than used before, which had therefore to be of higher power.'

[2] *Regional Scheme Report*, 20 June 1927.

[3] *Memorandum by the Chief Engineer in Relation to the Distribution of the Service*, Nov. 1926.

[4] *Regional Scheme Report*, 20 June 1927.

other stations' and that if the Company were 'to retain its control of broadcasting, conditions somewhat approximate to the American variety of stations would have to be instituted, but naturally without the American confusion'.[1] He went on to back Eckersley fully when the Chief Engineer was working out details of the Regional Scheme, even though he knew that the scheme would involve considerable dislocation of existing services, would seriously disturb the pattern of listening behaviour, and would take years to put into effect.

Don't try and communicate with your neighbours.

25. How Not to Use Wireless Equipment: A Bateman Cartoon

Choice had to be bought at a price. The dislocation would be considerable enough to entail abandoning most of the existing one-programme transmitters and acquiring new sites outside cities yet near to the populous areas. Disturbance of listening behaviour would be caused not only by the large-scale change in wavelengths—never a popular procedure—but by the enforced obsolescence of many cherished, if crude, pieces of wireless equipment. It was inevitable, indeed, in the new

[1] *Board Meeting, Minutes, 19 Mar. 1925.

conditions, that the owner of a valve set would have a great and increasing advantage over the owner of a cheaper crystal set. The 're-distribution of the service', as it was called at first, 'would encourage crystal users to adapt their sets to valves, since, under the higher powered scheme, they would be able to hear stations other than their own, and in addition those outside crystal areas would be given a choice of stations, the main stations being audible at much greater distances.'

For all these reasons the Board of the Company recognized in February 1925 that the 'scheme of redistribution' could only be put into operation slowly, and that 'plenty of time would have to be given for the adaptation of manufacturers' policy thereto'.[1] In particular, time was needed to develop equipment. There was no such thing as a high-power transmitter in 1925, and the BBC itself had to develop transmitter designs which were put into production by the Marconi Company.

The Board knew also that there would be considerable difficulty in securing the consent of the Post Office to the development of a large-scale scheme of high-powered stations. The Post Office had been 'concerned at the power demanded' when Reith first broached the proposals in very tentative form.[2] It asked for more details of the scheme and for an explanation of the reasoning that lay behind it. It also warned Eckersley of the perils of disturbing 'customers'. Each time a newer and better method had been introduced for calling a telephone exchange, the public had been 'vituperous' in their complaints against the innovation: 'people got into the habit of turning the magneto ringer when they called up, and the introduction of the central battery system was looked upon (particularly by infuriated colonels) as a definite deprivation'.[3]

In a letter of December 1925 Reith set out the main points of the BBC's case for the approval of the Post Office.

We, who formerly were the pioneers of broadcasting in Europe and of unified control in the world, are now losing our supremacy, since Germany is expanding her service rapidly in terms of higher power. Public and press criticism is accumulating against our pro-

---

[1] *Board Meeting, Minutes, 19 Mar. 1925.
[2] *R. A. Dalzell to Reith, 9 Nov. 1925.
[3] *Regional Scheme Report, 20 June 1927.

gramme policy. Alternative programmes give the only solution to
an otherwise insoluble problem. Alternative programmes can only
be given with more wavelengths or higher power. The former is
impossible owing to the international situation. . . . Objections to the
use of higher power within a defined waveband can only be raised
in terms of obsolescence of the apparatus or services which fear
jamming outside that waveband. We feel that a legitimate expansion
of a public service should not be hindered by difficulties which can
be eliminated. If specific objection is made that the harmonics of
our high-powered stations may interfere with existing services, we
trust that permission to carry out the scheme will be made con-
ditional, and not dismissed on the score of a potential difficulty.[1]

This powerful plea did not move the Post Office to speedy
action, nor did the recommendation of the Crawford Committee
that the Postmaster-General should continue negotiations
'which we understand have recently been initiated in connec-
tion with a scheme for new high-power stations'.[2] The newly
founded but short-lived Wireless Organizations Advisory Committee, set up in January 1927,[3] expressed disappointment one
month after its inception that 'no apparent progress had been
made' with the scheme, despite popular feeling that such a
scheme should have 'matured before now'. It asked the Postmaster-General to find 'an early opportunity to reassure listeners
that a system of distribution effective for the transmission of
alternative programmes, will be fully expedited so far as his
department is concerned'.

The most that the Post Office had been willing to do in 1926
was to authorize the start of further experimental broadcasting
at a new Daventry station, 'as a necessary preliminary to the
development of the whole scheme'.[4] Equipment for the new
station was ordered in the summer of 1926 and delivered in
March 1927. With the knowledge that the Post Office had been
willing to go as far as this, the BBC advised the Wireless Organizations Advisory Committee that it would be unwise to
press the Postmaster-General further. 'It was quite possible,
indeed, that any further pressure exercised on the Post Office

---

[1] *Reith to Sir Evelyn Murray, 24 Dec. 1925.
[2] Cmd. 2599 (1926), *Report of the Broadcasting Committee*, p. 12.
[3] See *The Birth of Broadcasting*, pp. 249–50.
[4] *Wireless Organizations Committee, Minutes, 14 Feb. 1927.

now might prejudice the position later on when there was really something to be gained.'[1]

More valuable at that point than outside public pressure, Reith and Eckersley maintained, were the recommendations of a detailed report on the technical side of the projected scheme. The report had been prepared by an independent committee of experts, appointed by the BBC, consisting of Dr. W. H. Eccles, the president of the Institution of Electrical Engineers and formerly a member of the Sykes Committee, Professor E. V. Appleton, then of London University, and Dr. L. B. Turner of Cambridge.

Throughout 1926 Eckersley had been perfecting the details of his 'regional plan'. He had finally reached the point where he offered a choice of four different ways of siting regional stations. Technical factors predominated in his detailed scheme. The siting of the stations had to be determined first by the power to be employed in the aerial, second by telephone facilities for simultaneous broadcasting connexions, and third by the routes of power cables under the new Central Electricity Grid Scheme. At the same time non-technical factors influenced final judgement. 'We had the choice of running along the line, London–Chelmsford–Colchester, or the line London–Derby. The Colchester route does not appeal, because so much of the field strength will be wasted over the sea, and so more interference (however little there should be) will be caused with the shipping in the estuary mouth. . . . We cannot come south of London, firstly because the wipe-out zone would prejudice the use of reaching-out sets in an area which is densely populated with well-to-do people, and also because of the non-existence of power and telephone facilities. It is furthermore doubtful whether the south coast represents numerically so important an area as that of the industrial Midlands.'[2]

Eckersley's plan, stated in the form of a timetable of development, won the approval of the Control Board and of the Board of the Company. In addition to objections from the Post Office, however, there was opposition from a powerful section of the wireless trade. 'Whilst no trade antipathy should stand in our way,' Control Board decided, 'it was desirable to have a paid

[1] *Wireless Organizations Committee, Minutes, 28 Feb. 1927.
[2] *Regional Scheme Report, 20 June 1927.

consultative technical committee to investigate the scheme, as the backing of such a committee unconnected with the trade and the Post Office would be of considerable value.'[1] The Eccles Committee was the result. It was asked to advise the BBC whether Eckersley's scheme was the most satisfactory and efficient method of achieving 'what was desired'. 'In the event of agreement', were the further plans for its extension approved and was it considered that there would be any justifiable opposition from the 'users of the ether'? 'In the event of disagreement', could any alternative methods or any 'lines of research to bring about the same end' be suggested? The experts soon produced an interim report strongly supporting Eckersley's proposals. They accepted also the long-term plan of opening five twin-wave stations, each costing up to £40,000.

No other 'users of the ether', they added, could justifiably object. This was a useful point, since the Post Office was naturally sensitive to the interests of the Armed Services, in particular. Eccles and his colleagues added also that in reaching their decisions they had given careful consideration to the listeners' point of view, realizing that the regional scheme 'affects a large proportion of listeners technically and also in what may be called "the civic sense"'. On both the technical details and the social implications they were fully satisfied.[2]

The unanimity of the Eccles Committee was useful to the BBC in strengthening its case with the wireless trade and the Post Office. So too was the experimental work at Daventry, where the new station (5GB) was operating very successfully, as Post Office engineers admitted, in its strictly limited broadcasts. Listeners who took their service from Daventry now had, at certain times of the day, a clear choice of programmes. The success of this arrangement for this limited section of the listening public meant that the arguments for delaying the further development of the scheme as a whole looked peculiarly flimsy. 'We believe that the inadequacy of the present distribution will shortly create real embarrassment if steps are not quickly taken to adapt the service to the enlarging requirements of the listening public', Reith wrote to the Secretary of the Post Office in July 1927.[3]

[1] *Control Board Minutes, 3 May 1927.
[2] *Report of the Eccles Committee.
[3] *Reith to Sir Evelyn Murray, 1 July 1927.

As a result of this letter a conference was held at the Post Office on 19 July 1927 at which the representatives of the BBC —Reith, Carpendale, and Eckersley—met four representatives of the Post Office—W. T. Leech, E. H. Shaughnessy, Lt.-Col. A. S. Angwin, and J. W. Wissenden—and representatives of the Admiralty, the Air Ministry, and the War Office Wireless Telegraphy Board. F. W. Phillips of the Post Office was in the chair. All the old arguments were rehearsed again. Phillips began by saying that the Post Office was 'rather perturbed' at the possibility of a large proportion of listeners being deprived of any coherent programme unless they modified their sets and of public outcry against the closing of the present main and relay stations, and Air Commodore Blandy, on behalf of the Services, expressed fear that there would be interference with their operations. Tall masts were particularly dangerous, he maintained, and for this reason the Post Office normally placed a total embargo on masts more than 150 feet high within an area south and east of the Wash and the Bristol Channel. Had this objection been sustained, there could have been no pattern of regional broadcasting.

A new argument for delay was also introduced into the discussion—that since there was to be a World Wireless Conference at Washington in 1927, a 'permanent scheme' would be difficult to approve before then. When Leech asked Eckersley whether the BBC was alone among European broadcasting organizations in making proposals of the kind they were advocating, Eckersley replied that while 'regional schemes' had already been adopted in Germany, Italy, Czechoslovakia, and Sweden, no proposals for twin-power stations had been formulated. 'The BBC', he added proudly, 'desired to be pioneers in this respect.'

Eckersley was intensely irritated at this late stage of the argument by what he thought was 'the silliness of the bureaucrats'.[1] He foresaw no difficulties in putting across the Regional Scheme if a patient policy of educating listeners in its implications were followed: 'The Regional Scheme must, of necessity, be introduced gradually even to the extent of giving alternate performances at a Regional Station and a Main Station for a

---

[1] *The Power Behind the Microphone*, p. 123.

time until the BBC and listeners were satisfied that they could obtain a satisfactory service under the new Scheme. Preliminary propaganda should be confined to generalities, such as enunciation of the general policy, "fewer stations, greater power", followed, when the Stations were nearly ready, by informative articles in the public press. . . . The alteration of a crystal set would cost only five shillings.' There would be no 'overwhelming complaint' if there were proper 'explanatory and educational work'.

Reith, who said nothing at the meeting for two hours 'and then dealt with the various points raised, and with some emphasis', felt that he 'altered things completely'.[1] His forceful contribution successfully overrode most of the objections expressed except that of the need to wait until after the Washington Conference.[2] Even though Reith pointed out in a letter to Sir Evelyn Murray six days after the meeting that he could not understand what possible bearing the Washington Conference could have on the implementation of the scheme,[3] the most that the Post Office would do in July 1927 was to authorize regular scheduled programmes for Daventry 5GB from 21 August onwards. On behalf of the Post Office, Leech insisted that no publicity should be given to the 'main Scheme', which was dependent, he said, on the building of high masts of 300 feet or more which could not at that time be authorized.[4]

The BBC was forced, therefore, to issue a statement in general terms about the better service that would ultimately be provided by a Regional Scheme. 'The progressive improvement in landlines attended by a corresponding development of programme technique and material synchronises happily with the present opportunity of improving the means of distribution.'[5] To Eccles, Eckersley was much more frank both about present frustrations and future intentions: 'The Post Office have temporarily turned down the Regional Scheme. Their attitude is that so much dislocation will be caused to listeners, that it will place the Postmaster-General in an invidious position

[1] Reith, Diary, 19 July 1927.
[2] *Post Office Conference, Minutes, 19 July 1927.
[3] *Reith to Sir Evelyn Murray, 25 July 1927.
[4] *'Basic Memorandum' attached to letter from Leech to Carpendale, 27 July 1927.
[5] *BBC Press Statement, 29 July 1927.

inasmuch as he will have to take the Parliamentary responsibility. We, naturally, cannot accept this over-cautious attitude,
more particularly in view of the recommendations of your Committee. I do not think there is a lot to be done particularly, but
I think we should proceed just as if the Regional Scheme was
going to take place, only allowing certain time for negotiations.
The Post Office, at any rate, have consented to the putting of
5GB into service as an alternative to Daventry 5XX.'[1]

The BBC did, in fact, go ahead just as Eckersley said. Even
before the Post Office Conference met, the Control Board had
decided to follow up 5GB with the building of new stations
near London and Manchester. Cardiff and other regional
stations were to follow later.[2] The formal opening of 5GB in
August 1927 gave a foretaste of some of the problems—and
opportunities—that lay ahead. The older Daventry Station
(5XX) was broadcasting the London programme at this time
on a long wavelength. Station 5GB, on a medium wavelength
and with greater power—30 kilowatts against 25—was used
to provide a 'contrasting' programme of the kind that Eckersley
had advocated and the Control Board had agreed upon.

To simplify wavelength problems, however, and to cut costs,
5GB replaced the older station of lower power (5IT) in Birmingham. Many of the programmes of the new station originated from the Birmingham studio. Listeners in Birmingham,
however, had to adapt their listening conditions in the new
circumstances. Eckersley knew that while they would be able
to receive adequate signals from 5GB, the signals would be
somewhat weaker than those to which they were accustomed.
Unfortunately on the night of the changeover, many Birmingham listeners, unaware of the technical subtleties of the transfer, heard nothing at all when the new station went on the air.
The result was a wave of public protest which only gradually
subsided. The Post Office received 3,000 complaints and
Eckersley himself estimated that 2 per cent. of the Birmingham
listening public gave up their wireless licences.[3] A Birmingham
clergyman made a particularly eloquent protest that his poorer

---

[1] *Eckersley to Eccles, 22 July 1927.
[2] *Control Board Minutes, 29 June 1927.
[3] *Report on the Proposed Regional Scheme by the Chief Engineer, 1929, p. 27; Post
Office Archives.

parishioners could not afford to buy sets good enough to pick up the new 5GB programmes. As late as February 1928 complaints were still being received by the Post Office 'at the rate of over 100 per week'.[1]

As the protests subsided, however, and alternative programmes (5GB and 5XX) could be picked up satisfactorily in Birmingham, the example of Birmingham could be held up both to the nation and the Post Office. 'We could cite a contented Birmingham as the justification of the Regional scheme and the chi-kying of the critics became less violent. But it had been "a damned close-run thing" as Wellington said of Waterloo.'[2]

The closing of 5IT and the opening of 5GB had nothing to do with the arguments for and against *regional* broadcasting as such. It was not until 1930, indeed, that the term 'National' programme was introduced to describe the older Daventry 5XX transmission. The argument was pursued in 1927 only in terms of 'alternative programming'. At first Eckersley himself had not anticipated the wholesale abandonment of the old local relay stations which had been built in 1923 and 1924. In a note prepared in November 1925 he had admitted that 'relay stations foster a provincial enthusiasm difficult to appreciate in London'.[3] In a later memorandum of November 1926 he had written that such local stations could be useful in the future in providing afternoon transmissions to schools, 'fostering local interest by means of the children's hour', broadcasting accounts of local dinners and 'speeches by local men', and providing 'local news'. Someone at Savoy Hill—unidentified—scribbled a large pencilled question mark against each of Eckersley's four points.

Eckersley had envisaged the local stations broadcasting local programmes for strictly limited hours and not being used to relay either 'Regional' or 'National' programmes. In fact, the relay stations were very quickly closed down as the Regional Scheme took shape—the first of them, Nottingham, in 1927. The crucial decisions were taken at a meeting of the Control

[1] Minute by F. W. Phillips (Post Office Archives).
[2] *The Power Behind the Microphone*, p. 122.
[3] *Unpublished Memorandum, 'The Distribution of the Service', Nov. 1925.

Board on 17 November 1926. It was at this meeting that the
BBC decided to substitute high-power twin-wave regional
stations for the existing main stations at Glasgow, Manchester, Cardiff, and London, to abandon the name 'relay
station', to restrict the time and range of programmes from the
newly styled 'local broadcasting stations' and ultimately to
abolish them altogether. 'It is decided that during the next five
years a gradual elimination of all stations other than Regional
will take place unless technical methods can be devised to meet
the problem of their retention.'[1]

The Control Board, however, went further than this. In all
its previous discussions of the Regional Scheme it had been
mainly concerned with technical questions and related questions
of finance. On 10 November 1926 and again on 17 November,
however, it wrote into the projected scheme cultural presuppositions which had nothing to do with technical factors, but a
great deal to do with finance. No provincial station, it was
decided, was to do anything which could be better done from
London, and in normal circumstances it was in London that
'the best talent and the greatest facility' were available.
'Occasionally a provincial hall or studio may be the originator',
but the scope of local programmes was to be narrowed drastically in the future. Although provincial orchestras were to
continue at the Manchester, Glasgow, Cardiff, and Belfast
stations, the orchestras at Newcastle, Bournemouth, and
Aberdeen would have to be reduced to octets on the completion of their contracts. 'The best can only be given where the
funds available are spent upon a few good programmes
sent S.B. [simultaneous broadcast][2] to many centres rather
than diluted to make every centre an originator of two programmes.'[3]

In 1926 London was thought of, almost without discussion,
as the cultural metropolis, the place from which 'the best'
was most likely to come. Eckersley might argue, as the scheme
took shape, that 'the Regional Scheme exists to give certain
Regions programmes having Regional significance, or, to put
it another way, local culture',[4] but finance inhibited Regional

1 *Control Board Minutes, 17 Nov. 1926.
2 For simultaneous broadcasting, see *The Birth of Broadcasting*, pp. 216 ff.
3 *Control Board Minutes, 10 and 17 Nov. 1926.
4 *Report on the Proposed Regional Scheme by the Chief Engineer*, 1929, p. 8. He had

Directors. Their 'local culture' was considered to be inferior, except in very special cases, to the 'universal culture' of the metropolis.

Eckersley's brother Roger, who was Assistant Controller of Programmes in 1927 and 1928, was particularly 'metropolitan' in his ideas and outlook. On 20 October 1927 he wrote to Reith suggesting that the 'local nights' at the relay stations should be gradually discontinued. 'I think it is difficult to draw a hard and fast line to apply to all of them, but we might at all events put the Stoke programmes to once a month instead of once a fortnight as at present. Do you think it would be a good moment, by way of gradually leading up to the Regional Scheme, to alter the rota to fortnightly instead of weekly at all or at any rate certain of the Relay Stations?'[1]

Reith had his answer ready. In a memorandum written earlier the same day he had pushed further the logic of the Control Board's discussions in 1926. He argued that it was desirable 'to produce a circular memorandum making it plain that it will not be interpreted as lack of initiative if fewer activities are conducted [by stations outside London], and pointing out that the interests of the service in general come first and that a separate show should justify itself as being efficient both economically and artistically'.[2]

This policy was later confirmed in a Control Board minute of great importance in November 1928. At Roger Eckersley's suggestion, 'the general principle was approved of provincial programmes being concentrated on purely local material, and, as far as possible, of eliminating provincial programmes of a similar character to those available in London at the same time'.[3] In a memorandum from Eckersley to the local Station Directors, this minute was interpreted to mean, 'Take from London what you cannot do better yourself, and do yourself what London cannot give you.'[4]

---

argued earlier that regional programmes should include 'Regional programmes of any sort reflecting a definite character of the Region they serve' ('The Distribution of the Service', 1925).

[1] *Memorandum from R. H. Eckersley to Reith, 20 Oct. 1927.

[2] *Memorandum from Reith to V. H. Goldsmith and R. H. Eckersley, 20 Oct. 1927.

[3] *Control Board Minutes, 21 Nov. 1928.

[4] *Memorandum from Assistant-Controller (Programmes) to Scottish Regional

The cultural consequences of their policy were considerable, particularly when, as we shall see, it became openly associated in 1929 with a doctrine of 'centralization'. The BBC was following all the other mass media of the early twentieth century in bolstering London's supremacy, and the proud 'provincialism' of the Victorian age, already in tatters in many parts of the country, continued to fade unlamented until long after the Second World War. Reith extolled the diffusion throughout the country of 'the amenities of Metropolitan culture'.[1] Roger Eckersley talked in 1928 of 'fostering local debates and discussions', but he saw the main work of the provincial stations as secondary, something which should be paid for only if there were adequate funds in the purse.[2]

Before long his brother Peter was complaining that the 'cultural side' of the Regional Scheme had been developed badly. He had hoped that regional programmes would 'reflect a definite character of the Region they served'. Just before he left the Corporation, indeed, he had prepared a very remarkable Report on the Regional Scheme, in which he envisaged the contrast between 'National' and 'Regional' programmes as a contrast between public and private enterprise. The regions should be left to develop independently under private enterprise. 'It is obvious that private enterprise broadcasting will come in some form or another. . . . How much better to make a bold and generous gesture now that it is possible to do so and let evolution decide the survival of the fittest.' Such heretical talk was a lively swan-song. 'With the responsibility for filling the second wavelength taken off his hands', Eckersley went on, 'the BBC programme builder is freed of a lot of harassing work, besides finding himself in possession of more funds for that work. He may receive a much wanted stimulus in listening to other people's work, he may in friendly rivalry put forward less jaded productions.'[3] Recollecting, not in tranquillity, how the scheme had developed after he left the BBC, he objected that 'in practice the extra wavelength' had served as 'an admini-

Director, North Regional Director, and Station Directors at Birmingham, Cardiff, Newcastle, Aberdeen, and Belfast, 28 Nov. 1928.
    [1] J. C. W. Reith, 'Broadcasting and a Better World' in *The Spectator*, 22 Nov. 1930.
    [2] *Memorandum of 28 Nov. 1928.
    [3] *P. P. Eckersley, *Report on the Proposed Regional Scheme* (1929), pp. 91–92.

strative convenience, not an extra facility to expand the scope of the service'.[1]

The Regional Scheme had come into operation on orthodox lines, with all the inevitability of gradualness, as 'a logical development of BBC policy'.[2] As if to emphasize the special place of London in the system, the first twin-wave station to be built was located near London. To the cultural and demographic arguments there was now added a political one. The Earl of Clarendon, the Chairman of the Governors of the BBC, told the Postmaster-General on his own initiative at a meeting at the Post Office in March 1928 that 'he did not want the Government to be unpopular in the London district because people could not hear the new station in the year of a General Election'. Reith commented tartly that 'there was much to fear for them the other way round if they kept holding the Regional Scheme up'.[3] It was now three years since the first discussions had taken place about Daventry 5XX. Permission to proceed with North London was given only after the Washington Conference had come and gone and a further round of talks at the Post Office had been completed.

The BBC went on to choose a 34-acre site, 400 feet above sea level on the Brookmans Park estate near the Great North Road, fifteen miles from Charing Cross. Work began in July 1928 and was planned to take a year. Among the special features of the station were two pairs of masts 200 feet high to support the two aerials necessary for double transmission.[4] The station was connected to the studios at Savoy Hill by four Post Office telephone cable circuits, specially arranged to avoid distortion.

Peter Eckersley had been 'very keen to have a building which expressed the spirit of our enterprise'. Although the building as it finally appeared, with Guthrie as architect, was in Eckersley's opinion far better than the 'Boys' Own Building Set in Sixteen Pieces' which had originally been sketched by an

---

[1] *The Power Behind the Microphone*, p. 127.

[2] *BBC Handbook* (1928) p. 68.

[3] Reith, Diary, 22 Mar. 1928; *Control Board Minutes, 24 Apr. 1928. There had been a meeting at the Post Office on 22 March.

[4] For a good description of the Brookmans Park Station, see *BBC Year Book* (1931), pp. 269–79.

architect who did not understand Eckersley's vision, it still 'fell short' of his 'imaginings'. Only the transmitter hall was, in his view, an unqualified triumph. Eckersley never got his way completely. He thought of but resisted the temptation to urge that a motto should be placed at the entrance, 'It is more blessed to send than to receive'.[1]

Because of the great frost of 1929 the building programme was delayed for six weeks, and it was not until 21 October 1929 that the station began to function. When it opened, the old London 2LO station, which had been located since April 1925 on the roof of Selfridges, was closed down. The problem of 'dislocation' which had arisen in Birmingham could have arisen even more acutely in London. Listeners in Central London within a narrow radius of the old 2LO transmitter now received a signal of only one-sixth the strength to which they were accustomed. Their new signal strength was more, incidentally, than East End listeners had enjoyed since the inception of broadcasting, but they were just as likely to be as upset by the change as those listeners situated very near the new transmitter, who found that they were 'wiped out' by the thirty-fold increase in signal strength and were now incapable of listening to 'foreigners'.

The example of Birmingham had been very useful to the BBC, however, and before the Brookmans Park station opened R. T. B. Wynn, then head of the BBC's Technical Correspondence Section, had prepared a series of pamphlets dealing with every expected question and complaint. Those listeners who feared 'dislocation' in 1929 were given immediate advice by the BBC. Crystal set listeners in Park Lane were told to rely on something more than a bit of wire round the living-room and no earth: listeners in Barnet were told to cut down the size of their aerials. The pamphlet *Crystal Sets and the Brookmans Park Transmitter* was distributed free of charge to large numbers of listeners. To make the transition easier still, a process of 'sliding-in' was adopted. At first the new station radiated on normal power only outside usual programme hours, for half an hour in the morning and from midnight until 1 a.m. The hours were gradually increased until the full take-over.

Although the main purpose in building the Brookmans Park

[1] *The Power Behind the Microphone*, pp. 124–5.

station was to permit London listeners to pick up two alternative programmes from the same station, it was not until 9 March 1930 that a full daily service of 'contrasted programmes' was introduced. This development also was heralded with a pamphlet, *The Reception of Alternative Programmes*, and a 'slide-in' arrangement. The second transmitter radiated a scheduled preliminary transmission for the first time on 9 December 1929 at a time when the first transmitter was not working: this procedure was followed to enable listeners to tune in easily to the second wavelength. Hours of dual transmission were increased first in the morning and late evening, and then for two evenings a week.

Correspondence about the changeover began to pour in to Savoy Hill in January 1930 after a questionnaire had been published in the *Radio Times*, asking for listeners' reactions to the reception of the dual programmes (see p. 312).[1] By 9 March, when the two programmes began to be broadcast regularly side by side, the correspondence had fallen off to a low level. The public relations side of the BBC had made the changeover as easy as possible. The experience gained, like the earlier experience of Birmingham, helped in the later development of regional broadcasting.[2]

The second instalment of the Regional Scheme followed soon afterwards. Moorside Edge, the North Regional station, was officially opened on 12 July 1931. Great care had been taken to choose the right site. If the station had been located on the Lancashire plain, the densely populated areas of Yorkshire would have been robbed of good signals: if the site had been placed near Leeds or Bradford, Lancashire would have suffered. Eventually a site was acquired at Slaithwaite, near Huddersfield. It was on a windswept moor 1,100 feet above sea level, but it was mid-way between the most densely populated areas of both Lancashire and Yorkshire. Two 500-foot masts were built to enable the station to serve a wider area than Brookmans Park. North Region broadcast on the longest medium wave allotted to the BBC in the European plan of agreed national allocation of wavelengths, which had been

[1] *Radio Times*, 17 Dec. 1929.
[2] See *BBC Year Book* (1931), pp. 387–92.

Number of letters and questionnaires in each week

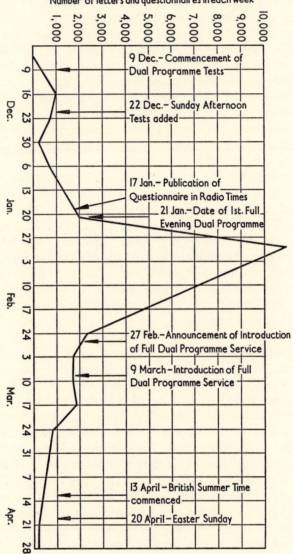

9 Dec.– Commencement of
Dual Programme Tests

22 Dec.– Sunday Afternoon
Tests added

17 Jan.– Publication of
Questionnaire in Radio Times

21 Jan.– Date of 1st. Full
Evening Dual Programme

27 Feb.– Announcement of Introduction
of Full Dual Programme Service

9 March – Introduction of Full
Dual Programme Service

13 April – British Summer Time
commenced

20 April – Easter Sunday

Dual Programmes from Brookmans Park: Listeners' Reactions, 1930.

accepted by all European broadcasting organizations, including the Soviet Union, at Prague in April 1929.[1]

Other regional stations followed at different times during the 1930s. The Scottish Regional Station was opened at Westerglen, near Falkirk, in September 1932, and the West and Welsh Regional Station at Washford Cross, Watchet, in August 1933. There were consequent changes in both cases. With the opening of the new high-power Scottish station, Aberdeen was converted into a relay station, with a changed wavelength, and the Edinburgh, Glasgow, and Dundee transmitters were closed. Soon after the opening of the West and Welsh Regional transmitter, the old Cardiff and Swansea transmitters were dismantled. The Plymouth and Bournemouth transmitters were retained, however, since there were special difficulties of reception in Cornwall, Devon, and Dorset.

Under the new arrangements, listeners in the remote Scottish Highlands still found reception difficult. The conversion of Aberdeen to a low-power relay-type station with a new exclusive wavelength, specially borrowed from Poland, did not help scattered listeners in north Scotland.[2] Some would-be Welsh listeners also had to wait until the division between West and Welsh Regional in 1935 and the building of a new Welsh transmitter at Penmon in Anglesey in February 1937. Other regional transmitters opened in the late 1930s were at Start Point and Clevedon—for West Regional listeners—in 1939; at Burghead and Redmoss, for Scottish listeners, in 1936 and 1938; and at Stagshaw in Northumberland, sixteen miles west of Newcastle, for North Regional listeners in Northumberland, Durham, Cumberland, and Westmorland, in October 1937. The Northern Ireland transmitter at Lisnagarvey, about nine miles south-west of Belfast, was opened in March 1936: it replaced an older low-power transmitter, and was the first 100-kilowatt medium-wave station to be built by the BBC.

With the building of these transmitters, the designs of which were prepared inside the BBC's own engineering department, listeners in most parts of the country now had the opportunity of listening easily to alternative BBC programmes. The

---

[1] See below, pp. 343–5.

[2] For details of Scotland, see *BBC Year Book* (1933), pp. 225 ff. For Wales, see the *BBC Year Book* (1934), pp. 161 ff.

network was greatly strengthened by the opening at Droitwich in October 1934 of a new National station of stronger power to replace Daventry 5XX. The power of 150 kilowatts which it employed was the maximum allocated under international regulations. Droitwich could be received throughout the whole country, although, on account of electrical interference in densely populated areas, the 'little Nationals' (the second of the twin-wave transmitters) were retained at some of the regional stations. Wavelength limitations continued to set the framework of necessity for the engineers: one long wave and ten medium waves were all that they could exploit. Within this limitation, however, the dream of the engineers had been fulfilled by 1939.

In the process, the number of users of crystal sets declined to a tiny minority. Exact figures are not available but an inquiry in Germany, where conditions were not very different, showed that in 1931 out of every hundred listeners there were eighty-one owners of valve sets and only nineteen owners of crystal sets. At the 1931 Radiolympia Exhibition there were only three exhibits of headphones.[1] Home-produced wireless sets also declined in numbers. By 1934 the home-made receiver was described as a 'comparative rarity'. 'It is no longer able to compete successfully either as regards price or performance with the product of a manufacturer who has adopted the press tool and the drilling jig to produce the metal chassis and quantity production methods which ensure minimum prices and maximum reliability.'[2]

Alongside technical changes, there were substantial changes of organization and outlook. The closing of local transmitters did not always imply the closing of local studios. The Cardiff and Swansea studios, for example, were retained when the Washford Cross transmitter came into operation, and in Scotland studio facilities in both Glasgow and Edinburgh were extended and modernized when the Westerglen station came into operation. Yet regional broadcasting altered the balance between local centres as much as it emphasized the cultural power of London. The cultural presuppositions, which had first been debated in 1926 and were re-examined by Siepmann

[1] BBC Year Book (1932), p. 30.
[2] BBC Year Book (1934), p. 427.

nearly ten years later, were always factors in the development. So, too, were finance and administration.

'The only authoritative criterion which he [Reith] had given —with respect to the inclusion of provincial matter', the Director-General wrote in 1932, 'had been on the basis of that which was justifiable in the artistic and economic sense.'[1] It was during the course of 1929 that BBC policy in London became more explicit than it had been in Reith's and Roger Eckersley's memoranda of 1926 and 1927, or even in the Control Board minute of November 1928. The key word in the policy was 'centralization'. It was used explicitly in a further Eckersley memorandum of February 1929, and figures in all the correspondence passing between BBC officials in London and the provinces.

After discussions by the Board of Governors, the Control Board, and a meeting of regional representatives, Reith sent round a private and confidential memorandum headed 'Centralization' in April 1929. 'Regional Directors are asked definitely', the memorandum stated, 'to accept the centralization policy, but to be assured that every consideration has been given to the problem. The disadvantages, of however definite a nature, such as those to which they have referred, have been in my mind all along. The local cultural loss should be, to a considerable extent, offset by the quality of the London programme, and to a further extent by the activities still open to Regional Directors.'[2]

As part of the policy, orchestras had to be cut in size, most of them to octets. Some local staff had to be declared redundant. As Reith's memorandum was implemented, many notes went out from London like that from Goldsmith, the Assistant Controller, to Edgar in Birmingham. 'There appears no doubt whatsoever that if the orchestral contracts are extended it will not be beyond the end of September 1930, and even that extension will be due to factors which are not at present apparent. As regards plays, the policy will be to do these only in London, except where better or different material can be produced locally, and in this case the play would probably be taken from an outside body of players. It would be uneconomic to

---

[1] *Memorandum of 30 May 1932.
[2] *Reith to the Regional Directors, 25 Apr. 1929.

maintain a special member of the staff for dramatic work at the Regional station for these rare occasions.'[1]

This was the policy of centralization at its most bleak. Yet Reith immediately qualified the bleakness in his memorandum. 'Whether it appears consistent or not,' he told the Regional Directors, 'I still believe that, in one way or another, it should be possible for Regional Directors as fully as ever to exploit the cultural significance and importance of broadcasting under the centralization system. The ways in which this can be done, however, will be different in many respects. I do not think it should be beyond the ingenuity and interest of Regional Directors to bring it about.'[2] In a further statement of January 1930 Reith made similar points. He distinguished between centralization of control and centralization of content and insisted that 'there would be a genuine attempt to make the transmissions on the Regional wavelengths genuinely Regional in point of view and in variety, providing a distinctive contrast to the more highly developed and standardised metropolitan programmes transmitted as "National". The organisation required in the provinces to achieve this purpose could be determined only in the light of experience.'[3]

Ingenuity was shown by some of the Regional Directors, although it was ingenuity within a framework which was at least as limiting as the technical framework of one long wave and ten medium waves was to the BBC as a whole. Some of the Directors genuinely interpreted the policy as an invitation to improve the quality of what they were doing, while reducing its range: others put up a spirited defence of some at least of the activities which it was suggested that they should cut. Edgar in Birmingham, for instance, putting himself into the position of the kind of independent entrepreneur whom Peter Eckersley had envisaged as the Director of a different kind of Regional Scheme, began several of his memos about staff with such phrases as 'if I were running these offices on a sub-contract' or 'I would unhesitatingly say that were I running broadcasting in the Midlands under ordinary commercial dividend paying conditions, I would certainly have such a man.'[4]

[1] *Goldsmith to Edgar, 12 Aug. 1929.
[2] *Reith to the Regional Directors, 25 Apr. 1929.
[3] *Control Board Minutes, 14 Jan. 1930.   [4] *Edgar to Reith, 19 Feb. 1929.

The development of regional programmes and regional networks did not await the building of the high-power regional transmitting stations. An interesting Control Board minute of September 1927, for example, states that the Director-General had spoken to E. G. D. Liveing, the Manchester Station Director and later Director of the North Region, concerning 'the desirability of gradually and tactfully acquiring ascendancy over the smaller stations in his area as E. R. Appleton had done over Swansea with a view to easier transference to the Regional Scheme'.[1] A month later Douglas Clarke, who was then concerned with liaison work between London and the provinces, wrote that he visualized in a few years, 'with the Regional Scheme in full working order, that the Central Station of each Region will have its Regional Director and under him in three parallel columns his Central Station staff, his outpost staff and his experts. Regional Director will be at the top of the line.' Clarke added that his picture was in line with 'that of Liveing and others'.[2] Local broadcasting was to be swallowed up in regional broadcasting.

The details of what happened in each region require separate monographs, but the story of the North of England illustrates many of the problems and the developments. As early as 1927, before the Control Board minutes on centralization and four years before the opening of Moorside Edge, there were efforts to group together some of the scattered stations in the North. The first move was to bring closer together the two Lancashire stations of Liverpool and Manchester, the former a relay station, the latter a main station since the beginning of broadcasting. Within a few months other northern stations were exchanging programmes. During the summer of 1927 there were frequent outside broadcasts heard throughout Lancashire and Yorkshire of programmes from northern resorts as scattered as Blackpool, Buxton, Morecambe, Scarborough, Southport, and Harrogate. There were even 'Huddersfield' nights. Events of special interest to northerners were given a regional coverage in 1928: they included the laying of the foundation stone of the University College at Hull, the opening of the Mersey Tunnel, and the 'Roses' cricket matches at Old Trafford and Sheffield.

[1] *Control Board Minutes, 6 Sept. 1927.
[2] *Note by D. H. Clarke, 'Relay Stations', 19 Oct. 1927.

During the late summer and autumn of 1928 the process of 'regionalization' went further. This was a time of 'intensive transition from the old individual stations to the collective grouping'.[1] The relay stations at Liverpool, Leeds–Bradford, Hull, and Stoke-on-Trent became subject increasingly to regional pressures. The orchestra at the Manchester studio, which had hitherto been engaged on weekly contracts, was made more permanent and took the name of the Northern Wireless Orchestra in August 1928: it consisted mainly of members of the Hallé.[2] Two BBC Adult Education Councils were formed in the North after a Conference at York in October 1928, the first under the chairmanship of the Vice-Chancellor of the University of Manchester, the second under the chairmanship of the chairman of the West Riding County Council Education Committee. Conferences of Station Directors were held to co-ordinate programme policy.

In September 1928 the title of 'North Regional Director' was first used, the earliest of the cluster of regional titles, and a month later administrative activities were concentrated in Manchester. Liveing's position of supremacy in the North had been expressed officially and in terms of organization. In a memorandum written some months after the change, Liveing spoke of the 'advantages of Regional concentration'.

While we have added three officials to the Regional offices, we have reduced officials at the relays by twelve. . . . Concentration has resulted in a greater efficiency of operation (a) through the opening up of interest in centres not hitherto touched and the improvement of local identification along specialist lines. . . . Our Education Assistant has opened up a lot of new territory, and, without his efforts, it is doubtful if, to mention School Broadcasting alone, the Education Authorities of Liverpool, Blackburn, Leeds and elsewhere, would have granted large sums for experiments in schools. Auditions at the various centres are now properly regulated, the Musical Director taking these. We have a wide knowledge of the Press, and Press personalities throughout the Region, through the travelling of the Information Assistant. We have given a valuable stimulus to the repertory movement in the North, including the Leeds Art Theatre, the Liverpool Repertory Theatre, the Hull Little Theatre, and the Sheffield Repertory Theatre, our Dramatic Assist-

---

[1] *BBC Year Book* (1932), p. 278.
[2] *Control Board Minutes, 1 Aug. 1928.

ant being employed for the purposes of such co-operation at the various studios. These are just a few of the results of our present regime, and are given at random.'[1]

Liveing was a supporter also of the switch from local news to regional news in November 1928.[2]

The North Region was thus recognized in some sense as having a cultural unity of its own, although there were doubts about the social and cultural relationship between the industrial areas of Lancashire and the West Riding, the 'old North' looking to Newcastle, and the Potteries to the south. In what the unity of the North Region consisted was never made fully clear. At times there were suggestions that there was a specifically northern bundle of qualities. 'The typical Northerner is shrewd or "jannock" in business, very outspoken in his opinions, sensitive to the opinions of others, and extremely warm-hearted and generous; he has a dogged determination, a very dry sense of humour, and, generally speaking, a more highly developed love of music than has the Southerner.' At other times there was emphasis on the economic differences between North and South: it was in the North that industrial products were made which were 'vital to the prosperity of England'.[3]

The special position of the 'old North' was recognized at last in 1938 when it became a kind of 'sub-Region': from 1932 onwards the experiment had been tried of transmitting a composite programme of National, North Regional, and London Regional material from Newcastle instead of the regional programme as broadcast from Manchester. This by no means satisfied local pride, and it was often pointed out not only that the North-East was very different from Lancashire but that Newcastle had been one of the oldest BBC stations.[4]

In the south of the area, the Potteries were a bone of contention between the North and the Midland Regions. They were 'transferred' from North to Midlands in 1935, and in 1936, when their fate seemed to be in the balance, a representative of the Midland Region stated strongly that 'the area is rightly assigned to the Midlands and it should remain Midland

[1] *Liveing to Reith, 18 Feb. 1929.
[2] *Control Board Minutes, 20 Nov. 1928.
[3] *BBC Handbook* (1928), p. 165.
[4] See below, p. 337.

territory'. 'All my evidence goes the other way', Siepmann retorted. 'The agricultural belt just south of them effectively cut them off from any real contact with the Midlands proper, and their activities brought them into much closer association with the North Region than the Midlands.' None the less, he yielded to Birmingham's claims. 'As the North Region is already larger than is convenient, we might, I suggest, let sleeping dogs lie.'[1]

The diversity of the North and the sense of local rivalry inside it—both between its distinctive component 'areas' and small, neighbouring communities within the same area—was reflected in an exceptionally large number of outside broadcasts. It was reflected also in music programmes. 'In other places music may be the crowning grace of the aristocracy, the plaything of the virtuoso, a spectacle for the idle, a commodity for the professional, but in the North it remains what it has been, a democratic institution, a supreme need of life.'[2] One big music concert was broadcast each week in 1933 from the Manchester studio: in one month in 1932 northern listeners heard the Huddersfield Choral Society in Bach's B Minor Mass, Sir Thomas Beecham conducting the Liverpool Philharmonic Society, and Act One of *Die Meistersinger* from the Theatre Royal, Halifax.

Good northern plays were not easy to find, but many light-entertainment programmes which later established a national reputation had their origins in the North. *Scrapbook*, for example, was first broadcast as an 'experimental' programme from Manchester in 1932: Liveing insisted on the adjective. At that stage it was not built up around an historical theme. Even earlier, Leslie Baily had prepared in the Leeds studio a programme called 'Hello, Yorkshire!' which contained the first germ of an idea which later developed into a characteristic feature of the *Scrapbook* series (and of so many other entertainment programmes)—the introduction of real-life 'celebrities' into the show. George Hirst, the cricketer, took part in such a local programme in 1926.[3]

---

[1] *H. J. Dunkerley to Siepmann, 13 Aug. 1936; Siepmann to Edgar, 14 Aug. 1936; Dunkerley to Siepmann, 19 Aug. 1936, with appended note in ink by Siepmann.

[2] Kenneth Adam, 'Music in the North', in the *BBC Year Book* (1934), p. 201.

[3] L. Baily and C. Brewer, *The BBC Scrapbooks* (1937), pp. 49–50.

While the story of the North Region is illustrative in many respects of what happened in the other regions, where both organization and titles were introduced later, in Scotland and Wales national as well as regional factors influenced background and response, and in the Midlands and London there was far less consciousness of separate identity.

Regional titles were decided upon at a Control Board meeting in July 1928—Scottish, West, Midland, and North Regional Directors, with the remaining Relay Station Directors to be known as 'Representatives'.[1] Earlier in 1928, D. Cleghorn Thomson in Scotland had been given the misleading title of Northern Area Director: this was changed after the Control Board's decision to that of Scottish Regional Director. It was not until September 1932, however, that the work of the four Scottish short-wave stations was fully co-ordinated and a Scottish Regional Service, covering most of the population of Scotland, was introduced; and it was not until 1937, after the Ullswater Committee had strongly backed the proposal, that the Welsh secured a region of their own. Shortage of wavelengths was the main reason for delay, and progress was made possible only by the synchronization of the Scottish National wavelength with the wavelength of London and the North Region. This provided the Corporation with an extra wavelength, and the two old West Regional transmitters could at last be treated as transmitters of two regions, one for Wales and one for a new West Region. Scotland thereby made possible the salvation of Wales.

Co-ordination in Scotland began with music and talks and was the subject of considerable local friction, centring both on personalities and on problems, on the future of the Aberdeen Octet, for instance, and the size of the Glasgow office. 'One's wings are being clipped and one is being debarred from flight in so many directions', Cleghorn Thomson wrote to Reith in March 1929 in a letter about 'the centralising trend which is observable in all spheres of our activities'.[2] He admitted that 'the speeding up of the process [of centralization] in Scotland is in the best interests of the service', but lamented the effects on

---

[1] *Control Board Minutes, 3 July 1928.
[2] *D. Cleghorn Thomson to Reith, 5 Mar. 1929.

'the atmosphere of Scottish broadcasting' and on 'those people who see their jobs vanishing'.[1]

Disputes about programme content followed somewhat later. 'What centralisation is going to do', Cleghorn Thomson told Eckersley, 'is to wipe out 60 per cent. of our programmes.' He added candidly—as a supporter of the scheme—that the 60 per cent. which would go had found few staunch friends and many enemies: it consisted of programmes which listeners had gradually come to know 'could be done better from London'.[2] Yet some of the 'few staunch friends' of Scottish programmes were very vociferous. From Aberdeen Neil McLean grumbled that 'the Scottish point of view is not adequately represented'; moreover, 'the difference between Scottish programmes involving Southern and Northern tastes is very considerable'.[3] On a visit to the Aberdeen studio in July 1929 Roger Eckersley found the BBC staff 'sad but philosophic'.[4] A few years later there were public protests in Scotland against the policy, as set out in the *BBC Year Book* for 1933, that even after both Westerglen transmitters were in operation there would be no '100 per cent. all-Scots programme on one of the alternative wave lengths'.[5]

The pattern of protest in Wales was muted by the fact that the BBC's programmes in the Welsh language were genuinely innovatory. Welsh services were broadcast from Daventry from January 1929 onwards, and Appleton in Cardiff gave frequent assurances that 'we shall be providing more Welsh programmes when the Regional scheme is ready'.[6] In March 1932 a Welsh Religious Advisory Council was set up, with Lloyd George as chairman. Reith, who travelled by train to its first meeting with Lloyd George, had a genuine appreciation of the role of the Welsh language: 'it constitutes a bond of enormous value and importance', he wrote in his diary; 'it is an immense pity that the whole of Scotland is not Gaelic speaking'.[7]

A number of big Welsh events received regular attention from the BBC. The Eisteddfod, for example, was regularly broadcast each year; so too was the St. David's Day Banquet in London.

1 *Cleghorn Thomson to Reith, 29 Apr. 1929.
2 *Cleghorn Thomson to R. H. Eckersley, 8 May 1929.
3 *N. McLean to Goldsmith, 29 May 1929.
4 *Notes on a Visit to Scotland, 9 July 1929.
5 *BBC Year Book* (1933), p. 246.
6 *Appleton to Goldsmith, 8 May 1929.   7 Reith, Diary, 8 Mar. 1932.

The fact, however, that the West Region covered both the West of England and Wales was a persistent source of grievance —not only on the Welsh side of the border. There were vigorous protests, for example, by 'West Country mayors' when the Plymouth studio was closed down in 1934. 'Our desire is for a greater proportion of items of local interest', the Mayor of Plymouth stated, somewhat weakening his case by adding, 'for we recognise the publicity value of these items'.[1] J. T. Sutthery, the BBC's spokesman, explained the BBC's case at a public meeting where, with Gladstone Murray's and Alan Dawnay's support, he expressed sympathy with the strong local feeling that 'residents in Devon and Cornwall are interested in having their own activities reflected through the broadcasting medium'.[2] When eventually the split between the West Country and Wales was about to take place in 1937, the BBC itself referred publicly to 'the zest with which the West Country and Wales have demanded separate treatment'. 'Nothing except technical difficulties', it added, 'has prevented the speedier dissolution of this mutually uncomfortable partnership.'[3]

From Northern Ireland, which first became a 'Region' in 1934, Beadle, as Belfast Station Director, remarked in 1929 that since he held that an orchestra was not worthy of the name unless it had at least thirty members, 'the policy of centralisation' had better be implemented by abolishing the Northern Ireland Orchestra instead of reducing it. 'Acting on the principle that we are to undertake no evening programmes which can be done as well from London, I believe that our local work will occupy on an average not much more than one night per week.'[4] Belfast continued to produce a considerable number of distinctively Northern Irish programmes—the Royal Ulster Show, for instance—and it also offered Ulster dialect plays. In the six years from 1926 to 1932 when Beadle was Station Director at Belfast the policy of centralization raised considerable difficulties and frequent 'clashes of interest', and Beadle has calculated that he crossed the Irish Sea about 150 times during this period

---

[1] *Western Morning News*, 30 Jan. 1934.

[2] Ibid.; *J. T. Sutthery to W. E. G. Murray, 30 Jan. 1934; Memorandum by W. E. G. Murray to A. C. Dawnay, 31 Jan. 1934 with Dawnay's reply, 1 Feb. 1934.

[3] *BBC Annual* (1937), p. 16.   [4] G. C. Beadle to Reith, 1 May 1929.

to discuss matters in London.[1] Because of lack of landline connexions with England, however, Belfast was spared drastic
cutting of local services, and the region developed many programmes of its own. 'The most characteristic tendency of the
year', it was stated in 1937, was 'the discontinuance of the
practice of importing cross-Channel material and the corresponding intensification of the search for local talent.'[2] This
policy had always to be qualified, however, in the knowledge
that Ulster, like the more outlying parts of the Empire, welcomed 'the constant relaying of the best of British programmes'.[3]

The remaining English region—Midland Region—did not
come into existence at once when 5IT (Birmingham) was
replaced by the new Daventry 5GB. The 5GB programme was
designed to be 'experimental, free and stimulating' rather than
'balanced', and it was to the 'National' programme (5XX)
that Midland listeners had to turn if they wished to follow
the kind of programme to which they had hitherto been accustomed. Percy Edgar, the Director of the old Birmingham station
5IT and the first Midland Regional Director, when the post
was formally so described in March 1930, wrote a most forceful
letter to Reith in February 1929 stating bluntly 'that the ever
growing policy of centralisation in London has clearly gone a
good deal further and more rapidly than public opinion here
is prepared to accept. . . . The policy of concentration requires
very patient exposition to local authorities as well as the Press.
Believe me, Sir John, I am not over-stating the case and frankly,
I feel not a little alarmed at the tendency of our policy today.'[4]

'Centralization' and 'Regionalization' went ahead, however,
side by side, and although some local programmes were cut,
by 1931 there was an increasing number of outside broadcasts
from the West Midlands. The Midland Regional Orchestra
was disbanded, but efforts were made to broadcast a range of
programmes 'which would to some extent reflect the life of the
central counties'. 'The Midlands', it was argued, 'has its own
personality . . . there is something there which can be found
nowhere else.'[5] How far the BBC was able to project that 'personality'—if there was or is one—is less clear. Indeed, the 1936

[1] G. C. Beadle, *Television, A Critical Review* (1963), p. 24.
[2] *BBC Annual* (1937), p. 36.   [3] *BBC Year Book* (1934), p. 235.
[4] *Percy Edgar to Reith, 19 Feb. 1929.   [5] *BBC Year Book* (1933), p. 203.

BBC Annual said of regional broadcasting generally, 'How far Regional listeners are as yet generally aware of the efforts made by the BBC to employ and foster the characteristic resources of each part of the country, is hard to say.'[1] The West Midlands enjoyed quite different economic circumstances during the 1930s from the older industrial region of Lancashire and Yorkshire, with which it had had strong social and political affiliations in the nineteenth century. There were differences, too, between the West and East Midlands. In relatively prosperous and cosmopolitan Birmingham, listeners may well have been less interested in specifically regional programmes than in an 'attractive' and popular 'alternative' bill of fare.

There was an uncertainty in other parts of the country on this issue too. How far did northerners, for example, wish to cling to what was distinctly northern? Jokes, yes: the latest dance tunes, no? Music by northern orchestras and shows, yes: specifically northern talks, no? The country as a whole was sharing a 'mass culture', and local differences were being reduced by other agencies of 'mass communication', particularly the press. If the BBC was to concern itself seriously with 'sub-cultures' rather than with (or as well as) 'the great audience' in which Reith believed, what about East Anglia, which was left outside the system, or the South-East which was curiously detached from the network, and even the London area itself, which had no BBC identity of its own except as a metropolis?

Given the wide range of social and cultural factors involved, it is scarcely surprising that there was some uncertainty about the Regional Scheme as a whole, not only in its inception but in its development. 'For some time all has not been well in the matter of programme activities at Head Office and in the Regions', an important memorandum of July 1932 stated. 'Neither has been sufficiently informed as to the other. There has not been enough collaboration, and misunderstandings have in consequence arisen. This is bad for programme work. . . . Both Metropolitan and Regional prejudices and bias must be eliminated, and ignorance on both sides lessened.'[2]

The writer of this memorandum recommended that Wellington, who had been concerned with programme policy and

[1] *BBC Annual* (1936), p. 26.   [2] *Internal Memorandum, 19 July 1932.

planning since 1924, should act as a co-ordinator, dealing with
simultaneous broadcasting, regional material taken on the
composite London Regional wavelength, regional programmes
shared between regions, and individual programmes in particular regions. Wellington took over the new post in the summer of 1932.[1] He was placed in the BBC hierarchy 'junior to
the Director of Programmes [Roger Eckersley] and the Director of Talks [Siepmann]', but 'his position with them was to
be advanced somewhat'—a gently nuanced phrase. 'By virtue
of the special charge to him in regard to matters affecting
Regional policy, D.P. and D.T. will in general be guided by his
advice, but retain over-riding powers upon considerations of
major policy.' The status of the Regional Directors was un-
altered: as in the past, they were to have direct access both
to the Controller (Carpendale) and to the Director-General.[2]
Reith encouraged them to look to him. Whenever he visited
regional offices, he asked the senior officers there how they were
getting on with head office. If they said very well indeed—'no
trouble'—he always replied that there must be something wrong.

Regional policies did not change after 1932, nor did the
formal limitations on the initiative of the Regional Directors or
the personal encouragement given them by the Director-General.
Awkward questions of hierarchy often arose, and there was a
regular tug-of-war between the regions and the Programme
Planning Department in London concerning the content of
regional programmes. The kind of question which often
arose may be illustrated from a correspondence in December
1933 between Sutthery in the West Region, Roger Eckersley
and Wellington in London, and Dawnay. It began with a lament
from Sutthery that the 'indigenous musical activities' of the
West Country were inadequate. 'Both variety and music have
become international, or at least national and the best stuff to
be found in the Region is brought there from outside.' Yet a
Rubinstein concert from Dartington Hall had been turned
down by head office 'on the score that Rubinstein has not yet
broadcast at all and that his first broadcast should be National
rather than West Regional'. Unless 'imported' activities were

---

[1] He was appointed in the first instance for a trial period of six months, but the
arrangement continued. (*Memorandum by Reith, 28 Feb. 1933.)

[2] *Control Board Minutes, 19 July 1932.

broadcast, the West Region would have to rely on South Wales choirs and West Country plays. 'As soon as we go into any other field and require a body of professional actors, I cannot reasonably contend that we can do better than London, unless I am to assume that we are more competent in production. And if this were true, there would be every argument for you to absorb our Producer in Head Office.'[1]

Eckersley wished Sutthery a merry Christmas and told him that his memorandum raised such important issues in relation to 'regionalism' that he proposed to discuss it fully with Dawnay. Two days later Dawnay replied that 'existing regional policy must be observed in principle'. 'Duplication of effort . . . is undesirable both on financial grounds and from the point of view of policy. What we want from the Regions is the sort of programmes which they can provide and we cannot (characteristic regional programmes) rather than a duplication of the programmes we do ourselves.' In fact, a quiet administrative answer was found on this occasion. The particular Dartington broadcast could be put on to the National programme 'if you can assure us that a first class broadcast can be given from Dartington from the technical point of view'.[2] A few days later Eckersley added, 'You asked for general permission to broadcast regionally any or all of the celebrity concerts from Dartington if they could not be done nationally. We cannot give any general sanction of this kind, but we will consider each case on its merits as it arises.'[3]

Details were to be left to negotiations between Sutthery and Wellington. The negotiations involved the same arts which Wellington associated with programme planning.[4] In February 1934 Sutthery was submitting a list of West Country programmes to be considered for the National or comprehensive Regional services. They included in addition to a running commentary on the Padstow 'Hobby Horse' ceremony and a short talk on Cornish wrestling—both superbly regional items—variety from Plymouth, organ music from Bath, and a symphony concert from the National Museum of Wales.[5]

[1] *J. T. Sutthery to R. H. Eckersley, 18 Dec. 1933. Copies to A. C. Dawnay and L. Wellington.
[2] *Dawnay to Sutthery, 20 Dec. 1933.
[3] *Eckersley to Sutthery, 7 Feb. 1934.
[4] See above, pp. 29–30.   [5] *Sutthery to Wellington, 22 Feb. 1934.

Wellington has given another example of discussion and negotiation with the regions, this time concerning the opposite situation, that of a region which was unhappy about taking a programme from London. At a time when two main symphony concerts were being broadcast from London each week—one on Wednesdays in the National programme and one on Sundays in the Regional programme—a Sunday concert, to be conducted by Casals, was given two 'phis', that is to say it carried the label, 'take this unless there is a strong reason for not doing so'.[1] E. A. F. Harding, then Programme Director in the North Region, planned instead to broadcast a concert given by a Merseyside Orchestra of unemployed musicians. Subsequent dialogue between Wellington and Harding ran as follows:

L. W. Surely you ought not to drop this Casals programme (a very important one) and substitute a lesser programme of the same kind.
E. A. F. H. Yes—I think it's right. To give a platform to this Merseyside orchestra is of great social importance.
L. W. I quite see that—but not on this date. Give them a special studio date or take another of their public concerts on a date when you don't have to pay such a price.
E. A. F. H. I'm most unwilling to change. I see the force of what you say, but I very much do not want to disappoint them.
L. W. All right: if you have committed yourself to them go ahead, but you know you ought not to have done so without knowing what you would have been dropping. Now you will have to keep faith with them but only at the cost of disappointing all the listeners in the North of England who would want to hear Casals conducting. I really do feel this is wrong.

'There', says Wellington, 'the argument ended.' Harding did not broadcast Casals, but this kind of difficulty never arose again between them. At best, he concludes, there was a sympathetic interplay between region and head office on matters of this kind. The periodic rows came and went, but there were long periods of mutual confidence.[2]

The general principles behind regional programme policy were restated in an undated draft memorandum which was

---

[1] For the 'phi' system, see above, p. 37.
[2] Note by Wellington, June 1963.

prepared in 1935 for the Ullswater Committee.[1] 'It is difficult to define precisely the criterion of Regional activity. It is understood in such terms as that no Region should embark on an activity which could be better done elsewhere, in any other Region or London. . . . Regional activity should be justifiable economically, politically, and artistically, although from the last point of view it would be permissible for a Region, for local reasons, to broadcast a second-rate artist or programme item to the exclusion of a first-class one from elsewhere, but not to lower the standard further than that.'

In 1935 the main features of London 'National' programmes were being circulated to the regions weeks ahead, and Regional Directors were left to work out the details of 'contrasting' regional programmes of their own and how much to broadcast of the London programmes or of programmes from other regions. There were few outside programmes which they were bound to take, but their ability to produce local programmes was limited not only by human resources but by programme finance. Naturally, the BBC in London laid most emphasis on availability of local resources, and in the evidence it submitted to the Ullswater Committee it was able to show that extra regional staffs were being recruited in 1934 and 1935.[2] 'The degree to which Regional Directors in the exercise of their discretion are able to include local material is illustrated by the divergence in the proportion of local material, which in 1934 varied from 23 per cent. in Northern Ireland to 40 per cent. in the Midland Region, a ratio which gives a rough representation of the comparative artistic resources of the two regions.'[3]

Regional programme staffs had, in fact, been doubled in 1934–5, but they were less strongly backed by executives and were still expected to show far more versatility than the more specialized BBC central staff in Broadcasting House. In some ways this was an advantage to the provincial producers: it led to greater freedom and initiative in production. In other ways it was a marked disadvantage, not least in that it involved frequent overwork. A 1937 note by Roger Eckersley on regional

[1] See below, p. 490.
[2] For the table of staff submitted to the Ullswater Committee, see below, p. 489.
[3] *Undated Draft Memorandum in the BBC's Ullswater Committee files, 'Regional Programme Policy: Content of Programmes'.

staff set out details of 'the amount of transmissions undertaken *per capita* of Regional staff, related to the same amount of work done at Head Office': the figures showed definitely that regional staffs were handling between them a greater number of programmes and that there were far fewer people involved than in London.[1]

Overwork has always been willingly accepted in the BBC if creative freedom has been secure. Whatever suspicious constitutional exchanges were going on in the 1930s between head office and regions, programme directors and producers found more excitement and fewer frustrations in their work than during any period in the BBC's history. At this level of activity E. A. F. Harding, Programme Director of the North Region from 1933 to 1936, was outstanding. Enterprising and exuberant, he treated what might have been regarded as exile in the North as a direct challenge to London. He raided the *Manchester Guardian*—from which he captured four journalists, Kenneth Adam, Donald Boyd, Robert Kemp, and E. R. Thompson—and with the full co-operation of W. P. Crozier, the editor, he drew upon the services of a number of the *Guardian*'s leader-writers and reporters as North Regional broadcasters. He turned also to the Northern Circuit, industry, the Civil Service, and the repertory theatres, amateur and professional, for talent, persuading Edgar Lustgarten to leave the Bar, encouraging Geoffrey Bridson and Francis Dillon to turn to writing and production, and nurturing the budding talent of Wilfred Pickles. At the centre of this little world, he attracted growing public attention in the North. His friends came from all walks of society. Mary Crozier, fresh from Oxford, became the radio critic of the *Manchester Guardian*, and on the other side of the Pennines the *Yorkshire Post* started a regular radio column. Harding himself, however, was his own most forceful critic. Weary casts were hauled off after performance for post-mortems which lasted most of the night and sometimes all of it. Whatever the official policy of the BBC, Harding's own motto was 'Anything London can do, we can do better'. The quality of Harding's work, particularly in the production of features, showed that despite financial limitations, regional broadcasting could offer listeners 'the best' that the medium could provide.

[1] *R. H. Eckersley, 'Regional Staff', 26 Oct. 1937.

Yet the position in the provinces in 1935 when Siepmann was suddenly moved from the important post of Director of Talks to become Director of Regional Relations was far from easy. The time was propitious for a large-scale critical survey both of what was happening in the regions and what was the relationship in practice between regions and centre. Siepmann provided a comprehensive and penetrating survey, which represented the fullest examination of regional problems that anyone inside the BBC had ever undertaken. Before writing the report, he visited all the regions, spending in each at least six days and at most three weeks. 'Apart from interviewing all members of the staff, inspecting premises and listening to evening transmissions,' he began his report, 'I have tried to give impressions of listeners' habits and of their reaction to our Regional programmes, and to secure from men of intelligence and experience greater knowledge of the needs and problems of the provinces insofar as these can be met by broadcasting.'[1] Siepmann's main concern was with programme policy: matters of administration were only lightly touched upon.

The provinces, Siepmann maintained—and he was writing as a man with little direct experience of provincial life—were either being denuded culturally or, through lack of resources and opportunity, were being deprived of 'self expression' and 'that richness and variety of experience which London enjoys and assumes as a matter of course'. Yet within the world of broadcasting the regions could have a creative part to play. 'Centralisation represents a shortsighted policy. The provinces are the seed ground of talent and the ultimate source of supply of our London programmes.' Examining the question from the other side, he concluded that while the regional services fostered a great variety of 'local interests and loyalties', they had not gone far enough in adapting their services fully to meet local needs. 'Most London material is out of tune to Northern and Western ears and the differential pace and tone of life and feeling in the provinces still require adequate expression. . . . Regions have been slow in the adaptation of their services. . . . Even now we are only on the threshold of effective action. Of the more or less uniform pattern of all Regional programmes and of the equivalent extent of their respective output, I am definitely critical.'

[1] *C. A. Siepmann, *Report on Regions*, Jan. 1936, pp. 1–2.

The same view of the regional opportunities which Siepmann set out in his report is presented in the introductory pages of the BBC's official 1936 Annual, covering the events and problems of 1935. Centralization on the business side was 'to a large extent inevitable and desirable'. It was 'in harmony with the common trend towards rationalisation as an aid to business efficiency'. It had both an economic and a technical basis— the need to make the best use of limited financial resources and the need to make the best use of a limited number of wavelengths. 'Once, however, these reasons of organisation have been allowed for, there still remains ample scope for diversity and individuality of programmes between the Regions. Some gloomy prophets have in recent years foretold the flattening out of regional characteristics under the steam roller of London tastes and ideas. . . . Happily, despite all warring forces, local life in the fullest sense of the word still flourishes up and down these islands. . . . The Corporation aims through its network of Regional stations at reflecting local life and local loyalties, and at strengthening associations and traditions which have their roots in the soil and history of our native countryside.'[1]

These lines may have exaggerated the strength of provincial forces, but they certainly marked a retreat from Roger Eckersley's policy. In his report Siepmann went further. The policy which had first been mooted in 1926 of doing nothing in the provinces which could better be done in London was at the heart of the difficulties. 'It is appropriate that National services should achieve as high a standard of excellence as possible, but the purist's concern for artistic integrity can be carried too far, and the case for Regional broadcasting cannot be measured by this single yardstick of artistic achievement. . . . The patronage of all the arts, the representation of local life and of local interests are limiting factors from a Head Office point of view, but need to be carefully weighed in the balance of advantage in considering the purpose on which our Regional policy depends.'[2]

Siepmann made a number of practical comments, criticisms, and suggestions. Regional Directors, he said, were uncertain of their position, some of them feeling like 'poor relations'. They often lacked adequate staff: in the country as a whole there was only 'a bare skeleton of what is necessary'. There was too

---

[1] *BBC Annual* (1936), p. 26.   [2] *Report on Regions*, p. 3.

much office work and too little field work. Head Office staff enjoyed 'a more leisurely pace' and 'more congenial conditions of work'. In all regions there was 'a marked deficiency in the preliminary training of newly appointed members of the staff'. Premises and equipment were below London standards. 'Our studio premises at Swansea and Plymouth are disgraceful.'

Among the proposals Siepmann made was a scheme for the regular exchange of BBC staff between London and the regions. He also suggested the setting up of a 'regular school of broadcasting for all members of the programme staff', and a developed programme of listener research. 'Regional correspondence is small and, great as is the collective knowledge of the staff of Regional characteristics and sentiment, I could not fail to be perplexed in my survey by the total lack of evidence as to the attitude of listeners to our Regional services.'[1] This was the prelude to the line of inquiry which was to end in Tallents asking for a 'Regional plan'.[2] Siepmann also pointed to the 'huge anomaly in our present system of Regional broadcasting—the absence of any interpretation of the country—excluding London —which extends from Norfolk to Sussex and Hampshire. . . . It is impossible to look at a map of England and to maintain the significance of our Regional policy . . . and yet be careless of the neglect of the great block of counties, mostly rural, it is true, and therefore limited in resources, but at any rate deserving of some measure of representation.'[3]

Turning in the last part of his report to the detailed work of the individual regions, Siepmann noted 'the differences of outlook and variety of interests and occupations' in the North Region alone, a region in which there was 'a real danger of over-centralisation', and 'the rather dreamy, backward feudal atmosphere which pervades so much of the West'.[4] He made tentative proposals for strengthening the North and reducing the area and output of the West. In Wales developments were to be gradual to give full time to a new and inexperienced staff 'to prove their capacities and to allow of the cooling of political and racial passions provoked by past controversies over Welsh policy'. In Scotland there was a 'self-consciousness' which was best left alone. In Northern Ireland, where he had had 'a long

---

[1] Ibid., p. 9.
[3] *Report on Regions*, p. 12.
[2] See above, p. 266.
[4] Ibid., pp. 14–15, 17.

and helpful conversation' with Ogilvie, the Vice-Chancellor of the Queen's University, Belfast, who was to be Reith's successor, he found 'a lamentable dearth of talent' and an energetic programme staff who 'valiantly attempt the hopeless task of making bricks without straw'.[1]

Siepmann's report was carefully studied by the Controller of Programmes, the Controller of Administration, and the Deputy Director-General. Appearing in the same year as the Ullswater Report, it focused attention on a subject which had interested the Ullswater Committee.[2] The Regional Directors had loyally backed the BBC in the public inquiry, but they were aware that changes were necessary. Graves said that 'he had always felt that we should do more to help the Regions': he urged the creation of a Southern Region, which would include the Midlands and counterbalance the North. At the same time, he and many other people who were prepared to make changes deprecated a full-scale attack on the policy of centralization. 'The object should not be to set up almost autonomous organisations concerned only with broadcasting to the inhabitants of their Regions': it should be 'to enable listeners throughout the country to have all that is best no matter whence it originates'.

There was obviously a difference in 1936 as in 1930 between those who believed, as Peter Eckersley had done, in regional distinctiveness, and those who believed, like Val Gielgud on the production side, that in a country as small as England broadcasting should aim at creating as large an audience as possible for the very best. The same difference runs through the recent history of the arts in England, and it was one of the themes of the Romanes Lecture by Lord Bridges in 1957.[3]

Nicolls, speaking for the administration, admitted that it was unfortunately true that some Regional Directors thought of themselves as 'poor relations'. 'It is arguable, of course', he went on, 'that a person who is confident in himself does not need assurance as to the future and that the reasons for Regional Directors worrying are probably subjective and personal.' He did not accept Siepmann's picture of understaffing, his demand

---

[1] *Report on Regions, Supplement on Northern Ireland*, p. 3.
[2] For the attitude of the Ullswater Committee to regional questions, see below, p. 499.
[3] Lord Bridges, *The State and the Arts*. See above, p. 37.

for a school of broadcasting, or his tentative suggestions, supported by Graves, for the creation of a new Southern or 'Home Counties' region. Much in Siepmann's report, he added, was not new.

Carpendale conceded that 'a case has most certainly been made out for Regional broadcasting as being necessary to reflect the local life and characteristics in the different Regions as well as to provide a valuable source of material for London programmes'. And it was he who formally set out a list of new appointments and staff changes which he thought would meet some at least of Siepmann's suggestions.[1] 'The accommodating spirit in which the Report is handled by the Deputy Director-General', Siepmann wrote, 'will, I know, be very welcome to Regions. The specific approval of staff adjustment provides a basis for development, and is, I think, as much as we can wisely tackle at present.'[2]

Regional comments on the report were mixed. Cardiff, for example, submitted a quotation from Havelock Ellis to the effect that there were 'three well-marked foci of individual behaviour in England', of which the south-western region was one (the northern was not). From Manchester, by contrast, there was a down-to-earth demand for better accommodation than the existing 'Board Room'.[3] The report, in general terms, was accepted by Control Board in July 1936 and by the Board of Governors a few days later.[4] Reith told Nicolls to do his best to ensure that there was no leakage of the document prepared after the Board meeting.[5] The document was carefully worded, but it accepted Siepmann's report 'in its broad outline', a report which, it is said, had already been 'foreshadowed by the Corporation in its evidence before the Ullswater Committee'.[6]

The document was precise in its attack on the centralization of cultural life. 'The Governors recognise the general tendency outside broadcasting towards centralisation in the metropolis and regard it as a bad tendency, which broadcasting can counter

---

[1] *Notes by the Controller of Programmes, the Controller of Administration, and the Deputy Director-General, 7 Apr. 1936.

[2] *D.R.R.'s Comments on D.D.G.'s observations, 14 Apr. 1936.

[3] *Appleton to Siepmann, 18 Feb. 1936; Liveing to Nicolls, 14 July 1936.

[4] Board of Governors, Minutes, 22 July 1936.

[5] *Reith to Nicolls, 23 July 1936.

[6] See below, pp. 487–90.

by representing the local point of view and encouraging local talent.' Regional programmes were needed not only for contrast with metropolitan programmes but 'to meet the legitimate demand for programmes suited to local tastes and humour'. All the same, there still had to be limits on regional autonomy. Staff conditions had to be comparable in different regions; 'artistic supervision is necessary to ensure a uniform standard in all the programmes'; and financial and technical factors still served as restraints. All in all, the Governors believed that they were setting out a policy which might be regarded as a 'Charter of Rights'. 'The Governors are satisfied that there should not be any uneasiness among the Regional Directors as to the future of Regional broadcasting. Adjustments may be necessary from time to time, but the essential function will remain intact.' As a pledge of faith, there was to be a meeting each month between the Deputy Director-General, the four Controllers, the Regional Directors, and the Director of Regional Relations; and Percy Edgar, as senior Regional Director, or any of the other Directors, was to be summoned to Control Board whenever regional matters were being examined.[1] Reith had always emphasized close personal relations with Regional Directors. Formal institutions were now being created to perpetuate personal conventions which he himself had established.

Conditions in the regions after 1936 did not change drastically, although there was a far wider range of activities than had been anticipated in 1930 and a far more specialized staff. The establishments of the various regions were not identical, the variations being designed 'to suit local requirements'. Relations with London still rested on informal consultation as much as on formal hierarchical patterns. Indeed, a fascinating set of contacts bound provincial staff with staff in London. 'While in theory contact with London is canalized through the Regional Director, in practice the various officials, notably the Regional Executive, Programme Director and Public Relations Officer correspond direct.'[2] They also used the telephone. One of the

---

[1] *Draft Memorandum for approval by the Board, accepting D.R.R.'s Report on the Regions, July 1936.
[2] *Note by D. H. Clarke for Regional Executives, 'Staff Organisation of Regional Offices', 8 Dec. 1937.

problems in every region was the 'drift of staff to London'. It particularly applied to regional announcers, who were in short supply in the two or three years before the war. 'I feel that the only answer to the "not leading anywhere" feeling', one BBC official wrote in 1937, 'is that the announcer should be trained in London, go to a Region, and be allowed to hope to transfer to London as vacancies occur.'[1]

Much loyal work was carried out in the regions both by people who felt that they belonged there and had no desire to move to London and by people who were conscious of the fact that regional work was one phase in their total BBC experience. It was varied work. A full report on the North Region, dated September 1937, forecast the 'increased independence and output of Newcastle'; Leeds, it went on, 'acts in almost all things directly under instructions from Manchester'. Music came from all parts of the region—the Huddersfield Choral Society, for example, and the Sheffield Philharmonic Society as well as the Hallé. At the same time, there was a Regional Orchestra, consisting of thirty-five players, serving under annual contract. Among the Regional Advisory Committees was a North Regional Music Advisory Committee, a North Regional Religious Advisory Committee, under the chairmanship of the Bishop of Wakefield, a North Regional Appeals Advisory Committee, a North-Eastern Appeals Advisory Committee, and a North-Western Area Council for Adult Education.

Money, however, was less abundant than advice, particularly towards the end of the BBC's financial year. Programme finance was governed by a weekly allowance, fixed quarterly in London after the budgetary proposals of all the regions had been examined together. The programme allowance varied considerably between quarter and quarter, a larger amount being allowed in the winter than in the spring and summer. 'This is owing to the fact that all heavy orchestral and choral commitments take place during the winter months, being replaced during the summer by the cheaper form of relay from seaside resorts and spas. Sporting outside broadcasts on the other hand increase during the spring and summer, and in the case of the Isle of Man are very expensive.' There was considerable pruning

---

[1] *Note by E. J. King-Bull, 20 Aug. 1937.

of estimates, and 'a deficit at the end of the year was frowned upon by all concerned'.[1]

In Scotland, to take a further example, the whole programme allowance when Andrew Stewart became Programme Director in 1935 amounted to £520 a week, reduced to £470 in the summer months. The differentiation disappeared in the later 1930s. There was a marked emphasis on the specifically Scottish element in programmes, but no attempt was made to pretend that they were solely Scottish. 'We do not, and I think should not, aim at filling up every minute of the Scottish Evening Programme with home performed entertainment', Stewart told Scottish listeners, but there was an emphasis on Scottish poetry, history, culture, and sport. For the rest, 'the Scot is and always has been a good European, liberally educated and with catholicity of taste. We therefore try to select such items of a cosmopolitan nature as we feel would interest or entertain a Scotsman, having regard always to this international cultural tradition, and not to current metropolitan appeal.'[2] In the same year that Stewart set out this objective, the BBC Scottish Orchestra was formed: it broadcast for over 150 hours in 1936.[3] Another interesting venture of 1936 was Geoffrey Bridson's remarkable feature programme, *March of the '45*, a joint enterprise of the Scottish and the North Regions: it has been hailed as the outstanding achievement of the features producers of the 1930s. In 1937 a lively discussion between two Scottish professors provided a remarkable ending to a series on *Scotland and the Empire*.[4]

There were interesting developments in other regions also. The BBC Welsh Singers were formed into a choir in 1936. North Region and Midland Region co-operated in a programme dealing with the legends of the mountains common to both: it was presented from Bakewell. Midland Region sponsored *Midland Parliament*, one of the very few examples in the inter-war years of relatively informal broadcasting on major industrial topics, including topics of great controversy. Along with North Region's *Cockpit*, it provided listeners with frank and outspoken

1 *Note on the Work of the North Region, Sept. 1937.
2 *'Coming Scottish Programmes', BBC Script, 20 Sept. 1935.
3 *BBC Annual* (1937), p. 26. See also G. Burnett (ed.), *Scotland on the Air* (1938).
4 *BBC Handbook* (1938), p. 19.

argument. In the West, there were lively rural programmes—
Farmer's Tales, *Village Opinion*, and *Roaming the Country*: they
were successful enough to direct attention to the BBC's remarkable—and continuous—success in interesting both urban and
rural listeners in the problems of the countryside.

Many of these programmes had more in common with the
BBC's post-war programmes than with programmes being
broadcast during the same period from London. There were
many signs in 1939 that, whatever the limitations imposed on
the Regional Scheme, it genuinely provided centres of initiative
and innovation outside London. And many of the men who
made their mark in the regional capitals were to make their
mark in the country as a whole later on.

4. Europe: Co-operation and Competition

DURING the late 1930s discussions of the Regional Scheme
centred mainly on questions of programme policy and organization. Yet the engineers, who had invented the scheme, were
involved at every point in its development. They had to take
into account not only the changing technology of radio but the
changing context of international regulation. The framework
for Eckersley's first regional proposals in 1926 and 1927 had
been the Geneva Plan for allotting European wavelengths,
which was accepted by the Council of the Union Internationale
de Radiophonie (UIR), also known as the International Broadcasting Union, in July 1926.[1] A year later the Washington
Conference, to which the Post Office had attached so much
importance,[2] had brought together representatives of national
administrations, of the IBU, and of other broadcasting organizations, and in 1929 a conference of governments at Prague
prepared a more complete and more effective framework for
broadcasting in Europe. So important, indeed, were these

---

[1] See *The Birth of Broadcasting*, pp. 316 ff. In Volume I of my History, the Union
is called by its French initials, UIR, which were generally used before 1927.
[2] See above, pp. 302–3.

deliberations that the *BBC Year Book* for 1930 stated firmly
that 'in the twelve months ending with August 1929 the international side of European broadcasting has outweighed the
national in the scale of importance'.[1]

The Washington Conference was the first International Radio
Telegraphic Convention to be held for fifteen years: previous
conventions had been held in 1903, 1906, and 1912.[2] Whereas
in 1912 there had been no talk of broadcasting, in 1927 it was
impossible to leave broadcasting out of the world-wide regulation of radio. Herbert Hoover, Secretary of Commerce and later
President of the United States, described 'the congestion of the
lanes on which communications are conducted' as the most
complex of all the problems which the participatory interests had
to consider; and the fifth article of the Washington Agreement,
signed in November 1927, allowed administrations of the eighty
contracting countries to assign any frequency and any type of
wave to stations in their territory, 'upon the sole condition that
no interference with any service of another country will result
therefrom'.[3]

The conference was concerned not with the allocation of
individual wavelengths but with the allocation of wavebands
between the different users of radio—ships, armed forces, commercial firms, and so on. It admitted the claims of broadcasting
to a medium band, some short-wave bands, and to long waves
between 1,000 and 2,000 metres. These claims had often been
fiercely contested by other users within individual countries.
The BBC's demand to be allowed to engage in long-wave broadcasting, for instance, had been opposed in the first stages by
both the Services and the Post Office.[4]

International interference was serious not only because it
brought broadcasting concerns into conflict with other radio
interests but because it led to conflicts among broadcasting
concerns themselves. The sufferer was the ordinary listener, and
Europe took the lead in seeking to eliminate the cause of his
suffering. The IBU's Geneva Plan, drawn up after protracted
argument, was designed to protect the ordinary listener and

[1] *BBC Year Book* (1930), p. 125.
[2] A National Radio Telegraphic Convention had been held in Paris in 1925.
[3] For details, see G. A. Codding Jr., *The International Telecommunications Union: An Experiment in International Co-operation* (Leiden, 1952), pp. 116–31.
[4] See *The Birth of Broadcasting*, p. 222.

went some way to regulate the situation while there was still time. In the United States, by contrast, little progress was made until February 1927 when Congress passed a Radio Act setting up a Federal Radio Commission. One hundred and ninety-four new American stations had gone on the air between July 1920 and February 1927, and there were serious problems and dangers analogous to those of traffic control. The five-man Federal Radio Commission was given power to classify stations, assign frequencies, and determine power. Within a few months of taking office it had taken steps to end 'bedlam on the air' and to exercise at least a measure of technical control over the 733 American stations seeking to operate on ninety wavelengths.[1]

The Geneva Plan, agreed upon in the far more difficult context of divided Europe, was an effort at self-regulation by the voluntary action of radio interests. The IBU had come into existence in 1925 with Reith as its initiator, Admiral Carpendale as its President, and A. R. Burrows, the first Director of Programmes of the BBC, as Secretary.[2] Carpendale was extremely successful as President. There was a rule in the original constitution that the president should be chosen for one year only and should not be reappointed, but Carpendale held the presidency for ten years. He did much to develop an atmosphere of trust and confidence. It was the engineers, however, who hammered out the details of the Geneva Plan and went on to modify it, through a Technical Committee, in meetings held every three weeks at Brussels.

The Control Centre at Brussels was the idea of Raymond Braillard, a brilliant young French engineer who had worked with Peter Eckersley on the details of the 1927 allocation. It would have been useless to allocate wavelengths if the stations did not stay strictly in their allotted channels. The Control Centre was a laboratory where the length of the wave of every European station was measured by a 'wave meter'. 'The laboratory started in an outhouse in Braillard's garden and grew into a large building on the outskirts of Brussels.'[3]

---

[1] See L. White, *The American Radio* (1947), ch. 7, 'The Government's Role'; C. A. Siepmann, *Radio, Television and Society* (1950), ch. i.
[2] See *The Birth of Broadcasting*, pp. 312 ff.
[3] P. P. Eckersley, *The Power Behind the Microphone* (1941), p. 94.

Peter Eckersley has described the whole 'Brussels phase' of European radio regulation as one in which the engineers took the initiative and reached the key decisions. It was succeeded, he has written, by the jurists' phase, beginning with the Prague Conference of 1929. This conference had been summoned by the IBU, which invited governments and administrations to participate in its deliberations and share in its decisions. 'Will you walk into my parlour?' had been the approach. 'We walked, some eagerly, some reluctantly', Eckersley adds. 'What, after all, is the loud bruha bruha of "authority". Anyway, off we went to Prague to hand ourselves over to "les administrations".'[1]

It is not clear that there was any alternative, nor is it clear that Eckersley himself was so conscious of the beginning of a new historical phase at the time. 'Carpendale, Eckersley and Hayes back from the Prague Government Conference', Reith wrote in his diary. 'Apparently quite successful, and the Union has emerged much more influential and authoritative than before.'[2]

For good or ill, by 1929 broadcasting was an affair of governments as well as of commercial concerns and public corporations. In France in 1928 and 1929 there were struggles between the group of stations controlled by the French Ministry of Posts and Telegraphs and French private stations, with the government being compelled to intervene. In Germany there was already a state-run service. The Soviet Union allotted an important role to broadcasting in its first Five Year Plan of 1928, promising 12 million receiving sets at the end of five years. In eastern Europe the practice had already begun of nations building stations—often high-power stations—close to frontiers. 'The word propaganda', a writer in the *BBC Handbook* for 1929 noted, 'has acquired an evil connexion.'[3] The declarations of the IBU were declarations of international good will in an age of power politics. 'Les administrations' held keys which opened or locked many front doors.

The Prague Conference, unlike the Geneva Conference, was one of governments and broadcasting authorities. There was British initiative behind it—and useful support from Poland—

---

[1] *The Power Behind the Microphone*, p. 97.
[2] Reith, Diary, 16 Apr. 1929.   [3] *BBC Handbook* (1929), p. 106.

and a resolution suggesting such a conference had been proposed by the Czech delegate at Washington.[1] The main effect of the conference, however, was to strengthen the agreements reached earlier at Geneva and Brussels, not to weaken them. Governmental authority was given to the 'unofficial' Geneva Plan, as modified by the Brussels Plan of 1928; and it was agreed that future modifications should be left to the IBU, with international inter-governmental conferences being called only when a majority of European governments so demanded. Braillard was again active behind the scenes, patching up differences. The decisions taken represented something half-way between 'non-governmental' and 'governmental' initiative, to use terms that have become more familiar since 1945. Any future changes in wavelengths negotiated by governments were to be put into effect only after an opinion had been given by the IBU. The IBU was thus recognized as the expert body for collective action.

The 'Prague Plan' did not allot definite waves to definite stations, except in a few exceptional cases. It left national administrations to make detailed alterations within a total of allotted waves. Many of the wavelengths, however, were those which had already been agreed upon at Geneva and Brussels. A number of wavelengths were permitted outside the Washington Conference bands. The Soviet Union, which had participated neither in the Geneva nor Washington Conferences, was provided with a number of wavelengths. Those countries with the oldest broadcasting systems—Britain, Germany, and Sweden—made a number of 'sacrifices' in exchange.

These and other arrangements made were fitted for the first time into a formal 'juristic' framework. The sanction behind the Prague Protocol of April 1929 was neither the interest of the engineer nor of the broadcaster, but the authority of government.[2] Administrations were expected to make the radio stations for which they were 'responsible' conform to the plan. Even the Brussels Control Centre was fitted into the new frame-

[1] J. D. Tomlinson, *The International Control of Radiocommunications* (Michigan, 1945), p. 181.
[2] International Telecommunications Union, *Documents de la Conférence Télégraphique Internationale de Prague* (1929). See also an article by P. Brenot, 'La Conférence Radioélectrique de Prague' in the *Journal Juridique Internationale de la Radio-électricité* (1929).

work by means of a neat diplomatic formula. 'The Belgian Administration shall be asked, provisionally and without cost or responsibility on its part, to be so good as to have measured, by organs chosen by itself, the wave lengths remitted by broadcasting stations and to communicate the results of these measurements to all Administrations through the intermediary of the International Bureau of the Telegraphic Union.'[1]

From 1929 onwards the IBU was caught up both in broadcasting and politics. There were difficulties under both headings. As the number of wireless stations in Europe increased rapidly, particularly in 1930 and 1931, problems of radio interference increased. 'Transmitting stations are being established everywhere. . . . Radio waves nowadays accompany one another, cross, meet, superpose, juxtapose, oppose, penetrate, mix and interfere with each other. Sent out together in all directions, they have great difficulty at times in finding their true destination.'[2] Engineers might have agreed—so Peter Eckersley thought—on a quite new plan to defeat 'cacophony', a plan including not only a reallotment of wavelengths but an increase in the separation between the medium waves, probably to 11 kilocycles. The solution of the problems of interference, he thought, lay in the IBU treating Europe as the BBC treated Britain—rationing wavelengths and accepting new shares.[3] Instead, there was no agreement. Wavelengths became precious commodities, and the agreement reached at Geneva and ratified at Prague became a solemn covenant which could not be broken. Precedent triumphed over logic.

The political difficulties were even more acute. The IBU held two principal meetings, the first in October 1931 at Rome and the second in June 1932 at Geneva. Because of the strains imposed on the effective implementation of the Prague agreement, the Union asked the Czechoslovak government as the official guardian of the Protocol to convene a European conference of governments to be held at Lugano in the autumn of 1931. It could not secure a majority of governments in favour of this course, however, and all that could be done was the

[1] 'The Protocol of Prague', clause x.
[2] Opening Address at the Lucerne Conference, 1933, by Pilet Golaz. Quoted in *The International Control of Radiocommunications*, p. 110.
[3] *The Power Behind the Microphone*, p. 101.

introduction of minor modifications. 'The European governments will hold a meeting in conjunction with the Union as
their expert adviser', it was promised, 'as soon as the World
Conference at Madrid has completed its labours and agreed
upon the extent of the broadcasting wave bands.'[1]

Soon after the fourth International Radio Telegraphic Conference had met in Madrid in September 1932 and created
a new International Telecommunications Union, an attempt
was made to reach a new agreement about European wavelengths. It had been hoped by the IBU that the Madrid Conference would lead to an appreciable increase in the number
and length of wavebands available for broadcasting stations,
but only four additional channels in the long wavebands were
reapportioned.

The ship-owners had triumphed over the less well-organized
broadcasting interest. 'At Washington there had been a measure
of respect for the needs of the various services. At Madrid,
Biblical examples were used to support the claim of one service
as against another, regardless of the technical aspects.'[2] Nor was
there unanimity among the broadcasters. The possibility of
allowing certain stations to broadcast outside the bands allotted
to broadcasting was admitted, but Russia stipulated that whilst
other European countries might wish to allot certain bands for
outside services she would reserve them for broadcasting. The
French, by contrast, in defending aviation and military interests,
made compromise with the broadcasting interests almost
impossible. The small powers left Madrid disgruntled and
uncertain, and as far as the European pattern as a whole was
concerned, far more variety of usage was anticipated at Madrid
than had been tolerated at Geneva or even Prague.

The Madrid Conference reiterated the case for national
sovereignty in broadcasting matters which had been stated at
Prague, but entrusted the IBU with the task of preparing for
a further conference about particular wavelengths. For its part
the IBU, following its own precedents, entrusted the prepara-
tory planning for the conference to a small Technical Committee. The committee began by undertaking an inventory of

[1] *BBC Year Book* (1933), 'The Year at Geneva', pp. 305–7.
[2] *The International Control of Radiocommunications*, p. 158.

all European broadcasting stations, including those contemplated or in course of construction, and drew up a catalogue of all power increases that had been made by European stations and all examples of persistent interference. It also listed the often contradictory criteria which would have to be taken into account in determining a new European allocation of wavelengths—the number of existing stations and those under construction or alteration; the necessity of providing minimum national services; the requirements of countries in which broadcasting was non-existent, just beginning its development, or in the course of expansion; technical and physical considerations, such as topographical and geographical conditions; political and national considerations, such as 'the co-existence of several national languages' and 'the importance of broadcasting as an instrument of government'; and 'conditions already established which it would be difficult not to take into account'.[1]

All these criteria had been considered when Braillard and Eckersley had worked out the 'logical bases' of a broadcasting formula in 1925. They were re-examined time and time again when the conclusions of the Technical Committee were debated at the European Broadcasting Conference called by the IBU at Lucerne in May and June 1933. Agreement could not be reached on a particular new formula, however, largely because different countries and different interests within countries wished to attach different weight to particular criteria. The question was fundamentally a political one, and the juggling of figures and formulae in technical jargon (like the juggling at the Disarmament Conference) was 'merely a diplomatic way of expressing a political interest'.[2]

Matters eventually had to be referred back to the Technical Committee, with the French even then protesting vigorously against the presence on the committee of a BBC engineer, L. W. Hayes. There had been persistent trouble between the British and the French in the talks leading up to the formation of the IBU,[3] and although Carpendale had a French Vice-President, Tabouis—the husband of the controversial French journalist

---

[1] See Codding, op. cit.; *Admiral Carpendale, Confidential Report on the Proceedings at Lucerne, May/June 1933.

[2] *The Power Behind the Microphone*, pp. 88–89.

[3] See *The Birth of Broadcasting*, p. 317.

of the 1930s, Madame Tabouis—this did not help matters. 'Tabouis was as famous in the Union for his speeches as Madame became later on in the larger world for her writings.'[1] French objections to the choice of Hayes were described by Carpendale as 'only one incident in the constant antagonism existing between France and England in matters of broadcasting'.[2]

There was also friction between the British Post Office, represented by F. W. Phillips, and the Soviet Union. The Russians pressed, as they had done at Madrid, for a large number of exclusive waves (Moscow alone wanted five wavelengths), while the representatives of air and shipping services objected to Russian stations 'encroaching into their wave bands'. British listeners knew nothing at all of all this elaborate bargaining, but Carpendale was ringing Reith up every night from Lucerne where, he said, they were 'having a dreadful time'.[3]

There was one moment in the talks, indeed, when they nearly reached an impasse.

Russia having refused to move sufficiently and the 'Services' having refused to have her stations in their bands in such large numbers, the only alternative was to 'increase the number of Russian stations in the long wave broadcasting band'. This was done, but thereby the next plan was made unacceptable to broadcasters, because in order to accommodate five Russian high power stations in the long wave band, it placed the stations too closely together— many of them being only 7 kilocycles apart. Daventry found itself actually 7 kilocycles from Moscow and 8 from Zeesen (Germany) which, of course, we refused to accept. The situation now was that the 'other Services' and Russia had scored at the expense of broadcasting in Europe.[4]

Four more 'plans' were put forward before the penultimate plan was produced in the middle of June. By this plan Britain found herself with no exclusive wavelength except Daventry and with several unsatisfactory 'shares', the power limit on the shares having been removed. At this point Carpendale resorted to high diplomacy, remembered Disraeli's threat at the Congress of Berlin, and actually left Lucerne for London. 'His departure surprised people', Reith wrote, 'but he thought it would have an effect, and he said he was returning to take instructions from me.'[5]

[1] *The Power Behind the Microphone*, p. 91.
[2] *Confidential Report, p. 2.   [3] Reith, Diary, 8 June 1933.
[4] *Confidential Report, p. 3.   [5] Reith, Diary, 11 June 1933.

A few days later agreement of a kind was reached, Daventry being separated from Minsk, its new Russian neighbour, by 8 kilocycles and from Zeesen by 9 kilocycles. 'Carpendale back at last from Lucerne', wrote Reith on 19 June, 'much delighted on having fixed on a plan of sorts for two years after a very rough passage indeed.'[1]

It was, indeed, only a 'plan of sorts'. After two months of deliberation, the conference had drafted and signed a European Broadcasting Convention with an attached plan for the distribution of frequencies throughout Europe, but eight of the thirty-five participating countries, led by Holland, Sweden, and Poland, refused to sign the draft, and nineteen of those who did sign made reservations about particular wavelengths.[2] 'Politics entered very largely into the final Plan.' Finland did not sign because of a dispute with Russia about the power of Radio Leningrad. Hungary was a non-signatory 'through not being able to get sufficient channels to counter her neighbours' propaganda'. There was also trouble with the shipping interests. 'The obsolete and unselective apparatus in ships was a factor which contributed to their excessive demands.'[3] While the nations divided on broadcasting wavelengths, the marine and air services were grouped together in peaceful subcommittees of all nationalities, 'and these formed a very strong opponent'.[4]

The best feature of the plan was that it provided wavelengths for three high-power long-wave stations yet to be built—in Spain, Roumania, and Turkey—and there was a hope, therefore, that it would be possible to have a two years' truce, and 'to fit things in during the next two years for the benefit of the non-signatory countries'. Britain agreed with Russia on a two-year scheme and France opposed, Britain and Russia winning by the barest margin, sixteen votes against fifteen.

The impact of these discussions on British listeners was not described to them in 1933 with the same colourful detail that Peter Eckersley had employed in his memorable descriptions of the discussions at Geneva and Prague. Yet three at least of

[1] Reith, Diary, 19 June 1933.
[2] *Confidential Report, p. 4.
[3] International Telecommunications Union, *Documents de la Conférence Européenne des Radiocommunications de Lucerne* (1933), pp. 809-66.
[4] *Confidential Report, p. 4.

the items on the agenda at this and subsequent meetings of the IBU—the 1934 meeting was held in London and the 1937 meeting, with Dr. Goebbels in the background, in Berlin—were of very real interest to listeners in Britain. The first was the problem of interference, the second the possibility of European interchange of programmes, and the third, more important than the rest, the fate of commercial radio stations in Europe, particularly Radio Luxembourg.

Interference at particular times was noted throughout the 1930s, particularly on the long wave, where there were too many claimants for the limited number of places available.[1] The separation between different stations was often inadequate to permit of good selective reception. Listeners often referred such problems, along with problems of domestic interference from electrical apparatus, to the Engineering Information Department of the BBC, earlier known as the Technical Correspondence Section. A further International Telecommunications Conference on these and other problems was held at Cairo from January to April 1938, and it was followed once more by the delegation of specific wavelength problems to the Technical Committee of the IBU.

Programme interchange raised quite different issues. Denmark, Germany, Holland, Hungary, and the U.S.A., for example, relayed the speeches at the opening of the Interim Round Table Conference in November 1930. A talk by George Bernard Shaw on *Saint Joan* was relayed to Norway, Sweden, Denmark, Finland, and the United States a year later. In December 1934 Henry Hall was heard in Czechoslovakia.[2] In 1935 British listeners could hear a Chopin recital from Warsaw, operas from Milan, Eskimo songs from Denmark, and a programme of Egyptian music from Cairo.[3]

The IBU frequently discussed such relays, attaching great importance to those which made for 'international understanding'. It also suggested other programme projects. At its 1932 Conference, for example, it discussed the possibility of assembling in each country a collection of musical scores typical of other nations.[4] It later sponsored 'National Nights' on which

[1] See, for example, *World Radio*, 10 July 1936.
[2] *BBC Annual* (1935), pp. 45–46.   [3] Ibid. (1936), p. 126.
[4] *BBC Press Release, 11 June 1932.

concerts were given in many parts of Europe 'dedicated to a specific country'. On Christmas Eve 1933 the bells of Bethlehem were heard simultaneously 'in all the continents of the world'.[1] Copyright questions figured frequently on the agenda, and there was a separate Legal Commission which in 1937 drew up a formal memorandum of propositions about copyright.[2] There were often bitter complaints against companies 'whose operations consist solely in picking up or tapping into transmissions of other organisations without previous consent in order to distribute these to their clientèle by wire, gramophone records or otherwise'.[3]

More important, however, than most of the other matters was the development of commercial broadcasting in Europe. All other questions dealt with by the IBU were in the last resort questions of co-operation: commercial broadcasting raised questions of competition, particularly for the BBC. British listeners were interested in the English programmes of Radio Normandie, Radio Luxembourg, and other continental commercial stations. The fate of these stations concerned not only the BBC but the Post Office, the press, and even the Foreign Office. It also interested the Ullswater Committee. 'It had been widely recognised that the practice of excluding advertisements from broadcast programmes in this country is to the advantage of listeners', the committee reported. 'In recent years, however, this policy has been contravened, and the purposes sought by the unified control of broadcasting have been infringed by the transmission of advertisements in English from certain stations abroad which are not subject to the influence of the British authorities except by way of international agreement and negotiation.'

The Ullswater Committee supported the effort to preserve the BBC's monopoly, while admitting that bodies like the IBU had limited powers to control or to redress the situation. 'We understand that the Post Office and the Foreign Office take all the steps which are in their power with a view to preventing the broadcasting from foreign countries in English of programmes

[1] *BBC Press Release, 7 June 1934.
[2] *BBC Press Release, 16 Mar. 1937.
[3] *BBC Press Release, 17 May 1933.

which include advertisements and to which previous objection has been taken. We approve this policy, but it is obvious that co-operation with foreign countries is necessary to make the policy internationally effective.'[1]

This man boasts he can get Timbuctoo on one valve.

26. Listeners to Foreign Stations, as seen by Bateman.

The first English-language commercial programmes from Europe made very little impression on listeners. In 1925 Captain L. F. Plugge persuaded Selfridges to sponsor a fashion talk from the Eiffel Tower station in Paris: three listeners wrote in to say that they had heard the broadcast.[2] Three years later a firm of radio manufacturers began a fortnightly series of Sunday concerts of light music by de Groot's orchestra from Radio Hilversum: the broadcasts, timed for a period when the BBC was off the air, lasted, with few interruptions, until 1930. They were supplemented by other broadcasts in 1929, 1930, and 1931 from Radio Toulouse. The broadcasts were advertised in the *Radio Times* and in *World Radio*, two BBC publications,

[1] Cmd. 5091 (1936), *Report of the Broadcasting Committee*, §§ 113 and 114. For the general conclusions of the Ullswater Committee, see below, pp. 498–504.
[2] *This is the IBC* (n.d.), p. 3.

and they caused little harm to the BBC. Indeed, when in 1928 there was talk of Baird Television buying time on Radio Hilversum, a note of warning from the BBC's Foreign Director, Major Atkinson, drew the uninitialed comment, almost certainly from Reith, 'My reaction is why worry when 10% of our listeners are affected? Are we so afraid of competition?'[1]

Competition quickened in 1929 and 1930. In 1929 a private company of radio advertising contractors was formed under the name of Radio Publicity Ltd. It canvassed business firms and arranged programmes on a number of foreign stations, including the powerful long-wave Radio Paris. In February 1930 it produced a pamphlet, 'How often have you thought—if only we could advertise by radio?' A number of gramophone-record firms, food-product firms, one toothpaste firm, and one cigarette firm had thought—and they arranged Radio Paris programmes, mainly recitals of gramophone records. Programmes were also arranged from the Irish Free State. R.P.L. changed its name to Universal Radio Publicity Ltd. in 1930. The BBC took no steps to interfere with these programmes, but it welcomed a Dutch ban on sponsored programmes in 1930 and a Belgian ban in 1932.

Two more serious commercial developments, scarcely noticed at the time by the BBC, were the registration in March 1930 of a new private company, the International Broadcasting Company, another and more ambitious venture of Captain Plugge; and the first concession to a French company, the Société Luxembourgeoise d'Études Radiophoniques, for a wireless station of not less than 100 kilowatts in Luxembourg in September 1930. The object of the IBC was to sell time on the air from foreign wireless stations. It had a curious contact, however, with the BBC. Plugge and one of his fellow directors were also directors of Radio International Publicity Services Ltd.: in this capacity they had been under contract to the BBC since 1927 to translate and sub-edit foreign wireless programmes for *World Radio*.

In October 1931 the IBC began arranging broadcasts from Radio Normandie, a 10-kilowatt station located near Fécamp and able to give a good service to the whole south coast area of England. The potential British audience for Radio Normandie

---

[1] *Note by C. F. Atkinson, 5 Nov. 1928.

was greater in size than the French audience. Again a firm of wireless manufacturers, this time an American firm, were IBC's first Radio Normandie clients: after the BBC had closed down, they began a Sunday-night gramophone programme of 'hit' records in what the BBC considered a 'blatant American manner'. For the first time in its history the BBC made a protest to the Post Office about foreign commercial competition, and the Chief Engineer suggested representations through the IBU.[1]

In the meantime the Luxembourg plan went ahead. The initial sponsors sold their concession to a new company, this time with a less innocuous name, the Compagnie Luxembourgeoise de Rediffusion, in June 1931. A majority of the Board of nine directors were to be of Luxembourg nationality, but most of the new capital, like the old, was French. Among the interests behind the venture were the Banque de Paris et des Pays Bas, the Compagnie Générale de Télégraphie Sans Fil, and the Agence Havas. The Banque de Paris was closely associated with the Société Française Radioélectrique, the great French wireless manufacturing company and owners of Radio Paris, and the C.G.T.S.F. was a sister company.

The new sponsors were to plan programmes under the direction of a Programme Commission to be appointed by the Luxembourg government. Advertising was to be allowed 'within limits fixed by the Luxembourg Post Office', and the power of the transmitter was to be not less than 100 kilowatts. The station was to operate on 'a wavelength of 210–500 metres in accordance with the Prague Convention or on a wavelength to be determined later by international convention'. The reference to the second possibility suggested that the sponsors were seeking to obtain a long-wave allocation, and Burrows from the IBU office in Geneva confirmed this. Both the technical details—wavelength and power—and the political pressures that lay behind the project for the new station created great concern in the BBC.

Knowledge of the 'congestion' in the long-wave band, coupled with the memories of the hard diplomatic bargaining about particular wavelengths at IBU conferences, led the BBC to ask the Post Office to write to Luxembourg concerning its future

[1] *Reith to the Postmaster-General, 16 Nov. 1931; Ashbridge to Reith, 16 Nov. 1931.

plans. An evasive reply was received which confirmed the worst suspicions.[1] Concern at the political level was enhanced by a brief paragraph in the *Wireless World* which quoted a tribute in the French *Journal Officiel* to one of the French sponsors of the venture who had just been promoted to office in the Légion d'Honneur. 'He has succeeded,' the *Journal Officiel* put it, 'in agreement with the French government, in founding the most powerful station in Europe, to be situated in Luxembourg under the absolute control of France.'[2]

Burrows made ominous supplementary points in two letters written to the BBC in December 1931 and January 1932. 'It looks as though the use of European broadcasting stations for advertising purposes will be unavoidable once Luxembourg has begun to shout with a loud voice all over European territory.' The power of the new station, he said, was to be 200 kilowatts and it would start broadcasting in the summer of 1932. It set an extremely dangerous precedent. 'If Luxembourg, which represents a certain financial group, is allowed by the governments of Europe to ignore the Prague Plan and the work of the Union, it will be extremely difficult, if not impossible, to prevent similar financial groups in other countries taking similar steps to suit their personal interests.'[3]

The BBC's first response was to work through Carpendale as President of the IBU. In January 1932 he wrote to Tabouis, his Vice-President, who was personally involved in the control of Radio Paris and the Compagnie Générale de Télégraphie Sans Fil. Carpendale began by pointing out that the BBC had not protested against English advertising from Radio Paris, Radio Toulouse, and Radio Normandie because these were French stations and their 'employment for non-French purposes was more or less exceptional'. This was an understatement, but the attitude underlying it was similar to that expressed at Prague and Madrid. Sovereignty was real and should not be challenged without powerful reason. Luxembourg, however, was a different matter, Carpendale insisted. Its power was vastly in excess of the needs of the Grand Duchy itself, and the people who had been granted the broadcasting concession had 'expressly and

---

[1] *Letter from G.P.O., 26 Nov. 1931; reply from Luxembourg, 2 Dec. 1931.
[2] *Wireless World*, 31 Oct., 21 Dec. 1931; *Journal Officiel*, 28 Aug. 1931.
[3] *Burrows to Carpendale, 21 Dec. 1931; to Atkinson, 6 Jan. 1932.

frankly confessed that their main object was to broadcast advertising programmes to neighbouring countries, particularly those
which do not allow advertising in their own national programmes'. Questions of principle were plainly involved. On the
technical question of wavelength, a precedent would be established if Luxembourg, 'under absolute French control' (as the
Journal Officiel had put it), were allowed to seize a long wavelength in defiance of international agreement. Did the French
intend it to make use of a long wavelength allotted to France?[1]

Tabouis in his reply made the most of the sovereignty of
Luxembourg. What could IBU do against a sovereign state?
He said that C.G.T.S.F. had not been involved in the first concession—conveniently overlooking its financial links with other
French organizations that were—and was only a minority holder
in the new concession. He tentatively hinted at compromises,
'results which shall be satisfactory in practice and remove your
fears'.[2] In fact, plans went ahead, and it was the British Post
Office which made the next protest, complaining in May 1932
that experimental broadcasts from Luxembourg on a wavelength
of 1,250 metres infringed the Washington Convention and
were interfering with British aircraft wireless services. The Air
Ministry supported this protest, which went through diplomatic
channels. F. W. Phillips of the Post Office also made it clear to
Carpendale that he did not approve of the 'threatened forcing
of advertising programmes into Great Britain' and that the
Post Office would not rent lines to advertising concerns.
Finally the IBU in June 1932 unanimously adopted a resolution
at its Montreux convention, condemning Radio Luxembourg's
'piracy' of a long wave. 'It expresses the universal opinion of
our members', Carpendale told Phillips, 'although one never
quite knows what certain countries who may benefit by these
arrangements really feel about it.'[3]

The Luxembourg government itself sent conciliatory replies
both to the IBU and to Britain, and a number of compromise
proposals were made in an effort to win British support for its
claim for a long wave. In September 1932, for example, Tabouis
suggested that Radio Luxembourg as 'a neutral and impartial

[1] *Carpendale to Tabouis, 29 Jan. 1932.
[2] *Tabouis to Carpendale, 2 Feb. 1932.
[3] *BBC Notes; Carpendale to Phillips, 16 June 1932.

station' could become 'one of the essential elements in that European co-operation which IBU had always desired': he conveniently did not refer to sponsored programmes at all.[1] Carpendale was rightly sceptical. Luxembourg could not be an 'international neutral post' unless it was managed by a 'non-commercial and truly international committee'.[2] He was willing, however, to meet representatives of the Luxembourg sponsors, CLR, in London, and did so in January 1933. Suggestions were made at this time that the BBC might be represented on 'an international advisory board consisting of several members per country'. Already German and Dutch broadcasting interests had expressed interest in such a proposal. It was pointed out also by the CLR representatives that unless the BBC came in, advertising interests would be completely free to 'counter the BBC's advertisement and Sunday policies very effectively indeed'.[3]

British listeners still knew nothing of the *haute politique* of all this. They did not even know much in general terms about the significance of the development of a third force between them and the commercial broadcasting interest—the British wireless exchange or relay trade. It is impossible to tell the story even of the *haute politique* without taking wireless-relay exchanges into the reckoning. The first relay exchange in Great Britain had been started in January 1925 in the village of Hythe near Southampton: its organizer, A. W. Maton, who owned an electrical shop, wired programmes to a number of local subscribers at a weekly rent.[4] Even earlier, in 1924, the Guernsey States Telephone Council had asked the BBC whether there would be any objection to 'the installation of a wireless receiving set near the switchboard in the Central Exchange so that the British Broadcasting Company's programmes could be intercepted and relayed to telephone subscribers on payment of a small charge'.[5] This idea, which was as old as the 1890s,[6]

---

[1] *Tabouis to Carpendale, 30 Sept. 1932.
[2] *Carpendale to Tabouis, 10 Oct. 1932.
[3] *CLR Memoranda of 12 Jan., 23 Jan. 1933.
[4] See R. H. Coase, *British Broadcasting, A Study in Monopoly* (1950), ch. 4, for a valuable general account of 'wire broadcasting'.
[5] *F. J. Brown to Reith, 1 Mar. 1924; Reith to Brown, 13 Mar. 1924.
[6] See *The Birth of Broadcasting*, pp. 42–43.

dazzled a number of people in different parts of the country in the later 1920s, and by 1929 there were thirty-four relay exchanges in Britain with 8,592 subscribers. 'A new industry had come into existence', and the number of exchanges more than doubled in the course of 1930.[1]

The operators of the first local relay exchanges took out a special licence from the Post Office: in addition, each separate subscriber had to take out a separate wireless licence. The nature of the owner's licence was changed by the Post Office in April 1930, two years after the BBC had sent to the Post Office a copy of German regulations which laid down that exchange operators had to promise not to relay 'private' or foreign programmes. In the new British licence of 1930 similar limiting conditions were imposed. First, in line not only with German precedent but with the Post Office's policy in 1922,[2] licensees had to promise not 'to originate at the stations [exchanges] or collect by wire any programme or item whether musical or otherwise or information of any kind for distribution to subscribers'. Second, the licences, like the BBC's Licence, were terminable. Third, the Post Office provided 'tramway terms' for compulsory purchase of private plant in 1932 at three months' notice and upon terms favourable to the State.

These limiting conditions did not, in fact, prevent the rapid growth of 're-diffusion'. By the end of 1931 there were 132 exchanges and 43,889 subscribers, and a year later 194 exchanges and 82,690 subscribers. The figures had risen to 343 and 233,554 by the end of 1935.[3] Following representations by relay interests, the Postmaster-General extended the period of the relay licences to the end of 1933 and later to the end of 1936, when the BBC's Charter was due to expire.

Relay reception had obvious advantages. Loudspeakers in houses were easier to operate than wireless receiving sets, and their hire was slightly cheaper and sometimes more convenient than the purchase of a set even on instalment terms. They were particularly suited to people living in large blocks of flats where individual reception was liable to electrical interference. They were capable, moreover, of providing better reception of foreign programmes than many low or even high-priced wireless receiving sets: a master set with special aerials at the relay

[1] Ibid., pp. 70, 76.   [2] Ibid., pp. 93–107.   [3] *British Broadcasting*, p. 76.

station had definite technical advantages. They were bound to be used, in a free market, for the rediffusion of foreign commercial programmes, if these programmes genuinely made an appeal to large numbers of listeners. The motive of the relay exchange owner was simple—to please the greatest possible number of subscribers.

The BBC was interested from the beginning in the development of relay exchanges. The system was seen as a potentially valuable supplement to broadcasting in areas of inferior wireless reception.[1] Peter Eckersley went further, and after he left the BBC quickly became one of the most active supporters of 'wire broadcasting', attempting in vain to convert the BBC to a policy of 'substituting wire for wireless'.[2] He pointed out as early as 1925 that wire broadcasting got round part of the difficulty of the limitation in the total number of available wavelengths, and in 1928 he joined with Goldsmith and Lochhead in preparing a memorandum on rediffusion in which he stated that the problem might involve the creation of 'an undertaking far surpassing the BBC in magnitude'.

This memorandum advocated the setting up of 'centrales', which would provide rediffusion by wire in towns and cities as 'an integral part of the BBC service'. 'It is not impossible', Eckersley added, 'to visualise, in say 20 years time, complete wire broadcasting, supplemented, it is true, but in minor part, by wireless broadcasting.'[3] To get the scheme going he envisaged co-operation with the Post Office, and went so far as to work out a scheme for an experimental BBC exchange at Norwich, the wiring to be done by the Post Office. The scheme broke down, one of the points of difficulty apparently being that the Post Office would not commit itself to the principle of BBC monopoly in the event of the scheme proving a success.[4] Eckersley left the BBC soon afterwards and in 1931 became associated with Rediffusion Ltd., one of the large companies by then engaged in the relay business. Sir William Noble, another of the pioneers of the BBC,[5] was also involved.

[1] *Memorandum on 'Relay Exchanges', 28 May 1943.
[2] See *The Power Behind the Microphone*, especially ch. xi.
[3] *Control Board Minutes, 6 Nov. 1928; Eckersley to Reith, 23 Oct., 5 Nov. 1928; Memorandum on Wireless Exchanges, 29 Nov. 1928.
[4] The detailed papers relating to this scheme have disappeared.
[5] For Noble, see *The Birth of Broadcasting*, p. 117.

Both the growth of the relay business and the expansion of commercial broadcasting between 1929 and 1932 gave force and urgency to the question of maintaining the BBC's monopoly control. It was no longer possible for the BBC to watch quietly what was happening. Relay stations putting across commercial programmes could break the BBC's monopoly with the ordinary British listener. Two conceptions of broadcasting, one explicitly agreed upon by Parliament as the basis of the British system—public service broadcasting by a public corporation—the other, commercial broadcasting, explicitly turned down inside Britain itself, were in danger of clashing without Parliament being consulted at all. In the conflict of conceptions the BBC had the full support of the press, which sent deputations on its own account to the Post Office to protest against foreign commercial broadcasts. It also agreed through the Newspaper Proprietors' Association and the Newspaper Society that newspapers would not make use of foreign stations for advertising or publicity purposes.[1]

With a view to avoiding an open clash, the BBC reached agreement in October 1931 with two of the largest relay exchange companies—Standard Radio Relay Services Ltd. and Radio Central Exchanges Ltd.—that in return for certain services from the BBC the relay exchanges concerned would rediffuse none but BBC programmes.[2] This was a fascinating development, but it broke down because of the attitude of the Post Office which, both parties agreed, had to give its consent to the scheme before it could come into force.

The Postmaster-General changed after the General Election of 1931, and Kingsley Wood, the new holder of the office, refused his consent to the scheme in June 1932. However firm the Post Office was in resisting the rise of Radio Luxembourg on the international front, it refused to buttress further the BBC's monopoly on the home front. It would be unfair, Kingsley Wood and his advisers argued, to impose restrictions on relay subscribers which were not imposed on the private owners of wireless sets. Most of the relay subscribers were, after all,

---

[1] *British Broadcasting*, pp. 107–8; *Advertisers' Weekly*, 22 Dec. 1932, 23 Feb. 1933.
[2] *Memorandum of 4 Nov. 1938, 'Relay Exchanges'. Among the services, the BBC promised to allow direct connexion between the exchanges and its control room by land-line.

listeners with limited means who should not be deprived of the freedom enjoyed by richer citizens. Kingsley Wood did not add, as he might have done, that relay subscribers also constituted a section of the 'mass electorate'. At this point broadcasting policy began to get caught up in the thickets of politics. Almost at the same time that Phillips was bemoaning 'the threatened forcing of advertising programmes into Great Britain', the Post Office was refusing to limit reception of these programmes from within.

When the agreement with the relay companies broke down, the BBC was left to work out its policy concerning commercial competition inside the IBU, this time along with the Post Office. As a result two important resolutions were passed by the Council of the IBU, on the initiative of the BBC, in May 1933. The first was aimed at Radio Normandie and stated that, in the light of the Madrid Convention, 'the systematic diffusion of programmes or messages, which are specifically intended for listeners in another country and which have been the object of a protest by the broadcasting organisation of that country, constitutes an "inadmissible" act from the point of view of good international relations'. Members of the IBU were asked to avoid such transmissions and to urge organizations outside the IBU to do the same.

The second was aimed at the projected Radio Luxembourg. 'The Union can have nothing to do with any developments in the technical field of broadcasting which do not pay the most scrupulous attention to the rules established by international conventions.' Moreover, 'the Union cannot sympathise with any type of programme which is essentially based on the idea of commercial advertising in the international field'. Lastly, 'the transmission of international programmes by a national organisation, which has not been internationally recognised, might give rise to such serious difficulties and disturb the good understanding between nations so profoundly that the transmission of such programmes despite the absence of international recognition must be considered by the Union as an "inadmissible" element in European broadcasting.'[1]

These resolutions were passed on by the IBU to the Bureau of the International Telecommunications Union, and the latter,

---

[1] The resolutions are printed in *British Broadcasting*, pp. 111–12.

in passing them on to national governments, added its own gloss. Commercial broadcasting was one way of organizing radio inside countries: there was no strength, however, in the case for broadcasting commercially to the inhabitants of another country 'in their own language, in order by this indirect violation of national laws, to give large profits to the organisers'.[1]

Unequivocal statements of this kind determined the atmosphere when Luxembourg's demand for a long wave was turned down at Brussels and Lucerne.[2] Yet it was clear that the pressure from commercial interests, including British interests, was increasing. The names of twenty-one British firms organizing programmes from foreign stations were published at the end of 1932: they were mainly in consumer-goods industries, including radio and gramophone records.[3] One newspaper was involved, the *Sunday Referee*, which in consequence was expelled from the Newspaper Proprietors' Association in February 1933.[4]

There was a close relationship between the *Sunday Referee* and Plugge's International Broadcasting Company (IBC) which considerably increased its strength in 1932: it even set up an 'International Broadcasting Club' in the summer of 1932 with the alleged object of 'bringing into closer relationship all listeners to IBC transmissions'. In April 1933 it began its own weekly programme sheet. Radio Paris was offering $2\frac{1}{2}$ hours of sponsored programmes on Sundays, Radio Normandie 12, Radio Toulouse $1\frac{1}{2}$, and Radio Côte d'Azur 1 hour. There were also $6\frac{1}{2}$ hours of sponsored programmes from Radio Normandie on weekdays. A new arrival among stations sending out commercial programmes in English was Radio Ljubljana in Yugoslavia.

Before Radio Luxembourg went on the air in the spring of 1933, in defiance of the IBU, the Post Office, and the BBC, the BBC had taken its first action to modify programme arrangements to prevent advertisers from foreign stations having a

---

[1] *Journal Télégraphique*, May 1933.

[2] For Brussels and Lucerne, see above, pp. 341–8. Phillips had also made a sharp attack on the long-wave proposal for Luxembourg at the Madrid Conference. See *The International Control of Radiocommunications*, pp. 159–60, where a portion of one of Phillips's speeches is printed.

[3] *British Broadcasting*, p. 101.

[4] *Sunday Referee*, 27 Feb., 12 Mar. 1933. It offered advertisers who bought space in its columns a broadcast advertisement of 100 words or more from Radio Paris. The *Sunday Referee* rejoined the NPA in Nov. 1934. Its use of Radio Paris had been anticipated by *John Bull* in Dec. 1931.

special advantage. It lengthened the hours of broadcasting on Sundays to include transmissions between 12.30 and 3 p.m. It did not change the content of the programmes, however—Reith said that it never would—and left Sunday variety and dance bands to Radio Paris and Radio Normandie.[1] When Radio Luxembourg began its broadcasts in English—on the forbidden long wavelength—it restricted them in the first instance to Sundays, and concentrated on light programmes, particularly the cheapest of all programmes to produce, gramophone records.

The object of the station was not to provide in any sense 'an international neutral point', but rather a communications centre of the 'world of pop', 'spots, pops and (in due course) old-time religion'.[2] The first studios were opened in the Villa Louvigny, set in a quiet park eleven miles from the city centre of Luxembourg. The BBC must have been extremely surprised when it received a letter in March 1933 from the first Station Director announcing that programmes in English would be sent out on Sundays and asking for BBC publicity on their behalf.[3] The response of the BBC was to ban the publication of Radio Luxembourg's programmes in *World Radio*.[4]

Radio Luxembourg, once established, remained on the air until two weeks after the outbreak of war in 1939, outlasting all other predominantly commercial stations. Further attempts at a 'compromise' with the BBC in 1933 (and 1935) failed completely, and the station went on alone, as it put it in a memorandum, 'with the work it assigned itself'.[5] Suppression was impossible. 'Non possumus', said Reith and Carpendale, with great reluctance.[6] In January 1934 Radio Luxembourg began to broadcast on the wavelength of 1,304 metres which had been allotted to Warsaw at the Lucerne Conference but had not yet been taken up. Post Office protests, many of them backed up by diplomatic representation through the Foreign Office, all failed,

---

[1] See above, p. 54.

[2] See the interesting article with this title written by P. Williams in *Time and Tide*, 15 Feb. 1962.

[3] *J. Martin to the BBC, 30 Mar. 1933.

[4] *World Radio*, 7 Apr. 1933.

[5] *Memorandum of 6 July 1933. There were talks in the Ardennes in 1935 between Carpendale and representatives of the Luxembourg government.

[6] *Memorandum to the Board of Governors, 27 Sept. 1937.

the Luxembourg Prime Minister repeatedly emphasizing that there was nothing he either could do or wished to do to stop CLR from conducting its affairs in its own way.[1] Protests from the IBU were similarly brushed aside as the comments of a 'private organisation'.

The amount spent by advertisers increased sharply in 1934 and 1935, as the football pools increased their share and more and more emphasis was placed on 'the lower middle and lower class market', as one advertiser put it.[2] Programmes consisted almost exclusively of variety, light music, and gramophone records. The British Post Office refused to allow Radio Luxembourg or any other foreign station the use of land lines for relay of their sponsored programmes from Britain, but with the development of improved methods of recording,[3] much of the presentation work could be carried on in London.

The BBC refused Radio Luxembourg permission to relay several big national events in Britain, such as the King's speech in February 1936, but it could not always stop the relaying of French commentaries on British events. Nor could it fully control its own broadcasters. Christopher Stone's contract with the BBC was cancelled when he broadcast regular programmes from the Continent, but some dance bands broadcast on both BBC and Radio Luxembourg programmes and the Programme Board had to recognize that it could not refuse BBC contracts to artists who broadcast from foreign commercial stations.[4]

The press remained suspicious of Radio Luxembourg. The odd situation arose, indeed, that the Communist *Daily Worker* could proudly announce, after the capitulation of the *Sunday Referee*, that 'no other daily newspaper in Britain gives the Luxembourg programme. The *Daily Worker* is now able to fill the gaps.'[5]

In the meantime, the number of British listeners to Luxembourg increased sharply, with the relay exchanges often acting as an intermediary. A survey made by the Institute of Incorporated Practitioners in Advertising in November and December

[1] There is a great deal of evidence on this matter in the Post Office Archives.
[2] For the marketing side of commercial broadcasting, see Mather and Crowther Ltd., *Facts and Figures of Commercial Broadcasting* (1938).
[3] See above, p. 99.   [4] See above, p. 55.
[5] *Daily Worker*, 29 Nov. 1935.

1935 showed that one out of two of the British listeners inter-viewed listened to Radio Luxembourg regularly on Sundays: on weekdays the figure dropped to 11 per cent. A London Press Exchange inquiry at the same time suggested that the Sunday listeners to Radio Luxembourg were 'loyal', that is to say they tended to listen at the same times each week.[1] Further inquiries were made by the BBC's own Listener Research section after the problem had been ventilated by the Ullswater Committee.[2] Among 2,000 members of the 'light entertainment' public, 22 per cent. listened regularly to foreign stations (not necessarily commercial stations) on weekdays and 66 per cent. on Sundays.[3]

The last big pre-war inquiries were made in 1938 by a Joint Committee of the Incorporated Society of British Advertisers and the Institute of Incorporated Practitioners in Advertising, with Professor Arnold Plant as chairman. Listening, it was clear, was still heaviest on Sundays, much of it during the extended hours of BBC transmission.[4] Over 1 million house-holds, it was estimated, were listening to Luxembourg between 1 o'clock and 2 o'clock on Sunday afternoons. The north-east of England, South Wales, and the London area provided the highest proportion of listeners—in that order. With minor exceptions, the BBC weekday service remained more popular than that of all foreign commercial stations combined, and British listening to foreign stations reached its peak when none of the Corporation's stations was transmitting.[5]

Of foreign stations other than Radio Luxembourg, Radio Normandie remained the most popular. Radio Paris was taken over by the French government in April 1933, and sponsoring stopped in November. Radio Toulouse had controls imposed upon it in July 1933, and there was talk of reducing the power of Radio Normandie later in the same year. Radio Toulouse was soon active again, however, and reopened with a blaze of trumpets (and addresses from Winston Churchill—and Peter Eckersley) in 1938. A new French commercial station, Poste Parisien, began broadcasting commercial programmes in Eng-lish in November 1933 and was followed by Radio Lyons, in

[1] *Material in BBC Archives.
[2] See below, p. 502.   [3] See above, p. 276.
[4] For the extension of hours, see above, pp. 25–26.
[5] *Survey of Listening to Sponsored Radio Programmes*.

which Pierre Laval had an interest, in 1936; and Radio Normandie actually increased the hours available for commercial broadcasting in the mid-1930s.

Captain Plugge, who was elected as Conservative Member of Parliament for Chatham at the General Election of 1935, talked of Radio Normandie as a 'thirteenth colony', which justified all the efforts of IBC. Its advertising revenue was considerably less than that of Radio Luxembourg, yet it had the backing not only of the IBC but of a number of big advertising agencies, some of them American. IBC ran a programme unit—the Universal Programme Corporation—in 1935, and Radio Normandie was consequently much less dependent on gramophone records than Radio Luxembourg has been in its post-war phase. Many of the programmes put across by Radio Normandie were of a distinctly American type. Three American 'soap operas' followed each other in a row, for example, on five days of the week in 1939.

Repeated efforts by the BBC to persuade the kaleidoscopic French governments of the 1930s to 'control' such broadcasting all failed. In 1934, for example, Pellenc, of the French Ministry of Posts and Telegraphs, told Carpendale that 'letters of recall' had been signed by his Ministry to stop English advertising programmes, but he did not know the outcome.[1] Three years later Jardillier, of the same Ministry, admitted that taxes imposed by the French government to act as a deterrent had been easily evaded.[2] Soon afterwards, in December 1937, it was reported from Paris that the Chautemps government was about to prohibit all English sponsored programmes by decree—and the reports rang so true that in London threatened commercial and political interests rallied with vigour[3]—but in January 1938 Chautemps resigned. The new Minister of Posts and Telegraphs did not seek to follow in the footsteps of his predecessor. Nor was the French Parliament any more effective than its Ministers. In April 1938 the Posts and Telegraphs Committee of the French Chamber reported in favour of suppressing English

[1] *Pellenc to Carpendale, 2 Oct. 1934.
[2] *BBC Note on a meeting of Dec. 1937.
[3] *The Times*, 28 Dec. 1937; see the *Advertisers' Weekly* for 6 Jan. 1938 for advertisers' comments. There were also letters to *The Times* in February and March and a protest in Parliament by Boothby. (*Hansard*, vol. 331, cols. 645–6.) The Incorporated Society of British Advertisers set up a Radio Defence Committee.

advertising programmes from French stations. Nothing came of its report.

Other countries were either more amenable to BBC pressure or were not tempted to yield to the pressure of British advertising interests, which was felt (and resisted) in Austria, Denmark, Hungary, Yugoslavia, and even Germany in 1936 and 1937. A limited amount of advertising was carried on from Radio Athlone, renamed Radio Eireann in February 1938, and for a short time Spanish stations were drawn into the British advertising network. By spring 1939, however, Luxembourg and the French pirate stations were the only ones still broadcasting advertising programmes to Britain. In Europe as a whole, a more serious problem was the extension of beamed radio propaganda, stirring up hate and distrust, particularly among ethnic minorities. With the opening of Radio Andorra in 1939, Monaco was the only country in Europe without an independent radio service,[1] but listeners' freedom was often severely limited. In Germany, for example, up to five years' imprisonment was the penalty for passing on to a third party 'detrimental news' picked up from a foreign station:[2] it was also an offence to decry in any way the activities or personnel of the German broadcasting system.[3] The People's Receiving Set was designed to receive German stations only. Three million of them had been sold by 1939, nearly 70 per cent. of them to 'workers'. Links with foreign countries were organized not through the IBU, but through bilateral pacts, like the cultural agreement with Italy in 1938, which provided for an exchange of music, talks, and descriptive broadcasts between the two countries.[4]

Against this background the BBC's battle against foreign commercial broadcasting lost some of its sting. The last unsuccessful international attempt to deal with it was made at the World Telecommunications Conference at Cairo in 1938, when all the participants at the Madrid Conference were present, along with representatives of nine new countries.[5] The conference increased the length of the waveband available for broad-

---

[1] *World Radio*, 29 Jan. 1939.
[2] Ibid., 14 Apr. 1939.
[3] See F. Gower, 'Broadcasting in Germany' in *The Spectator*, 24 Feb. 1939.
[4] *World Radio*, 9 Dec. 1938.
[5] See Codding, *The International Telecommunications Union*, pp. 160–80; Tomlinson, *The International Control of Radiocommunications*, pp. 210–12.

casting, yet refused to support the British Post Office in condemning commercial broadcasting for countries overseas.

The story of this last attempt, though dwarfed by frightening new developments in European radio, is exciting in itself. In February 1938 Colonel Angwin, the Engineer-in-Chief of the Post Office, moved a resolution in the First Sub-Committee of the Technical Commission of the Conference that 'because of the difficulty of allocating to the broadcasting service between 150 and 500 kilocycles, a sufficient number of waves to allow each country in the European region to assure a satisfactory national service, no wave of this band may be used by a country in this region for transmissions in the nature of commercial publicity sent in any other language but the national language or languages of that country'.[1] Angwin said that the British Parliament and press were 'aroused over this question, and the Post Office had even been requested to "interfere with the stations in question"'. Angwin was eloquent enough to win the support of his sub-committee which, after a brief discussion, passed the resolution. The French representative, however, was absent, and at the next meeting the whole question was re-opened with great feeling. The French challenged the jurisdiction of the sub-committee as well as the content of the resolution, and after a heated debate the matter was referred back to the Technical Committee as a whole. There was a tie in the vote in the full committee—fifteen on each side—with twenty-three abstentions. By the rules of the conference, the American chairman stated that the proposal had lapsed. The British had been supported by only eight European delegations out of twenty-seven. France had successfully defended French commercial interests not only in France but in Luxembourg. Phillips of the Post Office, unhappy about BBC Sunday programmes, had been somewhat restrained at the final session. 'Ashbridge', he wrote to the Director-General of the Post Office, 'came round in a very gloomy mood. He suggested that if I had been in my usual form I could easily have carried the meeting.'[2]

On the eve of the Cairo Conference the Post Office had

---

[1] International Telecommunications Union, *Documents de la Conférence Internationale des Radiocommunications du Caire* (1938).
[2] Phillips to Gardiner, 3 Mar. 1938 (Post Office Archives).

considered its policy towards commercial broadcasting from abroad in the light of changing circumstances. After Cairo there was considerable feeling that efforts to destroy foreign commercial broadcasting were, in the Postmaster-General's own words, 'very unpopular and achieving no results'. Britain, with its large home market and its public-service system of broadcasting, was the only country which had to face this particular problem, and the 'arguments for abandoning existing policy' were carefully rehearsed and canvassed.

Phillips favoured 'a vigorous reaffirmation of existing policy, coupled with an intimation that if and when sponsored broadcasting was permitted it would be undertaken by the BBC under State Control'. Others inside the Post Office—and other government departments—were clearly prepared to consider major changes of broadcasting policy. Sir Kingsley Wood, the former Postmaster-General and then Secretary of State for Air, was not averse to commercial broadcasting from inside Britain; Sir Robert Vansittart of the Foreign Office and Robert Boothby from the Conservative back benches, conscious of the stormy international scene, thought that Britain might actually sponsor advertising stations abroad from which British programmes could be disseminated; there were even voices in the Treasury hinting that the BBC's licence revenue was becoming insufficient to cover the amount required for the future development of television and overseas broadcasting, and that different ways of financing broadcasting might have to be considered. It is scarcely surprising that at the last pre-war international conference, the European Broadcasting Conference held at Montreux in the spring of 1939, the Post Office delegates were instructed not to raise the advertising question and, if consulted by other delegations, were to discourage them also from raising it.[1]

Some of these discussions point forward to the post-war debate. There was, however, a curious twist to the narrower Luxembourg story during the last few months before the outbreak of war. Given that Europe was being dominated more and more by propaganda, Vansittart, as chairman of the Committee for the Co-ordination of British Publicity Abroad, felt

---

[1] For Montreux, see *The International Telecommunications Union*, pp. 178–9. Post Office files give some sense of the background of discussions in 1938 and 1939.

that it would be better to make use of Radio Luxembourg than to continue to seek to destroy it. In September 1938, therefore, the unprecedented step was taken of providing Radio Luxembourg with special recordings of Chamberlain's speech on the Munich crisis. The BBC gave further help with the rebroadcasting of other speeches by Chamberlain in December 1938 and March 1939, and offered facilities to French and German commentators on President Lebrun's visit to London in March 1939.

All these changes were made at the specific request of 10 Downing Street and the Foreign Office. The feeling that war might be imminent was changing old relationships. Graves noted in January 1939 that there was 'a very definite desire on the part of the government that Radio Luxembourg should be used'.[1] The commercial radio interest, particularly Wireless Publicity Ltd., was aware of some of the possibilities of this new situation and supplied Vansittart with information and ideas, but the outbreak of war brought talk of further action to a close.

To the end, the style of Radio Luxembourg broadcasting remained unchanged—the continuous supply of the lightest and most ephemeral of all light and ephemeral fare. Yet the very last item broadcast before the station closed down in September 1939 was a march written by a Luxembourg composer with the title 'For Liberty'. 'It was played with considerable feeling,' a journalist reported, 'and the words were sung in none of Luxembourg's commercial languages, but in the national dialect which few but real Luxembourgers can understand.'[2]

5. Empire and Overseas

BY 1938 and 1939, therefore, the pattern of BBC attitudes was being modified under the threat of war as much as the pattern of programmes.[3] Broadcasts in foreign languages had begun with the inauguration of an Arabic Service—little more, at the start,

---

[1] *Memorandum by the Deputy Director-General, 9 Jan. 1939.
[2] *Daily Telegraph*, 23 Sept. 1939.
[3] For the details of the transformation, see below, pp. 645 ff.

than a daily news bulletin—in January 1938.[1] The Latin-American Service followed soon afterwards in March 1938, and from 27 September 1938 onwards, the day of Chamberlain's broadcast at the height of the Munich crisis, the BBC broadcast news nightly in French, German, and Italian: other languages were added in 1939.[2]

Throughout this impressive range of activities, which set the stage for the international role of the BBC during the Second World War, the chief object of the BBC was to provide honest news, not propaganda. Sir Robert Vansittart, at the Foreign Office, was never sure about the difference between the two:[3] the BBC, inspired by Reith, to its own glory and the glory of the country, saw the difference clearly. The perception of the difference depends not so much on subtlety of intelligence as on qualities of character. In the case of the BBC, the policy towards overseas broadcasting owed much to the public-service tradition in home broadcasting and, even more directly, to the Empire Service which celebrated its sixth birthday at the end of 1938, when overseas broadcasts were beginning to multiply. Long before the crisis came, Reith and some of his colleagues appreciated the significance of this service: they thought of it, indeed, as a natural development and not merely as the response to an emergency.

The first regular Empire broadcasts began on 19 December 1932. Long before that, however, Reith had taken up the subject with vision and enterprise, not only in relation to Empire broadcasting from the BBC in London but to the development of separate and autonomous broadcasting systems in the Dominions and Colonies. He had approached the India Office as early as 1924, and the Viceroy in 1925, about the great possibilities of broadcasting in India and he continued throughout the 1920s and 1930s to give his wholehearted support to separate ventures which would have started years earlier and on firmer foundations had his advice been taken.[4]

There would have been Empire broadcasting from London long before 1932 had it not been for technical and, even more important, financial limitations. These were described frankly

[1] See below, pp. 403–6.
[2] See below, pp. 645 ff.   [3] See above, p. 147.
[4] See *Into the Wind* (1949), pp. 113, 167; *The Birth of Broadcasting*, pp. 323–4.

at the Colonial Office Conference of May 1927, presided over by L. S. Amery, then Secretary of State, when Carpendale and Peter Eckersley attended a session on broadcasting along with Phillips and Lee of the Post Office and two representatives of the Department of Scientific and Industrial Research. Carpendale told the Conference that the BBC had been 'alive to the developments and the necessity for experiments in short-wave broadcasting' for Empire listeners: Eckersley, however, had been anxious not to go ahead until 'the quality of short-wave broadcasting' had improved.[1] He feared 'fading, distortion and unreliability'.[2] 'We stayed our hand so as not merely to put out noises combined with all sorts of atmospherics and inaccuracies and periods of silence and general unpleasantness, merely to satisfy what might be called the sentimental feeling abroad just to hear something from another country which is neither music nor intelligent speech.'

At this conference, W. G. A. Ormsby-Gore, then Under-Secretary of State for the Colonies, pressed Eckersley to go ahead. He had heard complaints, he said, that some listeners in the Empire could get Philadelphia but could never get Daventry or 2LO. 'Bournemouth they occasionally get, but it is pretty bad.' Could not the BBC aim deliberately at listeners outside Britain?

Carpendale then raised the financial difficulty in making costly experiments in overseas broadcasting. 'Our whole income is from listeners in England': could, then, large-scale overseas experiments be justified? He added also that there were serious copyright difficulties and problems of press suspicion and rivalry in relation to the possible broadcasting of 'Empire news'. Phillips backed him up on the last of these points. 'Judging from the experience when broadcasting was first floated in this country, we had an enormous struggle with the Press before we could get any settlement at all. When you raise this with the

---

[1] The first short-wave broadcasting service had begun in the United States in 1924, and Eindhoven in Holland, which began a regular three-day-a-week service in 1927, had started experimental broadcasts a year earlier. On 1 Sept. 1927 Gerald Marcuse, the well-known English amateur, was allowed to transmit material for two hours a day on wavelengths of 23 and 33 metres.

[2] *Memorandum by the Chief Engineer on Empire Broadcasting, 6 May 1927. See also a further Memorandum with the same title, 6 Dec. 1928. In a letter to Reith, 26 Feb. 1929, Eckersley rebuked critics who accused him of going slow on short-wave broadcasting. 'It is not enviable to be in a position where one feels that one has to be—in the general interest—apparently reactionary.'

Press, for broadcasting news to the whole world by telephone, you will have an enormous struggle, I think, before you get anything settled.'[1]

Despite these difficulties, however, the BBC was willing to go ahead, Carpendale concluded, 'and not say anything about paying yet'. 'It is difficult to ask a Colony to pay if they do not know in the least what they are going to get.' 'We want to put the thing into being', Eckersley added, 'and then talk about it as an actuality.' This approach was confirmed at a Control Board meeting soon afterwards, although it was still hoped that additional money would be 'specially granted by Government'.[2]

Trial broadcasts began in November 1927 from an experimental short-wave station (G5SW) working on a wavelength of 24 metres and situated at the Marconi Works at Chelmsford.[3] The results of the experiments were encouraging but reception was really good only in certain areas. This was partly because only one wavelength was used, and partly because there were no elaborate aerials to enable transmissions to be directed towards particular parts of the Empire. The first big transmission was on 11 November, when a special programme was broadcast to Australia.[4] This and following programmes were received with enthusiasm in many parts of the Empire and soon stimulated an overseas demand for regular Empire broadcasting. There might have been an even bigger demand had Reuters allowed news items to be broadcast.

The BBC believed that experimental Empire programmes, with all their limitations, had a twofold purpose—'to keep us in touch with the isolated man in the back of beyond to whom any contact with this country would be a very good thing' and 'to help the newly established broadcasting stations overseas against circumstances which we have not had to face here'.[5] It went on, however, to stress the importance of quality. 'Intelligi-

[1] *For the reasons for news bulletins not being included, see Reith to the Colonial Office, 11 Dec. 1928.   [2] *Control Board Minutes, 24 May 1927.

[3] *Colonial Office Conference, 15th meeting, 20 May 1927: stenographic record. For the origins of the BBC policy as put forward at this conference, see Control Board Minutes, 17 May 1927. For the decision after the conference to go ahead 'on an experimental basis at once', see ibid., 24 May 1927.

[4] In Sept. 1927 Australian messages from Dame Nellie Melba and the Australian Prime Minister, Bruce, had been picked up by the BBC.

[5] *C. G. Graves, notes of a lecture on 'Dominion and Empire Broadcasting', 9 Dec. 1933.

bility, continuity and quality are essential conditions, pre-requisite to successful broadcasting of this kind.'[1] Programmes, also, had to be of a high standard of interest. 'An Australian paper, commenting on the recent chance relay of the London station programme via the Australian stations, expressed dis-appointment in the artistic quality and interest of the items broadcast as compared with the fare provided by the local stations. Its opinion is a significant indication that the overseas programme cannot expect to enjoy a privileged status in point of acceptable quality.'[2]

The Chelmsford scheme would have been impossible without the full co-operation of the Marconi Company, which had useful experience in developing short-wave techniques even when transmission by short waves was thought to be freakish and unreliable. Meetings had been held with the Marconi Com-pany in August 1927 which led to a satisfactory agreement: the Radio Corporation of America came into the picture also, and two-way broadcasts were arranged from and to the American Station at Schenectady (2XAD). A receiving station at Terling in Essex was established by the BBC and the Marconi Company to test the success of this transatlantic interchange. By November 1928, however, the main Chelmsford transmitter was in a poor condition, and 'technical hitches' and breakdowns were frequent.

At a time, therefore, when the demand from overseas for regular broadcasts was becoming more insistent and foreign countries were beginning to devote increasing effort to short-wave services, the whole future of the BBC's experimental scheme seemed in jeopardy. Experiments cost money which the BBC could not easily set on one side. It had already spent £19,000 by the beginning of 1929. The Post Office, which had its own point-to-point telephone and telegraph station at Rugby, was interested in the problem but equally unable to do any-thing about it. There was no doubt that if sufficient money were available, a worth-while service could be achieved.[3]

This was the position in 1929 when the BBC once more approached the Colonial Office, first informally and then form-

---

[1] *BBC Handbook* (1928), p. 297.   [2] Ibid., p. 298.
[3] There is a useful article by Sir Noel Ashbridge, 'World Broadcasting on Short Waves', in *London Calling*, Special 21st Anniversary Number, 10 Dec. 1953.

ally, to take effective action.[1] In June 1929 Reith showed Leech of the Post Office an extremely interesting memorandum on 'Empire and World Broadcasting', prepared by Major C. F. Atkinson, the Foreign Director, and in September 1929 Leech said that the Colonial Secretary had written to the Postmaster-General concerning the need for Empire broadcasting.[2] The Colonial Secretary in the second Labour government was Lord Passfield (Sidney Webb), and he was anxious that some action should be taken before the Colonial Conference of 1930. He welcomed a long printed memorandum, prepared in draft by Atkinson and Ashbridge, the new Chief Engineer, which was submitted by the BBC in November 1929 and which stated boldly in its introduction that although the BBC was not responsible for providing an 'outgoing service', it was 'the only body fitted by constitution and experience for the management of such a service should it come into being'.[3]

The memorandum went on to state that although some technical problems still remained unsolved, 'something like a service' was technically possible, and that there was 'a real "listener's" interest, distinct both from the amateur's reaction and the ephemeral appeal of novelty'. It described the existing broadcasting facilities in Australia, Canada, New Zealand, South Africa, East Africa, India, Ceylon, Singapore, and Hong Kong, and the complete lack of facilities in the West Indies, Rhodesia, Colonial Africa, and the remaining parts of the Empire. There was a universal desire in all these countries, it said, 'to participate in great occasions and exciting events', although the right balance between what would and should be provided from London was difficult to decide. By the nature of things, decisions on such matters would have to be *a priori* and, in a measure, speculative.

Finally, the memorandum touched on foreign competition. 'Short-wave broadcasting stations are springing up everywhere, and some are under the direct control of governments, having as their objects: (1) the maintenance of touch with outlying

[1] *Control Board Minutes, 7 Aug. 1929, and a Note on them by Peter Eckersley, dated the same day.
[2] *Leech to Reith, 24 Sept. 1929.
[3] *For Passfield's interest, see a note from Reith, 10 Jan. 1930, and a letter from R. V. Vernon of the Colonial Office to Reith, 7 Feb. 1930. 'His Lordship has considered the scheme with interest, and is impressed with its merits, although it is not free from difficulties.'

nationals and (2) the world-wide presentation of the national viewpoint in terms of national culture.' Neither of these objects, it argued, was illegitimate, 'but the first assumes a principle that has already caused friction in Europe, while in the second the boundary between cultural and tendentious propaganda is, in practice, very indefinite'. The United States also, the largest English-speaking nation in the world and the one which had developed broadcasting on a larger scale than any other country, could not be ignored. In such circumstances, could the British Empire stay aloof? It was 'presumably entitled no less than others to diffuse its ideas and its culture': indeed, it was 'not impossible to conceive of a situation in which deliberate recourse to propaganda might become desirable'.

The rest of the memorandum was concerned with technical requirements, finance, and programme policy. The existing Chelmsford plant, on hire from the Marconi Company, would not suffice to provide a regular service, nor would the existing wavelength of 24 metres. At least two wavelengths were needed if all parts of the Empire were to be reached 'under varying conditions of light and darkness'. Daventry would be a good site for a new experimental station, which could then be replaced after five years with a permanent station. As for programme policy, 'a programme service provided for listeners overseas should be appropriate in scope, arrangement and timing to their respective positions in longitude, the broadcasting services already existing or planned, and other circumstances generally'.

At least four regular programmes should be provided— a 'Colonial' afternoon programme, 'culminating in a substantial news bulletin', and consisting of entertainment taken from home programmes, 'with Big Ben and various items of sentimental significance'; a 'South African' programme, coinciding in time with the home evening programme and containing little special matter, except a news bulletin in Afrikaans; an 'Australian and New Zealand' morning programme, performed specially in the day time but outside United Kingdom broadcasting hours; and a 'Canadian' small-hours programme, designed also for the West Indies, involving night staff and special terms for performers. In addition, there should be 'means of occasionally transmitting "peak" events or providing special programmes for relay'.

The new temporary station would cost £40,000 to build and £7,000 a year to maintain. The annual cost of programmes, apart from news, would be £34,000, assuming 1,700 hours of broadcasting. 'No new body, whether of public service or of commercial constitution, would be able to provide the service at lower cost, since such a body would not have the benefit of British Broadcasting Corporation general programme expenditure, not to mention its experience and organisation.'[1] An even cheaper scheme was suggested in an additional unprinted memorandum of June 1930. It would have cost £22,000 a year, but a new clause was added that 'colonial governments would be required to provide safeguards against any unreasonable commercial exploitation of the British Broadcasting Corporation's programme matter by re-broadcasters or re-diffusers in their particular territories'.[2]

The BBC's first scheme was discussed in March 1930 at the Colonial Office by representatives of the Colonial Office, the Dominions Office, the India Office, the Post Office, the Lord Privy Seal's Department, and the BBC. Sir Samuel Wilson, Permanent Under-Secretary of State for the Colonies, was in the chair.[3] The Dominions Office took the lead in arguing that the Dominions could not be asked to contribute financially: the most that they could do was to co-operate in the exchange of programmes. The Colonial Office then pointed out that it could not bear the whole cost of a service. It was in the light of this preliminary discussion, during which, Reith complained, the BBC had been made to 'show up in rather a bad light',[4] that the BBC's second and cheaper scheme was put forward.

Reith had found the Post Office unhelpful, too, both before and during this meeting. 'We are likely to be left with the baby to carry, because everybody else is too selfish and we are too decent to let it drown. Apart from ordinary instincts of humanity, we realise that it may have a great career in front of it.'[5]

---

[1] *'Memorandum on Empire Broadcasting submitted by the British Broadcasting Corporation to the Colonial Office in June 1930, and to the Imperial Conference in October 1930.'

[2] *Colonial Office Conference, 'Memorandum on Empire Broadcasting', June 1930.

[3] For the choice of chairman, see Passfield to H. B. Lees-Smith, 31 Dec. 1929 (Post Office Archives).

[4] Reith to Leech, 12 Mar. 1930 (Post Office Archives); *BBC Note on the Conference, 11 Mar. 1930.   [5] *Reith to Atkinson, 21 Mar. 1930.

27. Back from Munich
Chamberlain at the Microphone, Heston, Sept. 1938

28. King George V at the Microphone, 1934

29. Radiolympia (1933)

30. 5XX and Empire Stations at Daventry (1933)

31. J. H. Whitley (1931)   32. Sir Charles Carpendale (1938)

33. Reith
A Portrait by Sir Oswald Birley (1934)

The cheaper scheme was quickly prepared.[1] Among its other features was the regular transmission of news bulletins at 12 noon, 6 o'clock in the evening, and 12 midnight G.M.T. Reuters had at last expressed willingness to provide this service on a fee basis for a five-year period in April 1930: indeed, they provided an experimental news bulletin from Chelmsford for one month free of charge from 22 April onwards.[2]

At the Colonial Conference of June 1930 the BBC's revised scheme was approved in principle. 'The Conference recognises and appreciates the good will of the BBC in this matter. They are in favour of a scheme for Empire Broadcasting and generally agree with the proposals outlined.' A committee was set up to examine the scheme in detail, which by then had also secured the blessing of the Post Office.[3] The committee recommended that the cost of the scheme should be met out of a levy on colonial receiving-set licences, the income from which would be sufficient in the long run, it was held, to pay for practically the whole of the service.[4] In the meantime, the British Treasury was to be asked to provide funds to finance the service until the colonial contributions came in.[5]

With its usual lack of enthusiasm for interesting pioneer schemes,[6] the Treasury replied that the matter should be deferred until after the Dominions Conference in November 1930. 'If the British Broadcasting Corporation as part of its general policy of research and development likes to pay for a station and a service out of its existing revenue and make direct arrangements on its own with other broadcasting authorities overseas,' a Treasury official kindly noted, 'we shall have no objection.'

Unlike the Colonial Conference, the Dominions Conference, as had been anticipated, was far from enthusiastic. Reith, indeed, found its Communications Committee 'unsatisfactory and silly'.[7] For all the talk of Empire unity, the Dominions always wanted to go their own way, and control of broadcasting

[1] *Carpendale to R. V. Vernon, 24 June 1930.
[2] Reith to Leech, 10 Apr. 1930 (Post Office Archives); *BBC Press Release, 15 Apr. 1930.   [3] Phillips to Reith, 26 June 1930 (Post Office Archives).
[4] P. H. Morris to Phillips, 21 July 1930 (Post Office Archives).
[5] Minute of Imperial Conference Inter-Departmental Committee on Economic Questions (Post Office Archives).
[6] See also below, p. 564.   [7] *Note to Atkinson, 16 Oct. 1930.

seemed almost to be a test case of national sovereignty. The conference passed a resolution, therefore, directing attention to 'the technical and financial difficulties of the scheme' and demanding 'further information' to see whether the difficulties could be overcome.[1] It recommended 'as a first step that His Majesty's Government in the United Kingdom should suggest to the BBC that that body should communicate particulars of the scheme to the broadcasting organisations or other appropriate authorities throughout the Empire and should invite them to furnish their views (after any necessary consultation with their respective governments) as to the value to them of such a service and as to their readiness to make a contribution towards its cost in return for the right to relay any part of the service which they may require'.[2]

The British Treasury for its part flatly refused to accept the view that any part of the cost of an Empire broadcasting scheme should fall on the British taxpayer,[3] nor was it unduly concerned with the fact that the resolution of the Dominions Conference meant indefinite delay. Yet even the Post Office admitted that 'the proposal that the BBC should negotiate with the Dominion organisations' was 'rather a forlorn hope',[4] and the Lord Privy Seal's Office expressed regret 'at the inconclusive result which has been reached'.

The BBC, with no confidence in the outcome, was left to write round to the broadcasting organizations in Canada, Australia, New Zealand, South Africa, India, and other Empire countries.[5] The results were unfavourable,[6] and in the meantime

---

[1] *BBC Note on the Colonial Office Conference and its Outcome, 1 July 1930; Treasury Letters in the Post Office files, 16 and 17 Oct. 1930.

[2] *BBC Notes on the Dominions Office Conference and its Outcome.

[3] Treasury letter of 17 Oct. 1930 (Post Office Archives).

[4] Post Office letter of 21 Oct. 1930 (Post Office Archives).

[5] *Phillips to Reith, 6 Jan. 1931; Reith to Phillips, 16 Feb. 1931.

[6] *See, for example, the long, friendly, but unfavourable reply from the Australian Broadcasting Company (S. F. Doyle to Reith, 23 Apr. 1931), with the conclusion that Australia would not be warranted in making any heavy annual contribution to an Empire broadcasting service 'at this juncture', and the letter from E. A. Weir of Radio Services, Montreal, 30 May 1931. The Australian Broadcasting Commission was not set up until 1932, and the politics of Canadian broadcasting remained extremely complicated. See 'BBC Memorandum on the Broadcasting Systems of Canada, Australia and New Zealand Compared', June 1934, revised Oct. 1935. The Canadian Radio Broadcasting Commission, also set up in 1932, was the precursor of the Canadian Broadcasting Corporation of 1936.

the station at Chelmsford was felt to be in such a perilous state that it might break down 'at any moment'.[1] To make matters far worse, the financial situation in Britain itself had become extremely serious during the prolonged economic depression and the political uncertainty associated with the faltering Labour government. Sir Samuel Wilson of the Colonial Office told Reith in May 1931 that 'there is not the slightest chance of the Chancellor of the Exchequer agreeing to a special vote for the amount we require'. Passfield did not think that it was even worth while raising the matter with Snowden.[2] The most that could be hoped for was that the Treasury would permit the BBC to retain a larger share of its revenue from licences, and it was the Secretary of the Post Office himself, Sir Evelyn Murray, who suggested to the Treasury early in 1931 that if the Post Office's share of the licence revenue for 'management' was reduced from $12\frac{1}{2}$ to 10 per cent. the BBC 'might be induced' to 'throw in the Empire scheme without any *ad hoc* grant'.[3]

By the end of the summer the financial crisis had reached its alarming climax, and the Labour government had fallen. Just before its fall, which obviously surprised Passfield, Wilson told Reith that he was 'extremely depressed' that the Colonial Office had not been able to get the scheme put into effect: 'it is only another example of how difficult it is to get anything done, and especially in the Colonial Empire'.[4] Reith replied that he was equally disappointed, since broadcasting could provide 'a consolidatory element within the Empire, which in these days one cannot well ignore'. He still hoped that the Treasury would reconsider the matter favourably.[5]

All talk of the BBC getting a larger share of licence revenue was abruptly silenced, however, within the next two weeks. Instead, the notorious Report of the May Committee on National Expenditure, published in August 1931, suggested a cut in BBC expenditure without the BBC having once been asked by the committee for any information about its activities.[6] 'I made a formal and emphatic protest to Snowden, Chancellor of the Exchequer', Reith has written. 'He replied that he shared

[1] *Note by Reith on an interview at the Colonial Office, 1 May 1931.
[2] *Wilson to Reith, 2 May 1931. See also Control Board Minutes, 12 May 1931.
[3] Letter from Sir Evelyn Murray, 26 Feb. 1931 (Post Office Archives).
[4] *Wilson to Reith, 20 July 1931.
[5] *Reith to Wilson, 21 July 1931.   [6] Cmd. 3920 (1931).

my surprise that the May Committee had considered the BBC at all; it was clearly outside their terms of reference; he thought my rejoinder admirable.'[1] Yet after the fall of the Labour government, Snowden, who remained for a time as Chancellor of the Exchequer in the National government, asked the BBC for a 'voluntary contribution' to the National Exchequer. The new Postmaster-General and Reith agreed upon £50,000 by March 1932 and £150,000 in the course of the financial year, 1932/3. Murray, according to Reith, had thought of £100,000 in the first period, but Snowden thought that Reith's offer was 'a generous one'.[2]

As part of the agreement, the BBC expressed its willingness 'to carry the cost of Empire broadcasting'. Ormsby-Gore, in particular, welcomed this declaration: he too was conscious of the need for Empire broadcasting as a development 'of the utmost political as well as commercial importance to this country' and one which, in his view, was 'long overdue'.[3] Snowden wisely maintained, however, that it was inadvisable to mention the subject to the Cabinet at that stage, doubtless because he feared a bigger cut in BBC income. Yet the news was well enough known behind the scenes. Phillips of the Post Office wrote to a colleague in the Lord Privy Seal's office soon afterwards that 'as part of the settlement reached on the national economy proposals the BBC have undertaken to proceed with the plans for the creation of an Empire Broadcasting Station and the operation of a service therefrom without asking for additional revenue to finance the scheme'.[4]

In November 1931 the BBC publicly announced its intention of proceeding alone with an Empire Service.[5] 'The British listener's direct interest in the project is, of course, nil', it was stated. 'But the question of national interests had to be looked at more broadly.'[6] The decision was an important one, and it is

---

[1] *Into the Wind*, p. 154.

[2] Snowden to the Postmaster-General, undated (Post Office Archives).

[3] Ormsby-Gore to Snowden, 11 Sept. 1931 (Post Office Archives).

[4] Letter from Phillips, 20 Oct. 1931 (Post Office Archives).

[5] *BBC Press Release, 6 Nov. 1931. Reith had a letter of congratulation from Sir Samuel Wilson, 31 Oct. 1931: 'I am sure it is sound and that you will never regret it.'

[6] *BBC Year Book* (1933), p. 263. The BBC felt itself free to reopen the question of overseas contributions in the future. (Note by Ormsby-Gore, 9 Nov. 1931.)

a comment on the cautious and unimaginative political attitudes of the inter-war years that the BBC had been forced to take it unilaterally and on its own responsibility.

The first step necessary was the replacement of the old Chelmsford station by a new station at Daventry. The design of a broadcasting station to give effective world-wide coverage was a new concept. Ashbridge and his staff, with the manufacturers, developed a design to meet the requirements of the new service and an order for the transmitters was placed with Standard Telephones and Cables Ltd. The station was completed by December 1932. It had two transmitters which could operate on eight wavelengths and numerous aerials—some directional and some omni-directional. The Empire was divided into five 'zones', each zone being served by directional aerials. Programmes were 'beamed' to Australia, India, South Africa, West Africa, and Canada, the centres of the five zones. The six omni-directional aerials were designed for transmitting special programmes which Empire listeners could receive at any hour in any part of the world.[1] This was an entirely new concept in short-wave broadcasting. The first programmes of the new service were sent out on 19 December 1932, and they very quickly won a wide and scattered audience.

The programmes were expected to make their main appeal to Empire listeners equipped with short-wave receiving sets, and the new Chief Engineer, Ashbridge, was just as keen as Eckersley had been to ensure good quality. 'Feed back' information was essential to secure this: 'we said that we could get on only if listeners helped us'.[2] Relays by existing stations in the Empire were considered less important at this stage than they had been in 1927 and than they were to be in 1937. Emphasis was placed, however, on the need for a plentiful supply of recordings of BBC programmes for export, for transmission by local stations. This was still a field for experiment. 'Time differences and atmospheric conditions often put direct reception of a broadcast out of the question, while the physical export of discs is made impracticable by the weeks that must elapse in transit.

[1] There is a full description of the system in *BBC Year Book* (1933), pp. 275–83. For the opening of the station, see the *Radio Times*, 19 Dec. 1932.
[2] *C. G. Graves, Notes of a Lecture on 'Dominion and Empire Broadcasting', 9 Dec. 1933.

The expedient that has been adopted is to make, at the originating or receiving end, an electrical record for broadcasting at the first suitable moment after the event.'[1] It was in such guarded language that the BBC approached the beginnings of what was to become general practice in Britain, no less than in the Empire.

'Bottled' programmes had first been mentioned in November 1926:[2] they were then 'in their extreme infancy', as Atkinson put it. Progress had been slow between 1926 and 1932, although on the eve of the start of Empire broadcasting Blattnerphone tapes were coming into use,[3] a small specialist company, Colonial Radio Programmes Ltd., had been formed, and there had been meetings between the BBC and Electric and Musical Industries Ltd. about the recording of their artists for broadcasting from colonial stations. There had also been a discussion with Sir Stephen Tallents, then of the Empire Marketing Board, who watched over BBC interests at the Ottawa Conference in 1932 and was said by Reith to be 'most interested' in the development of Empire recordings.[4]

In announcing that special records of BBC programmes were to be made for the Empire, the BBC was at pains to insist that they were not for sale to members of the general public and that they would not be 'of a type likely to cause unemployment among local artists and musicians'.[5] The first BBC programmes specially recorded for overseas included *Cakes and Ale*, a programme of old English songs and choruses; Lily Morris, Bransby Williams, and Charles Coburn in vaudeville, with Henry Hall's Dance Orchestra; *Postman's Knock*, a British musical comedy written for broadcasting by Claude Hulbert; A. J. Alan telling a story; 'A Pageant of English Life from 1812 to 1933'; and, not least in the bill of fare, a Children's Hour programme. Such 'bottled programmes' were the first instalment in the development of what later became the BBC's

---

[1] *BBC Year Book* (1933), p. 266.
[2] See above, p. 98. *The idea was first put forward in a letter by Gerald Beadle, then Station Director at Durban, on 6 Apr. 1926. This was commented on by Atkinson in an undated memorandum, probably written in May 1926.
[3] See above, p. 99. *Control Board Minutes, 2 Feb. 1932; Notes on Director-General's Report for Board Meeting, 13 Apr. 1932; Supplement by V. H. Goldsmith, 11 Apr. 1932.
[4] Reith, Diary, 26 May 1932.
[5] *Radio Times*, 29 July 1932; *BBC Press Release, 21 July 1932.

'transcription service'. Future programmes, it was stated in 1933, would depend in very large measure on the criticisms and suggestions received from correspondents overseas. In other words, the Empire Service was to proceed on much the same lines as the parent BBC.

In one respect the new service was more fortunate than the BBC had been in the early days of domestic broadcasting. The Empire Press Union accepted the BBC's plan for news broadcasts. At an important meeting held in December 1931 representatives of the Empire Press Union, Reuters, and the Newspaper Proprietors' Association agreed to a plan of daily bulletins. 'Somewhat to my surprise,' wrote Reith in his diary, 'I got the whole thing across in 55 minutes, not only that there would be a News service on the new station but that it would start on the present station [Chelmsford] on January 4th 1932.'[1] Liaison meetings were held between the BBC and the Empire Press Union from the summer of 1932 onwards, and in October 1934, after the usual considerable discussion of financial questions and problems of copyright, agreement was reached with Reuters for the renewal of the Empire news service.[2] 'The news bulletins', it had been reported, 'seem to be the most generally appreciated items in the daily programme.'[3] Regular informal meetings with the Empire Press Union continued to be held throughout the first few years of the Empire Service.

In addition to news broadcasts, other early programmes for the Empire included vaudeville, light music, running commentaries, and dance music, although a number of correspondents in Canada complained that they already heard enough dance music from the United States. Symbolic items like Big Ben or 'the voice of the nightingale' were genuinely thought to be popular, but there was more doubt about talks. 'These are appreciated', it was felt, 'only if they are short and are given by the most eminent people.'[4] The BBC could not supply these in sufficient quantities. 'Once the man on the West Coast of Africa says, "Give us the big men—give us Winston Churchill or

[1] Reith, Diary, 11 Dec. 1931. *The minutes of this meeting of 11 Dec. 1931 also survive.

[2] *Minutes of a Liaison Meeting between the BBC and the EPU, 25 July 1932; Sir Roderick Jones to Reith, 16 Dec. 1932; Reuters to Graves, 4 May 1934; Reuters to Jardine Brown, 8 Oct. 1934.

[3] BBC Year Book (1934), p. 255.   [4] Ibid., p. 256.

Lloyd George", then we leave off.'[1] Established broadcasters in Britain soon began to win new friends in the Empire. 'Sir Walford Davies is now starting all over again to do in the Empire what he started to do ten years ago in this country, and he is proving extremely popular.'[2]

All these programmes cost little, most of them being prepared, in the first instance, for the home listener. Indeed, no special programme allocation was made for the first few weeks of the Empire Service, when there was ten hours of broadcasting each day, and the first week's programmes cost no more than ten guineas. It was thought to be quite a daring departure when soon after the success of the King's broadcast at Christmas 1932, a sum of £100 a week was allocated to Empire programmes.[3]

In return for British programmes to the Empire, there was a limited flow of programmes from the Empire to Britain. Representatives of the BBC made Empire tours in November 1932 and May and June 1933, and one of the results of the kind of liaison which was possible, if not always realized, was an Empire-wide broadcast in March 1933 from the top of Table Mountain at Cape Town. The South African Broadcasting Company arranged this broadcast. It was received in London by Post Office beam telephone service, electrically recorded, and rebroadcast by the BBC to Canada and other parts of the Empire. The first programme from India to be treated in this way was broadcast in December 1933.

Unfortunately, both beam transmission and electrical recording were expensive, and the number of such programmes, which were designed to make it easier for one part of the Empire to know what was happening in other parts of the Empire, was all too small. A less expensive 'imperial' service was the dissemination of information on industrial and commercial matters. After discussions with interested parties, a service of market intelligence reports produced by the Empire Marketing Board and a series of co-ordinated talks on business problems were arranged in 1933.[4]

---

[1] *Graves, Notes of a Lecture, 9 Dec. 1933.   [2] *Ibid.
[3] *Graves, Memorandum on The Empire Service, Apr. 1934.
[4] *Ibid.; *BBC Year Book* (1934), pp. 243–8. A conference on these matters was held at Broadcasting House on 16 Jan. 1933. Tallents, not then a BBC official, was among those present.

The organization of the BBC's Empire Department was placed from the start in the hands of Cecil Graves, who had been deputy to Roger Eckersley as Director of Programmes. To Reith, Graves seemed the natural choice: he had 'a fundamental soundness of outlook and judgement over the whole range of problems', along with 'powers of leadership and decision'.[1] His Deputy was J. B. Clark, who was brought from the North Regional offices at Manchester and was to have a long, varied, and active association with Empire broadcasting.[2] Graves effectively established the Service, and J. B. Clark, who was dedicated to his task and succeeded Graves in 1935, provided the Service with continuous direction through changing circumstances. He was helped by a staff, at first very small, later huge, the members of which were enthusiastic about their particular sphere of activity. In 1932 the staff engaged directly on the Empire Service numbered less than ten, and indirectly—primarily in the technical departments—twenty or thirty people at most were involved.

The setting up of a separate Empire Department—with all the engineering work remaining within the Engineering Division under Ashbridge—had repercussions for Major C. F. Atkinson, who had been Foreign Director of the BBC since January 1928 and had been charged with 'Foreign and Dominion liaison' since January 1927.[3] Graves took up his new appointment in September 1932, with full responsibility for programmes and planning,[4] and although Atkinson temporarily retained his responsibility for dealing with 'constitutional matters of Empire broadcasting', he later lost his influence. Even from the start Graves was made quite independent of the Director of Programmes and the Director of Talks (Siepmann). It was for Graves, if he wished, to ask them to construct special programmes for him.[5]

Few departments of the BBC enjoyed such autonomy in their

[1] *Into the Wind*, p. 298.

[2] Reith, Diary, 26 Sept. 1932, for his interview with J. B. Clark.

[3] *V. H. Goldsmith, Internal Memorandum on Foreign and Dominion Liaison, 12 Jan. 1927; Internal Memorandum of 26 Jan. 1928. 'The Foreign Liaison Office now becomes the Foreign Department, and Major Atkinson assumes the title of Foreign Director.'

[4] *BBC Press Release, 29 July 1932. G. C. Beadle, then Station Director at Belfast, took his place as Assistant Director of Programmes.

[5] *Control Board Minutes, 26 July 1932.

early years. Few also enjoyed such outside influence. Before
constructing any Empire programmes, Graves met nearly all
the High Commissioners and heads of government departments
concerned with Empire work.[1] Reith was invaluable at this
stage in arranging contacts and discussing with Graves the
great scope of his new post. Reith hoped that the King might
inaugurate the new Service. 'Saw Clive Wigram [the King's
secretary] about the King opening the Empire Service', he
wrote in his diary in October 1932. 'He said he had had two
sleepless nights about it, and was it a religious service?'[2]
Although the King did not open the Service, he gave his first
broadcast on Christmas Day 1932 to the whole of the Empire.
'The King spoke more personally and effectively than I had
ever heard him', Reith wrote. 'It was quite extraordinary how
quickly replies came from various parts of the Empire.'[3] It was
extraordinary also what a new emotional power—and personalization—had been added to twentieth-century monarchy.

Letters welcoming the King's broadcast and the inauguration
of the new Service poured in from the Empire in 1933. As
Empire interest grew, important changes were made both in
technical plans and in organization in London. The programme
allocation was raised to £200 a week in September 1933. This
was overdue, since some listeners, anticipating 'something
revolutionary' in the content of the programmes, had not been
completely satisfied.[4] The timing of broadcasts had raised many
difficulties also. The aim of providing programmes for successive
audiences in different countries of the Empire at convenient
listening times by their local clocks had not been fully accomplished. Indians complained that the broadcasts were too short,
Canadians thought that broadcasts started too late, and Austra-
lians grumbled about unsatisfactory conditions of reception.

Attempts were made to deal with all these criticisms. The
first result was that there was a sharp increase in broadcasting
hours. In November 1932 Empire broadcasting took 10 hours
out of 24. There were five periods of 2 hours each, spread
throughout the 24 to meet time differences across the world as

[1] Reith, Diary, 28 Sept. 1932.
[2] Ibid., 10 Oct. 1932.
[3] Ibid., 25 Dec. 1932. For the royal broadcast, see also above, pp. 112–13 and
Into the Wind, pp. 168–9.
[4] *N. Ashbridge, Memorandum on the Empire Station, 28 Feb. 1933.

the sun travelled from east to west. Within six months the 10 hours had risen to 14½. Fundamental changes were also made later in the year in the 'zonal pattern' of broadcasting. There had been a great deal of overlapping from zone to zone, with West Indian listeners picking up Indian programmes and the West African service being audible in New Zealand. Timing was particularly odd in this context. 'The announcement of "London calling the African and West African zones" was being heard at night in Africa, in the evening in South America, in the afternoon in the West Indies and at breakfast time in New Zealand.'[1]

To try to remove some of these anomalies, the geographical zones were converted into time zones. Former Zone One was converted into Transmission Number One, Zone Two into Transmission Number Two, and so on. Every overseas listener was then in a position to select any programme which he was able to receive and in which he was interested. Transmission One, which was radiated during early morning hours in Britain for late afternoon or evening listening in the Antipodes, could be picked up at earlier hours in the Middle East and India, and in Western Canada (especially in late spring and early summer) 'on the previous night'.[2] The overriding limitation in all these programme arrangements was that the BBC had at its disposal only two transmitters each with a power output of 15 kilowatts.

In addition to these changes, there was a further reorganization of the administration in June 1933, part of the larger set of changes in organization within the BBC.[3] Atkinson now relinquished his title of Foreign Director and became a 'Special Consultant', and Graves was given the title of Director of Empire and Foreign Services, with extremely wide powers.[4] The reasoning behind this change, which greatly strengthened Graves's position, was questioned by Siepmann, who felt that Empire and Foreign Services should not be managed by one Branch. The former was largely an indenting agency for home programmes, he argued, and would eventually become primarily a programme output department: the latter should be a genuine

[1] *BBC Year Book* (1934), p. 253. The detailed account given in this Year Book (pp. 249 ff.) of the first year's service is full and interesting.
[2] BBC, *The Empire Services* (1935), p. 13.
[3] See below, pp. 441–6.
[4] *Memorandum from the Director-General, 19 June 1933.

'service' department, helping all other sections of the BBC. Neither the Empire Service nor the future Foreign Service was, in fact, to develop along these lines, although neither Siepmann nor Graves could know this in 1933. Instead, Graves replied that he intended to take both Empire and Foreign work seriously, 'distributing his energy equally'. Both required a plentiful supply of 'intelligence' information. 'Where "operations" are concerned, which, when all is said and done, are the creative side of soldiering, no strategical or tactical scheme can be drawn up unless there is "intelligence" on which to base it.'[1]

Reith approved in 1933 of this conception of a 'Command' within Empire and Foreign work. A detached Branch Chief, concentrating largely on 'such international questions as those in which broadcasting could play a very important part', would help to make up for lost time, for the earlier failure of Government to respond to the opportunities he had sketched out to them. 'Past experience shows an extraordinary lag behind what I myself had anticipated in this respect.'[2]

Graves was certainly far more than an indenter or controller of programmes. Reith remained actively and powerfully interested in 'Empire operations' too, and both he and Graves were drawn into fascinating talks about strategy—about the future of Indian broadcasting, for example, which Reith believed had hitherto been overlooked, with tragic consequences. They were both very depressed after a meeting at the India Office in July 1934,[3] but when Lord Willingdon, the Viceroy, made a number of references to broadcasting in a speech in New Delhi a month later, Reith felt that frequent talks with him in London had been of some value.[4] They were interested also in broadcasting in Palestine, and when there were some home objections to the temporary secondment there in 1935 of R. A. Rendall, who was thought to be one of the BBC's most promising young men, Graves overruled objections with the sentence, 'The Director-General feels very strongly that when we are asked to do this

---

[1] *C. A. Siepmann, Memorandum on the Proposed Reorganisation of Empire and Foreign Affairs, 31 May 1933; comments by Graves, 31 May 1933. Both were addressed to Reith.
[2] *Reith to Siepmann, 7 June 1933.
[3] Reith, Diary, 5 July 1934.
[4] Ibid., 30 Aug. 1934. For Lionel Fielden's account of his experiences in India and a letter to him from Reith, see *The Natural Bent*, pp. 127 ff.

kind of job we should always give of the best, even if it means a certain inconvenience to ourselves.'[1]

Reith also took a lively interest in the future of South African broadcasting and went to South Africa in 1934, where he produced for General Hertzog, the South African Prime Minister, a report on broadcasting which he considers one of the most important documents he ever wrote. Graves also, after discussing the rich opportunities of broadcasting in Nigeria, was soon afterwards drawn, at Reith's suggestion, into a survey of broadcasting in Newfoundland.[2] It was Graves who wrote proudly in 1934 that he regarded himself, 'in my position as Director of Empire and Foreign Services, as the centre in the BBC to which all Imperial matters should be referred'. 'I regard it as my duty', he went on, 'to bring to the notice of the home people the possibilities of overseas relays, or even ideas of Imperial interest for inclusion in the home programmes. I hold the view that the development of the Empire service depends on reciprocity.'[3] This forecast was as wrong as some of the other forecasts of the period, but as a statement of intentions it was characteristic both of the man and of the period.

The sense of imperial interest was enlivened in the mid-1930s by fear that the unity of empire was being threatened not so much by the natural development of movements towards self-government inside it as by the machinations of other great powers. For this reason alone, Reith and Graves were in full agreement with Ashbridge, the Chief Engineer, that the Empire Service should be extended. From 1933 onwards the Germans were increasing the power of their short-wave transmitters and sending out programmes in English which gave a propaganda slant on national and international events.[4] 'Stayed to hear Ashbridge and Graves talking about the Empire Service', Reith wrote in August 1934, 'which I believe we must develop much

---

[1] *Graves to Nicolls, 18 July 1935. Rendall was then serving as West Regional Programme Director, and there were complaints that 'this is the worst possible moment for sparing him'. Rendall was later complimented by the Palestine Government for the way in which he had given 'broadcasting such a good start in this country'. *Sir Arthur Wauchope to Reith, 6 Nov. 1936.

[2] *Notes on visit of Mr. Hebden, Postmaster-General of Nigeria, 2 July 1934; Report on Broadcasting in Newfoundland, June 1935.

[3] *Note on Imperial Policy, Nov. 1934.

[4] *Ashbridge to Reith, 23 Aug. 1934; see also T. Grandin, *The Political Use of Radio* (1939).

more quickly, and intensively, because of competition in other countries, particularly Germany.'[1] A few months later the Federation of British Industries expressed alarm at foreign pressure and pressed the government to allow the BBC a larger share of licence revenue.[2]

The government, however, would not budge, and the BBC was left to proceed alone, seriously handicapped by continued shortage of funds. Other governments were not very co-operative either. For all the talk of colonial subventions in 1930, only Sierra Leone and the Gold Coast had set aside minute sums (£15) from their budgets as contributions to the Empire Service.[3] There is no evidence that the subventions were ever paid, and in both cases they were the work of one man, Sir Arnold Hodson, who had moved from the Governorship of Sierra Leone to the Gold Coast. 'I really think', Graves remarked without too much irony, 'that an official letter should be sent to the Secretary of State, suggesting that about every six months Sir Arnold Hodson should be moved to another Colony.'[4]

The whole range of the BBC's enterprise was pitifully small. Not only were Germany—and Italy—both taking their foreign services increasingly seriously, but American and Russian short-wave broadcasting was felt to be increasingly influential.[5] The opportunities for Britain were so great: the resources so meagre. The most that the BBC could do was to secure money for the extension of the Daventry station and a widening of the range of Empire broadcasting activities. In February 1935 the Post-master-General approved an extension of Daventry which would cost £170,000 and, along with further developments in

[1] Reith, Diary, 28 Aug. 1934.

[2] *Herbert Scott, President of the FBI, to Sir Philip Cunliffe-Lister, the Colonial Secretary, 19 Nov. 1934. See also *The Times*, 21 Nov. 1934.

[3] The Colonial Office sent round a memorandum about broadcasting to Colonial Governors in January 1933 which did not mention a subvention from licence revenue. It admitted, however, that the issue was not dead. *D. C. J. McSweeney to Graves, 2 January 1933. The memorandum, dated 7 Jan. 1933, was signed by Sir Philip Cunliffe-Lister and said that the Empire service, 'substantially due to the disinterested enthusiasm of the BBC, has my fullest support'. On 14 June 1933 McSweeney wrote again to Graves, 'We have by no means forgotten the question of contributions.'

[4] *Graves to Reith, 12 July 1934.

[5] R. E. Leeper of the Foreign Office told Graves as early as Sept. 1932 of the concern of the Foreign Office at the spread of Russian radio propaganda in Palestine and around the Persian Gulf.

engineering and in programmes, would entail an increased annual running cost of £80,000. The Treasury, through Sir Warren Fisher, endorsed the proposal, 'undertaking that due regard would be paid to this commitment in any future financial adjustments'.[1]

The setting in which this decision was reached is recaptured in two long reports on the work of the Empire Service which Graves prepared in 1934, the first in April and the second in December. In the first, he demanded more specifically Empire programmes and more programmes of high quality. 'We have established a short-wave service, but we have not been able to keep abreast of foreign short-wave development—development largely due to the vision of foreign governments who, appreciating the potentialities of our Empire Service, realised that we could not be allowed to take the lead.' Graves went on to compare the amount of 'exclusive material' prepared by the Empire Service with that of a regional station: the Empire came off worse.

He also compared, more pertinently in the light of history (though not of internal BBC politics), the action taken to that date in Germany and Britain. German short-wave stations did not re-broadcast programmes designed for the home listener: they sent out special performances, 'which presumably involved considerable additional expenditure'. Graves asked for more staff, some to deal with music, the others with drama and talks, and for more studio space. Carpendale scribbled in red pencil in the margin that the problem of studio space was harder than that of staff: 'where can they work?' Dawnay, in passing on Graves's memorandum to Reith, remarked fairly but gloomily that the recommendations amounted to little more than 'the raising of the Empire Service to the plane and status of a Regional Station'.[2]

In his second memorandum, written a few months later just after he had temporarily left Broadcasting House ill with tuberculosis, Graves further surveyed the resources at his command,

---

[1] *Note by Sir Donald Banks, 27 Feb. 1935.
[2] *Graves, Memorandum on the Empire Service, Apr. 1934. Note by A. C. Dawnay, 18 Apr. 1934. There was a parallel memorandum by Ashbridge, dated 2 May 1934.

human and material. He did not recommend that while he was away any one else should take over his post temporarily. J. B. Clark, he felt, could handle all Empire problems adequately: he would in time be 'one of the leading men in the Corporation'. He went on to argue that the policy of 'bottling' programmes for export to individual Empire broadcasting concerns, which he had hitherto advocated enthusiastically, should be dropped: 'All our energies should be directed on improvement of transmissions and reception and on inducing the Colonial Office to impress on Colonial Governors the ease with which receiving apparatus could be installed for the re-transmission of Empire programmes either through Wireless Exchanges or through local transmitters which need not necessarily be of great power.' More should be done, too, to diffuse commercial information, and the news service, which had become independent of home news in 1934,[1] should be developed 'as freely and as rapidly as possible' with more sub-editors and a greater output of topical talks. Turning to 'international relations', Graves strongly recommended that there should be a full-time BBC representative in the United States and that a willing response should be made to requests for help in starting broadcasting stations in the Colonies. In Palestine Rendall's work should be backed up. 'We shall be asked by Palestine to send someone to help them put their show in order at the time of the incorporation of their broadcasting service. I am very anxious that this shall be done if possible.'[2]

The development of Empire broadcasting was the subject of two official BBC memoranda to the Colonial Office in February and May 1935. Transmissions by then were up to 16 hours a day. An Empire News Editor, J. C. S. MacGregor, had been appointed with a staff of three sub-editors in September 1934. The service he provided was particularly appreciated: 25,000 letters and reports had been sent in to the BBC from various parts of the Empire. The number of listeners was increasing, particularly in places like Sierra Leone and the Falkland Islands, where Wireless Exchanges had recently been set up.[3] (However guarded was the attitude of the BBC to Wireless

[1] See above, p. 156.
[2] *Graves to Reith, 11 Dec. 1934.
[3] *J. B. Clark to Graves, 15 Feb. 1935; J. B. Clark to McSweeney, 19 Feb. 1935; BBC, *The Empire Broadcasting Service*, 8 May 1935.

Exchanges in Britain, it always gave them the warmest possible welcome in the Empire.) Some of the letters had been lyrical, and the *Sierra Leone Weekly News* had written charmingly of local reactions to the broadcast of the Duke of Kent's wedding in 1934; 'the excitement, commotion and bustle of listeners . . . called for an appreciation of the honour conferred on us by the installation of the radio in this Colony and the extent to which the monotony was relieved can better be imagined than described'. 'For this signal blessing,' it added, 'we doff our hats in genuine praise and raise three loud cheers to Sir Arnold and Lady Hodson.'[1]

Yet, for all the progress, German competition was always increasing. In 1933 the German Overseas Radio (*Reichssender*) had received 3,000 letters from listeners overseas. In 1934, the figure was 10,000, and in 1935 28,000.[2] 'It is possible for the German station to use a more concentrated type of beam transmission', Reith told the Colonial Secretary, 'than we can employ at Daventry, having regard to the wide geographical areas which our service must cover. This means that in certain areas where the danger of foreign political influence through these channels may exist (for example, in mandated territories in Africa) and in other big centres of population lying in the paths of the German beams, the transmissions in question can be picked up with the utmost facility. News bulletins, which we have reason to believe are prepared in the German Ministry of Propaganda, are read at fixed times in English and other languages.'[3]

The *Evening Standard* had already directed attention to 'the persistence and thoroughness of the German short-wave station' and had forcefully drawn the conclusion that 'we must not lag behind in a world where this is being done'.[4] The BBC knew just how much was being done. Kurt von Boeckmann was in charge of German short-wave broadcasting, which was given a high priority inside the Reichs Rundfunk Gesellschaft, and his staff were treated as being of equal importance to those in German home broadcasting. In July 1935 a German plan to put six new short-wave transmitters into use was announced,

[1] *Sierra Leone Weekly News*, 1 Dec. 1934.
[2] C. J. Rolo, *Radio Goes to War* (1943), p. 38.
[3] *Reith to Cunliffe-Lister, 22 Jan. 1935.
[4] *Evening Standard*, 12 Apr. 1935.

and Dr. Kurt Rathke, who was given charge of German international programme exchange, told J. B. Clark that Germany was particularly interested in South America. This was only partially true.[1] The Germans had also sent round a questionnaire to the Colonies and Dominions asking listeners to their programmes for information about quality of reception and programme preferences.[2] Clearly, the British Empire was well within their field of operations.

To counter this propaganda drive, the British government preferred exhortation to financial assistance for the BBC, and a private and secret circular on foreign programmes was sent by the Colonial Office to Colonial Governors in June 1935.[3] Malcolm MacDonald, the new Secretary of State for the Colonies, expressed the greatest interest in what was happening, and offered help for the future.[4] Reith told him that the German broadcasts, designed to give the world 'a favourable impression of conditions of all kinds in Nazi Germany', often involved 'definite distortion of British and other events with interpretations of them in a manner favourable to Nazi ideals', and that Italian broadcasts were 'particularly virulent'.[5]

All these considerations had been taken into account in the preparation of the BBC's evidence to the Ullswater Committee. 'The BBC (still deficient of authorisation and finance, but hopeful of Lord Ullswater's Committee) is doing all it can', it stated. 'In certain Colonies there is need to counteract the subversive propaganda of all foreign stations. In all Colonial territories it is vitally necessary to employ the instrument of broadcasting to its utmost extent.' Not for the first time, the BBC directed its pressure towards the British administration itself. 'A Department may need to be established in the Colonial Office, the functions of which would be the maintenance of close contact, on the one hand, with Colonial Governments and individual broadcasting officers, and, on the other, with the BBC.'[6]

[1] *Notes of interview between J. B. Clark and Dr. Kurt Rathke, 4 July 1935. Rathke had previously helped von Boeckmann with the Zeesen short-wave broadcasts.

[2] *Daily Telegraph*, 9 Apr. 1935.

[3] *Clark to Dawnay, 16 Apr. 1935; circular from Downing Street, 1 June 1935.

[4] *Letter from Malcolm MacDonald, 14 Nov. 1935.

[5] *Graves, Notes for the Director-General's Meeting with MacDonald, 1936.

[6] *BBC evidence to the Ullswater Committee, *Broadcasting and the Colonial Empire*, 25 Oct. 1935.

The Ullswater Committee responded to the BBC's appeal. It recommended unanimously that the Empire Service should be 'expressly authorised in the new Charter', that increased funds should be applied to its development (from an increased share of licence revenue), and that 'in the interests of British prestige and influence in world affairs . . . the appropriate use of languages other than English should be encouraged'.[1] In reaching these conclusions, it doubtless drew on other evidence besides that presented by the BBC. The press agencies had foreseen that in the future the Director-General might 'be anxious to exert the right of the BBC to broadcast in languages other than English', and the Federation of British Industries had stated that 'because the programme designers of the BBC had shown the ability to construct programmes second to none in the world', they should be granted adequate funds to do so for listeners outside the country. That this was not merely a businessman's view was shown in a later comment made by Sir Walter Citrine of the T.U.C. 'The BBC has a mission, without becoming propagandist, to tell the world what this country stands for.'[2]

There was a note of increasing urgency in this kind of comment, slow though the government's reaction was. The year of the Ullswater Committee was also the year of the Italo-Abyssinian crisis, and thereafter the international situation began to impinge more and more on the BBC's own plans and purposes. Talk of Empire broadcasting merely as an extension of 'sentimental ties' gave way increasingly to talk of the need 'to project England'.

In some ways the Silver Jubilee celebrations of 1935 marked the climax of Empire broadcasting as it had hitherto been largely conceived, even when foreign competition was known to be increasing. 'Tremendous enthusiasm in Australia', Sydney reported. 'Sydneyites were compensated for the rain which damped their own Jubilee celebrations by the satisfactory relay from London conveyed to their own firesides tonight.' 'Thousands of Canadians got up early this morning', Ottawa reported, 'and were rewarded by a very clear broadcast of the procession. The clattering hooves of the horses were heard quite clearly. . . .

---

[1] Cmd. 5091 (1936), § 115–24. See also below, p. 502.
[2] *General Advisory Council, Précis of Discussion, 16 June 1937.

The greatest cheers which have ever been heard to issue from the microphone echoed through many Canadian homes. For clarity and drama it was the greatest broadcast in history.'[1] Again it was the popular reaction within the home which counted. The success of Queen Victoria's telegraphed message to the Empire at her jubilee in 1897 had given a shadowy intimation of what wireless might do: 1935 was a triumphant demonstration.[2]

By the time of the Abdication in 1936 steps had already been taken to expand greatly the scope of the BBC's Empire Service. Four more short-wave transmitters of high power and modern design had been ordered for Daventry. It was recognized clearly at that time that what the BBC was saying was being listened to eagerly all over the world. 'During the speech of Edward VIII after his Abdication not a single call was received at one of the largest telephone exchanges in New York.'[3] The coronation of King George VI in 1937 marked another milestone. This was the kind of event the Empire Service could handle magnificently. How would it respond to new challenges with the whole world as the arena?

It responded vigorously. The year 1937 was a crucial one in the development of the propaganda war, and J. B. Clark was dispatched on an extensive Empire tour in May 1937, in the course of which he called at almost all British territories between Malta and Fiji. He was able to make a full appreciation of the situation and to answer criticisms about the scope of the Empire Service which were being made inside the BBC. From the United States, for example, Felix Greene, first BBC representative from late 1935 onwards in the New York office which Graves had suggested,[4] complained in 1937 that Empire programmes were 'flabby and uninspired' and had 'no real relation whatever with the needs and tastes of listeners in distant lands'.[5] It was no longer sufficient in Greene's opinion to talk of lack of funds: lack of ideas was handicapping work also. From Delhi,

    [1] *Reports on the Jubilee Programmes, May 1935.
    [2] For the Diamond Jubilee of 1897, see the report in the *Daily Telegraph*, 24 June 1897: for 1935 see H. Nicolson, *King George V* (1952), pp. 524–6.
    [3] *General Advisory Council, Minutes, 16 June 1937; see also, for the broadcast, BBC Press Release, 10 Dec. 1936.
    [4] *For his appointment, see BBC Press Release, 9 Sept. 1935.
    [5] *Control Board Minutes, 15 July 1937; additional notes by Greene.

Lionel Fielden noted that the small group of English listeners often turned off their sets in disgust because they found 'nothing worth listening to': 'Germany, Italy and Holland were rapidly out-stripping the BBC in the quality both of their transmissions and their programmes.'[1]

Both J. B. Clark and Graves, who had left the Empire and Foreign Department to become Controller (Programmes) and later in March 1938 Deputy Director-General, queried the representativeness of both these verdicts. Yet both recognized the need for change. 'Looking back over the past five years, I believe our policy to have been right,' Graves wrote, 'but the political situation now makes it necessary for us to study the question of competition with foreign short-wave programmes.'[2] Competition was, indeed, at the heart of the matter, and two years later Felix Greene, who was never satisfied, was to state even more caustically that 'it has not been fully grasped that in its international questions the BBC is not in the position of a protected monopoly'.[3]

Not all the difficulties related to programming. The continuing problems on the engineering side were well summarized by Ashbridge in October 1937. 'We are sending out a service, which is somewhat inferior to the German service, both technically and from the point of view of programmes. On the technical side this has been mainly due to the disgraceful way in which we have been let down by manufacturers entrusted with our transmitters.' It might even be necessary, he added, to use the Baird 'ultra-short wave television transmitter'[4] as a temporary high-power short-wave sound transmitter.[5]

The real test of resilience was the introduction of foreign-language programmes, a subject which had concerned the BBC before the Ullswater Committee directed public attention to it.[6] In this field Greene, for all his talk of 'competition', was more

[1] *Fielden to Graves, 14 July 1937.
[2] *Graves, Report on the Empire Service, 20 Aug. 1937.
[3] *'North American Representative's Report on the Empire Service', 14 July 1939.
[4] For the transmitter, see below, pp. 552–4.
[5] *N. Ashbridge, 'The Present Position of the Empire Service', Oct. 1937.
[6] *Memorandum 'The Use of Languages, other than English, in the Empire Broadcasting Service', June 1936; Control Board Minutes, 5 May 1936.

cautious than the Empire and Foreign Department chiefs he was criticizing. Afraid that such programmes would be interpreted as 'propaganda', part of a 'war of words' in which the British had hitherto refused to take part, he even sent the BBC a telegram to check up on the truth of a report in the *New York Herald Tribune* that they were about to begin.[1] Yet this was only one point of view. From County Hall, London, Herbert Morrison wrote in June 1936 to ask whether the BBC had ever considered broadcasting news bulletins in German and Italian, and to press for an early decision to start them. 'It is itself a terrible tragedy that millions of people abroad are receiving no impartial British news.'[2] Morrison, like Reith, was clear about the difference between news and propaganda, and another correspondent, arguing along similar lines, reminded the BBC of lines in President Roosevelt's inaugural address of 1937—'the time has come for democracy to assert itself'.[3]

The introduction of foreign languages was gradual, beginning with the Arabic Service, and the way ahead was never easy or clear. A few months after the publication of the Ullswater Report, a memorandum entitled 'The Use of Languages, other than English, in the Empire Broadcasting Service' was circulated to British representatives all over the world. They were asked for their views by the Dominion, Colonial, and Foreign Offices. This was a characteristically cautious approach by the government to a big subject, followed by what Reith described as 'several months of desultory talk' in the Cabinet.[4]

In April 1937 the same three government departments, along with the BBC and the Post Office, were represented on an official committee to discuss the question. Most of the replies from the Empire had urged the need not only for action but for speed. From Cuba, for instance, it was reported that 'British broadcasts would be welcome as a token of British interest in Spanish-speaking countries, and probably be accepted as evidence of British vitality'.[5] From the Middle East, where, since

[1] *Greene to Graves, 19 April 1936; telegram of 3 Dec. 1936.
[2] *Herbert Morrison to Reith, 17 June 1936; Reith to Morrison, 19 June 1936; Morrison to Reith, 24 June 1936.
[3] *E. Watrous to the BBC, 7 Jan. 1937. Watrous was an American living in Paris.
[4] *Into the Wind*, p. 290.
[5] *Note from the British Minister in Havana, June 1936.

1935, the Italian station Bari had established itself as a purveyor of inflammable propaganda, A. S. Calvert wrote that Arabic broadcasts should be introduced at once. While they would arouse some suspicion at the outset, 'a reliable service of appropriate items of News of a general nature, given with unfailing objectivity', would 'disarm suspicion'.[1] From Cairo Guy Pocock sent a message that he had been approached by the Director-General for European Relations at the Ministry of the Interior in an effort to urge him to counteract Italian radio stations. 'The Italians by their very virulence and volubility have over-reached themselves, and now is the time for the BBC to step in with broadcasts in Arabic from England, not in the nature of anti-propaganda, but just absolutely reliable news.'[2]

The Post Office told the BBC to call a meeting of all interested parties before embarking on foreign-language broadcasts[3]—it added, indeed, that this advice was based on a Cabinet decision —and a meeting was duly held on 13 April at Broadcasting House, at which the Dominion, Colonial and Foreign Offices were represented along with the Post Office. The Foreign Office pressed for broadcasts in Arabic, Spanish, and Portuguese, but the Dominions Office and the Colonial Office were less well disposed.[4] The result was the setting-up of a sub-committee within the BBC 'to consider how such a service could be introduced with the minimum amount of impairment to the Empire Service today and to its development in the future'.[5]

Graves himself seems to have been doubtful about future policy at this stage. All his experience in regard to the Empire Service and the contacts which he had made, he told Reith, convinced him that its success would be damaged and its improvement in future retarded if a policy of foreign-language broadcasts was adopted. 'British prestige and its reputation for integrity partly arose from the fact that we were adopting a different policy and were not doing something which other countries were doing lavishly.'[6]

[1] *Note from the British Legation at Jedda, 26 Oct. 1936.
[2] *Pocock to J. B. Clark, 30 Oct. 1936.
[3] *Gardiner to Reith, 5 Mar. 1937.
[4] *For Dominion Office doubts, see Sir Edward Harding to Graves, 26 Sept. 1936. See also Batterbee to Graves, 19 Feb. 1937.
[5] *Minutes of the meeting of 13 Apr. 1937.
[6] *Graves to Reith, undated note.

While the BBC's sub-committee was meeting, a Cabinet committee, on which the BBC was not represented, was considering
similar questions under the chairmanship of Kingsley Wood. It
was not until the autumn of 1937 that representatives of the two
committees met. Norman and Reith led the BBC contingent,
and Graves expressed the doubts and anxieties he had expressed
earlier in the BBC sub-committee. Reith, however, had no
doubts. 'I thought the BBC should have been in this field—and
all over it—two or three years earlier.'[1]

He insisted, however, on a number of necessary conditions.
Foreign-language services were not to prejudice the Empire
Service. They would have to be done on a considerable scale,
if they were to be done at all. Special finance would be required.
News would have to be supplemented by other programmes.
The BBC would have to be responsible, and would have to enjoy
the same freedom *vis-à-vis* government departments as in the
provision of its home service. The Foreign Office should not call
the tune or run broadcasting stations of its own, as it had been
planning to do in Cyprus. Any difficulties between BBC and
Foreign Office were to be settled informally without the sanc-
tions of a written agreement.

Less than three weeks later, on 29 October, the Postmaster-
General duly announced in the House of Commons that the
BBC would undertake broadcasts in 'certain foreign languages'.[2] He made it clear that when news was broadcast, it
would be 'straight' news and not propaganda. Unfortunately,
however, he referred to the new departure entirely in terms of
a government decision. This was bound to create consternation
both in the BBC and abroad. Reith rightly felt that an announcement in these terms prejudiced the new service before it began,
and that 'it was of cardinal importance that it should be known
that this was a BBC and not a governmental service'. 'The BBC
would be trusted where the Government might not be.'[3]
Kingsley Wood, to whom Reith complained at once by telephone when the news of the Postmaster-General's statement
came over the tape machine at Broadcasting House, soon
rectified matters. The Chancellor of the Exchequer, Sir John

---

[1] *Minutes of a meeting of 4 Oct. 1937 at the Ministry of Health; *Into the Wind*,
p. 291.

[2] *Hansard*, vol. 328 (1937), col. 501.   [3] *Into the Wind*, pp. 292–3.

Simon, followed up the Postmaster-General's statement with a further statement on the following Monday that the BBC had been 'invited' by the government to provide broadcast news services for South America in Spanish and Portuguese and for the Middle East in Arabic. South America was mentioned before the Middle East, certainly as a cover. Simon made three other points in his speech, which met Reith's stipulations. First, nothing would be done which might interfere with the Empire Service. Second, new transmitters were needed, and until they were brought into use, only a limited service would be available. Third, in operating the new service, the BBC would have 'the same full responsibilities and duties' as were laid down by its Charter in respect of its existing services.[1]

Having fought for its opportunity, the BBC lost no time. A committee, chaired by Tallents, was appointed two days after Simon's statement, and within a fortnight two new transmitters had been ordered.[2] The first staff for the Arabic broadcasts was appointed in the autumn of 1937, A. S. Calvert being seconded from the Consular Service to act as first sub-editor.[3] In November 1937 it was decided not to use classical Arabic, but rather 'a form of Egyptian Arabic'.[4] Discussions also began about what the scope of the Arabic Service should be.

The service was aimed at an audience nearing 40 millions, an audience which was already a 'vulnerable' target for Russian, German, and Italian propaganda—particularly Italian propaganda from the short-wave station at Bari. Already in the Middle East wireless sets were symbols of 'modernization', and there were some listeners, firmly entrenched in traditional culture, whose willingness to listen turned them into what have been called 'transitional' folk, people who are breaking partially with tradition without fully realizing it.[5] A. S. Calvert had reported before he joined the BBC that 'Arabs are insatiable for news . . . King Abdul Aziz receives the News at Riyadh

[1] *Hansard*, vol. 328 (1937), col. 674.
[2] *Control Board Minutes, 16 Nov. 1937.
[3] *Tallents Committee, Minutes, 11 Nov. 1937.
[4] Ibid., 25 Nov. 1937.
[5] D. Lerner (ed.), *The Passing of Traditional Society* (1958). Some wireless sets were distributed free to Arabs by EIAR, the Italian radio organization, before 1937. See *Radio Goes to War*, p. 41.

daily (and by a portable wireless set while travelling), and it is credibly reported that nowadays he employs a special official charged with the duty of noting down the news and conveying it to his royal master.'[1]

This was at the top of the feudal pyramid of Arab society. More important from the BBC's point of view were the listening habits of the populace. Here the reports were very encouraging.

Nearly every Egyptian home of some standing has its radio set [the BBC was told], but nobody is deprived of the pleasure of listening in, as every café boasts of a set, every barber's shop, every grocer's shop, and many others. I have even found them in workshops and factories. As the Egyptians and Palestinians like to get their money's worth out of their sets, it is not surprising to note that they tune-in their sets in the morning directly the station starts broadcasting, and they do not turn them off until the station closes down. This 'tap listening' is an infernal nuisance, and there is bound to be reaction against it sooner or later. If one walks up the Sharia Farouq in Cairo, one need not stop at one café or barber's shop to know what is on the programme; one merely walks along and there is a continuity of radio emission as though it were one set. In nearly every building there are three or four cafés where the working classes and the out of work sit for hours on end listening in to a badly tuned-in station, mostly Cairo.[2]

At the same time, almost all Arab listeners were interested in politics, and few could believe that the BBC broadcasts did not have a political purpose. 'Many enlightened Egyptians have stated that they are delighted that we are taking up Arabic broadcasts', a report went on: 'They are flattered on the one hand, and rather amused that the Italians have forced us into this counteraction. I must insist on this point of view, however, that no Arabic speaking person who is aware of our action can be convinced that we are not doing this except with a view to issuing propaganda. He is convinced that if we do not start actual propaganda now, we shall certainly work up to that in the future.'

This was the practical, operational problem of foreign-language broadcasting, as seen at a different level from that of

---

[1] *Note by A. S. Calvert, 26 Oct. 1936.

[2] *J. Heyworth Dunne, 'Report on Arabic Broadcasting in Egypt and Palestine with Special Reference to the Arabic Broadcasts from London', 20 Jan. 1938.

the Cabinet Committee and the BBC's sub-committee. Hitherto 'the Empire News had been prepared on the assumption that its listeners have sufficient faith in its accuracy to know that the BBC's silence is tantamount to a denial of a misleading report which may have been broadcast from elsewhere, and that a BBC News item automatically provides correction of any different story broadcast by a foreign organisation.'[1] Arab listeners did not know these conventions: they had to learn.

The BBC, for its part, had to learn what kind of programmes the Germans and Italians were beaming at the Arab world. It acquired this information in the first instance from the Foreign Office, which from the late summer of 1937 onwards had begun to monitor Italian news broadcasts in Arabic. The first monitoring of English news bulletins from foreign stations had begun during the Italo-Abyssinian War of 1935. The Foreign Office gave little sustained support to this venture, which went through a further phase of development at the time of the abdication crisis, when Whitehall was especially interested in knowing what American stations were saying about the King and Mrs. Simpson. In the case of Arab-language monitoring, the Foreign Office was genuinely interested from the start, and S. Hillelson, an Arabic scholar from the Sudan Civil Service, was engaged by the Foreign Office to monitor Bari broadcasts. The BBC took over Hillelson when it began to transmit its own programmes.

Fortunately for the BBC, monitored information suggested that the rival broadcasting organizations were not perfect. 'A new announcer—very much more of an Arab than the previous one', a monitoring official reported on a news reader from Rome. 'At the end he had to be hurried up, and consequently he tripped over himself.' When South American monitoring began four or five nights a week late in 1938, a German announcer speaking Portuguese was said to have 'a very woolly voice, to mumble badly, and to speak too close to the microphone'.[2]

The Arabic Service was inaugurated on 3 January 1938 by the Emir Seif-El-Islam Hussein, son of the King of the Yemen, who listened to the first broadcast in his palace in Sana'a. Messages of goodwill were broadcast on this occasion by the

---

[1] *BBC Memorandum, 'Monitoring of Foreign News Broadcasts', 27 June 1938.
[2] *Ibid.

Egyptian Chargé D'affaires in London, the Ministers for Iraq and Saudi Arabia, and the Governor of Aden, an easier collection to assemble in 1938 than in 1964. It was estimated also, unlike today, that 50 per cent. of the journals published in Arabic would be 'not unfriendly'.[1] In his speech the Egyptian Chargé remarked that 'while an Englishman might make a mistake, he is temperamentally always eager to get at the real truth'. This flattering statement was immediately put to the test for, difficult though it was to include, an item was broadcast in the first Arabic news bulletin relating to the execution that morning of a Palestinian Arab on the orders of a British military court.[2]

Only the BBC would have jeopardized the start of Arabic news bulletins by telling the truth in a bald, factual way. Protests were, in fact, received,[3] but a principle had been established. When Calvert, with his Consular Service background, suggested tentatively that 'there should be such selection and omission of items as to give a favourable impression of this country to the Arab audience', J. B. Clark replied with the authentic voice of the BBC—'the *omission* of unwelcome *facts* of News and the consequent suppression of truth runs counter to the Corporation's policy as laid down by appropriate authority'.[4]

There was liaison between the Foreign Office and the BBC, not least in the field of listener research,[5] but it did not influence programme policy. Every effort was made, instead, to create a viable 'Arabic programme unit' inside the BBC. Donald Stephenson, who was later to have a distinguished career in quite different branches of the BBC, was seconded from the Royal Air Force in the spring of 1938,[6] but great use from the start was

---

[1] *Undated memorandum, 'Publicity for Transmissions in Foreign Languages'.

[2] *First Arabic news bulletin, 3 Jan. 1938.

[3] *Telegram from *The Times* Correspondent in Palestine, 1 Apr. 1938; *Habazbuz* (Iraq), 11 Jan. 1938, 'Oh God help us against Satan. Accursed of God be the radio! Thus the London radio station inaugurated its Arabic programme by the broadcasting of reports of acts of terror in Palestine . . . a proceeding which even the most Zionist of Zionists would pronounce as representing a lack of taste, to say the least.'

[4] *Calvert to J. B. Clark, 18 Jan. 1938; J. B. Clark to Calvert, 19 Jan. 1938.

[5] Meetings were held at the Foreign Office from time to time (e.g. on 12 Jan. 1938) and Calvert was recognized as providing a link. 'Whilst we naturally recognise that Calvert, having been seconded to the BBC has only one master to serve,' Leeper of the Foreign Office wrote, 'we are anxious that his new master should let him keep in the closest contact with his old.' *Leeper to Graves, 5 Jan. 1937.   [6] *Arabic Service Committee, Minutes, 27 Apr. 1938.

made of Arabs, as use was to be made of foreigners generally as foreign broadcasting developed. A. K. Sourour and Aziz Rifaat were appointed direct from the Egyptian State Broadcasting Service in Cairo, where they had more than three years' experience. J. B. Clark signed them on, indeed, on his way back to London from his Empire tour.[1] Rifaat was a man of great imagination, a poet as well as a broadcaster, and Sourour had the reputation of being the best Arabic announcer in the world. They did as much to establish the BBC's Arabic Service as any of its more highly placed sponsors, for they were able to take account naturally of what Stewart Perowne called 'the ambivalence of the Arab mind when it is exposed to contact with the West'. 'It is an often remarked phenomenon', Perowne, the Arabic Programme Organizer, wrote in September 1938, 'that those who most ardently seek to possess themselves of the material equipment of the West are the most resolute champions and apostles of culture and religion of the East.'[2]

Scanning through the early Arabic programmes is an interesting historical exercise, and sometimes there are historical ironies. In August 1939, for example, it was decided to have an Englishman to speak on the anniversary of the Anglo-Egyptian Treaty, 'as one was given by an Egyptian last year'. It was agreed to recommend that Mr. Anthony Eden should be approached. The opening of an Egyptian short-wave station in the same month was hailed as 'an extension of the London–Cairo axis'.[3]

The Arabic broadcasters in Britain included journalists, politicians, diplomats, and students, among them a number of Arab students of drama at the Old Vic.[4] Two Arab ladies who introduced programmes regularly were known as 'readers', not as 'announcers'.[5] Sometimes Rifaat wrote a poem—as on the anniversary of the foundation of the BBC in 1939. Sometimes there were plays in Arabic, the first of them being broadcast in the spring of 1939 after hard work by Sourour.[6] It is not surprising that there were frequent requests from listeners for 'programmes in a lighter vein', like the running commentary

[1] *The Director-General of Egyptian State Broadcasting at this time was A. S. Delany.

[2] *Note by Stewart Perowne, 2 Sept. 1938.

[3] *Arabic Programme Committee, Minutes, 9 Aug. 1939.

[4] *Ibid., 14 Dec. 1938.   [5] *Ibid., 21 Dec. 1938.   [6] *Ibid., 26 Apr. 1939.

on the Grand National which was broadcast with an Arabic commentary in 1938.[1] There was also some doubt about the BBC's identity, however unique it seemed to itself. 'Identification announcements should be made more frequently throughout the programmes in order to avoid confusion with other stations broadcasting in Arabic.'[2]

The inaugural programmes of the BBC's Latin American Service were broadcast on 14 and 15 March 1938. A large group of guests was received by the Director-General in the Council Chamber of Broadcasting House at the very appropriate time of 11.30 p.m. on 14 March, and a champagne buffet supper was served at 2 a.m.

There is evidence that the BBC knew less about its potential listeners in Latin America than its listeners in the Middle East. It had been primed, however, with a great deal of information. 'Tap listening' was apparently as prevalent in Lima as it was in Cairo. 'Whatever views listeners might hold as to the News value of the Service, they would nevertheless listen. . . . And what is heard sufficiently often sinks in, just as heavy advertising can sell any article whether good, bad or indifferent.'[3] It is doubtful whether Reith—or the inhabitants of Lima—would have been impressed by this report. Other reporters were more searching. They pointed to the need for securing rediffusion rights through agreements with local stations, to the impossibility of winning the confidence of all sections of opinion in highly divided societies, and to the benefits which would accrue from linking news bulletins to more varied and colourful programmes. 'The demand for *personalismo* is probably the most characteristic and profound sentiment of the continent', one observer wrote. Another, a little later, remarked, 'My only criticism of BBC programmes is that you don't blow your own trumpet enough.'[4]

The urgent need for starting the service had been underlined by Felix Greene, who was sent by the BBC on a tour of Latin America in 1937. Latin America was just as vulnerable to out-

---

[1] *Arabic Programme Committee, Minutes, 8 Feb. 1939.

[2] *Ibid., 1 Mar. 1939.

[3] *Report from Lima, 21 Oct. 1936.

[4] *F. G. Lockwood to D. McCulloch, 17 June 1938; letter from T.P., 13 Oct. 1938.

side pressure as the Middle East. 'We are facing damaging propaganda in all its forms, propaganda concerted, skilful, highly
organized, and prosecuted with resourcefulness, energy and infinite diligence. . . . Countless Brazilians, Argentinians and
Chileans, in positions of influence and friendly towards our
country, have told me how difficult it is to stand by and watch
the effects of these activities and see Britain lift no finger to
protect her name and interests.'[1]

The Latin American Section confronted a huge task when it
was set in these terms, for most other British agencies did little
during the inter-war years—to the great annoyance of friends of
South America, like Sir Eugen Millington-Drake—to support
British cultural or political influence. Millington-Drake had the
closest relations with the new Section, which was small but com-
pact. Another Calvert, R. A., was Spanish-Portuguese Editor,
with T. Farrell as first Spanish Sub-Editor and C. E. Glass as
first Portuguese Sub-Editor. J. A. Camacho, who was to have
an outstandingly interesting later history with the BBC, was a
member along with M. A. Braune and A. Cortesao. Much of
the work of the Section would have been impossible without
good public relations, which were managed in the first instance
by R. J. Baker, R. A. Fusoni,[2] and R. E. Broughton. The engineering problems were considerable because South America
was—and is—a difficult area within which to provide an easily
receivable service from the United Kingdom.

It is possible, however, to exaggerate the distinctiveness of
response in South America and other parts of the world. As the
Latin American Service developed, many of the letters received
from Latin America were of the same pattern as letters received
from elsewhere. 'During the crisis, with the world on tiptoe,'
a BBC official wrote from Ecuador in September 1938, 'we
anxiously awaited the London news as the most authoritative
voice on these events.'[3] 'Sincere and cordial congratulations on
the impartiality, sound judgment and common sense with which
the London station has kept its innumerable Spanish speaking

[1] *Note by Felix Greene, Nov. 1937.
[2] Fusoni was in South America from October 1938 onwards. Another important
four-month tour was that of C. A. L. Cliffe, the Overseas Programme Director,
who arrived in South America just before Christmas 1938. He sent back a fascinating
report on his visit.
[3] *Note by C. A. L. Cliffe, Sept. 1938.

listeners informed of European events', wrote a listener in Cuba. There was always a minority who wanted more than just news. 'Authoritative talks on world affairs and interpretation of the News,' the same Cuban listener added, 'would be regarded as a valuable addition to the Service, and many listeners would like the programmes to carry a presentation of the English point of view and of English life in all its aspects.'[1]

The presentation of the news depended on the highly efficient Empire and Foreign News Section, which was later augmented to include foreign-language news experts. J. C. S. MacGregor was succeeded as Empire News Editor by C. A. L. Cliffe in September 1935, and the latter by J. F. G. Troughton, seconded from the Colonial Office, in 1937. In December of that year a new Overseas Intelligence Department was started under the direction of M. Frost. A. E. Barker was appointed Foreign Language News Editor in February 1938 and Overseas News Editor in December of the same year. A few months after the Latin American Service had been launched, European news bulletins began to be delivered in German, French, and Italian, and in January 1939 the European Language Service was made permanent.[2] In the meantime MacGregor had become Empire Service Programme Director in 1935 and Cliffe had become Overseas Programme Director in 1938.

We know very little of the new listeners who were recruited in the dark months of 1938 and 1939, but there is a limited amount of listener-research information about the listeners to the Empire Service. Indeed this chapter of the BBC's history comes round full circle with two detailed (but undated) reports, the first on public-relations aspects of Empire broadcasting, the second on an Empire Service Research Scheme based on information collected from a sample of 600 listeners in all parts of the Empire.

It was impossible to tell accurately how many listeners there were or how many potential listeners there might be. Estimates suggested that there were less than 100,000 wireless receiving sets in use in 47 Colonies—the Dominions were not included

---

[1] *Note by C. A. L. Cliffe, Sept. 1938.
[2] *Control Board Minutes, 27 Jan. 1939. See also below, pp. 645 ff.

in this reckoning—and less than 10,000 subscribers to Wireless Exchanges. Palestine accounted for more than a quarter of the receiving sets. In many Colonies, listeners were at the mercy of 'ignorant wireless traders'. Some manufacturers quite openly treated the Colonies 'as a dumping ground for out-of-date and faulty stock'.[1] The Dominions provided a large and

34. 'A Tour of Babel: Glances at some of the lesser-known BBC Departments' (1939).

highly critical audience. There were 927,481 licensed receivers in Australia, 226,476 in New Zealand, and 1,038,500 in Canada. All these countries had their own broadcasting systems with which the BBC had to compete as well as to co-operate. 'Although we may not want to pander to the programme requirements of Dominion listeners, we must recognise that if we do not give them for at least a proportion of the broadcasting programme time programmes of the type which they wish to hear, they will turn to other stations.' There was also an Empire over-spill audience outside both the Colonies and Dominions.

1 *Undated memorandum, 'Public Relations and Empire Broadcasting'.

A considerable proportion of the total correspondence received by the Empire Department originated in the United States.

How often did Empire listeners listen? In the sample survey, 21 per cent. listened up to 10 hours a week, 6 per cent. more than 40 hours a week. Whatever the appeal of foreign broadcasts to the Middle East or to South America, Empire listeners favoured Daventry by a large margin. Dutch stations came next in popularity, not Zeesen or Rome. Sixty-one per cent. of the sample in India, Burma, and Ceylon preferred Variety to any other kind of programme, 68 per cent. in the Near East, and 72 per cent. in British Colonies in West Africa. *Music Hall* was the favourite programme, followed by *In Town Tonight* and *Monday Night at Seven*. There was a marked lack of enthusiasm for Empire talks and little interest in features and drama, 'almost entirely due to the need for concentration and the poor quality of short-wave reception'. Few views on religious services were expressed.

This picture needs to be taken into account when the record of these years is finally assessed. The ideal of the great imperial servant relying on radio to strengthen his values and enliven his intelligence clashed sharply with the picture of the Empire listener which can be drawn from this sample. 'In the Colonies most of our listening takes place when we have done our day's work and (especially in the tropics) are sitting back and having a drink; therefore *light* entertainment is required, not programmes of educational value.' Or, as the wife of a colonial civil servant put it, 'it is very hot and wet, and light entertainment and interesting talks are all I can be bothered with'.[1] It is not fanciful to trace back some of the later difficulties in the Empire, both during the War and since, to the inability of any agency to change attitudes of this kind. The fact that the BBC as a public corporation tried more than any other is to its everlasting credit. It was serving itself well, too, in preparation, though for long it did not know it, for the enormous international task imposed upon it during the Second World War.

[1] *Undated memorandum, 'Empire Listener Research Scheme'.

IV

ORGANIZATION: THE GROWTH OF AN INSTITUTION

Ten years ago we hailed the new invention
  Just as a curious scientific freak. . . .
Those were the days of cramped accommodation
  For workers on the hillside of Savoy—
A Company, not yet a Corporation—
  Who spent laborious days, with little joy
And hasty meals, in long negotiation
  Before they gained permission to employ
Artists and actors, and allayed suspicion
  Of any undermining competition. . . .

. . . This giant is no drone that sleeps or dozes,
  Nor yet a monster armed with dragon's teeth,
And an impartial scrutiny discloses
  The workings of a steadfast soul beneath;
The BBC is not a bed of roses,
  But well has earned and well deserves its Wreath;
For here at last we safely can applaud
  One thing we manage better than abroad.

Lines taken from a poem of eight stanzas by CHARLES GRAVES in
Punch, 11 May 1932

1. Public Corporation

THE idea of a 'public corporation' influenced all aspects of broadcasting. Indeed, it had even wider implications. 'There is more in the BBC than just broadcasting', Reith told the assembled staff of the BBC just after they had moved to Broadcasting House. 'In this line you are not working to yourselves only, but showing what the BBC type of constitution can do, and the lessons it can teach with regard to other fields of activity.'[1]

Reith had a number of points in mind when he made this kind of statement, as he so often did during the 1930s. First and foremost, he wanted to emphasize that he and his subordinates were public servants: they did not require the incentive of making money to keep them energetic and enterprising. 'To the right kind of man, a dividend motive is unnecessary. More than this, the serving of public interest and the serving of financial interest are not normally fully compatible.'[2] For talking like this, Reith sometimes won the reputation of being 'something of a socialist'.[3] In fact, he was falling back on a different tradition—on a concept of 'duty' which was firmly rooted in his Christian upbringing. The sense of service sprang from within: it was nourished by introspection, heart-searching and seering self scrutiny, rather than taken for granted. 'A thorn in the spirit', he once told Baldwin, 'was worse than a thorn in the flesh.' Baldwin, who was never troubled by thorns, 'was much amazed and asked if I felt that I must burst'.[4]

Reith admired and trusted people who were clear what their duty was and did it unflinchingly, even though they knew it was hard. He felt that his own abilities were not always as fully tested or 'stretched' as they ought to have been, and that with his urge to serve, there might have been outlets for service in quite different walks of life. Frequently, however, he turned down opportunities of making far larger sums of money in other

[1] *J. C. W. Reith, Address to the Staff of the BBC, 3 May 1932.
[2] Address to the Royal Institution, 13 May 1932.
[3] Reith, Diary, 6 Feb. 1933.   [4] Ibid., 21 Feb. 1929.

organizations, including other branches of 'mass communication', than he was making in the BBC. And although he was often 'bored' by the BBC during the 1930s, as he admitted freely in his diary, he never treated it lightly. In 1932 he was referring to his 'over-burdened position', and over a year later was admitting that he 'should be very sorry to leave the BBC and . . . there are very few jobs indeed that would interest me at all'.[1] He did not shrink from talking about the need for 'idealism'. 'The broadcasting authority must not be afraid to postulate a policy or policies in which idealism plays a part, perhaps a determining part. . . . Idealism can be practical, and we have not far to seek for plans and policies which would be all the better for an infusion of idealism.'[2]

Reith's colleagues were expected to work in the same spirit. When he appointed them, he wanted to be sure that they genuinely *wanted* to be members of the BBC, that they were not merely looking for a job but for a particular job. Once appointed, they were not very well paid and their hours of work were long. 'I am convinced that all producers and their secretaries are most seriously overloaded and that a really dangerous situation exists', Rose-Troup wrote about the state of affairs in the Variety Department in June 1938:[3] the same comment had been made by Nicolls in 1935.[4] R. T. B. Wynn once went into Ashbridge's office at 6.50 p.m. and said, 'I'm sorry but I'm going a bit early tonight.' What was true of Variety or Engineering was true of many other departments during the same period, and what was true of Reith—his refusal to take outside jobs at far higher rates of pay—was true of many other people inside the BBC.

A genuine disinterestedness was one of the hallmarks of the organization, and Reith believed that it could set an example to the community at large. 'We have done our best', he once said, 'to found a tradition of public service rather than public exploitation. The broadcasting system of a nation is a mirror of that nation's conscience. . . . This is the trust which we have assumed and we did not assume it lightly. There are no loop-

[1] Reith, Diary, 15 Mar. 1932, 19 Sept. 1933.

[2] Address to the Royal Institution, 13 May 1932.

[3] *Memorandum by J. M. Rose-Troup, 'Variety Department, Staff and Output', 28 June 1938.

[4] *Nicolls to Reith, 31 Jan. 1935.

holes to duty, and no compromise is possible with what one considers to be right. The generation of tomorrow will judge us not just in terms of the amusement we have given, but by what we have stood for in the past and may still stand for in the future. If the day should come—and I don't think it will —when broadcasting should play to the lowest rather than the highest in man, then will the country itself have fallen very low.'[1]

At the same time, Reith was at pains to reiterate time and again that public service in a public corporation was something quite different from public service in the Civil Service—in the Treasury, for example, or in the Post Office. He and his colleagues were not government servants: they were genuinely managing their own business themselves, and they should manage it, he stressed, free from bureaucratic interference. There always was a danger of bureaucratic interference, of petty-mindedness stifling vision. Such petty-mindedness handicapped the development of the Empire Service, and tied up the development of television.[2] There was also a danger of political interference. Reith believed that many of the decisions of the Post Office were crudely political, particularly when Kingsley Wood was Postmaster-General. 'He was more party-minded than his predecessors: both ears to the ground.'[3] 'It is a sorry affair that a man should be so timid and his whole outlook be determined by considerations of popularity and avoidance of trouble', he noted in 1934.[4]

Free of politics and as far as possible free of red tape, the BBC needed a spirit of enterprise as well as a sense of duty.[5] 'Sir John Reith is the living proof of the truth of things in which he does not believe', wrote one right-wing critic of his views on public services and the irrelevance of the profit motive. 'There is no recent example that illustrates better than his the qualities of individualism and enterprise.'[6] Yet Reith never saw any antipathy between 'individualism' and 'institutionalization'. He believed, indeed, that the rapid creation of an accepted

[1] *Notes for Blattnerphone Record on Broadcasting (1931).
[2] See above, p. 376 for Empire broadcasting; see below, pp. 613 ff. for television.
[3] *Into the Wind*, p. 158.
[4] Reith, Diary, 25 June 1934.   [5] See above, p. 56.
[6] *The Independent*, 9 June 1934. The article was written by Sir Ernest Benn.

institution could be achieved only by outstanding individuals who could take speedy decisions and command genuine loyalty.[1] In the United States it was the 'absence of the institution which was preventing the best men in American radio from doing their best work and at the same time permitting others to operate without much idea of their responsibility to the public'.[2]

The parallels and contrasts between Britain and America fascinated him. Americans, however, did not always agree with his analysis. When in 1933 Reith sang the praises of the BBC as an institution in the presence of the American radio magnate, Owen D. Young of the Radio Corporation of America, Young replied that 'it was no good my [Reith] talking about the success of the BBC constitution and policy in general terms and as applicable elsewhere, since, according to him, it had been all done by me'.[3]

Reith was sure that the kind of 'public corporation' he had created was adapted to the needs of the age, offering at the same time authority, order, and enterprise. He was so sure, indeed, that he considered it to be 'a precedent for similar advances towards a better world in other domains where great services are handicapped by too definite State control or where the public is handicapped by there being too little State control'.[4] He mentioned as possible candidates for 'nationalised rationalisation' the railways, coal-mining, and the steel industry.[5] As early as 1929 he was delighted to find that Philip Snowden's 'conception of nationalisation was on BBC lines',[6] and a few days after he saw Owen Young in 1933, he had 'an interesting conversation' on the same subject with Stafford Cripps. 'I think I got him to agree that the Post Office should be de-nationalised to the BBC type of constitution', Reith wrote, 'but he persisted in trying to make out that the conduct of a service like the railways was different in nature from that of the BBC.' It was odd, Reith added, 'that I should be almost entirely socialist in my outlook in regard to the point on which the socialists put so much importance, namely the nationalisation of public

[1] See his Address to the Royal Institution, 13 May 1932.
[2] J. C. W. Reith, 'Broadcasting in America' in the *Nineteenth Century*, Aug. 1931.
[3] Reith, Diary, 14 Nov. 1933.
[4] Address to the Royal Institution, 13 May 1932.
[5] J. C. W. Reith, 'Broadcasting and a Better World' in the *Spectator*, 22 Nov. 1930.　　　　　　　　　　[6] Reith, Diary, 9 Apr. 1929.

services. Cripps had a good instance in his [broadcast] speech of the way in which roads used to be run on a capitalist system but became nationalised in the middle of the last century.'[1]

There was, however, a difference between railways—a means of physical communication—and broadcasting—a means of social communication—in Reith's mind as well as Cripps's. Reith was always interested, as he still is, in both forms of communication, but in the case of broadcasting he believed that 'economic and administrative arguments' were not the only ones to take into the reckoning. Efficiency of service and the 'right area' of operation were relevant to both, but there were additional arguments of 'an intellectual and ethical order' in the case of broadcasting.[2] 'Ethical policy cannot stand competition', he wrote in 1931. 'The only ultimate unfailing powers are, unfortunately, force and money. An ethical policy put across by one of these (our monopoly arises from the former) may be approved, but cannot establish itself on its own.'[3]

In a society where there were acute social divisions, competing political pressures, confusions of values and, above all, divergent assessments of individual worth, this approach did not always impress. It was certainly never likely to be unanimously accepted. The remarkable point was that through sheer strength of personality Reith won a substantial measure of confidence when he propounded his philosophy in public. In an age of little men, he had unmistakable moral stature. In an age when old institutions became sluggish or stagnant, as so many did in the 1920s and 1930s, the BBC was a new institution, growing faster than most institutions had grown before both in size and in influence. The vigour of Reith's philosophy is displayed in his interest in broadcasting overseas, in India, for example, Canada, or South Africa. He believed that the British idea of a public corporation—and the British ideal of public service that lay behind it—had wide relevance. In different times he might have been a great Empire builder, for he always longed to exert influence outside his own society as well as in it.

His power to impress was shown at its most striking in 1934. In March of that year there was a 'sustained' attack on the

---

[1] Ibid., 30 Nov. 1933.
[2] See also 'Broadcasting and a Better World'.
[3] Reith, Diary, 14 Dec. 1931.

BBC in the press, 'very much on personal issues'.[1] 'It seemed to be as much against me personally', Reith wrote, 'as against the BBC.'[2] At the height of the criticism, Reith paid a visit to the House of Commons to address the Conservative 1922 Committee;[3] he followed this up a few weeks later with an address in the same style to the Parliamentary Labour Party. Both visits were personal triumphs: they were also public demonstrations of a philosophy of conduct. Reith spoke briefly for five minutes, and went on to answer a battery of questions. He never flinched. 'I only wish the meeting had gone on for two hours longer', he wrote at the end of the 1922 Committee session. The following day, to his 'astonishment', the press 'executed an incredible *volte-face*'. There were fair accounts of the meeting in both the *Daily Express* and the *Daily Herald*, and among the headlines were 'Tables Turned on Critics', 'BBC Critics Converted', and 'Critics Turn into Supporters'. The Labour Party meeting, with Clement Attlee in the chair, was something of an anticlimax, but 'the result seemed equally successful and the meeting was on the whole very cordial'.[4] Very similar demonstrations of support were forthcoming when Reith left the BBC in 1938, and people and organizations of widely divergent views paid universal tribute to his achievement.[5]

The idea of a public corporation was not, of course, a monopoly of Reith. Many writers and politicians dwelt on the advantages of 'public corporations' at this time—notably Herbert Morrison, Sir Henry Bunbury, and W. A. Robson. American visitors came to Britain from the United States of Franklin D. Roosevelt to learn what 'public corporations' were. They went on conducted tours of the Central Electricity Board, the London Passenger Transport Board, and the BBC to see how large-scale institutions behaved when they were called upon to act as

[1] Reith, Diary, 19 Mar. 1934.
[2] *Into the Wind*, p. 184.
[3] See also below, pp. 454–5.
[4] *Into the Wind*, pp. 185–6; Diary, 19 Mar., 10 May 1934.
[5] See below, p. 634. Reith could also win over a difficult undergraduate audience, as he did in the Oxford Union in 1930. *Isis* wrote that he was impulsive and amusing. 'He says he is not a speaker, but if he is not, there are very few in the House who can call themselves so.'

'trustees for the national interest'.[1] There was no more eloquent protagonist of the system than Reith, and he was gratified by an American scholar's conclusion, after a detailed factual inquiry in 1936 and 1937, that 'the method of organising a public service, of which the BBC, the Central Electricity Board and the L.P.T.B. are conspicuous examples, represents a practical step of the greatest consequence towards resolving the conflict, inherent in a democratic system of society under existing conditions, between "democracy" and "efficiency"'.[2]

As early as 1905, A. V. Dicey had forecast that the time would come when 'every large business may become a monopoly, and [when] trades which are monopolies may wisely be brought under the management of the State'.[3] This trend of thinking had a definite influence on Conservative thought. Liberals also took up the idea of 'public enterprise' in their *Industrial Inquiry* of 1928, and J. M. Keynes gave it his blessing.[4] Finally, much Fabian argument pointed in the same direction, and the Labour Member of Parliament, William Graham, who had been a member of the Sykes Committee on Broadcasting in 1923, helped to popularize the term 'public corporation'.[5] Herbert Morrison gave it wide political currency.[6] W. A. Robson, who was quick to see the administrative significance of the phenomenon, pointed out in 1935 that the London Passenger Transport Act was introduced into Parliament by a Labour Minister, continued by a Liberal successor, and piloted through its final stages by a Conservative Minister of Transport.[7]

Influencing each of these strands of thought was the British desire to be 'practical', and it was Lord Allen of Hurtwood, whose own political attitudes were ambivalent, who described public corporations as 'accepted expressions of the British commonsense way of doing a technical job efficiently and with

[1] This was the language of the Crawford Committee Report of 1925. See Cmd. 2599 (1926), § 4. For the background and conclusions of the Crawford Committee Report, see *The Birth of Broadcasting*, pp. 327–48.
[2] L. Gordon, *British Experiments in Public Ownership and Control* (1937), p. 27.
[3] A. V. Dicey, *Lectures on the Relation between Law and Public Opinion in England during the Nineteenth Century* (1905), p. 248.
[4] J. M. Keynes, *The End of Laissez-Faire* (1926), pp. 41–42.
[5] See Hugh Dalton, *Practical Socialism for Britain* (1935), p. 94.
[6] H. Morrison, *Socialization and Transport* (1933).
[7] W. A. Robson, 'The BBC as an Institution' in the *Political Quarterly*, Oct.–Dec. 1935.

general consent'.[1] Allen thought of himself as 'a sort of unofficial spokesman for the BBC constitution', which he regarded as 'a new illustration of the singularly skilful manner in which the British race seems to develop the art of government'.[2]

Reith's main achievement was to create a public corporation rather than to write about it, but in a number of interesting articles he tried to set his own work in its administrative and historical context. The essential requirements of a public corporation, he stated, following Sir Henry Bunbury, were first, public control over major policy; second, absence of public interference in management; third, choice of the right field of operation; fourth, disinterestedness; and fifth, 'expertness'.[3]

Public control over major policy was exercised by the Postmaster-General and through him by Parliament. The Charter of 1927 gave the Corporation power to sue and to be sued, to hold property, real and personal, and to take other actions appropriate to its corporate nature. Yet it had to apply 'the whole of its surplus revenue (if any) and other income solely in promoting its objects'. It was not permitted to distribute a profit. Supplementary to the Charter was a Licence granted by the Post Office and running, like the Charter, for ten years from 1 January 1927.

Each year the BBC had to provide the Postmaster-General with a Report and Statement of Accounts. It also had to accept certain conditions which he laid down. The Postmaster-General, who had international obligations to consider, retained authority to approve the location, wavelength, power, and height of aerials of the broadcasting stations. He also had authority, which he did not use at this time, to specify hours of broadcasting. He could require the BBC to broadcast at its own expense

[1] Lord Allen of Hurtwood, *Britain's Political Future* (1934), p. 139. Allen of Hurtwood wrote to Reith on 24 Nov. 1932, 'I believe very few people even now fully understand that you have probably made a more remarkable contribution to human thought and the future of civilisation than any other living person.'

[2] Lord Allen of Hurtwood to Malcolm MacDonald, 23 Nov. 1932; *BBC Year Book* (1933), pp. 52–53. I owe the reference to Lord Allen's letter to Mr. W. H. Marwick.

[3] Sir Henry Bunbury, reporting on a discussion of problems arising out of the management of public utility services at the Institute of Public Administration in 1926. Reith saw Bunbury on 20 Nov. 1930, when they discussed this and other questions of administration (Diary, 20 Nov. 1930).

any message which a government department might wish to have transmitted. (Again, 'no improper advantage was taken of this clause'.) He could by written notice call upon the BBC 'to refrain from sending any broadcast matter (either particular or general) specified in such Notice'. He could take over complete control of BBC stations in case of emergency. Lastly, he could revoke the Licence at any time in the event of the BBC failing to observe any of the conditions laid down in the Charter or Licence or neglecting 'to send efficiently from the stations a programme of broadcast matter'.[1]

Reith would have preferred control over the BBC's operations —limited though it was in practice—to be exercised not by the Postmaster-General but by a senior Minister, like the Lord President of the Council, who would also be a member of the Cabinet.[2] This was to be the burden of BBC evidence to the Ullswater Committee.[3] He did not like major decisions to be taken by Post Office officials, who might be well equipped to deal with technical matters but knew little of the problems of programme building. He welcomed ultimate parliamentary control, however, as a check not only on the BBC but on the Post Office. Indeed, as we have seen, it was through his direct appeal to Members of Parliament that he won such a great personal triumph in 1934.

To serve as a counter-balance to public control, Reith laid great emphasis on the absence of public interference in management. He did not approve of the presence of elected representatives on the boards of control of public enterprises. Nor did he believe that ultimate public control involved daily scrutiny. 'Control should only be felt when the body was not carrying out its obligations, or had gone beyond its power, or had been guilty in some way or another of offending the letter, or even the spirit, of the constitution which had been duly considered and agreed.'[4] Reith was as averse to the detailed control of management by the members of boards as he was to its more remote control by Parliament.[5] He was, for the most part,

---

[1] See *The Birth of Broadcasting*, p. 358.

[2] See *Into the Wind*, p. 187; also below, p. 478.

[3] See below, pp. 482–8.

[4] J. C. W. Reith, 'Business Management of the Public Services', A Paper read at the Winter Conference of the Institute of Public Administration, Jan. 1930. Bunbury persuaded Reith to give this paper.   [5] See below, pp. 424–31.

extremely successful in his efforts to avoid detailed parliamentary control, and the Postmaster-General stated explicitly in Parliament in 1936 that while he was responsible for questions of general policy, he could not answer questions of detail about particular points of the broadcasting service.[1] There had been a debate on the subject in 1933 when the House of Commons passed a resolution stating that it would be 'contrary to the public interest' to 'subject the BBC to any control by Government or by Parliament other than the control already provided for in the Charter and in the Licence'.[2]

Reith described the procedure whereby parliamentary questions about the BBC were sifted. Of ten questions which a member might like to ask, quite likely four or five might not get through the Clerks of the Table. They would inform the would-be questioner that the matters concerned fell within the province of the Governors. The same answer might be given by the Postmaster-General to two or three out of the ten which actually got through. 'With regard to the other two or three, he might either say that he would draw the attention of the BBC to the matter or give the answer right off.'[3]

Some of the questions that did get through ring oddly today. In March 1933, for instance, G. G. Mitcheson asked the Home Secretary (not the Postmaster-General) if he would instruct the police to compel the BBC to remove immediately the statue recently placed over the front entrance of Broadcasting House, as it was objectionable to public morals and decency.[4] A few months later Robert Boothby asked the Postmaster-General if he would order the excision of all comments on foreign affairs from BBC programmes.[5] Finally—and most melodramatically —G. Buchanan asked the Postmaster-General in November 1934 if he was aware that 'a conspiracy had been made to take possession of the BBC and what steps were being taken to prosecute the individuals concerned'.[6]

The looseness of parliamentary control ensured the virtual autonomy of the BBC, which had been fought for so hard during

[1] *Hansard*, vol. 318 (1936), col. 2748.
[2] Ibid., vol. 274 (1933), cols. 1807–66 for the debate.
[3] *J. C. W. Reith, Talk to the BBC Staff Training School, 2 Oct. 1936.
[4] *Hansard*, vol. 276 (1933), col. 325.
[5] Ibid., vol. 285 (1934), col. 794.
[6] Ibid., vol. 293 (1934), cols. 1772–4.

the days of the General Strike.[1] On the third facet of a public
corporation, control over 'the right field of operation', Reith
was not dogmatic. He believed that since broadcasting was
nationwide, it should be controlled by a national organization,
which would take account of the interests of all parts of the
country and not merely of the densely populated areas. He
admitted, however, that there was usually much to be said for
and against centralization as against devolution of control, and
in the case of broadcasting there was no exception. 'It is in fact
one of the cases in which there is most room for an argument,
since it involves so many of the subtlest and most intangible
values, which cannot be subjected to the criteria of any customary or explicit scale.'[2] Another subtle point mentioned by Reith
was that there was a distinction between the BBC's work in
Britain and in the Empire. 'Although we operate an Empire
Service in addition to the Home one, we have no special rights
in that field, only a special responsibility.'[3]

On 'disinterestedness' and 'expertness' there was little to be
said. Reith did not suggest that 'disinterestedness' was incompatible with 'a fair return on capital invested'. He always
pointed out, however, that the change from Company to Corporation in 1927 had been designed in part to eliminate any
doubts about 'trade control' which might linger in the minds
of some people who would have no doubts about a public corporation. As for 'expertness', this could be taken for granted.
The BBC had always had expert engineers in its own organization, and expert technical argument had frequently determined
public policy just as it had influenced very powerfully the original
decision to grant a monopoly in broadcasting to the BBC.[4]

The concept of 'expertness' in programme matters took longer
to establish. The talented 'amateur' was at least as sure of a place
in the BBC during the inter-war years as he was in the Civil
Service. There was, indeed, a very special place for people who
would have found themselves dissatisfied in any other kind
of institution, Civil Service, business concern, or university.
They welcomed the 'contacts' the BBC provided and the close

[1] See *The Birth of Broadcasting*, pp. 360–84.
[2] 'Broadcasting in America', Aug. 1931.
[3] *Talk to Staff Training School, 2 Oct. 1936.
[4] See *The Birth of Broadcasting*, pp. 93 ff.; R. H. Coase, *British Broadcasting,
A Study in Monopoly* (1950), ch. i.

relationship between the BBC and the world of art and letters, and thought of themselves not as 'professionals' but as people enjoying a full, interesting, and varied life. Certain aspects of the work of engineers might not be very different from that of engineers in other concerns, the Marconi Company, for example —there was much movement to and from the BBC and the Marconi Company—but the work of the programme builders was quite different from work anywhere else. It is fascinating to trace the origins of what may be called 'professional wisdom' among programme planners and producers. Certainly by 1939 a professional ethos was already apparent, although it was by no means universally shared or approved.

Reith himself, as an ex-engineer, knew about this range of questions and motives. He was much more interested, however, in the bigger question of where 'expertness' of any kind should be found—in the Board of Governors or in the Executive? On this question, which was wrapped around in a blanket of personal issues, there was a tense conflict between 1927 and 1930. There has also been much public argument in more recent years.

The members of the Board of Governors of a public corporation have all authority, power, and responsibility vested in them. This was the language of the Charter. Until 1937 there were five Governors, all appointed by the King-in-Council— in practice, that is, by the Prime Minister and the Postmaster-General acting in the name of the Crown. They were to be persons of judgement and independence, who would inspire public confidence by having no interests to promote other than the public service. They were normally to be appointed for a period of four or five years. The Chairman was to receive a salary of £3,000, the Vice-Chairman £1,000, and each of the other Governors £700 a year.[1]

Reith had a very clear conception of what the relationship between himself as Director-General and the Board of Governors should be. All *de jure* authority lay with them, while, by contrast, the Director-General's power was *de facto*. Their role, he thought, should be that of 'trustees', exercising neither executive nor administrative functions. They should not seek to

[1] Cmd. 2756 (1926), *Wireless Broadcasting, Charter and Licence*, § 13.

be 'experts', certainly not experts in particular departments of broadcasting business. Their value lay in their 'general experience of men and affairs'. The Director-General had to manage the BBC, to co-ordinate the various activities of broadcasting, and take responsibility for the daily conduct of affairs.

This conception of the relationship between Director-General and Governors was accepted in the 1930s. It has been sharply criticized in print, however, by at least one subsequent Chairman of Governors, who has contrasted the 'Reithian' view of the relationship with that set out in the Beveridge Report of 1950.[1] It was criticized also in the period covered in this volume by two of the first batch of Governors appointed when the Corporation was formed in 1927, and during the 1930s it frequently formed the basis for an attack on Reith's 'autocracy'.[2] A careful study of the documents, however, justifies most of Reith's actions in relation to the Board, notably during his first troubled encounters with the Earl of Clarendon and Mrs. Snowden, the two most difficult members of his first Board. It would have been disastrous for the future of British broadcasting if Clarendon, basically a weak Chairman, and the ubiquitous and ambitious Mrs. Snowden—widely divergent though their views were[3]—had been able permanently to enhance the *de facto* powers of the Governors *vis-à-vis* the Director-General.

The exact balance of constitutional relationships always depends on the qualities of people. In the period from 1927 to 1930 Reith not only knew far more about the needs and opportunities of broadcasting than his Governors, but he had the strength of will to deal effectively with outside interests and the force of character to hold his own organization together. Clarendon gave him no help at all, and it is scarcely surprising that when Reith heard the news in February 1930 that Clarendon was leaving the BBC to become Governor-General of South Africa he could not resist the comment in his diary: 'What terrific news! We could not contain ourselves and did not know what to do to show our delight.'[4] With Mrs. Snowden

[1] Lord Simon of Wythenshawe, *The BBC From Within* (1953), ch. iii. See also Cmd. 8116 (1949), *Report of the Broadcasting Committee*, pp. 166–9.

[2] See, for example, E. Davies, *National Enterprise* (1946), pp. 66–67.

[3] 'I might have got on with Clarendon if Mrs. Snowden had not been a member of the Board', Reith has written, 'or with Mrs. Snowden if Clarendon had not been a Chairman.' *Into the Wind*, p. 117.   [4] Reith, Diary, 7 Feb. 1930.

his relations improved greatly after 1930, but when her period of office came to an end in December 1932 he wrote that he could not help feeling 'profoundly relieved that Lady Snowden [as she then was] was no longer on the Board'.[1]

The first Governors of the Corporation had hardly established themselves as a vigorous and determined band of people when they first met as a Board on 4 January 1927. They had shown what Reith regarded as 'appalling weakness' in not standing together firmly against the financial proposals of Sir William Mitchell-Thomson, the Postmaster-General, in 1926.[2] Their first meeting in January 1927 was characterized by a disagreement between Clarendon and Mrs. Snowden about the appointment of the secretary and the form of the minutes. Between then and the second meeting on 9 February Reith had seen both Clarendon and Mrs. Snowden separately without being able to improve relations. Part of the difficulty was that neither Clarendon nor Mrs. Snowden had great committee experience: they had never sat on a Board of this kind before. An even greater difficulty was that while the Postmaster-General had given none of the Governors any idea of what they were supposed to do, he had hinted to Clarendon that three-quarters of his time would be needed for his post as Chairman and to Mrs. Snowden that she would be 'almost fully occupied' by the BBC. She expected to have a room at Savoy Hill and believed that 'the Board should meet every day'.[3]

Two of the other Governors knew what boards were. Lord Gainford, the Vice-Chairman, had served with Reith in the old Company, and Sir Gordon Nairne was a former Comptroller of the Bank of England. The fifth Governor, Dr. Montague Rendall, knew something at least of one kind of Board of Governors: he was a former headmaster of Winchester. He wrote to Reith in 1928 that Reith was doing a 'superb' job of work at the BBC and that 'no one could do it better and more efficiently'.[4]

It is easy to attribute the strains and tensions of the period from 1927 to 1930 to Reith's distaste for the sharing of power.

[1] Reith, Diary, 10 Jan. 1933.
[2] See *The Birth of Broadcasting*, pp. 356–7; *Into the Wind*, p. 115.
[3] *Into the Wind*, p. 117.
[4] *Rendall to Reith, 14 Jan. 1928.

In his own autobiography, he admits frankly that he has always 'functioned best when responsibility for decision rested wholly and solely on me'. 'Every faculty', he goes on, 'is then alerted, mobilised. When, as on a committee, others are involved, it has often been otherwise. I can neither explain nor defend.'[1] An explanation of the troubles which concentrates on this personal attribute alone is, however, much too facile. Reith had enjoyed a smooth and harmonious relationship with the Board of the old British Broadcasting Company: he had led them quietly and with the minimum of difficulty to the most awkward of all decisions for a group of people to take—to abdicate in favour of others. After 1930 he was to enjoy good relations with all subsequent Boards of Governors.

There were two far more important causes of strain in the years between 1927 and 1930. The first was the personality of Clarendon and Mrs. Snowden; the second was the tension springing from the changing organization of the Corporation. The first cause was simple. Clarendon was neither sharp nor smooth: Mrs. Snowden was not popular in the Labour movement, where her husband occupied such a prominent position, and she revelled in the unprecedented prospect of power which the BBC offered her. The second cause was more complex. The BBC was growing fast and dealing with immensely varied problems between 1927 and 1930. In such circumstances, committees of any kind are subordinate to people. They must be so. And there may be so much to do on a big scale, so many big decisions to take, that personal authority is essential. In such challenging circumstances, the favourite British arts of committeemanship and sub-committeemanship appear very minor virtues. Yet just because new institutions cannot make all their strategic choices inside committee rooms, this inevitably makes committeemen restive. It was, of course, relevant in such circumstances that Reith himself was restive when committees spent hours discussing issues which he believed could and should be settled in minutes. 'The Chairman and Board are a humbug', he wrote in April 1927.[2] He was particularly annoyed at a meeting in 1928 when Mrs. Snowden said that she thought 'the Regional Scheme and the new

[1] *Into the Wind*, p. 260.
[2] Reith, Diary, 16 Apr. 1927.

Headquarters and everything should be abandoned unless I gave a guarantee that I would stay with them for three or four years'.[1] In Reithian language, 'the wells of satisfaction and inspiration' were being 'polluted'.[2] The result was an inevitable crisis, which again it is far too simple to call 'a badly conducted revolt against Reith's power'.[3]

In June 1929, after the monthly Board Meeting was over, Clarendon told Reith that there 'were three small things he wanted to mention'. They had obviously been discussed by the Governors at a meeting of their own. Governors wished to attend meetings of Advisory Committees sometimes; they wanted to be told of important resignations and appointments; and they felt that they would like to hear more of the work of 'Branch Chiefs'. 'They were all obviously 'frightened that I would make a scene about this,' Reith wrote in his diary, 'but they could have had all these things from the beginning and had frequently been reminded of the fact.'[4] When Reith said that there would be no difficulty about any of the three points, Clarendon bade him 'a most hearty farewell'. In stating the need for the third of the 'three small things', Clarendon had talked of Governors visiting 'collectively or in pairs Heads of Branches in their respective branches'. This odd statement, Reith felt, would make the Governors seem 'utterly ridiculous'. By their own ruling, 'a Governor was not to be allowed to see me alone or to enter the building alone—not even the Chairman'.[5]

This part of the ruling was not put into effect, but relations between Reith and the Governors deteriorated further in July and August, with the long-deferred question of Reith's salary injecting further complications.[6] The July Board meeting was 'negatively hostile'.[7] Clarendon told Reith that all the Governors were 'very disturbed' at Reith's attitude at this meeting: Nairne said flatly that he was not one of them.[8] Staff matters figured vaguely but ominously in the background. During the late summer, Clarendon became convinced that there was 'much discontent on the staff' of the BBC and that Reith was

---

[1] Reith, Diary, 14 Mar. 1928.
[2] Ibid., 14 May 1929.
[3] The BBC From Within, p. 50.
[4] Reith, Diary, 25 June 1929.
[5] Into the Wind, p. 121.
[6] Ibid., p. 122.
[7] Reith, Diary, 31 July 1929.
[8] Into the Wind, p. 122.

'a Mussolini'.[1] In conversations with Carpendale, he added vaguely that the Governors were 'not entirely satisfied with the administration'. It was not difficult to deal with such comments, but the atmosphere thickened. When Reith's secretaries heard that Clarendon had said that they were terrified of Reith, they were so incensed that they wanted to write to Clarendon themselves.[2]

Clarendon and Reith met at Clarendon's house in September 1929. It was an unpleasant interview, the tone of which can be deduced from the fact that Reith was not asked to sit down. Clarendon, who was nervous and ill at ease, began abruptly by asking Reith whether he did not admit that the Board of Governors was in the position of Commander-in-Chief of an army. Were not the Governors absolutely supreme and entitled to give any sort of order? Reith replied quietly—and it was surely a better analogy—that the Board was more like the Cabinet at home and the Chief Executive was more like the Commander-in-Chief in the field.[3] The references on both sides were hardly encouraging, considering the fierce conflicts that had raged during the First World War as to where the real *locus* of responsibility lay in military operations. Throughout the interview Clarendon adopted the posture of a high-ranking officer speaking to a subordinate requiring chastisement.

From generalities Clarendon and Reith passed to a few particularities. Clarendon said that Reith had objected to separate meetings of Governors and their lunching together at the Savoy Hotel. He also referred to Reith 'spying' on him, giving one alleged instance of a ludicrous kind. Yet before rushing off to another appointment, Clarendon had abandoned the military analogy and was comparing Reith's position to that of Permanent Secretary of a government department.

The meeting had accomplished little, and Clarendon suggested that Reith should put down his points in black and white. Reith left his chairman 'sure of our ground' and 'perhaps in a way spoiling for a row'. Nairne backed him, but urged him instead to send a conciliatory letter to Clarendon, regretting

[1] This was not the only time the phrase was used. See, for example, G. Allighan in *Ideas and Town Talk*, 25 Apr. 1931. See also below, pp. 509 ff., for staff problems.
[2] *Into the Wind*, p. 123.   [3] Reith, Diary, 24 Sept. 1929.

the difficulties, suggesting that the past be forgotten, and promising harmonious co-operation in the future. The letter was sent,[1] but did not clear the air. Nor did a memorandum. It was not until the end of October that Clarendon suggested that bygones should be bygones.[2] Even then Reith was unsure about the ultimate outcome. 'People here are pleased . . . and I suppose I should be too, but I have always said that there was no use in putting a patch on the sore until you have eradicated the poison.' He admitted that the state of affairs was very bad for the BBC. 'All sorts of things are going wrong now which are a direct result of my being sick with the Board, and all their muddling and wanting to interfere.'[3]

The Board meeting in November 1929 was peaceable, but difficulties continued in December and in January 1930. They ended abruptly in February 1930 when it was announced that Clarendon was to go to South Africa. After discussing the state of affairs inside the BBC with Reith, Ramsay MacDonald, the Prime Minister, asked Clarendon to leave his BBC post at once, and after a good deal of brain-racking H. B. Lees-Smith, the Labour Postmaster-General, suggested that he should be replaced by J. H. Whitley. Thereafter, says Reith, there was 'with him light, and understanding, and excellent wisdom'.[4]

Whitley was a man of genuinely wide experience. Born and brought up in Yorkshire as a Liberal and a Nonconformist, he had made his way in politics from local government to the House of Commons (in 1900) and through the House of Commons to the Speakership in 1921. He held this office until 1928. He had already given his name to the 'Whitley Councils', joint industrial bodies designed to secure regular consultation, co-operation, and conciliation in industry and the Civil Service.[5] His 'disinterestedness' was revealed by the fact that he had refused titles, and his power of conciliation was clearly demonstrated in his first letter to Reith. 'May I say with what pleasure I look forward to being associated with you in the great work of which you are the creator. I hope our association will be mutually helpful in the service to which you have given such

[1] *Reith to Clarendon, 26 Sept. 1929.
[2] *Clarendon to Reith, 30 Oct. 1929.
[3] Reith, Diary, 30 Oct. 1929.   [4] *Into the Wind*, p. 127.
[5] I am grateful to Mr. Oliver Whitley for letting me see a private memoir of his father.

unstinted devotion and to which I will bring my very humble contribution in the spirit of an admirer and a learner.'[1]

Reith soon learned that the letter was not mere words. Whitley chaired the Board with skill, and behind the scenes told Reith that he wanted to be treated as 'a friend'. He discussed with him the philosophy of broadcasting which had inspired all Reith's efforts and said how much he was in agreement with it. There could not have been a bigger contrast with Clarendon. 'Free from internal strife, suspicion and distrust,' Reith has noted, 'one was able, undisturbed, to get on with the job.'[2]

It was during this period that Reith set down most of his thoughts about the public corporation. He was able to take stock. It was during this period, also, that both he and Whitley prepared statements on the functions of Governors. Whitley accepted Reith's draft which was circulated to all new Governors until 1952. 'Their functions are not executive,' the statement read, 'their responsibilities are general not particular, and they are not divided up for purposes of departmental supervision. . . . With the Director-General they discuss and decide upon major matters of policy and finance, but they leave the execution of that policy and the general administration of the service in all its branches to the Director-General and his competent officers. The Governors should be able to judge of the general effect of the service upon the public, and, subject as before mentioned, are, of course, finally responsible for the conduct of it.'[3]

It is important to note that Reith did not hold that Governors should not intervene in matters of administrative detail.[4] Nor did he underestimate their importance in supervising the 'general administration of the service'. Long after the Second World War, indeed, he set out his views in a private letter to a newly appointed Governor. 'Whatever Governors may be prepared (under safeguards) to leave to the Executive, they must decide and direct policy; and they must have a lively, comprehensive, and continuing care for the product of the

[1] *Whitley to Reith, 3 June 1930. See also *The Times*, 3 June 1930.
[2] *Into the Wind*, p. 132.
[3] The document is printed in *The BBC From Within*, pp. 46–47.
[4] *Into the Wind*, p. 301.

organisation they are appointed to govern.' Above all, they had to watch 'programme policy'. 'Are we "giving the public what it wants", or have we any formulated and approved policy deriving from a sense of responsibility—general and specific?'[1]

Co-operation between Director-General and Governors must always depend on mutual confidence rather than on constitutional formulae. Until Whitley's death in 1935, Reith always felt that working arrangements were ideal. 'Whitley would never allow an announcement to be made in the name of the Governors or the Board. "We are one body," he said, "Governors, Director-General and staff. The Corporation; the BBC".'[2]

The same happy arrangement continued under R. C. Norman, who, at Reith's suggestion, had taken Lord Gainford's place as Vice-Chairman in 1933, and had continued in the office when Viscount Bridgeman replaced Whitley in 1935. There is a remarkable contrast between Reith's entries in his diary on the meetings of 1929 and 1930 and a meeting of January 1933. 'Norman came in and spent two hours asking all sorts of questions. He is very pleasant indeed. The Board Meeting was almost rowdy, certainly quite amusing.'[3]

Bridgeman was ill during his short period of office, and died later in 1935. Norman, who had been acting Chairman, formally succeeded him. He remained in the office until 18 April 1939, when he was succeeded by Sir Allan Powell. Norman was a distinguished Chairman who lasted longer than any other, even though he had been told at the start that he would probably be quickly replaced by someone else. 'Mr. Norman's extended term of service (over six years instead of the usual five)', a BBC official publication noted, 'covered perhaps the most striking period of expansion in the BBC's history.'[4] It did not add that it also included the moment of most difficult choice in the history of the BBC to that date—the finding of a successor for Reith.[5]

Finding successors for the Governors was never an arduous task. There was always a queue of people anxious to serve. In 1933 R. C. Norman, Lord Bridgeman, and Mrs. Mary

[1] I am grateful to Lord Reith for showing me a copy of this letter written in 1952.
[2] *Into the Wind*, p. 176.   [3] Reith, Diary, 11 Jan. 1933.
[4] *BBC Handbook* (1940), p. 11.
[5] For the complicated story of the choice of a new Director-General, see below, pp. 636 ff.

Agnes Hamilton replaced Rendall, Gainford, and Lady Snowden. Nairne had already been replaced at the end of 1931 by
H. G. Brown, a company lawyer in the City and senior partner
of Linklater and Paines. When he was appointed, it was suggested in the popular press that the BBC had picked him out of
a mass of Browns as representing 'the typical suburban listener'.
In fact, his was one of the shrewdest appointments made, and he
proved a tower of strength to the BBC. Lord Bridgeman was a
Conservative politician who had held ministerial office in successive Conservative governments, and Mary Agnes Hamilton,
like Lady Snowden before her, was felt to 'represent' at the
same time both the feminine and the Labour point of view. Reith
found her a particularly valuable member of the Board. Not
only did she provide a useful link with Labour politics, but at
the personal level her advice came to be greatly appreciated.
She, for her part, found Reith 'the most interesting individual'
she had met 'for long'. 'Says he believes in democratic aim, not
in democratic method', she wrote in her diary. Later she was
to add that he had 'a swift and powerful brain, and a strong
will. There is a fire within; something capable of greatness, but
impatient, intolerant and for co-operation ill adjusted.' Her
complaint in retrospect was that 'while I was at the BBC, we
talked and thought too much about the D.G. and too little
about broadcasting'.[1]

On Whitley's death MacDonald had recommended Bridgeman rather than Norman as Chairman,[2] and H. A. L. Fisher
came in as a new Governor, bringing with him experience not only
of Oxford but, as he was wont to boast, of the Cabinet. He was
keenly interested in the immense possibilities of broadcasting,
yet he did not take a major part in decisions about policy, and
he willingly acquiesced, it has been stated, when the voting went
against him. 'Fisher was too deeply imbued with the central
doctrines of liberalism', his biographer tartly notes, 'to despise
the voice of the majority.'[3] He strongly backed Reith, however,
when he was attacked in Parliament, and thought Norman 'an
ideal Chairman'.

[1] M. A. Hamilton, *Remembering My Good Friends* (1946), pp. 281 ff.
[2] *Into the Wind*, p. 216. 'In neither of MacDonald's appointments to the chair
had he chosen a member of his own party.'
[3] D. Ogg, *Herbert Fisher* (1947), p. 128.

When Norman replaced Bridgeman, the Vice-Chairman-ship passed to H. G. Brown, and Viscountess Bridgeman became a Governor in her husband's place. At the end of 1936 Mrs. Hamilton was given a fifth year of office, and the Board of Governors was increased to seven. The two new Governors were Sir Ian Fraser, who had taken great interest in broadcasting and had served on the Crawford Committee in 1925—he realized that broadcasting would be important in time of war and gave up his parliamentary seat when he took the governor-ship[1]—and Dr. J. J. Mallon, Warden of Toynbee Hall. Other changes before the war were the substitution of Margery Fry for Mrs. Hamilton and the replacement of Brown by C. H. G. Millis, Managing Director of Baring Brothers. Millis became Vice-Chairman of the Board in June 1937.

The issues centring on the appointment of Sir Allan Powell as Chairman in 1939 and the role of the Governors in war-time belong more properly to the third volume of this History. There were questions in Parliament, however, about Powell's quali-fications which provide an epilogue to the 1930s rather than a prologue to the 1940s. 'We have considered a great number of names, and we think this gentleman is eminently suitable for the position', Chamberlain replied. He would not, however, list any of the necessary qualifications. Nor did his questioners reveal that they understood much about the scope and re-sponsibilities of his office. 'Will the Prime Minister tell us', Jimmy Maxton asked, 'which of these bits of experience qualify this gentleman to arrange variety programmes?[2]

Reith did not always find that the new Governors were in sym-pathy with his views. While Norman had been in full agreement with him about 'the rule against specialist Governors' and had written forcefully to the Postmaster-General in support of the rule,[3] Mallon, for example, thought that Governors might 'departmentalise'.[4] Fraser, moreover, had ideas which clashed with those of Norman, and there were open disagreements about who should be appointed as Deputy Director-General when Carpendale left. 'The present Governors are absurd',

---

[1] I. Fraser, *Whereas I Was Blind* (1942), p. 156.
[2] *Hansard*, vol. 345 (1939), cols. 31–32.
[3] *R. C. Norman to Major J. C. Tryon, 1 Oct. 1935.
[4] Reith, Diary, 10 Feb. 1937.

Mallon wrote to Tallents in a most unconstitutional letter of October 1937.[1] 'These new Governors and another one to come are an infernal nuisance',[2] Reith had commented a few months earlier. Yet by the end of 1937 Reith was more uncertain than ever about his own place in the BBC, let alone the place of his Governors. 'Fifteen years since I went to the BBC', he wrote in his diary on 31 December. 'What a time, and how doubtful I am about staying much longer.'[3] By the time that Powell was appointed, the BBC was under new management.

When Reith talked about a public corporation, he was thinking not only of Governors responsible to the public but of 'Controllers' responsible to the Director-General. Just as the Governors had *de jure* authority and the Director-General *de facto* power in the structure of the BBC as a whole, so the Director-General had *de jure* authority and the Controllers *de facto* power in the internal working of the administration. As early as 1923 there was a weekly meeting of the chiefs of departments, and in 1924 this was given the title of the Control Committee, later the Control Board.[4] The Control Board remained in existence in 1939, although its name was changed to the Director-General's Meeting in March 1933.[5] The name was changed back again in October 1935 after Dawnay's departure, and one further change was made in the spring of 1938 when a distinction was drawn between Control Board Meetings at which major matters of policy were discussed and Controllers' Meetings at which detailed decisions would be taken about operational matters.[6] The last Controllers' Meeting was on 12 May 1939, after which the familiar and established pattern was restored.

Reith saw the pattern in simple terms. At most, five or six people were directly responsible to him. This narrowed 'the span of control'. The five or six individuals who were in charge of major units of broadcasting constituted an executive or control board. 'Here was in operation an ideal combination of co-operative management and definite leadership and direction. There was nothing statutory about it. It might be said to have

[1] J. J. Mallon to Tallents, 28 Oct. 1937 (Tallents Papers).
[2] Reith, Diary, 20 Jan. 1937.   [3] Ibid., 31 Dec. 1937.
[4] See *The Birth of Broadcasting*, p. 207.   [5] See above, p. 33.
[6] *Controllers' Meeting, Minutes, 1 Apr., 14 Oct. 1938.

begun as a convenience to myself—a weekly meeting at which I could have the several and collective views of senior officials, and at which problems that affected them all might be discussed. It was more than that, however; I had in mind from the earliest days that it should function as a real management committee.'[1]

There was never any suggestion, however, that the Control Board was settling BBC policy by democratic vote. 'The situation as between Controllers and Director-General', Reith maintained, 'was the same as that between Director-General and the Governing Board.' 'They might be surprised if the Director-General intervened in a particular matter—this or that—but there would be nothing more than that to it. In other words, the Director-General cannot give a Controller what he does not expect the Governing Board to give him'; but *de facto* there was great authority and responsibility vested in them. 'And Control Board functions more and more effectively and comprehensively.'[2]

Reith said that he liked to think that the Governors could feel secure that what had been recommended to them came not from the Director-General only, but from the Control Board; in other words, that what he was telling the Governors had had the careful scrutiny of six senior BBC officials working together. Indeed, the Chairman of Governors and other members of the Board could attend meetings of the Control Board by invitation, thereby expressing 'the unity of the whole organisation'.

There was also, in his view, a continuity of process. Just as the Governors devolved specific duties on him as Director-General, so he in his turn devolved authority on others. He hoped that this process of devolution would operate in all branches of the BBC. 'The four Controllers can give their subordinates no more than they themselves get from above, but increasingly they too are devolving authority and responsibility on their Departmental Directors. . . . There are, therefore, a great many people party to and concerned in management at the BBC. . . . What the BBC does, therefore, is more and more not what one individual thinks: more and more, it comes from a consensus of opinion and experience.'[3]

---

[1] *Into the Wind*, p. 300.
[2] *J. C. W. Reith, Talk to the Staff Training School, 2 Oct. 1936.   [3] Ibid.

This was Reith's account of the public corporation in action. It left out many imponderables, however, and was very much the view of an organization as seen from the top. The most important element behind the 'consensus' of the BBC was the informal discussion of issues, which continued daily, with secretaries usually acting as intermediaries,[1] whether or not committees were in session, and which was more free and unrestrained than the discussion which went on at the rather formidable Control Board or Common Room tea party, to which senior staff were invited. A different imponderable was concerned not with group consensus but with individual motivation. To some members of staff, at least, the keenness to serve the Corporation had its origins in the desire to belong to an organization which allowed for a very substantial measure of unrestrained personal initiative. They were frustrated, sometimes, by what they thought of as the gulf between themselves and the 'men at the top'.

Even the committees sometimes seemed artificial. It was not a 'rebel', but one of Reith's greatest admirers inside the BBC who wrote that he was sceptical of committees like the Control Board unless they were required for policy reasons, 'as a shield against outside, or even Government, criticism'. 'The members are at best exercising a remote control over what their executive staff are in fact doing and many of the decisions reached are really quite wrong ones.' 'You can't sack a Control Board *en bloc*', he went on, 'if they make a mistake, but you can sack an individual Director or Head of Department. To my mind the test of suitability for Headship of any group or activity is the willingness to accept responsibility; once you have a Board or Committee, which is technically responsible for *your* opinions, either you despair of getting things done *as you know they should be* or, if you are that type, you nestle snugly down behind the protective screen of high level decision and become a "Yes" man.'[2]

This was how part of the structure seemed to a man who had an important part in it, attending the Control Board from time to time as a deputy. Sir Stephen Tallents also—as a new-comer

---

[1] R. Wade, typewritten manuscript, 'Early Life in the BBC'. 'Secretaries could bully their chiefs without feeling they were committing *lèse-majesté*.'
[2] Ibid.

—wrote in his diary after first attending a Control Board meeting of 'the triviality' of its proceedings.[1] It is difficult, however, to see how the BBC could have proceeded on lines other than of Control Board procedure. A system of personal devolution of all power to Heads of Departments would have led to intensive and possibly rigid departmentalism, and it would have left Reith with a wider span of control at the top than he wished to manage. Critics who complained that the constitution of the control system was modified to meet the absorption of Colonel Dawnay into the staff as Controller of Programmes missed the essential fact that Dawnay was appointed quite definitely to relieve Reith from a mass of harassing detail.[2]

Reith, indeed, was never fully satisfied with the organizational shell which surrounded broadcasting activity. He knew that many experiments were necessary to achieve effective internal organization, and that just as effective action had to be taken to deal with the strains of the 1930s as had been taken to deal with the external threats of the 1920s. The fact that the BBC was a public corporation was often overshadowed in practice by the fact that it was a rapidly growing organization, subject to all the stresses which growth entailed. And criticism of what was happening inside Broadcasting House, much of it based on malicious gossip, was sufficiently widespread at various times during the 1930s to provoke barrages of press comment. It was also one of the factors which had to be taken into account when the Ullswater Committee inquired officially into the future of broadcasting in 1935.

Reith himself knew how difficult the problems of organization were, and often he took Mrs. Hamilton into his confidence. 'One of the points I discussed with her', he wrote in his diary in January 1934, 'was the extent of my control. I told her that it required a good deal of renunciation on my part to avoid giving categoric decisions, so that people could learn by experience and be wiser next time; that often I would have vetoed things had I been going still on my original line. I said that I thought that

---

[1] Note by Tallents, 15 Oct. 1935. He complained two weeks earlier of 'the dreadfully closeted' atmosphere of the Common Room tea party where there was too much 'mutual admiration in the air'. Note of 30 Sept. A later verdict on the Control Board was that it was 'intrinsically not good enough for its job'. Note of 17 Oct. 1937 (Tallents Papers).

[2] See below, pp. 443 ff.

even if this meant trouble for the BBC it was perhaps wiser from the BBC point of view in the long run.'[1] A few months before he left the BBC, he also noted, 'Controllers' Meeting will do far more than in the past, so still less for D.G. to do, which is as it should be.'[2]

2. The Logic of Growth

As an institution grows, it creates difficult problems both of control and communication. During the late 1920s and 1930s the BBC faced problems caused by two kinds of growth—first, growth in the size of staff and the extent of premises; second, growth in the areas of activity. To existing lines of activity were added new ones—notably the Empire Service and television. Each kind of growth by itself entailed new responses. Together, they called for bold decisions and well-regulated machinery.

The second kind of growth has acquired a special interest in the light of what happened to the BBC during the Second World War, when its Empire and Foreign Service expanded beyond all pre-war dreams, and of what has happened since 1945, notably the emergence of an Independent Television Authority and of a system of competitive television. Although the first kind of growth—in staff and buildings—was thought of during the 1920s and 1930s as the main factor creating both new problems and new opportunities, it was problems associated with structural organization which set the frame for decision making.

There were limits to what could be done with the frame. 'In a business which covers so many different lines of activity', Reith told a Conference in 1930, 'it is impossible to enunciate one comprehensive policy. There should in fact be as many lines of policy as there are lines of activity, and with every policy, subsidiary and derivative ones as well.'[3]

Yet, at any given time, within a broadcasting organization, there have to be 'groups', 'branches', 'divisions', 'departments',

[1] Reith, Diary, 10 Jan. 1934.   [2] Ibid., 5 Apr. 1938.
[3] *J. C. W. Reith, Address to the University of Cambridge, Board of Extramural Studies, Summer 1930.

or whatever they are called, within which 'lines of policy' can be determined and followed. 'Engineering' is one obvious 'group', whether the broadcasting organization is big or small: 'Programmes' is another. Was there any logical basis in the 1920s and '30s, however, for also having groups labelled 'Administration', 'Finance', or 'Public Relations'? Clearly the structure of 'groups', like the names they were to be given, had to allow for change as the size of the whole organization changed and, just as important, as the people (with their varying abilities and temperaments) changed. There was a further problem associated with growth. If new services arose, like Empire broadcasting or television, which could organizationally be split up as between say 'Engineering', 'Programmes', 'Finance', and 'Administration', was there any case for making them into separate 'groups' in such circumstances?

It is easy to poke fun at the elaborate cycles of nomenclature which can be discovered in the records of the BBC during its process of organizational growth. Two memoranda of different dates reach quite different conclusions about names, each apparently for quite sound reasons. In January 1928, for instance, a BBC memorandum was circulated saying that 'in order to avoid the confusion which has existed in the past between sections and sub-sections, the only designations to be used in future will be Branch, Department, and Section. The five Departments of the Corporation which have hitherto been designated as such will be known as "Branches" [i.e. Administration Branch, Engineering Branch, Information Branch, Programme Branch and Accounts Branch] and the allocation of the titles "Department" and "Section" will be carried out by the Head of each Branch concerned.'[1] Seven years later, in August 1935, a BBC memorandum was circulated reading that the term 'Branch' would be abolished and that in future there would be four 'Divisions' (i.e. Administration Division, Engineering Division, Programme Division, and Public Relations Division) and that the component units of the 'Division' would be called 'Departments'. There was a complication, however, which obviously baffled the title makers. 'In some of the bigger Departments, having Departments within them, the distinction in status will be maintained, except in the Engineering Division, by the position of

[1] *BBC Internal Instruction, no. 61, 9 Jan. 1928.

the word "Director" etc. in the title of the Head of the Department: it will precede the name of the independent Departments and follow that of the dependent ones.'[1]

Seven years in broadcasting history is as long as seventy in the history of many institutions, and the changes in nomenclature mentioned above may be treated seriously as an expression of the sociological law that 'large groups devote a larger proportion of their resources to their own operation than do small groups'.[2] Behind issues of this kind, however, lies the criticism that the BBC during the 1930s was becoming 'too hierarchical'. There was, indeed, considerable confusion over titles throughout the last years of the period, and although all the titles were historically related to function, a number of them were residues, survivals of previous abandoned states of organization. The titles often baffle the reader of memoranda years later. Fortunately a system was fairly generally applied whereby the authors of memoranda, however embalmed in titles, had their initials typed (along with the initials of their typist) at the foot of their papers. This makes names on outgoing memoranda easy to identify, but the names of recipients are often far from easy to place in periods of rapid change of office.

Before the major 'reorganization' of 1933, which has been referred to on several occasions in other contexts, Reith became increasingly unhappy about the BBC's organizational structure. Changes made, for instance, in the organization of Talks or Drama[3] were piecemeal, and there were only limited changes in Administration.

From 1927 to 1932 there were five Assistant Controllers, each in charge of what was called after January 1928 a 'Branch'. The first Assistant Controller, W. E. Gladstone Murray, was Assistant Controller (Information), dealing with a 'group' of activities which included Publications, Publicity, and 'External Relations'; V. H. Goldsmith was in charge of the Administration; P. P. Eckersley (and after 1929 Noel Ashbridge) was Assistant Controller (Engineering), although the title 'Chief Engineer' was normally used; the fourth Assistant Controller

---

[1] *BBC Internal Instruction, no. 315, 30 Aug. 1935.

[2] See T. Caplow, 'Organisational Size' in the *Administrative Science Quarterly*, June 1950, and F. W. Terrien and D. L. Mills, 'The Effect of Changing Size upon the Internal Structure of Organisations' in the *American Sociological Review* (1955).

[3] See above, pp. 89 ff., 124–6.

was R. H. Eckersley, who was also called Director of Programmes; and the fifth, T. Lochhead, Assistant Controller (Finance), was usually called Chief Accountant. Between the five Assistant Controllers and Reith was the Controller, Admiral Carpendale, and one officer, Major Atkinson, the Foreign Director, was directly responsible to him. The position is set out in the simplified chart below.

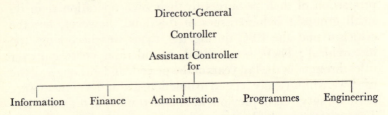

Within the lower echelons of the system there were changes in relationships, like that between News and Talks, and in titles. The Programme Executive, for example, was given the title of Assistant Director of Programmes in 1929. New jobs were created also, like that of General Editor (Publications), which came into existence in 1928 and was filled by Nicolls, the former London Station Director. One of the most difficult tasks during this period was the reorganization made necessary by the gradual substitution of the Regional Scheme for the cluster of local stations. The acceptance of regional primacy before the local stations closed was doubtless an attempt to narrow the span of central–local relationships.[1]

A number of short-lived changes, some of them quite sweeping, like the abolition of the title of Assistant Controller (with the exception of that of Goldsmith), followed in 1932. It seems that 'Administration' was deliberately being separated out at this stage, with all other posts in the BBC being considered as 'functional'. It was not until August 1933, however, that a really comprehensive reorganization was carried out, resting on a crucial distinction between 'blue tab' and 'red tab' which was to last until 1942. Reith called—and still calls—the reorganization 'a development of the existing system'.[2] In fact, however, an attempt was being made to express relationships logically

---

[1] See above, p. 314.
[2] *Draft Notes of a Meeting held in the Board Room, 21 Mar. 1933. Reith, Carpendale, Goldsmith, Graves, and Nicolls were present.

in such a way that formal patterns of responsibility took the place of the previous procedures. In this sense there was a real 're-organization' in 1933. There was a careful and detailed examination of the role of every officer in the BBC and of almost every operational process.[1] Considerable thought was given to the 'placing of each department' in the structure—including 'difficult departments' such as Outside Broadcasts and Programme Booking.

There is no doubt that the changes were felt to be necessary in the first place because Reith considered that he was being given too much work to do under the 'unreformed system'. 'I have been thinking for several weeks of reorganising things', he wrote in his diary in January 1933. 'Tonight I took Goldsmith to dine at the Athenaeum and gave him the outline of it.'[2] Thereafter, the entries in his diary on the subject multiply. 'Today Carpendale, Goldsmith and I got down to the reorganisation business at 6.45', he wrote on 8 March, 'and with a short interval for dinner at the Langham worked in my room until a quarter-to-one. I made notes about conclusions throughout and felt at the end that at last we had got on to the straight road.'[3] When Reith met his senior officers to discuss his plan at the end of March 1933, he said specifically that one of its main purposes was 'to free the D.G. of a good deal of work he is now doing in dealing with officials direct'.[4]

The biggest single new idea in 1933 was not so much the separation of the 'creative' and the 'administrative', although this was fundamental, as the establishment of a new top post, that of 'Output Controller'. In addition to talking to his colleagues, therefore, from February 1933 onwards Reith began to scour the country for the right man to fill what he believed would be one of the most important jobs in the BBC. Eventually, after many names had been considered and quite a number of people informally interviewed, Colonel Alan Dawnay was given the post. Among the other names considered by the Board was that of Sir Stephen Tallents, who was to join the BBC three years later in quite a different capacity.

---

[1] *See, for example, Notes prepared on the Procedure for organizing a Mozart Concert.

[2] Reith, Diary, 6 Jan. 1933.   [3] Ibid., 8 Mar. 1933.

[4] *Notes of a Meeting, 21 Mar. 1933.

Dawnay came from the War Office to the BBC. In other circumstances, the post might have gone to a don or even to a politician. Reith was surprised, indeed, that one of Dawnay's backers was an Oxford don, J. C. Masterman, who had originally been offered the post himself, but had turned it down for 'the decisive reason' that he did not feel 'the sort of crusading zeal—the missionary impulse to do something great which you would be entitled to expect from your second-in-command'. Reith accepted this reason as decisive, adding that 'for this job, a man would not merely have to be free from any doubt as to whether he had "crusading zeal", but he would very positively need to feel certain that he had'.[1] Reith liked Dawnay and believed he would do a useful job of work, yet he was not entirely happy either in general terms about the outcome of the quest or in particular terms about the range of Dawnay's qualities. 'It is dreadful to have been in the position of having so magnificent a job in one's gift. I could not help taking account of the fact that an incalculable amount depends on this decision, to me personally, to the BBC, and to the country generally.'[2]

The reorganization long outlasted Dawnay, who left the BBC on his doctor's orders in 1935. His tenure of office was never easy, and the experiment could not be described as successful. The more general aspects of reorganization were fully outlined in two internal memoranda of August and September 1933 before coming into effect in October. 'The object of the reorganisation', the first memorandum stated clearly, 'is to secure (1) the better co-ordination of authority and responsibility, (2) the clearer definition and separation of administrative and creative functions and (3) the freeing of the Director-General from much of the detail with which he is at present dealing.' The 'main innovation', it went on, 'is the separation of administrative and creative functions. The purpose of this is to enable creative staff to concentrate on their creative work.' An earlier note had stated succinctly that 'the main idea behind the reorganisation is that the Administrative Division should

[1] J. C. Masterman to Reith, 17 Mar. 1933. Reith to Masterman, 20 Mar. 1933. I am grateful to Sir John Masterman for showing me these letters.
[2] Reith, Diary, 26 May 1933.

not merely administer the staff as at present but should administer Programmes and Publications'.[1]

The transferred administrative staff will work, under their administrative chief, to the requirements of the creative staff, who will be relieved of all immediate and direct responsibility in administrative matters. It is intended that the transferred administrative staff shall form something in the nature of an Output Secretariat, carrying out the smallest administrative functions on behalf of the creative staff, e.g. taking the minutes of and making all arrangements for their meetings. The system implies that Heads of Branches, Departments and Sections in the Output Division will work direct to their corresponding Executives and through them to the Director of Internal Administration and Controller (Administration), the referring of administrative questions to their creative superiors not being contemplated as part of the normal procedure.[2]

By the reorganization, two Controllers were to be responsible directly to the Director-General for the whole work of the BBC. Carpendale was to be Controller (Administration) and Dawnay Controller (Output). Each would be in charge of what was called a 'Division'. In each Division there were to be four Branches. In the Administration Division the Branches were to be Internal Administration (under Nicolls), Business Relations (under Goldsmith), Finance (under Lochhead), and Engineering (under Ashbridge). It was explicitly stated, however, that Ashbridge's 'direct responsibility in certain respects to the D.G. is unaffected by the reorganisation'. In the Output Division, the four Branches were to be Programmes (under Roger Eckersley), Talks (under Siepmann), Empire and Foreign Services (under Graves), and Publicity and Publications (under Murray). The new position is set out in simplified form in the chart below which may be compared with the chart on p. 442.

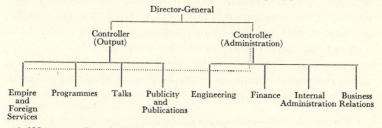

which may be compared with the chart on p. 442.

[1] *Notes on a Proposed Programme Executive Department, 27 Mar. 1933.
[2] *BBC Internal Memorandum, no. 233, 29 Aug. 1933.

In fact, before the reorganization came into effect on 2 October 1933, two important changes of nomenclature were made. The Programme Branch was re-named the Entertainment Branch and the Output Division was re-named the Programme Division. Dawnay's title, therefore, was Controller (Programmes).

The new system marked a definite strengthening of central control and got rid of such objections to the old system as 'too many people working direct to D.G.', 'five separate provinces reporting directly to D.G.', and 'too much responsibility spread all over the Corporation'. It had weaknesses, however—most of them concerned less with formal hierarchy than with informal attitudes. An attitude of guarded suspicion on each side made for a division of outlook between 'output' and 'administration'. It became an article of faith that 'programme people' should not be bothered with administration—they certainly did not fully free themselves from it[1]—and this could lead all too easily into irresponsibility. On the other side, administrative staff could all too easily come to regard themselves—and even more easily come to be regarded—as the 'policemen' of the system.

As far as 'the ladders of control' were concerned, it proved very difficult in practice to restrict communication about 'administrative matters' to the vertical hierarchy of administrators without some of these matters being referred to a higher level by a member of staff on the output side. The same was true of output matters. There might even be divided loyalties. Some administrative matters were, in fact, referred upwards through the Programme Division via the Head of Branch to Controller (Programmes) who then dealt direct with Controller (Administration). There was, moreover, a further proliferation of titles. Necessity rather than virtue was given as the reason for this. 'For convenience in both internal and external identification of writers and for sorting purposes, it is better to have titles and not to have everyone signing for Controller.'[2]

The system remained intact until the Second World War, when the various branches of the BBC were scattered throughout the country, but some of the criticisms which were made of

[1] For example, they usually had to make many detailed arrangements for the booking of studios for rehearsals and transmissions.
[2] *Paper for the Reorganization Committee, 'Titles', 24 Mar. 1933.

it during its last years had been anticipated before it came into operation. 'I feel that the happy working of a scheme which separates so definitely administrative from creative responsibilities', Roger Eckersley wrote, 'is too dependent for its smooth working on personalities.'[1] 'I was influenced by the fact', he went on, 'that after consideration over the weekend, each departmental head definitely asked for the retention of their own executives within the creative division.' Music, for example, had asked for the retention of booking and orchestral management on the grounds of 'the delicately specialised nature of the work'. Ashbridge emphasized the need for small informal committees. 'Very large weekly meetings would not meet the need. It is not always advisable to talk fully with a large committee.'[2] A few weeks after the system had been put into effect an unsigned note was prepared for Carpendale about what was happening. 'If reorganisation were working properly D.E. [Director of Entertainment]', it stated, 'would be spending most of his time in three ways (1) outside creative contacts (2) internal programme conferences (3) attending rehearsals, listening to transmissions etc. He told me a few weeks ago that his office work had not decreased at all and that he had not been able to get near the studio. I think', the writer added, 'that this is really because his general outlook is not really creative.'[3]

There were further changes within the system in October 1935 after Dawnay's departure.[4] The post of Deputy Director-General was then created, with Carpendale as the obvious man to fill it. Nicolls took his place as Controller (Administration). At the same time, Engineering became a Division, and Ashbridge was called Controller (Engineering). Two further Assistant Controllers were appointed to assist Graves, the new Controller (Programmes). Roger Eckersley was to assist him on the entertainment side, and Gladstone Murray was to move over from Publicity and Publications to a vaguely defined sphere of programme duties. It was further stated that an important new post in Public Relations would be created, with an officer,

[1] *R. H. Eckersley to Reith and V. H. Goldsmith, 11 May 1933.
[2] *N. Ashbridge to Reith, 10 May 1933.
[3] *Notes for Controller (A), 5 Jan. 1934.
[4] *BBC Internal Instruction, no. 308, 12 July 1935.

still to be found, 'working in collaboration with both Controllers and to the Director-General'.[1]

The changes, when they came, went further. In 1936, after Gladstone Murray had left the BBC to direct the newly formed Canadian Broadcasting Corporation, Sir Stephen Tallents was made Controller (Public Relations) on the same level of the hierarchy as Graves, Nicolls, and Ashbridge. Tallents's appointment was suggested by the Board of Governors, Reith had no alternative candidate in mind, and he accepted the name with reservations. The new structure was as follows:

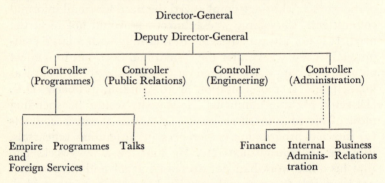

By 1936 it had become obvious that the structure was imposing very heavy burdens not on the Director-General, but on the Controller (Programmes). Television did not emerge as a separate Division, however, and even after the development of foreign-language broadcasting, the Empire and Foreign Services did not pass completely out of the domain of the Controller (Programmes).[2] Nor had regional relations ever been completely tidied up. In the 'centralizing' phase, Lindsay Wellington had been Liaison Officer linking them with London, but with the reorganization of 1933 it had been specifically stated that regions should work primarily through the Controllers and their Divisions, as the 'Branches' did in London. Siepmann's appointment in 1935 as Director of Regional Relations marked the beginning of the process of mild decentralization,[3] but its organizational results were very difficult to assess. Regional staffs had been standardized, as far as possible, in 1933,[4] but

[1] Ibid.
[2] See above, p. 445; below, pp. 601–2.   [3] See above, p. 331.
[4] *BBC Internal Memorandum, no. 233, 29 Aug. 1933. See below, pp. 489–90.

as they grew substantially from 1934 onwards, more and more power inevitably passed into the hands of the Regional Directors. This shift was, in any case, in line with that recommended by the Ullswater Committee.[1]

It was the increase in the numbers of staff more than any other factor which posed problems for the Corporation. How were they to be appointed, promoted, and organized? As early as 1932 Nicolls, with Reith's blessing, was suggesting something in the nature of an Appointments Board to allay complaints amongst the staff, who did not realize that their qualifications for vacancies that arose were being considered without their knowledge.[2] Until then, staff vacancies had not been advertised internally as well as externally; and Reith, Carpendale, and Goldsmith had discussed names and qualifications on the basis of knowledge available to them from within the organization. About the same time, Reith drew attention to the shortage of staff with the right qualifications. He had always attached great importance to 'motive' as a necessary qualification at every level and to the willingness to work for the BBC with enthusiasm and not simply for 'the sake of a job'. By 1932, however, staffing was becoming more formalized. It was a landmark in the history of the BBC as an organization, as it is in the history of most growing business firms, when Reith argued that 'without too much regard for actual positions, we should endeavour to get half-a-dozen first-class men who would be posted in various training places in Head Office and the provinces to learn the business'.[3]

From the angle of the 'Branches', 'Departments', and 'Sections', changes in the demand for staff—at all levels—sometimes tended to be jumpy rather than smooth, influenced by outside decisions as much as decisions from within. The process was well described in a letter of December 1934 to Dawnay from Harold Bishop, who always kept well in order the organization of the BBC's Engineering Service. 'The progressive increase in programme hours', he wrote, 'eventually and inevitably means that we have to ask for more staff. This increase in staff is usually a smooth one, but, of course, staff must go up in

[1] See below, p. 499.
[2] *Control Board Minutes, 19 Apr. 1932.   [3] Ibid., 15 Dec. 1932.

jumps. When the jump becomes necessary, it is difficult for me to explain why one apparently small addition to the work means more staff. It is a case, however, of "the last straw breaking the camel's back".[1]

The growth of total numbers of staff between 1926 and 1939 is set out below in tabular form. The table shows a considerable jump in numbers in the first year of the Corporation—while still at Savoy Hill—a steady growth from the end of 1927 to the end of 1931, the slowest growth in the Corporation's history, and then an upward rise until the Second World War, the annual rate of increase only once falling below 10 per cent. and on one occasion rising above 30 per cent. It is interesting to note that the movement of staff numbers increased faster than the number of wireless licences issued to listeners. This was not an illustration of Parkinson's Law, but an indication of the greater range of broadcasting activities, of the operation of the kind of forces described in Bishop's letter.

THE GROWTH OF BBC STAFF, 1926–39

Year	Staff	Wireless licences	Staff and licences in each year on 31 December % increase in year	
			Licences	Staff
1926	773	2,178,259	32·4	17·5
1927	989	2,395,183	10·0	27·5
1928	1,064	2,628,392	9·7	7·6
1929	1,109	2,956,736	12·5	4·2
1930	1,194	3,411,910	15·4	7·7
1931	1,287	4,330,735	26·9	7·8
1932	1,512	5,263,017	21·5	17·6
1933	1,747	5,973,758	13·5	15·6
1934	2,031	6,780,569	13·5	16·3
1935	2,518	7,403,109	9·2	24·0
1936	3,350	7,960,573	7·5	33·1
1937	3,673	8,479,900	6·5	9·6
1938	4,060	8,908,900	5·1	10·6
1939	5,100	9,082,666	2·0	23·1

Source: Figures in the Finance Division

The breakdown of staff numbers in terms of occupations is impossible for this period, although at the time of the Ullswater

[1] *Bishop to Dawnay, 3 Dec. 1934.

Committee in 1935 the biggest single professional group consisted of engineers. There were 800 of them scattered about
the country, performing different kinds of tasks at very different
levels.[1] The staff was very roughly graded, at least from 1925
onwards, with five grades of employment, but there was no
automatic incremental system and no publicity was given to
salary scales.[2] 'Normal' increments had to be earned. Not to
earn the 'normal' rise indicated, in Reith's words, that 'there
was a query about the man', but there were also 'above normal'
rises. From 1927 to 1933 the details of staffing matters were
dealt with by V. H. Goldsmith, the Assistant Controller. Nicolls,
then the Director of Internal Administration, took over these
duties from 1933 to 1935, and from 1936 onwards W. St. J. Pym
served as the BBC's first Director of Staff Administration.
Pym was a wise and shrewd administrator, and his first main
task was to overhaul the salary and grading system. In the
process of doing this, he quickly ironed out a number of personal discontents.

The BBC, by current standards, had been a 'good employer'
long before 1936. From the earliest days it had a Medical
Officer and from 1932 a Surgery, and at Broadcasting House
it had a cafeteria restaurant operating (not to the satisfaction
of every one) on a twenty-four-hour basis. A BBC Club had been
founded in the days of the Company, and in 1929 a Club
Ground and Pavilion were opened at Motspur Park. A Pro-
vident Fund had been started in 1925, and in 1931 a large-scale
Staff Pension Scheme was introduced.[3] A special feature of the
1931 Scheme was that after comparatively short service, staff
resigning voluntarily could receive the moneys contributed on
their behalf by the Corporation in addition to their own contributions. The intention was to provide for easy movement out
of the Corporation by 'creative staff' who might wish to occupy
themselves in broadcasting for a relatively short period.

Reith always realized that BBC staff were quite different
from those of a civil service department. They needed, in his
view, not absolute security but relative security. By 1935
monthly-paid staff whose service with the BBC was terminated

[1] *BBC evidence to the Ullswater Committee, 1935.
[2] *First Report of the Director-General to the Board of Governors, 13 Jan. 1927.
[3] A Benevolent Fund was introduced in Apr. 1934 by Trust Deed.

received one month's pay for every year's service less the number of months' notice, and weekly-paid staff one week's pay for every year's service. No payment was made, however, in cases of summary dismissal. This scheme was deliberately designed to enable the Corporation to get rid of people, especially on the programme side, who for one reason or another had not lived up to expectations, and, equally important, to enable such people to be free of the Corporation. In fact, the BBC lost very few staff of any kind, as the following table shows:

TERMINATION OF APPOINTMENTS

Year	Died	Resigned	Employment terminated
1927	2	25	6
1928	2	19	16
1929	3	38	24
1930	2	10	7
1931	3	6	6
1932	3	10	5
1933	3	9	9
1934	..	9	11

Source: BBC's evidence to the Ullswater Committee,
specially requested by Major Attlee.

The high figures for 1929 were accounted for by the starting of 'talkies', which attracted some of the Corporation's Engineering and Programme staff, and by the closing of relay stations and the policy of centralization under the Regional Scheme. Many of the people who left for the former reason subsequently tried to get back. Thereafter, the figures were smaller than for most organizations of comparable size. There was, indeed, relatively little staff discontent inside the BBC, as compared with other bodies, although the glare of publicity was focused upon it. Most of the many press 'stunts' on this subject do not usually stand up to historical scrutiny. Behind some of them, at least, was something more than the pressure of publicity: there was also the resentment of people who had left the BBC. The resentment often led to distortion. There were certainly few, if any, other concerns—definitely not the universities—which were as generous as the BBC in making *ex gratia* payments or in allowing employees to have 'Grace Terms' overseas, with assistance for both subsistence and travel.

The 'good employer' policy was an aspect of management which developed naturally and without strain both at Savoy Hill and Broadcasting House. In 1929 and 1930, however, under Mrs. Snowden's pressure and with encouragement from Horace Wilson, then Permanent Secretary of the Ministry of Labour, the Governors began to turn their attention to staff matters.[1] In February 1930 Mrs. Snowden suggested the formation of a Staff Association consisting of five councils, which could make representations direct to the Board of Governors, short-circuiting management altogether.[2] She, Clarendon, and Sir Gordon Nairne were appointed as a committee 'to report on the procedure which they recommend should be adopted to enable the staff to make direct representation to the Board on any matter concerning their work, conditions of service, status etc.'.[3] Reith queried both the policy and the accuracy of this minute, but the committee—with Nairne increasingly unhappy about his association with it—sought to find out how staff organization was conceived in the Bank of England, the Post Office, and the Admiralty. Eventually a plan for a Staff Association was produced by Lord Gainford. It had many similarities with a scheme in operation at Lloyds Bank.

Reith, proud of his personal approach, refused to believe that either Post Office or bank experience could help the BBC. He felt, indeed, that there was already far more genuine 'accessibility' and 'communication' in the BBC than in banks or the Post Office.[4] He asked the heads of all BBC Branches to express their opinion on the arguments for change. Carpendale, who for a time had served as a go-between when relations between Reith and two of the Governors had been so strained, felt that the proposed new scheme would do positive harm. It had its origins in 'misconception' and 'misrepresentation'. Goldsmith and Ashbridge both said that the 'morale' of their own staff was 'excellent' and that staff members were satisfied with the BBC's 'personal approach'. 'It has always

[1] *Board of Governors, Minutes, 12 Feb. 1930.
[2] *Clarendon to Reith, 14 Mar. 1930, enclosing Draft Scheme.
[3] *Minute of the Board of Governors, 12 Feb. 1930.
[4] *Note by Reith on the Proposed Staff Association, 14 May 1930.

been my own policy', Roger Eckersley wrote, 'to beg staff not to bottle up their grievances, but to be open and direct about them, and I always encourage a policy of direct access upwards.'[1]

Control Board collectively endorsed these opinions and expressed no interest in a Staff Association. 'In Head Office', it was stated, 'there are 173 in the Programme Branch and 105 in the Information Branch (together including 121 typists and clerks). This total is no aggregate mass which could be dealt with largely upon common lines. It is made up of men and women, a few of whom are administrative and business people. Others are musicians, dramatists, educationists, novelists, journalists, artists, and some who might have been *dilettanti* had they not found their *métier* in the BBC. The majority of these are individualists, and any form of representative council would be alien and repugnant to their whole outlook. These individuals require direct and personal approach and no other way —and this they have.' There were also 243 Head Office staff, labelled Administration, and 246 in Engineering. In neither case, it was claimed, were there any signs of wage earners 'being dissatisfied with their lot' or of salary earners seeking new kinds of machinery.[2]

When Whitley became Chairman of the Board of Governors, he examined the question of staff representation for himself and came to the expert conclusion that there was no immediate case for setting up a representative council. If Whitley himself did not want a Whitley Council in the BBC, this was clearly a complete rebuff to Mrs. Snowden's ideas of 1930. The matter did not come to the surface again until 1934, this time on a different plane, when there was a lively press campaign, led by Jonah Barrington, who had just left the BBC and was supported by Oliver Baldwin, who was then the BBC's Film Correspondent.[3] The campaign was part of a bigger press attack on the BBC, and it spilt over into Parliament, where BBC staffing policy provided one of several anti-BBC themes. It was on this occasion that Reith went across to the Commons and left both

[1] *Memoranda by Controller, Assistant Controller, Chief Engineer, and Director of Programmes, 28 May 1930.

[2] *Control Board, Statement on Proposed Staff Association, signed by C. D. Carpendale, V. H. Goldsmith, N. Ashbridge, R. H. Eckersley, W. E. G. Murray, and T. Lochhead, 27 May 1930.

[3] See also above, p. 474.

Conservative and Labour members convinced that there was no need for a public inquiry into the BBC's attitudes to staff questions.[1]

On this occasion also, about 800 members of the staff, organized by Miss L. Taylor of the Accounts Branch, signed a memorial expressing disgust at the press allegations which had been made against Reith and the Corporation and affirming their loyalty to the BBC. This was a very serious response. More light-heartedly, a writer in a magazine of the BBC Club, *The Heterodyne*, poked fun at the whole episode with verses which began:

> The Colonel and the Admiral
> Were in an awful state;
> They said it was disgraceful
> That the staff arrived so late.
> They ground their teeth and bit their nails,
> And rung their well-washed hands.
> 'Will nobody obey,' they said,
> 'Our very just commands?'
> 'Would thrashings do', the Colonel cried,
> 'Or even boiling lead?'
> 'I doubt it,' said the Admiral,
> And shook his heavy head.'[2]

Another lampoon in the same number took the form of a sketch in which Reith instructed Nicolls to administer the oath to a batch of new BBC staff—'Do you, newcomers to the BBC, most solemnly swear that you will serve the Corporation night and day—will read, remember and observe all rules, instructions, memoranda, and notices, that have been or shall be devised and issued; will every detail of your private lives reveal to us at all times—and, last, will do, say, think nothing that is not approved?'[3]

The form of these comments hardly suggests the existence of 'Prussianism' or of a 'Reithian dictatorship' inside the BBC. Some outside complaints continued, however, and were taken up (and found to be wildly exaggerated) by the Ullswater Committee. Yet with the growth of staff numbers there was a powerful case for more systematized procedures, and the committee

[1] See above, pp. 417–18. [2] *Heterodyne*, Apr. 1934.
[3] Ibid.

went on to make a number of important recommendations, which influenced future BBC policy. When Reith asked whether

35. One Image of the BBC (1931)

these staffing matters would be raised by the committee, he was told categorically by the secretary that 'both the issue of trade unionism and that of some form of independent internal staff organisation will inevitably arise in the deliberations of the Committee'.[1]

On the trade union issue, the BBC had never sought to prevent members of its staff from becoming members of trade unions, but it did not normally take part in collective bargaining procedures. On the issue of 'independent internal staff organisation', decisions were being taken before the committee met. Besides the questions of trade unionism and staff representation, there had also arisen once more the more fundamental question of recruitment and promotion, which Nicolls had raised in 1932.[2] Reith had always taken an active interest in appointments, as many of the successful applicants have recalled in their memoirs, and in the autumn of 1933 he came to the conclusion that an independent committee should be appointed to advise the Board of Governors about both recruitment and promotion procedures.[3] Professor Ernest Barker

---

[1] *H. G. G. Welch to Reith, 15 Oct. 1935.

[2] See above, p. 449.

[3] *Director-General's Meeting, Minutes, 9 Jan. 1934.

37. 'The Transit of Mercury' (22 June 1938)

36. Max Beerbohm Cartoon of Reith (1938)
'Here, dear Sibyl, is what I meant about Sir John Reith's appearance—his essentially poetic (and queerly *Pre-Raphaelite*) appearance. This I have caught, I think. But I seem to have missed the steely practical look that is there too.'

38. Reith locking the door after the last Programme at Savoy Hill (1932)

(a) As it might have been: An Artist's Drawing of 1928

(b) Near completion (1931)

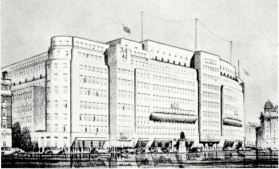

(c) As it might have been: An Artist's Drawing of 1938

39. Broadcasting House

40. Savoy Hill: Studio 9 (1928)

41. Eric Gill at work on *Prospero and Ariel* (1933)

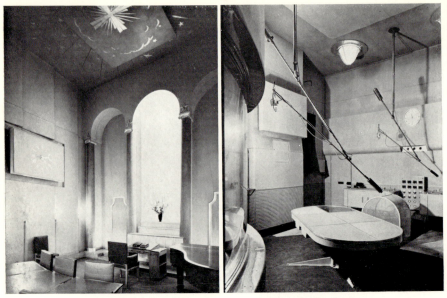

(a) Studio 3E   (b) Studio 6D

(c) Studio 3B

42. Broadcasting House: Interiors (1932)

and D. B. Mair, a retired Civil Service Commissioner, agreed to serve, and they produced their report in February 1934.

The BBC's 'collecting of candidates', Barker and Mair reported, had been well done and posts had been filled 'with a sole regard to the capacity and promise of the applicants'. There were five main sources of supply—independent application, recommendation by friends, recommendations by outside expert bodies like University Appointments Committees, public advertisement, and transfer of existing staff. The only changes Barker and Mair suggested were that the method of public advertisement should be used 'as widely as possible' and that a system of interviewing boards should be set up, with representatives present of 'the particular branch of the service concerned'. 'The BBC', they concluded, 'seems to us to stand half way between a great commercial concern and a public authority which manages an undertaking. It will therefore naturally combine some features of both—the elasticity of appointment of the commercial concern and the responsibility to the public which belongs to the public authority. It is on this basis that we have made our recommendations.'[1]

Barker and Mair also noted that there was 'a good proportion of women to men' on the staff. There was, in fact, a separate Women Staff Administrator, Miss G. M. Freeman, in the BBC, whose main concern was with the secretarial and clerical staff. Women, indeed, were employed at many different levels of the BBC, far more than in comparable organizations. No history of the BBC would be complete without reference to the key part they played in the daily running of the organization. Caroline Banks, first head of the General Office, was responsible between February 1923 and April 1931 for the selection, training, and promotion of all the women clerical staff and the conditions of their work. When she left the BBC—to return later as Mrs. Towler—Reith said of her that she was 'big enough to increase with increasing responsibility',[2] and this was surely the real test of personal contribution in a period of rapid growth. Miss Isa Benzie was a key figure in the development of overseas broadcasting. Mrs. Esmond was a genuine pioneer of

---

[1] *E. Barker and D. B. Mair, Report on the Recruitment of the Staff of the BBC, 8 Feb. 1934.

[2] *Heterodyne, Mar. 1931.

the early News Service, and Janet Adam Smith of *The Listener*, Florence Minns, Kathleen Lines, and Elise Sprott all moved over from secretarial work to posts of considerable responsibility; Miss Shields was succeeded as Reith's secretary by Miss Nash in 1928, and Miss Nash by Miss Stanley in 1936. These secretaries were at the very heart of the organization. Miss Edwin, Carpendale's secretary, was the BBC's first archivist, collecting invaluable notes of early problems and procedures; and Florence Milnes was responsible for one of the biggest and best executed tasks in the BBC's history, the creation of a Library, on which every one else, including the writer of this history, came to depend.

The later development of staff relations after the publication of the Ullswater Report belongs to a different period in the Corporation's history, a curious twilight period before war swamped the staff and brought in thousands of new recruits to the BBC's service. It was then that the real revolution occurred in the system of relationships which made the BBC such a distinctive institution. The beginnings of these changes are best considered, as they are below, in the light of the Ullswater Committee's survey.[1]

Before these changes, however, there was what seemed at the time to be an almost equally important revolution. It was associated with the move from Savoy Hill to Broadcasting House in 1932, which soon acquired a kind of symbolic significance. Before the move, all was 'intimacy and harmony'. After the move all was 'bureaucracy and conflict'. This extreme version of what happened indicates what a powerful hold buildings have on the imagination. Savoy Hill was cramped and congested, yet the very limitations of the building made for improvisation, a valuable ingredient in broadcasting, and for personal contacts and relationships which cut right across departmental dividing lines. Savoy Hill was associated also with pioneer experiences, the first of everything in broadcasting—except for the excitements of Writtle—and around such experiences the mists of nostalgia always gather. The memory of Savoy Hill was frequently more powerful than all the hopes of new endeavours.

[1] See below, pp. 513 ff.

Broadcasting House, by contrast, was thought by some to be a kind of status symbol, 'formal, cold and pretentious', representing in its architectural form the big organization on display. It is interesting to note how all the 'rebels' against the conventions of the BBC during the 1930s vent their wrath first against the building. 'A Leviathan of a building', R. S. Lambert calls it: 'not the dove or the eagle but the white elephant should be its crest.' 'Savoy Hill was suitable for the pioneering stage of the BBC, and maybe Broadcasting House is suitable for its bureaucratic stage.'[1] Maurice Gorham associated it with Reith crossing the entrance hall with a sense of triumph. 'When the lift doors closed behind him, a sort of sigh swept across the hall as everybody let his breath out and got to work again.'[2]

The language evokes far more than it should, in the case both of Savoy Hill and Broadcasting House. Hierarchy did not suddenly settle on the BBC in 1932: it was there, as Gorham himself points out, at Savoy Hill, expressed not only in titles, as we have seen, but in the trays and carpets.[3] It was, indeed, a necessary concomitant of growth, not a symptom of bureaucracy. Nor did Reith himself warm at once to the environment of Broadcasting House. He was as nostalgic as anyone about leaving Savoy Hill, for, after all, he had been there from the first, and he did not like the new Broadcasting House building any more than the 'rebels'. 'I was not happy about the new Broadcasting House', he has written since, 'but had not urged my own view against that of others. It was really too early to contemplate a comprehensive headquarters for British broadcasting, and I did not like the building.'[4]

'There was publicity,' he adds, 'much of it probably sarcastic, about the dedication *Deo Omnipotenti* from Philippians iv. 8 in the entrance hall. It was Rendall's composition; the inclusion of my name [in the inscription] was his doing. The sentiment was magnificent; I entirely approved of it; but was not sure if the BBC could live up to it.'[5] Indeed, he asked Marmaduke Tudsbery, who had been Civil Engineer of the BBC since 1926, whether his name could be eliminated.

---

[1] R. S. Lambert, *Ariel and All His Quality*, p. 150.
[2] M. Gorham, *Sound and Fury*, p. 42.
[3] Ibid., p. 30.
[4] *Into the Wind*, p. 159.
[5] Ibid.

Although the contrast between Savoy Hill and Broadcasting House so quickly became symbolic of two phases in the natural history of the BBC, there had been plans to move from Savoy Hill during the earliest months of the Corporation. Tudsbery was asked to search at once for a new site or building in London, and in the spring of 1927 directed attention to the freehold site of Foley House in Portland Place on which Broadcasting House now stands. At that time the BBC was not in a position to purchase so large a freehold, and the plan was abandoned. Tudsbery went on to examine a number of other sites—Dorchester House, an island site in Adelphi Terrace, the present site of Grosvenor House, the Grand Hotel in Trafalgar Square, 40,000 square feet in Exhibition Road and 31,000 square feet in Haymarket, and so on. He even looked carefully at the present site of Bush House, where the BBC was eventually to transfer first its European Service and later all its External Services, and took the site sufficiently seriously to have sketch development plans made. Eventually, however, he returned to Portland Place, and the site, which had been acquired by a financial syndicate, was leased in February 1928.[1]

A consideration of the list of rejected sites leads to the same kind of 'if only' historical speculation as the consideration of a list of rejected Director-Generals. A more useful historical comment is that the BBC was prepared to go ahead with the acquisition of the site in 1928 only on condition that parts of the future premises were let. The bottom floor of the building was to be used for a garage, for example, and for shops, and the entrance hall for a bank (see opposite page), while the first and second floors were not to be taken over at once, but to be reserved for later expansion.[2] G. Val Myer, the architect for the syndicate, and Tudsbery drew up preliminary plans, of which 'the guiding principle was to exploit to the utmost the peculiar advantages in shape and size of the site'. 'Offices and similar departments to which daylight is essential' were to be arranged around the whole of the exterior of the building. 'On the other hand, the studios and their suites, for which insulation from external noise

---

[1] *M. T. Tudsbery, 'The Search for a Site for Broadcasting House, London', 20 Feb. 1959. Foley House, built by the architect James Watt on the site of an older house, was demolished in 1928.

[2] *Joint Report by the Architect and Civil Engineer, 3 July 1928.

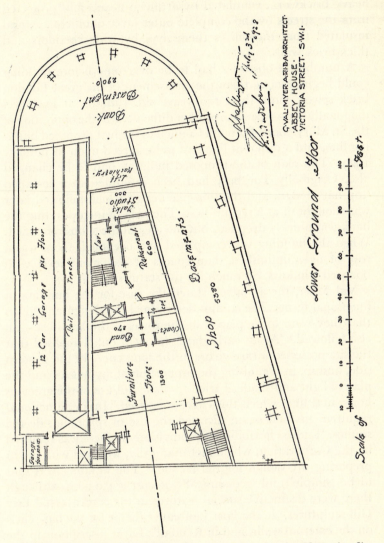

43. Sketch Plan of the Proposed New Premises at Broadcasting House (1928)

is the first need, have been grouped in a vast central tower of heavy brickwork, ventilated by artificial means and protected from the streets by the complete outer layer of offices . . . and insulated from the offices themselves by wide corridors and thick brick walls.'[1]

A number of obstacles had to be overcome before building could begin, among them the encasement of the great London brick sewer, more than 130 years old, running at low level diagonally across the site. Another difficulty was the opposition of the St. Marylebone Borough Council to the first proposed building line, and a different line had to be agreed upon in January 1929.[2] The plan of the proposed building had to be changed also. Originally Tudsbery had been interested in a so-called 'top hat' design, and the ship-like design which followed later was thought of as a second-best. The idea of incorporating the bank was quickly dropped, but the idea of the shops remained. When the building was completed and occupied, there was a row of ugly unfinished shop spaces at pavement level with boarded windows. So much for the status symbol.

Val Myer, the architect, stated the case for the building in functional terms. The studios determined the design and given that they were to be placed in the tower—'the key idea'—all else followed.[3] 'At an early date', he went on, 'I realised that the site possessed a rare virtue in the long curve of the western side, and so, in organising the proportion of my masses and the play of light and shade, I tried to make full use of the gracious horizontal lines which this curve suggested.' Inside, functional requirements had again dictated the use of space outside the studios. 'Endless flexibility of subdivision of offices was required by the Corporation, which fact, naturally, weighed with me in preparing my design for the façade.'[4] The building was said to be 'simple' and 'economical'—it cost £350,000—although there were distinctive special features in the controversial Eric Gill sculptures,[5] in the Poet Laureate's theme for the bas-reliefs on the external walls, and in Rendall's Latin inscription in the entrance hall.

[1] *Joint Report by the Architect and Civil Engineer, 3 July 1928.
[2] Minutes of a BBC Deputation to the L.C.C. Building Acts Committee, 14 Jan. 1929; *Report of the Civil Engineer to Reith, 23 Jan. 1929.
[3] See G. Val Myer, 'Notes on the Building' in *BBC Year Book* (1932), pp. 57–63.
[4] Ibid.   [5] See above, p. 422.

The first press announcement reflected the architect's conception very accurately and clearly. 'The design of the building will be simple, almost severe, depending for its effect more upon the grouping of masonry masses than upon profusion of detail.'[1] Professor Reilly, however, directed attention to the symbolic nature of the building. 'These great stone cliffs . . . rising, as it were, one behind the other from a base modulated by a range of larger windows, a band of wave ornament, and a central strongly marked balcony, but with no crowning cornice, give an aspiring look to the building well in keeping with its central function.'[2]

To the historian of taste, the original décor of the building is more interesting than its architecture or even the Latin appellation *Templum Hoc Artium et Musarum*. The décor caught a mood in the history of English taste and deserved, which it never could have been, to be preserved intact. The Gill sculptures themselves, particularly 'Ariel between Wisdom and Gaiety', were an expression of the mood, which was also very well displayed in such different parts of the building as the studio for religious services and the Director-General's suite. Pictures of the Concert Hall Green Room should have a place in any history of twentieth-century styles.

A Studio Decoration Committee was constituted at a Control Board meeting in November 1929,[3] and Raymond McGrath was chosen as special consultant. Several different decorators were employed but there was a remarkable unity about their work, possibly because of the pressure of the committee, more likely because of the presence of Dr. Rendall, 'the Representative of the Governors and the ultimate authority in matters of decoration at Broadcasting House'.[4] There is evidence, indeed, that the Decorating Committee, like all decorating committees, ran into difficulties. 'Several of the Programme Departments —Talks Department, for instance—were of the opinion that each Studio should be done by a separate Decorator to give it individuality. Mr. [Roger] Eckersley, on the other hand, did not favour this as he thought that continuity would be kept in the work by the employment of as few minds as possible.'[5]

[1] *BBC Press Release, 27 Nov. 1928. [2] *Broadcasting House* (1932), p. 12.
[3] *Control Board Minutes, 12 Nov. 1929.
[4] *Carpendale, 'Report on the Decoration of Broadcasting House', undated memorandum. [5] *Ibid.

The main comments of the staff on the new premises at Broadcasting House were concerned more with space than décor. For many people the move was a disappointment on these grounds. Some of the offices were long and narrow, many of the studios were far too small. The *Architectural Review*, which referred to 'the labyrinthine pokiness of the interior', was frequently quoted.[1] From the point of view of the Corporation, the most serious deficiency of the building was that it was too small from the start. Very shortly after the removal from Savoy Hill there was only one spare office left, on the third floor, and small offices had to be subdivided, as in Savoy Hill days, to ensure privacy. Expansion began almost at once both in nearby houses and further afield. St. George's Hall, as we have seen, was taken over in 1933 and the Maida Vale premises in 1934.[2] The BBC was never able before 1939 to have enough buildings to house either its staff or its activities.

There is a wonderful account in *Punch*—'a moving commentary by an actual Eye Witness'—of the BBC's 'march' from Savoy Hill across London to Broadcasting House. The procession, heralded by the Greenwich time signal, was accompanied by the strains of 'Land of Hope and Glory'. It included M. Stéphan, the well-known teacher of French, *sur un petit cheval*, and Father Ronald Knox on a white elephant. Gillie Potter was the Hogsnorton representative of Reuters, the Press Association, the Exchange Telegraph Company, and Central News, and Vernon Bartlett the representative of the League of Nations. 'A modest little display of Chamber Music' was accompanied by the Wireless Correspondents of 'the cheaper papers, bleating and wailing'. Also in the procession was an ordinary listener captured by Sir Walford Davies and feeding out of his hand, and Sir John Reith, last of all, except for the Epilogue. 'Actually,' *Punch* added regretfully, 'the BBC moved quietly, almost stealthily, by instalments and in plain vans.'[3]

When the staff was assembled in Broadcasting House, Reith did, in fact, deliver to them one of his most interesting addresses, which deserves to be quoted exactly as it was given.

---

[1] *Architectural Review*, Aug. 1932. See also the description in *The Architect* and a commemorative book, *Broadcasting House* (1932).

[2] See above, p. 175.   [3] *Punch*, 13 Jan. 1932.

You came in response to an order issued [he began], and you came as a staff. Would you try and listen to me as individuals, for I am going to try to talk to you for a very few moments as such; not as staff in the mass but as individuals? Now, in the front row there are the eighteen veteran survivors of the thirty-one who accompanied me into Savoy Hill on March 19th 1923. I felt I should like to have their moral support in the front row. . . . If there is anyone in this room who regrets leaving Savoy Hill, and who had a melancholy feeling on the last day there, I suppose it should be I, as I was the first to enter it, and actually it was I who found the place. But I have no regrets. I have an affection for the old place; it was the scene of great labour and some achievement on the part of those who worked there; but I do not regret the past, because regretting the past is a great mistake. I look forward, and nothing but forward.

He then went on to state his main purpose in gathering the staff together.

I suppose I have had three main functions since I joined the BBC: one is to resist attacks on the organization from without. They were considerable, and they are not altogether non-existent today. Another is to be on the look-out for ways and means of progress in our work. And the third is to ensure, if I can—and I mention it third accidentally,—it is of no less importance, to say the least of it, than the others—to ensure, if I can, the health and happiness of each one of you. With a big staff spread over several buildings I could not come in contact with a great many of you. It has been a perpetual distress to me, and some of you know me well enough to know that I don't say what I don't mean, to pass people in corridors and in the vicinity of our offices wondering whether or not they were members of our staff.

During the next few weeks, he said, he proposed to visit everyone in his office.

I will certainly know your names before I come in, and I shall know something about your work. Have you ever heard people say, or seen them write, that the BBC is a vast organization [he concluded], and a pretty efficient one at that, but that there is rather too much of the machine—not quite enough soul? Well, we certainly are a big organization, but I am going to substitute for that word another and a better one. I prefer to look upon this Corporation as an organism rather than an organization; an organization may have little of the human element; not so an organism.

We exist to provide programmes—that is why we were started and why we work, but no branch or department works to itself; no branch or department can do well without others, in fact the whole, benefiting; and no branch or department can do ill without affecting the whole. And an organism is a collection of individuals, and the health of one can affect, and mind you, does affect, the health of the whole.

This was the essence of Reith's attitude towards staff relations, and it should be treated not as the epilogue but as the prelude to any account of what happened in the 1930s. What Reith was anxious to secure above all else was a feeling of loyalty to the BBC. Given this, he felt that everything else would follow. He also wished personally to know who every one in the BBC was, just as every one knew him. Broadcasting House did not provide, however, the kind of milieu where these objectives were easy to realize. Nor with a very considerable annual intake of staff was it easy to take for granted a feeling of common participation in a single enterprise. Even had there been no questions concerning staff representation or trade union organization, as there were bound to be in the national social circumstances of the 1930s, it would have been difficult to have guaranteed the continuance of the staff relations which Reith most desired.

In any event, he was given one more demonstration of support for his views in November 1935 when the Ullswater Committee was finishing its work. The question of forming staff associations, which Reith felt he did not wish to force on the staff, however much pressure there was from outside, was put to a free vote by ballot: 9 per cent. were in favour of an association of some sort, 11 per cent. thought that association should be further considered, and 80 per cent. were opposed.[1]

3. Public Images

ONE aspect of the BBC's organization has been left out—the role of advisory committees. The staff was responsible for daily operations, the Governors for 'public trusteeship', and advisory

[1] *Into the Wind*, p. 230.

committees were expected to keep the BBC in touch with 're-presentative' 'specialist' opinion. It was through the work of the committees that a small but influential circle of people outside broadcasting were permitted an entry to Broadcasting House. Each separate committee had its own history, and some, like the Central Council for School Broadcasting, had a considerable measure of genuine autonomy.[1] The main committee, however, which to some extent knew of the activities of all the rest, was the General Advisory Council, which was not set up until 1934.

The oldest of the committees, the Central Religious Advisory Committee, had been formed in 1923,[2] and exercised a continuous influence over the BBC's policy. It was followed up by the Music Advisory Committee, which first met in 1925. 'Such committees are awfully difficult to handle', Reith wrote after its first meeting,[3] and Boult, after becoming Director of Music, was highly critical of its members for their complete lack of co-operation.[4] Many of the members of the committee were all too willing to pursue their sectional interests rather than to serve the interests of music, and they were usually far more cautious and protectionist in their outlook than the BBC's own Music Department.

A characteristic minute of 1936 reads, 'Sir Landon Ronald expressed apprehension of the unfavourable effect in many quarters of the decision to include two pianos of foreign makes in the Corporation's equipment. . . . Mr. Norman said that the . . . Music Advisory Committee had no responsibility for the Corporation's decision, which was reached by the Board after careful consideration of the report of the subcommittee of judges. After some discussion the Chairman read out the actual marks awarded by the judges to the various makes included in the tests.'[5] The Advisory Committee on Spoken English, which was formed in April 1926, also caused difficulties, which led Reith on more than one occasion to contemplate relying solely on the expert advice given him by Professor A. Lloyd James. It had a distinguished membership, however, and at least in its early days the BBC profited greatly from the association with it of men like Bridges, Shaw, and Kipling.

[1] See above, pp. 196–7.   [2] See above, p. 227.
[3] See *The Birth of Broadcasting*, p. 244.
[4] See above, p. 183.   [5] *Music Advisory Committee, Minutes, 12 Nov. 1936.

Only one minute-book of this most interesting committee survives, and the first meeting reported—in September 1934—had Shaw in the chair, with Professor Lascelles Abercrombie, Lord David Cecil, and Mr. Kenneth Clark as the first three people mentioned in the list of members present. This was an important meeting, since the committee had just been enlarged and reconstituted 'to include a larger body of authoritative opinion over a wider range of scholarship'.[1] Among the words which the committee solemnly discussed (with the aid of experts like Lloyd James, Daniel Jones, H. C. K. Wyld, and Harold Orton) were 'acoustic' (to be pronounced ăcówstic), 'aerated', 'decorous', 'disputant', 'garage', 'ordeal', and 'ukelele'. Logan Pearsall Smith signed the minutes.[2]

New standing orders for the committee were drafted in 1934, and Lloyd James made a statement about the history of the committee. It had decided from the start to direct its attention to a limited number of problems. 'At all meetings, the leading English and American dictionaries were consulted, every member being provided beforehand with the pronunciations in all these dictionaries.' Although the conclusions it reached had not always been put into effect, the committee had done much, Lloyd James claimed, to improve the standard of spoken English. 'Southern announcers cannot treat the r sound in the Northern manner, and very few English born speakers give to the unaccented vowels the flavour that Mr. Bridges recommended. But the BBC very definitely concerns itself with checking ultra-modern tendencies in the language, and in carrying out the injunctions of the Committee with regard to the so-called purity of English vowels.'[3]

Here was a BBC committee dealing with fascinating questions concerning the language which no other committee, public or private, was examining. It was a committee also which had the power, through the publication of *Broadcast English* pamphlets, the first of which appeared in 1928, and the system of training announcers, to put its decisions into effect, and thereby to influence popular habits. Lloyd James, its inspiration, was not only an erudite scholar but a man who believed passionately in

1 *Statement by the Chairman of Governors, 29 Jan. 1937.
2 *Advisory Committee on Spoken English, Minutes, 20 Sept. 1934.
3 *Statement on the History of the Advisory Committee, 20 Sept. 1934.

the power of broadcasting. Yet the problems which most directly concerned him did not always admit of easy answer, and is encouraging to note that a resolution was carried (again with it Shaw in the chair) in January 1937 that 'before a pronunciation could be recommended to the Corporation a two-thirds majority of the full Committee was necessary'.[1] 'Many scholars have had to confess', the Chairman of Governors remarked, 'that the spoken word is a matter of human behaviour in which few have had that scientific training that alone makes possible calm and dispassionate judgements.'[2] It would have been interesting to have had the comment of the author of *Pygmalion* on this.

We have one of Shaw's comments, however, on the work of the committee as a whole just after the enlargement and reconstitution in 1934. 'The new Committee so far is a ghastly failure. It should be reconstituted with an age limit of 30 and a few taxi-drivers on it. The young people WONT pronounce like the old dons, and Jones and James, who are in touch with the coming race, are distracted by the conflict. And then, are we to dictate to the mob or allow the mob to dictate to us? I give it up.'[3] He did not. One man who did was Dr. C. T. Onions, co-editor of the *Oxford English Dictionary*, who joined the committee with 'misgiving', made a solemn protest to Lloyd James in 1932 against 'insufficiently rigorous procedure', and wished to bow himself out 'silently without giving you any trouble'.[4] 'It is odd that in no other department than language—one's own language,' he added, 'would the distinguished amateur be tolerated.'[5] Bridges also had once expressed a doubt, before Onions joined. 'Our own Committee of Six was open to the objection that it had two Welshmen, one Irishman and one American. If Onions is taken on, they may say there are three Welshmen.'[6]

While the Advisory Committee on Spoken English was considering how to pronounce 'acoustic' and 'aerated', steps were

---

[1] *Advisory Committee on Spoken English, Minutes, 29 Jan. 1937.
[2] *Statement by the Chairman of Governors, 29 Jan. 1937.
[3] Quoted in *Into the Wind*, pp. 235–6.
[4] *C. T. Onions to A. Lloyd James, 3 Jan. 1932.
[5] *Onions to Lloyd James, 12 June 1932.
[6] *Robert Bridges to Lloyd James, 11 Dec. 1929.

being taken to constitute the General Advisory Council, a completely new institution. Ernest Barker, one of its first members, called its creation 'an act of statesmanship', very specifically relating its existence to the theory of the public corporation. 'The attachment of consultative bodies, representing both public opinion and expert knowledge, to departments of State and to great public concerns which have something of the character of a department of State, is a policy in which I profoundly believe.'[1]

At Mrs. Hamilton's suggestion, Reith invited William Temple, the Archbishop of York, who was already Chairman of the Central Council for Broadcast Adult Education, to become chairman of the new committee.[2] The intricate game then started of thinking of names and crossing off names of which other people had thought. It was decided from the start not to invite people on a 'constituency basis', but to expect that they should be 'broadly representative of most, if not all, of the main interests—corporate and individual—which Broadcasting serves or affects'.[3] The list of such interests drawn up by the Chairman of the Board of Governors reads like a list of interests represented in the chamber of a corporative state—'literature, philosophy, music, art, drama, science, medicine, economics, law, journalism, history, religion, international affairs, imperial affairs, politics, trade unionism, trade, industry, public services, social services, universities, teachers, and rural interests'. Norman also added touchingly at the foot of his list, 'No category—Lord Derby'.

Two of the most interesting points made about the first draft list of highly distinguished people were first, in Dawnay's words, that it had 'too many of the elderly and venerable as opposed to the younger and more active',[4] and second, in Temple's view, that a representative of 'the extreme left' should be included 'because it would tend to allay the bitterness of feeling always characteristic of the Left Wing'.[5] The Board of Governors would not permit the inclusion of Harold Laski, however, or of Lord

[1] *Memorandum by Ernest Barker, 'The General Advisory Council', 3 Apr. 1936.
[2] *Mrs. Hamilton to Reith, 28 Apr. 1934.
[3] *Note by R. C. Norman, 19 Apr. 1934.
[4] *Dawnay to Reith, 29 June 1934.
[5] *Temple to Reith, 9 July 1934.

Lloyd on the extreme right.[1] Nor did they include J. B. Priestley, who had been suggested by Siepmann 'partly to get something more rugged into the personnel of the Council and partly to escape from the rather academic quality of the members'.[2]

The General Advisory Council held its first meeting on 20 February 1935. Reith, who had proposed the new Council with high hopes of what it might do, was immediately doubtful about its 'utility'.[3] The Council met on two further occasions in 1935. It submitted its own evidence to the Ullswater Committee,[4] and in the years down to the outbreak of the war considered, however sketchily, most of the major issues relating to broadcasting policy. Temple was chairman only for the first year, being succeeded by Lord Macmillan.

The BBC's view of the Council, in so far as there was one single view, was that it had a twofold purpose—'to secure the constructive criticism of representative men and women' and to create a kind of pressure group or rather an opinion group, the members of which would 'use their influence in helping towards a fuller understanding of the BBC's problems and policy'. There was no intention of making the Council a really active agency. It was expected to be 'detached' and 'non-expert', and in 1937 it was decided that it should concentrate on 'at least one question of wide general debate' at its meetings. Care was taken to de-limit the scope of its work in relation not only to that of the Board of Governors but that of 'the network of specialist advisory committees, which are tending to develop in response to disclosed needs'.[5]

The General Advisory Council was rather too much like the House of Lords even for some of its members, and Ernest Barker at least would have preferred it to have been more like the Consultative Committee of the Board of Education. He wanted a smaller body, with a maximum size of twenty, in touch with 'the general body of consumers' and with fewer 'distinguished members'.[6] His views received some support—Carpendale pointing out, for instance, that the 'undue weight' of the Council

[1] *Reith to Temple, 19 July 1934. For Laski's comments on Reith, see *Into the Wind*, p. 143.   [2] *Siepmann to Reith, 2 July 1934.
[3] Reith, Diary, 20 Feb. 1935.   [4] See below, pp. 486–7.
[5] *Memorandum on the Future of the General Advisory Council, Spring 1937.
[6] *E. Barker, Memorandum on the General Advisory Council, 3 Apr. 1936.

arose to some extent because it was the successor to the old Central Council for Adult Education. In general, however, internal opinion inside the BBC held that the Council should be above all else 'ambassadorial', and it was Sir Stephen Tallents, the new Controller of Public Relations, who summed up the feeling best by writing unctuously of the Council guaranteeing that questions of broad policy could be examined by 'some of the best and most experienced minds in the country, and in a detachment from the emergencies and compromises of the day-to-day conduct of a broadcasting service'.[1]

When Tallents wrote these words, he and the BBC were already being drawn, although Tallents did not know it, into a most complex tangle of public relations. The 'public image' of the BBC was to be upset more, indeed, by a curious sequence of private events than it was ever enhanced by the 'ambassadorial' influence of the General Advisory Council.

R. S. Lambert, the editor of *The Listener*, decided in February 1936 to demand an unqualified apology from Sir Cecil Levita, an eminent public figure in London politics, for statements he had made about Lambert's credulity. The difference between Lambert and Levita had its origins in disputes within the Film Institute, of which Lambert was a Governor, but the BBC was involved from the start in that Lambert argued that Levita's statements about him, which were made at a lunch with Gladstone Murray, tended to show that he was unfit to hold his post in the BBC. The words to which Lambert took exception included the phrase 'belief in the occult, notably the talking mongoose', and it was the Isle of Man mongoose, 'answering to the name of Gef', which gave the popular name to the case when Lambert's charges reached the Courts—and the press—in November 1936.[2]

The mongoose soon became less important than allegations concerning the BBC's attitude towards Lambert after his decision to take legal action. Sir Stephen Tallents had warned Lambert that if he proceeded with his case he would be doing two dangerous things—first, making the Corporation doubt his

---

[1] *Notes on Professor Barker's Memorandum, Apr. 1936.

[2] The story of the mongoose is described in the book by R. S. Lambert and Harry Price, *The Haunting of Cashen's Gap* (1936).

judgement, and second, 'placing his own interests in priority to those of the Corporation'. The Chairman of Governors, R. C. Norman, who was a political colleague of Levita, also told Lambert much the same. Reith was in the background. The issues were delicate, and he was irritated that Lambert had not approached him first.

The BBC background came out in the press during the case and undoubtedly did the BBC harm. Lambert, who was awarded heavy damages—£7,500—had appeared as a solitary individual fighting for his reputation and his rights not only against Levita but against the BBC, the Big Corporation. There had often been talk of the BBC interfering with the private lives of its employees: now it was said to have interfered with the civil freedom of one of them.

In an attempt to redress the damage done to it by the revelations of the Lambert–Levita case, the BBC asked the Prime Minister on 9 November for an official inquiry into the role of the BBC from the time that Lambert had first expressed his grievance. A week later the inquiry began before Sir Josiah Stamp, Sir Maurice Gwyer, and Sir Findlater Stewart, and after a number of witnesses had been examined—Lambert came last—the Board of Enquiry produced a report which was far more favourable to the BBC than Lambert had expected. It exonerated the BBC from some of the most serious allegations of undue exertion of pressure, but admitted that warnings given to Lambert had been neither well couched nor based on a full realization of the merits of Lambert's case. It also criticized strongly the tone and language of a memorandum Lambert had sent to Reith. Finally, it urged the BBC to re-examine its staffing arrangements. 'A tradition and a technique in dealing with staff matters has to be established in the controlling authorities: on the staff side a code to determine how far individual freedom of opinion and action are consistent with the paramount responsibilities of the Governing Body must be built up and accepted *ex animo* by the staff.'[1]

The timing of the Lambert–Levita case was almost as significant as its content. It followed hot on the inquiry of the Ullswater Committee, which was something in the nature of

[1] Cmd. 5336 (1936), *Report of the Special Board of Enquiry.*

a grand inquest on the BBC, and it could not have been calculated to do more harm in the public eye. The BBC had won many plaudits during the 1930s, often from the most unlikely quarters, but there was also a current of criticism running through the period, not so much criticism of the BBC's monopoly as of its internal power structure. Against Reith's picture of the twentieth-century public corporation, well adapted to the needs of the age, Raymond Postgate, for example, set the picture of a revived Chartered Company, 'encouraged and authorised to seek the extension of its power . . . with the knowledge that if its immoderation in so doing led to serious trouble, the state would rescue it'. 'Although the BBC may equally plausibly be regarded as an experiment in a wholly new form of social organisation', he went on, 'or as a revival of an old, there is at least reason to inquire whether the diseases of the old Chartered Companies are not developing again in the new body.'[1]

The charges were put in milder form in a special broadcasting number of the *Political Quarterly* in the autumn of 1935 which has to be placed alongside the laudatory Special Broadcasting Number of *The Times* of August 1934. 'The BBC', Reith had written in *The Times*, 'is the focus of many incoming and outgoing rays, and if (wilfully or even unwittingly) it changes position the optical scheme may be greatly modified thereby.'[2] The writers in the *Political Quarterly* represented several incoming and outgoing rays. W. A. Robson, who called the BBC 'an invention in the sphere of social science no less remarkable than the invention of radio transmission in the sphere of natural science', praised its successes and defended its constitution, but criticized its Board of Governors as being too old and respectable, its staffing policy as being too personal, its regional policy as being too centralizing, and its 'controversial' programmes as being too cautious. 'The BBC is almost overburdened with a sense of responsibility. One sometimes has the impression that because it is not answerable to one particular body it feels itself to be answerable to everyone for all its actions.'[3] Ivor Thomas, however, in the same number, tried to see the BBC in inter-

[1] R. Postgate, *What to Do With the BBC* (1935), pp. 10, 11–12.
[2] J. C. W. Reith, 'Evolution of Broadcasting: A Social Need Supplied' in *The Times*, Broadcasting Number, 14 Aug. 1934.
[3] W. A. Robson, 'The BBC as an Institution' in the *Political Quarterly*, Oct.–Dec. 1935.

national perspective and praised it with few reservations. 'The most important question which can be asked about any broadcasting organisation is: What is the ideal it sets before itself?' Thomas had no doubt: 'The BBC has faced this question courageously, and it has achieved a greater degree of success than any foreign broadcasting institution.'[1]

Internationally, indeed, as the international scene darkened, the BBC was standing more and more on its own. In Germany Dr. Goebbels had already fashioned radio into an effective instrument of propaganda. Each of the thirty-eight party regions (*Gaue*) had a *Gaufunkwart* or regional radio officer and under them were *Kreisfunkwarte* in each of the thousand districts into which Nazi Germany was divided. It was their business to see that when *Gemeinschaftsempfang*, community listening, was ordered, every factory, public square, and school was fitted with receivers. The People's Wireless Set was designed to receive German stations satisfactorily and to receive nothing else. Between 1935 and 1939 several other countries followed, less systematically, the same line of development. The defenders of the Alcazar in Toledo during the Spanish Civil War were prevented by jamming from receiving messages saying that relief was on the way: Queipo de Llano made his reputation as a 'broadcasting general'. 'The voices of the national stentors are now so loud that the ordinary listener to international broadcasting now feels his pleasure spoiled by competing political broadcasts', wrote a foreign critic of radio in 1938.[2]

Few people understood the full implications of what was happening in Europe until it was too late, and a far more serious objection to BBC policy than that advanced at the time was that the BBC itself was slow in informing people of the danger. 'The policy pursued was evasive', Mrs. Hamilton wrote later; 'we ought to have given a positive direction—we did not. . . . What the BBC did do was faithfully to reflect a quite general outlook.'[3] Viewed in this light, the Talking Mongoose was as much a creature of escape as the Loch Ness Monster, and talk about the 'Prussianism' of the BBC was an excuse for not understanding what was happening in Prussia.

[1] Ivor Thomas, 'Systems of Broadcasting', ibid.
[2] C. Saerchinger, 'Radio as a Political Instrument' in *Foreign Affairs*, Jan. 1938.
[3] M. A. Hamilton, *Remembering My Good Friends* (1944), p. 287.

What the BBC did do—and it was to do much in the international sphere—is the subject of a later chapter. In the meantime, while Postgate was attacking the BBC as a 'Chartered Company', while the *Political Quarterly* was praising and blaming it, and while Tallents was resolutely defending it in *John Bull*,[1] the Ullswater Committee was sitting and subjecting the BBC to its third official scrutiny. It was this Committee which was to lay down the conditions under which the BBC was to operate in the next long stage of its history until Beveridge took up the charge again after the Second World War.

4. The Ullswater Committee

THE Charter of the BBC was due to expire on 31 December 1936. As early as December 1933 Reith touched on the subject at a meeting with Kingsley Wood. This was long-term strategy. The Postmaster-General told Reith that a public committee would have to be appointed, and Reith replied that he presumed that 'certain changes' would have to be discussed beforehand.[2] Reith had in mind financial changes and a greater measure of 'liberty'.

In fact, it was not with Kingsley Wood personally that Reith tried to reach an early agreement but with the new Director-General of the Post Office, Sir Donald Banks, who replaced Sir Evelyn Murray in February 1934, and Sir Warren Fisher, the active and extremely influential Secretary to the Treasury. Fisher was an outstanding civil servant, and one of his Treasury colleagues told Reith that 'he would have considerable influence in the matter'.[3] Banks was friendly and co-operative. 'With him at the Post Office,' Reith wrote, 'things will go much more simply with respect to our future constitution.'[4]

There were many meetings between the three men to discuss what Reith called 'our best tactics for getting our new Charter and Licence'. Despite Kingsley Wood's remark in December

[1] Sir S. Tallents, 'The BBC's Sins—the Answer' in *John Bull*, 14 Dec. 1935.
[2] Reith, Diary, 12 Dec. 1933.   [3] Ibid., 21 Dec. 1933.
[4] Ibid., 19 Jan. 1934.

1933, Reith still hoped for some time that the matter might be settled by a small committee of the Cabinet which would then take its recommendations direct to the Cabinet and on to the House of Commons, and by February 1934 he had produced draft proposals which, if acceptable, would have eliminated all public discussion.[1] He quickly came to the conclusion, however, that there were some 'public issues' which could best be aired in a public committee. He wanted it to consist of about five members, 'of such a sort as we would be quite happy with and sure of'.[2] One of the most important of the 'public issues' was the question of the future of the Wireless Exchanges. For the Exchanges, as for the BBC, the key date was 31 December 1936, when their own Licence from the Post Office was due to expire.[3]

Reith, Banks, and Warren Fisher were able to agree on the kind of terms which would appear in a new BBC Licence and Charter, but Kingsley Wood had his own ideas on how to proceed. He knew about the meetings which had been held between Reith and the two senior civil servants, and he obviously did not intend to leave Reith free to determine national broadcasting policy after discussing matters with them. For political reasons also he was anxious that there should be as few changes as possible in the existing arrangements. When he saw the draft agreement which had been prepared by Reith, Banks, and Fisher, therefore, he was by no means as co-operative as Reith wished. A meeting at the Post Office on 25 June 1934 was described by Reith as 'most unsatisfactory'. 'I have never seen such political expediency as the Postmaster-General showed at this meeting', he wrote in his diary. 'I said it was quite unnecessary to appoint a Committee if there were to be so few changes in the present documents. There is no courage or determination.'[4] The first time Reith had met Kingsley Wood he had formed similar impressions. There was, indeed, a sharp clash of temperament, involving complete incompatibility of outlook. It was not simply that the Postmaster-General was seeking to impose his authority over the Director-General of the BBC. 'He talked a lot about giving the public what it wants and said that no member of the Board really knew what the public wants.'[5]

---

[1] Ibid., 26 Jan. 1934.   [2] Ibid., 2 Mar. 1934.
[3] Ibid., 16 May 1934. For the position of the Wireless Exchanges, see above pp. 356–60.   [4] Reith, Diary, 25 June 1934.   [5] Ibid., 5 Apr. 1932.

One of the points that Reith wanted and had included in the 'Analysis of Proposals' paper, drafted with the help of Banks and Fisher, was the transfer of constitutional control over the BBC from the Postmaster-General to the Lord President of the Council. This idea, in particular, did not appeal to Kingsley Wood. Nor was it made an easier idea to canvass by the notorious unwillingness of the then Lord President of the Council, Stanley Baldwin, to add to his responsibilities. There is little doubt also that Kingsley Wood disliked the active participation of a representative of the Treasury in the drafting of the proposals, even though BBC difficulties so often began not in the Post Office but in the Treasury. Reith had made sure before starting his conversations with Warren Fisher that he had the approval of the Prime Minister, MacDonald, and they had talked frankly of the need to improve liaison between the BBC and the wide range of government departments with whom it was concerned.[1] There is no evidence that the Prime Minister's approval automatically carried with it the wholehearted approval of Kingsley Wood.

It was clear after the meeting of June 1934 that there would be a public committee to look into the future of broadcasting, yet it was not until Easter 1935 that the membership of the committee was publicly announced. The months between were spent—intermittently—in a discussion about possible membership, but when the final names were announced, there were some names added which had not been discussed either with Reith or, more surprisingly, with Banks.[2] Reith thought that Lord McKenna would be a good chairman:[3] it soon became obvious, however, that he was not a *persona grata* with the government. Reith's suggestion that Ernest Barker should be a member of the committee was also very quickly turned down, probably on the grounds that he was 'too much of a Liberal'.[4] Eventually the chairmanship was offered to Lord Ullswater, an ex-Speaker of the House of Commons, who was then seventy-nine years of age. Kingsley Wood felt that he had the right kind of 'judicial or quasi-judicial status'.[5]

---

[1] Reith, Diary, 2 Feb. 1934. MacDonald quite agreed with Reith's view 'that we could have a much better liaison without any prejudice to our autonomy'. See also *Into the Wind*, pp. 182–3.   [2] Ibid., p. 219.

[3] *Reith to Banks, 9 July 1934.   [4] *Reith to Warren Fisher, 14 Aug. 1934.

[5] *Reith to Warren Fisher, 26 Nov. 1934.

The members, whose names were decided upon in 1934, included Sir William McClintock, an expert on finance whose claims had been pushed by Warren Fisher, and Lady Reading. Before the end of the year McClintock had already gone through all the existing papers on BBC finance, past, present, and future. Within six weeks he had gone back to Reith and said that he was 'immensely impressed with the financial statements, with the methods of financial control, and with the financial state itself'. Reith was naturally happy about this. 'The credit for this lay with Lochhead, the Chief Accountant. It was comforting to reflect that in this respect at least—a most important one —the Committee's findings were likely to be satisfactory.'[1]

Reith was anxious that no names of members of the committee should be announced until just before the committee got down to work. 'It would be a pity to have an interval ... giving an opportunity for lobbying etc.'[2] The politicians taking part in the committee's work were not approached, indeed, until 1935. They represented all three parties, thereby following the precedent set by the Crawford Committee in 1925. The Conservative member was J. J. Astor, who had been a member of the original Sykes Committee of 1923. Before Reith had addressed the 1922 Committee, Astor had pointedly gone up to him to shake him by the hand.[3] The two Liberal members were Clement Davies, then a National Liberal but, more important in this context, a Welshman, and H. Graham White. Labour was represented by Attlee, and the committee was completed with Lord Elton, an Oxford don and National Labour peer, and Lord Selsdon, the former Postmaster-General who was better known inside the BBC under his original name, Sir William Mitchell-Thomson.[4]

Selsdon was approached at the last minute, as was Clement Davies. Reith was very angry indeed about the choice of Selsdon, who had just produced his Report on Television,[5] nor did he have sympathy with the view that the committee should be representative enough to cover Welsh interests as such. (After

[1] *Into the Wind*, p. 215.   [2] *Reith to Banks, 3 Jan. 1935.
[3] *Into the Wind*, pp. 185–6. For the meeting with the 1922 Committee, see above, p. 418.
[4] For the difficult relationship between the BBC and Mitchell-Thomson, see *The Birth of Broadcasting*, pp. 353 ff.
[5] See below, pp. 591 ff.

all, there was no representative for Scotland.) More seriously, he was concerned at the over-weighting, as he saw it, of Post Office experience. After he had learned of the final composition of the committee while he was on holiday, he wrote frankly to Banks that he thought 'for a matter of this sort there is far too much of the Post Office about it—appointed by the P.M.G., two Postmaster-Generals [Selsdon and Attlee] and one Assistant Postmaster-General [Graham White]'. Selsdon was particularly unwelcome for the part that he had played in 1926 and 1927. 'Everything that bothers us in the Charter and Licence he is responsible for.'[1]

Given the composition of the Ullswater Committee and the way its membership was announced, Reith rightly felt that it would be impossible to maintain the close personal relations he had enjoyed with Banks while they had been discussing future tactics with Warren Fisher. 'I think you will see the difficulty', he wrote candidly to Banks. 'If relations are entirely official, or, to be more definite, if we have to regard the Post Office as being against us, then we know what to do, and, however regrettable, it is straightforward. But it is different if we imagine them to be friendly, act accordingly, and then discover that, whether for "political" considerations or for any other reason, we have been led up the garden and all our plans frustrated.'[2] Private talks duly ceased. Indeed, Kingsley Wood telephoned Warren Fisher to say that he would prefer that no mention be made to the members of the committee of the meetings or agreements between Reith and the two civil servants in 1934.[3] Nor was the BBC to have access to committee papers.[4]

Relations between the BBC and the Post Office became distinctly cool during the early weeks of the committee's life. 'He will sacrifice the interests of this great public service to his own miserable political ends', Reith wrote after he had had another interview with Kingsley Wood on 30 April.[5] Unfortunately, we

[1] *Reith to Banks, 26 Apr. 1935. Reith also sent a frank statement of what had happened in 1926 to Warren Fisher on 15 May 1935. 'It shows', he said, 'pretty clearly that Selsdon put our present Charter and Licence across us in 1926.'
[2] *Reith to Banks, 26 Apr. 1935.
[3] *Into the Wind*, p. 220.
[4] *Banks to Reith, 2 May 1935. Reith, nonetheless, got them. Note of June 1963.
[5] Reith, Diary, 30 Apr. 1935; *Reith to Banks, 30 Apr. 1935. 'This meeting', Reith told Banks, 'was different from previous ones. . . . There was this afternoon, on both sides, as unfriendly a feeling as there could be.'

do not have Kingsley Wood's comments on Reith, but we know that at this time the Post Office did not propose to include a BBC representative on an inter-departmental committee to advise with respect to the control and use of broadcasting in time of war. For its part, the BBC had little respect for Ullswater. 'He is over eighty', Reith wrote, 'and I think it is extraordinary that they should appoint a man of this age to be Chairman of the Committee. He seemed quite friendly, but the whole affair is quite outside his comprehension, I am afraid.'[1]

The terms of reference of the committee were 'to consider the constitution, control, and finance of the broadcasting service in this country and advise generally on the conditions under which the service, including broadcasting to the Empire, television broadcasting, and the system of wireless exchanges, should be conducted after 31 December 1936'.[2] Reith was consulted about the terms, and had the word 'constitution' substituted for the word 'management'. The terms, like the membership, were settled at the last moment, while Reith was on holiday, and it was by telegram that he learned that the word 'constitution' had been substituted.[3]

Reith was anxious, above all, to draw a distinction between the task of the new committee and the task of the Crawford Committee in 1925. 'The situation was very different then,' he told Banks, 'as there were doubts about the old Company and radical change was assumed. The present Committee is presumably more to recommend respecting the future than to investigate the past . . . [and] there is little doubt, if any, that the present system will be maintained.'[4] There was little doubt, as Banks confirmed. 'So far as I could judge Ullswater's disposition,' he told Reith before the committee met, 'he was not in the least inclined to turn the world upside down—and "the shorter the better" seemed to be his attitude to the Committee.'[5]

After its appointment had been announced in the House of Commons on 17 April 1935, the committee quickly got down to work. It decided to hold its sittings in private and not to

[1] Reith, Diary, 28 Mar. 1935.
[2] Cmd. 5091 (1936), *Report of the Broadcasting Committee*, § 1.
[3] *Telegram from Banks to Reith, 15 Apr. 1935.
[4] *Reply by Reith, 15 Apr. 1935.
[5] *Banks to Reith, 17 Apr. 1935.

publish its evidence.[1] This severely circumscribes the work of the historian even today. The committee agreed, however, to issue a press statement on 1 May, notifying individuals and organizations that evidence or representatives would be welcome, and much of this evidence inevitably made its way not only to St. Martin's-le-Grand but to Broadcasting House. In all, seventy-nine witnesses gave oral evidence, almost four times the number giving evidence before the Crawford Committee. The witnesses included directly interested parties, such as the Relay Services Association of Great Britain and the International Broadcasting Company; representatives of powerful outside interests, such as the Newspaper Proprietors' Association and the Empire Press Union; and spokesmen of other government departments, including the Foreign Office and the Board of Education.[2] 'Opinion Groups' were not very actively involved for, as Banks had told Reith, there was little doubt that the basic principles behind the organization of British broadcasting would remain unchanged.

The BBC was formally asked to give its own evidence early in May 1935[3], and it duly submitted a brief but comprehensive memorandum setting out its views.[4] 'It has purposely been made as brief as possible', Reith told Welch, 'on the assumption that this would be to the liking of the Committee.'[5] The memorandum stated firmly in its introduction that while the BBC was 'a monopoly with an assured income, independent of ordinary commercial obligations', it always endeavoured to keep in close touch with public opinion. As far as its programme policy was concerned, it had been shaped from the outset 'by the conviction that listeners would come to appreciate that which at first might appear uninteresting or even alarming'. The Corporation had, in fact, 'aimed at providing a service somewhat ahead of what the public would demand were it possible for such demand to be made articulate and intelligible'. As far as engineering policy was concerned, 'national coverage' had been the objec-

---

[1] *Reith to Banks, 30 Apr. 1935, stating the position as H. G. G. Welch, the Post Office secretary of the Committee, had described it to him.

[2] Cmd. 5091 (1935), Appendix A.

[3] *Welch to Lord Bridgeman, 3 May 1935.

[4] *'Memorandum of Evidence submitted to the Broadcasting Committee by the BBC', May 1935.

[5] *Reith to Welch, 3 May 1935.

tive, 'first with one programme and then with alternative programmes'.

On the finance of the service, a lucid statement was drawn up, which set out the main headlines of income and expenditure (Table I). Capital expenditures, it was shown, had been met

TABLE I

BBC Income and Expenditure, 1927–34

	Income		Expenditure		Accumulated surplus or deficiency at 31 December
	Licences	Publications, &c.	Revenue, excluding depreciation	Capital	
	£	£	£	£	£
1927	801,000	100,000	747,000	14,000	140,000
1928	872,000	130,000	847,000	69,000	226,000
1929	944,000	153,000	918,000	151,000	254,000
1930	1,043,000	181,000	989,000	97,000	392,000
1931	1,179,000	246,000	1,128,000	933,000	−244,000*
1932	1,306,000	323,000	1,288,000	279,000	−182,000*
1933	1,460,000	392,000	1,455,000	273,000	−58,000*
1934	1,710,000	349,000	1,656,000	260,000	85,000
TOTAL	9,315,000	1,874,000	9,028,000	2,076,000	85,000

* The deficiencies in the years 1931, 1932, and 1933 were met by short-term borrowing.

from income. This had been wise policy in a period when income from licences was still expanding, but the Corporation would soon cease to have any surpluses available for capital purposes. Nor could it easily borrow 'without carrying a liability not represented by corresponding assets'. Attention was directed, therefore, to the basic question of the share of the Post Office and the Treasury in gross revenue from wireless licences, and figures relating to the respective shares were set out as in Table II. The moral was clear. If the BBC was to develop Empire work and television, both of which were treated briefly but adequately in the memorandum, then far greater financial provision was absolutely necessary. Five specific points were made. First, the Postmaster-General should undertake not to alter the licence fee without the agreement of the Corporation. Second, the retention by the Post Office of a fixed percentage of the total revenue from licences was undesirable: it was manifestly absurd to think of it as payment for the service of collection. Third, the whole income from licences, subject to allowing for the real cost of collection, should be received by the Corporation. Fourth, exemption from income tax should be granted, since the BBC was not by its constitution allowed to make profits. Fifth, borrowing powers should be increased to £2 million.

TABLE II

Gross Licence Income, 1927–34, and Effective Allocation Thereof

Year ending 31 December	Approximate gross licence income	Allotted to post office for service of collection	Post Office and Treasury share				BBC net effective share after allowing for income tax
			Treasury				
			Normal share including increases	Special subsidies	Income tax	Total	
	£	£	£	£	£	£	£
1927	1,192,000	12½% 149,000	242,000	..	20,000	411,000	781,000
1928	1,307,000	12½% 163,000	272,000	..	20,000	455,000	852,000
1929	1,470,000	12½% 184,000	342,000	..	60,000	586,000	884,000
1930	1,696,000	12½% 212,000	441,000	..	50,000	703,000	993,000
1931 {	714,000	12½% 89,000 }	714,000	25,000	74,000	1,046,000	1,105,000
	1,437,000	10% 144,000 }					
1932	2,614,000	10% 261,000	910,000	137,000	110,000	1,418,000	1,196,000
1933	2,968,000	10% 297,000	986,000	225,000	121,000	1,629,000	1,339,000
1934	3,369,000	10% 337,000	1,135,000	187,000	113,000	1,772,000	1,597,000
	16,767,000	1,836,000	5,042,000	574,000	568,000	8,020,000	8,747,000

Little was said in the memorandum about constitutional questions as such. It was submitted simply that the 'relationship between the State and the Corporation, evolved as a result of practical experience, is satisfactory . . . [and] that no change should be made either in the direction of reducing or of extending the measure of autonomy now enjoyed by the Corporation'. Two important issues were raised, however, as they had been in the talks between Fisher, Banks, and Reith. First, the Lord President of the Council should assume ministerial responsibility, in place of the Postmaster-General, for all matters pertaining to direction and policy arising under the Charter. Second, if only to make this transfer possible, a clear differentiation should be made between the respective functions of the Charter and the Licence. The Charter should deal with direction and policy; the Licence should deal with matters which the Postmaster-General had to control and should continue to control by virtue of his powers under the Wireless Telegraphy Acts —such matters as the regulation of wireless wavelengths and traffic and the collection of licence revenue.

The memorandum suggested that the main reason for seeking to transfer authority over 'cultural and general matters' from the Postmaster-General to the Lord President of the Council was that it would ensure Cabinet 'control' at the highest level. It hinted that this would be the best way of perpetuating the pattern of broadcasting along the lines which had been followed since 1927. 'The Lord President's control should be so expressed as to ensure that the Corporation gives an adequate and satisfactory service, and (e.g.) [a disarming e.g.] to prevent its whole character being changed to the sponsored system of the United States.'

The only other section of special interest related to Wireless Exchanges.

These exchanges are numerous abroad [the memorandum stated], and are increasing in this country. In December 1934, there were about 318 of them, with 192,707 subscribers. In their comparatively unregulated state the proprietors are in a position materially to damage the Corporation's programme policy by taking a large proportion of programme material from foreign sources (as in fact they do) and so upsetting the balance upon which the Corporation's programmes are constructed. They may, for instance, omit talks of one political colour from a series which has been carefully balanced. [This was probably one of the least likely of contingencies and was not the BBC's main ground of alarm about the Exchanges.][1] The Corporation seeks some measure of control over the programmes by Wireless Exchanges and urges that the existing rights held, and restrictions imposed, by the Post Office, should be maintained and enforced.

This short statement of BBC policy, even when backed by a brief supplementary memorandum,[2] did not suffice, but it provided a most useful background to Reith's oral evidence to the committee. It also provides, along with memoranda

---

[1] See above, p. 359.
[2] *'Supplementary Memorandum', submitted to the Broadcasting Committee. This Memorandum dealt mainly with the proposed constitutional changes.

submitted later, a most useful survey for the historian of the BBC's attitudes in 1935, a kind of summary of much of the material which has been set out in detail in previous chapters.

Reith himself, accompanied by Bridgeman and Norman, gave oral evidence for the first time on 8 May. 'I was examined for over two hours and got on quite well, supplying a vast amount of information apparently out of my head and being treated in quite a friendly way until . . . Selsdon got on to our proposed changes in the constitution.'[1] All Reith's irritation at his appointment bubbled to the surface, but he was sure that Selsdon's hostile questioning irritated the members of the committee as much as or even more than it irritated him. There were two further interviews during the following week, which 'tremendously pleased Norman, who thought they went very well'.[2] At these meetings it was agreed that Regional Directors and chief officials from Broadcasting House should also give evidence. Reith had no objections to this, although he believed that Selsdon expected 'to find some criticism of me within the organisation'.[3] Reith also urged the General Advisory Council of the BBC to give separate evidence, and a sub-committee was appointed to draft a report. It included Lloyd George, Citrine, and Beveridge.

The report provided powerful backing for Reith's view that ministerial responsibility should be transferred to the Lord President of the Council. 'We are convinced that the independence of the Corporation must be fully respected, and we emphasise the importance of avoiding the assumption—not uncommonly made on the Continent and in this country—that the Corporation is an organ or agency of the Government.' The BBC should be allowed to extend facilities for political discussion—particularly at a time when 'political speeches are hardly reported at all in the popular press. It should be a senior minister who dealt with whatever criticisms were made in the House of Commons, not the Postmaster-General. . . . On problems connected with universities, higher education and research generally, the Lord President is now acknowledged as the guid-

---

[1] Reith, Diary, 8 May 1935; *Into the Wind*, p. 227.

[2] Reith, Diary, 15 and 16 May 1935. At these meetings it was decided that the Committee should see the draft Charter and Licence which Reith had discussed with Banks and Fisher. See *Reith to Fisher, 10 May 1935.

[3] *Into the Wind*, p. 227.

ing authority of the State. By analogy, as well as owing to the prospective relations of the Corporation with British communities overseas, it would seem fitting that the Lord President should announce the opinions of the Cabinet, and be the minister to whom the Corporation can turn for counsel.'[1]

On Wireless Exchanges also the report backed Reith vigorously. 'No commercial organisation should be allowed to destroy the unity of programmes, and to introduce elements which have hitherto and with public approval been deliberately excluded. . . . We therefore feel strongly that in future no Exchange should be allowed to transmit programmes inconsistent with the general policy and principles followed in the programmes of the Corporation [no reference was made here to what should happen in the BBC's silent hours] and that to this end the Corporation should be given control over the programme activities of all Wireless Exchange systems in the United Kingdom. At the same time, we suggest that the technical work of the Exchanges be undertaken by the Post Office.'[2]

Among the signatories to this report were William Temple, as chairman of the General Advisory Council, Beveridge, Margaret Bondfield, Citrine, Lloyd George, Lord Macmillan, Lord Rutherford, Arthur Salter, George Bernard Shaw, Sybil Thorndike, and Lord Tweedsmuir.[3] It is not easy to dismiss this list as a cross-section of the 'Establishment' of the 1930s.

The BBC officials who gave evidence to the committee did not provide it with the kind of ammunition that Reith believed Selsdon wanted. Three Regional Directors were interviewed—Edgar, Liveing, and Dinwiddie. Edgar was pointedly asked by Selsdon whether he would prefer no notes to be taken of his evidence, but he and the other two Directors vigorously defended the regional system as it operated at the time.[4] Dr. Adrian Boult also was asked questions about the case for greater decentralization both functionally and geographically. 'Some of us', Ullswater told him, 'feel that there should be a great deal more de-centralisation than there is. . . . We have rather been snubbed about that and damped down and told that the thing is not

[1] *Report from the General Advisory Council, June 1935.   [2] Ibid.
[3] Reith had hoped that Lord Tweedsmuir (John Buchan) might be a member of the Ullswater Committee, but MacDonald said 'he would never do'. Reith adds, 'I expected this'. (*Reith to Fisher, 14 Aug. 1934.)
[4] Reith, Diary, 14 and 20 June 1935.

possible, and so on, but we cannot help thinking that it is possible.'

Boult stood up boldly to this leading question and defended current BBC policy. He had pointed out in his written evidence that Regional Directors and their Music Directors had always enjoyed complete freedom to choose the musical programmes they wished and that they had been under instructions to co-operate as much as possible with musical enterprises within their regions. The 'big disparity' in the amount of music—other than dance music—broadcast from each region was 'in itself a proof' that these matters were 'left to the discretion of the local Directors who decide just what music within their regional boundaries is fit for broadcasting and what is not'. Midland Region, he told Ullswater, originated 41 per cent. of its musical programmes, no other region more than 28 per cent. (Northern Ireland reached that proportion), and West Region originated as little as 22 per cent. 'If these matters were directed from an office in London, remote and ill-informed of local conditions,' Boult said, 'there would almost certainly be a much greater degree of uniformity.'[1]

Boult was able to point out that much of the evidence in favour of decentralization came from musicians' organizations. 'The agitation for Regional autonomy obviously has at the back of it the belief that this means a cessation, or at any rate a substantial reduction, in simultaneous broadcasting, which in turn would mean the broadcasting of more performances by second and third-rate societies, and more work for the music profession generally.' Leaving on one side the probability that 'autonomous' regional broadcasting would rely on 'net-working' devices, Boult unashamedly said that if more work were really to be provided, 'the Corporation's programme standards would go down'. The argument amounted, therefore, to 'a suggestion that the Corporation should no longer run its service in the best interests of the public but that these interests should be subservient to the somewhat narrow interests of the music profession itself'.

It was the music profession, particularly the Incorporated Society of Musicians, which emerged as one of the fiercest

[1] *Oral examination of Dr. Boult; written evidence submitted to the Ullswater Committee.

critics of the BBC in 1935. There was irony in this in that the BBC prided itself above almost all else on the contribution it had made to the diffusion and enjoyment of music.[1] It was the charges made by the Incorporated Society of Musicians in what Reith called 'a monstrous document'[2] which made the Ullswater Committee feel that they would like to see Boult. 'He so flabbergasted them by saying at once that other witnesses had been telling lies,' Reith wrote later, 'that they let it go at that.'[3]

They did not quite let 'regionalism' go as easily as that, and rightly so, for there were important and controversial issues here which needed to be sorted out. One of the most interesting statistical tables submitted by the BBC gave details of programme staffing arrangements in London and the provinces to show that the regions were not under-staffed.[4]

REGIONS

	Midland	North	Northern Ireland	Scottish	West	Welsh	Total	London
Music	4	3	3	3	$1\frac{1}{2}$	$1\frac{1}{2}$	16	19
Drama and Features	2	2	2	2	2	2	12	9
Variety	1	1	1	$\frac{1}{2}$	1	1	$5\frac{1}{2}$	13
Talks	1	1	$\frac{1}{2}$	1	1	1	$5\frac{1}{2}$	9
Outside Broadcasts	1	1	1	1	1	1	6	4
Children's Hour	1	1	1	1	$\frac{1}{2}$	$\frac{1}{2}$	5	3
Announcers	2	2	2	2	$1\frac{1}{2}$	$1\frac{1}{2}$	11	8
Studio Assistants	2	2	2	2	2	2	12	13
Totals	14	13	$12\frac{1}{2}$	$12\frac{1}{2}$	$10\frac{1}{2}$	$10\frac{1}{2}$	73	78

Figures by themselves are silent, and the most frank account of the historical record of the BBC's centralization policy and

---

[1] See above, pp. 171 ff.

[2] Reith, Diary, 20 June 1935. 'I saw Walford Davies in the afternoon', Reith added, 'and he rang up the Secretary [of the I.S.M.] to get a copy of it, but Eames refused to give it to him. He sent a wire to the President who signed it, but he had got no reply by Saturday. This shows what a dirty game they are playing if they are not prepared to let an ex-President of the Society see it.'

[3] *Into the Wind*, p. 229.

[4] *Note on the Staffing of the Regions, 24 June 1935.

the reactions against it was given by Reith himself.[1] In a memorandum which he used in giving oral evidence, he stressed three points—that central control and supervision were quite essential as part of 'a nation-wide responsibility'; that the Corporation had 'taken full cognisance of the desirability of developing Regional activities' and had 'conferred as great a degree of independence as is possible or desirable upon its Regional Directors with a view to this being done'; and that 'the process of Regional devolution has in fact proceeded, and is proceeding, as quickly and as comprehensively as is compatible with efficiency in the broadest sense of the term'.[2] He admitted that there had been far more centralization 'in the early days' than there was in 1935, for many reasons, not least the need to establish 'a settled policy and the beginnings of a tradition of public service'. Within the previous year, however, regional programme staffs had been practically doubled and 'the quality of personnel' considerably improved. A new post of Director of Regional Relations had been appointed 'to develop the policy of independence between the Regions and London'. (Siepmann did not give evidence.) 'The *de facto* independence of the Regions' was proceeding, indeed, at a rate which could not be accelerated 'without injury to the interests not only of the country as a whole, but of listeners in any of the Regions'.

It was a frank and forceful memorandum, although it said little about the cultural aspects of the question, and admitted that it was difficult 'to define precisely the criterion of Regional activity'. A more precise definition would have been helpful. Regional Directors, Reith stated, had to be satisfied that local material possessed local justification, that it was of a kind which could not be produced elsewhere—there were difficulties in interpreting this—and that it should conform to the principle of contrasting alternative programmes on which the Regional Scheme was based. 'Contrast' by itself, however, was the most inadequate of criteria by 1935, nor, as we have seen, was it always adequately achieved.[3]

Boult's and Reith's rebuttal of the evidence given by the Incorporated Society of Musicians—it led into areas far

[1] For the problems associated with the policy, see above, pp. 314 ff.
[2] *J. C. W. Reith, undated Note on Regional Policy.
[3] See above, pp. 51 ff.

removed from music—was part of a pattern of rebuttal which characterized the inquiry. As statements of other people's evidence reached Broadcasting House, 'many of them', Reith thought, 'devoid of foundation or sense', a 'document of rejoinder' was prepared.[1] When the Publishers' Association, for example, submitted a memorandum, the BBC protested that it had made a false assumption about future BBC publications policy.[2] Finally two sizeable printed memoranda, the first of thirty-three pages and the second of ten pages, dealt with almost all the evidence in turn, hostile, friendly, or neutral.[3]

The statements are interesting and cover many points. In reply to the National Federation of Music Societies it was stated that 'the Corporation has no desire to monopolise concert-giving, and recognises that the concert-giving societies of the country have been and ought to remain, the backbone of musical culture. The Corporation has therefore avoided unfair competition and has co-operated whenever and so far as programme and financial limitations will allow.' Sir Thomas Beecham, who had given evidence complaining that the Corporation's public concerts damaged the enterprise of London music societies, was said to have presented 'many grave inaccuracies in his evidence'. The Royal Philharmonic Society, by his own admission, had not suffered, and if experience from the whole country was taken into account, the number of music festivals had increased from 150 in 1923 to 220 in 1934 and within the previous twelve months twenty new Chamber Music Societies had been formed. There was no foundation for Beecham's assertion that the BBC Symphony Orchestra had made a 'very serious inroad into the volume of work hitherto done by other orchestras, as the Corporation is most particular to prevent the acceptance by members of its orchestras of outside engagements which might otherwise accrue to other orchestras or to individual musicians'.

The evidence from music societies, unions, and musicians did nothing *in toto* to damage the BBC before the Ullswater

---

[1] *Into the Wind*, p. 228.
[2] *Rejoinder to Memorandum by the Publishers' Association of Great Britain and Ireland.
[3] *Rejoinder to Written and Verbal Evidence of Various Parties; Further Rejoinder to Written and Verbal Evidence of Various Parties.

Committee, and it does nothing *in toto* to move the historian nearly thirty years later. Behind much of the evidence, which at its best was evidence not against the BBC but against broadcasting, was a tacit assumption that all had been well with British music before the advent of the BBC—a parody of the truth—and that there was a certain lump of musical activity which had to be fairly shared out between a number of existing interests. The BBC was an interloper, and what it did was to disturb the shares. Some of the proposals made by the BBC's critics would have done great damage to music—the protectionist argument, for instance, that all those engaged on the 'administration side of music' should be completely 'divorced from all active performance of the art'. This was almost as wild a protectionist remark as the assertion that Children's Hour broadcasts had destroyed the sale of children's books.[1]

Other remarks about music were plain nonsense—the remark, for instance, that it was impossible as a result of the intervention of the BBC to run in one year more than one-third or one-fourth of the opera which had been possible previously. How could this statement be reconciled with the fact that there was an eight-weeks' season at Covent Garden, a six-months' season at Sadler's Wells, a five-weeks' season at Glyndebourne, and various miscellaneous operatic enterprises? If opera was still inadequately provided in 1935, it was not because of anything that the BBC had done but because of more fundamental causes far beyond the BBC's control.

Reith's reaction to such remarks was that it would be 'salutary' if the critics were given a taste of the American system of broadcasting. Indeed, they did not need to look so far. 'An examination of the International Broadcasting Company's programmes will show whether or not the competition which the Corporation has to face from sponsored programmes broadcast in English is likely to raise the standard.'[2] The I.B.C. itself gave evidence in 1935 which forced the BBC to state firmly that 'to concede the claim for a wave-length dedicated to advertising would be to upset the broadcasting system as now constituted'. This was one of the few direct references to arguments that were to swell in the post-war period. Another reference was made in

[1] *Rejoinder to Memorandum by the Publishers' Association.*
[2] Ibid., p. 18; *Into the Wind*, p. 228. For the work of I.B.C., see above, pp. 352-3.

reply to a suggestion of Philco Ltd. that there should be limited hours of sponsored programmes on the American model and that American programme practice and presentation should be employed in the peak programmes.

Sponsoring, Philco suggested, was to be limited to 'radio manufacturers of standing', and it was on this point rather than on the bigger point of principle that the BBC chose to object.[1] It still did not completely rule out sponsoring, although it contended that 'the suggestion that in the compilation of sponsored programmes the final word should rest with the sponsors is surely absurd'.[2] Another block of evidence came from various press and publishing interests, which at this stage were bitterly opposed to 'commercialism' in broadcasting.[3] They were still anxious, however, to set limits to the BBC's own activities, as they had done since the early days of the Company. The BBC reiterated its earlier policy of seeking the co-operation of press interests, while at the same time safeguarding the developing interests of its own listeners. 'The Corporation is ready to co-operate with the Empire Press Union as hitherto', it declared, 'and has no desire to prejudice the activities of the overseas press. At the same time the Corporation does not wish to have its news bulletins stripped of all human interest. It is denied that the broadcasting of news bulletins damages the press . . . and the suggestion that news bulletins should not contain last minute news is unacceptable.' On publications, the BBC strongly objected to a suggestion of the Periodical Trades Press that the BBC should confine itself entirely to the 'spoken word'. 'Broadcasting created new demands and its publications are an integral part of the broadcasting service. It is suggested by the Corporation that private enterprise cannot meet this want in so consistent, reliable and disinterested a fashion as the national organisation, which has special knowledge and which in its programme planning takes account of the complementary part that the publications play.'

[1] *The Managing Director of Philco wrote to Reith on 12 June 1935 enclosing a copy of the Philco written evidence. 'You will recall that some two years ago I wrote to you in the same strain', he told Reith, 'but I am sure that you will appreciate that the suggestions we have made are solely dictated by what we consider to be best for the community at large.'

[2] *Rejoinder to Written and Verbal Evidence of Various Parties, p. 28.

[3] See above, p. 359.

On what was probably the most contentious of all the issues in 1935, that of the future of the Wireless Exchanges, there was a sharp confrontation of views. After the failure to reach agreement both with the Wireless Exchange companies and the Post Office on this question,[1] much time was spent on seeking to formulate an intelligent policy not for the present but for the future. At the back of the policy was invincible suspicion. 'Each exchange may increase to the stature of a BBC in miniature, and furthermore the possibility must be visualised of several enlarged exchanges being merged under a single financial control. Concerns with sufficient capital would be in a position to buy time on the several continental stations which will sell it, and produce their own programmes abroad on the existing American system.'[2]

The Post Office seemed less concerned about the growth of relay listening than the BBC, and there were times when Post Office officials suggested that the Corporation was making 'a great bother about a little matter'.[3] In October 1933, however, Jardine Brown produced a paper once again suggesting joint control of the Wireless Exchanges by the Post Office and the BBC. 'The Post Office has a new Public Relations Department under Sir Stephen Tallents', Jardine Brown added, 'which might be readily adapted to look after Wireless Exchanges.'[4] Ashbridge thought that the BBC might take over all existing Exchanges of appreciable size 'only if the Post Office were prepared to carry out the work of installing and maintaining the wiring and possibly the collection of the weekly subscriptions'.[5] He set out powerful arguments against the BBC being drawn into the venture, but added on the other side that 'we may have to face the fact that the Post Office may gradually relax their regulations in order to satisfy various political influences. Again, various municipal bodies may get control of exchanges and endeavour to obtain the right to broadcast local politics direct to exchange listeners.' This had seemed to be the issue at stake in 1933 when the Middlesbrough Corporation introduced a bill which, *inter alia*, empowered the Corporation to run a relay exchange. The relevant clauses were defeated on a free vote in

[1] See above, p. 359.   [2] *BBC Year Book* (1933), p. 72.
[3] *Notes on an interview between L. Simon and R. B. Solomon.
[4] *Memorandum on Wireless Exchanges, 10 Oct. 1933.
[5] *N. Ashbridge, 'Wireless Exchanges', 8 Nov. 1933.

the House of Commons by 144 votes to 48. The Labour Party
opposed the deletion, but it was perhaps more significant that
Kingsley Wood gave no lead to Conservatives.[1]

A. M. Lyons, a Conservative back-bencher who moved the
deletion of the clauses, argued that the Relay Exchange system
would lead to 'unbalanced programmes',[2] and Lord Mount
Temple, moving deletion in the Lords, spelt this out more fully.
'The Wireless Exchange may, and probably will, completely
upset [BBC] balance. Either the exchange may broadcast an
excessive amount of entertainment, to the detriment of the
entertainment industry, or it may broadcast an excessive
amount of one-sided controversial matter. The capitalist companies may select only items which express their economic views,
and the Socialist municipalities those items which further col-
lectivism.'[3] It is not certain how much views of this kind determined the ultimate vote. More stress was laid by most speakers
on unfair competition with private enterprise. All similar Corporation Bills failed, and interestingly enough their opponents
included the existing privately owned Relay Exchanges.[4]

BBC policy in 1935, when the Ullswater Committee was considering the question, continued to rest on the case for regulation
in the interests of public service. Wireless Exchanges were
admitted to have 'public value', yet their owners had power,
'by substituting transmissions from abroad in place of items of
the Corporation's programmes, to alter entirely the general
spirit of the BBC's programme policy. They can, for instance,
select the lighter items from British programmes and replace
talks and other informative matter with light relays from
abroad, thereby reducing programmes to the level of entertainment interest only. The BBC has always regarded entertainment
as an important part of its work, but it has declined to devote
its programmes entirely to amusement. This policy has been
upheld by public opinion, and has already resulted in an
acknowledged improvement in public taste.'[5]

The existing system, the BBC suggested, was unstable. Small
Exchanges might be linked together. There might even be

---

[1] See *Broadcasting, A Study in Monopoly*, p. 82.
[2] *Hansard*, vol. 280, cols. 98–99.   [3] Ibid., vol. 87, col. 188.
[4] *Broadcasting, A Study in Monopoly*, pp. 82–83.
[5] *Wireless Exchanges, Amplifying Memorandum supplied at the request of the
Broadcasting Committee.

unified financial control. 'A Press magnate, or other person with large finances, may obtain control of the whole system, artificially popularise it by relaying as far as possible amusement programmes only, and then use it to mould public opinion to his own way of thinking by a discriminating selection of programme items.' He might claim that he was acting in the cause of freedom, although the freedom in which he was interested was not freedom for the individual but freedom for the relay management. Even if such dangers were not to materialize, there was always the possibility of collusion between advertisers and Exchange owners. 'Exchange managements can contend that what they give is what their subscribers want; but the matter may actually be determined by what the managements receive as a consideration.'

Successful regulation of the system depended, the BBC argued, on tightening Post Office limitations and vesting control of programmes in the BBC. In other words, the BBC was seeking the same arrangement which Jardine Brown had advocated in 1933 —close co-operation between BBC and Post Office. There was one sop. 'The Corporation would be willing, within practical limits, to allow Exchanges to be connected direct by wire to the appropriate BBC Control Room (at the expense of the Exchanges), which would give subscribers an interference-free service.'

The Relay Services Association, which had been registered in April 1934 and claimed to represent 90 per cent. of Wireless Exchange proprietors, stated a diametrically opposed point of view. It claimed that the relay system was much more efficient and economical than the scattering of individually owned wireless sets, and that the Postmaster-General should give it greater freedom to develop in private hands. The threat of compulsory purchase should be withdrawn, and the service should be recognized as 'a natural concomitant of the operations of the BBC'. The BBC should supply it with programme details well in advance, and there should be direct land-lines between BBC stations and Exchanges. Perfect reception of BBC programmes would wean subscribers away from foreign programmes, but there should be continued freedom to transmit foreign programmes and, indeed, to originate local programmes relating to local affairs. The Postmaster-General already had power to veto absolutely the relaying of any particular programme, and the owners of Exchanges were prohibited by their Post Office licence from receiving any money or other consideration from any person for the distribution to the subscribers of any programme or message received by the station. In other words, there was adequate ultimate control.

The BBC queried a great many of the statements issued by the Relay Services Association and prepared a detailed 'rebuttal' of some of the points. In addition to this work of submitting criticism and counter-evidence, care was taken, particularly by Reith, to secure positive support of BBC policy from outside bodies, including government departments. It was at his suggestion, for example, that the Board of Education gave evidence. 'I went to the Board of Education at twelve and was there for one-hour-and-a-half', Reith wrote in his diary on 18 June. He saw there the President of the Board and the Chief Inspector and 'stimulated them' into appearing.[1] A few days earlier he had spent two and a half hours at Transport House talking to the T.U.C. about its evidence.[2]

Reith always considered that work of this kind was a basic task for the Director-General. The best case, as he saw it, still needed the most careful handling. Public relations could not be left to chance. Soon after the committee had begun its meetings he lunched with Mrs. Hamilton and Attlee, who told him that no damage was being done to the BBC by 'the procession of more or less hostile and axe-grinding witnesses'.[3] He talked to McClintock at an interesting and enjoyable party given by Lord Beaverbrook.[4] With Welch he had a running correspondence, making it clear from the outset that 'a little encouragement would do both us and the cause a lot of good': 'about the most we ever get in newspapers is something rather patronising to the effect that on the whole the BBC has discharged its responsibility with commendable vision and efficiency.' 'As I said, one gets rather bored at times.'[5] Such exchanges continued, and towards the end of the year, when the Report was completed, he had a long and informal chat with Lady Reading.[6]

[1] Reith, Diary, 18 June 1935.   [2] Ibid., 7 June 1935.
[3] Ibid., 19 June 1935.   [4] Ibid., 4 July 1935.
[5] *Reith to Welch, 24 June 1935.   [6] Reith, Diary, 6 Dec. 1935.

He also gave evidence once more in the middle of July before the summer adjournment. Selsdon tried to move him on the Lord President issue. 'It was the voice of Kingsley Wood as well as of Mitchell-Thomson', Reith believed.[1] By the end of the year he was suspecting Selsdon even more. 'He is against our having Wireless Exchanges and is playing a dirty game about Luxembourg and advertising generally.'[2] Other rumours from the committee were that Attlee was insisting on the publication of BBC accounts in full—this goaded Reith into sending him a note about the importance of freedom in the management of public corporations[3]—and that both Attlee and other members were worried about staffing arrangements. There were press rumours about Reith also. The one that annoyed him most was a *Daily Mail* report that he had asked the Ullswater Committee to combine his post with that of Chairman. 'Not only untrue,' he commented, 'but I completely disapprove of this combination.'[4]

Waiting for a committee report requires patience. By the end of August 1935 Reith heard that the Report was circulating in draft.[5] It was not until December, however, one day before Christmas, that he received a copy of the Report a few months before it appeared. 'It gives us all we want', he wrote, 'but it is a wretched document with several silly and annoying things in it; also the summary is deplorably misleading.'[6] Within a few months, this initial reaction had taken far more precise form.

A great debt of gratitude, the 53-page Report began, was owed to the wisdom which founded the BBC 'in its present form' and 'to the prudence and idealism which have characterized its operations and enabled it to overcome the many difficulties which surround a novel and rapidly expanding public service'. The constitution of the BBC had been taken as a model in other countries and there was no reason for changing it in any of its significant clauses. 'Our recommendations are directed towards the further strengthening and securing of the position which the broadcasting service of Great Britain has happily attained in the few years of its history.'[7]

---

[1] *Into the Wind*, p. 229.
[2] Reith, Diary, 6 Dec. 1935.
[3] Ibid., 17 July 1935; *Into the Wind*, p. 229.
[4] Reith, Diary, 10 Sept. 1935.
[5] Ibid., 23 Aug. 1935.
[6] Ibid., 24 Dec. 1935.
[7] Cmd. 5091 (1936), *Report of the Broadcasting Committee*, § 7, 'General Approval'.

This was a good start, although Reith was not mentioned personally, as Mrs. Hamilton was to tell him, at any point in the Report.[1] The Charter, the Report went on, should be extended for ten years. Governors, as Reith had always argued, should not be specialists or representatives of particular interests or localities. Some of them, however, might be younger, particularly when 'new scientific developments' were constantly occurring and 'changes of opinion and practice' were so rapid that 'each successive generation is brought up in a different world of experience'.[2] This sounds more like the comment of old men regretting their youth than of young men seeking power. There might be seven Governors instead of five, the Report continued, but they should not interfere too closely with the work of the BBC's own officials. They had a joint responsibility, 'not divided for purposes of departmental supervision', and they were to 'leave the execution of . . . policy and the general administration of the service in all its branches to the executive officers'.[3]

Within the Corporation, there was scope for continuing regional devolution. Instead of criticizing under this heading, the committee chose to welcome trends which were already apparent within the BBC. 'The position of the Regional Directors in relation to Broadcasting House has just been strengthened by the appointment of a Director of Regional Relations. We approve the gradual enlargement of their responsibilities, subject to the maintenance of a consistent policy for the service as a whole and to ultimate control by the Corporation itself and a very small group of its highest officers whose duties are of national scope.'[4] The extreme case for 'regionalism' was rejected. 'Listeners are by no means exclusively interested in their own districts.' This and other factors affected 'the proportion of Regional programme time' which could with advantage be devoted to material of local origin.[5]

On staffing questions, which had been of particular interest to Attlee, the committee accepted the verdict of the Barker/Mair Report that there was a fair field and no favour in recruitment. Posts had been filled with sole regard to the capacity and promise of the candidates. Major staff appointments should,

[1] Reith, Diary, 6 Jan. 1936.   [2] *Report of the Broadcasting Committee*, § 12.
[3] Ibid., § 16.   [4] Ibid., § 21.   [5] Ibid., § 23.

however, be advertised in the future, and appointments made on the recommendations of a specially constituted Selection Board. Facilities should also be granted for a representative organization of the staff if they should wish it. 'As the BBC is one of a number of new and recently created forms of public institution standing between Government Departments on the one hand and commercial undertakings on the other, its practice may have some influence in each of these directions and be looked upon as a pattern for future institutions.'[1]

The BBC's suggestions about constitutional changes were approved in general terms, although with far less precision than the BBC had stated the case in its own memoranda. Managerial independence in the conduct of daily business was taken for granted, and it was accepted that overall responsibility for 'the cultural side of broadcasting' should be transferred from the Postmaster-General to 'a senior member of the Government . . . free from heavy Departmental responsibilities'. The Lord President of the Council was not, however, mentioned by name. 'We refrain from specifying any individual office and we think that it should rest with the Prime Minister to select a suitable Minister for the purpose.'[2]

As for finance, after the Post Office had covered costs, 75 per cent. of the remaining revenue from wireless licences should go to the BBC for purposes other than television, and the balance should be available if it was required. Only if all broadcasting expenses had been covered, should any surplus go to the State. These proposals followed very closely an additional memorandum on finance which had been submitted to the committee by the BBC. Capital expenditure, the committee went on, should be paid for out of revenue, as in the past, but borrowing powers should be increased to £1 million. On the question of the form in which the Corporation presented its annual accounts, the committee upheld the reticence of the BBC in face of much adverse criticism. 'We accept the view that publication of details (whether of payments to individual artists or of staff salaries or of any other category of expenditure) would tend to impair independence of day-to-day management and would serve no useful purpose unless Parliament wished to withdraw that independence from the Board of Governors and to establish instead

---

[1] *Report of the Broadcasting Committee*, § 30.   [2] Ibid., § 53.

a system of direct control as in the case of a Government Department.'[1] After all, the Corporation's accounts, despite all the adverse criticism, were open to investigation at any time by the responsible Minister. They had also been kept in 'complete form and good order', and all that was needed in addition in the future was a slight breaking down of sub-headings and sub-totals.

A long section on programmes followed before brief separate sections on Empire broadcasting, television, and Wireless Exchanges. 'Having regard to the immense number of listeners, the infinite variety of taste, and the many types of programme which are being broadcast at all times', the balance of programmes was right. More freedom should be permitted in relation to the broadcasting of news, and although it was necessary, as in the past, for the Corporation to refrain from broadcasting its own opinions by way of editorial comment on current affairs, it was 'vital' that there should be a 'strong and impartial editorial staff'. Television had to be free from restrictions as to hours, and it is possible that at some future date news bulletins would be wanted 'at times when they are not now given'. Above all, 'controversial topics should continue to be discussed'. 'If broadcasting is to present a reflection of its time, it must include matters which are in dispute. If it is to hold public interest, it must express living thought. If it is to educate public opinion, it must look upon the questions of the hour from many angles.'[2]

Further points were made about political broadcasts, music, and schools broadcasting, but there was nothing about talks, drama, variety, or light entertainment. The numerous critics of the BBC's music policy were given no encouragement. 'We support the policy of a full development of studio performances by the BBC orchestras', the committee affirmed, 'and their judicious use in public concerts not necessarily confined to London, together with the relaying of the best performances of outside organisations in any important class of music.'[3] Broadcasting could serve 'as one of the strongest forces aiding the active cultivation of music generally'. Schools broadcasting had proved its value, and the councils concerned with it 'should be given independent status, with power to determine the school educational programme to be broadcast and the ancillary

[1] Ibid., § 75.   [2] Ibid., § 85.   [3] Ibid., § 96.

leaflets and pamphlets to be issued'.[1] Receiving apparatus should be part of the basic equipment of every school.

Direct advertising should continue to be banned. 'We . . . are most anxious that the intellectual and ethical integrity which the broadcasting system in this country has attained should be preserved.'[2] Sponsored programmes, however, should not be banned, provided that they were used 'discreetly'. 'While recommending the continuance of the power, we hope that any increase in its use will be limited to the initial stages of Television broadcasting.'[3] Foreign commercial broadcasting should be discouraged by every available means, although it was 'obvious that co-operation with all foreign countries' was 'necessary to make the policy internationally effective'.[4]

Finally, the Empire Service should be expressly authorized and developed, and 'in the interest of British prestige and influence in world affairs, the appropriate use of languages other than English should be encouraged'.[5] Television also should be provided with necessary funds, since 'no hard and fast line can be drawn between Television broadcasting expenditure and ordinary broadcasting expenditure'.[6] 'Ownership and operation of Relay Exchanges should be undertaken by the Post Office and the control of their programmes by the Corporation.'[7] On all these matters, the Corporation's case was accepted *in toto*. In relation to publications also, the committee found the existing system quite satisfactory. 'The BBC has hitherto observed reasonable limits in the exercise of its powers and we have no reason to suppose that it will do otherwise.'[8]

Favourable as the Report was to the BBC, there were a number of private reservations. McClintock, pro-BBC, argued that as there had been no criticism of BBC capital expenditure in the past, the BBC should not have to submit capital schemes to Parliament in the future.[9] Selsdon, pro-Wireless Exchanges, held that they should not be owned by the Post Office or their programmes controlled by the BBC. 'The owner of an ordinary wireless set has—within the limits of the power and selectivity of his set—full freedom to receive BBC or foreign programmes at will, and I do not see why, within reasonable limits, a similar

[1] *Report of the Broadcasting Committee*, § 102.   [2] Ibid., § 109.   [3] Ibid., § 111.
[4] Ibid., § 114.   [5] Ibid., § 122.   [6] Ibid., § 128.
[7] Ibid., § 134.   [8] Ibid., § 137.   [9] Ibid., p. 52.

freedom should not be vicariously enjoyed by subscribers to exchanges.'[1] Obviously, Selsdon had been left unmoved when BBC witnesses had talked of different kinds of freedom. His philosophy had little in common with that of the BBC. 'After all, the relay Companies, if they are to succeed, must give their public what that public wants and, in trying so to do, they have the advantage that, by measuring the relative loads, they can estimate with some approximation to accuracy how many of their subscribers are listening at any given moment to one or other of two alternative programmes.'

Elton, Astor, and Graham White wanted to see sponsored programmes disappear completely, even as far as the early stages of television were concerned. 'The costs of a public service such as Television should be met out of public funds.'[2] They foresaw a 'real danger that advertisement may intrude itself over the whole range of BBC programmes' and believed that 'this would be contrary both to the public interest and to the wishes of a great majority of listeners'. Attlee did not sign this reservation. He concentrated rather on party questions than on general questions of public policy. It was undesirable that Governors should be drawn solely from persons whose social experience and background was that of the well-to-do classes. (This had never been a problem.) It was necessary inside the BBC that 'the Staff should be given full opportunities for ventilating any grievances collectively, that the BBC should definitely recognise the right of every employee to join an appropriate union, and that a proper system of consultation and collective agreement should be instituted'. (These matters, however important, created relatively little interest inside the BBC.) In political broadcasting, although the BBC had endeavoured to hold the scales even between the various political parties, there had been outstanding instances to the contrary. During the economic and political crisis of 1931, there had been tendentious talks supporting the National government. Even in the General Strike the BBC had been 'used' to back the government of the day. Attlee does not seem to have carried out much research on these questions, but his general line of argument that 'the BBC should have sufficient independence to resist

[1] Ibid., p. 53.
[2] Ibid., p. 48.

being made the instrument of one side in a national controversy' corresponded very closely to BBC objectives.[1]

When Reith read the Report, he saw much of this kind that appealed to him, but he has admitted that he felt little enthusiasm. The summary, as he realized, was too brief and superficial to be sustaining. Christmas 1935, therefore, was not a very happy time for him. 'I went through it all [the Report] critically, hypercritically; made a hundred notes where the wording might have been different; eliminated ninety and wrote a memorandum for the Governors about the residual ten.'[2] The Governors were pleased with the Report, yet by the time they had read Reith's careful memorandum they must have been conscious of the fact that he felt that Ullswater and his colleagues had not recognized how much British broadcasting had owed to his energy and independence. The Ullswater Report suggested no drastic changes in the life of the BBC, but it hinted, for those who had eyes to read and ears to hear, that one day drastic changes might come.

5. After Ullswater

WHEN the Ullswater Report reached Reith, Kingsley Wood was no longer Postmaster-General and Ramsay MacDonald was no longer Prime Minister. There were substantial Cabinet changes in June 1935, following an exchange of posts between Baldwin and MacDonald. From the BBC's standpoint the changes marked more than a reshuffle, for Kingsley Wood left the Post Office for the Ministry of Health, almost taking Banks with him. Wood was replaced by Major Tryon, a less adept politician and a less ambitious Postmaster-General. He soon took the opportunity of telling Reith that 'the personal publicity which his predecessor had indulged in was not at all in his line'.[3] The new government was confirmed in power at the General Election of October 1935, in which the BBC played a prominent

---

[1] *Report of the Broadcasting Committee*, pp. 48–51.
[2] *Into the Wind*, p. 247. Of his first 105 comments 103 were critical. Tallents, Diary, 6 Jan. 1936 (Tallents Papers).
[3] Reith, Diary, 25 June 1935.

part. Indeed, while the Ullswater Committee was still sitting, Reith sent Welch a note of the political arrangements the BBC had made.[1]

The change of government was followed by the death of King George V in January 1936, only a few months after his Silver Jubilee. On both these occasions, days of mourning and days of rejoicing, the BBC enhanced its national prestige. 'The most potent means of unifying behaviour', a long and detailed Mass Observation Report on Jubilee Day remarked, 'was the broadcasting of the ceremony and processions and of the King's speech. It meant that a very high proportion of the population spent the day listening in and thus partaking in the central events.'[2] As for the days of illness and mourning, it was a wireless phrase which perfectly caught and still evokes the mood— Stuart Hibberd's memorable rendering of the bulletin signed by the doctors, 'The King's life is moving peacefully towards its close'.[3]

The Ullswater Report was published on 16 March 1936, and was hailed at once as a further tribute to the BBC. At Reith's suggestion Tallents, the recently appointed Controller (Public Relations), saw Beaverbrook and found that he was 'strongly with the BBC'.[4] 'Now the test is over', the *Daily Express* commented, 'and the BBC emerges triumphant. There should have been a twenty years' Licence extension instead of ten. The constitution of the BBC, which combines the best elements of public and private control, has in fact served as a model in some foreign countries; in others which have followed different paths, the contrast is all in favour of the British system.'[5] Newspapers of quite different political views took the same line. So did *The Times*, which noted that the fact that the Ullswater Committee took the BBC's existence so much for granted was the highest tribute that could be paid.[6] 'You have certainly achieved a very friendly press these days', Dawnay wrote to Tallents.[7] 'I

[1] *Reith to Welch, 1 Nov. 1935.
[2] Mass Observation, *May the Twelfth* (1937), p. 267.
[3] See S. Hibberd, *This—is London*, p. 125. Large numbers of letters poured into the BBC saying how well 'broadcasting was managed' on this occasion, yet since the public never agrees about broadcasting at times like these there was also a critical minority. See a letter to *The Times* from C. G. Graves, 27 Jan. 1936.
[4] Note by Tallents, 12 Mar. 1936 (Tallents Papers).
[5] *Daily Express*, 17 Mar. 1936.   [6] *The Times*, 17 Mar. 1936.
[7] Letter from Dawnay to Tallents, 16 Mar. 1936 (Tallents Papers).

think we have had as good a press . . . as we could reasonably expect', Tallents replied. 'No monopoly can expect to be loved.'[1] It was left to the *Spectator*, fulfilling the proper function of a weekly, to write, 'There is no need to praise again the virtues of the BBC, they are too well known. But is the note of self-satisfaction not a little too strong?'[2]

This last criticism, which was quite exceptional, was directed not so much at the Ullswater Report as at a press statement which the BBC had had time to prepare between Christmas 1935 and March 1936. This statement, written by Reith, was given to the press a quarter of an hour after the Report came out. Fifty reporters were present when Tallents issued the document.[3] It noted the endorsement by the committee of the constitution and work of the BBC and the approval of the committee for 'all the major points' in the BBC's recommendations, but went on, as Reith had done privately, to complain of the summary, which, 'if read without continuous reference to the text', might prove 'in several places misleading'. There were also points in the Report itself, the document went on, 'which, while made as part of a declared policy of strengthening and securing the existing position', might have 'a contrary effect'.

Fifteen specific points were made. Ten years was too short a period of Charter extension. There was no need to have more Governors: 'Collective wisdom does not grow with numbers, and a small Board is generally more efficient than a large one.' Arrangements for the appointment of staff, at least since the time of the Barker–Mair inquiry, had been satisfactory and there was no need for further changes. 'There will always be a considerable percentage of appointments which it would be useless to advertise' and 'the compulsory addition of a Civil Service Commission representative or of an independent member to BBC Appointments Boards [as the Committee had recommended][4] would be incompatible with its independent status and productive of no good results.'

There was still no pressure from inside the BBC for the formation of a staff association, and a recommendation in the

[1] Letter from Tallents to Dawnay, 20 Mar. 1936 (Tallents Papers).
[2] *Spectator*, 20 Mar. 1936.
[3] *'Observations by the Board of Governors of the BBC on the Report of the Broadcasting Committee.'
[4] *Report of the Broadcasting Committee*, §§ 34 and 35 and Summary (d).

Report that BBC staff 'should be free from any control by the Corporation over their private lives'[1] was unwarranted. 'The Corporation does not concern itself with the private lives of its employees, except in so far as their personal conduct affects or may affect the performance of their duties as servants of the Corporation. The State itself is not indifferent to the private activities of those who serve it. No good private employer can afford to disregard conduct of an employee which may affect the efficiency of himself or his colleagues, or the good respect of his concern. Still less can such a public authority as the BBC with a service whose activities enter the great majority of the homes of the country, disregard such conduct.' This was the fullest statement that the BBC had ever made on this thorny subject. It ended with the words, 'Every such case which the Corporation feels obliged to consider—and in thirteen years there have been very few—is examined individually and sympathetically on its merits.'

Objection was also taken to a clause in the Report dealing with the BBC's attitude to critics. The committee had rightly directed attention to the danger of a monopoly excluding critics of BBC programmes from ever obtaining engagements to broadcast. This has always been the strongest kind of argument against the BBC's monopoly of broadcasting, and the committee wanted the BBC to 'make it clear that it welcomes criticism and that on no consideration would it exclude any person from an opportunity of engagement merely because he had expressed adverse opinions on its activities'.[2] The BBC replied, a little tartly, that it welcomed criticism, and quite deliberately brought critics to the microphone if only to protect itself against those who sought to create for themselves 'a nuisance value'. There were instructions, however, that the employment of critics was to be judicious lest the critics felt that the BBC was trying to ingratiate itself with them or that a sure way to be invited to broadcast was to be unpleasant about the Corporation. Perhaps it would have been more helpful here if the point of principle had been taken more directly.

On advisory committees, the BBC was doubtful whether it was necessary to extend the system throughout all the regions; and on capital expenditure, McClintock's reservation was fully

[1] Ibid., § 39 and Summary (d).   [2] Ibid., § 40 and Summary (d).

endorsed. 'An obligation to submit annually to Parliament the major items of contemplated capital expenditure would, as Sir William McClintock states, tie the BBC's hands and involve an undesirable encroachment on its independence, which else-where the Committee seem anxious to preserve and to which the Corporation attaches the utmost importance.' On political broadcasting there was a tilt at Attlee's personal note, a quite deserved tilt. 'The dissatisfaction expressed in Mr. Attlee's Reservation with the opportunities afforded to members of his Party was at least equalled by that of his opponents.' Finally—or rather with a warm welcome for the committee's suggestions about Wireless Exchanges conveniently following it and bringing the document to a close—there was a reaffirmation of the Corporation's Sunday policy. 'Sunday programmes have been progressively lightened, and the process continues. The Corporation knows, however, that there are great numbers of listeners who desire that the character of the Sunday programmes should not be assimilated to those of weekdays.'

Before the government announced its views on the Ullswater Report, there were questions and answers in Parliament and a not unexciting debate, during which both the Report itself and the BBC's comments on it provided ample material for discussion and argument.

Sir Percy Harris, Liberal member for Bethnal Green, asked the Postmaster-General in March why an 'interested party' had been allowed to see the Report and make comments on it before it had been submitted to Parliament first. Tryon replied that the Broadcasting Committee was a departmental committee, not a Committee of the House, and that as soon as its recommendations were known he had considered it essential 'to consult the BBC in order to facilitate the Government's consideration of certain recommendations of the Committee'. He resisted further pressure from H. B. Lees-Smith, Sir Archibald Sinclair, and other supplementary questioners who pressed the point. 'The Report was not handed to the BBC for their information', he said neatly, 'but to obtain information.'[1]

Indeed, although he did not tell the House so, a small Cabinet committee had already been appointed to 'brood on' the

[1] *Hansard*, vol. 310, col. 53.

Report. It consisted of Sir John Simon, the Home Secretary, as chairman, Neville Chamberlain, the Chancellor of the Exchequer (when he was required or available), Sir Kingsley Wood, Oliver Stanley, the President of the Board of Education, Ormsby-Gore, the First Commissioner of Works, and Tryon. Malcolm MacDonald was added when Empire broadcasting was discussed.

Tryon began by stating his own view to the committee that the Ullswater Report had been right in concluding that there should be no radical change in the existing system and that any modifications should be directed to strengthening and securing it. He also supported the BBC's proposal that whenever government guidance 'or control' of the BBC was needed, it could best be exercised by a Cabinet minister of high rank in touch with Cabinet policy and with full access to the most secret information. He did not believe, however, that the Charter could be renewed for a longer period than ten years. Attlee was against a long renewal, and the House would obviously divide on the proposition.

The House discussed the Report on 29 April 1936 with no government statement to guide them. It was an unsatisfactory debate in which more heat was generated than light. Lees-Smith, for the Labour Opposition, said that the experiment of running broadcasting by a public corporation had been fully vindicated. There was great need, however, for the BBC to reform its staffing and to establish representative staff associations. The point was taken up with vehemence by later speakers, particularly by Sir Stafford Cripps, who referred to the Lambert–Levita case which was then *sub judice*. 'What right have they [the BBC] to use their economic power over Lambert', he asked, 'to make him discontinue an action against Mr. X?' The BBC was likened to 'an unlimited dictatorial autocracy', one member going so far as to add (a few months later) that it had become 'an autocracy which had outgrown the original autocrat. It is a despotism in decay, and it bears all the marks of that autocracy.'[1] Rumours of the wildest kind were freely circulated on the floor of the House, driving Reith to comment —'incredible credulity; serene malignity'.[2] One newspaper,

[1] Ibid., vol. 311, col. 974; vol. 318, col. 2740.
[2] *Into the Wind*, p. 199.

which had been highly critical of the BBC, expressed much the same kind of reaction. 'To criticise, freely and frankly, the policy of administration of a public servant is the right of democracy. To make him an object of savage attack is altogether wrong. Such attack dishonours public service, reduces its prospects of recruiting able men, and plays into the hands of vested interests in constant search of opportunity to convert public services into private monopolies.'[1]

Apart from vituperation and platitude, the House had little to offer. The Front Bench was silent, and Wavell Wakefield, one of the few speakers to touch on a main point at issue, the Wireless Exchanges and their future, was himself a director of one of the largest national relay concerns. Only one speaker, Richard Law, directed the debate from talk of personal dictatorship to possible dangers of the BBC exercising a 'cultural dictatorship', and he cut little ice. 'Are we to understand', he asked, 'that the only way in which the Corporation can achieve a balanced and good programme is to have everybody in the country listening to the BBC's programme, and nothing else all the time?' Law wanted the Relay Exchanges to be 'free' to broadcast what they wished. 'It is not a question of whether the programmes are good or bad, but it is undesirable that any one body should have the power, not only to say what should be broadcast in this country, but to say what should be listened to, not by the country as a whole, but merely by the poor and less fortunate listeners.'[2]

It is doubtful whether the government was influenced one way or the other by any of the speeches in the debate. There is evidence that Kingsley Wood's own view coincided with that of Richard Law on the 'freedom' of the Relay Exchange proprietor to broadcast just what he wished, and that he agreed with members who had criticized BBC staff conditions. The Cabinet Committee must have agreed not to inform the BBC of its plans, for when Norman and Reith went to see Tryon a fortnight after the debate he gave them no information concerning what the government proposed to do. Instead, he produced a six-page document about detailed work inside the BBC and asked for comments. It was not until June 1936 that the government's White Paper was issued.

[1] Quoted in *Into the Wind*, p. 248.   [2] *Hansard*, vol. 311, col. 1008.

Most of the recommendations of the Ullswater Committee were accepted, but not all of them.[1] The proposal that Wireless Exchanges should be taken over technically by the Post Office and executively by the BBC was shelved. In other words, Selsdon's reservation counted for more than the committee's Report on this matter. The licences of the Exchanges were to be renewed for another three years, that is to say until 31 December 1939, and in the meantime the Post Office was to undertake experimental work on wire broadcasting. Two new conditions were to be attached, however, to the relay companies' licences. First, the Exchanges had to reach 'a reasonable standard of efficiency in technical and other aspects'. Second, those Exchanges which distributed two programmes had to distribute a BBC programme as one of them when the BBC was on the air.

The proposal that a senior minister, such as the Lord President, should be responsible for policy matters concerning the BBC which were raised in Parliament, was also turned down. This proposal had had a poor press, many of the newspapers claiming that it would tie the BBC politically and make it seem both at home and abroad more like a government department. Most of the criticism along this line was based on ignorance of the fact that it was the BBC itself which had made the proposal initially. It was no less effective criticism for all that. 'This Cabinet Minister', wrote the *Morning Post*, 'will soon come to regard the BBC as his Department. Then goodbye to the independence and the cultural entertainment of wireless.'[2] 'Not everybody would relish the idea of intimate political control under a functionary who would resemble in a suspicious degree a Minister of Propaganda', wrote the *Western Mail*.[3]

The other points of difference between the Ullswater Report and the government's White Paper were only minor ones, although the ban on 'editorializing' was to be applied to publications as well as to programmes—in fact, publications always had been treated in this way—and 'sponsored' programmes as well as direct advertising were to be excluded. The press made little of these points, concentrating almost exclusively on staff

---

[1] Cmd. 5207 (1936), *Broadcasting: Memorandum by the Postmaster-General on the Report of the Broadcasting Committee.*

[2] *Morning Post*, 17 Mar. 1936.   [3] *Western Mail*, 18 Mar. 1936.

difficulties and losing much of the 'equability' which it had shown when the Report itself first appeared. On this occasion Reith was annoyed with Tallents. 'It seems to me that we have had an extraordinarily unsatisfactory press. . . . We have had a very raw deal from the government and there is only one paper of any importance—and perhaps only one of any sort— which realizes this.' He ended with the question, 'Can you lay plans against this sort of thing in future?'[1]

After a further debate in the House of Commons in July 1936, with a somewhat milder atmosphere than had characterized the debate in April, Government and BBC set to work on the final draft of the Charter and Licence. Although the Corporation had submitted drafts at the beginning of the Ullswater inquiry, these were not used as the basis for the new documents and everything had to start again. Yet just because the new Director-General of the Post Office, Sir Thomas Gardiner, who had replaced Banks, insisted on taking every point in detail with Reith, the final document was far more acceptable to the BBC than it had once seemed likely to be. 'Jardine Brown [the BBC's lawyer] is amazed at the alterations I have got', Reith wrote.[2] 'Post Office share of the licence fee was reduced to 9 per cent. If the PMG ever exercised the right of veto, at least he had to say whether or not its exercise could be made public, which implied that it normally would be. Many objectionable points were taken out of the official documents and included in a memorandum of agreement which could be modified without difficulty when desired and agreed.'[3]

Soon after the new Charter was granted, there was the last of the three debates of 1936—with the ammunition of the Lambert–Levita case and the Stamp inquiry to add to the previous inflammable materials. It was in this debate that Lees-Smith excelled himself by referring to the BBC as 'the nearest thing in this country to Nazi government that can be shown'.[4] Everything was out of perspective when language of this kind was used, and it did nothing to induce genuinely rational inquiry. Yet at the end of the debate the Postmaster-General promised that there would be reforms in staffing arrangements at the

[1] Memorandum from Reith to Tallents, 9 July 1936 (Tallents Papers).
[2] Reith, Diary, 27 Nov. 1936.   [3] *Into the Wind*, pp. 254–5.
[4] *Hansard*, vol. 318, col. 2370.

BBC. A Staff Association would be set up and—*pace* Reith's views on 'non-departmentalized' governors—J. J. Mallon, one of the two new Governors, was especially adept in his handling of the machinery of industrial conciliation.

When Tryon made this statement Reith had already taken the most important decision in relation to new kinds of staffing arrangements that he had ever made. W. St. J. Pym was appointed as Director of Staff Administration in November 1936, and for the first time there was a section on staffing arrangements in the BBC's *Annual Report* to Parliament.[1] Pym was an admirable choice for the new post. He was affable yet dignified, and he had wide experience of how to handle the multitude of problems the BBC was facing. He could also influence Reith, who liked him from the start.[2]

Pym's first report was on staff representation. He began with the position of the trade unions, which he said had been content hitherto for the most part to satisfy themselves that the Corporation was observing their basic conditions. The Electrical Trades Union was exceptional in having asked for right of access and organization in the Engineering Division. There was, in fact, no great urge inside the Corporation either for militant trade-union action or a staff association. 'There seems to be little incentive—even in the absence of any other form of collective representation—for the staff, or any section of it, to start an Association.'[3] In other words, Pym, writing with genuine independence, corroborated the general point made by Reith about the state of staff feeling in Broadcasting House.

At the same time, Pym went on, there was a case for setting up a Joint Council, not so much to 'protect' staff as to serve the Corporation. 'The staff may not feel the need for protection. But the protection of individuals is not the concern of a Joint Council, and the protection of groups is only one and not the most important of its functions. Moreover, the result of the recent referendum cannot be regarded as altogether conclusive; to some extent it probably represented not so much a straight vote on the general principle as a vote of confidence in the

[1] Cmd. 5688 (1937), *BBC Eleventh Annual Report*, p. 24.
[2] Reith, Diary, 18 Dec. 1936.
[3] *W. St. J. Pym, *Report on Staff Representation* (1937), p. 7.

present management.' There was a final point, and it was probably the most important. 'The Corporation will no doubt continue to be exposed to hostile criticism, so long as no form of staff representation exists. Such criticism, however ill-founded, is bound to have an irritant effect on the public and also on the staff.'[1]

Pym's report, with useful information about the way in which other bodies managed their staffing arrangements, was referred by the Board of Governors to the Treasury for the advice of a small informal committee, consisting of Sir James Rae of the Treasury, J. W. Bowen, former Secretary of the Union of Post Office Workers, and G. L. Darbyshire, the Establishment Officer of the London, Midland and Scottish Railway. This committee proposed the setting up of Joint Councils of the Whitley type.[2] Again, however, it substantially backed the BBC's claim that the staff had been far less interested in these matters than Attlee, Cripps, or Lees-Smith had suggested. 'Normally a system of Joint Councils is built up on the existence of representative Associations or Unions and an expressed desire for the introduction of such machinery. This position does not obtain in the Corporation's service.'[3]

The report of the Rae Committee was referred to the BBC's staff in September 1938, by which time Pym had prepared a draft scheme for a Joint Council. H. Parker, later Sir Harold Parker, of the Treasury, to whom it was referred, thought that 'given a desire to make the system work' it would 'be well worth the time involved'.[4] The next step was a new ballot held in November 1938 in which 79·6 per cent. of the eligible staff voted: 77·7 per cent. of those voting said that they were in favour of a Joint Council, 11·6 per cent. were opposed, and 11·3 per cent. did not express an opinion. Most 'yeses' came from the Midland Region, most 'nos' from the North: occupationally the male clerical workers were the most interested, and the catering staff the least. 'The result of the ballot', Pym concluded, 'points to the introduction of a Joint Council Scheme for all sections of the staff.'[5] He also told the new Director-General,

---

[1] *Report on Staff Representation*, p. 10.
[2] *Staff Representation Report by Sir James Rae, J. W. Bowen, and G. L. Darbyshire, Jan. 1938.
[3] Ibid., p. 8.   [4] *H. Parker to W. St. J. Pym, 5 Oct. 1938.
[5] *Note by Pym, 28 Nov. 1938.

Ogilvie, that the details of the ballot were 'quietly and seriously reported in the Press'.[1] Ogilvie himself addressed a 'meeting of delegates' from various BBC 'groups' in February 1939, telling them that 'we are not bound in advance by the details of the Rae Report. In view of the diversity of staff the scheme cannot be a copy of any other scheme. It must be pliable. Probably the right course for us is to start with a simple form of organisation, letting it develop naturally rather than handicap ourselves by constructing something elaborate in advance.'[2]

Negotiations and meetings continued throughout the spring and summer, and it was not until after the outbreak of war that the first Staff Association came into being. In the meantime, however, there had been a number of other changes in staff policy. Long before Ullswater reported, increasing use had been made of advertising and appointments boards in the recruitment of new staff. From January 1937 procedures were further formalized. Reference was made to the Civil Service Commission on the rare occasions when it was proposed to fill a vacancy for a monthly-paid staff post with an outside candidate without public advertisement; and for appointments above a certain grade the Assistant Commissioner and secretary of the Civil Service Commission joined the BBC's appointment committee. There were so many applicants for jobs on a weekly wage basis that advertisement was never necessary during this period. Another interesting development was the setting up of a Staff Training School in October 1936. Courses held there attracted broadcasters from all over the world, including the United States, India, Turkey, and Nigeria.

Many of these changes can be paralleled in the natural history of any great organization when it passes a certain point in its development. Reith himself was very conscious in 1936 and 1937 of the way in which conditions inside the BBC were changing, and set out to persuade his Controllers to recognize the significance of what was happening. 'It is essential', he told them, 'that you should satisfy yourself that any individual who is meant to be carrying responsibility in however small a measure is in fact carrying it. . . . No Controller can today be in touch with every member of his Division directly. But he can

---

[1] *Pym to Sir S. Tallents for the attention of F. W. Ogilvie, 7 Dec. 1938.
[2] *Notes of a Meeting of Delegates, 24 Feb. 1939.

and should be indirectly, whether there are a hundred or a thousand, members of it.'[1] Against this background of institutional change, in some respects the BBC was becoming less distinctive: in other respects, it seemed to offer less of a challenge to Reith himself at the apex of the pyramid. Yet there were new challenges, particularly that of television. The story of development in this new world of communication leads back from the 1930s to the very beginnings of the BBC.

[1] Memorandum by Reith, 18 May 1936 (Tallents Papers).

V

THE NEW WORLD OF TELEVISION

My time having been occupied with many other matters, I find that I have not been able to devote as much consideration to Television as I would have wished; and while convinced that it will have a very definite place in the future, I do not feel any useful purpose would be served by discussing the subject at the present time.

MARCONI
In a letter of 30 Oct. 1928

I believe that television is destined to become the greatest force in the world—I think it will have more influence over the lives of individuals than any other force.

H. A. LAFONT, *American Federal Radio Commissioner,* 1931

1. Back to Baird

TELEVISION LIMITED, the earliest concern of its kind in the world, was formed before the British Broadcasting Corporation —in June 1925—with a capital of £500. Its sponsor, John Logie Baird, 'a son of the manse', like Reith, had first experimented with television in an attic at Hastings in 1923 and 1924. He was then thirty-four years old. In June 1923 he inserted a notice in the Personal Column of *The Times*: 'Seeing by Wireless—Inventor of apparatus wishes to hear from someone who will assist (not financially) in making working model.'[1] In fact, he did need financial help, and through the advertisement was brought into touch with W. J. B. Odhams. He offered Odhams a 20 per cent. interest in his 'Television inventions' for £100, an offer which Odhams turned down. Through Odhams, however, necessary apparatus was provided by Captain A. G. D. West, then Research Engineer at the BBC, and later one of Baird's most loyal and zealous helpers.

Television was only one of Baird's interests at that time, but it was an interest which obviously meant much to him. Marconi in his generation had turned 'the wonder of wireless' from dream into reality: could not Baird do the same with the even greater wonder of television? He had a good general grasp of the principles and practice of electrical engineering, which he had first learned as a student, again like Reith, at the Royal Technical College, Glasgow, and later at Glasgow University. Even before that, as a boy, he had installed single-handed an electric-light plant in his home. The current was generated by a home-made dynamo, driven by a water-wheel worked from the water main and a symposium of accumulators made out of old jam jars and sheet lead.[2] Baird was still improvising at Hastings in 1924. 'His first "televisor" had the ingenuity of Heath Robinson and a touch of Robinson Crusoe.'[3] An old tea chest formed a base to carry the motor which rotated a circular

[1] *The Times*, 27 June 1923.
[2] R. L. Tiltman, *Baird of Television* (1933), p. 30.
[3] S. A. Moseley, *John Baird, The Romance and Tragedy of the Pioneer of Television* (1952), p. 63. Both these biographies are lamentably weak on exact chronology.

cardboard disc. The disc was cut out of an old hat box, and a darning needle served as a spindle. An empty biscuit box housed the projection lamp. The necessary bull's eye lenses were bought from a bicycle shop at a cost of fourpence each.

With such crude apparatus, held together with glue, sealing-wax, and string, Baird achieved exciting results. Early in 1924 he was able to transmit the flickering image of a Maltese cross over a distance of two or three yards. 'I myself saw a cross', a visitor to the Hastings attic wrote in a magazine, 'and the fingers of my own hand reproduced by the apparatus across the width of the laboratory. The images were quite sharp and clear, although perhaps a little unsteady. This, however, was mostly due to mechanical defects in the apparatus and not to any fault of the system.'[1]

Baird's experiments have a genuine romance about them. They were not, however, the first of their kind. The pre-history of television began with the discovery by Edmond Becquerel of the electro-chemical effects of light in 1839, and entered a new phase with the announcement in 1873 of the discovery of the photo-sensitive properties of selenium.[2] This announcement led to 'a glut of schemes and proposals' for 'seeing by electricity'. The projects, like the early wireless projects which were being devised soon afterwards, were being advanced in different countries.[3] Senlacq in France experimented with transmitter screens; Ayrton and Perry in England were inspired by a cartoon in *Punch* and the fear of an American monopoly, under the control of Graham Bell, to 'intimate that complete means of seeing by telegraphy have been known for some time by scientific men';[4] George Carey of Boston introduced the idea of a practical mechanism for scanning images in an article in *Design and Work* in 1880; and in 1881 Shelford Bidwell actually demonstrated apparatus for transmitting silhouettes (with an

[1] F. H. Robinson, 'The Radio Kinema' in *Kinematograph Weekly*, 3 Apr. 1924.
[2] Selenium itself had been discovered in 1817. Willoughby-Smith drew attention to its properties in the *Journal of the Society of Telegraph Engineers* in 1873. For details of this and other developments, see the important article by G. R. M. Garratt and A. H. Mumford, 'The History of Television' in the *Proceedings* of the Institution of Electrical Engineers, vol. xcix (1952).
[3] For the history of wireless, see *The Birth of Broadcasting*, pp. 25–36.
[4] Letter to *Nature*, 22 Apr. 1880.

ingenious scanning system) which has been preserved in the London Science Museum.

Many of these experiments belong more to the history of photo-telegraphy than of television—Senlacq's and Carey's, for example—but it is difficult to separate the two strands in early technical history. The next crucial development, however, directly influenced Baird. In 1884 a German scientist, Paul Nipkow, first conceived the idea of a scanning disc, spirally perforated, and rotating. Nipkow's projected transmitter also made use of a selenium cell, but the small currents passed by the cell were not strong enough, in the absence of an amplifier, to give practical results. The theory was simple. Objects placed in front of the transmitter would be 'scanned' by a series of concentric curved lines corresponding to the path of the holes in the disc. There is no evidence, however, that Nipkow put his theory into practice. The picture he would have obtained would have been very small in relation to the size of the disc. A different scanning device, also to be used by Baird, was developed in 1889 by Lazare Weiller. The image to be transmitted was scanned not by perforated discs but by revolving mirrors, the light reflections being projected on to a selenium cell.[1]

The 'glut of schemes and proposals' came to a halt at this stage, largely because of a technical difficulty. The time lag of selenium and its consequent insensitivity to rapid changes in the intensity of light proved discouraging, and inventors moved over to other fields in the 1890s. Even after the first commercial cathode ray had been produced by Braun in 1897, it took ten years before Boris Rosing, working in St. Petersburg, conceived the first television system to use cathode-ray tubes. Rosing used two mirror drums in his apparatus. These scanned the image and played the light reflection upon a photo-electric cell. Rosing lacked an amplifier, however, and ran into what he called 'practical difficulties'.

While Rosing was experimenting in Russia, A. A. Campbell-Swinton in England suggested quite independently that by the proper use of cathode-ray tubes, 'high-definition' television was possible. Drawing upon Shelford Bidwell's work, he saw no insuperable difficulties in the way of 'distant electrical vision'.

[1] According to Garratt and Mumford, loc. cit., the device had been tried out even earlier in 1882 by Atkinson.

The absence of efficient thermionic valves, however, limited the development of television transmitters.[1] Campbell-Swinton, who was one of the keenest members of the Röntgen Society and later of the Wireless Society of London and the Radio Society of Great Britain, was to be a member of the deputation which pressed for the beginning of regular sound broadcasting in 1922.[2] With characteristic restraint, however, he stated in 1911 that his 'idea' about television was 'an idea only and the apparatus has never been constructed. Furthermore, I do not for a moment suppose that it could be got to work without a great deal of experiment and probably much modification.'[3]

Although no further practical developments were made before 1914, and the First World War did not serve to stimulate television in the way that it stimulated practical advances in wireless, it is clear that before 1914 two possible future lines of development had been sketched out. The one looked back to Nipkow and forward to Baird. The other looked back to Rosing and forward to the present. The second line of development depended entirely on undiscovered or undeveloped electronic devices—particularly, the efficient thermionic valve and the multi-stage amplifier. It is an important fact both in the history of technology and in the history of television as a 'medium' that mechanical means of scanning developed before all-electrical systems were evolved. The resourceful individualist antedated the organization man. Baird was an example of the first type. So too was the American, C. F. Jenkins, who in 1925 demonstrated the transmission and reception by wireless of the image of a slowly revolving model windmill.[4] The television technology both of Jenkins and of Baird was incapable of providing what we now call 'high-definition' television. This could be achieved only by all-electrical methods.

Because of the timing of development, the controversy between two 'television systems' embittered the early history of organized television in much the same way—although at the level of science rather than empiricism—as the conflict between

---

[1] For the development of the thermionic valve, which was invented in 1904 by Fleming, see *The Birth of Broadcasting*, p. 28.

[2] See ibid., p. 129. He also gave evidence before the Sykes Committee.

[3] See *The Birth of Broadcasting*, p. 214. Presidential Address to the Röntgen Society, Nov. 1911, printed in the *Journal of the Röntgen Society*, vol. viii (1912), p. 1.

[4] *Wireless World* (1926), vol. xviii, p. 642.

two gauges bedevilled the early history of railways. Associated with this controversy was a second and all too familiar one concerning the nature of Baird's contribution to television history. To some commentators he has been *the* genius: to others, a clever and persevering man, not so much the inventor of television as the first person to see clearly what its possibilities were. Although the popular controversy is not dead, it is difficult to dissent from Peter Eckersley's verdict that Baird is to be honoured not because of his inventions but because he belongs to the company of men 'who see past immediate technical difficulties to an eventual achievement'. Comparing him with Marconi, Eckersley argues that while neither man was pre-eminently an inventor or a physicist, they both had 'that flair for picking about on the scrap-heap of unrelated discoveries and assembling the bits and pieces to make something work and so revealing possibilities, if not finality'.[1]

Such an achievement is an invaluable one in an age of science, and few scientists rise to it. Whether or not Baird made a genuinely 'original' scientific contribution, he was as skilful and as persistent as most other great inventors of the industrial revolution, and, like them, he ran into every kind of financial and psychological obstacle. The promotion of his enterprises caused him far more pain than pleasure: the enterprises themselves were often bold and visionary, although limited seriously at their technical boundaries. Unlike the earlier inventors, however, Baird was drawn into a blaze of publicity and surrounded by sponsors who often promised more than could possibly have been performed. In consequence, Baird occupies an important but curious position in history. He publicized television more effectively than any other individual, but eventually when television established itself it was not on the lines he had for long envisaged.

Not surprisingly, it has been all too easy to surround both Baird's achievement and his failures with an aura of legend. It has also been all too easy to simplify the attitude of other people and institutions towards his work. The BBC did not come into the story until 1926, but having come into it, there was ample scope for even darker legend, for what Baird's most

---

[1] Letter to Sydney Moseley quoted in S. A. Moseley, *John Baird* (1952), p. 250. Compare my account of Marconi in *The Birth of Broadcasting*, pp. 31–32.

recent biographer has called 'tragedy' as well as 'romance'. Listening to a radio announcement that Baird had died in 1945, the biographer, Sydney Moseley, noted tersely that 'the BBC which had failed to acknowledge John Baird's existence, had at last announced his passing'.[1] This was both dark and wild legend. The BBC and John Baird had been only too aware of each other's existence: their relationship, indeed, is the main theme of British television history until the mid-1930s.

While making his early experiments in Hastings, Baird was in urgent need of money and, like most pioneers, he found it very hard to get. A press demonstration of his apparatus got him a mention in the *Daily News* and a gift of £50.[2] Soon afterwards he sold a one-third interest in his invention for £200 to Will Day, a London cinematograph proprietor, who had read a magazine article about the success of Baird's experiments. With the money in his pocket, Baird bought several hundred flashlamp batteries. Later he disposed of another share of a sixth to Day.[3] Having completed these extremely insecure financial arrangements, Baird moved to London in August 1924.

In March 1925 he discovered a richer backer, Gordon Selfridge jun., who was the first of the publicity seekers with whom Baird was to have so many complicated dealings. Selfridge put him on display in his store, taking pains to state in his advertisements that he was not financially interested: 'we know that our friends will be interested in something that should rank with the greatest inventions of the century.' Selfridge also compared Baird with Edison, a comparison which was to be drawn frequently in the future. 'The picture is flickering and defective, and at present only simple pictures can be sent successfully; but Edison's first phonograph announced that "Mary had a little lamb" in such a way that only listeners who were "in the secret" could understand—and yet, from that first result has developed the gramophone of today. Unquestionably the present experimental apparatus can be similarly perfected and refined.'[4]

[1] *John Baird*, p. 7.   [2] Ibid., p. 64.   [3] *Baird of Television*, p. 67.
[4] The advertisement is reproduced in *Baird of Television*, pp. 74–75. A full description of the apparatus was printed in *Nature*, 14 Apr. 1925. 'Mr. Baird has overcome many difficulties,' the writer in *Nature* added, 'but we are afraid that there are many more to be surmounted before ideal television is accomplished.'

From the glare of publicity, Baird passed yet again into the twilight world of insecurity. Selfridge gave him only a brief engagement, Day would not back him further, the Marconi Company was uninterested in acquiring his patents, and the newspapers to which he turned were for the most part unsympathetic. Again, following the footsteps of eighteenth- and nineteenth-century inventors, he had to fall back on relatives to give financial backing to the tiny Television Company he founded in 1925. His only other help came from Hart Accumulators and General Electric, who provided him with free batteries and valves. He was overjoyed, in such circumstances, when in October 1925 he managed to produce a convincing image. Unlike the images demonstrated at Selfridges, it was something more than a black and white 'effect' and had definite outlines and features.

Business prospects soon improved also. By January 1926, when Baird successfully demonstrated 'original television apparatus' at the Royal Institution,[1] he had been joined in his enterprise by an old business associate, Captain Oliver George Hutchinson. Together with a friend, Broderip, Hutchinson bought out Will Day's interest in Baird's concerns. He took charge of the 'management' of the Television Company, and in February 1926 moved Baird into an office and laboratory at Motograph House, near Leicester Square.

The first reference to Baird's experiments in the Post Office Archives relates to Hutchinson. The Television Company first wrote to the Post Office on 4 January 1926, and a month later F. W. Phillips reported that Hutchinson had called to talk about a 'television service'. With the kind of absurd exaggeration which was to do Baird so much harm, Hutchinson said that Baird's invention was 'practically out of the experimental stage'.

A shrewd member of the audience at the demonstration at the Royal Institution—E. G. Stewart, a group engineer for the Gas Light and Coke Company—had written at the time that it

---

[1] See *The Times*, 28 Jan. 1926, for the account of the successful televising of the ventriloquist's doll. The *New York Times*, 6 Mar. 1927, paid early tribute to Baird. 'No one but this Scotch minister's son has ever transmitted and received a recognisable image with its graduations of light and shade.'

would be 'an error of judgment' if the inventor did what Hutchinson wanted and placed his apparatus immediately on the market. 'The apparatus as now developed', he went on, 'gives a crude image which is not even physically pleasant to view. Again distortion is present, whilst only comparatively small fields of view (e.g. the face) may be presented. Whilst the existing type of apparatus would undoubtedly achieve a temporary market, the public would quickly tire of the results and either expect a rapid improvement or, failing such improvement, leave the idea in disgust. . . . Those well-known personalities whom the public would most desire to see would be scared of television by the present reproductions so that deserving developments later on would be hampered in securing support.'[1]

Hutchinson, from whom Baird soon became estranged,[2] was not the kind of businessman who calculated carefully about long-term results. His project was one of a cluster of highly speculative ventures which titillated the Stock Exchange in Britain's pale imitation of the American boom of the 'roaring twenties'. He did not intend to be put off either by cautious engineers or Post Office 'bureaucrats'. When he saw Phillips he did not admit that a Post Office Licence was necessary for television, but he asked that the Post Office should grant the Television Company some kind of concession for a public service. He had only the vaguest ideas of what a public service meant, talking airily of transmitting photographs of speakers from London to Paris or installing television apparatus in theatres.[3]

When the Post Office had not made up its mind by June 1926 as to what it wished to do, Hutchinson took the matter up again, stating that the Television Company was losing money and that powerful American interests had approached them about a take-over. He suggested that it would be unfortunate for Britain if Baird's apparatus had to be transferred to the United States.[4] A few days later the Post Office gave its approval to experimental television transmissions, and a licence (2 TV) was issued in August. A further licence for 2 TW (Harrow)

[1] This fascinating account by E. G. Stewart is in the files of the Gas Light and Coke Company, and I am grateful to Mr. L. Hardern for drawing attention to it.
[2] *John Baird*, pp. 96 ff.
[3] Minute by F. W. Phillips, 4 Feb. 1926 (Post Office Archives).
[4] Hutchinson to Phillips, 29 June 1926 (Post Office Archives).

followed. On the strength of the issue of the licences the Baird Company advertised a 'televisor' for sale at a price of 30 guineas.

These moves were associated with important financial changes, which were to set the pattern of Baird finance for the next few years. Television Ltd. remained as a parent company, with Baird and Hutchinson as sole directors and a small nominal capital, but Baird Television Development Company Ltd. was formed as a public company in April 1927 with an authorized capital of £125,000, all issued, and an outside chairman, Sir Edward Manville, the then chairman of the Daimler Company.[1] Television had passed from its experimental stage into the arena of high finance and business speculation, and the price of TV shares moved with many other factors besides the progress of technical invention. A year later, in June 1928, when the formation of a third company, Baird International Television Ltd., was announced, the authorized capital was £700,000 and there was a heavy over-subscription.

Baird himself was uneasy about all these financial ramifications at the time, and even more so in retrospect. He objected to Manville booming at him 'through a cloud of cigar smoke' and making 'impossible suggestions'. 'I was busy with wheels and pulleys', he wrote in notes on his life, 'and soon came to regard Board Meetings as analogous to going to church— functions to be slept through. Sometimes I awoke with a start at some of the proceedings at these meetings, but after a few questions I relapsed again into dreams of further permutations and combinations of wire and mirror drums and lamps.'[2]

Through all the vicissitudes of business—and they were to be many—Baird continued his experiments. In December 1926 he showed his 'Noctovisor', a piece of apparatus which permitted transmissions of images from a dark room with infra-red rays.[3] In May 1927, after the American Telephone and Telegraph Company—possibly the 'powerful American interest' to which Hutchinson referred—had staged the first public television demonstration outside Britain and thereby broken what

[1] *John Baird*, p. 96. Hutchinson wanted the Company to be called 'British Television Ltd.' and actually had stationery printed with this title. Baird insisted on his own name being kept in.
[2] Quoted in *John Baird*, p. 98.
[3] For 'Noctovisor', see *Nature*, 5 Feb. 1927.

Hutchinson had loosely talked of as a 'monopoly',[1] Baird arranged a demonstration of television over the 438 miles of telephone wire between London and Glasgow.[2] He also co-operated in experiments with H. L. Kirke, the lively and enterprising BBC engineer.[3] In September 1927 he gave a demonstration at the British Association meeting at Leeds. A Post Office engineer who was present indicated that 'the invention has not reached a very advanced stage yet'.[4] Other observers were more enthusiastic. After witnessing one of the 1928 demonstrations a Glasgow University professor commented that 'the chief difficulties connected with television have been overcome by Mr. Baird, and the improvements still to be effected are mainly matters of detail'.[5]

Soon after the Leeds demonstration, a Television Society of Great Britain was formed, with Lord Haldane as its first President. By 1928 Baird was experimenting with colour and stereoscopic television: he also succeeded in transmitting pictures which were received on the other side of the Atlantic.[6] These were 'heroic' achievements which no historian can overlook. Baird's work was all the more remarkable, as the *New York Times* put it, because he was pitting 'his inventive wits against the pooled ability and the vast resources of the great corporation physicists and engineers'.[7] A similar point was made by Sir Ambrose Fleming, the inventor of the thermionic valve, who wrote after a visit to Baird in June 1928 that he was sure Baird's laboratory was 'the birthplace of new, interesting and very important inventions'.[8]

[1] There were, in fact, several interesting foreign developments. In 1926, for example, work began in the Bell Telephone Laboratories. The successful demonstration of Apr. 1927 used both wire and radio, and pictures were transmitted 22 miles from a station in New Jersey to New York.

[2] *Nature*, 18 June 1927.

[3] *John Baird*, p. 81. For Kirke's co-operation with Baird, see Post Office Archives. Hutchinson told H. G. G. Welch of the Post Office on 23 July 1927 of the extent of the co-operation. The use of BBC stations for Baird broadcasts was felt by the Post Office to be 'premature' at this stage.

[4] Minute by W. E. Weston, 9 Sept. 1927 (Post Office Archives).

[5] *Nature*, 18 June 1927.

[6] For colour, see *Nature*, 18 Aug. 1928. For stereoscopic television, see a note by C. Tierney in *Television*, Sept. 1928. For the transatlantic transmission, see the *New York Times*, 11 Feb. 1928. The successful transatlantic broadcast was followed by the foundation of the Baird International Television Company. Baird also transmitted pictures to a ship at sea. See *Television*, Apr. 1928.

[7] *New York Times*, 11 Feb. 1928.   [8] *Baird of Television*, p. 122.

At this juncture in events—with new companies being created and new experiments being carried out—Baird met Sydney A. Moseley, the journalist, who thereafter made it one of his 'causes' to hail Baird as a genius and his inventions as the greatest of the century. Moseley was proud of the fact that he was, in his own phrase, 'Britain's first radio critic'. He enjoyed broadcasting as an 'adventure', and wrote about it in Sunday newspapers and *Amateur Wireless*, not always to the liking of Reith or his colleagues:[1] he was also an unsuccessful speculator and the author of a widely read popular treatise on how to make money quickly.[2] The date of Moseley's first meeting with Baird was 1 August 1928. By then Baird had moved his office to 133 Long Acre. He told Moseley that 'he was having a bad time with the scoffers and sceptics—including the BBC and part of the technical press' and that he wanted Moseley to test his claims.

Moseley, who found Baird 'a model for the schoolboy's picture of a shock-haired, modest, dreamy, absent-minded inventor', soon felt that he had discovered not only a man but a cause. He became Baird's 'self-appointed champion'. 'Once more into the fray', he exclaimed with his usual zest. By October 1928 he had publicized Baird with all the energy that he could command: 'the last few weeks have been a whirlwind of frenzied activity'.[3] In the course of these weeks, he took particular pleasure in persuading himself that the BBC was the chief target of the 'attack'. 'I wish to protest at once against the unfair attitude which the BBC appears to be adopting towards television', he wrote in a letter to the BBC; 'I think you will recognise in me a friend of the BBC from No. 1.'[4]

Soon he was talking in more lurid terms. 'The struggle to put Baird over with the BBC is more or less a *guerre à mort*, no

---

[1] His published *Private Diaries* (1960) describe the story of his association with broadcasting in detail, from his first letters to the BBC in Nov. 1925. By Apr. 1926 he had broadcast often enough for J. G. Broadbent of the BBC to write to him, 'I expect you feel by now that you have thoroughly mastered the peculiar but by no means easy art of broadcasting.' 'I believe I have!' Moseley commented (p. 275). One 'outspoken' article on the BBC that Reith did not like was called 'The Napoleon of the BBC' (ibid., p. 278). Another article was called 'If I Ran the BBC' (ibid., p. 288).

[2] *Money Making in Stocks and Shares* (1927). A large part of this book was written on Southend Pier.   [3] *John Baird*, p. 109; *Private Diaries*, pp. 292, 295.

[4] *Moseley to W. E. G. Murray, 13 Sept. 1928.

holds barred.'¹ The Report of the Directors of the Television Company in 1929 stated the purpose of the war in more diplomatic language. 'Today the apparatus required for the successful transmission and reception of living scenes both by wire and wireless has reached such a stage as, in the opinion of most of them who have witnessed demonstrations, warrants broadcasting facilities being accorded so that the "listening-in" public might be afforded the opportunity of enjoying this new application of science.'²

Baird had not met Reith in October 1928—indeed Reith's diary for this period is silent on all matters relating to television—and by the BBC Moseley meant Peter Eckersley, the Chief Engineer, and Gladstone Murray, the Assistant Controller in charge of Public Relations. Murray seemed 'sympathetic': Eckersley, for the best of reasons, was sceptical. Not averse to publicity himself, he liked publicity to be backed up by practical achievement. In his first talks with Baird and Hutchinson he asked for genuine 'scientific investigation' without publicity. He knew, from Murray, that the *Daily Mail* had backed the Glasgow demonstration of 1927, and he had a healthy dislike of what were then called 'stunts' and now would be called 'gimmicks'.

In an undated memorandum, he expressed views to which he held consistently. Television was interesting and important, yet before it could become a new 'public service' there would have to be prolonged scientific experiment:

The advisers of the Baird Television Company believe that this apparatus is sufficiently developed to have a public service value. They contend that the attitude of the BBC is obstructive and irrational. The advisers of the BBC believe on the other hand that the Baird apparatus not only does not deserve a public trial, but also has reached the limit of its development owing to the basic technical limitations of the method employed.³

¹ *John Baird*, p. 294.
² *Baird Television Development Company Ltd., Report of the Directors, 11 Feb. 1929. It also stated that as soon as facilities were accorded, radio manufacturers would be ready to produce 'televisors' manufactured under licence from the Baird Television Development Company.
³ *Undated memorandum, 'Terms of Reference'. This memorandum was probably written after 1928, but the same ideas were expressed at a Control Board meeting as early as June 1927. Control Board Minutes, 21 June 1927.

Eckersley thought that however interesting Baird's work might be as laboratory work, it would be 'an insult to the public' to put on low-definition television pictures within the very narrow channel allowed to the BBC for medium-wave transmission. He also thought that it would be quite deceptive to encourage the idea—so confidently taken up by Moseley—that broadcast pictures would quickly 'improve'. Clear, detailed pictures required a wide television channel, and one effective television station working on medium waves would occupy more of a waveband than all the broadcasting stations, all the ships' stations, and all the long-wave stations were to occupy at the outbreak of the Second World War. Even if Baird's pictures were to 'improve' in 1928 and 1929, it would still not be possible to transmit them successfully through the narrow channels permitted on the medium waveband: if they did not improve, they were not worth transmitting.[1]

This categorical statement provided the basis for a clear, coherent, and sensible policy for the BBC to follow at that stage. If Baird and his technicians could show good pictures, the BBC would be glad to try and broadcast them, but it had to be recognized that it would be impossible to do so on existing wavelengths. Eckersley never tried to mislead the public about this policy. Indeed, in the same number of *Popular Wireless* in which Moseley first advertised Baird's work to what was thought of as a 'hostile' technical audience, Eckersley wrote an article on the opposite page stating his own views of the significance of television development.[2] In July 1928 the BBC issued a press statement in which it stated clearly that it had not 'so far been approached with apparatus of so practical a nature as to make television possible on a service basis'. 'When the development of the science has reached the stage where some form of service which will benefit listeners may be guaranteed, the BBC will be prepared, subject to the co-operation of the Postmaster-General, to co-operate in this matter.'[3]

Moseley made little effort to understand the BBC's point of view. With his fondness for a fight, he imagined himself

[1] P. P. Eckersley, *The Power Behind the Microphone* (1941), pp. 238-9.
[2] *Popular Wireless*, 14 July 1928; see also *John Baird*, p. 103. *Popular Wireless*, sceptical of television, had issued an offer of £1,000 in Mar. 1928 to anyone who could transmit within seven days more recognizable faces, various simple objects in action, and the hands of a clock. [3] *Manchester Guardian*, 16 July 1928.

championing the lone individual against the great monopoly, the inventor against the organization, the man without power and influence against those with 'the trappings of rank and title and high office'.[1] He was a 'no stuff and nonsense' man. This kind of fight is a favourite British pastime, hallowed by the popular press, but it does not necessarily achieve results.[2] Nor does it become more convincing when men of rank and title as well as journalists are used to support it. Moseley was very proud of the fact that Herbert Samuel maintained that 'it is not a happy position when any great monopoly can impede progress'.[3] There is no evidence that Samuel made any effort to discover the facts. Nor did some others whose names Moseley used.

Fortunately there were people who did. Baird's critics, indeed, included men who were far more outspoken than any sceptics inside the BBC. Campbell-Swinton, who, as we have seen, made his own contribution to the technical history of television, believed that Baird and Hutchinson were misleading an ignorant public. He felt that articles in the press in the late summer of 1928 stating that the Baird Television Development Company were going to 'broadcast their own programmes' were 'impudent'.[4] So, too, did some sections of the press. 'Known television systems are not capable of sufficient development', the *Daily Telegraph* noted, 'to warrant great optimism with regard to their early utility for television in the home.'[5]

This public debate was in the background in the autumn of 1928 when the question of relations between the Baird Television Development Company and the BBC was suddenly pushed to the forefront. Unfortunately the exact chronology of the story is far from completely clear. Not only does Reith's diary remain silent, but Moseley, for all his flurry of excitement, has left few precise comments in his own published diary. Even in the remarkably full BBC Archives some key documents are

[1] *John Baird*, p. 107.   [2] Ibid., p. 111.
[3] *There was a persistent attack on the BBC in the press 'for doing nothing about television' in 1928. Rather inadequately, the BBC decided that the best way to deal with it was to publish three articles in the *Radio Times*. See Control Board Minutes, 15 May 1928.
[4] *A. A. Campbell-Swinton to Peter Eckersley, 4 Aug. 1928.
[5] *Daily Telegraph*, 10 Mar. 1928.

missing. One point about the approach to relations is clear: far more than mechanical considerations influenced the argument, then and at later dates.

The prelude to the story was the publication in the late summer of 1928 of a series of Baird Television Development Company advertisements to which Campbell-Swinton objected. Their themes were 'Television For All' and 'Practical Television in the Home', and they suggested that regular television transmissions were about to start.[1] Very quickly, therefore, the question arose as to the attitude of the BBC towards the independent development of television.[2] Reith knew little of Baird or of television, but he believed from the start that speech transmissions and visual transmissions were part of the same technical and social complex and should not be separated. Broadcast telephotography and television were 'bound to come', he argued, 'and it would be a mistake to allow others to hinder them'.[3] Preoccupied as he was in 1928 and the early months of 1929 with other matters—mainly relationships with the Governors[4]—he did not consider that the BBC could ignore television developments. Nor, of course, could television interests ignore him. On at least one occasion in 1929 he was sounded as to whether he would head a television combine, 'at practically any figure'.[5]

It was the Post Office rather than the BBC which first took up with the Baird Television Development Company the question of the misleading advertisements.[6] It had been pressing Baird in vain since August 1927 to allow Post Office engineers to see a completely independent scientific demonstration,[7] and it refused to consider any question of regular 'broadcasting' until such a demonstration had been held.[8] Baird replied somewhat breathtakingly that there was unanimity of opinion among prominent radio manufacturing companies that his

---

[1] *The Times*, 22 June 1928; *Daily Chronicle*, 4 Aug. 1928. The first 'television' had been advertised much earlier in the year. See the *Daily Chronicle*, 21 Feb. 1928.

[2] *Control Board Minutes, 25 Sept. 1928. The advertisements were discussed on this occasion.

[3] Ibid., 14 July 1928.   [4] See above, pp. 425-30.

[5] Reith, Diary, 26 Apr. 1929.

[6] Letter of 7 Aug. 1928 (Post Office Archives).

[7] The first formal request had been made in a letter of 18 Aug. 1927 (Post Office Archives).

[8] Letter of 30 Aug. 1928 (Post Office Archives).

television system was more advanced than radio reception was when a public service was first instituted in 1922. The manufacturers now wanted to obtain licences to make and sell television apparatus as the radio manufacturers had wanted to make and sell wireless sets then.

The misleading precedent was hammered home. 'May I direct your attention to the fact that the licence to manufacture this apparatus will be of little avail unless coincidentally some sort of broadcasting at stated intervals can be assured to producers of television.'[1] Rumours of such 'broadcasts' freely circulated at the Radiolympia Exhibition. Christmas was mentioned vaguely as the date of the beginning of the broadcasts, and 200 metres as the wavelength.[2]

While approaching the Post Office, the Baird Television Development Company also approached the BBC with a formal request that one of its stations should be made available for Baird television transmissions. The wavelengths which the Post Office had assigned Baird in 1927, the Company claimed, were technically unsatisfactory. Moreover, the Services were grumbling that Baird transmissions were interfering with their work.[3] Confronted with this definite request, the Corporation temporized—doubtless for the kind of varied reasons that Eckersley had stated—and Baird was then reported in the press as saying that he intended to go ahead and apply for a station of his own with rights similar to those already granted to the BBC. 'Frankly,' he is said to have added, 'we regard the BBC as a rival organisation.'[4]

Before considering Baird's request further, the Post Office temporized too, suggesting quietly to Reith that if genuinely scientific demonstrations of Baird television, which both the G.P.O. and the BBC were demanding, proved that the invention had possibilities, the BBC should do as Baird had first asked and allow experimental transmissions from a BBC station.[5]

[1] Baird to Sir Evelyn Murray, 8 Sept. 1928 (Post Office Archives). For the precedent of 1922, see *The Birth of Broadcasting*, ch. III.

[2] *J. H. Whitehouse to W. E. G. Murray, reporting conversation with Bowyer Lowe, 25 Sept. 1928.

[3] The wavelengths had been assigned in the first instance in Aug. 1926 only after consultation and negotiations with the important Wireless Sub-Committee of the Imperial Communications Committee.

[4] *Evening Standard*, 10 Sept. 1928.

[5] *Sir Evelyn Murray to Reith, 12 Sept. 1928.

Reith agreed that before the BBC decided what to say to Baird the comments of Post Office engineers on Baird's work would be extremely useful. At long last, therefore, on 18 September 1928 a Post Office demonstration took place at Long Acre and at the Engineers' Club about 600 yards away. The 'televisor' receiver at the club was in a cabinet about the same size as a pedestal gramophone, and the objects shown included faces of individuals speaking and singing. The image was only $3\frac{1}{2}$ inches by 2 inches, although, with the help of a lens, it could be doubled in size. The mechanical scanner worked well, but the image flickered and was distorted by interference. An unfriendly observer complained that the image of the human head was 'grotesque rather than impressive', 'curiously ape-like, decapitated at the chin, and swaying up and down in a streaky stream of yellowy light'.[1] The Post Office engineers were sufficiently impressed, however, to urge the BBC to allow one of its stations to be used for further Baird experiments.[2]

Now came a crisis which only in the light of later events was not *the* crisis in the troubled relations between the Baird Television Development Company and the BBC. Eckersley was not satisfied with the Post Office report and insisted on the long-awaited independent BBC demonstration. This took place on 9 October 1928. It was attended by Reith, Peter Eckersley, Gladstone Murray, Roger Eckersley, Major C. F. Atkinson, and Noel Ashbridge, and it was agreed beforehand that no opinion was to be expressed either at the time of the demonstration or in reply to questioners afterwards.[3] Perhaps unfairly, although this was not a game of cricket, Peter Eckersley warned the party beforehand that all they would see would be the head and shoulders of a man. He added tersely that if they thought 'listeners' wanted to see the head and shoulders of a man, they would have to sacrifice an all too precious wavelength to do so. 'The question remains can the full length of a man be given adequately, or two men standing together talking, or a lot of men playing football, or a liner arriving at Plymouth, or any topical event? Can they, in fact, inadequately possibly, give

---

[1] *Whitehouse to W. E. G. Murray, 1 Oct. 1928.
[2] Post Office Report, 19 Sept. 1928; *Sir Evelyn Murray to Reith, 19 Sept. 1928.
[3] *Control Board Minutes, 9 Oct. 1928.

running commentaries? If they say that they cannot at present but will be able to do so later, our reply should be "then we will wait until you can before we do experiments".[1]

This was prejudging other people's opinions, and Eckersley was speaking with the weight of great technical authority. He did not hesitate to answer his own questions. 'They can polish up the head and shoulders, but they can never give a complete man. . . . They will never do anything approaching a running commentary, and to say that they can do so by experiment with our stations is perfect nonsense.'

The conclusion for him was plain. 'If it is thought by the Control Board that what they see demonstrated, i.e. what has been done by Baird, justifies in itself a service, then let us go ahead, but I warn everyone that in my opinion, it is the end of their development, not the beginning, and that we shall be for ever sending heads and shoulders. Are heads and shoulders a service?'[2]

With the words of this document ringing in their ears, the members of the Control Board saw the demonstration. It was worse than they anticipated. Gladstone Murray, whom Moseley had considered 'sympathetic,'[3] thought that 'from the angle of service' the demonstration 'would be merely ludicrous if its financial implications did not make it sinister'. 'Keeping in mind the fundamental fact that the intrusion of Baird transmissions into the broadcasting band will gravely disturb our normal service and prejudice the Regional Scheme, I think it is our duty to resist or delay the suggestion in every reasonable and possible way.' Murray did not fear a clash with the Post Office on the issue. 'It is obviously the intention of the Post Office to dump the blame for further obstruction on our shoulders. This does not worry me in the slightest. We can carry well-informed and disinterested opinion with us. This is all that matters.'[4]

[1] *Peter Eckersley, 'Note on Suggested Attitudes Towards Television', 8 Oct. 1928.
[2] Ibid. [3] See above, p. 530.
[4] *W. E. G. Murray, Note on 'Yesterday's Television Test', 10 Oct. 1928. Murray wrote round to a number of newspapers warning them 'to avoid accepting rumours of the favourable attitude of the BBC towards the Baird Television Scheme': e.g. Murray to R. M. Barrington-Ward, 15 Oct. 1928. Many of them shared the BBC's doubts. See a letter from the editor of the Daily Express to Murray, 15 Oct. 1928.

44. J. L. Baird at Work (1925)

(a) *The Man with the Flower in His Mouth* (1930)

Left to right. George Inns, Lance Sieveking, Gladys Young, Earl Grey, Denis Freeman (kneeling), Lionel Millard, and Mary Eversley

(b) *The Man with the Flower in His Mouth* (1930)

Standing, Lance Sieveking with his Fading Board; *seated*, Val Gielgud

(c) Experimental Television from Broadcasting House (1935)

45. Early Television

(*a*) Ready for the Camera   (*b*) As seen by the Viewer

46. Early Images

Jane Carr made up for Television by E. Robb (1932). 'The face is whitened, and blue black is applied to the eyebrows, lashes, side of nose and lips—Heavy white is applied between lids and eyebrows'

47. The First Transmission (1932)
Left to right. J. L. Baird, S. Moseley, and Sir H. Greer

48. Preparing for Televising the Coronation (1937)
On the plinth, Sir Noel Ashbridge. Also in the party, Carpendale, Graves, Tallents, Selsdon, F. W. Phillips, and Shoenberg

There was, however, one other fact that mattered, and it was a fact that Moseley appreciated. The BBC had allowed and was allowing experiments with vision. It seemed to be treating Baird and the initiators of the other experiments in contrasting ways: moreover, the other experiments did not necessarily point forward to technical perfection. Moseley was quick to notice the willingness of the BBC to co-operate with Wireless Pictures, a company formed in January 1927 and reshaped in August 1928: indeed, on his side, he saw something 'sinister' in this.[1] Wireless Pictures Ltd., unlike the Baird Television Development Company, was interested only in still pictures—not television—but it had been granted rights to an experimental service (with Post Office approval) in July 1928.

The 'Fultograph', invented by Otto Fulton, the Technical Controller and Adviser of the Wireless Pictures company, cost £22 and printed a picture of only 4 inches by 5 inches. Sales were not very great, and yet the BBC continued to allow the 'experiments' in October 1928, just at the time when the Baird issue came to a head.[2] Technical specialists—a somewhat smaller body than Murray's 'well informed and disinterested opinion' —might know that the Fultograph broadcasts did not raise the same technical difficulties and dilemmas as Baird's television. They might know also that the process had been tried and tested and was in use in Vienna and Berlin. The public, however, knew nothing of this, and for its part the Post Office did not consider that Baird ought to be treated differently from Wireless Pictures Ltd. In view of the facilities offered to Fulton, the Post Office told Reith, it would be difficult to refuse Baird.[3]

Yet this is precisely what the BBC did do after the unfavourable demonstration of 9 October 1928. It drew up a statement which the Post Office regarded as too 'uncompromising', and continued to stand by it after Reith had telephoned the Post Office.[4] The statement as issued by the Governors on 17 October read that 'the opinion of the BBC representatives was that, while

[1] *Private Diaries*, p. 294. It was a fact that when the BBC allowed experimental transmissions in 1929, a share issue made by Wireless Pictures was over-subscribed.

[2] *Control Board Minutes, 3 and 17 July, 15 Aug., 2 Oct. 1928.

[3] Letter of 25 Sept. 1928 (Post Office Archives). Baird bought out Wireless Pictures in Apr. 1929.

[4] Reith to Phillips, 15 Oct. 1928; Phillips to Reith, 16 Oct. 1928 (Post Office Archives).

the [Baird] demonstration was interesting as an experiment, it failed to fulfil the conditions which would justify trial through a BBC station. The Board of the Corporation has decided that an experimental transmission through a BBC station shall not be undertaken at present. The Corporation would be ready to review the decision if and when development justified it.'[1]

Manville protested at once to the Post Office that the BBC was arrogating to itself functions which had never been delegated to it,[2] and Moseley told Murray that the statement was 'a terrible mistake'. In face of this barrage, the BBC did not shrink. Murray replied briefly to Moseley that the statement was the result of extremely careful thought. 'It would have been far easier and a more popular course for our people to have gone ahead with co-operation now, but they felt it their duty to adopt the more difficult course.' In the heat of the moment, however, Murray went much further than this and far further than Reith had done. 'For the future,' he added, 'I am not sure whether broadcasting as it is now established should ever absorb television even in a state of development that would justify general application. It is more probable that television will evolve a new art form in its own way and for its own public.'[3]

The crisis had almost reached its climax, and by the middle of November 1928 Murray as well as Moseley was talking of 'hostilities'. On the one side, the Baird Television Development Company had formally asked the Postmaster-General for a licence to operate its own broadcasting station.[4] On the other side the BBC was almost as suspicious of the Post Office as it was of the Baird Television Development Company. Reith and Clarendon, the Chairman of the Board of Governors, saw the Postmaster-General, Sir William Mitchell-Thomson, and were 'threatened' that if the BBC did not 'let' Baird have 'a private show' the Post Office 'would give an experimental licence to Baird for higher power' and 'for speech as well'.[5] It was doubt-

[1] The original copy of this note is missing from the BBC Archives.
[2] Manville to the Postmaster-General, 19 Oct. 1928 (Post Office Archives).
[3] *Moseley to W. E. G. Murray, 22 Oct. 1928; Murray to Moseley, 23 Oct. 1928.
[4] Letter to the Post Office, 25 Oct. 1928 (Post Office Archives).
[5] Reith, Diary, 6 Nov. 1928. Reith added of the Postmaster-General that he was 'a feeble and blustering creature: thought less of him than ever'.

less in the light of this meeting that Control Board decided the same day that should the Baird Television Development Company be given an experimental station for itself—which it clearly considered to be a possibility—the BBC monopoly of sound should be 'strenuously upheld'.[1]

The BBC had no intention of abandoning television lightly. In a further and longer statement of November 1928, 'The Truth About Television', it emphasized that 'without the introduction of some new and revolutionary principle', television, in which it was genuinely interested, could not become a visual counterpart of sound. All existing television systems were incapable of producing pictures up to the standard even of newspaper photographs and drawings. Campbell-Swinton was quoted to the effect that future realization of this standard was beyond 'the possible capacity of any mechanism with moving parts'.[2] There were other problems in 1928, however, besides mechanical scanning. The requirement for television purposes of a large number of twin-wave stations ran counter to the policy, associated with the Regional Scheme, of building a smaller number of high-power stations.[3] 'What would be given to the millions of listeners to compensate them for the loss of the alternative programmes for which they have been waiting for years?' A few 'viewers' might enjoy a curious spectacle but large numbers of others would suffer. 'Such a move would upset the democratic foundation of British broadcasting and disturb its basic tradition of the greatest good for the greatest number.'[4]

After this statement was issued, Murray met Moseley and Hutchinson 'in the middle of hostilities' to go over the events of the previous few weeks. Hutchinson felt that the BBC's attitude towards the Baird demonstration had been 'perfunctory, casual and frivolous' and that subsequent statements had been 'a gross breach of faith and manners'. He purported to detect 'sinister' influences behind the Corporation's attitude, and was unconvinced by Murray's reply that there were no extraneous or hidden motives. He also attacked Peter Eckersley

[1] *Control Board Minutes, 6 Nov. 1928.
[2] Campbell-Swinton had stated this in a letter to *The Times*, 20 July 1928.
[3] See above, pp. 293–5.
[4] *BBC statement of Nov. 1928, 'The Truth About Television'.

for his personal share in condemning Baird's work. Murray in reply insisted that all the Corporation's officials from the Director-General downwards were determined to implement a common policy, which was 'to resist television while it is still premature and to welcome it and give it every encouragement once it has reached a stage where it may fairly be regarded as being available for general service as an adjunct [*sic*] to broadcasting'.[1]

In acknowledging a copy of Murray's notes on this meeting, Moseley showed how strained relations were. He agreed that 'Broadcasting and Television must come together', but did not feel that Murray's methods offered the best way of achieving the union. He would have been even more suspicious had he heard Peter Eckersley report to Control Board at the end of November that there were rumours that the British Thomson-Houston Company and the Marconi Company had 'competitive schemes under way'.[2] This had been very vaguely hinted at during the conversations with Hutchinson and Moseley and was, of course, implicit in much that Campbell-Swinton was saying. Not all the suspicions, however, were on Moseley's side. The BBC itself was highly suspicious of rumours that Hutchinson had been approaching continental broadcasting authorities, Dutch, German, and French, to relay Baird transmissions: it seemed very odd that 'repeated efforts to get from France the truth about the reputed Tour Eiffel arrangement for television and English hours next February have drawn no *réponse* or *démenti*'.[3]

Given such suspicions on both sides, the Post Office was determined, none the less, to seek reconciliation. The main reason was political. The Postmaster-General made it clear to the BBC that he was finding it difficult politically to defend an entirely negative attitude to television. He did not suggest that the BBC engineers were wrong in their pessimistic forecasts of the future of Baird's inventions, yet he went on to say that he felt it was necessary that there should be still another scientific

---

[1] *'Notes on a meeting with Captain Hutchinson and Sydney Moseley in Long Acre at 11.30 a.m. on the 19th inst.' The notes were sent to Moseley so that there would be no misunderstanding (W. E. G. Murray to Moseley, 20 Nov. 1928). Moseley did not fully accept them and felt in any case that they should not have been taken at all (Moseley to Murray, 21 Nov. 1928).

[2] *Control Board Minutes, 27 Nov. 1928.

[3] *Notes by C. F. Atkinson, 11 Dec. 1928.

demonstration under stringent conditions. This time there should be a panel of independent judges including himself, Sir Evelyn Murray, Reith, Carpendale, some of the Governors of the BBC, and a few selected Members of Parliament. The panel should be split into two groups, one to witness the reception of television at Savoy Hill, the other to be stationed at the Post Office in St. Martin's-le-Grand. The demonstration and tests were to be held in complete secrecy.[1]

Reith, Manville, and Mitchell-Thomson agreed on this procedure,[2] but it was impossible to maintain the secrecy on which the BBC had insisted. The proposed test was the subject of general gossip in the lobby of the House of Commons as early as the first week of December, and in the first fortnight of January it broke out into the newspapers. 'Further trials of the Baird television apparatus will take place, it is understood, in February,' the *Daily Telegraph* stated, 'and one or more of the BBC stations will be used for this purpose. It is part of the agreement, however, between the BBC and the Baird Company that these tests shall take place secretly and that no publicity shall be given to them until the BBC has thoroughly considered the results of the trials.'[3]

The Baird Television Development Company denied any responsibility for the leak or for a similar statement in *Popular Wireless* four days later.[4] People inside the BBC believed, however, that it inspired an article in *The People* a few days later with the banner headline 'The Great Wireless Mystery'. 'The attitude of the BBC in regard to this amazing British invention is absolutely incomprehensible', *The People* thundered. 'What justification has the BBC for denying to the British public the same opportunities which are now open, or very soon will be open, to wireless enthusiasts in other parts of the world?'[5]

It was known that Baird had been receiving a stream of foreign visitors in the last few weeks of 1928 and that some of

[1] *Sir Evelyn Murray to Reith, 13 and 26 Nov. 1928.
[2] *Reith to Sir Evelyn Murray, 3 and 11 Dec. 1928; Hutchinson to Reith, 18 Dec. 1928; Reith to Sir Evelyn Murray, 18 Dec. 1928.
[3] *Daily Telegraph*, 1 Jan. 1929.
[4] *Popular Wireless*, 5 Jan. 1929. 'There are to be trials from the BBC stations, presumably conducted with guarantees of secrecy. It is believed that these will take place in February.'
[5] *The People*, 6 Jan. 1929.

their views were very similar to those expressed in *The People*. 'Unquestionably the Baird system is increasingly in advance of any system on the Continent', one of them wrote; 'it seems to be extraordinary that a British invention should be unable to obtain facilities for its development in the country of its birth.'[1] 'I have no doubt in my mind from what I have seen here in London', the Technical Manager of the Czechoslovakian Broadcasting Service added, 'that television has definitely reached a commercial stage.'[2] The feeling that the BBC would eventually co-operate was communicated to Moseley by E. J. Robertson of the Beaverbrook Press who told him that after several interviews with people inside the BBC he was sure that the Corporation would 'give your people the chance for which they have been waiting'.[3]

Three days after the article in *The People*, the *Financial Times* published the categorical statement that there was a *rapprochement* between the BBC and the Baird Television Development Company, and the *Manchester Guardian* stated that Baird transmissions would be given by the BBC in February.[4] As the price of Baird shares rose on the Stock Exchange, the BBC's reaction was to republish the original brief statement the Governors had drafted on 17 October. Baird retaliated with a statement complaining that the BBC had violated a pledge of secrecy.[5] The two messages were published simultaneously. Indeed, just after the BBC's Control Board had decided to send a copy of its statement to Baird's company, a messenger from Baird's company arrived during the discussion with a copy of the company's statement.[6] The struggle seemed to have begun all over again.

In fact, negotiations for a further test continued along the lines discussed in the earlier tripartite correspondence. The Baird Television Development Company cultivated a 'progres-

[1] Note by F. Gradenwitz in *Television*, December 1928, quoted in *Baird of Television*, pp. 136–7.

[2] Quoted ibid., p. 137. For a favourable British viewpoint, see Sir Ambrose Fleming's article in *Television*, Nov. 1928. 'There is no reason to despair of the possibility of television being carried on with mechanical movements. . . . All invention progresses by steps of evolution and we cannot at one jump attain the ideal perfection.' For two more cautious articles, see M. P. Davis, the Vice-President of Westinghouse, and Dr. A. N. Goldsmith in the *New York Times*, 16 Sept. 1928.   [3] *Private Diaries*, p. 298.

[4] *Financial Times*, 9 Jan. 1929; *Manchester Guardian*, 9 Jan. 1929.

[5] Ibid., 10 Jan. 1929.   [6] *Control Board Minutes, 9 Jan. 1929.

sively friendlier attitude towards the BBC' in the last half of January,[1] and Baird International shares rose sharply, partly on rumours of imminent foreign deals, partly on rumours of a forth-coming merger between the Baird concerns and Wireless Pictures Ltd. On the last day of the month Reith met Hutchinson for the first time, noting briefly and unemotionally in his diary that 'they are supposed to be giving us a demonstration in February'.[2] By a curious coincidence, this was the day that Reith first realized that domestic difficulties were jeopardizing the position of Peter Eckersley within the BBC. Although Eckersley carried on protracted and often acrimonious negotiations with the Baird Television Development Company until his resignation in the autumn of 1929, his role inside the BBC had been weakened. The way was prepared for what he later described, with exaggeration, as a 'reversal of policy'.[3]

At his meeting with Hutchinson, Reith began by asking about the financial pattern of Baird interests, being answered by Hutchinson that he and his colleagues were 'in no way market jugglers'. They went on to discuss foreign interests in the project, and the details of the further demonstration. Reith has often been depicted as the arch-enemy of Baird,[4] but in his last words to Hutchinson he said without equivocation that 'it was a pity they should prejudice their technical case by exaggerated and unwarranted statements concerning immediate commercial and public use'. And although he had been upset after his own meeting with Eckersley, he told Hutchinson that it was 'absurd' to blame Eckersley for the BBC's attitude to Baird.[5]

The 'reversal of policy' owed much to what Gladstone Murray called 'political pressure'. Questions were asked and answered in the House of Commons on 29 January and 5 February which seemed to link the BBC directly with the Baird

[1] *W. E. G. Murray to Reith, 28 Jan. 1929.

[2] Reith, Diary, 31 Jan. 1929.

[3] *The Power Behind the Microphone*, p. 238.

[4] Notably in Moseley's book, where the position is overpersonalized. See particularly ch. viii, 'The Monopoly says No'. Moseley also described the 'conflict' as 'a classic illustration of what may happen in any clash between Private and National enterprise' (p. 113).

[5] *Note by Reith to Carpendale, Eckersley, and Gladstone Murray, 31 Jan. 1929.

interests.[1] The most that the BBC could do was to suggest that the picture of an 'enlightened' Postmaster-General disposing of reactionary resistance was quite inaccurate. The demonstration did, in fact, take place—a little later than had been first suggested—on 5 March. One of the 'performers' was Jack Buchanan, an old friend of Baird.[2] As a result of it the Postmaster-General reiterated his earlier opinion that the Baird system was capable of producing an image of sufficient clarity and definition to justify regular experimental BBC transmissions. He called it a 'noteworthy scientific achievement', adding that while the system was not sufficiently developed to justify television 'programmes' within regular listening hours, he would assent to a BBC station being made available outside regular broadcasting hours. He made two further points—first, that since medium waveband broadcasting was seriously congested, the Company should press on with requirements 'on a much lower band', and second, that neither the Postmaster-General nor the BBC should accept any responsibility for 'the quality of the transmission or for the results obtained'. People who bought 'televisors' were buying them at their own risk.[3]

On receiving this welcome news from the Postmaster-General, Hutchinson wrote at once to Eckersley.[4] He did not get an immediate reply, for Eckersley was in Prague.[5] There was an air of procrastination, indeed, inside the BBC which, given the decision of the Post Office, was scarcely a helpful contribution to the further development of experiment. For the first time in

[1] Colonel Malone asked the Postmaster-General about the 'secret' demonstration, and the Postmaster-General robbed it of its secrecy by giving the date. Thurtle asked Sir Philip Cunliffe-Lister why the Baird Television Development Company had not held an annual meeting or issued any accounts since the Company was formed in 1927 and was told that only now were negotiations in progress with the BBC which would clarify the Company's future.

[2] *Baird of Television*, p. 144.

[3] *Sir Evelyn Murray to the Baird Television Development Company, 27 Mar. 1929. For a quite different opinion of the demonstration, see *Popular Wireless*, 16 Mar. 1929.

[4] *Hutchinson to Eckersley, 4 Apr. 1929.

[5] *Ashbridge to Hutchinson, 5 Apr. 1929. There were many further delays and further reasons given for delay on this and other issues during the next few months. On 2 May 1929 Hutchinson was still protesting at 'the seeming delay in making definite arrangements' (letter to Eckersley, 2 May 1929). He pointed out that the delay was hampering foreign deals with European and Colonial interests. He enclosed a note of the German Reichs-Rundfunk-Gesellschaft, which backed up his case.

the story the BBC was behaving in a manner which it is difficult to justify. The only real reason it could give for delay—and unfortunately the reason was not advanced at once—was that until the overdue Brookmans Park transmitter was available the Corporation was extremely short of transmitters.[1]

No attempt was made to offer temporary help, and after Hutchinson had written an important letter setting out his complaints about the BBC's attitude on 15 May, he had to send a second letter on 24 May asking why he had not received a reply.[2] It was not until 26 June 1929 that the BBC promised in a very grudging letter the use of 2LO for certain limited periods outside broadcasting hours—three morning broadcasts weekly of one-quarter of an hour.[3] Carpendale's grim list of conditions contrasts sharply with the enthusiasm and excitement about experiments which rang through some of Hutchinson's earlier letters. Not surprisingly, Hutchinson refused the offer and said that it would be necessary to reopen the matter with the Postmaster-General.[4] Accordingly, Ampthill and Manville wrote a long letter to the Post Office setting out the position as they saw it.[5]

On 6 August Reith saw Sir Evelyn Murray at the Post Office —television was only the third item on the 'agenda'[6]—and the following day the BBC more generously considered granting the Baird Television Development Company five half-hours a week outside programme hours.[7] Reith, who was not responsible personally for the earlier delays,[8] formally offered the increased allocation of hours on 12 August,[9] and the Post Office advised

[1] See above, pp. 309–10. The point about Brookmans Park was made clearly for the first time only on 6 May. *Eckersley to Hutchinson, 6 May 1929.
[2] *Hutchinson to Eckersley, 15 and 24 May 1929.
[3] *Carpendale to the Baird Television Development Company, 26 June 1929.
[4] *T. W. Bartlett (Secretary of the B.T.D. Co.) to Carpendale, 9 July 1929.
[5] Ampthill and Manville to the Postmaster-General, 9 July 1929 (Post Office Archives).
[6] Reith, Diary, 6 Aug. 1929.
[7] *Control Board Minutes, 7 Aug. 1929.
[8] In a scribbled note on an account of a meeting between W. E. G. Murray and the Secretary of the Television Society, Reith complained, however, of the 'gross misrepresentation' by the Society in suggesting that the BBC had delayed matters. 'I don't like either personally or the BBC officially to be called evasive or dilatory, etc.' (8 Aug. 1929). Nonetheless, it seems that the charges in this particular case were justified.
[9] Reith to Phillips, 12 Aug. 1929 (Post Office Archives).

Hutchinson to accept. 'The Postmaster-General considers that in present circumstances these periods should be sufficient for the proposed experimental service.' He did not accept a proposal from Hutchinson that the experiments should be guaranteed for a period of years, maintaining that 'the BBC should be free to use their stations for whatever system may ultimately prove to be the most suitable. . . . It is hardly, however, necessary to point out', he concluded, 'that if the proposed experimental service proves a success and meets with widespread appreciation, there will be a public demand for a regular and permanent service: and the conditions under which such a demand should be met will then be considered.'[1]

Hutchinson accepted the offer on 4 September, although he called it inadequate. It was a 'temporary measure', to which there was no alternative.[2] After a long meeting at the BBC on 11 September, at which both Hutchinson and Baird were present for the first time, it was agreed that transmissions should begin on 30 September. (Reith was not present.) They would start from the Oxford Street transmitter and later be transferred to Brookmans Park. Transmission times were normally to be from 11 to 11.30 in the morning on weekdays, excluding Saturdays, with the possibility of occasional broadcasts after midnight.[3]

Two riders were of special interest—one in relation to what was to happen in 1936, the other in relation to what was to happen in 1954. 'We desire to make it clear that no monopoly can be created for any proprietary system of television': this left the way open for the rival system that eventually triumphed in 1936. 'In accordance with the Corporation's Charter, no advertising matter can be transmitted': this left one way firmly closed until 1954.

[1] *W. T. Leech to Hutchinson, 14 Aug. 1929.
[2] *Hutchinson to H. B. Lees-Smith, 4 Sept. 1929.
[3] *Carpendale to Hutchinson, 11 Sept. 1929.

2. The Experiment

ECKERSLEY left the BBC a few weeks before the 30-line 'experimental broadcasts' began. A joint statement of the BBC and the Baird Television Development Company, announcing that they were to take place, was issued two days after his last attendance at the Control Board. 'The object of the demonstrations', the statement read, 'is to afford the Baird Company wider opportunity than they have hitherto possessed for developing the possibilities of their system of television and for extending the scope and improving the quality of reproduction.'[1] The Baird Television Development Company had agreed to all the BBC's conditions.[2] A period of co-operation began, often cautious, sometimes cordial, which was to last until the first official inquiry into television in 1934.[3]

The first transmission 'was a great day for Baird and for all of us', Moseley has written.[4] In all the complex negotiations between GPO, BBC, and BTDC, Baird himself had been a shadowy figure in the background, an eccentric who lived in a world of his own rather than dreamed of a new world of television opening up for millions of viewers. There were no millions of viewers when a letter from William Graham, President of the Board of Trade in Britain's second Labour government, was read on 30 September: had he appeared, he would have made the maiden broadcast of any British politician on British television. The 'performers' who did appear were Sydney Moseley, Sir Ambrose Fleming, Professor E. N. da C. Andrade, Sydney Howard, the comedian, Miss Lulu Stanley, the singer, and Miss King. When Baird, who spoke extremely briefly, was asked how many people he thought had been able to receive the programme, he put the total at under thirty. 'There is one receiving set at my home on Box Hill, and I believe the BBC and the Post Office each have one. That makes three and I should say there are half a dozen other sets in the

[1] *Joint Press Statement, 11 Sept. 1929.
[2] *Hutchinson to Carpendale, 26 Sept. 1929.
[3] See below, pp. 582–94.
[4] *John Baird*, p. 118.

country. Add to them the receivers which clever amateurs may have built for themselves from our directions and you might count another twenty. That makes twenty-nine in all.'[1]

Technical conditions were appalling. Because only one BBC transmitter was available, sound and vision could not be synchronized and the sound and the pictures had to be transmitted alternately in two-minute sequences. The transmitting apparatus was imperfect, and because two wires were badly connected, viewers in the early stages of the broadcast saw only a waving silhouette instead of a recognizable human face. At the receiving end, even with the help of a lens, the picture was only as big as a saucer. 'The general effect', one viewer put it, 'is similar to that of looking into an automatic picture-machine as installed in amusement halls.'[2]

This was far from the 'candy floss' with which television came to be associated. Baird had the vision to see into the future as Sarnoff and Burrows had seen into the future of sound radio before the BBC came into existence.[3] 'Television from the BBC station will begin modestly, with turns such as a single singer. But it is only a question of time before "lookers-in" will see the Derby or the Cup Final.'[4] Yet even when technical conditions were so appallingly bad—and no high official of the BBC had graced the opening transmission—Baird was still proud enough to claim that 'it is a great day for Britain that she is the first country to give official recognition to television'.[5]

The first big step forward was dependent not on Baird, but on the BBC. Synchronization of sound and vision was achieved on 30 March 1930. The second circuit at Brookmans Park was brought into use a few weeks after the opening of the new station. R. C. Sherriff, the author of the 'hit' play, *Journey's End*, and Gracie Fields were among the performers, and a 'televisor' was installed at 10 Downing Street to enable the Prime Minister, Ramsay MacDonald, and his family to enjoy the programme. Before this historic occasion the BBC had already extended the hours of television transmission. The withdrawal

[1] Quoted *John Baird*, p. 19.   [2] *Amateur Wireless*, Oct. 1929.
[3] See *The Birth of Broadcasting*, pp. 39–40.
[4] *Evening News*, 30 Sept. 1929.
[5] Quoted in *John Baird*, p. 128.

of the Fultograph experiment in November 1929 permitted, without strain, an additional half-hour on Tuesdays and Fridays after the end of regular broadcasting.[1]

The synchronization of sound and vision, which the Baird Television Development Company felt was a necessary technical pre-condition of their selling 'televisors' to customers, followed logically. The price of 'televisors' was set at 25 guineas, although very few of them were sold. MacDonald hailed the transmission as a 'wonderful miracle', telling Baird that he had 'put something in his room which would never let him forget how strange the world was—and how unknown'.[2] There were other observers, however, who pointed to the many technical flaws. 'The general reproduction reminded me considerably of the early "movies", in which the characters lived, moved and had their being in a heavy and persistent shower of rain. A black smudge at the bottom of the picture was an incidental flaw caused by some technical defect either at Brookmans Park or Savoy Hill.'[3]

In the negotiations about these developments Ashbridge, the new Chief Engineer, wrote and argued sensibly and in a co-operative spirit. He warned Bartlett, the secretary of BTDC, as also did Reith, that good sound might actually handicap the appreciation of faulty vision.[4] Other people inside the BBC were less co-operative. R. Gambier-Parry, the Information Executive, told Bartlett in December 1929 that if sound and vision were synchronized and full programmes were transmitted, 'they would have to be subject to rigorous censorship by ourselves, and they would have to be submitted to me at least two weeks ahead'. Such an attitude is antipathetic to all experiment. Bartlett, however, tried to be helpful. 'He was prepared to go further in advance than two weeks,' Gambier-Parry wrote, 'but I did not want this as I was anxious to avoid any excuse for including his programmes in the *Radio Times*.'[5] The gracelessness of this attitude is also revealed in the *BBC Year*

[1] *Bartlett to Reith, 11 Nov. 1929; Control Board Minutes, 12 Nov. 1929. Bartlett to Reith, 22 Nov. 1929; Reith to Bartlett, 27 Nov. 1929. See also *Private Diaries*, pp. 303–4.

[2] MacDonald to Baird, 5 Apr. 1930, quoted in *Baird of Television*, p. 153.

[3] Quoted in *John Baird*, p. 131.

[4] *Note by Ashbridge, 'Television Tests', 25 Nov. 1929.

[5] *Gambier-Parry to W. E. G. Murray, 18 Dec. 1929.

Book for 1931 where no reference is made to the historic date of 30 March 1930.[1]

Fortunately at a different level there was some understanding of what the term 'experiment' really meant. In an article on 'The Future of Broadcast Drama' in the *BBC Year Book* (1931) Tyrone Guthrie, who, as a bright young man, had already produced many experimental productions for sound radio, stated that the future inevitably lay with television rather than with sound radio. 'In fusion with the visual arts,' he went on, 'I believe the broadcast drama will lose most of its individuality and its virtue, but will only then for the first time come into its own in popular esteem: will only then take its place as the most popular method of entertainment, and consequently as the most forceful medium of propaganda in the history of the world.'[2] This was not a one-sided verdict, and it displayed genuine imagination. So, too, did R. C. Sherriff's statement at the end of the first broadcast of combined sound and vision: 'I am afraid if this invention becomes too perfect, it will cause most people to spend their evenings at home instead of visiting the theatre.'[3]

It was in a mood of excitement and with a desire to experiment that Val Gielgud asked for permission in May 1930 for Lance Sieveking to produce the first television play, Pirandello's *The Man with the Flower in His Mouth*.[4] The idea of a play may have come from Moseley, who was scheduled as joint producer.[5] Again the BBC's consent was grudging. 'There was some discussion as to whether this co-operation was desirable, and it was decided that the collaboration should be made free of charge, A.C.(I) [Murray] restraining the Television Company from using it for undue publicity.'[6]

Behind the grudging language was the nagging fear, never dispelled, that to build up publicity was to lead the public along the garden path. In *The Man with the Flower in His Mouth* only one figure could be projected at a time and that figure could scarcely move. The focus was still uncertain and variable. George Inns, who arranged the effects, felt that it was

[1] *BBC Year Book* (1931), p. 66.
[2] Ibid., pp. 185–90. See above, p. 58.
[3] Quoted in *John Baird*, p. 133.
[4] *Control Board Minutes, 6 May 1930.
[5] For Moseley's account, see *John Baird*, pp. 133 ff.
[6] *Control Board Minutes, 6 May 1930.

all very primitive and that television had no future.[1] He certainly did not foresee that in the distant future he would win the Premier Award at an International Television Festival. Yet the press gave the performance an enthusiastic reception. Val Gielgud considered the whole experiment 'most interesting' and Sieveking wrote 'a full production report'.[2]

The play, in which Gladys Young took part, was a fascinating artistic experiment, but Control Board, ignoring the enthusiasm, hoped that it was the kind of experiment which would not be repeated. 'Whilst this play provided material of interest to the Productions Department and no doubt to the Baird Company and showed our willingness to co-operate to the limits of which their system was capable, no material technical progress has been made such as would justify our Programme Branch co-operating any further. Such co-operation, with attendant publicity, would mislead the public as to the possibilities of the system now or as now foreseen. Our future action therefore would be only that the Engineering Branch holds a watching brief.'[3]

In fact, Baird himself was always exploring the fringes of his imperfect medium, taking up one experiment after another, more with the passion of an artist than the prudence of a scientist, and with Moseley acting as an omni-present impresario and calling himself 'Director of Television Programmes'. In July 1930 Baird introduced a big television screen to the public, and each evening for a fortnight a part of the performance at the London Coliseum was devoted to a 'tele-talkie' demonstration in which eminent men and women, including George Robey and George Lansburg, were seen projected upon a television screen measuring five feet by two feet.[4] The form of the big screen, made up not of neon tubes and Kerr cells but of a honeycomb of over 2,000 cells into each of which a peanut-type filament lamp was placed, marked technical regression rather than progress, yet the performance was warmly applauded in Berlin, Paris, and Stockholm as well as London.

Early in 1931 he went on to demonstrate 'zone television', with as many as eight full-length figures projected on the

[1] *Television Programme, *Window on the World*, 7 Nov. 1961.
[2] *John Baird*, pp. 138–9.   [3] *Control Board Minutes, 22 July 1930.
[4] *Baird of Television*, pp. 166–7; J. Swift, *Adventure in Vision* (1950), p. 46.

receiving screen and a cricket lesson by Herbert Strudwick.[1] In May 1931 he showed street scenes in normal daylight,[2] and one month later televised the Derby. On that occasion the Nipkow discs were abandoned and mirror drums used. 'The broadcast is important', *The Times* noted, 'in that it is the first attempt which has been made, in this or in any other country, to secure a television transmission of a topical event held in the open air, when artificial light is impossible.'[3] In spite of poor definition, viewers could see the parade of horses and all the excitement of the race itself. 'The result astonished us all', another journalist put it. 'We had found the stepping-stone to a new era in which mechanical eyes will see for us great events as they happen and convey them to us at our homes.'[4]

More important perhaps than these 'public demonstrations' was the series of experiments with short-wave television transmissions, culminating in April 1932 with what was described as 'the world's first demonstration of ultra-short-wave television'.[5] Baird did not know that the BBC had already undertaken ultra-short-wave experiments in 1931.[6] Eckersley had been doubtful of their usefulness on the grounds that they would cover only a limited area,[7] and Baird himself had expressed the same view on a visit to the United States in September 1931.[8] Yet Baird was willing, when occasion demanded, to change his mind. After securing permission from the Post Office to use a separate wavelength for this and further experimental broadcasts independently of the BBC,[9] he began to work co-operatively with the BBC from December 1932 onwards.[10]

[1] *The Times*, 5 Jan. 1931.

[2] *Daily Mail*, 9 May 1931.

[3] *The Times*, 4 June 1931.

[4] *Daily Herald*, 4 June 1931; see also the *Daily Telegraph*, 4 June 1931.

[5] *BBC Press Release, 29 Apr. 1932.

[6] *Control Board Minutes, 6 Oct. 1931. R.C.A. had also carried out tests.

[7] *The Power Behind the Microphone*, p. 239.

[8] *John Baird*, pp. 210–11.

[9] *Letter of Agreement 1931, quoted ibid., p. 159. The BBC was annoyed that Baird had been given permission to use ultra-short waves (*Carpendale to Phillips, 28 Apr. 1932). Phillips replied on 7 May that the BBC had only been consulted in the past 'if the proposals raised the question of a public service or of the use of the Corporation's stations'.

[10] *BBC Press Release, 5 Dec. 1932. A wavelength of 7·3 metres was used and the pictures were stated to have 'much more detail and no flicker'. Baird wrote to Reith (6 Dec. 1932) attaching the highest importance to this work, which he said was more advanced than that carried on by the American Radio Trust.

He showed complete inflexibility, however, in relation to non-mechanical methods of scanning—partly, perhaps, because the financial and technical resources for large-scale experiments were beyond his reach. 'There is no hope for television by means of cathode ray tubes', he told the Americans in September 1931. Limitations of outlook quickly became prejudices, and the fatal flaw in Baird's work was his inability to see beyond these limitations. The result was that for all his ingenuity and enterprise, he was doomed to be what Rebecca West aptly called 'the man who sows the seed and does not reap the harvest'.[1] With Moseley's aid he was publicizing television in 1931 and 1932, not ensuring that his own system would be the technical basis of a new service.

Yet it is difficult in retrospect not to catch the excitement of all that he was doing. He had abundant vision even if his techniques were limited. The BBC did not always appreciate the vision. There had been rumours that permission to transmit would not be granted in 1931,[2] and even when these rumours were shown to be unfounded, there was a feeling that the BBC's facilities were not being fully offered to Baird. In November 1930 Lord Gainford, the Vice-Chairman of the Board of Governors, had a long talk with Lord Ampthill, the chairman of Baird International Television Ltd. Ampthill asked for a bold BBC policy of active encouragement of television, and was not put off when Gainford talked of flickering images and bad reception. Gainford replied in guarded language that 'we were not a Corporation which had to cater for Empire, or inventions, though we naturally wanted to help Empire and trade interests. Our duty was to 3,200,000 listeners who paid 10s. to listen to programmes, and for us to deprive those people of one alternative programme for longer intervals than were now conceded was unreasonable.'[3]

Repeating his views in a long letter, Ampthill stuck to his points. Viewing hours were at the most inconvenient times, and the scale of activity did not encourage the sale of 'televisors'. Laboratory 'televisor' models were more impressive than the

[1] Quoted in *John Baird*, p. 159.
[2] *Lord Gainford to Lord Ampthill, 9 Dec. 1930; BBC Press Statement, 4 Dec. 1930.
[3] *Gainford to Reith, 8 Nov. 1930.

models on sale, and experiments were continuing at Hendon on ultra-short-wave television transmission. The Baird companies were having to do all their development work themselves and pay the BBC for the limited services they received: this was a much more unfavourable situation than their competitors faced in, say, Germany. Could not the BBC assist the Baird companies to develop their world-wide interests? 'The inventions we are developing are purely British and will if successfully developed provide increased trade and work for this country.'

Summing up, Ampthill said that what his company most wanted were 'extended facilities and a closer co-operation of your Corporation'.[1] Gainford replied that the BBC was prepared to co-operate as best it could but that its primary concern remained the interests of listeners. 'Anything which even temporarily cripples or reduces this service must be avoided if we would observe our tradition and practice.'[2] The correspondence ended with Ampthill telling Gainford neatly that it was his confident hope that television would in due course 'become an important part of the practice of the BBC and add to the lustre of the traditions you are rightly observing'.[3]

Any coldness in the BBC should not be exaggerated, and where it existed, it should be studied in relation first to the comparative lack of public interest in the programmes, outside the press, and second to the BBC's knowledge that other systems were being developed with what was felt to be a better technical future. In January 1931 Baird told the Postmaster-General that the number of television sets sold was less than a thousand:[4] this was hardly the basis for large-scale immediate expansion, although Baird added that by his calculations ten times as many people had constructed their own sets.

As far as other systems of television were concerned, the Gramophone Company was experimenting with mechanical methods from 1930 onwards, and the Marconi Company set up a research group in August of that year with the deliberate purpose of examining alternative systems. 'It was generally realised', a Marconi Company historian has written, 'that much

---

[1] *Ampthill to Gainford, 17 Nov. 1930.
[2] *Gainford to Ampthill, 9 Dec. 1930.
[3] *Ampthill to Gainford, 15 Dec. 1930.
[4] Report of Meeting of 2 Jan. 1931 (Post Office Archives).

higher standards were necessary if commercial interests were to be served, and investigations into the many involved problems in systems employing the scanning of a photo-image of the scene by cathode ray were being pursued, particularly in America.'[1]

Given this background and the desire to give viewers a real 'service', if they were to be provided for at all, relations between the Baird interests and the BBC improved in 1930 and 1931. As Eckersley faded out of the picture on the BBC's side, Hutchinson also disappeared from the scene on the opposite side, and Baird himself came increasingly into prominence, still with Moseley as a trusted adviser. In September 1930 Moseley commented to Gladstone Murray on how friendly relations had been of late:[2] in January 1931 Reith told Baird that there was the 'maximum good will' towards him 'personally', and that the BBC was 'anxious to be as helpful as possible in the solution of your difficult problems'.[3] He met Baird in person in the same month after Baird had asked for an interview,[4] and told him that there were various directions in which the BBC could help the Baird Television Development Company to make more effective and more economical use of existing facilities 'within the limits of present policy'.[5] The limits of that policy were clear, and Reith never pretended otherwise. The BBC still took the view that the development of television had not reached a stage where the public could be provided with regular 'service' transmissions.[6]

What the BBC would not do was to 'subsidize' Baird—a term he resented[7]—or to provide more convenient and longer hours. Information coming in from Germany and America seemed to suggest—though Baird queried it violently[8]—that the BBC's cautious policy, which Ampthill had questioned, had been fully justified. The Bell Telephone Company, it seemed, had cut

[1] Marconi Company, *Chapters of Marconi History*, no. ix, 'The Development of Television in Great Britain', p. 2. See also N. E. Davis, 'Television Transmitter Development, 1931–1936' in *Sound and Vision* (1961).
[2] *Moseley to W. E. G. Murray, 10 Sept. 1930.
[3] *Reith to Baird, 15 Jan. 1931.   [4] *Baird to Reith, 2 Jan. 1931.
[5] *Control Board Minutes, 6 Jan. 1931, followed by 'Draft Recommendations'.
[6] *Baird to Reith, taking up these points, 27 Jan. 1931.
[7] *Baird to Reith, 27 Jan. 1931.
[8] *Moseley to W. E. G. Murray, including observations by Baird and Moseley, 25 Feb. 1931.

down its experiments after spending a huge sum, and the German Post Office had spent 200,000 marks on television in two years, quite in vain. The *Berliner Tageblatt* had warned all television pioneers that they should not put a bad thing before the public, label it 'good', and reply to complaints that it was 'good enough' except that people could not see it properly.[1]

Quite apart from these particular facets of international television history, many of which Baird could dispute, it should be remembered that 1930 and 1931 were years of economic depression and that the BBC's finances were so severely strained that the Corporation could not contemplate even modest expenditure on the creation of an Empire Service.[2] Two sets of financial considerations were clashing. At the very moment that Reith was arguing with the government about the BBC's contribution to national solvency, Baird was pleading with MacDonald to give financial help to save television from falling 'into American hands'. 'It is not possible to rely on the promises of the BBC', he complained. 'They have outward friendliness, but have inwardly maintained a hostility which is difficult to understand.'[3]

Baird and his backers felt, as Ampthill stated it, that they could not hope to sell British 'televisors' until they had more regular broadcasts at more convenient times: the BBC did not feel that it could embark on a vast and unknown expenditure, particularly when there was a fundamental doubt about the future of the system. To dramatize this difference as a personal contest between 'two sons of the Manse' is to see it completely wrongly. Yet it is undoubtedly true that the Baird interests were severely shaken by their failure to offer more to their potential clients. The boom days—in so far as boom days had ever existed in Britain during the 1920s—were over. The price of Baird shares fell on the capital market and a series of elaborate financial changes followed, largely inspired by Sydney Moseley.

[1] *Cutting from the *Berliner Tageblatt*, 28 Jan. 1931; *Control Board Minutes, 17 Feb. 1931. The cutting was sent to Baird.

[2] See above, pp. 375 ff.

[3] For Reith's difficulties, see above, pp. 379–80. The letter from Baird to Mac-Donald is in the Post Office Archives. Baird got no response from the Prime Minister, whose secretary told him he was too pressed to reply and referred him to the Post-master-General. Nor was Herbert Samuel much help to Moseley at this time, for all his talk. As Home Secretary, he doubted whether it 'would be practicable' to engage the Prime Minister's attention. *Private Diaries*, p. 313.

The Baird Television Development Company and Baird International Television Ltd. amalgamated to form Baird Television Ltd. in June 1930; this change was made probably because it was no longer considered desirable on strategic grounds to suggest that television was still under 'development'.

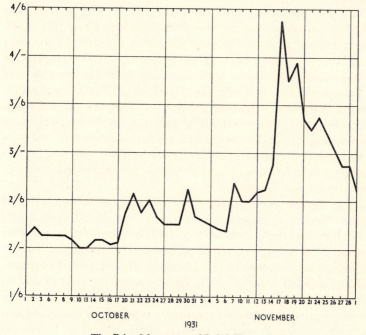

49. The Price Movement of Baird Shares (1931)

The new company had a capital of £825,000 of which about £700,000 had been spent, sometimes with little restraint, on various kinds of development. The amalgamation was followed in September 1930 by the 'agreed' voluntary liquidation of the so-called 'parent company', Television Ltd., which held a million deferred shares in the new amalgamation. At the time of liquidation of the 'parent company', the shares of the public company had fallen to about 4d.: not long before, in January 1929, shares in Baird International Television had reached more than 14s. and shares in the Baird Television Development Company 30s.

The million deferred shares in the public company, which had been allotted to the 'parent company' in return for the surrender of original rights, constituted a controlling interest, and when the 'parent company' voluntarily went into liquidation, Moseley had the task—congenial to the author of *Money Making in Stocks and Shares*—of ensuring that these shares passed from the liquidators into the right hands. The answer was simple: he had to acquire the shares himself. To do this, however, he had to secure enough shares in the dying Television Ltd. to control its policy. This he managed to do, in face of considerable opposition both from big financial interests and from people who 'believed' that the shares he had done so much to publicize were a genuine gold-mine. 'The time arrived when Moseley held, either himself or through his friends, sufficient voting strength in Television Ltd. to carry a resolution authorising the joint liquidators to accept his offer of £16,500 for the 997,300 deferred shares, and he signed a contract *undertaking to complete the deal in a month*.'[1]

The significance of this transaction was not so much that it gave Moseley temporary control of the Baird companies, which he had done so much to create, but that within a matter of weeks this large block of shares was acquired by Isidore Ostrer, the President of the Gaumont-British Film Company. Ostrer assisted Moseley while he was acquiring control and in making his final payment: Ostrer's own acquisition of control was announced publicly in January 1932.[2] To Moseley he was a 'millionaire with ideals',[3] the perfect *deus ex machina*: Reith was more sceptical about the extent of Ostrer's idealism. 'Lunched with Murray and Isidore Ostrer', he wrote in his diary in December 1932. 'He said a great deal about Television and I wondered how much was genuine, and how far it would take him against commercial motives.'[4]

Before Ostrer took control of the Baird interests in January 1932 there had been a marked improvement in Baird's relations with the BBC. The Derby Day demonstration of 1931 has some-

[1] Notes by W. H. Knight, quoted in *John Baird*, p. 175.
[2] *Private Diaries*, p. 311.
[3] *News Service Release, 28 Jan. 1932. Maurice Ostrer, a Vice-Chairman of Gaumont-British, was to be a Director of the new concern along with Moseley.
[4] Reith, Diary, 15 Dec. 1932.

times been held to have impressed the BBC so much that it changed its policies,[1] and certainly it is true that in August 1931 the BBC allowed the Baird Company to install one of its new portable transmitters in Studio 10 at Waterloo Bridge and to transmit a BBC sound programme.[2] More important, however, in modifying attitudes was a favourable report by Ashbridge in October 1931 on the technical aspect of Baird's work. 'On the 12th October I paid a visit to the Baird Television Laboratories in Long Acre', Ashbridge wrote. The first picture he saw there was 'easily the best television I have seen so far and might be compared, I think, with a cinematograph "close-up" of say fifteen to twenty years ago. . . . Were it possible for the ordinary public to buy an apparatus of this kind and to run it without difficulty or undue expense, I think we should just have reached real programme value.' This was by far the most encouraging assessment ever made inside the BBC of Baird's work. 'At present', Ashbridge went on, 'this apparatus is not in a fit state to develop commercially, but there is, I think, reason to assume that this will follow in a comparatively few years' time.'[3]

Moseley, who was present when Ashbridge saw Baird, did not help Baird's case, 'although he did practically all the talking'. 'While not being impressed very much with what Moseley said, because a good deal of it was contradictory, I was much more impressed by the technical results which I saw, because I now think that a good deal of development has been made in the past nine months or so.' The conclusion was clear. 'We ought to take steps to carry on Television transmissions and development by some means or other, including the Baird Company. I would be inclined to encourage the Baird Company to a reasonable extent in what they are doing now, because I feel that someone must develop Television for broadcasting, and if they do it adequately so much the better. If not, sooner or later, the BBC will be forced to do it, and at great cost to the listening public.'

[1] See, for example, *John Baird*, p. 153.
[2] The portable transmitter went astray after it had left Long Acre in April 1931. 'Nothing has arrived at No. 10 Studios,' Murray wrote to Moseley, 'so perhaps the portable transmitter was sent to No. 10 Downing Street, instead. I gather the current there is quite appropriate.' (*W. E. G. Murray to Moseley, 17 Apr. 1931.) For the first studio broadcast, see *The Times*, 20 Aug. 1931.
[3] *Memorandum of Ashbridge to Reith, 'Television', 14 Oct. 1931.

Gladstone Murray recognized at once that this memorandum changed the situation. 'One always had in mind that sooner or later there would arrive the right moment for the BBC to take the strategic initiative about television. But a prerequisite condition was an intimation from the Chief Engineer that progress was being recorded and that the service stage was not indefinitely remote. It seems to me that this condition has now been fulfilled.'[1] Two months earlier—after the Derby—Murray had suggested flatly to Moseley that the period of experimental transmission had lasted long enough to yield all possible data and that 'a better scheme had to be evolved' if the BBC were effectively to assist further development.[2] The result of discussions at this time had been a wide-ranging talk between the Chairman of the Board of Governors of the BBC and Baird on 17 August 1931. 'He seemed extremely well disposed and anxious to help us', Baird had written to Sydney Moseley, who was in America at the time, seeking financial help to complete his purchase of the Baird Television shares.[3]

Before Ashbridge presented his 'favourable' report, therefore, there had been signs of *rapprochement*, with further talks about a closer co-operation and a wider range of programmes.[4] Midnight transmissions were to be replaced by one half-hour weekly feature beginning with Jack Payne, and there were to be television tests in the North Region.[5] Yet tension remained and could flare out, as always, with considerable bitterness. Before Ashbridge's memorandum of October, the discussions, friendly

[1] *W. E. G. Murray to Reith, 19 Oct. 1931.

[2] *W. E. G. Murray to Moseley, 12 Aug. 1931. Moseley welcomed this letter in his reply of 12 Aug. 1931: 'I think it is vital in the interests of this country, that the one great force which is able to help it should come to an arrangement with the Baird Company to safeguard the interests of British television.'

[3] Letter from Baird to Moseley, quoted in *Private Diaries*, p. 313. For the meeting, see *'Chairman's Notes on his interview with Mr. Baird on 17 Aug. 1931'.

[4] *Notes on a Television Meeting between Baird, Ashbridge, and W. E. G. Murray, 1 Sept. 1931. See also Control Board Minutes, 3 Sept. 1931; Murray to Baird, 8 Sept. 1931.

[5] Gladstone Murray had been very irritated when in the previous year there had been newspaper talk of 'television coming to Yorkshire'. See the *Yorkshire Weekly Post Illustrated*, 18 Oct. 1930. According to oral evidence, engineers in the BBC thought Baird had his eye on the second of the twin-waves at the regional stations for television purposes. Gladstone Murray told Moseley tartly then (*a letter of 23 Oct. 1930) 'that there is no possibility whatsoever of television being broadcast in December or January from the North Regional station at Slaithwaite [Moorside Edge]'.

though they often were, had not cleared the air. Baird, indeed, had confessed to Gladstone Murray that he found the BBC's communications dominated by 'a note of suspicion'. 'One might deduce that the Baird Company was a kind of predatory monster engaged only in trying to embarrass or demolish the BBC.'[1]

Back from America, Moseley, who had dreams at this time of the BBC taking over the Baird interests,[2] added that 'there is no doubt that the BBC regards television as a nuisance and would be glad to see it "fade out".... The venomous hostility of the former Chief Engineer has crystallised into a kind of cynical indifference.'[3] The 'co-operation' had been too limited. Since the hours of transmission remained unchanged and no provision was being made for television studios in the new Broadcasting House, he intended to press ahead 'for separate independent broadcasting facilities, both visual and aural'.

Ashbridge's report was prepared, therefore, with talk of 'independent broadcasting facilities' once more in the air. It ended with a definite comment that the granting of separate wavelengths outside the broadcasting band 'might be unsound from our point of view'. Gladstone Murray took up the point. 'The right direction for the future seems to be for the Baird people to concentrate on their commercial operations, leaving us to look after the programme work and either to absorb or supervise the technical development of the transmitting end.... Once the initiative is passed to us, we should be in a position not only to counter any hostile use of television but also to determine the rate and the manner of applying it to broadcasting.'[4]

Control Board—or rather 'a majority of opinion' on Control Board, backed by Reith—supported a 'policy of co-operation' with Baird, and details were worked out in October and November 1931.[5] The Baird Company was to provide and install complete television equipment in a studio in the new Broadcasting House; the BBC was to pay a nominal rental fee; there was to be consultation and association between the engineers of the Corporation and the Company; and the BBC itself was to provide a weekly one-hour programme from

---

[1] *Baird to W. E. G. Murray, 9 Sept. 1931.   [2] *John Baird*, p. 202.
[3] *Moseley to W. E. G. Murray, 5 Oct. 1931.
[4] *W. E. G. Murray to Reith, 19 Oct. 1931.
[5] *Control Board Minutes, 27 Oct. 1931.

11 o'clock to 12 o'clock on weekday mornings and 12 o'clock to 1 o'clock on Saturdays. These suggestions, sent to Lord Ampthill and approved in principle by the Baird interests, marked a major change in policy. There was, however, a crucial escape clause. 'We should be free to give transmissions by other Television methods, whether the Baird transmissions were continued or not.'[1]

Before the negotiations between the Corporation and the Baird interests were completed, Ostrer had taken over control of the Baird interests and Ampthill had resigned from the chairmanship of Baird Television.[2] The detailed negotiations had been left to a small 'expert' committee of representatives of both sides, which seems to have worked amicably and constructively.[3] This committee was supplemented inside the BBC from February 1932 onwards by a 'Television Committee' dealing with programmes and programme research. It consisted of Graves, in the chair, Gielgud, Wellington, Mase, and Fielden.[4]

Prospects not only for a legal agreement but for effective co-operation on programmes seemed very favourable when the Postmaster-General, Kingsley Wood, 'inspected' the Baird laboratory at Long Acre in March 1932. 'The demonstration was good', Ashbridge wrote, but, once again, Moseley, he thought, had not helped matters by his rhetoric. He delivered 'a long harangue about the development of a great British industry, suggesting that the whole question was more than a mere commercial proposition, and [was] concerned [with] the building up of a great public service. He suggested that there was a potential market of 4 million television sets, in fact most of what he said was hopelessly exaggerated. . . . He hinted at some kind of Post Office or Governmental Enquiry, which, however, he left in a very nebulous state. He seemed almost to hint that there should be some enquiry similar to that which

---

[1] *Reith to Ampthill, 19 Nov. 1931. Ampthill accepted the plan in principle in a letter of 24 Nov. 1931. There was, however, a further correspondence about details: Reith to Ampthill, 22 Dec. 1931; Ampthill to Reith, 11 Jan. 1932; Reith to Ampthill, 13 Jan. 1932. Control Board Minutes, 12 Jan. 1932.

[2] *John Baird*, p. 214.

[3] Baird's independent pursuit of ultra-short-wave experiments did not help the negotiations, however. See above, p. 552.

[4] *Minutes of the First Television Committee, 22 Feb. 1932.

took place prior to the starting up of the British Broadcasting Company. The Postmaster-General did not comment on this, and I commented very sparingly.'[1]

Agreement between Baird Television Ltd. and the BBC was reached over a period of time, culminating in September 1932.[2] The BBC promised to provide at least two television programmes a week until 31 March 1934—a much later terminal date than had originally been envisaged[3]—and the Baird Television Company promised, for its part, to issue a notice with all television and kits of parts that it sold, stating without equivocation that transmissions by the Baird system might cease after March 1934. A BBC engineer, Douglas Birkinshaw, was appointed to the first BBC post in television—that of Research Engineer, later to be joined by D. R. Campbell and T. H. Bridgewater, engineers of the Baird Television Company, who were responsible for the installation of Baird equipment. It was felt to be a good omen that their initials spelt 'BBC'. On the programme side, Eustace Robb, a former Guards officer, was the first television producer, and George Grossmith was an adviser.

Baird was less successful in his negotiations with the Post Office than he was in his negotiations with the BBC, even though he had the BBC's backing. Kingsley Wood rejected two specific proposals—first to allow him one penny from the revenue of each wireless receiving licence, second to provide him with an annual subsidy of £10,000 a year towards research.[4] The second idea, based on the opera subsidy, had been Reith's, and Reith wrote to Kingsley Wood to support it.[5] He had added—and it was in line with his whole philosophy of broadcasting—that if such a subsidy were paid, 'it might necessitate some

[1] *Ashbridge, 'Note on the Visit of the Postmaster General to the Baird Television Laboratories, 29 Mar. 1932'. See also Control Board Minutes, 6 Apr. 1932.

[2] *Note of 28 Oct. 1932. There was no final signed agreement even at this date, but what had been agreed was set out in a document in December of that year.

[3] This date had first been discussed at a meeting on 22 Jan. 1932. It was made clear from the start that 'the assurance of continuance until 31 Mar. 1934 does not imply continuance of the four or five programmes a week . . . but only that there will not be entire discontinuance before that date'. (*Note of meetings of 22 Jan. and 4 Feb. 1932.)

[4] For the penny rate, see Baird to Kingsley Wood, 12 Apr. 1932; Kingsley Wood to Baird, 21 Apr. 1932 (Post Office Archives). For the subsidy, see *Reith to W. E. G. Murray, 15 June 1932.

[5] *Reith to Kingsley Wood, 23 May 1932.

reconstitution of his company, for instance to the extent of a limited dividend', noting that the Company had hitherto never paid any dividend. Baird had regarded Reith's intervention as of 'the utmost importance' and thanked him warmly for it,[1] but it drew no response from Kingsley Wood, even when the BBC offered to augment the subsidy out of its own revenue.[2] 'I have felt bound to refuse the application,' the Postmaster-General wrote to Reith in June 1932, 'leaving the question of a payment by the BBC for settlement between the Company and your Corporation.' No explanation was given to Reith. To Baird it was pointed out simply that it was impossible at that stage to add to the nation's expenditure on research: there would be many other claimants, some of whom 'might seem to deserve prior consideration'.[3]

Baird had made his big bid and failed. The BBC was co-operating with him more fully than ever, yet he himself was increasingly conscious of what he bitterly called 'years of un-remunerative labour'.[4] There were very few viewers for his programmes, and the sale of sets remained extremely low.[5] The press might take up his programmes as 'stunts', but in a highly competitive radio industry, where there was no unwillingness to produce radio sets, there was no commercial company prepared to manufacture 'televisors'. The BBC was basically right in very cautiously assessing the permanent value of his work.[6]

[1] *Baird to Reith, 18 May 1932.

[2] Baird had characteristically asked for a far bigger sum from the BBC than it could hope to pay. For the use of his patents he asked an annual sum larger than that paid by the BBC for the whole of its wireless patents owned by the Marconi Company, Standard Telephones, the Radio Corporation of America, and other wireless interests. *See Reith to W. E. G. Murray, 15 June 1932.

[3] *Kingsley Wood to Reith, 20 June 1932; Kingsley Wood to Baird, 20 June 1932 (Post Office Archives).

[4] *Baird to Kingsley Wood, 9 June 1932.

[5] He told Reith in Dec. 1932 that only about 500 manufactured 'televisions' were in use (*Baird to Reith, 2 Dec. 1932).

[6] A quite independent writer on the BBC's attitude towards Baird sums up as follows: 'The delay imposed by the BBC [on Baird] was right, both from the point of view of public entertainment and of progress in the television art. The only thing open to question was whether the delay was long enough.' See S. G. Sturmey, *The Economic Development of Radio* (1958), p. 199. *Cf. Ashbridge in a note of 9 June 1952 on Moseley's book: 'Looking back over the years I do not think the BBC did anything wrong, nor did it hold back excessively. It might, of course, have handled the situation more adroitly, but this applies to so many things and is to some extent unavoidable with an organisation like the BBC when so many people are concerned inside and outside the organisation.'

The Ostrer interests, as Reith had prophesied, gave Baird less support than he had anticipated, looking for quick results rather than extended experiments and paying no attention to his suggestions about the business side of development. Finally in June 1933 Moseley resigned from the Board of Television Ltd., ostensibly on the grounds that he could help television more from outside the company than inside it.

'Experimental broadcasts' continued, sometimes with a flourish. In November 1932 Carl Brisson, the Danish film star, introduced by Baird himself, was televised from Broadcasting House to the Arena Theatre in Copenhagen 600 miles away. Among the items of fare in 1933 were a television revue, *Looking In*, presented by John Watt and Harry S. Pepper, with Anona Winn as one of the performers, a boxing contest, and the first of a continuing sequence of animal programmes, including greyhounds and sea lions. There were 76 transmissions in 1932 and 208 in 1933.[1] There was even an article by Baird himself in the *BBC Year Book* for 1933.[2]

All these broadcasts enabled the BBC to gain valuable experience of television far ahead of any foreign broadcasting concerns, but they were viewed with suspicion by many people inside Broadcasting House, who felt that the interests of a tiny handful of people were jeopardizing the interests of the many. 'The BBC is most anxious to know the number of people who are actually seeing this television programme', a remarkably early broadcast 'listener-research' request stated in the summer of 1933. 'Will those who are looking in send a postcard marked "Z" to Broadcasting House immediately?' A year earlier Graves had complained that those immediately concerned with television were demanding 'ideal conditions' which would lead to great expense being incurred, and Control Board held that 'expense and interference with Broadcasting progress was unjustified in view of the extremely limited public for television and its present limited powers'. It was decided that Graves and Ashbridge should tell Robb and Birkinshaw that 'they could go so far and no further and must view the matter in its right proportion'.[3] The 'right proportion' is never easy to decide.

---

[1] *Note on Television Programmes to 31 Dec. 1934, Plant Costs prepared for Carpendale. [2] *BBC Year Book* (1933), pp. 441–7.
[3] *Control Board Minutes, 9 Aug. 1932.

Only £2,225 was spent by the BBC on television in 1932, including producers, engineers, studios, artists, scenery and costumes, and £7,129 in 1933. The figure fell to £6,617 in 1934.[1] It is difficult to imagine 'experimental broadcasts' being financed for any less than this.

Even at this level, the axe fell. In September 1933 a brief formal notice was served on the Baird Television Company that the BBC intended 'to terminate the arrangement between us at 31 March 1934 in accordance with the terms of our letter of 21 March 1932'.[2]

3. The Rivals

THE letter of notice had less to do with dissatisfaction with Baird or with the costs of television programmes than with the exciting progress made in developing other systems of television. In Britain the first television experiments within a big business organization had been made along 'mechanical' lines by the Marconi Company: in 1932 the company had displayed 'head and shoulders television'—with Nipkow discs and light-beam scanning devices. The displays included demonstrations at the British Association meeting at York.[3] On the other side of the Atlantic the competitors whom Baird most feared, the big American radio and gramophone companies, were experimenting with 'electrical' instruments from the mid-1920s onwards. V. K. Zworykin had begun to develop electronic methods of scanning in the research laboratories of the Westinghouse Electric and Manufacturing Company as early as 1925, and in 1930, at David Sarnoff's suggestion, had transferred his experiments to the associated laboratories of the large Radio Corporation of America—which in 1929 had amalgamated with the Victor Talking Machine Company.[4]

[1] *Note on Programmes and Costs to 31 Dec. 1934.
[2] *Letter of 22 Sept. 1933.
[3] Marconi Company, 'The Development of Television in Great Britain', p. 2. See also *The Marconi Review*, September to October 1932.
[4] V. K. Zworykin, 'Television with Cathode-Ray Tubes' in the *Journal of the Institution of Electrical Engineers*, vol. 73, 1933, pp. 437 ff. For the story of Zworykin's dealings with Westinghouse, which did not permit him the full freedom to develop

Zworykin, who had been a pupil of Rosing in St. Petersburg, made a major 'break-through' with his invention of the 'ionoscope', a charge-storage type of transmitting tube. Details of this invention were announced publicly in 1933. Zworykin also designed viewing tubes which incorporated grid modulation, a hard vacuum, and electro-static focusing.[1] After modification, the 'ionoscope' served as a model for the 'Emitron Camera', developed in Britain by Electric and Musical Industries Ltd.—E.M.I.[2]

E.M.I. was the most important new British combination of the period covered in this volume. It was incorporated in 1931 as the result of a merger between the Gramophone Company Ltd., which had begun to carry out television research a year earlier under the direction of G. E. Condliffe and C. O. Browne,[3] the Columbia Graphophone Company, and other interests. Each of the two main firms had a long history. The Gramophone Company had been founded as a private company in 1898 with purely British capital; the Columbia Company had operated in Britain from 1898 to 1922 as a branch of the American Columbia Gramophone Manufacturing Company, but had been a purely British concern since 1922. There were changes in the structure of control in the 1920s. In 1925 the British Columbia Company actually acquired the whole of the issued capital of the American Company: in 1920 the Victor Talking Machine Company of the United States acquired a controlling interest in the Gramophone Company, and when Victor was merged with R.C.A. in 1929, the Gramophone Company thus became a subsidiary of the huge American corporation. E.M.I., the new combination, not only spanned, therefore, the whole range of radio, including both production and distribution,[4] but it had direct links with other American business interests.

The importance of these links in relation to the history of television was that when E.M.I. was founded it did not have to

television that he required, see J. Jewkes, D. Sawers, and R. Stillerman, *The Sources of Invention* (1958), pp. 385–6.

[1] *The Economic Development of Radio*, p. 200. See also W. R. Maclaurin, *Invention and Innovation in the Radio Industry* (1949).

[2] For the merger, see *The Economic Development of Radio*, p. 176. See also above, p. 76.

[3] C. O. Browne, 'Multi-Channel Television' in the *Journal of the Institution of Electrical Engineers*, vol. 70, 1932, p. 34.

[4] In 1931 it founded its own hire purchase company, the Retailers' Trust Ltd.

start from scratch in the process of invention. Zworykin's early work could be used in British development. There were also business links between E.M.I. and the Marconi Company. In 1919 the Marconi Company of America had been wound up, and the Marconi Company had given the Radio Corporation of America all its American patent rights: in return R.C.A. had granted rights in its patents to the Marconi Company in Britain. Ten years later, in 1929, the Marconi Company sold all its interests in radio-receiver patents and other 'home entertainment apparatus' to the Gramophone Company, thereby indirectly, when it was formed, to E.M.I.

There was to be a final deal in 1934 when the Marconi Company joined with E.M.I. to form the private company, Marconi–E.M.I. Television Company Ltd.[1] After 1934 it was possible to combine the experience of the Marconi Company in designing high-power transmitters and aerials with the experimental acumen of E.M.I., which had been demonstrated in the process of perfecting the Emitron Camera. These interlocking relationships were expressed on the Board of E.M.I. which had as its only two non-British Directors David Sarnoff and Marconi himself.

The manipulation of Baird financial interests could not produce results comparable with those achieved through genuine technical co-operation within and between large firms. The real reason why Baird was outstripped by E.M.I., it has been suggested, was not because E.M.I. was a powerful Anglo-American combination, the kind of 'sinister' combination he and Moseley had painted in deep black for the benefit of the Postmaster-General, but because E.M.I. had at its disposal the laboratory facilities for developing television which Baird lacked. 'The character of the direction of research may explain why it was E.M.I. and not any other large company, which produced the world's first high-definition television system.'[2]

Such an explanation, doubtless true as far as it goes, leaves out genius. E.M.I. was fortunate enough, under the general direction of Isaac Shoenberg who had formerly been an executive of the Marconi Company, to acquire a team of brilliant

---

[1] For some of these manœuvres, see *The Economic Development of Radio*, ch. x, *passim*. The BBC were informed of the new development: *H. A. White (of the Marconi Wireless Telegraph Company) to Reith, 23 Mar. 1934.

[2] Professor Sturmey's verdict in *The Economic Development of Radio*, p. 212.

research engineers. Shoenberg had been educated in pre-war Russia with Zworykin and Sarnoff and had worked closely with S. M. Eisenstein in the laboratories of the Ruskoje Company, founded in 1907 and later controlled by the Marconi Company.[1] He left Russia in 1914 to join the parent Marconi Company, and joined E.M.I. when it was founded. Some of his new colleagues had been employed previously by Columbia; they included G. E. Condliffe, A. D. Blumlein, C. O. Browne, J. D. McGee, P. W. Williams, and E. L. C. White. Blumlein and Browne were killed in an air crash during the Second World War: they were outstanding scientists in any company, men of originality, resourcefulness, and vision. They and their colleagues were willing to think afresh about the practical implications of the kind of theory Campbell-Swinton had sketched out twenty-five years before, and they took their first practical step in December 1931 when they obtained their experimental licence.

At first the group worked, as the Marconi Company had done, on mechanical scanners for test transmissions, restricting the use of cathode-ray tubes to receivers. By the end of 1932, however, they were concentrating on electronic systems, drawing on Zworykin's early work but going far beyond it. The way ahead was not easy. The signals obtained from the early ionoscopes tended to become submerged in spurious signals associated with 'secondary-emission effects', and there was a temptation to continue with mechanical scanning. 'Instead,' Shoenberg has written, 'we decided that the potentialities of the electronic scanning tube justified a great effort to overcome the problems it presented at the time.'[2] Research went ahead. Improvements to the electronic scanning tube made the spurious signals more manageable, and after Blumlein, Browne, and White had devised ingenious circuits to deal with unwanted signals, Blumlein and McGee went on to reach the ultimate solution to the problem—stabilization of cathode potential.

It was in November 1932 that E.M.I. first approached the BBC to ask representatives to witness a demonstration of high-definition television,[3] and in December 1932 Ashbridge reported

[1] *J. W. Wissenden to E.M.I., 8 Dec. 1931; Wissenden to Ashbridge, 17 Dec. 1931.
[2] Shoenberg drafted an account of what he and his engineers had accomplished in the *Proceedings of the Institution of Electrical Engineers*, vol. xcix (1952).
[3] *I. Shoenberg to Ashbridge, 29 Nov. 1932. 'In my humble opinion,' Shoenberg wrote, 'the results would be of quite considerable interest to you.'

with guarded approval of what he had seen.[1] The E.M.I. apparatus, he stated, differed considerably from the Baird system: in particular, there were three times as many lines per picture and twice as many pictures per second. Definition was much better than with the Baird system and flicker greatly reduced. The apparatus, however, had so far been developed only for the transmission of films, and there were doubts about its future in relation to studio performance. All in all, however, it offered prospects of steady improvement. Although the pictures 'are hardly likely at the present stage of development to command sustained attention over long periods, they represent by far the best wireless television I have ever seen, and are, probably as good as, or better than, anything that has been produced anywhere else in the world'.

Ashbridge added a few comments of his own on the general problems of television development. Neither Baird nor E.M.I. yet offered technical facilities as highly advanced as sound radio engineers had offered the BBC in the distant days of 1922 and 1923. Whereas it had been possible then to hear a talk and catch the personality of the speaker, Ashbridge could not imagine anyone looking at a 'home projector' with sustained interest for a period of much more than an hour in 1932. Even when television reached a higher level of technical achievement, it would not supplant sound radio. There would still be 'a number of important items'—orchestral music, for example—in which there would be no obvious advantage in adding television to sound.

Moreover, during the first stages of development, television, unlike sound radio, would be a 'luxury service', hardly likely to arouse 'steadily increasing enthusiasm such as sound broadcasting has enjoyed'. There was no parallel to the crystal set. Yet, given all this, Ashbridge wisely added that he did not think that the BBC could 'hold back' in developing a new invention of this type to its greatest extent, provided that 'the financial commitments on the programme and technical side' were examined with the utmost care. From the start, the Corporation would have to accept 'the financial risk of another method superseding the one under review at the moment'.

[1] *Ashbridge, 'Report on Television Demonstration at E.M.I.', 6 Dec. 1932. For Ashbridge's views in retrospect, see his article 'Twenty-five Years of BBC Television' in *Sound and Vision* (1961).

E.M.I. did not want to hold back. Its directors soon showed that they wanted to secure apparatus for broadcasting, and they had no interest 'in the possibility of collaboration of some kind between themselves and Baird'.[1] Reith put this possibility to Alfred Clark of E.M.I. when they had preliminary discussions in January 1933 about terms for co-operation, and Clark immediately turned it down. Minor alterations to the BBC's ultra-short-wave transmitters would be necessary, Clark said, but H.M.V., a part of the E.M.I. complex, would lend all necessary apparatus and films sufficient for about a year. E.M.I. was anxious, Clark concluded, to go almost immediately into the commercial production of sets to be ready for the seasonal upsurge of demand in the autumn of 1933.[2] The BBC thought that this last ambition was precipitate: 'I feel very strongly', Ashbridge wrote, 'against trying to dump another doubtful service on the public as early as next autumn.'[3]

While the BBC was learning of E.M.I.'s plans, the Baird Company was proposing to go into mass production of its own receivers. This alarmed Ashbridge, who felt that though there had been an improvement in the Baird techniques in ultra-short-wave broadcasting, it might still be necessary to terminate the Baird experimental broadcasts altogether in March 1934.[4] For his part, Baird was sufficiently alarmed about the development of cathode-ray tubes in television to start experimenting in this field, although he was at pains to add that he did not think that they 'by any means supersede mechanical systems'.[5]

During the course of 1933 he completely abandoned the Nipkow disc as a scanner for the televising of interviews and films, but in his anxiety to do things which his rivals could not do he was driven to develop many extremely cumbrous devices. For studio scenes, for example, which Ashbridge encouraged him to concentrate upon, he made 'intermediate' films, which were developed very quickly and, while still wet, were scanned by a 'flying spot scanner'. The time delay of sixty seconds made

1 *Notes by Reith on a conversation with Alfred Clark, 4 Jan. 1933.
2 *Control Board Minutes, 3 Jan. 1933.
3 *Ashbridge to Reith, 5 Jan. 1933.
4 *Ashbridge to Reith, 5 Jan. 1933; Control Board Minutes, 31 Jan. 1933.
5 *Baird to Ashbridge, 13 Jan. 1933.

this elaborate device far more unwieldy than instantaneous methods of television transmission.

Recognizing the bother and messiness of the intermediate film process, Baird borrowed under licence from the Farnsworth Television Laboratories of Philadelphia an electronic system which had been developed by R.C.A.'s rivals. Philo Farnsworth, its inventor, was as much of an individualist as Baird, preferring to work on a small scale with relatively simple equipment, and as early as 1927 he had demonstrated a complete electronic system of television, involving the use of cathode-ray tubes both in transmitters and receivers. His camera, greatly improved by 1931, was known as an 'image-dissector tube', and, unlike other cameras, it did not employ the principle of charge storage.

Farnsworth was taken up for a time by Philco, but, like Baird, he was not at his ease about either financial entanglements or the desire of his 'supporters' to make money quickly. His role in America may, indeed, be compared with that of Baird in Britain, although his methods were so different. 'Farnsworth's almost single-handed battle to develop a practical television system before the R.C.A.', it has been argued, 'may have driven the latter to increase the tempo of research—just as the achievements of Baird with the mechanical system may have hastened the development of the electronic system and the beginning of television broadcasting in England.'[1] Yet Baird's willingness to secure the use of Farnsworth's inventions from the United States—with the help of Ostrer's capital—shows the extent of his uneasiness in 1933 as E.M.I. seemed to be increasing its hold over the BBC. The decision was late and reluctant, and it was not until 1940, when all his concerns were in ruins, that Baird admitted in a memorandum to Moseley that 'cathode ray tubes are the most important items in a television receiver'.[2]

Baird's immediate reaction in January 1933 to the news that the BBC was negotiating with E.M.I. was to challenge any agreement between BBC and E.M.I. on three grounds. First, it would be contrary to the agreement between Baird and the BBC: the BBC had pledged itself not to transmit by any method other than the Baird system 'unless the proposed new method showed an improvement of a revolutionary nature'. There was

[1] *The Sources of Invention*, pp. 387–8.   [2] Quoted in *John Baird*, p. 238.

nothing 'revolutionary', he claimed, about E.M.I.'s work. Second, if the BBC were to work with E.M.I. it would be dealing a heavy blow at British industry and directly assisting an American concern: this was the argument which Moseley loved and which Baird tried out at various times with MacDonald and Baldwin.[1] 'The development of television was a matter of concern not only for the BBC but for this country.' It was of the utmost importance that 'broadcasting in this country should not be under foreign influence—directly or indirectly'.[2] Third, Baird held that he could produce as good television of the high-definition type as E.M.I. could.

The BBC replied very firmly that it would and could support or encourage research in any quarter. 'As a monopoly concern it is the duty of the BBC to endeavour to determine what is the best method of doing television from a technical point of view, wherever the system might originate. The question would afterwards arise as to whether the best system could be adapted from other points of view.' Why did Baird fear comparative tests of his own performance and the performance of rivals? 'If the Baird system were better, no possible harm could be done to it by doing tests with another system.'[3]

Receiving little satisfaction from the BBC, Baird and Moseley turned back again to the Post Office. 'I am not satisfied that the BBC realises its duty to the country', Moseley wrote to Kingsley Wood. 'My own relations with the executives are of the friendliest, but I think it is a matter for the Government rather than for the BBC to lay down a policy with regard to the future of British television. The BBC, which holds a monopoly by virtue of a Charter granted by H.M. Government, seems to me to be extraordinarily cynical where the rights of a British sister service are concerned.' It would be a 'public scandal' if the Radio Corporation of America, through one of its 'controlled' companies in London, were to 'march in' through the back doors of

[1] *On 27 Jan. 1933 Moseley wrote to Baldwin: 'I wonder whether, in the welter of cynicism of modern politics, there is any sincerity in the plea of "British first".' Baird also wrote to the Prince of Wales in February 1933, and his letter was referred to Roger Eckersley by Sir Godfrey Thomas on 21 Feb. 1933. 'I am afraid I know very little about the present situation in regard to television', Thomas wrote, 'and cannot pass any opinion on the suggestion that the BBC are "wasting a pioneer British industry"—or "giving secret encouragement to alien interests".'   [2] *Baird to Reith, 31 Jan. 1933.
[3] *Minutes of a Meeting held with the Baird Company on 27 Jan. 1933.

the BBC.[1] The Post Office immediately sent a copy of this letter to the BBC,[2] and Reith personally supervised the draft of the reply.[3] The same question was repeated. Why was Baird afraid of comparative tests? The claim to superiority over rival systems could best be demonstrated in a trial by ordeal.[4]

Evidently the Post Office shared this view, for two Post Office engineers, Gill and Faulkner, were sent to Hayes in February 1933 to study E.M.I. transmissions. They reported favourably that the picture was good and the film shown easy to follow. On the international aspect of the question, they added that only 27 per cent. of the E.M.I. stock was held in America and that Sarnoff was the only American director.[5] The E.M.I. system had been wholly developed and manufactured by English staff in English workshops.

Notwithstanding this evidence, however, the Post Office pressed the BBC to postpone E.M.I. tests from Broadcasting House until further demonstrations of Baird's work had taken place.[6] It would be wiser 'politically', Gill told Gladstone Murray, not to conduct E.M.I. experiments in Broadcasting House.[7] The BBC protested against this advice, but had to yield to a Post Office suggestion that there should be two new 'competitive' demonstrations of ultra-short-wave television on consecutive days, the first from Long Acre and the second from Hayes.[8] The demonstrations were held on 18 and 19 April 1933, and once again there was general agreement among Post Office representatives (including Phillips, Wissenden, Lee, and Angwin) and Ashbridge and Bishop of the BBC that 'the results of the E.M.I. demonstrations were immeasurably superior to those obtained by Baird's and that the E.M.I. equipment was far in advance of its competitor'.[9]

[1] *Moseley to Kingsley Wood, 28 Jan. 1933.
[2] *Phillips to Carpendale, quoting Moseley, 1 Feb. 1933.
[3] *There is a pencilled note by Reith to Ashbridge attached to Phillips's letter, reading 'Urgent. Please give me a reply to sign explaining the whole thing.'
[4] *Reith to Phillips, 3 Feb. 1933. See also *Reith to Baird, 3 Feb. 1933.
[5] Report of 13 Feb. 1933 (Post Office Archives).
[6] *The BBC had asked for permission to broadcast by the E.M.I. system on 7 Feb. 1933 (letter of Harold Bishop to Phillips). The reply was given in a letter of Phillips to Reith, 13 Mar. 1933.
[7] *W. E. G. Murray to Reith, 8 Feb. 1933.
[8] *Phillips to Reith, 10 Apr. 1933.
[9] *Note of a Meeting held at the General Post Office on 21 Apr. 1933.

THE RIVALS   575

In spite of this agreement, the Postmaster-General, who was not present at the meeting of engineers, continued to rule that the BBC should not give facilities to E.M.I. which might prejudice Baird's case. Phillips, who usually saw all the difficulties ahead, had stated bluntly after the tests that the Post Office was afraid that if the Baird Company were prevented from installing high-definition equipment, questions would be asked in Parliament and in the press. These would be difficult to answer, and the Post Office (mainly) and the BBC (to a lesser extent) 'would be blamed for the inevitable bankruptcy of the Baird Company'. 'The Post Office wanted to protect themselves against any such trouble, and this was the real reason for their anxiety.'[1] Ashbridge argued in vain that Baird's inability to demonstrate effective apparatus of a high-definition type was a sign that he had not listened to persistent BBC advice and that if any blame were to be apportioned it should be on Baird himself.

Commercial as well as political questions were involved in the argument at this stage. It was clear that whichever concern first obtained facilities from the BBC for the development of high-definition television would automatically acquire a very considerable advantage in the manufacture and sale of receivers, since it would possess patents which might be essential in the manufacture of receivers suitable for the particular transmission process which had been adopted.[2] The trade in receivers was the magnet. It was because of this that Reith refused an invitation from Bush Radio, an associated company of Ostrer's Gaumont-British group, to attend a dinner to inaugurate the placing on the market of a new consignment of 'televisors'. 'I am afraid I cannot associate myself', he replied, 'with the launching of a receiver by any particular company.' Any BBC dealings with the receiver manufacturing industry should be with associations of manufacturers rather than with particular firms.[3]

Reith also raised the question of Bush Radio's plans with Kingsley Wood. 'For some time past it has been highly unlikely', he said, 'that we should be able to see our way to continue Baird transmissions beyond March 1934, having regard

[1] Ibid.
[2] For the economics of the matter, see *Wireless World*, 14 Apr. 1933.
[3] *Reith to Moseley, 21 Apr. 1933.

576 THE NEW WORLD OF TELEVISION

to their programme value and to the limited interest which they
have evoked.' Bush Radio advertising, therefore, could create
a difficult situation, particularly when the BBC (along with the
Post Office) had made it clear that it preferred the E.M.I.
system.[1] It was planned to introduce the Bush Radio receiver,
costing £25, to the press in May 1933, but the demonstration
did not take place.

At the same time it was announced that Captain A. G. D.
West, formerly Chief Research Engineer at the BBC and
latterly an engineer in the cinema industry at Ealing, was to
join Baird's technical staff.[2] This was the best move made so
far by the new controllers of the Baird concerns. 'There is no
doubt', Ashbridge wrote after seeing West, 'that the Baird Company has received a fresh fillip and is now in entirely new hands
from a technical point of view. Whether, however, this will lead
to anything tangible or not, it is impossible to say.'[3] The change
of direction was followed by a transfer of the Long Acre studio
to the top of South Tower at the Crystal Palace.[4]

The idea of getting round the difficulties between the two
rivals by trying out rival schemes in Broadcasting House side by
side or on consecutive nights originated inside the BBC—
from V. H. Goldsmith. Baird objected at first, but later came
round to the idea: Shoenberg remained adamant on the grounds
that Baird had nothing to offer.[5] Kingsley Wood supported the
idea after discussions with Whitley and Reith, during which he
made it quite clear that his attitude to rival television claims
was 'entirely political'.[6] 'I am sure it is wise', he told Reith, 'to
have the Baird and the E.M.I. apparatus installed at Broadcasting House simultaneously, assuming, of course, that Mr.
Baird so desires, and to carry out the trials of the two sets of

[1] *Reith to Kingsley Wood, 27 Apr. 1933. Baird agreed to a form of wording
to be placed on all 'televisors' saying that the BBC reserved the right to discontinue
transmissions after 31 March. (*Baird to Goldsmith, 25 May 1933.)
[2] *H. Bishop, Note on the Baird Press Demonstration, 30 May 1933. For West,
see above, p. 519.
[3] *Ashbridge to Reith, 13 July 1933. West told Ashbridge on 13 July and in a
letter of 14 July that they were actively pursuing experiments in 120-line cathode-
ray work.
[4] *Wissenden to Reith, 20 July 1933.
[5] *Ashbridge to Reith, 12 May 1933.
[6] Reith, Diary, 15 May 1933.

apparatus over the same period. I am prepared to stipulate with Mr. Baird that his apparatus should be ready within a reasonable time, say two months.'[1] The BBC formally accepted the idea in June 1933,[2] and eventually Shoenberg agreed, stating that he was not in the least concerned whether Baird's apparatus would be installed in Broadcasting House along with his own. The best system, whichever it was, 'would win in the end'.[3]

After protracted discussions and many practical setbacks E.M.I. decided, however, not to install apparatus in Broadcasting House and carried on further experiments between Hayes and their receiving studios in Abbey Road. The Baird Company had almost finished the installation of new high-definition apparatus on the eighth floor of Broadcasting House when it received the formal notice to terminate existing arrangements for 'experimental broadcasts' on 31 March 1934.[4] By a curious twist in the history of publicity, it was now the turn of the Baird Company to accuse the BBC of leaking information to the press without first consulting Sir Harry Greer, the new chairman of Baird Television Ltd.[5]

In fact, the BBC remained quiet during these interesting months of discussions and negotiations. 'A discreet silence is maintained by the authorities at Broadcasting House', the newspapers proclaimed.[6] Until a public statement was issued in October the world was dependent on rumour and leakages.[7] 'No reference is to be made in any of our periodicals to television without previous reference to Controller or Chief Engineer through me', Goldsmith had ordered in May 1933.[8]

---

[1] *Kingsley Wood to Reith, 22 May 1933.

[2] *Reith to Kingsley Wood, 14 June 1933; Kingsley Wood to Reith, 15 June 1933.

[3] *Note on telephone conversation between Bishop and Shoenberg, 24 June 1933.

[4] *Bishop to Carpendale, 19 Sept. 1933: for the letter terminating the agreement, see above, p. 566.

[5] *Greer to Reith, 27 Sept. 1933. The Baird Television Company made all its employees sign a 'secrecy' pledge in Nov. 1933. See Greer to Whitley, 29 Nov. 1933.

[6] *Daily Independent*, 22 Aug. 1933; *North Eastern Daily Gazette*, 17 Aug. 1933, 'BBC refuses to Talk'.

[7] It had been intended originally to get the statement out on 27 Sept. but eventually, after long discussions about its contents, it was decided to make it into a 'lowest common denominator' statement agreeable to all television interests, including E.M.I. It finally appeared on 12 Oct.

[8] *Note of 8 May to the editors of the *Radio Times*, *The Listener*, and *World Radio*.

The order followed an article by Filson Young, to which Reith had taken exception.[1] In it Filson Young had prophesied that 'within a short time—a few years or even less—it will be possible for the millions to see in their own homes an image of events actually in progress elsewhere. The Grand National, the Boat Race, the Cup Final, now listened to in the form of descriptive ejaculations by an eye witness will be actually seen on the glass panel of some parlour cabinet a thousand miles away.' 'Before you have learned to be perfect listeners', he went on in characteristic vein, 'you will have to begin to learn a new technique—the art of looking.' This was too much for Carpendale. Correcting a draft statement which read that it was probable that television would become a practical proposition during the next few years, he remarked, 'I think this is too optimistic. I would change the first two lines to read, "It is *possible* that television *may* become a practical proposition during the next few years."' And then, as a heartfelt cry—'But in view of the graft and intrigue etc., is it not best to drop the subject in our publications?'[2]

There was neither graft nor intrigue in the success story of E.M.I.'s experiments in the autumn of 1933 and the spring of 1934. Outside observers noted that the freedom from mechanical inertia and from difficulties of synchronization which the use of cathode-ray apparatus permitted was a technical advantage which would enable it to establish its supremacy.[3] While Baird engineers floundered, unhappy at the prospect of carrying out public experiments in Broadcasting House,[4] E.M.I. was spending £100,000 a year on research.

The outlook of Shoenberg and his colleagues was diametrically opposed to that of Baird. 'In deciding the basic features of our system', Shoenberg wrote years afterwards, 'we frequently had to make a choice between a comparatively easy path leading to a mediocre result and a more difficult one which, if successful, held the promise of better things.'[5] The atmosphere in which

[1] *Radio Times*, 28 Apr. 1933; *Note by Reith, 30 Apr. 1933. See also above, p. 71.   [2] *Note of 2 May 1933.

[3] Leader, 'The Progress of Television' in *The Electrician*, 25 Aug. 1933.

[4] *Notes by Ashbridge, 8 Dec. 1933, on a letter from Greer to Whitley, 6 Dec. 1933. The Baird engineers did not like Kirke or Bishop even to 'look in' at what they were doing. *Bishop to Ashbridge, 18 Dec. 1933.

[5] *Proc. Inst. Elect. Eng.* (1952).

choices were made was 'very rare because of the complete absence of any kind of frustration, of red tape', Shoenberg added. 'Complete confidence in each other was the reason why we were able to do a very complicated job in such a short time.'[1]

The choice of the more difficult path was soon justified when in January 1934 representatives of the BBC saw a further E.M.I. demonstration at Hayes, and pronounced the results 'extremely good'. 'Programme value' was thought to be considerable and 'the receivers appeared to be in practical form and looked very much like large radio gramophones'. 'The important thing about this demonstration', Ashbridge added, 'is that it was far and away a greater achievement than anything I have ever seen in television.' Kirke agreed with him: they were both clear, too, that E.M.I. meant to develop television 'energetically'.[2]

Everything was pointing to the eventual triumph of E.M.I. over Baird, yet the BBC did not immediately abandon Baird even after the termination notice had been sent. It was decided that a limited number of transmissions would continue, as of grace, after 1 April 1934,[3] and a further Baird demonstration in Film House, Wardour Street, was attended on 12 March by representatives of the BBC—and by the Prime Minister.[4] Ashbridge, who attended, was scrupulously fair in his comments. 'The film transmission given by E.M.I. is appreciably better than that shown by the Baird Company. On the other hand, however, no opportunity has been available so far to compare a demonstration under absolutely strictly comparable conditions. Moreover, the E.M.I. Company have not so far attempted a demonstration with living objects.'[5]

To try to settle between the rivals clearly involved the BBC in issues which they were unable fully to settle for themselves. On 15 March 1934, therefore, Reith wrote to Kingsley Wood

---

[1] *Television programme, *Window on the World*, 7 Nov. 1961.

[2] *Ashbridge to Reith, 17 Jan. 1934.

[3] *A BBC Press Statement offering the possibility of this had been issued on 4 Dec. 1933: see Notes exchanged between Beadle and Goldsmith, 20 Feb. 1934; Note by Beadle, 7 Mar. 1934, definitely stating that there would be two programmes a week; Carpendale to Greer, 13 Mar. 1934. Saturday afternoon broadcasting started in Oct. 1934.

[4] *Greer to Carpendale, 7 Mar. 1934.

[5] *Ashbridge, 'Report on Demonstration of Baird Television at Gaumont-British Studios, Wardour Street on 12 March 1934'.

asking for a conference 'between some of your people and some of ours to discuss the future arrangements for the handling of television'. There were three aspects to consider, Reith stated—the political ('using the term in the policy sense and for want of a better one'), the financial, and the technical.[1] Kingsley Wood agreed, and nominated Phillips and Angwin to meet Carpendale and Ashbridge.[2]

Doubtless Reith had political aspects in a wider sense in his mind also, for in March 1934 the BBC was being subjected to a sustained attack in the press for not moving faster with television.[3] At the fifth annual meeting of the Baird Television Company on 20 March Greer was careful not to attack the BBC, but a number of shareholders did.[4] Greer himself was content to put the problem into historical perspective. 'Last week the Prime Minister came to view this miracle. . . . He was aghast. So stunned was he by the marvel which had been shown to him that he spoke in alternate admiration and fear—admiration for the genius that had created it, fear that mankind might not be wise to use it for its good. I do not share that fear. The instinct which has prompted this invention is just as fundamental as the instinct which drove Marconi on.'[5]

The representatives of the Post Office and the BBC met at St. Martin's-le-Grand on 5 April. They compared the work of the Baird Television Company and E.M.I., noting that while the latter, as manufacturers, were producing 'well constructed and workmanlike apparatus', the former produced much that was 'distinctly amateurish in construction and finish'. Only the cathode-ray tubes used by Baird and produced by General Electric were superior, especially in colour, to the apparatus of E.M.I. Both Baird and E.M.I., it was noted, were pressing the BBC to provide further facilities, Baird threatening, as always, that he would otherwise take independent action, E.M.I. urging the building of a separate television transmitting station on a high position overlooking 'the populous parts of London'. Carpendale said that 'the BBC were loth to take such a step

[1] *Reith to Kingsley Wood, 15 Mar. 1934.
[2] *Kingsley Wood to Reith, 20 Mar. 1934. J. W. Wissenden was later added to the Post Office side.
[3] For the general attack, see above, pp. 454–5.
[4] *Greer to Reith, 21 Mar. 1934.   [5] *The Times*, 21 Mar. 1934.

until the major questions of policy, probable development, finance and technique were settled'.

The meeting then went on to discuss a number of general questions, including the best method of financing a public service; the use of such a service for news items and plays; the relative methods of other systems, such as Cossor and Scophony;[1] arrangements to prevent one group of manufacturers from obtaining a monopoly of the supply of receiving sets; and the possible use of film television to serve a chain of cinemas. It is unfortunate that no full record survives of what was said under each of these headings, some of which remain topical in 1964. As it was, the meeting concluded by agreeing that a government-appointed committee should be set up to advise the Postmaster-General on questions concerning television. The weight of authority of such a committee, Carpendale declared, would greatly strengthen both the BBC and the Post Office in the decisions they would have to take.[2]

The idea of such a committee had already been put to Kingsley Wood by Reith a few days before the meeting of 5 April.[3] 'I am sure that something by way of a Public Committee is required,' he had written in his diary on 27 March, 'with the Post Office and ourselves represented.' Alfred Clark of E.M.I. approved of the suggestion.[4] Reith thought of Eccles as a possible chairman, although the Postmaster-General had never heard of him.[5] At the meeting of 5 April the question of who should be chairman was left open, Phillips remarking that 'the Postmaster-General would probably have strong views on this'.

On 16 May Kingsley Wood told the House of Commons that he had set up a Departmental Committee 'to consider the development of television and to advise the Postmaster-General on the relative merits of the several systems and on the conditions under which any public service of television should be provided'.[6] The chairman of this important inquiry into the great medium of the future was Lord Selsdon, formerly Sir William Mitchell-Thomson, who had been Postmaster-General when the Corporation came into existence. It was he who, in

[1] The BBC corresponded with Cossor in 1933. Scophony Ltd. had been founded in 1932, and developed optical-mechanical methods, known as 'split focus' scanning.
[2] *Comments on a Conference held at the Post Office, 5 Apr. 1934.
[3] Reith, Diary, 29 Mar. 1934.   [4] Ibid.
[5] *Reith to Carpendale, 4 Apr. 1934.   [6] *Hansard*, vol. 288, col. 1450.

Reith's considered opinion, had so mismanaged matters in 1926 that the public control of sound radio had been given a most inauspicious start.[1] Indeed, Reith considered the appointment of Selsdon so 'shocking' that it gave him no confidence in the outcome of his inquiry.

4. The Inquiry

THE committee took its first evidence on 7 June 1934, when it interviewed on successive days representatives of the Baird Company and E.M.I. Choosing between them was at least as fascinating as choosing between George Stephenson's *Rocket* and its jaunty competitors on a distant day in 1830. Before the committee met, however, it was solemnly warned by a member of the general public that the choice was not simply between two rival systems already in existence. 'I have written to you with all respect', the correspondent began, 'to warn the BBC that the systems now before the public, however interesting, are not the last word in practical television. The BBC should wait a while before committing itself to an expensive outlay involving the use of short wave transmission with limited effective range.'[2]

Lord Selsdon and his colleagues proceeded with their inquiries. His colleagues were mainly experts who already knew a great deal about the problem of television—Phillips and Angwin of the Post Office and Carpendale and Ashbridge of the BBC. O. F. Brown of the Department of Scientific and Industrial Research was added to the inner team, and the vice-chairman was Sir John Cadman, who was to be chairman in 1938 of the Committee on Imperial Airways, which reported just before Reith took over his first post after leaving the BBC. Such is the tangle of historical connexion. The secretary was J. Varley Roberts of the Post Office. Thirty-eight witnesses were examined—some of them on more than one occasion—and many written statements were received. Baird himself was not among

---

[1] See above, p. 480.
[2] *J. B. King to Ashbridge, 15 May 1934; Ashbridge to J. Varley Roberts, the secretary of the Television Committee, 16 May 1934.

the witnesses, but Blumlein of E.M.I. was. Every business organization interested in television was represented, and a small number of other interests, far smaller in number than the interests which had been represented at the Crawford inquiry into sound broadcasting in 1925 or the subsequent inquiry presided over by Ullswater in which Selsdon took part.[1]

The formal evidence was felt to contain 'secrets of commercial value', and was not published. Likewise appendixes on the rival British systems and on developments in the United States and Germany, which had been examined on the spot by deputations led by Selsdon and Brown, were also left unpublished. Yet the international dimension of the Report was particularly interesting. Technical progress at this date was at least as advanced in the United States as it was in Britain, but there was no television service. Television stations were licensed only on an experimental basis, as in Britain, and their programmes were not very attractive to the business interests who were managing radio as a commercial proposition.[2] They were to claim later on, in a very un-American way, that the industry had been given a chance to profit 'by experience abroad';[3] and even at the time Sarnoff told Reith that he was not going to start a regular television service until both competitive pressure and technical experience had increased. In Germany the State itself was soon interested in technical progress in television. Goebbels had spoken to one of the Baird Television directors about it, and had told him what a wonderful thing it would be to show Hitler and himself in every home.[4]

No British politician seems to have had similar ambitions, nor was there any reference to politics in the final report of the committee. The issues centred on techniques, finance, and organization. In the second of these matters the Treasury set the pace. In the first, however, and to a lesser extent in the third, the position of the Post Office was of strategic importance, as it had been at the time of the initiation of sound broadcasting. It was the Post Office which felt the pressure of contending

[1] See above, pp. 476 ff.
[2] D. G. Fink, 'Television Broadcasting Practice in America, 1927–1944' in the *Journal of the Institution of Electrical Engineers*, vol. 92 (1945). See also *Adventure in Vision*, ch. ix.
[3] *Heinl Radio Business Letter*, 20 Jan. 1939.
[4] *Evidence to the committee by Major A. G. Church.

claimants for television facilities, which was expected to give sound and independent opinions on all technical matters, and which was called upon to judge and decide in the 'public interest'. In the case of television, however, there was a worrying minor doubt about the extent of its authority. Its power to exercise some measure of control over television was derived from the provisions of the Wireless Telegraphy Act of 1904, under which no person could establish or work a wireless station without a licence issued by the Postmaster-General. The Act also prescribed that the Postmaster-General could decide the conditions attaching to any such licence. In submitting the Report of his committee to the Postmaster-General, Selsdon admitted, however, that there were doubts as to whether television without any accompanying matter, written or spoken, was covered by the 1904 Act.[1]

The point was academic. Explanatory written or spoken matter was already an essential part of a television service; the Post Office had intervened persistently from the start in television development; and new legislation, if necessary, could always be passed. Post Office policy before 1934 had been to issue television licences to 'qualified persons or firms' who applied for them, but the licences were confined to research and experimental work and did not carry with them any authority to conduct a form of public service. It had also been a part of Post Office policy to confer with the BBC about all future developments and to rely upon it to test new techniques by organizing broadcast transmissions on a limited scale. 'The view has been held that when television has reached such a stage of development that it would be suitable for a public service, it would probably be found preferable that such a service should be undertaken by the BBC as an adjunct) to their broadcasting service rather than that a separate organisation should be established for the broadcasting of television.'[2]

This was certainly the view of the BBC also,[3] although it was recognized before the committee met that there were genuine financial problems attached to the development of television by

---

[1] *Selsdon to Kingsley Wood, 14 Jan. 1935. A note by the Post Office Solicitor had been drawn up on 27 June 1934.
[2] *Television Committee, Introductory Memorandum, 15 May 1934.
[3] See above, p. 533.

the Corporation. In his memorandum of January 1934 Ashbridge had suggested that it might not be 'practicable' to
finance a television scheme out of the ordinary licence fee. 'The
financial difficulties may become so serious that the only way
of getting enough revenue would be by sponsored programmes.
This is, of course, mainly because it must be started as a luxury
service and continue as such for some years. In the case of
ordinary broadcasting this was not the case.'[1] On at least one
occasion before 1934 the question of sponsored television programmes had been raised. There had been talk of a 'fashion
parade' in 1932, and it had been decided as a matter of principle
that there should be no mention by name of the dress houses
responsible.[2]

The wireless press, as represented by Dr. J. H. T. Roberts of
Liverpool University, speaking for *Popular Wireless* and the *Wireless Constructor*, backed the claim of the BBC to develop and
control television before the Selsdon Committee. Roberts
believed, however, that 'part of the cost should come from the
present revenue of the BBC, as television is a natural outcome of
broadcasting. . . . Given improved facilities, and with the whole-
hearted co-operation of the BBC, Television would develop
more in twelve months than it has done since its inception and
would soon reach a stage at any rate of practical utility.'[3]
Popular Wireless had always deprecated exaggerated claims for
television systems, so that this statement was a gesture of faith
and confidence.

The other interested party, the Radio Manufacturers'
Association, representative of 119 manufacturers and at least
90 per cent. of total production in the radio trade, considered
that the future of television was 'assured'. 'The greatest progress
is to be expected', its memorandum stated, 'if development
takes place on lines parallel with those of acoustic broadcasting.'
Recalling the part played by the 'joint action of certain independent individual firms' in the foundation of the BBC, the
Association looked to the BBC in the future. It insisted, however,
that the cost of development should not be a new charge on the

[1] *Ashbridge to Reith, 17 Jan. 1934.
[2] *Control Board Minutes, 23 Aug. 1932; note from Roger Eckersley to Robb,
24 Aug. 1932.
[3] *J. H. T. Roberts, 'Outline of Evidence to be presented to the Committee'.
Unfortunately none of the synopses or memoranda are fully dated.

BBC. The Treasury should find the money out of that proportion of licence revenue which it had hitherto retained.

One precedent, the R.M.A. went on, should not be followed —that of collecting income from royalties on receiving apparatus. The system had quickly been found unworkable in the case of sound radio and it would be unworkable again. The Association said little about the technical side of television, although what it said was important. First, there should be no 'exclusive long term contracts' with the owners of existing transmitting systems, 'which would prevent or delay the adoption of any new system which might be developed on more satisfactory lines'. Second, 'in the opinion of the R.M.A., the present thirty-line transmissions are of no value whatever and should be discontinued forthwith'.[1]

Alone among the biggest manufacturers, the General Electric Company, a member of the consortium of firms which had brought the British Broadcasting Company into existence in 1922,[2] considered that 'the analogy' between beginning a television service and the 'easy birth of broadcasting' was quite misleading. 'We must be prepared for a greater measure of disappointment and the use of greater persistence and salesmanship if so great an experiment is to be successful.' General Electric had entered into a gentleman's agreement with Baird Television Ltd. and was thereby committed to the development of Baird's systems. It did not believe that the BBC would provide the necessary 'persistence and salesmanship' which, it argued, was as essential in programme building as in engineering. 'The standardised and ordered machinery and organisation which we have come to associate with broadcasting' was inappropriate in the case of television. Instead, there should be 'responsible and substantial companies' operating 'on certain wavelengths or in certain areas'. A 'Central Television Board' should be created, including representatives of the Post Office and six to eight independent members selected from public life, industry, and commerce and unconnected with any financial interests in television. Alongside the Board there should be an Advisory Committee which would include a representative of

---

[1] *Synopsis of Evidence to be submitted by the Radio Manufacturers' Association.

[2] See *The Birth of Broadcasting*, pp. 107 ff.

the BBC and representatives of the 'approved television trans-mitting companies'. The companies should also have the right of direct access to the Board.[1]

The 'line-up' on this issue is interesting, for the Newspaper Proprietors' Association came out strongly in favour of a BBC monopoly, 'in accordance with the terms of the present BBC Charter', and added that there should be 'no forms of advertising by means of what are known as sponsored programmes'. Any television organization outside the control of the BBC would lead to 'confusion and a lack of proper balance'.[2]

The Newspaper Proprietors' Association wished severely to limit the scope of television, whoever managed it: General Electric was thinking not so much of a permanent 'settlement' for television as of a satisfactory working arrangement during the first years of research and experiment. The BBC made the same point in one of its memoranda. 'The fact has to be faced that it is probable, so far as one is able to see at the moment, that many years must elapse before even a majority of present-day listeners will be able to make use of the proposed television service, if only because of geographical coverage. It must be remembered also that the majority of listeners at the present time do not pay more than £7 to £10 for a receiving set and that were the minimum cost of a sound receiving set at the present time as much as £25, the possible effect on licences would be to reduce the number by some 50%.'[3]

The Selsdon Committee had to examine both the technical merits of the rival television systems and future finance and organization of a television service. Much of the technical evidence was necessarily secret, since it related to patents: the problems of finance and organization, however, raised major matters of public policy. On the technical side, there was tacit agreement between the Baird Television Company and E.M.I. that 'low-definition' television of the 30-line or 180-line type was obsolete. The old theoretical debate about scanning had thus come to an end before the inquiry began, even though the Baird Company had not yet produced an efficient direct scanner

[1] *General Electric Company, Synopsis of Evidence.
[2] *Memorandum from the Newspaper Proprietors' Association.
[3] *Memorandum from Carpendale.

of the 'electric eye' or photomosaic type. The future, both sides recognized, lay with television of much higher definition.

Disagreement started at the points where questions of technique and questions of policy overlapped. The Baird Television Company made much of the fact that it had been first in the field and that it was a British company. The Film Quota Act had been passed in 1933: surely television needed similar protection. Moreover the Federal Radio Commission, after a two-day hearing in 1931, had rejected the use of the Baird system in the United States simply because it was 'alien'. E.M.I. for its part insisted that all its equipment, including cathode-ray tubes and photo cells, everything down to the last screw, was home-manufactured, and that most of its key patents were British.

Evidence about other 'systems' and organizations was given by A. C. Cossor Ltd., Ferranti Ltd., General Electric, and Scophony, some of it suggesting that the differences between systems were not as great as the contestants maintained. There was also some pressure for a 'patent pool' of the kind that had emerged in the wireless manufacturing industry.[1] Ferranti in its evidence directed attention away from systems and patents to the likely future appeal of television in the north of England, where its main works had been located since 1897. 'Imagine how many people in Lancashire would have liked during this last week to look at the Test Match.'

The BBC's main evidence was given by Reith, appearing alone on 30 November 1934. By then the committee had made up its mind that since 'the relationship between sight and sound broadcasting' was so close as to be 'absolutely indissoluble', it was 'impossible to conceive' any authority controlling visual broadcasting other than the authority which controlled sound broadcasting. Selsdon made this clear to Reith at the outset. The reasoning was set out in the final Report. 'We have, of course, considered the possible alternative of letting private enterprise nurture the infant service until it is seen whether it grows sufficiently lusty to deserve adoption by a public authority. This would involve the granting of licences for the transmission of sound and vision to several different firms who are pioneering in this experimental field. We should regret this course, not

[1] See S. G. Sturmey, *The Economic Development of Radio*, ch. xi, *passim*, for the detailed history of pool arrangements.

only because it would involve a departure from the principle
of only having a single authority broadcasting a public sound
service on the air, and because the subsequent process of "adoption" (which we believe would be inevitable) would be rendered costly owing to the growth of vested interests, but also
because we foresee serious practical difficulties as regards the
grant of licences to the existing pioneers as well as possibly to
a constant succession of fresh applicants.'[1]

This cumbrous sentence was concerned more with past and
current contingencies than with long-term agreement. In telling
Reith, before he gave his evidence, that this was the committee's
view, Selsdon went even further. He went as far, indeed, as any
one could go. 'I cannot think that there can be any objection in
any quarter—except perhaps on grounds of private interests—
to the BBC being entrusted with the task. I cannot see that any
rational being could object.'

Reith told the committee that the BBC was quite prepared to
organize a television service with one station in the South and
one in the North of England and an ultimate network of fourteen stations,[2] and that he would welcome the formation of
a Television Advisory Council or Committee to operate during
the experimental phase. He added tersely, however, that the
term of life of such a council or committee ought to be defined:
'some committees are not always ready to die when other people
think their usefulness has come to an end'.

The main part of the interview was taken up with a discussion
on finance, both the committee and Reith agreeing that it was
'quite impossible', as Selsdon put it, 'to disintegrate television
finance itself from the general question of the BBC revenue'.
The committee had already concluded that advertising should
not be considered as a form of revenue, and Reith consented:
yet he left the issue of sponsoring quite open. 'I have no objection in principle to the sponsor system and we do in fact do
something which is near to that, and might do it in the future.'[3]
Taxes on retailers were ruled out, but not levies on the manufacturers of television sets.

[1] Cmd. 4793 (1935), *Report of the Television Committee*, § 40.
[2] *The willingness of the Corporation 'to prepare seriously to assume responsibility for the new service' was put into writing in a letter from R. C. Norman, then
the Vice-Chairman of the Governors, to Selsdon, 13 Dec. 1934.
[3] *Evidence of Sir John Reith, 30 Nov. 1934.

These matters had been discussed by the committee on its return by ship from the United States, but had not been finally settled in November 1934. Nor was the crucial question of what contribution the Treasury should make to future finance. Was the BBC to pay from its existing level of income the greater proportion, the smaller proportion, or no proportion of television costs? Reith was in no doubt that this unresolved question was the crucial one. 'Entertainment as we know it in our sound service, is very costly, and it is only in terms of real interest and entertainment that the new service will succeed.' A 'quite new studio technique' would have to be evolved, and there would be an immense demand for outside television broadcasts.

In this statement Reith was far more realistic than Brown and Phillips, who seemed to suggest that the service could be kept working on the basis of 'old classic films', which could be 'picked up' cheaply, and 'trailers' for films showing currently in the cinemas. Yet Selsdon saw further than Reith in one essential respect. He asked Reith whether he envisaged a day on which BBC programmes would be so 'enhanced in value' by television that a number of people who did not then have sound broadcasting sets would go off and buy a combined licence. When Reith replied simply, 'No, I do not ever envisage that', Selsdon commented, 'I frankly do. I think the time will come, it may not be so far off as it may look at the moment, when you will be having people definitely asking to see a football match, and when that arrives I am sure you will tap a whole reservoir of people.' Reith was less enthusiastic about the prospects of television than he had been about the prospects of sound radio. He found Selsdon 'very genial', but felt that the committee as a whole was a 'poor one'.[1]

In saying this, he was probably still thinking about the vexed question of finance which had been left open at this hearing. Indeed, he wrote to Selsdon a few days later taking up again the unfinished question. 'The members of the Committee cannot know anything about the state of our finances, and I was not asked whether we had, so to speak, any surplus funds for this or for any other purpose.' Far from having any surplus funds, Reith insisted, the BBC lacked the funds to develop existing services adequately. 'As a matter of fact, for your private infor-

[1] Reith, Diary, 30 Nov. 1934.

mation, we propose in due course to present a case for an increase of revenue, irrespective of television, feeling that our present revenue is insufficient for our expanding needs, e.g. in such matters as the very important Empire Service.' Reith reiterated that the BBC wished to take up television, but that the 'real entertainment value' which was absolutely necessary would cost a large sum. Television could not be provided on the cheap. 'The standard must be infinitely higher than anything we have done up to the present.'[1]

The committee's Report appeared on 31 January 1935, twenty-eight pages in length, and price 6d. To the finance of television it devoted its last five critical pages. The BBC's responsibility was recognized, and a Television Advisory Committee was recommended—with Post Office, BBC, and D.S.I.R. representation—for a period of five years, without power to deal with the compilation of programmes, the detail of the construction of stations, or day-to-day operations. These were to be left to the BBC itself. The 'ultimate establishment of a general television service' was recommended, with an immediate start in London. '*Solvitur ambulando.*' The cost of constructing a national network was conjectured: so too was the cost of programmes. 'We have not budgeted', the Report read, 'during this early stage for a programme comparable in duration, variety or quality with existing sound programmes, although the service should be amply adequate to provide interest and entertainment for the public, as well as opportunity for daily demonstrations by retailers of sets.'[2]

Direct advertising was ruled out for the same reasons that the Sykes Committee of 1923 had ruled it out:[3] sponsored programmes, 'for which the Broadcasting authority neither makes nor receives payment', were permitted. An increased licence fee was felt to be unfair to those millions of listeners who would be outside the range of television stations, and a separate television licence was ruled out on the grounds that if it were high it would 'strangle the growth of the infant service' and if it were low it would be 'purely derisory as a contribution towards the cost'.

[1] *Reith to Selsdon, 6 Dec. 1934.
[2] *Report of the Television Committee*, § 63.
[3] Cd. 1951 (1923), *The Broadcasting Committee*, Report, §§ 40–41.

It was easier to reject formulae than to find acceptable ones, and the recommendation about BBC and Treasury 'shares' of expenditure was almost as vague as it had been in November.

We are left with the conclusion that, during the first experimental period at least [until December 1936], the cost must be borne by the revenue from the existing 10s. licence fee. The determination of the allocation of this contribution as between the British Broadcasting Corporation and the Treasury naturally presents a wide field of controversy, which we should have had to survey at length were we attempting to lay down a permanent basis. Since, however, we are dealing with only a relatively limited sum (£180,000), for a very limited period (less than two years), we suggest that the best course would be for a reasonable share of the amount to be borne by each of the two parties—the Corporation and the Treasury—and we think that the matter should be considered and determined in this light by the Treasury after consultation with the Postmaster-General and the Corporation.[1]

This was hardly a clarion call. Nor were the paragraphs relating to the committee's careful consideration of the technical merits of the rivals, particularly the Baird Television Company and E.M.I. 'The task of choosing a television system for a public service in this country is one of great difficulty. The system of transmission governs in a varying degree the type of set required for viewing, and it is obviously desirable to guard against any monopolistic control of the manufacture of receiving sets.'[2] It had proved impossible, however, to persuade manufacturers to form a 'patent pool' into which all television patents should be placed for the benefit of the 'operating authority', which would then choose which patents it wished to employ. The government had no power to compel an owner of television patents to put them into a pool against his will and, 'with the best will in the world' (which was lacking), 'patent holders might find it exceedingly difficult to agree among themselves on a fair basis for charging royalties and sharing the revenue so obtained'.[3] Failing agreement, there had to be competition. Whichever system or systems were adopted at the outset, 'it is imperative that nothing should be done to stifle progress or to prevent the

[1] *Report of the Television Committee*, § 70.   [2] Ibid., § 51.
[3] Ibid., § 53.

adoption of future improvements from whatever source they may come'.[1]

Low-definition television, which had served as 'a path along which the infant steps of the art have naturally tended', had no real future,[2] but low-definition 30-line pictures should be maintained for the benefit of 'pioneer lookers' until a high-definition service began to operate.[3] Such a service should be established at once, with a single transmitting station in London working with two systems of television in parallel. Baird and E.M.I., tried so often, should be given yet another 'extended trial', 'under strictly comparable conditions': their systems should be used 'alternately—and not simultaneously' for the new public service from the London station.[4]

A number of conditions were set out. The transmitting companies were to grant licences 'to any responsible manufacturer' to produce television receiving sets on payment of royalty; the Advisory Committee was to have power to recommend that devices could be introduced by the BBC other than those covered by the transmitting companies' patents; 'transmissions from both sets of apparatus should be capable of reception by the same type of receiver without complicated or expensive adjustment'; 'definition should not be inferior to a standard of 240 lines and 25 pictures per second'; and 'the general design of the apparatus should be such as to satisfy the Advisory Committee, and, when it has been installed, tests should be given to the satisfaction of the Committee'.[5]

By the time the Selsdon Committee reported early in 1935 E.M.I. had developed its system to the point where it could give demonstrations on a standard of 405 lines and 50 pictures per second. An Emitron type of camera was being used in conjunction with a radio transmitter developed by the Marconi Company. The transmitter had a peak power of 12 kilowatts. Only the modulator was in need of further specialized development. The Baird Television Company's techniques remained inferior. The intermediate film wasted time: it required, moreover, that the performer should be made up heavily with a thick yellowish foundation, grey eye shadow, and bright red lips. The spotlight method, which produced Baird's best close-up head and

---

[1] Ibid., § 51.   [2] Ibid., § 26.   [3] Ibid., § 34.
[4] Ibid., §§ 51–55.   [5] Ibid., § 56.

shoulder effects, entailed complete darkness in the studio while the programme was being transmitted. The Farnsworth camera was not perfected, and in this kind of technique the Emitron camera was manifestly superior. The doom of Baird was anticipated in September 1935 when the BBC finally closed down the old 30-line broadcasts. All the 'televisors' still in existence suddenly became obsolete, and there was a lull before anything new went over the air.

Just before the lull started, the BBC announced that it had chosen Alexandra Palace as the home for its new London transmitting station.[1] With the Baird Television Company ensconced in the south tower of the Crystal Palace and the BBC in Alexandra Palace, the Victorians were coming into their own again. Both edifices recalled the exhibitions of the mid-nineteenth century. 'Television is incongruously housed', *The Times* complained. 'Gaunt and unlovely, the Palace dominates part of North London, with only the 220 ft. mast to indicate the marvel in the south-east corner. An inadvertent entry by the back door brings the visitor over a desolate branch terminus of the L.N.E.R. into empty, echoing halls, where the assorted objects might have been gathered by a surrealist.'[2] Yet there was a kind of aptness in the fact that the home of one of the great nineteenth-century exhibitions was to become the first centre of the greatest exhibition of the twentieth century—a continuous one. The exhibition was not yet ready in 1935. 'Nevertheless,' as the Report put it, 'the time may come when a sound broadcasting service entirely unaccompanied by television will be almost as rare as the silent cinema film is today.'[3]

5. The Service

REGULAR BBC television broadcasts, the first in the world, began on 2 November 1936. Between the publication of

[1] The *Daily Herald* anticipated the news, 17 May 1935. The lease ran for twenty-one years as from 1 June 1935. Contracts for building work were not sent out until Oct. 1935. T. C. Macnamara was given the task of planning the station.
[2] *The Times*, 7 Jan. 1938.   [3] *Report of the Television Committee*, § 36.

Selsdon's Report and the official opening, much had happened to determine the shape of things to come. First, the Television Advisory Committee came into existence, meeting for the first time on 5 February 1935, only a few days after the Report had been laid before Parliament.[1] Second, the Baird Television Company and E.M.I. hurried forward with their technical developments. Third, the BBC began to order equipment and to make appointments in connexion with its new service. The technical problems of running a regular daily service were new, and it was also necessary to examine the problems and opportunities of new kinds of studio work.

The Television Advisory Committee had exactly the same membership as the Television Committee, except that Sir Frank Smith of the Department of Scientific and Industrial Research replaced Cadman. At its first meeting it decided on the minimum of publicity, turned down an offer by the *Sunday Express* to provide the first television programme, and agreed on the appointment of a Technical Sub-Committee, consisting of Smith, Angwin, Ashbridge, and Brown. It also approved the first steps towards the acquisition of the Alexandra Palace site. It was some time, however, before the BBC was able to go ahead with the building and equipment of the station. The question of site itself remained open until May, and tenders did not go out until the summer of 1935.

There were difficulties, too, as between the various companies. It had been anticipated that the Baird Television Company and E.M.I. would not wish to use any apparatus in common,[2] but, in addition to this long-standing difference, the Radio Manufacturers' Association found it impossible to agree with either of the two contending companies on a standard form of licence covering the use of television patents.[3] When the matter was at last settled in July 1935 the idea of a standard licence had to be dropped, and the two companies were left 'to

---

[1] The Report was laid before the Cabinet on 31 Jan. See *The Times*, 1 Feb. 1935.
[2] They did in fact use aerials, high-frequency feeder lines, and sound transmitters in common.
[3] *See the *Report of the Television Committee*, § 56 (d). The R.M.A appointed a Television Negotiating Committee to meet representatives of the Baird Television Company and E.M.I. early in March 1935. See Minutes of the Television Advisory Committee, 5 Mar. 1935. Clause 56 (d) had to be withdrawn when the two sides could not agree. (Minutes of the Television Advisory Committee, 30 Apr. 1935.)

licence any responsible manufacturer to use their patents for making television sets on payment of a *reasonable* royalty'.

The two companies were unequally placed in the last stages of their duel, and Birkinshaw, appointed Engineer-in-Charge at Alexandra Palace, had the difficult diplomatic task of keeping peace between them. West of the Baird Company reported to Ashbridge in October 1935 that the Baird Television Company's use of Farnsworth apparatus was still imperfect and that intermediate film processes would have to be used at least until March 1936.[1] The variety of apparatus employed did not make matters easy for the BBC: when, for example, it was decided that a small experimental 'portrait studio' should be opened 'at or near Broadcasting House', it was agreed that it would be impossible to accommodate Baird's intermediate film apparatus as well as an E.M.I. ionoscope.[2] And when all the necessary apparatus had been installed at Alexandra Palace, both companies still needed two months to make preliminary programme tests with their apparatus before public transmissions could begin.[3]

Not all the difficulties were on Baird's side. E.M.I. had to run a shuttle service from Hayes to replace cathode-ray tubes at short notice. It insisted also on complete and what seemed at times 'unreasonable secrecy' as to what its engineers were doing.[4] Relations between the two contestants were so strained that Ashbridge suggested that the only fair way of deciding which one of them should bat first when transmissions began was to invite the two companies to toss for it.[5] Accordingly, a coin was tossed by Lord Selsdon at a meeting held at St. Martin's-le-Grand on 23 July 1936, and H. Clayton, the vice-chairman of the Baird Television Company, had the luck.[6]

Before either company was ready, the BBC's new Director of Television had taken a bold initiative of his own. He was Gerald Cock, a man given to bold initiatives,[7] and he had taken up his new post in February 1935, almost immediately after the committee reported. When he was first appointed he had 'not the slightest appreciation of what would be needed', but he very

---

1 *Minutes of the Television Advisory Committee, 2 Oct. 1935.
2 *Ibid., 19 Dec. 1935.   3 *Ibid., 20 Jan. 1936.   4 *Ibid., 20 Feb. 1936.
5 *Ibid.   6 *Ibid., 23 July 1936.   7 See above, pp. 80 ff.

quickly came to the conclusion that he was concerned with 'the greatest medium for communication the world had ever seen'.[1] Cock decided in the summer of 1936 that the long and inevitable delay in providing a television service could best be brought to an end by a burst of activity that would capture public attention. Television could best be given a new boost by the BBC organizing television transmissions from Alexandra Palace to the Radiolympia Exhibition in August 1936. The Radio Manufacturers' Association was felt to be somewhat 'half-hearted' about this—only seven manufacturers showed television receivers—and the Baird Television Company was doubtful whether, given short notice, transmissions would be as good as they ought to be.[2] Cock went ahead vigorously, however, with the full support of the Television Advisory Committee.

The programmes were planned by Cecil Madden, who was to have a long and successful career with the BBC. Madden, with ample theatrical experience, was given only ten days' notice to commission lyrics and music and to find stars and arrange films. He was at the mercy not only of the engineers of the two companies but of what were known to be difficult reception conditions at Olympia. Yet, with every kind of technical difficulty to harass him, and Cock's two highly publicized lady announcers—Jasmine Bligh and Elizabeth Cowell—both ill, Madden at last succeeded in presenting what one newspaper called 'real television'.[3]

Leslie Mitchell was the announcer: he had been employed in sound radio as an announcer and as a member of Maschwitz's Variety Department, and he had to carry out his first duties for the Radiolympia transmissions in the pitch dark which Baird's spotlight system necessitated. He managed both to catch the excitement of the occasion and to remain visibly unruffled even when it was suspected that sabotage as well as technical hitches were responsible for some of the irritating disturbances and breakdowns. Cock, Birkinshaw, Madden, Mitchell, and Elizabeth Cowell, who returned from her illness to Alexandra Palace in time for the last few days of Radiolympia, helped to raise the

[1] *BBC Television Programme, *Window on the World*, 19 Mar. 1962.
[2] *Minutes of the Television Advisory Committee, 2 May 1936; Clayton to Carpendale, 17 July 1936.
[3] *Morning Post*, 26 Aug. 1936.

spirits of the radio manufacturers far more than Baird had ever been able to do, and they were relieved to discover that there was an even slightly bigger demand for sets capable of receiving both systems than they had anticipated. They even raised Baird's spirits too. There had obviously been a wide enough range of programmes and sufficient signs of promise of future technical quality to attract a public. The range included not only live performances, but films of the *Queen Mary* docking at Southampton, of Arsenal playing Everton, and of Baird, in what was to be the last of his big 'stunts', 'televising' aboard a Royal Dutch airliner.

The entry of Gerald Cock into the picture marks a shift of emphasis in the story of pre-war television. Hitherto almost everything had depended on techniques: after Radiolympia 1936 it depended on programmes also. It is true that there was a deliberate pause between the end of Radiolympia and the official opening of the new television service on 2 November 1936 because plans were not completed. Yet pictures were being sent out during this period and at least one programme with a long future ahead of it, the magazine *Picture Page*, was first broadcast, with Madden as producer, during the pause, on 8 October 1936. Joan Miller, the Canadian actress, was the commentator, shown sitting at a telephone switchboard and plugging the viewers—they were still called 'lookers' in 1936—through to the celebrities. 'They were very adventurous wonderful days', she has reminisced since. 'It was rather like "covered wagon work" and we were homesteading as we went along, finding out everything. Every programme was a way of finding out how to do the thing. And the cameramen also were finding their way.'[1] The engineers too were learning every day about the capabilities and limitations of the new equipment.

Before Radiolympia, Cock also had been finding his bearings in the new world of television, a world which was quite alien to many of the senior officials in Broadcasting House. The premonition that the world was about to change can be noted first in a memorandum written by Roger Eckersley in July 1934, while the Selsdon Committee was beginning its inquiries. 'It may be a long time before Television is perfected', Eckersley wrote, 'and I suppose that at the beginning television sets will

[1] *Window on the World*, 19 Mar. 1962.

be so expensive as to be the toys of the favoured rather than pieces of furniture in the homes of the proletariat.' Yet 'given practical television, the general public will wish to see as well as hear. . . . Is there anything we can do to prepare for it?' Building schemes should be changed, Eckersley implied, and dressing-rooms and stages built. Broadcast drama would soon cease to appeal. So would visionless Variety.[1]

No one seems to have replied directly to this memorandum, although a few months later Gerald Beadle, who was to end his long and distinguished BBC career as Director of Television, was writing notes on the exceptionally high cost of television Variety.[2] Carpendale, seeking to impress upon Reith the importance of his evidence before the Selsdon Committee, could not hide his own scepticism. Watching at home in semi-darkness to see what was happening on a tiny screen did not seem to him ever to be likely to enthral the millions. 'If television had come before the movies I might think otherwise, but the cinema today is so cheap and so perfect and so universal in its appeal that I doubt if television can stand up to it for a long time to come.'[3] Its only hope of success—and Eckersley agreed with him about this—was to develop a costly television service, running in parallel to the sound broadcasting service. 'It is impossible to forecast any independent programme which will be adequate for the purpose, without the expenditure of a large sum of money. We feel that we have led the public to expect too much from broadcasting . . . for us to envisage the possibility of our continuing with the television service on the elementary lines along which broadcasting itself originally started.'[4]

This was where Cock came in. His first report, written in March 1935, envisaged a separate programme staff, including a film expert, a first-class executive, and a permanently attached technical adviser with wide and not circumscribed functions. He also envisaged—in the short run only—'provided' or 'sponsored' programmes, with brief acknowledgements at the beginning and end of the programme but with 'no selling of time on

[1] *Roger Eckersley to Dawnay, 12 July 1934.
[2] *Beadle to Carpendale, 3 Dec. 1934.
[3] *Carpendale to Reith, 20 Nov. 1934.
[4] *Eckersley to Dawnay, 29 Nov. 1934.

the U.S.A. or Luxembourg model'. He felt that the suppliers of 'ladies' hats, dresses and jewellery' and motor-car and aeroplane manufacturers would be interested in mutual co-operation 'without strings'.[1] There was strong opposition to this proposal inside the BBC on the grounds that 'the principle was bad', and when Cock pointed out that 'sponsoring' would raise the quality of programmes, it was insisted that 'considerations of economy should not be the reason for accepting a principle which had never been accepted by the BBC in the past'.[2] The Board of Governors took the same view, and insisted that during the experimental period 'the same criteria should apply to the Television service as to sound broadcasting'.[3]

'Sponsoring' of a strictly limited kind was, in fact, occasionally employed, although names quickly dropped out.[4] New car models, for example, were displayed for half an hour in October 1936, 'driven slowly along the terrace of Alexandra Palace' and 'halting in turn on a special concrete apron adjoining the ramp on which the television "camera" is manipulated to provide near or distant shots'.[5] Nothing much more daring or contentious than this was attempted, and even this provoked protests.[6]

Cock was also determined, if he could, to forge new links with the 'entertainment world'. Recalling the tough negotiations with outside interests in which he had taken part as Director of Outside Broadcasts,[7] he urged the need, in particular, to reach an agreement with the cinema industry. 'It is suggested that a special tuning-in film should be made to our order by Gaumont-British as the first co-operative effort between BBC Television and the Film Industry.' It would be a special 'show', lasting about three or four minutes, 'with an A. P. Herbert or Maschwitz lyric set to music'. Film technique would inevitably begin to influence many types of programmes where the 'artists' of sound radio had hitherto had a free field. There would be a great increase in 'actuality' and 'news-topical' programmes,

---

[1] *Minutes of Television Policy Committee, 4 Dec. 1935.

[2] *Note on Sponsored Programmes, 5 Dec. 1935. The note, written by Nicolls, followed a Controllers' Meeting on 4 Dec. 1935.

[3] *Board of Governors, Minutes, 11 Dec. 1935.

[4] *Note by Goldsmith, 1 Dec. 1936.

[5] *BBC Press Release, 6 Oct. 1936.

[6] *A. P. Ryan to Tallents, 5 Oct. 1936.

[7] See above, pp. 80 ff.

and in the preparation of these, too, 'much of the present pain-fully acquired broadcast technique is bound for the scrap heap'.[1]

Ashbridge scribbled comments freely on Cock's draft, adding in pencil the urgent practical note—'must get a horse race or boat race or something as soon as humanly possible'. With his experience of outside broadcasts, Cock immediately agreed. He warmed to his new job as its range of possibilities became clear to him, and he was quite at home in a brief battle with film interests in October 1935, when Western Electric, a subsidiary of the powerful American Telephone and Telegraph Company, and R.C.A. both refused leave for the televising in Britain of any sound films licensed by them—virtually 90 per cent. of the American talking-film output. Reith appealed direct by tele-phone to David Sarnoff, and R.C.A. waived its prohibition 'until further notice'.[2] Western Electric also waived its ban for as long as television had not 'actually passed out of an experi-mental into a commercial stage'.[3]

Cock's vision enabled him to move forcefully through such obstacles. In one statement, indeed, his imagination ran ahead of what has actually happened since. 'The growth of a Tele-vision Service will see a revolutionary change in the gramo-phone record industry. "Telegram" sets will replace radiograms and long-running film records will be used instead of discs, the picture track being shown on the home television screen.'

Reith was worried that Cock might move too fast and too independently in the position of 'comparative autonomy' in which he found himself:[4] this was to be a worry of other Director-Generals in other circumstances, and it explains much in the subsequent history of television. He approved, however, of the kind of organization Cock had suggested, with a skeleton tele-vision staff augmented by 'borrowed' producers. Cock himself was to be responsible in the BBC hierarchy to the Controller (Programmes), and Television was to be a department of the Programme Division.

These decisions went much further than any which had been hinted at before 1935, but it was clear that television, which, after all, was still in the 'experimental' stage, was not to have complete freedom to develop on its own. It was to be treated as part of a complex, a complex within which relationships were bound, almost by the nature of things, to be difficult and uncertain. What was to be the link between Broadcasting House and Alexandra Palace? Were the two media to be treated as 'integrated' elements in the same whole or as parallel services? Reith fell back on the analogy of the Empire Service. 'Cock and his staff are in the same position as Beresford Clark and his staff of the Empire Department. This means that they are subject to A.C.(P) supervision, but it would be as unreasonable to have a [separate] A.C.(P) for Television as to have an A.C.(P) for the Empire Service. It would be no less unreasonable for one suddenly to appoint an Assistant Director-General for programmes.'[1]

This was a supremely logical conclusion, which derived from Reith's conception of functional organization. It was in the light of such argument that Control Board laid down in January 1936 that all television programmes should be subject to the functional control of the broadcasting departments and in particular that talks should be properly 'censored', whatever 'the actual expedients or procedure in regard to manuscripts'.[2] The decision was reiterated a few months later when Control Board stated that 'the Television Department should be dealt with definitely in future as other Departments of the Programme Division, and subject to the same clear authorities'.[3]

Yet there was another side to the question. The disadvantages of this policy were, first, that it was almost impossible to enforce, and second, that the 'clear authorities' within the hierarchy were not always clear about the special needs of television as a medium. Graves, who was one of the main architects of the policy, argued cautiously, for example, not in terms of opportunity but of precedent. 'In my opinion, the present plans of the Television Director are too ambitious. With his characteristic keenness and enthusiasm, he is planning to start a service at a level which I feel need not be reached for some months after the actual date of the start of the regular transmissions.'[4]

---

[1] *Reith to the Controllers, 28 July 1936.
[2] *Control Board Minutes, 14 Jan. 1936.
[3] *Ibid., 15 Sept. 1936.　　　　[4] *Graves to Carpendale, 26 Mar. 1936.

Such attitudes, expressed or merely felt, can stifle creative initiative at critical moments of broadcasting history. Graves was comparing the early days of Empire broadcasting with television and getting the terms of the comparison wrong. He wanted a succession of 'repeats' rather than a burst of ideas. 'It is the novelty of being able to see that really matters at the start, not what can be seen.' To try to exercise a measure of control over Cock, therefore, he arranged that Roger Eckersley, at this date Assistant Controller of Programmes, should be given a special watching brief in relation to television.[1]

Control Board approved this arrangement, although it also approved an interesting four-month plan which Cock had prepared.[2] Many ideas were sketched out in this plan which are crucial to the whole use of television as a medium. The announcers were to have 'a pleasant personality and informal manner'. There was to be a Television Orchestra led by Hyam Greenbaum. A range of regular series of programmes was suggested, including 'Press Personalities', 'From the Theatre', 'In the News', 'The World of Sport', and 'The Zoo Today'. Short excerpts of old and silent film classics were to be offered, and an organization was to be formed for collecting 'People in the News' each day.[3]

Until film supply was assured, it was impossible to say whether or not there would be an independent BBC Newsreel Service: there would be problems here deriving from news agreements concerned with sound broadcasting. It was also difficult 'to know how to deal with Religion with brevity and dignity at present'. Lastly and, in retrospect, not least interesting, the programmes were to be interrupted with what might be called 'natural breaks'. 'To avoid eye strain, there should be interval signals between individual programme items, lasting not more than half a minute. These intervals should be marked by means of a modern clock, the dimension of whose face should be roughly the same as the dimensions of the received picture.'[4]

[1] *Graves to Reith, 3 Apr. 1936.
[2] *Control Board Minutes, 26 Mar. and 7 Apr. 1936.
[3] *There were difficulties with film companies throughout 1936 and 1937, but permission was received to show British Movietone News in Sept. 1936 and the Gaumont-British News Reel in Nov. 1936. Twentieth-Century Fox agreed to lease its 'Magic Carpet' series in Oct. 1936.
[4] *G. A. Cock, 'Notes on Television Programme Service', 5 Sept. 1936.

It was along the lines of this memorandum that Cock prepared for Radiolympia. Jasmine Bligh and Elizabeth Cowell
were chosen from the large numbers of women from all parts
of the world who applied for announcers' posts: the one, in
Margaret Lane's words, was 'tall, statuesque, really beautiful
in the dignified Edwardian manner', and the other 'slight,
quick with a lively face which one would call "chic" '.[1] Leslie
Mitchell was chosen as third announcer from a list of 600 applicants. Cecil Madden, the programme organizer, had considerable experience of 'show business': he was soon to become a
'Mr. Television' in himself.[2] Leonard Schuster, the former
Executive Officer of the Outside Broadcasts Department, was
the administrator whom Cock wanted.

Among the others who joined the team, then or soon after-
wards, were D. R. Campbell, who dealt with lighting, Peter
Bax, formerly assistant stage manager at Drury Lane, who
dealt with design, D. H. Munro, George More O'Ferrall, Dallas
Bower, a film director, and Stephen Thomas in presentation.
The engineering operation was under the over-all control of
Ashbridge, with assistance from all departments. At Alexandra
Palace the team on the spot was led by Birkinshaw, who had
among his engineering lieutenants T. H. Bridgewater as senior
maintenance engineer and H. W. Baker and H. F. Bowden as the
two senior engineers-in-charge of transmitters.[3]

Cock's ambitions and dreams were dependent not only on
the goodwill—or ignorance—of administrators, but on the skill
—and knowledge—of engineers. In the month of Radiolympia,
just after Reith had warned the Controllers of the dangers of
'staff troubles in Television',[4] Ashbridge prepared a long paper
on the engineering side of the new television service. First, there
was a real limit to its extension. There was no surplus of 'wavelength space' on the ultra-short waves, which had been chosen
for the new service: there was almost as keen competition for
the limited number of waves available as there was in the
medium-wave band, and the most that the BBC could legitimately promise on the current line of definition was a network of

[1] Quoted in G. Ross, *Television Jubilee, The Story of Twenty-Five Years* (1961), p. 32.
[2] Ibid., p. 37.
[3] For the trio, Birkinshaw, Bridgewater, and Campbell, see above, p. 563.
[4] *Reith to the Controllers, 28 July 1936.

four stations. There was also a problem of power. The power of Alexandra Palace (about 17 kilowatts) would give an average range of transmission of twenty-five miles. It was about the highest power that engineers could then achieve: if power were to increase to, say, 100 kilowatts, masts would have to be built of at least 500 to 600 feet in height, and there would be powerful Air Ministry objections to this.

These were major transmitting difficulties. So too was the construction of co-axial cable, essential for distributing television programmes more than a few miles, and the perfecting of outside broadcast apparatus, which depended on an efficient link between the outside broadcasting point and the transmitting station. At the receiving end, there was a serious but as yet unmeasured danger of interference, particularly from motor-cars. 'This is the most virulent type of known interference for transmissions by ultra-short waves, and this may conceivably cause a serious set-back since legislation is not likely to be rapid, and may be difficult to apply to existing motor-cars.'

All technical problems in broadcasting history overlap with other problems, and Ashbridge passed in the second half of his memorandum to the 'programme side'. There, the central point was 'the reaction of the public to viewing'. This would be difficult to assess at first, because of the need to separate the interest due to novelty from that created by 'genuine entertainment'. The reaction would also depend on the quality of reception. 'We must avoid making decisions in committee or elsewhere as a result of looking at a picture on a receiver which not only may have cost say £150, but is in perfect running order, with no trace of interference, and has been adjusted by expert engineers. All important decisions which are affected by the quality of the programme must be judged on home receivers receiving the broadcast at a medium range.' Those types of programmes in demand might involve greatest cost and most new technical development. In general, technical costs might be two or three times greater than for sound broadcasting, and programme costs would be correspondingly higher too. Studio provision at Alexandra Palace would not be big enough for more than a year or two, and the BBC would have to build 'elaborate studios apart from the Alexandra Palace of a size and type which at the moment are quite unknown'.

The distant shape of Television Centre may have formed a misty image in Ashbridge's mind. He was certainly more long-sighted in his brilliant forecast than those of his contemporaries on the programme side who envisaged the total decay of sound radio. 'At the beginning, the television service will be only loosely related to the sound service', but, however it was ultimately organized, 'blind broadcasting' would still remain, at least for certain kinds of music and certain kinds of talks and news. 'One must not assume that the analogy applying to talkies and silent films will apply to television and broadcasting.' Ashbridge went on to foresee that there would ultimately be the same 'local' or 'regional' question arising in relation to television as had already arisen in relation to sound radio. Indeed, 'it is likely that there will be far more separate stations associated with cities than in the case of sound broadcasting'.[1]

Few of these issues, so cogently explained by Ashbridge, complicated the brief history of pre-war television. Had there not been a war, however, they would have arisen urgently and inescapably long before the late 1940s. As it was, Radiolympia came and went, and Ashbridge felt that 'very considerable technical progress all round is necessary before the service can be looked on as definitely and firmly established'.[2]

After the pause,[3] the official opening of the new service took place on 2 November, with speeches on both systems from Major G. C. Tryon, the Postmaster-General, the chairman of the BBC's Governors, and Lord Selsdon. Sir Henry Greer, the chairman of the Baird Television Company, and Alfred Clark, chairman of E.M.I., were each televised by their own systems. Norman found the right words for the occasion. 'We believe that these proceedings will be remembered in the future as an historic occasion, not less momentous and not less rich in promise than the day, almost fourteen years ago, when the British Broadcasting Company, as it was then, transmitted its first programme from Marconi House.'

[1] *N. Ashbridge, 'Notes on the Television Service for the Alexandra Palace', 10 Aug. 1936.
[2] *N. Ashbridge, Report on Radiolympia, Sept. 1936.
[3] *Control Board Minutes, 7 Sept. 1936. 'Programmes for the next month should be as simple and flexible as possible; and the main programme effort should be concentrated on research.'

The speeches were followed by light entertainment, provided by Adèle Dixon and Buck and Bubbles, two coloured American comedians and dancers, and in the evening Madden presented the second edition of his *Picture Page*. It was introduced by Jasmine Bligh, and included Jim Mollison, the aviator, a breathless and extremely difficult person to interview, Kay Stammers, the tennis star, and 'Bossy' Phelps, the King's Bargemaster, who was interviewed by John Snagge.

It was Cock's object to provide television programmes for two hours daily, from 3 o'clock until 4 o'clock and from 9 o'clock until 10 o'clock, 'with the finest artists' and the briskest possible camera work. 'Every day we are learning something new. We discovered recently that the television eye is more sensitive than a camera. It registers details the camera does not see.' New techniques would be explored in every kind of programme. 'Informality and brightness will be the keynotes.'[1] Every effort was made to exploit not only the studio space in Alexandra Palace but the amenities of the surrounding park, with its grassy slopes, woods, and lake. Early studio programmes included revue, variety, ballet, illustrated talks and demonstrations, and film excerpts from West End shows. From outside the studios came demonstrations of golf, riding, boxing, and other sports. By the beginning of December 1936 Reith admitted that he had been more impressed by television than he had expected and that it would develop quicker than had been anticipated.

Tallents went further. He said that he felt no doubt about the popular appeal of the new service, particularly among 'the less educated', who would derive special advantage from the double support of sight and sound impressions. Development would be controlled by factors of cost and technique, and not by lack of public demand. He thought that television would demand a new technique, different from that of either sound broadcasting or film production. To some extent at least a specialized television staff was likely to be required, and the proposal to give functional control over it to the producing staff engaged in sound production needed much further examination.[2]

An extraordinarily interesting and percipient memorandum from Val Gielgud brought out the 'creative' implications of discussions of administration and policy. It was as far removed

[1] *BBC Press Release, Oct. 1936.   [2] *Control Board Minutes, 1 Dec. 1936.

from Graves's memoranda as any statement of intentions could be. If Reith's desire to keep the 'two services' together was to be realized—and Gielgud hoped that it would—then there would have to be a complete change of outlook in Broadcasting House. Otherwise television would become 'more and more divorced from ordinary sound broadcasting' and would take on 'the shape of a rival organisation, competing for artists, finance and equipment'. 'Would it not be possible for us', Gielgud asked, 'to try to jump ahead of mere process by trial and error? . . . Television should concentrate upon those aspects of broadcasting which in due course it will be called upon to serve, and the programme departments which are bound, before long, to have to cope with Television as part of their normal activities should face up to that problem now.'

This was the only way, Gielgud thought, of retaining what Reith believed to be absolutely necessary—a sense of unity in broadcasting and an 'integration' of the two media. Gielgud admitted honestly that he was to some extent dismayed with the prospect: 'it implies for my own work a degree of sudden and violent return to the absolute simplicities which is bound to be both difficult and rather disheartening'. Doubtless he was thinking back to *The Man with the Flower in His Mouth* when he added that he feared that within a very few years the radio play for sound only will be 'as defunct as the dodo'. In the light of this, he went on, it seemed 'an irrational and mistaken dispersal of effort' to have two or three comparatively raw producers considering television production problems at Alexandra Palace, while his own staff continued to expend most of its energies on forms of programme 'doomed to the scrap heap'. 'Even if it were necessary for our actual programme output to be to some extent limited as a result of such a change, I still feel', he concluded, 'that by taking the public into our confidence, and by a clear statement that we were regarding the implications of the not-too-distant future in a practical way, we could achieve credit for a far-sighted policy and at the same time lay the foundation for being able to tackle Television properly as soon as it becomes available as a service over a very wide area.'[1]

Gielgud looked fearlessly across space into the new world of television. Graves responded constructively a few months later

1 *Gielgud to Reith, 2 Dec. 1936.

by telling departmental heads to take a more active share in and responsibility for what was being transmitted from Alexandra Palace. He closed with Gielgud's argument, that since outside broadcasts would soon be very largely, if not entirely visual, and talks, features, drama, and schools broadcasts would be attempted by television, there would have to be a 'considerable adjustment in duties and responsibilities'. The longer it was delayed, the more difficult it would become to enforce it.[1]

There was further delay, however, before Carpendale issued a general directive in January 1938 stating that the progress of the television service made it desirable that there should be 'much closer contact with the sound broadcasting service'. 'Heads of Departments are requested to . . . bear in mind the possibility of eventual amalgamation in some fields of Television and Sound broadcasting activities as well as the parallel operation of the two services.'[2]

Before this directive was issued in January 1938, the television service had made considerable progress. In February 1937 the contest between the Baird system and the Marconi–E.M.I. system at last came to an end. The Baird system was dropped. On 30 November 1936 there had been a cruel fire at the Crystal Palace which destroyed a great deal of the Baird Television Company's equipment. It was not the fire, however, which destroyed the Baird Television Company, but the undoubtedly superior achievement of E.M.I.

Fortunately for the BBC the decision, when it came, had to be made not by itself but by the Television Advisory Committee. The committee had already been told by Ashbridge in October 1936 that Baird's system of spotlight transmission was unsuitable for the official opening in November, and Selsdon had declared that since the public service should not be allowed to start with an inferior production of television, E.M.I. might have to be called in first.[3] In fact both systems were used at the opening but when the committee re-examined the question after the opening, there was 'general agreement that the results

[1] *Graves to Heads of Departments, 20 Aug. 1937.
[2] *Memorandum from the Deputy Director-General, 'Television and Sound Broadcasting', 7 Jan. 1938.
[3] *Minutes of the Thirty-Second Meeting of the Television Advisory Committee, 15 Oct. 1936.

obtained with the Baird system were distinctly inferior to those obtained with the Marconi–E.M.I. system and that the Baird spotlight and Intermediate Film methods in particular had proved to be unsatisfactory in operation'.[1] Cock stated his view firmly that the BBC should make exclusive use of the Marconi–E.M.I. system, and Selsdon agreed.[2]

The result was that what were called 'London television standards' were laid down: 405-line pictures only were approved with 50 frames per second, and Baird's 240-line picture with 25 frames per second became sub-standard. The only point that held up an announcement along these lines until February 1937 was fear inside the Post Office—by no means a new fear —that unless adequate safeguards were secured, 'the adoption of the Marconi–E.M.I. standards would put the Company in a very strong monopolistic position, which in the light of past experience with the Marconi Company should be avoided if possible'.[3] Adequate guarantees were given, and the Post Office and BBC announcement of E.M.I's victory, when it came, created far less friction than it might have done. Even Moseley in his championship of Baird did not question the rightness of this final decision.

Baird himself was completely isolated. His colleagues did not seem to understand what a terrible blow it was to him personally 'to be thrown out of the BBC', and argued that the sale of receivers mattered far more than facilities for transmission. Before long Moseley was back again with a new plan and a new company, Cinema–Television, associated with Gaumont-British and designed to fit big television screens into Gaumont cinemas.[4]

The BBC was able to profit directly from the withdrawal of the Baird system. More studio space became available, and there was no longer the handicap of moving everything round at the end of each week, as in a provincial repertory company. It was

[1] *T.A.C. meeting of 16 Dec. 1936.
[2] *Ibid., meeting of 23 Dec. 1936.
[3] *Ibid., meeting of 11 Jan. 1937. For what was thought to be relevant 'past experience', see *The Birth of Broadcasting*, pp. 30–34, 107 ff.
[4] S. Moseley, *John Baird*, pp. 219–23. *The Television Advisory Committee recommended that independent Baird transmissions to cinemas on a wavelength of 8·3 metres should not be allowed in view of the shortage of wavelengths. See Minutes of the Forty-Second Meeting of the Television Advisory Committee, 2 June 1937; Phillips to Baird, 19 June 1937. The BBC also objected to Baird using Post Office land-lines.

a sign of changing times that from April 1937 onwards the BBC began to invite distinguished visitors to watch television in the Listening Hall at Broadcasting House: 150 privileged people watched television in this style in May 1937.

In the same month came the great public event of 1937—the Coronation. Permission was not forthcoming for the installation of television cameras in Westminster Abbey[1] but three cameras, part of a total complement of twenty-two, were installed in the rain at Hyde Park Corner. A special eight-mile cable was laid by the Post Office between Hyde Park Corner and Alexandra Palace, and a huge new portable transmitter made its first public appearance in the BBC's first four-ton television van. Freddie Grisewood was the commentator and it was estimated that several thousand people saw the transmission, while a few lucky 'viewers' picked it up over sixty miles away.[2]

One of the highlights of the programme, to which the press gave headline treatment, was a special smile by the King into the television camera. There was also the inevitable near-technical hitch. Two channels had been provided in case of breakdown, and to the consternation of the engineers both channels went dead just before the transmission was due to start. E. L. C. White, an E.M.I. engineer, found out what was wrong and reassembled the apparatus for one channel with only a few minutes to spare.

Even with the Coronation, the beginning of a monthly sports review, tennis at Wimbledon, the Lord Mayor's Show, the ceremony at the Cenotaph on Armistice Day, Mr. Middleton with his 'television garden', and Pet's Corner at the Zoo, sales of television sets increased only slowly. About 400 had been sold by the end of January 1937:[3] at the end of the year the figure was estimated at just over 2,000.[4] Yet in the early days of

[1] *T.A.C., meeting of 26 Feb. 1937. Ashbridge said that 'in all the circumstances he was not disposed to regard the decision not to allow the actual Coronation ceremony to be televised as being altogether a matter for regret'.

[2] Ross, op. cit., p. 52, writes of 50,000 viewers: the *BBC Handbook* (1938) more modestly suggests 10,000 (p. 42).

[3] *Investors' Chronicle*, Feb. 1937. A Listener Research Report of 26 June 1939, Appendix F, suggested that 280 sets had been sold by the end of 1936.

[4] Listener Research Report. According to figures calculated by the Statistical Department of Murphy Radio Ltd., the total number sold by the end of 1937 was no more than 1,600.

February, in good time for the Coronation, the price of receivers had fallen by about a third. E.M.I. and H.M.V. sets fell in price from 95 guineas to 60 guineas, and Baird 85-guinea sets to 55 guineas. Further cuts were made for the 1937 Radiolympia which opened on 25 August, but sales remained sluggish.

Three reasons were usually given for the slow progress. First, the long years of exaggerated Baird Company publicity had led to a recoil or at least to a popular reluctance to realize just how much standards (though still inadequate) had improved. Second, there was still some doubt about 'systems'. The fundamental design of television receivers, unlike wireless sets, depends on the technical standards in use at the transmitting end, and some would-be buyers seem to have feared that a change in transmitting standards was imminent which would render current sets completely obsolete. Third, the BBC was not transmitting for a big enough number of programme hours. A quarter of a million people visited a Television Exhibition at South Kensington between 10 June and 20 September 1937, and although there was a fall of about a quarter in the total attendance at Radiolympia in 1937 from the figure of the year before, the television section was always crowded.

Jonah Barrington, writing in the *Daily Express*, expressed a widespread feeling when he said that the BBC was holding a 'thriving lusty baby called television' and it was 'too heavy for them'. 'Consider the lesson of Radiolympia. There we saw manufacturers making magnificent gestures by dropping the price of television receivers and increasing their efficiency. But do the BBC reciprocate by increasing their programme service? There is no definite news. They may do this and they may do that. Gentlemen—we need action. And quickly. Because the present programme allowance—two hours daily and a demonstration film in the morning—is woefully, ridiculously inadequate.'[1]

Barrington's solution—the complete amalgamation of sound broadcasting and television, that is to say the televising of all sound programmes—was being widely canvassed in 1937,[2] even though it rested on a confusion between the technical and

---

[1] *Daily Express*, 6 Sept. 1937.

[2] *Sir Ian Fraser to Reith, 20 Oct. 1937; Reith to Fraser, 21 Oct. 1937; Graves to Reith, 22 Oct. 1937.

artistic features of two different media. The BBC's response was slightly to increase transmitting hours (after a total break from 26 July to 18 August) and in February 1938, after the Post-master-General had answered a question on the subject in the House of Commons, to introduce for the first time an hour's transmission on Sundays. The Postmaster-General stated at the same time that the existing standards of transmission would remain unchanged until January 1941.[1]

There were various obstacles in the way of the BBC respond-ing to public appeals to engage in a more adventurous tele-vision policy. One of them was the old difficulty with outside interests—not only film companies, but music publishers and theatres. George Black refused to release his artists even after Reith had met him, for the first time, at lunch in December 1937.[2] Attempts to televise other artists from the BBC's own stage in St. George's Hall also failed. Some artists disliked wholeheartedly either the very idea of appearing on television or the 'long journey' of five miles from the West End to Alex-andra Palace. The Jockey Club was opposed to broadcasts of racing, although the Epsom Grandstand Association allowed broadcasts of the Derby. Despite, or because of, one particularly successful televised—and rediffused—prize fight, that between Boon and Danahar in February 1939, the Boxing Board of Control became very suspicious of televised boxing. More important, however, than this kind of difficulty was the con-tinuing problem of finance. Television, it was known, could absorb money at an alarming rate. How was it all to be paid for?

The Selsdon Report of 1935 had left open the vexed question of the size of the Post Office and BBC 'shares' during the first 'experimental' period of development between January 1935 and the expiry of the BBC's Charter on 31 December 1936.[3] Selsdon himself thought that a fifty-fifty arrangement was right —£90,000 each.[4] Cadman, who was absent when the committee discussed finance in detail, felt that the Treasury should pay the full £180,000.[5] Before this difference could be settled, the Ulls-water Committee had reported.[6] Its proposal that the BBC's

[1] *Hansard*, vol. 331, col. 32, 1 Feb. 1938.   [2] Reith, Diary, 1 Dec. 1937.
[3] See above, p. 592.   [4] *Selsdon to Kingsley Wood, 14 Jan. 1935.
[5] *Selsdon to Kingsley Wood, 17 Jan. 1935.   [6] See above, p. 498.

share of licence revenue should be increased to 75 per cent. was accepted, but its suggestion that an extra proportion should be provided for television development was watered down by the government to read that if after the renewal of the Charter in January 1937 'the Treasury should hereafter be satisfied that the income of the BBC is insufficient to support their services, including Television and Empire broadcasting, it should be open to the Treasury to approve such increase as they may think appropriate in the circumstances in the proportion of licence revenue payable to the BBC'. Once again everything was left vague, and no specific guarantee was given in relation to television.[1]

When it was clear in March 1937 that the allocation of 75 per cent. would not cover the adequate development of the television service, even after drastic economies had been made both in sound radio and television estimates, Reith approached the Postmaster-General for an extra 7 per cent. of licence revenue, a sum of £261,000.[2] The request was too late to affect the government's estimates, and the Board of Governors decided in May 1937 that television expenditure in future should be determined by the sum the government was prepared to release. A memorandum written by Ashbridge in the same month made it abundantly clear that even if the whole balance of 25 per cent. were paid to the BBC (about £950,000) it could not finance more than three or four television stations. As it was, the Alexandra Palace studios were hopelessly small and inadequate for any considerable increase in the output of programmes.[3]

In the light of Ashbridge's statistics, Reith wrote again to the Postmaster-General in June, stating that the financing of television in 1938 and afterwards would have to depend entirely on 'sources outside the present revenue available for sound broadcasting'.[4] Given the small number of owners of television sets, there was surely no justification for financing television in any way that would be detrimental to the best interests of the sound broadcasting service.

In July 1937 Reith met Sir Warren Fisher and Sir James Rae

[1] For the government's general attitude to the Ullswater Report proposals, see above, pp. 510–12.
[2] *Reith to Tryon, 23 Mar. 1937.
[3] *N. Ashbridge, 'Television Finance', 31 May 1937.
[4] *Reith to Tryon, 8 June 1937.

of the Treasury and Sir Thomas Gardiner of the Post Office to discuss television finance. The Treasury representatives began by praising the BBC's system of financial control and by agreeing with Reith that the 75 per cent. was needed exclusively for sound broadcasting. 'They expected me to be grateful for this', Reith wrote in his diary. 'I said it would have been unjust otherwise.' On political grounds, however, they refused to consider the idea of a separate television grant. 'Television they wanted us to finance from a loan for two years or so and then work with the Advisory Committee, agree a percentage which would eliminate this loan (over a long term if they have their way, but they won't), and take care of expenditure, capital and maintenance for say five years. Quite ridiculous and irritating to us, but they urged political reasons and I said I should have to accept it, but I argued with every emphasis against it.'[1]

Official intimation of the Treasury's attitude was given in October, after Reith had told a Cabinet sub-committee of the impossibility of financing either television or foreign service costs out of 75 per cent. of licence revenue, and no one had demurred.[2] The Treasury letter of October accepted the fact that the 75 per cent. would not cover the costs of television, but once again refused to set any particular additional percentage to cover costs. It dropped the idea of loans on grounds of 'constitutional accounting propriety' and agreed to provide a supplementary estimate for 1937 and a new estimate for 1938 on the basis of figures submitted by the BBC.[3]

When the press campaigned for more television programmes, few people had any idea of these difficult and often frustrating discussions behind the scenes. They did not know, for example, about a battle which was raging on the issue of whether or not to convert the old theatre at Alexandra Palace into a large studio at a cost variously estimated as between £70,000 and £140,000.[4] The scheme eventually had to be turned down on

---

[1] Reith, Diary, 28 July 1937.
[2] *Notes of a meeting held on 4 Oct. 1937.
[3] *Letters of 25 Oct. and 3 Nov. 1937.
[4] The idea was tentatively put forward in April 1937, was approved by a number of BBC committees in the summer of that year, was included in the Television Advisory Committee's recommendations of 23 Dec. 1938, and was finally turned down, on account of Treasury opposition, in Feb. 1939.

grounds of cost, although Cock, who opposed it on opposite grounds, argued tenaciously that 'the improvisation of facilities by reconstructing buildings designed for other purposes can never be really satisfactory and must be considered in the nature of stop-gap action. Television demands a functional plant designed for that purpose alone.'[1] The failure to provide even a temporary scheme was really an example of the influence of Treasury parsimony on broadcasting policy.

It was only after the Treasury had declared its willingness to provide extra finance[2] that the BBC came to the decision that it could slightly increase hours of transmission and consider Sunday programmes, which the radio trade was extremely anxious to have started. From 3 April 1938 onwards, therefore, Sunday programmes from 9.5 p.m. to 10.5 p.m. were broadcast, and from the end of 1938 to July 1939 an extra hour in the afternoon. Early in 1936 twenty programme hours each week had been assumed to be the minimum basis of a television service. The figure had only just been achieved when the imminent outbreak of the Second World War closed the service down.

Finance remained a serious problem until September 1939. Supplementary income was provided in February 1938 to help meet the BBC deficit on television programmes as set out in the figures submitted by the BBC after the correspondence of the previous October, and an additional estimate for 1938/9 was carried through Parliament—without debate—in March 1938.[3] The BBC was to receive an extra 15 per cent. of licence revenue, making up 90 per cent. in all, the extra percentage being granted to cover the costs both of television and foreign-language broadcasting.

Yet the greatly increased expenditure on foreign-language broadcasting[4] did not make television development easy, and the financial position had become very serious again by October 1938 when the BBC submitted a detailed *Report on Television Development in 1939 and 1940* to the Television Advisory Committee.[5] A 50-per-cent. increase in television expenditure was

---

[1] *Control Board Minutes, 22 Feb. 1938; Note by Cock.
[2] *This was announced at the Forty-eighth Meeting of the Television Advisory Committee on 14 Jan. 1938.
[3] There was a debate on the supplementary BBC estimate: see *Hansard*, vol. 332, cols. 1897–2022, 9 Mar. 1938.   [4] See above, pp. 397 ff.
[5] *Minutes of the Fifty-Fourth Meeting of the Television Advisory Committee,

50. The Television Studio: A Drawing for *The Listener* (1936)

51. Alexandra Palace (1936)

52.
Gerald A. Cock,
First Director of
Television
(1937)

53.
Elizabeth Cowell,
Television
Announcer
(1939)

54. F. W. Ogilvie, Director-General, 1938

envisaged in 1939, even though this did not allow for any increase in the hours of programmes. The main items of expenditure were the long overdue provision of 'theatre' facilities and the extension of television to four provincial centres. Long-term development demanded an order of expenditure far higher than that which the Television Advisory Committee itself had thought necessary. 'An annual income of £1,000,000 would not cover the needs of an acceptable Television service on a national scale for more than a few years', the Report concluded. Further revenue for television would have to be sought, therefore, either from the introduction of a separate television licence or from sponsoring.[1]

The acting chairman of the Television Advisory Committee congratulated the BBC on 'an admirable document which took a right view of the position', but the Post Office representatives expressed the view that the BBC should devote a larger share of its own resources to television. This division within the committee came at the end of a year when it had been seeking, at the Postmaster-General's request, to work out a long-term programme of television development and the probable order of television expenditure for a period of some years ahead.[2] The division of opinion became academic, however, when in February 1939 the Treasury flatly refused to sanction either the 'theatre' expenditure or the extension of television to the provinces.[3] The reason given had nothing at all to do with television. 'Heavy demands for essential expenditure on rearmament and defence' were felt to be sufficient reason in themselves.

27 Oct. 1938. The BBC's report was also considered at the next meeting of the committee on 2 Nov. 1938.

[1] 'Sponsoring', which had been discussed so generally in 1935, had been considered by the Ullswater Committee (Cmd. 5091 (1936), § 110–11). They did not rule out the practice, but stated (§ 111) that there was 'an obvious danger' that television might come to rely more and more on sponsored programmes. The government forbade the BBC to make use of sponsored programmes in the new Charter of 1937. The Director-General of the Post Office in a note to Reith (15 Mar. 1937) said that this was meant to preclude programmes 'provided' by commercial firms.

[2] *The Postmaster-General had asked them to do this in Jan. 1938. See Television Advisory Committee, Minutes, 14 Jan. 1938.

[3] *The Postmaster-General passed on to the Treasury the BBC's proposals, as supported by the Television Advisory Committee, on 2 Jan. 1939. The Treasury's reply was sent to the Post Office on 18 Feb. 1939 and passed on to the BBC on 25 Feb. 1939.

In the few months that remained before war was declared, there was a searching review of television expenditure along with a discussion as to the extent to which a greater share of BBC funds should be diverted to it.[1] There were also fruitless efforts from inside the BBC and the Television Advisory Committee to persuade the Treasury to change its ruling.[2] Ogilvie, the new Director-General, even made a speech at Liverpool in April 1939 telling the public that delays over technical research were not the most important handicap to television development in the provinces: since 1923 'nearly forty per cent of licence revenue had gone in indirect taxation for purposes other than broadcasting'.[3]

The appointment of Lord Cadman to replace Lord Selsdon as chairman of the Television Advisory Committee in March 1939—Selsdon had died in December 1938—led to a further initiative. Cadman believed that 'sponsored programmes' might be the answer to the financial difficulties,[4] and continued to express this view when the BBC officially came out against them.[5] The Treasury was drawn into this discussion, and made new proposals in August 1939.[6] It suggested a stable grant of $87\frac{1}{2}$ per cent. of licence revenue for the next few years and offered help to start television in Birmingham. While the arguments against sponsored programmes in sound broadcasting might be 'considerable', it went on, entirely different considerations applied in the case of television where the service was very experimental and had little prospect of becoming self-supporting

[1] *The official position on this point was reaffirmed in a memorandum of 10 Mar. 1939: 'The suggestion that sound revenue should be employed to develop television is contrary to the recommendations of the Ullswater Committee, and quite apart from the fact that 75% is needed for sound broadcasting, it seems improper that licence buyers outside London should have still further to subsidise the entertainment of those people in the London area who are able to afford to buy a television set.'

[2] *BBC statement on its licence revenue with particular reference to television; Sir John Simon to Ogilvie, 3 Apr. 1939, referring to the meeting of 6 March.

[3] *The Times*, 5 Apr. 1939.

[4] *Minutes of the Television Advisory Committee, 14 Mar. 1939.

[5] *The first BBC statement was completed on 24 Mar. 1939. The Television Advisory Committee referred the matter back again to the BBC at its meeting on 18 May. Control Board reaffirmed opposition to sponsoring at its meeting of 25 May and the Board of Governors on 31 May. The Television Advisory Committee continued to support sponsoring in a long memorandum approved at its meeting of 23 June 1939.

[6] *Letter of 11 Aug. 1939, sent on by the Post Office on 16 Aug. 1939.

within a 'reasonable period'. 'If, indeed, the BBC share the general view of the Television Advisory Committee as to the desirability of giving a really stirring and immediate impetus to television', the Treasury offer concluded, 'My Lords find it difficult to understand their reluctance to adopt the measure which is, of all measures, most calculated to secure this result.'

The debate about how to deal with this matter was still raging inside the Control Board of the BBC—with sharp divisions of opinion—when war brought it to an abrupt end.[1] There was a note of gloom in Ogilvie's comment that 'the arguments against sponsoring such as they are (independence, artistry, the attitude of the press, etc.) are hardly likely to appeal to the Treasury'.[2] For his part, Cock stated his position unequivocally. 'May I record my conviction that the two greatest disasters that could happen to television', he wrote to Nicolls in March 1939, 'would be (1) sponsored programmes and (2) delivery of the Television Service in any shape or form to cinema interests.' Both these ideas were in the air 'only because of the restrictive attitude of the Treasury to expansion'.[3] The kind of sponsoring the Treasury had in mind was very different from that which he had advocated on a limited basis in 1935.

The small number of 'viewers', as they began to be called, had little idea that such fascinating discussions were going on behind the scenes. Slowly and undramatically, however, their numbers were increasing. Moreover, as the technical arts of transmission improved, so too did the quality of reception. Cock was able to claim in a broadcast in February 1938 that 'thanks to the continual co-operation of engineers and research workers . . . friction has disappeared and Television is now a really efficient medium'.[4] 'The qualified optimism of two years ago has given place to a profound belief in this miraculous medium.' At the 1938 Radiolympia, television was the main feature of the show. Sixteen firms displayed receivers, and prices had been sharply reduced. Serviceable twelve-inch receivers could be bought from 37 guineas upwards, and efficient small sets for as little as

[1] *Control Board Minutes, 26 Aug. 1939.
[2] *Memorandum by Ogilvie, 'Television Finance', 11 Aug. 1939.
[3] *Cock to Nicolls, 22 Mar. 1939.
[4] *Cock, Broadcast in the National Programme, 1 Feb. 1938.

21 guineas. With Munich intervening between the end of the Exhibition and the advent of winter, more sets were sold between the beginning of October and Christmas 1938 than had been sold in the whole previous period of television history. The exact figure is unknown but it was probably between 5,000 and 6,500. Sales during the eight effective months of 1939 are harder to estimate, but must have been somewhere between 8,000 and 10,000. Estimates of the number of sets in use in August 1939 vary between just under 20,000 and 25,000.[1]

The members of the Radio Manufacturers' Association campaigned very vigorously, a few singly and all collectively, to achieve this result. In March 1938 they formed a Television Development Sub-Committee which sent fortnightly detailed criticisms of programmes and suggestions for improvement first to the Television Advisory Committee and in copy form to the BBC. C. O. Stanley of Pye Radio was the chairman of the sub-committee. Many of the requests they made were impossible to achieve for technical reasons: most were impossible to achieve for financial reasons. Their attitude, however, was almost uniformly friendly to the BBC.

Their tastes were undisguisedly lowbrow. They did not like 'morbid, sordid and horrific plays'; they were sceptical about foreign cabaret and ballet; and they were unmoved by Handel's *Acis and Galatea*. They objected to studio items being presented twice, a practice which was necessitated by the meagre programme allowance. Yet in the last year of pre-war television, they organized joint publicity campaigns with the BBC. At their suggestion, for instance, a series of talks on television began on sound radio in November 1938, with Howard Marshall as the speaker. During the next four weeks lectures were given in London and the provinces, large advertisements appeared in the *Radio Times* and the national dailies, and a thousand poster sites were bought on the London Underground.[2] In December 1938 Gerald Cock answered questions in front of the camera, while viewers rang him up and were connected to a telephone at his desk.

High quality transmissions provided more effective propa-

---

1 *The Listener Research Report of 26 June 1939 and the Murphy figures suggest a total sale of just under 20,000. C. O. Stanley of Pye Radio estimated 25,000.
2 *These comments are taken from the Minutes of the Sub-Committee.

ganda than lectures about the medium or even lectures to dealers about the sets. The Boon–Danahar fight of February 1939 was such a programme. So, too, were the televised Boat Races. Permission to use land near the Thames for the 1938 Boat Race was granted by the Chiswick and Brentford Council to the BBC in return for a small fee only after a vote had been taken and carried by thirteen votes to eleven.[1] The Test Match at the Oval against Australia in August 1938 caused no problems; the only problem at the Cup Final between Preston North End and Huddersfield Town a few months earlier was that after he had unhesitatingly predicted the wrong result (a Preston defeat) Thomas Woodrooffe, the commentator, had to eat his hat.

Among the plays broadcast, *Clive of India* exploited many arts of the cinema, while J. B. Priestley's *When We Are Married* was the first play televised direct from a theatre, St. Martin's, in November 1938. *The Parnell Commission* was one of the first feature programmes; *Tristan und Isolde* the first opera. The lake in the Alexandra Palace grounds was used for a reconstruction of the naval attack on Zeebrugge. Bertram Mills's Circus was an immediate success. Cicely Courtneidge, Lupino Lane, Tommy Handley, Tommy Trinder, Basil Radford and Naunton Wayne were among the comedians televised; Beverley Nichols was the first after-dinner speaker. Margot Fonteyn also appeared, as did Laurence Olivier and Ralph Richardson. Behind the scenes there were many new names—Mary Adams, Jan Bussell, Eric Crozier, Reggie Smith, Moultrie Kelsall, Harry Pringle, Philip Dorté, and Royston Morley. There were also two complete mobile film units, bought in August 1938.

In the same month, a new Central Control Room was opened in Alexandra Palace. The producer could now work in his own control gallery separately from the engineers. *Cyrano de Bergerac*, an early classic of sound broadcasting, was the most ambitious television programme hitherto attempted in October 1938. A few weeks before, one of the first politicians, after Tryon, had appeared on the screen—Neville Chamberlain, arriving at Heston from Berchtesgaden.

There was little doubt that this range of programmes, limited though it was by finance, gave Londoners not only the first

[1] *Television Jubilee*, p. 56.

regular television service but also the best television service in the world in 1938 and 1939. The United States was well behind. It was not until 1939 that N.B.C. announced that it was ready 'to make the art of television available to the public', with two hours of programmes a week which could be received on sets constructed by R.C.A.: the first sponsored programmes were not given until 1941.[1]

Announcements of future prospects have a note of irony about them, at least in retrospect. Early in 1939 the Americans made a bet with the British Radio Manufacturers' Association that before the end of 1939 there would be more television sets in use in the United States than in Britain. The losers were to pay for a dinner in Paris in the spring of 1940, a dinner which would itself be televised. Finland, it was announced about the same time, was planning a service by 1940 in time for the Olympic Games.[2]

Not only did Britain stand out in the international scene but, according to listener research, British viewers liked what they saw. In February and March 1939 nearly 60 per cent. of viewers questioned thought that television programmes were satisfactory and only 6 per cent. did not. Nearly 80 per cent. thought that the programmes were getting better, and only 4 per cent. thought they were not.[3] The world outside was darkening, but the world of television seemed (for all the arguments behind the scenes) to be growing brighter and brighter every day. Then came the sudden blow. On the morning of 1 September 1939, 'Black Friday', Birkinshaw, the engineer in charge at Alexandra Palace, received a message at 10 o'clock that the station should be closed by noon. The last item to be televised for the benefit of visitors to Radiolympia was a Mickey Mouse film. The last words spoken—in the style of Greta Garbo—were 'Ah tink ah go home'. There was no closing announcement.

---

[1] L. White, *The American Radio* (1947), p. 24. The NBC programmes did not begin until 30 Apr. 1939. *Fortune* magazine commented (May 1939) that 'it is natural that television should not have come to stay before 1939'.

[2] *BBC, Notes on Television, sent to *Fortune* magazine, 8 Mar. 1939.

[3] *Listener Research Survey, 'Viewers' Opinions on Television Programmes', 26 June 1939. A total of 4,806 elaborate questionnaires were sent out to viewers and 4,024 viewers (84 per cent.) replied. Forty-four per cent. of the viewers were indifferent as to whether the announcers should be men or women: of the rest, an overwhelming majority preferred women. This preference was in marked contrast to that of the audience for sound radio at that date.

VI

FROM PEACE TO WAR

———

How I wish that every few years we could build a big bonfire of these millions of inter-departmental memos—a bonfire which would blaze to the memory of red tape.

Remark attributed to F. W. OGILVIE,
Autumn 1939

1. A Change of Director-Generals

TELEVISION was closed down for the duration of the war. Sound broadcasting, however, was about to have its finest hour. The shadow of war had begun to hang over the BBC long before 1939, and when Reith left the BBC in June 1938 it was realized by observers that the Corporation might be called upon before very long to change itself almost out of recognition. The Ullswater Committee had 'recognized' in its Report that in 'serious or national emergencies . . . full governmental control [over the BBC] would be necessary'. 'We recommend that this should be announced as soon as possible,' the Report went on, 'and that the action taken should at once be reported to Parliament.' This was one of the clauses in the Report on which neither Postmaster-General nor BBC made any comments. Yet Attlee stated in his dissenting note that he thought that even in war-time 'the BBC must be allowed to broadcast opinions other than those of the Government'.[1]

The issue of war and peace had been raised so often behind the scenes during the 1930s that it is perhaps surprising that so much was left vague in the Ullswater Report. The reason lay, in part, in the elaborate security precautions which were taken for granted behind the façade of appeasement in the Britain of the 1930s. The first reference to future war in Reith's diary came as early as September 1933 when Sir Maurice Hankey told him that he thought that 'some time ago the Government should have taken some steps to prepare the country for what they would have to do in the event of air raids, and that he thought the best means of doing this would be through a series of talks on the BBC'.[2] Thereafter references multiply. A few years later, Reith, on a four weeks' holiday, was writing a fascinating book, *Wearing Spurs*, on his experiences as a young officer during the First World War. The memories of the last war were still vivid when the next war was being taken for granted.

---

[1] Cmd. 5091 (1936), *Report of the Broadcasting Committee,* § 57; Reservations by Mr. Attlee, p. 49.
[2] Reith, Diary, 19 Sept. 1933.

Almost exactly a year after the first reference to the possibility of war, Reith took up the matter very seriously, nominating Ashbridge, Tudsbery, and Colonel F. W. Home, the latter a former chairman of the Services Wireless Board, to deal with questions of defence, civil disturbance, and air raids.[1] He had further talks with Hankey, General Sir John Dill, then the Director of Military Operations and Intelligence at the War Office, and with Wing-Commander E. J. Hodsoll of the Home Office Air Raid Precautions Department. Dill proved particularly co-operative and there was 'complete understanding and confidence' from the start.[2]

It was Hodsoll who sent a copy of a letter, which he had just written, to Dawnay in October 1934, explaining the position as it then was. 'Censorship arrangements are already in train', Hodsoll said, 'and need no further comment, as also are emergency regulations.' The three matters which did require consideration were 'the question of the general policy of the use of the BBC in time of War', the physical protection of the BBC against hostile air attack, and the physical protection of the BBC against sabotage.

The first of these questions was—and is—the most interesting. 'I have always felt,' Hodsoll said, 'and my conversation with General Dill confirms my opinion, that the BBC will be one of the most important instruments in time of War, more particularly, if we are subject to air attack on a large scale, in helping to keep up the morale of the civil population. . . . The first question that would naturally arise is as to whether the Government should take over control of the BBC or not. After thinking over this matter a good deal and discussing it with various people, my own opinion is strongly that it would be better if the BBC were left as they are, although naturally there would be extremely close liaison between the Government and the BBC officials.'[3]

While the position of the BBC was being discussed in Ministerial Committee, with a view to proposals going forward to the Committee of Imperial Defence and the Cabinet, the Home Defence Department was asked to decide what answers to give

[1] Reith, Diary, 17 Sept. 1934.
[2] *Into the Wind*, p. 192.
[3] *Copy of a letter by E. J. Hodsoll, 29 Oct. 1934.

to the other two questions Hodsoll had raised.[1] Within the BBC itself precautions were being taken which would relieve some of Hodsoll's anxieties. 'The real essence of the problem', Hodsoll told Reith, 'is one of organisation; that is to say, to face the fact that very heavy damage might be experienced, and to have plans prepared which will reduce the disorganisation which such damage might cause to a minimum and will enable the services to be maintained in as great a state of efficiency as is possible in the circumstances.'[2]

This was the kind of assignment Reith appreciated, and he initiated a series of inquiries which led to the preparation of a long memorandum on 'Protection Against Air Attack'.[3] He also helped Hodsoll with the final drafting of the text of a 'short, simple and concise handbook for the general population, giving them some simple rules for their own protection in case of air raids'.[4] Within the BBC itself Colonel Home visited all regional studio centres and transmitting stations early in 1935 and made arrangements for the erection of fences, steel shutters, and other defences.

While Ashbridge worked closely with Hodsoll, Bishop began to draft a report on the technical operation of the broadcasting service in time of war.[5] At the same time, Reith sat on a sub-committee of the Imperial Defence Committee, along with Dill, Warren Fisher, Vansittart, and others—'as strong a C.I.D. Committee as had ever been called'[6]—in which the main matter under discussion was the organization and role of a war-time Ministry of Information.[7] John Colville, the Minister-Designate of Information, was in the chair. Reith was particularly glad to be invited to sit on this sub-committee since a few months earlier Kingsley Wood, when Postmaster-General, had snubbed the BBC by suggesting that it would be possible to have a committee to inquire into the control and use of broadcasting in war on which there would be no BBC representative. Reith in return had snubbed Kingsley Wood by refusing to provide him with a memorandum stating the BBC's views, but he willingly co-operated with Tryon.[8]

[1] *Copy of a letter by Hodsoll, 30 Oct. 1934.
[2] *Hodsoll to Reith, 4 June 1935.   [3] See below, pp. 629–30.
[4] *Hodsoll to Reith, 1 Oct. 1935.   [5] *Ashbridge to Reith, 16 Oct. 1935.
[6] Reith, Diary, 25 Oct. 1935.   [7] Ibid., 28 Oct. 1935.
[8] *Reith to Tryon, 9 July 1935; Into the Wind, pp. 220–1. See above, pp. 480–1.

The sub-committee offered him the post of Director-General of the Ministry of Information, which he turned down.[1] He felt that there was something ominous in a Foreign Office suggestion, made at the first meeting of the sub-committee, that one of the existing Foreign Office departments should form the nucleus of the new Ministry and that the Minister should be housed in the Foreign Office.[2] Further difficulties arose later in relation to the position of the Admiralty. By insisting that the chief naval censor should be located in the Admiralty and not in the new Ministry, the Admiralty was restricting the power of the Ministry of Information before it came into existence. Reith remembered all this on a grey morning in January 1940 when he told Chamberlain, the Prime Minister, that he had imagined Chamberlain was about to offer him the Ministry of Information and that he had hoped that it would not be so.[3]

It was doubtless because he knew more than Attlee of the negotiations that were in progress in 1934 and 1935 that Reith did not refer publicly in 1936 to Attlee's note of dissent. Already, indeed, he had submitted to the Postmaster-General in July 1935 a long paper on 'The Position of the BBC in War'. Other writers of memoranda on this subject were to lay emphasis on 'morale'. Reith began, quite differently, by laying emphasis on integrity. 'It is essential that the responsibility and reliability of the BBC's News Service should be established beyond doubt, even though in practice accuracy could not amount to more than the nearest approach to absolute truth permitted by the overriding war conditions including censorship.' He went on to say that the Board of Governors would not find it easy to take collective responsibility in time of war. Decisions and executive action must as far as possible rest with individuals. There would have to be very close liaison between the BBC and the Ministry of Information, and no constitutional machinery should impede the process of reaching quick decisions.

Reith told Tryon that with the good offices of Dill he had regularized censorship arrangements. Colonel Home would be Chief Executive Censor of the BBC, working in close liaison with the War Press Bureau.[4] This would safeguard 'the negative side'. On the 'positive side', proper working arrangements had to be made with the future Ministry of Information. Reith was less prescient in his picture of the content of war-time broadcasting. He foresaw, as some writers did not foresee, that Empire broadcasting would probably continue—as he put it, 'adequate, discreet and apparently objective'—but he did not foresee that there would be a great proliferation of overseas broadcasting. And in his account of the pattern of home programmes, while he recognized that there would probably have to be one single service, if only to save costs, he thought that talks would have to be largely of a 'utilitarian character to hold the interest of the public on that basis'.

In the 'Memorandum on Protection Against Air Attack' the position was stated somewhat differently. Here it was remarked that 'whether the existing organisation of the BBC would continue to function in time of war on existing lines, so long as this remains possible, is a matter for decision at the time. . . . It is, however, assumed generally that broadcasting will play such an important part in any future emergency that it will be essential that services of some kind should continue, even if on a basis more restricted than in normal times.'[1]

The dots concealed a technical problem, the answer to which was not fully known. How far would or could 'broadcast emissions' be used to guide hostile aircraft along the wireless beams to their targets?[2] Until the answer to this question was known, the answers to all further questions about broadcasting in war-time were necessarily obscure. From January 1936 onwards Ashbridge and Bishop sat on a technical sub-committee of the Imperial Defence Committee which sought an answer. These were conflicting requirements. A scheme was proposed by the BBC for synchronizing radio transmitters in three groups, each using a single wavelength, to ensure that enemy aircraft could not use broadcasting stations for navigational guidance. The Air Ministry began by turning the scheme down, as it also turned down modified proposals that there should be two groups instead of three and that radio stations should be closed down when enemy aircraft were near to them. The Home Office had made

---

[1] *BBC Memorandum, 'Protection Against Air Attack' (undated).

[2] See H. Bishop, 'War-time Activities of the Engineering Division of the BBC', Paper read to the Institution of Electrical Engineers, Mar. 1947.

it clear at a meeting in April 1937 that it wished broadcasting to continue during war-time air raids, but in the light of the Air Ministry warnings the government—as late as June 1938—was seriously contemplating that it might have to stop all broadcasting in war-time.[1]

It was not until July 1938 that the technical sub-committee finally accepted the BBC's modified plan to limit home broadcasting to two groups of medium-wave transmitters, each synchronized on a single wavelength, with a proviso that any or all transmitters might have to be closed down on orders from Fighter Command.[2] The inevitable effect of the scheme was a poor service to listeners in some areas of the country, particularly since the Air Ministry required that the long-wave Droitwich transmitter would have to close down when war was declared. Nevertheless the scheme proved highly successful in achieving its important objective.

The decision also implied that while there would be one single 'home service' in the event of war, at least there would be a service. It would have two specifically war-time purposes—first, to issue instructions to the public and second, to 'maintain morale', a hideous phrase, which everyone immediately understands. 'It is not improbable', the 'Memorandum on Protection against Air Attack' stated, that 'the fortitude of the population, particularly in crowded and urban areas, may be severely strained and any measures which may be taken to help maintain their morale will be of inestimable value. It is conceived that the broadcasting of programmes of music [sic] may be a very valuable factor to this end, and is another reason why great importance is attached to the maintenance of the broadcast service.'

A number of BBC committees considered all these questions during the last few months of Reith's Director-Generalship. A Broadcasting in War-Time Committee met nine times, for example, between October 1937 and September 1938, with Carpendale (and then Graves) in the chair, along with Nicolls, Ashbridge, Tallents, and Lochhead; and a Sub-Committee on War-Time Programmes, appointed in March 1938, drafted the sombre details of the single programme which would have to

---

[1] *Minutes of a Meeting at the General Post Office, 19 June 1938.
[2] See the article by L. W. Hayes in the *Radio Times*, 14 Dec. 1945.

be put out. Two sub-committees on Defence worked out the logistics of staffing, given the curtailment of services, dividing staff into categories, and leaving a large number in Category C —'those who would not be required in war-time and who should at once find war-time service which could be approved by the Corporation'. They also had to deal with the acquisition of sites outside London and the best ways of equipping them, but they had not yet reached this stage of their activities when Reith left.

Apart from Reith, the key man in the story was Sir Stephen Tallents, who was appointed Director-General Designate of the Ministry of Information when Reith refused. A second appointment of interest was that of Colonel R. S. Stafford, who joined the BBC in May 1936, took up work on defence arrangements in October 1936 and was later appointed Defence Director,[1] and served on the various war-time and defence committees. Stafford had prepared the draft of an A.R.P. plan for Broadcasting House within a month of arrival. Meanwhile from October 1936 to the beginning of 1938 Tallents maintained his curious dual role, dealing with some matters where there was a divergence of opinion between the BBC and the government, and always being in the anomalous position of acting as a subordinate inside the BBC to people who would be his own subordinates if war broke out.[2]

The difficulties did not come to a head, however, until the autumn of 1938, after Reith had left the Corporation. Tallents had told the other Controllers in September 1937 that it was essential that he should have full information about BBC plans for war since he would be very directly involved in deciding what to do about them. For the first time they learned directly that the Committee of Imperial Defence in October 1935 had decided 'that in time of War or when the threat of an emergency was imminent the Government should assume effective control over broadcasting and the BBC'.[3] During the next year Tallents was so fully drawn into his prospective duties that the new Director-General had to ask either for his release or for his

[1] *Control Board Minutes, 15 Sept. 1936; 29 May 1937; 6 July 1937.
[2] *For the BBC's approval of Tallents's appointment, see Reith to Warren Fisher, 28 Oct. 1936.
[3] *Controllers' Meeting, Minutes, 22 Oct. 1937. The meeting of the Committee of Imperial Defence had been on 4 Oct. 1935.

full-time secondment to a government post. 'He wished to make it clear', Ogilvie added, 'that the BBC was always glad, within limits, to co-operate with the Government but that there came a point beyond which it was undesirable from every point of view to continue with a joint arrangement.'[1] Tallents was, in fact, released soon afterwards from the Director-Generalship designate of the Ministry, and was plunged deep in the debates which raged in Broadcasting House on the eve of the war.

As for the exact pattern of relations between the new Ministry of Information and the BBC, this was more or less settled before Reith left. The government had decided that in the event of war the Ministry of Information, in the course of its ordinary duties, would be responsible for censorship control over the programmes of the BBC. As a consequence, the Board of Governors would go out of commission. An Order-in-Council would probably be promulgated, reducing the number of Governors to two, appointing the Director-General and the Deputy Director-General as the two Governors in question, and making them Chairman and Vice-Chairman of the BBC. There would also be a Supplementary Licence in the event of war, enabling the Postmaster-General to transfer certain of his powers to the Minister of Information.[2] Reith felt that this arrangement would guarantee the independent role of the BBC. It was dependent, however, on the strength of his own personality, and the plan was to generate considerable opposition among Governors in 1939.[3]

Reith left the BBC in the midst of all these preparations, at the express behest of the Prime Minister, Neville Chamberlain. 'Fifteen years since I went to the BBC', he had written in his diary on 31 December 1937. 'What a time, and how doubtful I am about staying much longer.'[4] He had been writing very similar things as early as 1927,[5] but this time he was really unsettled—so unsettled, indeed, that he had offered his resignation to the Board of Governors a month earlier. It was turned down

[1] *Minutes of a Meeting between the Home Secretary and the Director-General of the BBC, 10 Nov. 1938.   [2] *Unsigned Paper, 27 July 1938.
[3] See I. Fraser, *Whereas I Was Blind* (1942), pp. 162 ff.; D. Ogg, *Herbert Fisher, A Short Biography* (1947), pp. 128–9 ff. The problem will be discussed fully in Volume III of this History.   [4] Reith, Diary, 31 Dec. 1937.
[5] See for example an entry in the diary for February 1927, 'Beginning to feel that I ought not to be long with the BBC, but it is extremely difficult to know what the next job is to be.'

by the Governors almost before it had been made. 'Please feel assured', they told him, 'that you have in the fullest measure the
unstinted confidence of every member of the Board.'[1]

There was talk of a number of important jobs in the spring of
1938, including very tempting talk from Hore-Belisha about
a new post of 'director of organisation' in the War Office.[2] None
of this materialized, however, and Reith was left with only one
definite offer, that of the chairmanship of Imperial Airways.
The offer was made in June 1938 by Sir Horace Wilson, who
acted as an intermediary between Reith and Chamberlain. The
affairs of Imperial Airways had been a subject of official inquiry,
and there was need for a strong personality to give a new lead.
Reith did not want to go to Imperial Airways, and felt that he
could only leave the BBC if the Prime Minister gave him something in the nature of a definite order. He never quite got such
an order, yet he went to Imperial Airways, with what was called
in the House of Commons the government's 'full concurrence'.

A study of his papers on the eve of this great turning-point
both in his own life and in the life of British broadcasting leaves
the impression that Reith did not feel like a really free man in
1938. He did not so much make a choice, therefore, as reach the
conclusion that a decision had been forced upon him.[3] From the
time of the publication of the Cadman Report on British Airways in March 1938—and it was not a report which made good
reading—Reith seems to have been drawn towards his ultimate
fate. He was forty-eight years old, and he wanted a job where
he would be 'fully occupied quantitatively and qualitatively,
fully stretched'. He did not want to sever all connexion with
broadcasting, but he was tired of the Director-Generalship of
the BBC, tired of its committees, of some of its Governors, of a
few of his subordinates, above all of the way in which he had
been attacked by people outside the Corporation. He felt that
he had completed his task at Broadcasting House, rounding off,
as he told L. Marsland Gander of the *Daily Telegraph*, 'a fifteen
years' task of organisation'.[4] Work had been devolved to other

---

[1] *Into the Wind*, p. 296.   [2] Ibid., p. 310.

[3] The whole episode is treated fully in *Into the Wind*, pp. 306 ff. In a letter to
Tallents, dated 4 July 1938, he spoke of being to some extent 'under a kind of
anaesthetic—which is perhaps as well' (Tallents Papers).

[4] See the interesting article in the *Daily Telegraph*, 27 Jan. 1938. The main headline was 'Sir J. Reith completes BBC organization'.

people, and the only way he could make himself busy again was to withdraw 'some of the responsibilities and authorities devolved'. He did not want to do this. 'He has in fact reached a stage in his career', Marsland Gander wrote, 'when the vehicle of his creation promises to travel on smoothly to further success.' When Woods Humphery, the Managing-Director of Imperial Airways, bobbed in and out to see him, it was as if he were a messenger from the gods, not really a friendly messenger, but one who could not be cast aside.

When Reith told the Board of Governors that he intended to take over the chairmanship of Imperial Airways on 8 June they were 'all much shocked'. 'Could he not be seconded,' they asked, 'or take Norman's place as Chairman of the BBC when Norman resigned?'[1] To the first question, he said no, but he went so far in relation to the second as to take soundings as to whether Imperial Airways might relax its rule that its chairman should hold no other post. He had changed his mind, however, about whether to go further with the soundings by the time he actually left the Corporation on 30 June.

There were many twists of the emotions in the three weeks which followed the Board Meeting of 8 June. The first was on the same evening, when the Governors and Senior Executives were giving a party for Carpendale, who had retired in March after long and dedicated service. 'Melancholy and rather ironic', Reith wrote, 'that I should have to make a farewell speech when I myself was departing.' The second twist came after the announcement of his new appointment had been made. When he read the morning papers and the masses of letters which flooded in, particularly letters from the staff, he was left in no doubt of the personal hold he had acquired in his years with the BBC. There was affection as well as respect in much that was said. 'Sir Ariel Takes Wings', wrote the *Birmingham Daily Mail*.[2] 'You have created one of the greatest organisations in the world', wrote Maurice Hankey, 'which will continue on your lines for centuries.'[3] 'The news came as a great shock to the Corporation itself', said Norman, the chairman of Governors, 'as a shock I am sure to the whole body of listeners. Nothing but a sense of urgent national importance would have taken him away, and

---

[1] Reith, Diary, 8 June 1938.   [2] *Birmingham Daily Mail*, 15 June 1938.
[3] *Maurice Hankey to Reith, 7 June 1938.

he would never have consented to leave his great work here
except from the highest motives of public duty. But with "the
country calling", Sir John would never fail to respond.'[1]

'Taking wings' or 'responding to a call'? Reith is a complex
character, as great men are, and neither verdict is totally true.
When Reith left the BBC, he hoped for something bigger than
Imperial Airways. Yet he was drawn towards the new and the
untried, and behind his decision there was an element of
perverse obstinacy, along with all his other motives, including
the sense that a job had been done. Yet he was not the only
character in the story. J. J. Astor grumbled at the 'inversion of
values on the Prime Minister's part'. Just why did Chamberlain
want Reith, with whom he had never been friendly, to go to
that particular post at that particular time?[2] Did the shadows
of war influence Chamberlain's will and Reith's choice?

What was most unfortunate and unpremeditated in June
1938 was the disturbed manner of Reith's going. When on 29
June the Governors chose his successor, they did not invite Reith
in. This hurt Reith badly. One or two of them felt also, Norman
told him, that it would not be wise for him to continue to sit on
the Board. Reith was already overwrought with emotion when
this final twist came, and he did not feel that he could attend
any part of the Board meeting after what had happened. The
following morning he rang Chamberlain telling him not to
pursue any further the idea of his sitting on the BBC Board
while serving at Imperial Airways. He also gave instructions
for both his BBC receiving sets—one for television—to be
recovered from his home that day. That evening he left Broadcasting House, without ceremony, not to enter it again, except
in dreams, for many years. With three or four friends he drove
down to the high-power transmitting station at Droitwich, and
at midnight switched off the transmitter and generating plant.
It was an engineer's job, like the job he had before he joined the
BBC. He then signed the Visitor's Book—J. C. W. Reith,
late BBC.[3]

[1] *BBC Press Release, 2 July 1938; see also Norman's address to the General
Advisory Council of the BBC, 15 June 1938.
[2] For an earlier incident involving Reith, Wilson, and Chamberlain, see *Into the
Wind*, pp. 307–8; M. Gilbert and R. Gott, *The Appeasers* (1963), pp. 69–70.
Chamberlain complained to Reith that the BBC gave undue prominence to
political attacks on him.   [3] See *Into the Wind*, p. 319.

There were no demonstrations thereafter, for there was too much pain and too much restraint. There was, however, a farewell message to all section and departmental heads in London and the regions: 'When this reaches you I shall have left the BBC. In the short time since I knew I was going it has not been possible to take leave even of heads of departments individually, but the mere going is painful enough so I am not altogether sorry. I cannot leave, however, without sending this note to wish you and your staff every happiness and good fortune. If your work and personal contacts here bring you as much satisfaction as mine have to me, you will realise when your time comes how I am feeling today. Goodbye and thank you.'[1]

Reith left on 30 June, but it was not until 10 July that the name of his successor was announced.

It was not the name of the favourite candidate, certainly not the favourite of the press, where two names were very generally quoted—Sir Cecil Graves, the Deputy Director-General, and Sir Stephen Tallents, the Controller of Public Relations. 'As the BBC continues on its leaderless way,' the *Star* pontificated a week after Reith's departure, 'the conviction is growing that Sir John Reith should never have been allowed to leave until his successor had been announced. That mistake having been made, the new appointment should have been decided on with despatch.'[2] Sagittarius in the *New Statesman*, in a poem 'The Air Presumptive' that deserves to be quoted in full, was irreverential:

> Who shall succeed departed Reith?
> To whom, in all sublunar space,
> Can Britain suitably bequeath
> His place?
> Breathes there a being fit to sway
> Reith's self-made Empire of the Air?
> The Talking Mongoose is, they say,
> Less rare.[3]

Apart from Graves and Tallents as 'insiders', a number of outsiders were mentioned, some of them obviously at very long odds. The *Daily Express* put forward the name of Maconachie

---

[1] *Message of 30 June 1938.   [2] *The Star*, 6 July 1938.
[3] *New Statesman*, 16 July 1938.

from inside, the *News Chronicle* Sir George Gater from outside. Four papers, including the *Star*, even mentioned Lord Selsdon. Among the names referred to once in the bundle of leading national and provincial papers were Sir John Anderson, Sir William Beveridge, Sir Andrew Duncan, Sir Ian Fraser, Sir Robert Vansittart, and Lord Winterton. Tallents, however, was mentioned twenty-six times, and Graves, who was a Roman Catholic, as all the papers pointed out, twenty-three. The *Glasgow Evening News* had its own favourite son, Sir Hector Hetherington, but it also mentioned Professor F. W. Ogilvie. He was referred to also in two other papers, the *Daily Herald* and the *Evening Standard*, but the *News Chronicle*, which was consistently unreliable in its reporting of broadcasting matters during the 1930s, published what it called a denial from Ogilvie on 5 July. 'Mr. F. W. Ogilvie, Vice-Chancellor of Queen's University, Belfast, denies that he is a candidate for the Director-Generalship.'[1]

Ogilvie was in fact chosen. It was he whose name had been discussed by the Governors at their meetings of 22 June and 29 June. At the first of these meetings Reith had been present, and the Governors asked him to telephone Ogilvie in Belfast to see whether he would be interested. He said that he would, and came over to London on the 27th to meet first Reith, then Norman, and next the other Governors. 'He had high academic and intellectual qualifications,' wrote Reith, 'a man of fine character and outlook; of personal charm; thus far an exceptional candidate.' Then he adds, as he told Norman, 'I was quite sure he was not the man for the BBC.'[2]

He did not prove the man for the BBC in the difficult years which lay ahead, and his tenure of office was short, stormy, and in some ways calamitous. Yet he had, as Reith said, the kind of background that would make him highly commendable to the Warden of All Souls and highly presentable both to the Governors and to the public. He had been educated at Clifton College and Balliol, served for five years during the First World War and was wounded, and became a Fellow and Lecturer at Trinity College, Oxford, before moving to the Chair of Political Economy at Edinburgh in 1926 and from there to the Presidency of Queen's University, Belfast, in 1934. His work there had

[1] *News Chronicle*, 5 July 1938.   [2] *Into the Wind*, p. 318.

been highly successful, involving tact and strength of character as much as academic prowess. He had also written books as different as *Industrial Conflict* and *The Tourist Movement: an Economic Study*. Like Reith, he was the son of a Scottish Presbyterian and a regular church-goer. He knew a great deal about music, and was said to have a passion for Bach fugues.[1] At Belfast he had instituted lunch-time concerts, which were known as 'lunch-time pops'.

Norman, who took responsibility for Ogilvie's appointment, said later that Ogilvie had every quality except that of being able to manage a large organization, the one quality which was indispensable. In appointing Ogilvie Norman had not taken into account the likely imminence of war and the effect that it would have on the shape of BBC organization. The situation needed a strong man who could manage an institution that would grow almost out of recognition. Far from the BBC being a settled institution, as Reith had believed when he moved to Imperial Airways, there were just as many problems ahead as there had been during the previous decade. Ogilvie himself knew little of these problems, but he believed that war was imminent, and took the position of Director-General quite deliberately with this in mind. Chamberlain seems to have had it in mind also: he welcomed Ogilvie's appointment, as did Baldwin. Perhaps none of them had the imagination quite to realize what a new war would mean to the BBC.

Reith would have preferred Graves, who, as Deputy Director-General, acted the full part until Ogilvie arrived on 1 October.[2] Reith felt that he was better than any of the outside candidates whose names had been suggested. Graves had been chosen as Deputy Director-General in October 1937, with Tallents as his chief rival. Thereafter Tallents was extremely unhappy about the shape of the organization and his own future place within it. He believed rightly that Reith was against him, and drew a distinction between 'the old gang' inside the BBC and newcomers like himself. He was also keenly ambitious, and often said that he was puzzled by the fact that he was thought good enough to be Director-General of the Ministry of Information yet not good enough to be Director-General of the BBC.[3]

[1] *Evening Standard*, 20 July 1938.   [2] *Into the Wind*, pp. 321–2.
[3] Notes on a Meeting with the Governors, 13 July 1938 (Tallents Papers).

Tallents saw the Governors at his own request on 13 July, and had a very friendly reception, telling them what he thought the qualities of a good Director-General should be. They included the gift of understanding 'the creative spirit', of being able to harmonize 'a various and largely immature staff'; above all, of having the tenacity and courage 'to hold out against pressure to make the Corporation more like a Government Department'. He said that he had never subjected himself to as much self-restraint as he had done in his spell at the BBC. 'What you did today', Fraser told him later, 'was forceful, appropriate and in perfect taste and enhanced your reputation with all.'[1] Norman, however, wrote simply to thank Tallents for the quality of his services to the Corporation and to tell him that Ogilvie had been chosen.[2] There is no record of Graves's interview with the governors, but it is known that Reith had advised Norman that if Graves was not acceptable as Director-General, the post should be offered to an 'outsider'.

The most interesting letter was from Ogilvie himself to Tallents on 19 July: 'It ought to have been you or Graves.'[3] He thanked the two of them for the kind reception they had given him at Broadcasting House when he had visited it the previous day. There was, as yet, no talk of the future. The news of the appointment had not been very well received inside the BBC: in the popular press it came as a complete surprise. Ogilvie was bombarded by reporters and received over 1,100 letters of congratulation. He also gave an informal talk to reporters about 'his plans' for the BBC. 'Why Ogilvie?' the *Star* headed another of its ponderous articles. 'This is the question on everyone's lips. The new Director-General bears a name unknown to the public.' It ended the article, however, with the soothing words, 'The success of Ogilvie will depend not on the flattery of the rich and the powerful, but the confidence that he evokes from the ordinary people. If they come to trust and believe in him, he can become a second Reith.'[4]

[1] Fraser to Tallents, 13 July 1938 (Tallents Papers).
[2] Norman to Tallents, 13 July 1938 (Tallents Papers).
[3] Ogilvie to Tallents, 19 July 1938 (Tallents Papers).
[4] *The Star*, 22 July 1938. Cf. a note by Tallents, 8 July 1938. 'If Ogilvie fails, a real dog fight.' (Tallents Papers.)

2. Preparations for War

No one could have become a 'second Reith', nor would it have
been good for the BBC, in 1938 or at any other time, for a new
Director-General merely to have moved in his predecessor's
footsteps. The post required initiative and leadership as well
as powers of conciliation and adjustment. Ogilvie had little
experience of the world he was entering, but he did his best to
discover its contours for himself. Unfortunately, he had little
time. Patient exploration was not permitted in the last few
months of 1938 and the months leading through the crises of
1939. It would have been difficult to have followed Reith at any
time. In 1938 and 1939 the difficulties could turn into night-
mares. Patience and a willingness to listen courteously and carefully to the views of other people were qualities that Ogilvie
possessed in abundance, and to some at least of his new colleagues he soon appeared in a favourable light—simple,
friendly, and unassuming. These very qualities, however—and
some of them Reith did not possess—were limitations in the
circumstances of the time. Managerial power was needed more
than patience, and willingness to listen could suggest weakness
instead of strength. Ogilvie was possessed of a stubborn tenacity
which he had displayed successfully in his previous post: it did
not help him, however, in many of the situations which he confronted before and after the outbreak of war.

There were three aspects of the world of broadcasting which
set the terms of Ogilvie's life in 1938 and 1939. First, there was
the organization itself, big, bulging, and inevitably in places
bureaucratic. Ogilvie had a healthy dislike of bureaucracy, yet
there was very little he could do about it. 'I believe that one of
the minor tragedies of a gigantic organisation such as the Corporation is its utter impersonality', he said to Jack Payne. 'If
you want to talk business with another department it is not just
a simple matter of telephoning; you have to write "memos" and
have them passed from hand to hand.' This was not the way in
which a university worked. It was then that Ogilvie added the

words about building a bonfire of inter-departmental papers which would blaze to the memory of red tape.[1] Much went up in flames during the Second World War, yet Ogilvie never had the bonfire of which he dreamed. There was no 'reorganization', indeed, until after he had gone, nor were there any memoranda about reorganization in his neat, attractive hand. 'Why can't we all get on with our jobs without raising wretched questions of definition and of seniority?' he asked Graves once in a moving letter after war had begun.[2]

There was no shortage of talk by others, however, about the need for reorganization. The second aspect of the world of broadcasting with which Ogilvie had to deal was the multiplication of duties and functions in the last few months of peace, particularly as a result of the introduction of foreign-language work. As early as November 1937 there had been discussions about the creation of a new post of Director of Overseas Services, a 'Captain of the Ship', Carpendale described him.[3] The post should go to the Director of Empire Services, it was felt, and there should be an overhaul of the Programme Committee. In addition, recommendations of a committee headed by Sir Stephen Tallents were also accepted, and two new departments were created—one for Home Intelligence, headed by Maurice Farquharson, and the other for Overseas Intelligence, headed by M. A. Frost.[4]

There was much talk about symmetry at this time—about the lack, for example, of a post on the home side comparable in scope and grade to that of Director of Overseas Services,[5] and of the need for full 'functional control' of both Empire broadcasting and television.[6] Eventually it was decided to leave the shape of final organization on the Overseas side 'until after the actual experience of operating the foreign languages service'.[7] The changes that were made did not satisfy J. B. Clark, who

[1] J. Payne, Signature Tune, p. 34.   [2] *Ogilvie to Graves, 27 Jan. 1940.
[3] *Carpendale to Reith, 10 Nov. 1937. See also Reith, 'Notes and Queries on Organisation', 5 Nov. 1937; Nicolls to Reith, 8 Nov. 1937, and Graves to Reith, 8 Nov. 1937.
[4] *BBC, Internal Memorandum, 30 Nov. 1937.
[5] *Control Board Minutes, 12 Nov. 1937; 'Report on Reorganisation Agreed at Control Board', 12 Nov. 1937; Carpendale to Reith, 10 Nov. 1937.
[6] *J. B. Clark to Graves, 14 Jan. 1938.
[7] *Note on Organisation, Feb. 1938; BBC, Internal Instruction, No. 420, 1 Mar. 1938.

described them in March 1938 as having been made in a 'peremptory manner'.[1]

Such difficulties were merely a foretaste of much greater difficulties to come in April 1939, when the creation of two new posts of Assistant Controller provoked considerable indignation among many of the departmental heads. They felt that they were losing rights of direct access to the Controllers, and that these rights were fundamental to the 'Dawnay settlement'.[2] 'The main point of danger to my mind,' Mary Somerville wrote on behalf of herself and some of her colleagues, 'is that we Programme Department Heads, who, in the nature of things, have the clearest grasp of the detail of programme work and of the differing types of activity and conditions of work required in our several Departments, seem to be getting further and further removed from the counsels of those who on the one hand formulate and interpret external policy, and on the other hand the internal policies which affect our conditions of work.'[3]

There were other difficulties, too. Whereas the Programme Department Heads felt that the machinery for making organizational changes was so cumbrous, undemocratic, and morale-shattering that 'the less change of organisation there is, the better',[4] Tallents, not Ogilvie, was trying to think out completely new patterns of organization. 'I have tried the approach', he began a memorandum of April 1939, 'of attempting to see how the BBC would best be organised if it were being started anew with all its present work in view, and with provision for the addition of some extra work in the future.'[5]

No one could act as a really effective mediator in these altercations, and what Ogilvie said did not appease, although his intentions were known to be admirable. In Savoy Hill days, he remarked, there was a small organization which permitted a much closer co-operation. 'It was more difficult today to run a show like the BBC on quite the same family lines, though he was entirely in favour of the Director-General and Heads of Divisions keeping as close a contact with individuals as possible.'[6]

1 *J. B. Clark to Graves, 2 Mar. 1938.
2 *Mary Somerville to Graves, 30 May 1939.
3 *Minutes of Informal Meeting of Programme Heads, July 1939.
4 *Unsigned note of Apr. 1939.
5 *Tallents, Memorandum on BBC Organisation, 13 Apr. 1939.
6 *Notes by Graves of a meeting on 12 June 1939.

His nostalgia for the small informal organization was to grow. In the meantime, he hoped that 'the machinery for putting forward suggestions or complaints' would become as efficient as possible. If there could not be forceful leadership, there could at least be good communications.

The difficulties did not disappear, and they affected two levels of staff in particular: first, the old-timers, those who could really remember Savoy Hill and objected to serving the interests of what Mary Somerville once described very powerfully as 'lay Ministers' and a 'lay Cabinet';[1] and second, the junior staff, who often felt that they were outside the picture altogether. When J. B. Clark had accused the Control Board of reaching decisions in a 'peremptory manner', Graves noted tartly that 'we could not consult junior staff as to their views on proposed changes of organisation or policy'.[2] He was not, of course, thinking of J. B. Clark himself, whom he regarded as a close colleague, but the remark was of the brand that sticks. In Ogilvie's time much of the 'restlessness and disquiet below' had its origin in suspicions of other people's attitudes and in the rumours which circulated around them. 'Rumours of impending changes circulate, and garbled versions of the truth upset people who are most likely to be affected.'[3]

Graves was in favour not of a 'bonfire of red tape', but of sharper definitions of responsibility. 'With a D.G. taking decisions on nearly everything that happened', he said of the 'old days' at Savoy Hill, 'there was necessarily very close co-operation, but as we grew larger there was gradually and inevitably a devolution of authority and a consequent growth of departmentalism. . . . I firmly believe that the difficulties we are experiencing today are due to the fact that not enough people are clear as to where their responsibilities begin and end, and where authority lies. Definition of responsibility may possibly have had insufficient attention in the process of devolution.'[4] In the same memorandum Graves argued strongly for the Reithian conception of the Control Board as the body which had 'to study and determine programme policy in general

---

[1] *Minutes of Informal Meeting, July 1939.
[2] *Graves to J. B. Clark, 7 Mar. 1938.
[3] *Graves to Nicolls, 19 Jan. 1938.
[4] *Note by Graves on 'Programme Division', 5 June 1939.

terms'. He deprecated the tendency of Programme Board and Control Board to clash with each other.

The third aspect of the world of broadcasting, relations with government, was just as uncertain and difficult in 1939 as the internal relations between personalities and committees. By far the most difficult problem was the finance of television, although the development of propaganda, even on the hated Radio Luxembourg station, raised problems also.[1] Some of the details of the television debate of 1939 have already been discussed.[2] The last two documents before war broke out are extremely interesting. The first is a minute of the Television Advisory Committee in June 1939 stating that in view of the great difficulty of financing the television service and providing for its extension to the provinces, 'we consider that the inclusion of sponsored programmes and even direct advertising in that service would be fully justified'. It added that 'the BBC could be trusted to carry out the new policy judiciously and in a manner which would not offend the susceptibilities of viewers'.[3] The second was a memorandum by Nicolls setting out a number of inevitable repercussions of such a proposal on sound broadcasting, including an increase of fees and a lowering of the standard of care taken to censor commercial allusions and to select programme items. 'The question of sponsoring in Television', he concluded, 'raises that of sponsoring in Sound, and that in turn raises the far wider and ultimately more important issues of the comparative prestige abroad of the present "incorruptible" system as against the sponsoring system. . . . The estimate of the revenue to be anticipated from sponsoring does not affect the principle but it may influence the decision.'[4]

On this and many other matters Ogilvie took the same line as Reith would have done, and held it even more tenaciously, perhaps, than some of his rivals for the Director-Generalship. He was unhappy, however, about the concentration of power in his own hands, so much so that he eventually came to distrust the whole argument for monopoly. His principles were severely tested in an organization where events and personalities moved at a far faster pace than that to which he was accustomed. Nor

[1] See above, p. 369.   [2] See above, pp. 618–19.
[3] *Report of the Television Advisory Committee, 23 June 1939.
[4] *B. E. Nicolls, Note on Sponsoring for Television, 17 Aug. 1939.

did he keep in close touch with Reith about his problems. 'I know well that I shall be coming to you for unofficial advice and help, if I may, for many, many a long day to come', he wrote to Reith on 16 July, but no personal relationship of this kind ever blossomed out.[1]

In one important respect he—or rather the BBC—succeeded in gaining a more favourable institutional settlement than Reith had thought possible. Reith's conception of war-time relations between government and BBC, which depended on the strength of his own personality, was considerably modified between September 1938, the time of the Munich crisis, and September 1939, when war was declared.

The Munich crisis provided a useful dress rehearsal for the bigger crisis of September 1939. It was the first stage, indeed, in a sequence of events which was to lead through into the Second World War and which will be dealt with in more detail in the next volume of this History. The most important development was the inauguration of news bulletins to European countries in three languages—French, German, and Italian. M. Stéphan read the French bulletin, Walter Goetz, the artist, read the German, and Francis Rodd (later Lord Rennell) the Italian. The bulletins displaced domestic programmes on some of the medium wavelengths. Indeed, many regional programmes were cancelled or postponed from 28 September until the end of the crisis, and a single regional programme was broadcast from 7 o'clock in the evening onwards. Many government messages were broadcast, and Chamberlain's movements to and from Germany were carefully covered both on sound and television. Richard Dimbleby was one of the commentators at Heston when Chamberlain returned from Munich.

Summing up the role of broadcasting in the crisis, *The Listener* concluded:

Broadcasting . . . satisfied that hunger for news which seizes the population during critical hours. . . . [It also] scotches rumour, and thereby helps to create that steadiness of nerve which is bound to be a principal asset of any civilized people subjected to war conditions in the future. On the practical side the announcement of last Thursday night's plans for evacuating the children of London gave further

[1] *F. W. Ogilvie to Reith, 16 July 1938.

proof of how broadcasting can be used to maintain order and guide action. In pre-radio days what length of time must have elapsed, and what output of energy been expended, in conveying to thousands of parents and children all over the Metropolis information of the plans devised by authority for their orderly transference to security in the country! But now, through wireless, it is possible to give them all simple directions where to go, what to take with them, and what to do on arrival—without lapse of time and with the certainty that the mass movement thus initiated will take place without panic.[1]

Some of the detail of the crisis is recorded in J. B. Clark's Day Book. 'Discussions about emergency plans' were the main item on the day's agenda for 26 September. The following day Clark attended an overseas announcers' meeting in the afternoon to explain war-time plans, and went on to visit the Foreign Office with Nicolls to discuss the details of the inauguration of European language bulletins. The only heading for 28 September reads: 'Abnormal rush of emergency work.' Ogilvie took up his post at Broadcasting House earlier than he had intended to watch how things developed. By 5 October it seemed likely that the foreign-language bulletins would continue even if the crisis ended. Halifax soon asked officially for them to be continued, and there were discussions on the pattern of future news broadcasts in November.[2] The anti-gas doors in Broadcasting House were taken down on 12 October and the sandbags in the entrance hall were removed on 17 October, but there was to be no full return to the 'normal' for many years.

The crisis revealed the double role of broadcasting: first for the home audience—to give orders and to maintain morale; and second for the world—to spread reliable news and views. On the first front the BBC mobilized its resources fully, with dozens of government messages, prayers from the Archbishop of Canterbury, serious talk from Harold Nicolson, whose highly successful programme *The Past Week* had begun in July, and Major Wakelam addressing staff on 'The Anti-Aircraft Defence of Britain'. (John Hilton had broadcast on A.R.P. in April 1938, earning Maconachie's praise—'great stuff'.)[3] After the crisis

[1] *The Listener*, 6 Oct. 1938, 'Crisis in the Machine Age'.
[2] *Minutes of a Meeting held at the Foreign Office, 1 Nov. 1938; Halifax to Ogilvie, 10 Nov. 1938. [3] *Sir R. Maconachie to Hilton, 20 Apr. 1938.

ended there was a fascinating series of anonymous talks, arranged by Christopher Salmon, called *Everyman and the Crisis*. J. T. Christie, then headmaster of Westminster, summed up at the end. In the widest sense of the word, these broadcasts were educational, and perhaps the main effect of the crisis on the public was that it extended national education. Never again would a listener write to the BBC along the lines of a letter received soon after the first German and Italian news bulletins had been transmitted: 'I consider it against public policy to allow the Germans and Italians to take over radio at 7.00 p.m. They are both against the British.'[1]

Overseas listeners, including listeners in Germany, paid tribute to the international role of the BBC. Empire countries re-broadcast news bulletins, and Raymond Gram Swing told British listeners after the crisis had ended that in the United States the Columbia Broadcasting System alone had taken thirty-six talks from London as against fifteen from Paris and twelve from Berlin.[2] Typical of overseas comments was a letter from the Superintendent of the Colombo Broadcasting Station: 'If I may say so, the privilege of relaying the Daventry News Bulletin during the tense political situation in Europe was very, very greatly appreciated.' A listener in Canada added that 'the London news was far more interesting, apparently more dependable and more impartial than that from other sources'.[3]

During the next year the various Overseas and European services were expanded, and new services were started for Spain and Portugal, and in Afrikaans. This extended activity was made possible only by the provision, somewhat falteringly, of increased financial grants from the government and by the building of four more high-power short-wave transmitters in 1939. By the summer of 1939 plans had been completed for a composite European service with music and other programmes as well as news bulletins. This 'consolidated service' continued for a few weeks until the outbreak of war.[4]

The efficient development of this service from the hastily improvised news bulletins at the time of Munich provides one

---

[1] *BBC Record, Bulletins in Foreign Languages, Oct. 1938.
[2] *Raymond Gram Swing's American Commentary, 15 Oct. 1938.
[3] *Summary of Overseas Comments, Nov. 1938.
[4] See *BBC Handbook* (1939), pp. 118 ff.

of the most remarkable stories in the history of the BBC. Already
on 24 September 1938 J. B. Clark was prepared to create a full
German service 'on exactly the same plan' as that followed in
developing the Arabic and Latin American services,[1] and public
pressure was building up from outside encouraging him to do
so. 'Broadcast in German day or night' and 'tell people of the
universal desire for peace' were two of the insistent messages
being received from all parts of the country.[2] Dr. Wanner,
a friend of Reith, who had been head of the South German
Broadcasting Organization before the Nazis took over, was telling Clark as a German that 'an antidote to their own propaganda is more precious to them than their food'.[3] That the
Germans took the broadcasts seriously was shown by the fact
that within two minutes of the start of the first British bulletin
in German, the German stations abandoned their normal programmes in favour of a re-broadcast speech by Hitler.[4]

The BBC's experience in running Arabic and Latin American
broadcasts was particularly valuable at the meeting on 1
November when Halifax, as Foreign Secretary, was discussing
with the BBC what should be done in the future. Ogilvie
argued that it would be desirable for the bulletins to be prepared and edited by the BBC without direct Foreign Office
responsibility, as in the case of the existing foreign-language
broadcasts. At first Halifax 'demurred slightly', pointing out
that 'the relationship between ourselves and Germany was much
more delicate and that the BBC could hardly be expected to
possess sufficient knowledge of facts to enable it always to be the
best judge of what should or should not be included in a bulletin'.[5] He yielded, however, in the light of the BBC's experience
of running the Arabic service, and agreed that regular but informal contact with the Foreign Office should be substituted for
direct Foreign Office control. A fortnight later Halifax reported
to Ogilvie a message he had received from a recent visitor to
Germany. 'Most important of all is the BBC news in German.
It is eagerly listened to because it is and is known to be straight

[1] *Note by J. B. Clark, 'Continental Service—German', 24 Sept. 1938.
[2] *Note by J. E. H. Forty (North Region), 28 Sept. 1938.
[3] *Note by J. B. Clark, 5 Oct. 1938.
[4] *Note on Broadcasting of News Bulletins in European Languages, submitted
to Board of Governors, 12 Oct. 1938.
[5] *Notes of a Meeting at the Foreign Office, 1 Nov. 1938.

news, with no propaganda.' The main difficulty was that British broadcasts lacked adequate power to be picked up on 'the ordinary German small wireless set'.[1]

Rex Leeper of the Foreign Office formally raised the question of Portuguese broadcasts to Portugal in January 1939.[2] 'It is strategy with which we are dealing now and nothing else,' the British Ambassador in Lisbon told Tallents, 'and only quick action will serve so far as this place is concerned.' He added that it was a long time since he and Tallents had been associated with each other, and then it was in connexion with 'the liquidation of the last war'.[3] Spanish broadcasts to Spain were first discussed in February.[4] It was not until April, however, that financial help was forthcoming from the Treasury.[5] In the meantime the scope of the German service was being extended, with more expression of views as well as straight news. Local and 'experimental' jamming of broadcasts to Germany was reported in April,[6] as detailed reports began to come in about German attitudes and listening behaviour.[7]

The shift in mood in 1939 is well reflected in changes of content and approach in the 'views' programme broadcast to Germany under the title of *Sonderbericht*. During the period from 27 January to 15 March the content of the 'Sonderbericht' service was consistent with a continuing policy of appeasement: there was only one political talk out of four. The period from 15 March (the German occupation of Czechoslovakia) to 10 April saw the proportion of political talks rise to one in two, and 'Sonderbericht' writers were able to permit themselves a far greater measure of plain speaking. From 10 April to the summer of 1939 there was an extension of the policy pursued during the second period, with intensive research into German propaganda techniques, as carried out both in the German press and on the German radio. This development of policy was carried

[1] *Lord Halifax to Ogilvie, 14 Nov. 1938.
[2] *R. Leeper to C. G. Graves, 31 Jan. 1939.
[3] *Sir N. Selby to Tallents, 2 Feb. 1939.
[4] *Note by C. G. Graves, 16 Feb. 1939, after a telephone conversation with Leeper; F. W. Ogilvie to Sir Alexander Cadogan, 17 Feb. 1939.
[5] *Cadogan to Ogilvie, 25 Apr. 1939.
[6] *M. A. Frost to C. F. A. Warner, 12 Apr. 1939.
[7] *See, for example, a Memorandum on 'Reception of BBC Broadcasts in German in the Consular District of Dresden', June 1939.

out smoothly and with little strain. It was a sign of the adaptability and resilience of the BBC.[1]

Between the time of Munich and the outbreak of war, expansion of services was coupled with the revision of a number of unworkable and vexatious regulations. The idea of abolishing the Board of Governors altogether was scrapped; censorship, it was decided, was to be left to the Director-General—it was in fact delegated to Nicolls as Controller (Programmes) in August 1939—with the exception of news and political censorship, which was to be indirect, informal, and voluntary, based on liaison with the Press Division of the Ministry of Information;[2] and, in face of great initial opposition, it was agreed that there would be no compulsory censorship of broadcasts to America by N.B.C., Columbia, or other American broadcasting companies.

All these were gains for autonomy and freedom. Some were the result of BBC pressure, others of second thoughts, at least one of government anxiety. In late August 1939 the Prime Minister's Office asked the BBC not to broadcast a message from the National Council of Labour to the German people. The BBC did, however, broadcast a summary of the message in the Home News, and went on, after the Foreign Office withdrew objections, to broadcast the message in German—in full. The incident left the T.U.C. and other Labour bodies full of resentment at government handling of the BBC, and it confirmed Chamberlain's government in its fear of interfering too closely in the affairs of the Corporation.

Sir Samuel Hoare, who was put in charge of the planning of the Ministry of Information in June 1939, was strongly opposed to any plans for the government taking over the BBC in wartime,[3] and he was the first Minister to state publicly what government policy towards the BBC would be. In an important speech of 28 July 1939 he said that the government did not intend to take over the BBC, but rather 'to treat broadcasting as we treat the Press and films and leave the BBC to carry on . . . with a very close liaison with the Ministry of Information . . . and

[1] *A. E. Barker, 'The BBC's German News Talks', 21 July 1939.
[2] *Nicolls, Memorandum of 28 Aug. 1939.
[3] *Hansard*, vol. 352, cols. 394–5, 11 Oct. 1939.

with definite regulations as to how the work should be carried on'.[1]

Many of these regulations were set out in an important document—BBC Document C—which filled twenty-two foolscap pages of typescript. Incredible though it may seem, the draft of this basic document is undated, but it appeared in its final form as late as August 1939. It provided a comprehensive operational instruction both to engineers and to programme staff about exactly what to do when the order was given. The proposals for the synchronization on two wavelengths of home broadcasting were set out, along with the list of stations to be closed down completely. Droitwich long-wave was to be used only for navigational warnings from the Admiralty, if required, and at certain specified times after synchronization. Details were also given in the document of how and when the Prime Minister should speak to the country. The last section, foreseeing all emergencies, was headed 'Action to be Taken if a War Emergency should arise when the Home Transmitters are closed down'.

'Document C' was fully discussed in a sub-committee of the Committee of Imperial Defence, which included Bishop.[2] At the same time W. K. Newson, the BBC's Defence Assistant, was attending meetings of a BBC sub-committee concerned with the 'Protection of Points of Importance Against Air Attack'. It was agreed to plant trees at some of the transmitter stations, to darken buildings and roads, and to provide additional protection. The first sandbags outside Broadcasting House did not appear until the last days of August 1939.

The implications of these measures fall within the next volume of this History. Three points, however, fit into the pattern even at this stage. First, the BBC was inspecting sites and buildings outside London which were to be used in time of war, and plans for evacuation and dispersal were already far advanced by the time war broke out. Second, some essential war-time services, like Monitoring, had their origins in time of peace. Third, where relationships with outside bodies as well as with the government were concerned, the BBC had clarified most outstanding problems before war broke out.

[1] Ibid., vol. 350, col. 1838, 28 July 1939.
[2] *The sub-committee produced two reports, on 4 Aug. and 29 Aug. 1939.

It was in December 1938 that Ogilvie first saw Sir John Anderson about buildings. Anderson then told the Director-General that while he felt that in principle big public organizations should choose stand-by headquarters outside London, he could give no advice about possible locations. A month earlier the BBC had begun looking for outside properties, and Tudsbery and Ralph Wade, accompanied by an estate agent and sometimes by Bishop, began exploring the Home Counties. Their net spread wider and wider, and eventually in March 1939 Wood Norton Hall near Evesham was acquired. By April 1939 arrangements had been made to billet 600 people in Evesham.[1] The setting of the Hall was impressive: it was said to have been 'reconstructed' in the 1890s by the Duc d'Orléans at a cost of £100,000, and the fleur-de-lis was the omnipresent *motif*. The grandeur of the surroundings did not mean that there was any lavish redeployment of BBC finance. One minute of the Defence Sub-Committee reads: 'A.R.P. Woodnorton, Re 533. An estimate of £20 for a trained dog for use at Woodnorton was turned down and D.O.A. was requested to obtain a suitable animal from the Battersea Dogs' Home.'[2]

The Monitoring Service had its origins in the mid-1930s,[3] but it was not until March 1939 that an 'enemy propaganda' organization was set up under Sir Campbell Stuart. There was loose Foreign Office control, and A. P. Ryan was the BBC's liaison officer. It was envisaged that in the event of war Ryan would be dividing his time equally between Campbell Stuart and the BBC. During the same month Graves was in correspondence with J. B. Beresford, who had been designated head of the 'Collecting Division' of the Ministry of Information, and various different schemes were put forward by the BBC for monitoring. The first, not conditioned in any way by finance, envisaged the setting up of a number of monitoring centres on the lines of the existing centre at Tatsfield, 'with a total number of receivers sufficient to monitor programmes of all countries in which we were interested on a twenty-four hour basis'. The second envisaged the supply to selected experts of short-wave receiving sets which they could use in their own homes.

---

[1] *Stafford to the Secretary, the Ministry of Health, 20 Apr. 1939.
[2] *Defence Sub-Committee, No. 2, 24 May 1939.
[3] See above, p. 403.

On this occasion, Graves for the first time seemed to have envisaged an expansion of BBC staff during the war. He told Beresford that 'our present foreign languages staff were fully occupied on their own jobs and would be taken over to similar work in War time'. If an 'enlarged scheme of monitoring' were put into effect, it would require new sources of highly specialist manpower which was already in short supply.[1] Proposals were put forward a fortnight later for a 'monitoring unit' which would work on a three-shift basis for twenty-four hours a day.[2]

In this period of preparation for war, the main outside body with which the BBC had to concern itself was the press. Plans were made early in 1939 for a twenty-four-hour service of BBC news bulletins throughout the day, and this upset some sections of the press, 'as they felt that there would be serious competition with the newspapers, to their detriment'. It was even suggested that frequent news bulletins would be inadvisable, 'particularly if news were bad'. The BBC stood its ground, and was ready when war broke out to broadcast far more news than had ever been broadcast before. In this connexion, at least, prophecies were correct. 'People would be getting home at all hours of the day, and the first thing they would want to do would be to hear the latest news.'[3]

3. The Last Months of Peace

WHILE all these preparations were going on, the ordinary daily programmes were continuing also. It is true that the extension of foreign-language broadcasting ate into the listening week—news in French at 10 o'clock on the Regional Programme, for instance, followed by news in German (with news talks) and Italian—but there was also a regular run of favourite series. Listeners' letters had a familiar ring. 'I am so disappointed to find that *The Thirty-Nine Steps*, which I had been looking forward to, is being given during Church time on Sundays. As

---

[1] *Graves to J. B. Clark, 30 Mar. 1939, describing visit of J. B. Beresford.
[2] *Graves to J. B. Beresford, 14 Apr. 1939.
[3] *Record of interview between Graves and Waterfield, 18 July 1939.

a few of us still attend Church or Chapel, it means that most of us will miss it.'[1] 'When will the BBC cease to hail every new Variety production as a successor to *Band Waggon*? The blight that has descended over all light programmes since that fatal March 15th, when *Band Waggon* ended, has not been lifted.'[2]

Band Waggon was, indeed, the big 'hit' programme of the winter before the war. First broadcast on 5 January 1938, it caught the spirit of the times and proved an unprecedented success.[3] So too did Sandy McPherson, who joined the BBC as Theatre Organist in November 1938 and immediately established his reputation as a friend of his listeners, 'a homely man', the very reverse of the anonymous BBC stereotype. The music he played was a *pot-pourri* of old and new, sacred and secular. Among the new popular music was 'All The Things You Are', a hit song of 1939. Together with 'I Get Along Without You Very Well', 'South of the Border', 'In an Eighteenth-Century Drawing-Room', and 'Scatterbrain', it set the background for the last months of peace.

At the other end of the musical spectrum Toscanini broadcast in May 1939, and the King and Queen with Queen Mary paid a visit to Broadcasting House to listen. There was controversy in the same month about a possible broadcast by the Duke of Windsor. In the end, Ogilvie, after hours of anxiety, decided not to permit it. Other broadcasts of 1939 recalled the controversial issues of the past rather than pointed forward to the problems of the war. There was a debate on municipal trading, for example, in March 1939, and even a debate on unemployment—with Florence Horsbrugh, William Whiteley, and Megan Lloyd George—a month later.

On 20 June 1939 an informal, confidential conference was held at Broadcasting House at the suggestion of Dr. Welch, the new Director of Religious Broadcasting. Among those present were Professor T. S. R. Boase, Mary Trevelyan, the Rev. Donald Soper, and the Rev. Eric Fenn. 'There was unanimous feeling in the group that the strict puritan Sunday could no longer be enforced and general agreement that this was to the good.' Sunday broadcasting, however, the group felt, should be clearly distinguished from broadcasting on other days of the week. The

---

[1] *Radio Times*, 4 Aug. 1939.   [2] Ibid., 18 Aug. 1939.
[3] See above, pp. 117–18.

broad criterion was to be that Sunday programmes should 'serve the purpose of making men and women more truly and fully *human*'. Anything, therefore, which enabled people better to 'appreciate beauty, apprehend truth, and live fuller and more constructive lives', it was held, 'should be welcomed and should find fullest expression (but not exclusive expression) in the specifically "religious" items'.[1]

This new emphasis collided with the grim facts of 1938 and 1939 as much as with traditional BBC policies. Beauty and truth were not always compatible in 1938 and 1939, and the likelihood of war lent irony to the phrase about living 'fuller and more constructive lives'. The restless spirit of the times has been well caught in an entry in Stuart Hibberd's diary for the week of 12 to 19 March 1938: 'During this week we heard of (*a*) Hitler's triumphal march into Vienna as he annexed Austria; (*b*) Sir Samuel Hoare's speech on A.R.P. requirements; (*c*) Barcelona devastated by bombs, hundreds killed and injured; (*d*) Dr. Mess's broadcast on "Can Progress be traced in human history?" '[2]

The news could not fail to break through, and it broke through more and more insistently between March and September 1939. In January 1939 President Roosevelt's broadcast, with its attack on dictatorships, was given in full—forty-one minutes instead of the scheduled thirty—and Tallents was writing in his diary on the eve of a Hitler speech that the government was at last convinced that war was 'inevitable'.[3] Government pressure on the BBC was mounting steadily, and Ogilvie had to tell Sir John Anderson, when he went to see him about evacuation, that he could only broadcast about government defence policy if similar facilities were given to the Opposition. Parliament was debating the subject, and even after it had finished the debate the BBC would have to watch carefully the amount of time that was given to government speakers.[4]

There was one curious discussion inside the BBC which showed some of the problems as the country moved relentlessly towards war. In April 1938 Graves asked his colleagues to offer suggestions for 'programmes to give a fillip to the morale of this

---

[1] *Minutes of Informal Conference on Sunday broadcasting, 20 June 1939.
[2] *This—is London*, p. 157.
[3] Diary, Jan. 1939 (Tallents Papers).
[4] *Notes on meeting between Ogilvie and Anderson, 7 Dec. 1938.

country'.[1] Moray McLaren suggested four programmes called *The Defence of Christendom*, which would start with the Mongol invasion of the twelfth century, along with programmes about British heroes, including *Henry V* and *Scott in the Antarctic*; de Lotbinière said that he could not be very explicit, but that 'broadcasts on royal occasions, e.g. the state drive through Brussels—if it comes off—are also likely to give an impression of foreign good will towards this country and of belief in its future';[2] and no one said anything about *Band Waggon*. Maconachie wrote the most telling reply and the one which showed the difficulties which the BBC faced when it operated in this new atmosphere. 'I have been thinking over this proposal since you mentioned it to me, and feel that propaganda of this kind is full of pitfalls. If, for instance, we were dealing with subjects of real public importance, such as the military strength of the country, it would surely be futile, if not dishonest, to leave out the black spots, and emphasise merely the bright ones.' So long as comments like this were made inside the BBC, its own morale was not in real danger.

Maconachie, in fact, went on to make two specific suggestions—'the creation by Features and Drama or Variety Departments of a character on the lines of Mr. Penny but, unlike him, a confirmed pessimist, who through a series of adventures is made to look ridiculous—the idea being to kill pessimism by ridicule'—and 'a series of monthly talks by John Hilton'.'These', he added, 'would be crude and emotional, and would appeal probably only to the working class, but with this class would probably be very effective.'[3]

There was also an interesting reply from R. T. Clark, the Home Service News Editor. 'As far as the News is concerned, it is very difficult for me to put up any suggestions on the matter of improving the morale of the country. I am afraid that at present the majority of people would admit that the main items of news are, in themselves, depressing.' Again, Clark drew the right conclusion, which was to be the foundation of the BBC's war-time policy: 'It seems to me that the only way to strengthen

[1] *The memorandum itself is missing, but the first reply to it was by Moray McLaren on 27 Apr. 1938.
[2] *Reply by S. J. de Lotbinière of 27 Apr. 1938 to a memorandum by Graves.
[3] *Maconachie to Graves, 27 Apr. 1938.

the morale of the people whose morale is worth strengthening is to tell them the truth, and nothing but the truth, even if the truth is horrible. After all, what is horrible is a matter of taste or conviction, and depression is as often as not caused, not by the news itself, but by the peculiar conditions, physical or otherwise, in which the recipient hears it.'[1]

This emphasis on the bare truth was qualified by a strong feeling inside the BBC that the Corporation itself should do as much as it could to explain to listeners what the crisis was and what effects it would have on them. Reith had little interest in the discussion on morale, which he called an attempt at 'national heartening', but he rightly pointed out that 'the initiative is with us. The Labour Party want more politics. Governors want more politics. And I think we all do.'[2] A year later, under the new régime, Siepmann was asking for broadcasting definitely designed to meet the demands of an emergency. 'Only a few old ostriches still question that we face an emergency. On the other hand, the ignorance, unawareness and even unreadiness to serve is depressingly evident on every side.' In his view, the BBC had to exploit the appeal of 'personalities like Churchill and Eden', the illustrative resources of feature programmes, and the educational possibilities of talks.[3]

There was no unified campaign, although special programmes were devoted to the Services and their needs, a recruiting drive by radio was planned, and Churchill and Eden were thought of as broadcast speakers on 20 June and 27 June. This last idea, the most interesting of them all, was turned down by the government, not formally but in informal talks behind the scenes that led up to the final arrangements for the recruiting drive. The account of just how it was turned down is interesting. A discussion took place at the Ministry of Labour on 5 June 1939 between representatives of the BBC, the Ministry of Labour, and the Lord Privy Seal's Office. The government's point of view was stated by S. H. Wood, speaking as Sir John Anderson's representative. 'The Lord Privy Seal was grateful to the BBC for its suggestions, but his general feeling was that it was taking a steam hammer to crack a nut. He objected to having in all the

[1] *R. T. Clark to Graves, 28 Apr. 1938.
[2] *Reith to Graves, 27 Apr. 1938.
[3] *Siepmann to Nicolls, 20 Apr. 1939.

big guns: Churchill, Lloyd George etc., because he said that it would make people think that the Government was in a hole and must have mismanaged its recruiting campaign in the past. . . . Moreover, the Lord Privy Seal objected to the proposed "crisis" programme as being likely to give people the idea that they might be involved in a war in a few months' time, say September.'[1]

Maconachie dealt with Wood as fiercely as he had dealt with the Afghans, but he could not move him. 'We did not believe', Maconachie said, 'that they would get their recruits except by authoritative public men telling people that there was still real danger and real need for them, and that on a purely broadcasting plane they would not get, for example, stretcher bearers, by substituting Walter Elliot (or Mrs. Chamberlain) as an appellant for the Churchills and the Lloyd Georges.'

War did, in fact, come in September. On 23 August Tallents was opening the 1939 Radiolympia and prophesying that British television would be 'a world winner'.[2] The same evening the *Star* claimed that the size of Broadcasting House was to be doubled. It published a sketch of the new building and described it as likely to rank as 'one of the finest buildings of its kind in the world'.[3] The 23rd of August, however, is remembered not for these statements but for the Russo-German Non-Aggression Pact; and one day after news of the Pact was published the BBC's advance party set out for Evesham. For another week the BBC's National and Regional Programmes were broadcast as usual, and the *Radio Times* appeared for 3 to 9 September as if the world would remain exactly the same. Then the changes began to come, starting on Friday 1 September, the day Hitler announced that he would enter Poland. Additional news bulletins were broadcast, a programme from Broadstairs was cancelled and gramophone records played in its place, and on the Regional Programme a concert of light music from Holland was not transmitted. On the same day orders were signalled to every transmitting station and studio of the BBC to make the changeover to war conditions. 'Document C' was being put into effect.

1 *Report of interview at Ministry of Labour, 5 June 1939.
2 Notes for Speech, 23 Aug. 1939 (Tallents Papers).
3 *The Star*, 23 Aug. 1939. See also illustration no. 39.

Saturday was a gloomy day. War had not been declared, but the BBC was already behaving as if it had been. The single synchronized Home Service programme consisted mainly of gramophone records, punctuated by announcements. This was not good for morale, nor was the government's ominous silence about its intentions. Rumours were even spreading that Britain was not going to fight. History seemed to be standing still, both for the listeners and for the broadcasters. At midnight, however, there was a thunderstorm, and the Cabinet began preparing its ultimatum to Germany. The following morning, 3 September, Chamberlain made the most effective broadcast speech of his career, because it was the simplest and most heartfelt. 'Now may God bless you all. May He defend the right. It is the evil things we shall be fighting against—brute force, bad faith, injustice, oppression and persecution; against them I am certain that the right will prevail.'

BIBLIOGRAPHICAL NOTE

THE main source used in the writing of Volume II of this history, as in the case of Volume I, has been the BBC's own records. The BBC's Registry houses past and current papers of the Corporation, and these are well indexed. The collection of papers is subject to systematic review, and papers of permanent importance are subsequently transferred to the Archives Section. The large number of BBC files covers the various aspects of broadcasting at home and overseas, broadcasters' personal dealings with the BBC, the institutional history of the BBC and its committees, and the relations of the BBC with outside bodies, the government and the public. Some of these files duplicate material in the Post Office Archives, with which they must be studied in close conjunction. Other sources inside the Corporation include volumes of press cuttings collected by the News Information Service; the Play Library of scripts of sound drama broadcasts; the Television Drama Script Library; the Recorded Sound Archives; and the *Radio Times* Hulton Picture Library. The files of *Ariel* are also useful.

General books on the BBC and broadcasting include:

(1) COASE, R. H. *British Broadcasting: A Study in Monopoly.* Longmans, 1950.
(2) CROZIER, M. *Broadcasting: Sound and Television.* O.U.P., 1958.
(3) GORHAM, M. *Broadcasting and Television since 1900.* Dakers, 1952.
(4) PAULU, B. *British Broadcasting: Radio and Television in the United Kingdom.* O.U.P. 1957.
(5) PAULU, B. *British Broadcasting in Transition.* Macmillan, 1961.
(6) SIEPMANN, C. A. *Radio, Television and Society.* New York, O.U.P. 1950.
(7) STURMEY, S. G. *The Economic Development of Radio.* Duckworth, 1958.

Among the books on broadcasting written between 1927 and 1939 the following are informative:

(1) BRITTAIN, SIR HARRY. *The ABC of the BBC.* Pearson [1932].
(2) CHESMORE, S. *Behind the Microphone.* Nelson, 1935.
(3) GOATMAN, W. *By-Ways of the BBC.* King & Staples, 1938.
(4) MAINE, B. S. *The BBC and Its Audience.* Nelson, 1939.
(5) MATHESON, H. *Broadcasting.* Thornton Butterworth (Home University Library), 1933.
(6) MOSELEY, S. A. (ed.) *Who's Who in Broadcasting.* Pitman, 1933.

(7) MOSELEY, S. A. *Broadcasting in My Time*. Rich & Cowan, 1935.
(8) ROBINSON, E. H. *Broadcasting and A Changing Civilisation*. Lane, 1935.
(9) SMITHERS, S. W. *Broadcasting From Within*. Pitman, 1938.
(10) THOMSON, D. C. *Radio is Changing Us*. Watts, 1937.
(11) THE TIMES. Special Broadcasting Number, 14 August 1934.

The following autobiographies have proved, in their various ways, to be illuminating and important:

(1) BEADLE, SIR GERALD. *Television: A Critical Review*. Allen & Unwin, 1963.
(2) BREWER, C. *The Spice of Variety*. Muller, 1948.
(3) DUNCAN, P. *In Show Business Tonight*. Hutchinson, 1954.
(4) ECKERSLEY, P. P. *The Power Behind the Microphone*. Cape, 1941.
(5) ECKERSLEY, R. *The BBC and All That*. Low, Marston, 1946.
(6) FIELDEN, L. *The Natural Bent*. André Deutsch, 1960.
(7) GIELGUD, VAL. *Years of the Locust*. Nicholson & Watson, 1947.
(8) GORHAM, M. *Sound and Fury*. Marshall, 1948.
(9) GRISEWOOD, F. *The World Goes By*. Secker & Warburg, 1952.
(10) HALL, H. *Here's To The Next Time*. Odhams, 1956.
(11) HIBBERD, S. *This—is London*. Macdonald & Evans, 1950.
(12) LAMBERT, R. S. *Ariel and All His Quality*. Gollancz, 1940.
(13) MASCHWITZ, E. *No Chip on My Shoulder*. Jenkins, 1957.
(14) PAYNE, J. *Signature Tune*. Paul [1947].
(15) REITH, J. C. W., 1st Baron. *Into the Wind*. Hodder & Stoughton, 1949.
(16) SIMON OF WYTHENSHAWE, E. D., 1st Baron. *The BBC from Within*. Gollancz, 1953.

For other selected aspects of sound radio, the following are useful:

(1) BAILEY, K. V. *The Listening Schools*. BBC, 1957.
(2) BBC. *New Ventures in Broadcasting*. BBC, 1928.
(3) BBC. *Wireless Discussion Groups*. BBC, 1931.
(4) BBC. *Broadcasting House*. BBC, 1932.
(5) BBC. *A Technical Description of Broadcasting House*. BBC, 1932.
(6) BBC. *The Empire Broadcasting Service*. BBC [1933]; rev. edn., 1937.
(7) BBC ADVISORY COMMITTEE ON SPOKEN ENGLISH. *Broadcast English*, 7 vols. BBC, 1928–39.
(8) BOARD OF EDUCATION. *Adult Education: Wireless Listening Groups*. HMSO, 1933.
(9) FOORT, R. *The BBC Theatre Organ*. BBC, 1938.
(10) JAMES, A. LLOYD. *The Broadcast Word*. Kegan Paul, 1935.
(11) KENT EDUCATION COMMITTEE. *Educational Broadcasting: Report of a Special Investigation*. Carnegie Trust, 1928.

(12) PALMER, R. *School Broadcasting in Britain.* BBC, 1947.
(13) PEAR, T. H. *Voice and Personality.* Chapman & Hall, 1931.
(14) RUSSELL, T. *The Proms.* Parrish, 1949.
(15) SIEVEKING, L. *The Stuff of Radio.* Cassell, 1934.
(16) TURNER, W. J. *Facing the Music.* Bell, 1933.
(17) YOUNG, FILSON. *Shall I Listen?* Constable, 1933.

On particular programmes there are a number of books, including:

(1) BAILY, L., and BREWER, C. *The BBC Scrapbooks.* Hutchinson, 1937.
(2) CANNELL, J. C. *In Town Tonight.* Harrap, 1935.
(3) GIELGUD, V. *British Radio Drama, 1922–1956.* Harrap, 1957.
(4) HILTON, J. *This and That.* Allen & Unwin, 1938.
(5) PEACH, L. DU G. *Broadcast Sketches.* French, 1927.

On television the books already published include:

(1) ASHBRIDGE, SIR N. *Television.* Institution of Mechanical Engineers, 1938.
(2) BOGART, L. *The Age of Television.* New York: Frederick Ungar, 1956; 2nd ed., 1958.
(3) BBC. *The London Television Station: Alexandra Palace.* BBC, 1937.
(4) BBC. *A Picture Book of Television, 1930–50.* BBC, 1950.
(5) DINSDALE, A. *Television.* Pitman, 1926.
(6) GARRATT, G. R. M., and MUMFORD, A. H. 'The History of Television' in the *Proceedings* of the Institution of Electrical Engineers, Vol. 99, 1952.
(7) HORTON, D. *Television's Story and Challenge.* Harrap, 1951.
(8) MOSELEY, S. A. *Private Diaries.* Parrish, 1960.
(9) MOSELEY, S. A. *John Baird.* Odhams [1952].
(10) ROSS, G. *Television Jubilee.* W. H. Allen, 1961.
(11) SWIFT, J. *Adventure in Vision.* Lehmann, 1950.
(12) TILSLEY, F. *Television Story.* BBC [1949].
(13) TILTMAN, R. F. *Baird of Television.* Seeley Service [1933].
(14) TWENTIETH CENTURY. Special Number on *Television*, Nov. 1959.

The constitutional position of the BBC is discussed in:

(1) DAVIES, E. *National Enterprise.* Gollancz, 1946.
(2) DIMOCK, M. E. *British Public Utilities and National Development.* Allen & Unwin, 1933.
(3) GOODMAN, E. *Forms of Public Control and Ownership.* Christophers, 1951.

(4) GORDON, L. *The Public Corporation in Great Britain*. O.U.P., 1938.

(5) O'BRIEN, T. H. *British Experiments in Public Ownership and Control*. Allen & Unwin, 1937.

(6) POSTGATE, R. *What To Do with the BBC*. Hogarth Press, 1935.

(7) POLITICAL QUARTERLY. Special Number on *The BBC*, Oct.-Dec. 1935.

(8) ROBSON, W. A. (ed.) *Public Enterprise*. Allen & Unwin, 1937.

The key official sources for the period, apart from *Hansard*, which has been very fully used, are:

(1) Cmd. 4793 (1935), Report of the Television Committee. The Selsdon Report.

(2) Cmd. 5091 (1936), Report of the Broadcasting Committee, 1935. The Ullswater Report.

(3) Cmd. 5207 (1936), Memorandum by the Postmaster-General on the Report of the Broadcasting Committee, 1935.

(4) Cmd. 5329 (1936), Broadcasting. Drafts of (i) Royal Charter ... for the Continuance of the British Broadcasting Corporation; and (ii) Licence and Agreement between H.M. Postmaster-General and the British Broadcasting Corporation.

(5) Cmd. 5337 (1936), Report of the Special Board of Inquiry appointed by the Prime Minister to inquire into certain Statements made in the Course of the Recent Case Lambert *v.* Levita affecting the BBC.

(6) Cmd. 5405 (1937), Minute by the Prime Minister on the Report of the Board of Inquiry. . . .

(7) House of Commons, Committee of Public Accounts. Interesting material relating to the BBC is given in the Reports for 1927, 1929, 1932, 1937, 1938, and 1939.

(8) The BBC's *Annual Reports and Accounts* published by H.M.S.O. These may be supplemented from the invaluable BBC *Handbooks* and *Year Books*. Most of these are well illustrated and cover most aspects of BBC policy. Unfortunately, however, the amount of information given each year varied considerably, as did the format.

Among the periodicals which have been consulted for the period covered in this volume the *Radio Times*, *The Listener*, *Popular Wireless*, *Wireless World*, and *The Economist* have been especially useful. The files of *The Times*, the *Daily Express*, the *Daily Mail*, the *Daily Herald*, the *Manchester Guardian*, and *Punch* have also been used.

INDEX

Note. A diagonal stroke has been used to indicate intermittent references over a number of pages: thus, Adult education 217/27 infers that various references to this subject may be found in pages 217 to 227; whereas 217–27 would indicate a connected narrative concerning this subject. The illustrations are indexed according to their numbers, such references being in italics.